Mul

D0229920

HOUSE OF LO

Over
becou
and
mode
libera
actua
theor
appro
direct
"state

Anth
Philo
Reaso
(2001

Davic
Divis
Soutl
Nietz

Multiculturalism and Political Theory

Edited by

Anthony Simon Laden and David Owen

CAMBRIDGE UNIVERSITY PRESS
Cambridge, New York, Melbourne, Madrid, Cape Town, Singapore, São Paulo

Cambridge University Press
The Edinburgh Building, Cambridge CB2 8RU, UK

Published in the United States of America by Cambridge University Press,
New York

www.cambridge.org
Information on this title: www.cambridge.org/9780521670906

First published 2007

Printed in the United Kingdom at the University Press, Cambridge

A catalogue record for this publication is available from the British Library

Library of Congress Cataloguing in Publication data
Multiculturalism and political theory / edited by Anthony Simon Laden and
David Owen.
    p. cm.
Includes bibliographical references and index.
ISBN 978-0-521-85450-4 (hardback)
ISBN 978-0-521-67090-6 (pbk.)
1. Multiculturalism. 2. Pluralism (Social sciences) 3. Minorities–Civil rights.
I. Laden, Anthony Simon, 1967–II. Owen, David, 1964–III. Title.

HM1271.M843151 2007
305.8001–dc22

2007003516

ISBN 978-0-521-85450-4 hardback
ISBN 978-0-521-67090-6 paperback

Contents

Notes on contributors   *page vii*
Acknowledgments   *xi*

Introduction   1

Part I Trajectories   23

1 The new debate on minority rights (and postscript)
   Will Kymlicka   25

2 Structural injustice and the politics of difference
   Iris Marion Young   60

3 Multiculturalism as/and/or anti-racism?
   Charles W. Mills   89

4 Feminism and multiculturalism: mapping the terrain
   Ayelet Shachar   115

Part II Approaches   149

5 Egalitarian liberalism and universalism
   Simon Caney   151

6 Contextualism, constitutionalism, and *modus vivendi*
   approaches
   Jacob T. Levy   173

7 Negotiation, deliberation, and the claims of politics
   Anthony Simon Laden   198

Part III Critical issues   **219**

8   Multiculturalism and the critique of essentialism
     Andrew Mason   221

9   Liberalism, multiculturalism, and the problem of
     internal minorities
     Daniel M. Weinstock   244

10   Redistribution and recognition: two approaches
     David Owen and James Tully   265

11   A critical theory of multicultural toleration
     Rainer Forst   292

Part IV New directions   **313**

12   Law's necessary forcefulness: Ralph Ellison vs.
     Hannah Arendt on the Battle of Little Rock
     Danielle Allen   315

13   Imagining civic relations in the moment of their
     breakdown: a crisis of civic integrity in the
     Netherlands
     Bert van den Brink   350

14   Democracy and foreignness: democratic
     cosmopolitanism and the myth of an
     immigrant America
     Bonnie Honig   373

     Index   408

Notes on contributors

Danielle Allen is Dean of Humanities at the University of Chicago. Her research interests include classical Greek literature, political philosophy, the history of rhetoric, the philosophy of punishment, democratic theory and history, and twentieth-century American poetry. She is the author of *The World of Prometheus: The Politics of Punishing in Democratic Athens* (2000) and *Talking to Strangers: Anxieties of Citizenship since Brown v. Board of Education*, as well as numerous articles and chapters in edited volumes.

Bert van den Brink is Research Fellow of the Royal Netherlands Academy of Arts and Sciences and Associate Professor of Philosophy at Utrecht University, the Netherlands. He is the author of *The Tragedy of Liberalism: An Alternative Defense of A Political Tradition* (2000), coeditor of *Bürgergesellschaft, Recht und Demokratie* (1995), and *The Problem of Reasons of One's Own* (2004). He is on the editorial board of the journal *Philosophical Explorations* and on the advisory board of the journal *Contemporary Political Theory*.

Simon Caney is Professor in Political Theory, Oxford University, and Fellow and Tutor in Politics, Magdalen College. He has published articles on liberalism, perfectionism, human rights, climate change, international distributive justice, national self-determination, multiculturalism and intervention. He is the author of *Justice Beyond Borders: A Global Political Theory* (2005). He has also has co-edited *National Rights, International Obligations* (1996) and *Human Rights and Global Diversity* (2000). He is currently writing books entitled *On Cosmopolitanism* and *Global Justice and Climate Change* (co-authored with Dr. Derek Bell.)

Rainer Forst is Professor of Political Theory and Philosophy at Johann Wolfgang Goethe-University in Frankfurt/Main. He is the author of *Contexts of Justice: Political Philosophy beyond Liberalism and Communitarianism* (2002), *Toleranz im Konflikt: Geschichte, Gehalt und*

Gegenwart eines umstrittenen Begriffs (2003; English translation forthcoming with Cambridge University Press), and *Das Recht auf Rechtfertigung: Elemente einer konstruktivistischen Theorie der Gerechtigkeit* (forthcoming).

Bonnie Honig is Professor of Political Science, Northwestern University, and Senior Research Fellow, at the American Bar Foundation, Chicago. She is the author of *Democracy and the Foreigner* (2001) and *Political Theory and the Displacement of Politics* (1993), as well as editor of the *Oxford Handbook of Political Theory* (with John Dryzek and Anne Phillips) (2006), *Skepticism, Individuality and Freedom: The Reluctant Liberalism of Richard Flathman* (with David Mapel) (2002), and *Feminist Interpretations of Hannah Arendt* (1995). Her most recent work includes "The Time of Rights: Emergent Thoughts in an Emergent Setting," in *The Politics of Pluralism: Essays for William Connolly*, ed. Michael Shapiro and David Campbell (forthcoming, 2007) and "Bound By Law? Alien Rights, Administrative Discretion, and the Politics of Technicality: Lessons from Louis Post and the First Red Scare," in *The Limits of Law*, ed. Austin Sarat, Lawrence Douglas, and Martha Umphrey (2005).

Will Kymlicka is the Canada Research Chair in Political Philosophy at Queen's University, and a visiting professor in the Nationalism Studies program at the Central European University in Budapest. He is the author of five books: *Liberalism, Community, and Culture* (1989), *Contemporary Political Philosophy* (1990; second edition 2002), *Multicultural Citizenship* (1995), *Finding Our Way: Rethinking Ethnocultural Relations in Canada* (1998), and *Politics in the Vernacular: Nationalism, Multiculturalism, Citizenship* (2001).

Anthony Laden is Associate Professor of Philosophy at the University of Illinois (Chicago). He works in moral and political philosophy, where his research focuses on liberalism, democratic theory, feminism and the politics of identity, and the nature of practical reason and reasoning. He is the author of *Reasonably Radical: Deliberative Liberalism and the Politics of Identity* (2001). His recent articles include "Outline of a Theory of Reasonable Deliberation" (*Canadian Journal of Philosophy*, 2000), "The House that Jack Built: Thirty Years of Reading Rawls" (*Ethics*, 2003), and "Reasonable Feminists, Radical Liberals: Reason, Power and Objectivity in the Work of MacKinnon and Rawls" (*Journal of Political Philosophy*, 2003).

Jacob T. Levy is Tomlinson Professor of Political Theory at the Department of Political Science, McGill University, and Secretary-Treasurer of the American Society for Political and Legal Philosophy. He is the author of *The Multiculturalism of Fear* (2000), and numerous articles and chapters on minority rights, indigenous rights, nationalism, federalism, and the history of liberal thought, that have appeared in *Ethics, Nomos, History of Political Thought, Social Philosophy and Policy,* and edited collections including *Citizenship in Diverse Societies, Language Rights and Political Theory,* and *Nationalism, Liberalism, and Pluralism.* He has been a Fulbright Scholar (1993–1994) and a visiting Mellon Fellow at the University of Chicago Law School (2004–2005). He is currently writing on rationalism and pluralism in liberal thought.

Andrew Mason is Professor of Political Theory at the University of Southampton. He is the author of *Explaining Political Disagreement* (Cambridge University Press, 1993) and *Community, Solidarity and Belonging* (Cambridge University Press, 2000), and the editor of *Ideals of Equality* (1998). His most recent book, *Levelling the Playing Field* was published in 2006.

Charles W. Mills is Distinguished Professor of Philosophy at the University of Illinois at Chicago. He works in the general area of oppositional political theory, and is the author of three books: *The Racial Contract* (1997), *Blackness Visible: Essays on Philosophy and Race* (1998), and *From Class to Race: Essays in White Marxism and Black Radicalism* (2003). Currently he is working on a joint book with Carole Pateman, tentatively titled *Contract and Domination* (forthcoming).

David Owen is Professor of Social and Political Philosophy at the University of Southampton. He is the author of *Maturity and Modernity* (1994), *Nietzsche, Politics and Modernity* (1995), and *Nietzsche's Genealogy of Morality* (2007), and co-editor of *Recognition and Power* (Cambridge University Press, 2007). Recent articles in political philosophy include: "Political Philosophy in a Post-Imperial Voice" (*Economy and Society*, 1999), "Cultural Diversity and the Conversation of Justice" (*Political Theory*, 1999), "Criticism and Captivity" (*European Journal of Philosophy*, 2002), and "Culture, Equality and Polemic" (*Economy and Society*, 2003). He is currently writing a book on the ethics of migration.

Ayelet Shachar is the Canada Research Chair in Citizenship and Multiculturalism at the Faculty of Law, University of Toronto and the Leah Kaplan Visiting Professor in Human Rights at Stanford

Law School. Her research focuses on citizenship theory, immigration law, multilevel governance regimes, state and religion, and the rights of women within minority cultures. She is the author of *Multicultural Jurisdictions: Cultural Differences and Women's Rights* (Cambridge University Press, 2001); and Winner of the 2002 Best First Book Award, American Political Science Association, Foundations of Political Theory Section. Her new book, *Citizenship as Inherited Property: The New World of Bounded Communities*, will be published by Harvard University Press.

James Tully is a Professor of Political Science, Law, Philosophy, and Indigenous Governance at the University of Victoria, BC, Canada. Before the University of Victoria he taught Political Science and Philosophy at McGill University and was the inaugural Henry N. R. Jackman Distinguished Professor of Philosophical Studies, in Philosophy, Political Science and Law, at the University of Toronto 2001–2003. He has published eight books and many articles on topics in contemporary political philosophy and the history of political philosophy, including *Strange Multiplicities: Constitutionalism in an Age of Diversity* (Cambridge University Press, 1996). He is a Fellow of the Royal Society of Canada and a Fellow of the new Canadian Trudeau Foundation.

Daniel Weinstock holds the Canada Research Chair in Ethics and Political Philosophy in the Department of Philosophy of the Université de Montréal, where he is also a Full Professor. He is the founding director of the University's Ethics Research Center. He has published many articles on the interface between culture and justice. He is presently working on a book project exploring the complex relationship between children, families, and the liberal-democratic state.

Iris Marion Young was Professor of Political Science at the University of Chicago. Her research interests covered contemporary political theory, feminist social theory, and normative analysis of public policy. Her books include *Justice and the Politics of Difference* (1990), *Throwing Like a Girl and Other Essays in Feminist Philosophy and Social Theory* (1990), *Intersecting Voices: Dilemmas of Gender, Political Philosophy, and Policy* (1997), and *Inclusion and Democracy* (2000).

Acknowledgments

The original thought for this volume arose in a conversation with John Haslam at APSA in 2000. In this respect, John has seen the project through from glint in the eye to conception to, finally, gestation. Throughout this process, he has been encouraging, helpful across a range of issues, and – above all – patient (despite the temptations to the contrary). We are deeply grateful to John for all his support as well as his editorial acumen.

Early versions of the chapters by Laden, Levy, Mills, and Young were given as papers at a Chicago Political Theory Network conference in November 2004. The editors are grateful to all who attended and in particular to Peg Birmingham, David Ingram and Paul Gomberg, who served as discussants, and to Stephen Engelmann, who helped to organize the conference.

We would also like to thank our respective colleagues in Chicago and Southampton who have provided a working environment within which these issues are fiercely debated in an utterly non-dogmatic spirit, and, in particular, Chris Armstrong, Russell Bentley, Chris Brown, Samuel Fleischacker, Andrew Mason, and Aaron Ridley. We are both much in debt over several years to the intellectual generosity of James Tully. Andrew Brearley was of great assistance in putting the final manuscript into a consistent form.

Finally, we would like to thank our respective Carolines for – yet again – covering the father-shaped holes in family life that occurred in the course of constructing this volume with their characteristic grace and good humor. This volume is dedicated to our children, Arthur, Miranda, Clara, Raphaël, and Jacob who will, in their turn, engage with a world where (we hope) the debates discussed herein have made a difference. Several of the chapters in this volume have been previously published, and we gratefully acknowledge the permission to republish them here. "The New Debate over Minority Rights," by Will Kymlicka, was previously published in Will Kymlicka, *Politics in the Vernacular* (Oxford: Oxford University Press, 2001), and is reprinted here with the permission of Oxford University Press. "Law's Necessary Forcefulness," by Danielle Allen, previously appeared in the *Oklahoma City University Law Review* 26(3) (Fall 2001), pp. 857–896, and is reprinted here with permission of the Oklahoma City Law Review. "Democracy and foreignness" by Bonnie Honig was published in a slightly different form as "The Foreigner as Citizen," chapter 4 of her *Democracy and the Foreigner* (Princeton: Princeton University Press, 2001) and is reprinted here with permission of Princeton University Press.

Iris Young died as the final touches were being made to this volume. Those who knew her, even slightly, will feel the loss of a vibrant, humorous, and passionate human being whose commitment to justice made a difference. Those who knew her work will feel the loss of one of political philosophy's most practically grounded and theoretically imaginative voices. We hope that those who will meet her for the first time in this collection will understand why we join so many colleagues and friends in missing her.

Anthony Simon Laden, Chicago

David Owen, Southampton

Introduction

For almost twenty years, the re-emergence of political philosophy's engagement with the culturally diverse character of political communities in the modern state has been characterized by fierce debate and continuing controversy, during which time an impressive variety of philosophical approaches, theoretical positions, and practical judgments have been elaborated, attacked, defended, revised, and (occasionally) abandoned.[1] There are a number of reasons, however, for thinking that this is an appropriate juncture at which to take half a step back from these debates.

First, the field of inquiry is now sufficiently well established for it to be possible to review its development and, in so doing, to draw attention to significant trajectories within this process, highlight central problems, interrogate unnoticed assumptions, and elucidate its current limitations. In other words, it is now possible to take the field of inquiry itself as a relatively well-defined object of reflection and evaluation. Second, reflections on cultural diversity within analytical political philosophy have established three major approaches within which – and, to a lesser extent, between which – critical dialogues have flourished. In this context, an "approach" is not to be seen as a theory but as something like *an orientation in thinking*, a framework of argument within which a number of different theoretical positions are situated against a broadly common background of basic commitments concerning the appropriate character or shape of arguments in political philosophy. Third, in the course of the theoretical debates concerning multiculturalism, a number of critical issues have emerged as pivotal; topics ranging from the concept of culture itself and, more specifically, whether defenses of multiculturalism appeal, despite their protestations to the contrary, to an objectionable *essentialist* understanding of culture, to the position of minority groups within cultural minorities or within the territory of a

---

[1] See Jeremy Waldron, "What is Cosmopolitan?," *Journal of Political Philosophy*, 8 (2), 2000, pp. 227–243.

(partially) self-governing national minority. Fourth, the delineation of this field of inquiry helps to make visible new directions for research in this field and, in particular, theoretical innovations that have emerged either through an immanent process of critical reflection on the development of the field or by way of the application of heterodox theoretical approaches to this domain.

These reasons provide *prima facie* grounds for taking this half step back from the debates in order to *review* the development of this field of inquiry, *survey* the major approaches established on this terrain, *address* the critical questions posed in the debates, and *highlight* new directions in research. Attending to these four tasks provides the rationale for the structure of this volume in which each part takes up one of these tasks. This introduction will provide contexts for each of these endeavors by sketching the background to the relevant debates and role of each of the chapters in the collection. In the course of doing so, it will also highlight certain methodological and philosophical developments that the debates over issues of cultural diversity have fostered, developments whose relevance cuts across the organization of the volume and whose importance spreads beyond the engagement with cultural diversity.

I

Reflection on the rights of peoples is contemporaneous with the emergence and development of modern Western political thought. While the issue of religious toleration was brought acutely to the fore as a topic for philosophical and political reflection by the confessional conflicts that ravaged Europe in the sixteenth and seventeenth centuries,[2] it is equally true that, at the same time, the European encounter with the New World and the colonial empires that emerged from this encounter raised the issue of the rights of peoples.[3] Debates concerning the legitimacy of rights *over people* in the Spanish case and *over things* (primarily land) in the French and English cases served as crucial loci for the development of European legal and political thought.[4]

With the emergence of nationalism within post-revolutionary Europe, this issue ceased to be a topic related primarily to colonial contexts and

---

[2] See Stephen Krasner, *Sovereignty: Organized Hypocrisy* (Princeton: Princeton University Press, 1999), p. 77.

[3] See Robert A. Williams Jr., *The American Indian in Western Legal Thought: The Discourses of Conquest* (Oxford: Oxford University Press, 1990) and Anthony Pagden, *Lords of All The World: Ideologies of Empire in Spain, Britain and France c.1500–c.1800* (New Haven: Yale University Press, 1995).

[4] See Williams, *The American Indian* and also S. James Anaya, *Indigenous Peoples in International Law* (Oxford: Oxford University Press, 1996), p. 23.

became an issue for internal European politics, a shift marked at the Congress of Vienna (1815) in which, for the first time, protection was granted by an international peace treaty to an ethnic or national group as well as to religious groups. Castlereagh's successful argument "that the rights of the Poles ought to be guaranteed by the great powers within the three states that participated in the partition of Poland (Prussia, Russia and Austria)" was grounded on the claim that efforts "to make the Poles 'forget their existence and even language as a people has been sufficiently tried and failed.' Institutions had to reflect the desires of the population; otherwise it was impossible to maintain stability."[5] This argument represented one side of what became a central debate in nineteenth-century liberalism between the advocates of rights for national minorities such as Castlereagh, Leonard Hobhouse, and Lord Acton, and advocates of the liberal nationalist position represented by John Stuart Mill and T. H. Green, who argue that political stability requires the "common sympathies" brought about by shared language, culture, and history; in other words, "cultural homogeneity."[6] This liberal debate concerning national minorities was given further impetus by the shift in the Balkans from rule by the Ottoman Empire to a plurality of independent successor states (Greece, Romania, Serbia, Montenegro, Bulgaria, and Albania) addressed in the Treaty of Berlin (1878) as well as by the post-First World War emergence of a plurality of successor states to the Austro-Hungarian Empire addressed by the League of Nations' system of minority guarantees.[7]

Thus, from Vitoria's innovative articulation of a largely desacralized Law of Nations in 1532 via the disparate but related arguments of Grotius (1604), Pufendorf (1688), Locke (1690), Vattel (1758), and Blackstone (1765) concerning property rights and the law of nations to the classic liberal texts of the late nineteenth and early twentieth centuries, the issue of the rights of indigenous peoples and national minorities has been a significant element in the articulation of the tradition of Western legal and political theory.

From this historical perspective, then, the puzzle is twofold. First, why is there such a paucity of engagement with the topic of minority rights between the end of the Second World War and the later years of the

---

[5] Krasner, *Sovereignty*, p. 83.

[6] Will Kymlicka, *Multicultural Citizenship* (Oxford: Oxford University Press, 1995), pp. 49–74. The phrase "common sympathies" is from John Stuart Mill, *Considerations on Representative Government*, ch. 16.

[7] See Jennifer Jackson Preece, *National Minorities and the European Nation-States System* (Oxford: Oxford University Press, 1998), pp. 55–95 and Krasner, *Sovereignty*, pp. 90–104.

twentieth century? Second, what triggered the theoretical re-engagement that has proliferated over the last twenty years?

In response to the first of these questions, we can note that there are a number of different political developments that supported the marginalization of the topic. The failure of the minorities regime established by the League of Nations and the justifiable sense that it had contributed to the outbreak of the Second World War led the Allies to develop the alternative policy of massive forced population transfers as a way of dealing with the immediate post-war problem of national minorities. This policy was explicitly legitimated by the 1950 UN Report *Study of the Legal Validity of the Undertakings Concerning Minorities* which argued not only that the pre-war minority treatises were no longer in force (so could not justify claims to the illegality of Allied policy) but also, and crucially, that "the protection of minorities in the post-war era was governed by a new philosophy: the promotion of the fundamental human rights of all human beings."[8] This new philosophy expressed through the Universal Declaration of Human Rights ensured attention was focused on the issue of universal rights and human dignity; as Musgrave notes, "[a] proposal to include a provision protecting minorities in the Declaration was expressly rejected by the General Assembly, which concluded that it would be too difficult to formulate a provision applicable to all minorities"[9] and, at the multilateral level, "there was clearly a reluctance in the early post-war period to grant special rights to minorities."[10]

It also seems likely that the fact that the ideological terrain of the Cold War was rapidly expressed in terms of the issue of civil and political vs. social and economic human rights helped divert attention from the rights of minority cultures or peoples. The formation of this ideological terrain was undoubtedly facilitated by the fact that both of the major Cold War blocs shared a commitment to a vision of cosmopolitanism underwritten by a developmental account of history that legitimated coercive projects of assimilation with respect to "pre-modern" minority peoples in these blocs or states. This may have been more visible and violent in the case of the figure of New Soviet Man and the policies of Russification legitimated in its name or in the continuing case of the Han Chinese repression of nomadic groups such as Kazakhs and Uighurs as well as "pre-modern" societies such as that of Tibet, but such a view equally informed the child-removal policies that produced

---

[8] Thomas Musgrave, *Self-Determination and National Minorities* (Oxford: Oxford University Press, 1997), p. 129
[9] Ibid., p. 130.   [10] Ibid., p. 133.

the "stolen generations" of indigenous peoples in Australia and Canada as well as of the Roma in Switzerland. It is also the case, we may recall, that it was the United States of America and France who blocked the proposal of the Ad Hoc Committee which drafted the 1951 Convention on Genocide to include "cultural genocide" as a prohibited category.[11]

Alongside these political developments, we can also identify contributing academic developments. Will Kymlicka has argued with some plausibility that the neglect of the topic of cultural minorities owes much to the specific history of liberal thought in the USA. Kymlicka points out that American liberals in the nineteenth and early twentieth centuries were not impelled to address two of the major motivations for discussing national minorities – governing colonized peoples and negotiating nationalist conflicts in Europe. Moreover, we can add, since the USA was, given its own historical self-representation, understandably sympathetic to the liberation struggles of colonized peoples (other than those of its own domestic nations) and also deeply suspicious of the role played by national minorities issues in leading to two "European" wars in which the USA had reluctantly become a late entrant, it is unsurprising that neglect of this issue continues into the post-war period in which "American theorists have become the dominant interpreters of liberal principles."[12] On a less sociological note, we can also suggest that a specific intellectual development in political philosophy may have played a (largely inadvertent) role in marginalizing the topic of minority rights. The publication of John Rawls's *A Theory of Justice*[13] not only marked the re-emergence of analytic political philosophy but also shaped its methods and agendas. In particular, much subsequent work in analytic political philosophy followed Rawls in reflecting on ideals of justice at a relatively high level of abstraction and also, critically, making a number of idealizing assumptions such as the closed character of the polity (entered at birth, left at death) and its cultural homogeneity. These idealizations acted, at least initially, to deflect philosophical attention from the related topics of migration and cultural diversity.

Among the developments that no doubt led to a re-engagement with issues of cultural diversity were the character of two predominant types of political struggle in the 1950s and 1960s – national liberation struggles on the part of the colonies of European empire-states and equal rights struggles by blacks and women. The story here is, however, somewhat complicated, as one strand of both those movements encouraged a normative picture of a world of equal states in which

---

[11] Ibid., p. 131.   [12] Kymlicka, *Multicultural Citizenship*, p. 56.
[13] John Rawls, *A Theory of Justice* (Cambridge, MA: Harvard University Press, 1971).

citizenship denotes the effective enjoyment of an identical set of rights and opportunities on the part of all adult members of the polity. That is to say, the sort of idealized picture that led liberal political philosophy to ignore issues of cultural diversity. However, a different, perhaps more radical strand of these movements challenged liberal notions of equality as similar treatment for all, demanding not similar treatment but an end to domination and oppression. The first wave of such radical action in Scotland and Wales, in the Basque Country and Catalonia, and in Quebec as well as among North American Indians, manifested itself in the rise of nationalist independence organizations (some peaceful, some violent) for whom the initial goal and spur to political action was to redress the balance in their relationship to a culturally dominant other within the nationalizing state by forcing that other to acknowledge their own equal status as independent nations or distinct societies.[14] As these movements have developed second waves, the demands for independence and against domination have been disentangled, and this has generated both political action and philosophical reflection on the possibility of relations of non-domination between national minorities and majorities that do not take the form of independent statehood for national minorities but, rather, of self-government rights within a state (or within and across states in the case of groups such as the Kurds), whilst simultaneously requiring the recognition of the relevant parties in international and not merely domestic law.

During the same time period, social movements for racial and gender equality also challenged the liberal ideal of equal citizenship as an identical set of rights and opportunities. While these movements emphasized the idea of equality as non-domination clearly from the beginning, and were not, for the most part, making demands for political independence, they can also be seen as making two intertwined demands that succeeding generations of "ethnocultural" activists and theorists have more clearly distinguished. The first is a demand for equal power, for an end to domination and oppression. The second is a demand that the non-necessary differential burdens that members of diverse cultural groups bear as citizens should be acknowledged by the state.[15]

Thus, by the later years of the twentieth century, it was manifestly clear that both of these forms of political struggle were directed to a goal of equality as non-domination that could not be adequately captured in

[14] See M. Monserrat Guibernau, *Nations without States* (Oxford: Polity Press, 1999).
[15] See the chapters by Young and Mills in this volume for discussions of the relationship between oppression and diversity.

terms of either a model of equal nations as independent sovereign states nor of equal citizenship as an identical set of rights and opportunities.

Just as the flowering of feminism and critical race theory in the academy occurs within the context of political struggles against gender and racial inequality, the political struggles by indigenous peoples, national minorities, and immigrants provide the background against which the sudden re-emergence and rapid development of engagement with the topic of culturally diverse peoples and the modern state takes place. The suddenness of this re-emergence can be seen in the fact that following the publication of James Crawford's important edited collection *The Rights of Peoples* (1988), there emerges a plethora of work across a number of disciplines focused on this topic. In political theory, the crucial standard-bearers were Will Kymlicka's *Liberty, Culture and Community* (1989), Andrew Sharp's *Justice and the Maori* (1990), and, in a less direct way, Iris Marion Young's *Justice and the Politics of Difference* (1990); works that were rapidly followed by, among others, Charles Taylor's influential essay "The Politics of Recognition" (1992), Yael Tamir's *Liberal Nationalism* (1993), and James Tully's *Strange Multiplicity* (1995). The late years of the twentieth century also saw the publication of significant studies in law such as Antonio Cassese's *Self-Determination of Peoples: A Legal Reappraisal* (1995), Thomas D. Musgrave's *Self-Determination and National Minorities* (1997), and S. James Anaya's *Indigenous Peoples in International Law* (1996) and in history, with texts ranging from Robert Williams Jr., *The American Indian in Western Legal Thought: The Discourses of Conquest* (1990) to Anthony Pagden's *European Encounters with the New World* (1993) and *Lords of all the Earth: Ideologies of Empire in Spain, Britain and France c.1500–c.1800* (1995) presenting significant studies on how European thought is transformed through Europe's engagement with the New World. Whatever the precise explanation for this eruption of interest, the salience of the issue of cultural diversity for political theory was rapidly established and entrenched in the final years of the twentieth century.

II

As suggested by this brief historical overview, within analytic political philosophy and political theory, discussions of cultural diversity have largely taken place in a context where the dominant political theory was some form of liberalism, and thus much of the debate has involved identifying aspects of liberalism that obscure or distort questions surrounding culturally diverse political societies. It is thus possible to chart some of the more theoretical developments of this debate by seeing how they arose in response to various features of traditional liberal thought. At first glance, however, that the issue of cultural diversity rose to theoretical prominence in the form of *criticisms* of liberalism strikes many liberals as surprising. After all, liberalism, at least according to its own self-understanding, was itself a philosophy developed partly in response to issues of diversity.

Liberals generally see the origins of the relevant liberal doctrines about diversity as a response to the religious wars of the sixteenth and seventeenth centuries in Europe. Liberalism is thus seen as a theoretical response to the fact of religious diversity (albeit narrowly defined as a diversity of Christians). That response involves three characteristic features. The first is an idea of religious tolerance that ultimately develops into liberal ideas of the separation of church and state, and, more generally, state neutrality.[16]

The second feature involves the strong protection of individual liberties. A state can conceivably remain neutral between competing religions while nevertheless allowing each religion unbridled authority over its believers. Liberalism, however, justifies state neutrality by conceiving of religious belief as a matter of individual conscience. Individual citizens, it is claimed, have particularly strong and deep ties to their religion, and these ties generate non-negotiable ends.[17] The state can only adequately respect its members, then, if it gives them the space to pursue those ends. It does this by protecting a variety of individual liberties, from liberty of conscience to freedom of assembly and speech. These liberties then allow members of a religion to band together free from the influence of the state, but also allow members of different religions to organize their religious lives in peaceful coexistence within a single state.

Finally, liberalism offers a theoretical justification for the protection of individual liberties via an argument about human equality and similarity. The ultimate ground for the protection of individual liberties, then, is not the merely pragmatic matter of ensuring social peace, but a claim about the importance and even necessity for mutual respect as a matter of justice. Although this argument takes a number of different forms in the hands of different liberal theorists, the basic idea is that although people may belong to different religions, and thus have, as John Rawls famously put it, a variety of "conceptions of the good," beneath these differences, citizens are basically the same, in that they have a claim and

---

[16] See Rainer Forst's chapter in this volume for a more detailed discussion of the forms of tolerance and their implications for broader forms of diversity.

[17] See, for example, Rawls, *A Theory of Justice*, pp. 206–207.

a desire to be treated equally, where this involves having a fair share of the same basic goods, like liberty, opportunity, income, and respect.

Thus, liberalism's response to religious diversity involves a general theoretical solution to the problem that emphasizes human equality as a result of human similarity, and thus conceives equality in terms of similar treatment, treats religious belief as a matter of individual conscience, and advocates state neutrality and the protection of individual liberties as the just response to diversity.

Many philosophers and political theorists who have turned their attention to issues of cultural diversity have found this basic liberal framework inadequate for handling questions of diversity that are broader and touch on different matters than those that stem from doctrinal disputes among European Christians. They have thus developed new philosophical ideas and analyses whose value and power extend beyond the particular debates in which they originated.

While liberty of conscience and freedom of assembly have served to protect and preserve certain forms of religious diversity and religious minorities rather well, they turn out not to be very good one-size-fits-all remedies for other forms of diversity. Linguistic minorities, for instance, do not merely need the freedom to speak and think in their own language in the privacy of their own homes and clubs, but the ability to interact with the state and wider social institutions in their own language. They may need the government to provide free public education in their language as well as that of the dominant linguistic group. Non-Christian religions may require forms of dress or diet or activity that go beyond issues of thought, speech, and assembly protected by standard liberal liberties. The attention to forms of cultural diversity beyond the Protestant–Catholic divide, then, led many theorists to develop a greater sensitivity to both social context and the particularities of different cultural demands. Rather than trying to shoehorn all issues of diversity into the model developed to handle one form of religious pluralism, these theorists have urged political theorists to pay more attention to the specific form various cultural needs take. This has resulted in two related developments within political theory. The first is a greater engagement with more empirical disciplines, and a greater attention to the complexity of actual political societies.[18] The second is a theoretical engagement with the question of the relevance of context to doing political theory at all.[19] If we are going to reject once-size-fits-all remedies, then this opens the question of just what kind of theory we

---

[18] See, for example, the chapters by Will Kymlicka and Daniel Weinstock in this volume.

[19] See, for example, the chapter by Jacob Levy in this volume.

need to develop. Thus, the attention to cultural diversity has led to philosophical discussions about the place and role and aims of political theory itself.[20]

Second, many theorists have criticized liberalism's reliance on a norm of equality that takes similar treatment as an ideal. In a culturally diverse society, members of a majority and minority culture may have greatly differential needs and access to resources that might enable them to support and reproduce their culture. Treating these individuals equally, it is thus argued, may require treating them differently, either by allowing exceptions to general rules to make space for particular cultural practices, or by subsidizing or regulating activities that either support or undermine the flourishing of minority cultures. The idea that cultural diversity may require adopting differential treatment as a means of producing equality has generated some of the most strident debate between liberals and those who criticize liberalism's capacity to address issues of cultural diversity adequately.

It is important to distinguish this debate about differential treatment from a different criticism of liberal norms of equality. Here, critics have charged that liberalism turns a blind eye to inequality that takes the form of domination, especially when that domination is carried out through social structures and actions, rather than directly via state action. Critics have thus charged that the idea of state neutrality turns out to cover up a variety of ways that states favor majorities, especially cultural, national, or linguistic majorities. As a consequence, they have focused our attention on the workings of social power, power that does not rest directly in the control of the state, but which can serve to systematically disadvantage minority or other socially oppressed groups. The recognition of the importance of social power is of course not new in theoretical discussions of cultural diversity; it is a longstanding theme of radical political theory of all stripes. But advocates of what Iris Young calls a politics of difference have done much to expand our understanding of how that power functions, and its role in undermining the possibility that state neutrality could provide a proper path to justice in a culturally diverse political society.

Both those theorists who criticize liberalism for failing to take sufficient heed of inequalities in social power, and those who criticize liberalism for its insensitivity to the difference that cultural difference makes direct their criticisms against liberal norms of equality. As a result, it has been

---

[20] For a discussion of this point in the context of feminist theory, see María Lugones and Elizabeth Spelman, "Have We Got a Theory for You!" reprinted in *Hypatia Reborn*, ed. Margaret Simons and Azizah al-Hibri (Bloomington: Indiana University Press, 1990), pp. 18–33.

common to conflate these lines of criticism, and this conflation has had the effect of muddying both the conceptual terrain and the philosophical battle lines. One can thus find liberal theorists who are attentive to questions of power but do not attend to issues of cultural difference, and theorists who are sensitive to cultural difference but fail to take heed of the workings of social power.[21] Nevertheless, a better appreciation of what equality might require and of how to conceive of equality is a further consequence of the recent attention to cultural diversity.

The final development generated by attention to the cultural diversity we want to highlight turns on the liberal adoption of what has been called a theoretical approach. Many liberal theories ground claims about human equality on the basis of claims about human similarity. If human beings are, beneath all of their differences, essentially similar, then it is possible to build up a theory about how such individuals, given their various surface differences, can best organize their collective life. And then political theory is naturally seen as the discipline involved in producing such theories. Once we attend to cultural diversity, and recognize the diversity of that diversity, however, it becomes less plausible to think that such a theory might profitably be derived from something like an account of human nature. This recognition has led some writers in this collection to adopt what is sometimes called a political approach to questions of cultural diversity.[22] The idea is to see the point of political philosophy as engaging with and clarifying the terms of the actual demands made by particular citizens on behalf of cultural groups, rather than developing highly abstract theories into which those demands are then shoehorned. As with the move to contextualism, the development of a political approach involves putting political theory into conversation with more empirical disciplines, but it also challenges theorists to leave more space for actual political and social movements. In this way, attention to cultural diversity has helped to fuel productive reflection on both the nature of democratic politics and what, if any, role political philosophy might play in a culturally diverse society.

III

Since debates about how political philosophy should properly take heed of cultural diversity have been of increasingly central importance to political theory for almost two decades now, those debates themselves

---

[21] See the chapters by Iris Young and Charles Mills in this volume. The issue is also touched upon in the chapters by Anthony Laden and Bert van den Brink in this volume.
[22] See the chapters by Anthony Laden and by David Owen and James Tully in this volume.

have a history. In the first part of the volume, important contributors to that debate reflect on that history, and draw lessons about its evolution and possible future. In "The new debate over minority rights," originally written in the late 1990s, Will Kymlicka identifies what he takes to be the three main stages of the history of debates about minority rights. In the first stage, the minority rights debate was regarded as just another instance of the liberal-communitarian debate. Those who defended minority rights were assumed to be adopting a communitarian viewpoint that rejected liberal individualism in favor of some form of collectivism. So-called liberal culturalists (Kymlicka among them) ushered in a second phase, by arguing that some minority rights could be defended within a liberal framework. Rather than seeing minority rights as the rights of groups, these authors argued that many rights to cultural protection and autonomy were best thought of as individual liberal rights to contexts, forms of identification, and conscience that traditional liberals valued. Kymlicka then goes on to identify a third stage that he saw as emerging in the late 1990s: what he calls minority rights as a response to nation-building. The key shift here is to recognize that the liberal state itself has not been neutral on cultural matters, but has historically often been engaged more or less explicitly in forms of nation-building. In this context, the key question about minority rights is not whether they are justifiable in universal terms, but whether they are necessary in specific historical and political contexts to balance the nation-building power and projects of majorities. This final move increases the importance of specific context, as well as re-emphasizing the "minority" part of minority rights.

In a new "Postscript" written specifically for this volume, Kymlicka updates his original account, and reflects on the recent apparent retreat from multiculturalism in theory and practice. He argues that in fact the retreat, where it has happened, has been confined to questions concerning immigrant groups, and in particular to immigrants in certain contexts (those where large numbers of immigrants are illegal, Muslim, and/or unskilled). He suggests that in fact, multiculturalist theorizing has been remarkably successful in changing the terms of political debate on questions of cultural diversity, though there are still challenges, both theoretical and political to be faced.

Whereas Kymlicka sees the recent history of political theory and philosophy in terms of progress made, Iris Young and Charles Mills paint a more ambiguous picture. Both suggest that to a large extent the recent focus on what Young calls a "politics of cultural difference" has tended to obscure issues of what she calls "structural inequality." While both acknowledge the importance of questions of cultural diversity, and the value of much theoretical work in this domain, both challenge us to recognize that not all problems of difference are best thought of in this manner. Young's contribution, "Structural injustice and the politics of difference" draws precisely and explicitly a distinction between two forms of a politics of difference. Both challenge the dominant liberal view that treating everyone equally involves treating them similarly. What Young calls the "politics of positional difference" addresses groups who are formed primarily as a result of various social hierarchies. It is thus concerned with issues like the social division of labor, the power to decide institutional actions, and the construction of social norms. The politics of cultural difference, on the other hand, focuses on the interaction within political states of multiple cultural or ethnic or religious groups, and how they might accommodate one another, and how one group's status as minority or majority might affect its claims to justice. Since both lay claim to the title "politics of difference," and both are critical of difference-blindness in much liberal theory, there has been a tendency to conflate them, both by their champions and their critics. Among the lamentable consequences of this conflation, Young suggests, is the failure to distinguish structural racism from non-racial cultural misrecognition, the over-emphasis of state actions as both a source of problems and the locus of possible solutions, and a normalizing use of the model of toleration, which assumes that there is a well-constituted "we" who should or should not tolerate "them."

Mills raises similar, though more focused, worries, in his "Multiculturalism as/and/or anti-racism." The place of race in discussions of multiculturalism has been a complicated, and Mills suggests, generally not very illuminating one. For the most part, discussions of cultural diversity, criticisms of traditional theories for their insensitivity to difference, and developments in what is often called the politics of recognition have taken their analyses to cover racial injustice as well. Mills argues that such multiculturalism as anti-racism has largely rested on the mistaken conflation of race with either culture or ethnicity. Rather, he suggests, we need to follow the increasing body of literature on race itself which regards racial categories as essentially hierarchal and social, to be analyzed not in terms of recognition, but in terms more familiar from political economy, such as exploitation, domination, and inequality. To the extent that multicultural theorists can restrain their ambitions and allow such discussions of race to proceed on a separate track, Mills suggests we can do with multiculturalism and anti-racism side-by-side. But to the extent that multicultural theory fails to distinguish between questions of cultural difference and racial hierarchy, multiculturalism itself may stand in the way of racial justice.

Gender, like race, is seen by many theorists as a site of what Young calls "structural inequality," and yet unlike race there has been little serious effort to treat gender differences and inequalities under the rubric of cultural difference. Nevertheless, questions of gender and gender-based inequality have impacted on debates about cultural diversity and led to the development of a sort of sub-field within debates over multiculturalism. As Ayelet Shachar explains in her overview of these debates, "Feminism and multiculturalism: mapping the terrain," they center around whether and how multiculturalism might be bad for women, given that the accommodation of some cultural diversity can include the accommodation of sexist practices and norms. Shachar distinguishes three theoretical positions that have developed in the last ten to fifteen years. Liberal feminists have argued that women's equality always trumps cultural accommodation, but they have often combined this commitment with a rather caricatured view of (especially non-Western) cultures, failing to note both the internal diversity of all cultures and turning a somewhat blind eye to the deep sexism of Western cultures. Post-colonial feminists have reacted to these liberal shortcomings, insisting on a more critical account of Western culture, and pointing out the racialized and racist tropes that stand behind much of the liberal feminist critique of various cultures. Finally, multicultural feminists bring together what Shachar claims are the best of each tradition, treating women as both culture- and rights-bearers, and examining the impacts of particular cultures on women and women on those cultures from a more explicitly political context. After summarizing the basic tenets of these three views, Shachar goes on to discuss how they each might react to a recent proposal by Canadian Muslims to set up private religious courts to handle family law under the rubric of the Canadian Arbitration Act. Whereas Mills and Young raise worries about the impact of debates over cultural diversity on questions of structural inequality, Shachar ends on a more upbeat note, suggesting that the interaction between feminists and multiculturalists has generated and continues to generate valuable insights and creative approaches to resolving admittedly thorny questions.

A survey of the current state of debates in political theory about issues of cultural diversity could focus either on the various main approaches or the various main issues of contention. Part II of the volume takes up the major approaches, and part III looks at some of the main issues. Over the course of the last ten years, three main approaches have emerged. An "approach," as used here, is a kind of orientation in thinking, rather than a full-blown theoretical apparatus, and so people who disagree with one another on many or all issues relating to cultural diversity can nevertheless share an approach. The approach one takes to issues of cultural diversity will affect how one initially sees a variety of questions, and indeed, which issues and questions one takes to be worth addressing at all. Seen this way, the histories Kymlicka and Shachar relate involve shifts in approach. Part II offers discussions of each of the current major approaches: liberal universalist, contextualist, and political.

Liberal universalists hold that the issues raised by cultural diversity do not require that we abandon universal political theories, and in particular, defend the universal reach of liberal principles. Within this approach, there are a wide variety of reasons for adopting this position. Authors like Brian Barry, for instance, maintain liberal universalism on the grounds that the issues of cultural diversity ought, for the most part, to be ignored by political theory: our various cultural attachments should be seen as no more than personal tastes. Others, however, like Simon Caney, are not dismissive of the political claims made on behalf of cultural minorities. They argue that though such claims need to be taken seriously, they do not require us to abandon a commitment to universal political theory: they can be accommodated within a universalist liberalism. In his contribution to this volume, Caney lays out a central reason for adopting a liberal universalist approach: that any less robust defense of rights is incoherent. He focuses his attention on those who have recently defended liberalism at home, but thought that those arguments weakened in the face of cultural diversity among states. He argues that once we recognize the deeply interrelated nature of various basic human rights with more robust liberal ones, we cannot coherently affirm only the minimal set of human rights. Thus, any commitment to minimal rights, along with a concern for the overall coherence of our views, requires the adoption of an egalitarian liberal universalism.

Contextualists argue that the variety of claims of culturally diverse communities require that we abandon to some degree the bold claims of liberal universalism. Just what role context should play in political theorizing, and at what point that role signals a departure from universal theorizing to a new style of political theory that might be called contextualism is the subject of Jacob Levy's "Contextualism, constitutionalism, and *modus vivendi* approaches." Levy attempts to disentangle a variety of uses of context in recent work on multiculturalism, to as it were apply the methods of contextualism to contextualism itself. The key distinction Levy draws is between roughly universalist theory that uses an attention to specific context to illustrate, test, or possibly revise universal claims and genuinely contextualist theorizing that allows the context to generate and determine the theoretical conclusions, conclusions that of necessity will be more modest than those that arise from universalist approaches. Within the contextualist camp, Levy argues for a kind of modesty: one that recognizes some role for universal claims but that nevertheless takes there to be a great deal of room left open for questions such as those of institutional design, permissible but not mandatory schemes of rights, duties, and distributions, and forms of accommodation whose justification begins with an acknowledgment by all of a fact of diversity without an acceptance of that fact as itself desirable. Within these bounds, Levy argues, there is plenty of important work to be done where consideration of specific context should lead the way. One can thus be a contextualist on this ground without succumbing to relativism, a more extreme form of contextualism that Levy suggests cannot help us sort out issues arising from cultural diversity.

Both universalists and contextualists take up what Anthony Laden characterizes as a theoretical approach, one that sees questions of cultural diversity as theoretical problems to be solved. Laden contrasts this theoretical approach with a political approach, that analyzes these questions in terms of the political claims they generate and how we, as citizens rather than theorists, ought to respond to these claims. In his "Negotiation, deliberation, and the claims of politics," Laden argues that the approach we take (whether theoretical or political) will to a large degree shape the view we take of questions of cultural diversity, and the framework within which we analyze them. He argues that a theoretical approach leads to the analysis of debates among culturally distinct groups in terms of what he calls the logic of negotiation, whereas a political approach allows us to see these same debates as potentially taking up what he calls the logic of deliberation. He argues that approaching the demands of cultural groups as moves in deliberation rather than negotiation offers us a broader set of accommodating responses, and allows us to be more sensitive to a number of factors often obscured by the logic of negotiation, including the specific context in which a claim is made, and the relations of power among those by and to whom the claims are made.

Part III focuses on four topics that have become pivotal to contemporary debates on multiculturalism: the question of whether multiculturalism is dependent on an objectionable essentialist view of culture; the problem of protection for "internal minorities," that is, minorities within minorities; the relationship of redistribution and recognition; and the nature and limits of toleration in contexts of cultural diversity.

Multiculturalists are often accused of peddling an "essentialist" view of culture, sometimes even when they explicitly repudiate such a view. The debate that is generated can descend into a slanging match: multiculturalists accuse critics of failing to read their work with due scholarly care; their critics respond that multiculturalist arguments must rest upon an essentialist conception of culture whatever view of culture is officially espoused. Progress can be made here only if we become clearer about precisely what it means to hold an essentialist view of culture, why essentialism about culture is bad (if indeed it is), and how essentialist assumptions are supposed to figure in the arguments of multiculturalists. To address these issues, Andrew Mason considers three of the main interpretations of what it means to say that a conception of culture is essentialist. First, a conception of culture is essentialist if it assumes that when a group shares a culture, they do so in virtue of sharing characteristics which make it the particular culture it is. Second, a conception of culture is essentialist if it supposes that cultures are separate, closed, and internally uniform. Third, a conception of culture is essentialist if it assumes that cultures can be authentic and inauthentic, or change in authentic and inauthentic directions. Mason argues that these views are genuinely distinct, and that each is problematic – except for a version of the first one which maintains that a group shares a culture in virtue of sharing a way of life that makes it the particular culture it is. He maintains that if this idea is essentialist, then it is an unobjectionable form of essentialism. Mason then examines a number of the most influential multicultural arguments in order to see whether they must rely upon essentialist assumptions. In particular, he addresses arguments for group representation; arguments based upon the idea that recognition of cultural identities is a human need; arguments that appeal to the way in which the flourishing of members of cultural groups depends upon the prosperity of those groups; and arguments for providing exemptions from laws and policies on cultural grounds. He concludes that although some versions of these arguments may employ essentialist assumptions, none of them need do so.

If multicultural policies are to be implemented, then an immediate issue of concern will be the duties of a liberal state towards minorities within those minorities who enjoy forms of multicultural recognition or accommodation. Daniel Weinstock argues that taking this topic seriously raises difficult questions for the attempt to reconcile liberalism's commitment to individual rights with the granting of cultural autonomy. He draws attention to two key issues in this debate. First, to adopt Kymlicka's strategy of appealing to an analytical distinction between rights that secure external protections and rights that allow internal restrictions fails to sufficiently register the problem that this distinction is often hard to sustain in practice; most measures taken will turn out to have both internal and external dimensions. Second, to adopt the alternative stance of focusing on a right of exit raises a central dilemma: either they are characterized by an empty formalism that does not adequately ground the claim that non-exit is equivalent to consent or they require large-scale intervention by the liberal state to ensure that the substantive conditions needed for the autonomous exercise of the right of exit are in place. Having indicated these problems with the orthodox approaches to the topic of the rights of minorities-within-minorities, Weinstock offers a proposal for recasting of the terms of the debate by jettisoning two assumptions central to the debate thus far: the *independence* assumption which claims that people's cultural identities are formed largely independent of the social and political structures they inhabit and the *completeness* assumption which claims that individuals' identities are completely shaped by their membership of a cultural group. Undermining the sociological basis of these claims leads Weinstock to propose that the experience of individualism is common to members of modern political societies in that their identities are to be seen as achievements formed from their membership of diverse groups and plural forms of engagement with social and political life. The significance of this shift in the understanding of the terrain of the debate is that, first, it suggests that those costs of exit which the state can effect may be lower than the literature tends to assume and, second, it allows various restrictive interpretations of cultural traditions to be seen as choices made by (some of) the members of a community rather than as matters of fate and, hence, allows states to widen the policy options for acting beyond the focus on toleration and rights of exit to a broader concern with the incentives guiding the dominance of more restrictive or more liberal readings of cultural traditions.

A concern that has accompanied the development of multiculturalism in both theory and practice is the worry that it may, in various ways, weaken the liberal egalitarian project of redistributive or social justice. David Owen and James Tully address this issue by surveying what they term, following Laden, theoretical and political approaches and, in the course of this discussion, arguing for the priority of the political approach. They focus first on the debate within luck-egalitarianism concerning whether cultural identity – or the preferences and commitments shaped by that identity – is appropriately conceived as an expensive taste and, if so, what implications follow for the relation of recognition and redistribution. In the second section of their chapter, they set out reasons for moving from a theoretical to a political approach. Arguing that the theoretical approach is marked by two orienting presumptions: monologicity and finality, they argue that both presumptions should be rejected in favor of a dialogical orientation such that we move from theoretical abstraction towards an engagement with actual political "multilogues" of recognition, and a processual orientation that takes reasonable disagreement to be a permanent and essential feature of democratic and political life. They then proceed to develop this political approach in terms of a commitment to dialogical or civic freedom that is spelt out in terms of the idea that conditions of reasonable political deliberation should be such not only that all citizens have an equal opportunity to advance public reasons concerning the character of their civic relationship to one another, and to their trusted and accountable representatives all the way up or down, but also that the reasonable acceptance or rejection of a claim expressed as a public reason makes a difference to the course of the deliberation through which we shape and reshape the content of our shared identity as citizens.

The topic of toleration is at the forefront of political concerns with cultural and religious diversity, yet, as Rainer Forst demonstrates, contemporary debates concerning the nature and limits of toleration in relation to such diversity draw on two very different conceptions of toleration: the *permission* conception and the *respect* conception. The former presents toleration as a permit to difference granted by a majority to a minority on condition that the minority acknowledge their dependent position; the latter, by contrast, is one in which the tolerating parties adopt a stance of reciprocal recognition, respecting each other as moral and political equals. Developing an account of the respect conception from Bayle and Kant, Forst argues for an account of toleration grounded in the moral idea of the person as a reasonable being with a *right to justification* based on the recursive principle that any morally salient interference with the actions of a person needs to be justified in terms that can be accepted by the person concerned if it is to be legitimate. Forst then applies this view to a number of controversial multicultural cases before linking it to the development of a critical theory of toleration.

Part IV takes up the recent emergence of perspectives on the issues raised by the culturally diverse character of democratic constitutional states that build on, or move away from, the relatively well-established positions within these debates to pose different questions. This section offers three significant examples of such heterodox interventions.

In "Law's necessary forcefulness," Danielle Allen attends to the problem of the variable distribution of harms and benefits throughout a citizenry by addressing the debate between Ralph Ellison and Hannah Arendt over how to reflect on the "Battle of Little Rock." Central to Allen's argument is Ellison's account of democratic *sacrifice*, that is, the requirement that those who suffer loss in the context of particular political decisions but nonetheless accede to these decisions are acknowledged as having engaged in a form of sacrifice that makes possible stable and enduring forms of collective political action, where such acknowledgment underwrites a normative commitment to the equitable distribution of the diverse negative effects of collective political action over time. In contrast to Arendt, whose sharp distinction between social and political action led her to argue that the events of Little Rock betrayed a struggle for social advancement by the black community in which they were abusively prepared to demand that their children be heroes, Ellison saw the demands made on the children as a form of, and an initiation into a life of, democratic sacrifice that links social and political realms. Through a close analysis of the events of Little Rock and the contrasting political perspectives of Arendt and Ellison, Allen provides an illuminating perspective on issues of social and political invisibility, citizens' interaction with law, the necessary costs of democratic disagreement in pluralistic societies, and the fair distribution of civic burdensomeness, that is, the burdens assumed through maintaining attachment to one's civic identity and its demands. In using Ellison's concept of sacrifice to articulate a way of addressing the question of what may be asked of whom, Allen attends to, and provides an original way of reflecting on, one of the most central issues raised by multiculturalism.

Like Danielle Allen, Bert van den Brink focuses on issues of pluralism and diversity through attention to a concrete exemplification of the stakes of debates over such issues. His chapter "Imagining civic relations in the moment of their breakdown" begins by reflecting on the crisis of civic identity generated in the Netherlands in the aftermath of the murder of the Dutch film director and columnist Theo van Gogh by a young Dutch-Moroccan, Mohammed Bouyeri. Van den Brink draws attention to, and focuses critical scrutiny on, the plurality of ways in which this crisis was described and evaluated by politicians, public intellectuals, and media commentators, and what these constructions disclose of the dominant patterns of expectation and evaluation with regard to citizenship in culturally diverse Dutch society. In adopting this strategy, van den Brink is able disclose the *informal* politics of citizenship in Dutch society as organized in terms of a commitment to unity and substantive consensus on cultural norms and values as prerequisites of a well-ordered political society, and to reveal the role played by this informal politics of citizenship in the generation of the crisis of civic identity. Reconceptualizing this crisis as one of *civic integrity* rather than *civic identity*, van den Brink draws attention to (1) the centrality of both disagreement and the need for agreement to democratic politics (Waldron's "circumstances of politics") and (2) the unequal distribution of effective power in democratic political societies. He does so in order to argue for the importance of the practical acknowledgment of the normative status of the marginalized and the dissident as free and equal democratic citizens, such an acknowledgment grounding a commitment to the accountability of agents of power not only in formal public legal contexts *but also* in the informal politics of social life. He goes on to outline the demands of civic integrity in terms of the requirements appropriate to meet the need for accountability in the informal politics of social life.

Both Allen and van den Brink draw attention to the role of political rhetorics in relation to the reflection on citizenship and this dimension is further developed in Bonnie Honig's analysis of the literature on American exceptionalism in the context of the myth of immigrant America. Honig addresses the work that this myth performs across the political spectrum in depicting the foreigner as "a supplement to the nation, an agent of national re-enchantment that might rescue the regime from corruption and return it to its first principles." She identifies four variants on this argument:

1. In the capitalist version of the myth, it is the figure of the hard-working immigrant success story – the immigrant who arrives with nothing but achieves material affluence through their manifestation of the capitalist virtues – that reassures citizens that anyone can make it, that the American dream remains a viable notion.
2. In the communitarian version of the myth, it is the figure of the immigrant as exemplifying the virtues of family and community that guides the citizen back to these core values where they have lapsed under the pressures of capitalism and liberal individualism.
3. In the familial version of the myth, it is the figure of the immigrant as defender of the patriarchal family who exemplifies and orients citizens to their appropriate sexual and gender roles.
4. In the liberal version of the myth, it is the immigrant as explicit agent of consent who in choosing America manifests to its citizens the choice-worthy character of America and reminds them through ceremonies of naturalization of the legitimacy and universality of America's liberal-democratic principles.

In each of these versions of the myth, the foreigner as new citizen is valorized as a re-enchanting supplement but, as Honig persuasively shows, this xenophilia is doubled by (and, in a certain respect, produces) a xenophobia in which foreigner-citizens are figured as crass materialists, as cultural aliens who reject American values, as instrumental manipulators, and as welfare scroungers. In other words, in all variants of the myth, the (xenophiliac) picture of the (good) immigrant as giving to America is doubled by a (xenophobic) picture of the (bad) immigrant as taking from America – and the same person or group may be presented as simultanously good and bad in different versions and uses of the myth. In opposition to these oscillating narratives, Honig proposes a democratic cosmopolitan version of this myth which valorizes the immigrant as democratic taker, as one who does not possess rights but takes them by acting as if they possessed rights – this is one who gives by taking. Honig's strategy thus draws attention to the need for political theorists to engage the role played by the civic imaginary in political life.

The last twenty years have been a remarkably fertile and fruitful period for political theory and this volume attempts to reflect on, and exhibit, some portion of that fertility in order to orient and encourage the future development of both the style and substance of political theory in its engagement with cultural diversity. In elaborating various accounts of how we got here, where we are now, and where and how we might move on from here, the half-step back from current debates taken by this volume aims to support the development (if not resolution) of these debates. It is, after all, not least in our ongoing arguments concerning who and what we are as citizens, that the relationships between our diverse ethical, political, and cultural identities are woven into the tapestry of civic life.

Part I

Trajectories

1   The new debate on minority rights (and postscript)

Will Kymlicka

The last ten years have seen a remarkable upsurge in interest amongst political philosophers in the rights of ethnocultural groups within Western democracies.[1] My aim in this paper is to give a condensed overview of the philosophical debate so far, and to suggest some future directions that it might take.

As political philosophers, our interest is in the normative issues raised by such minority rights. What are the moral arguments for or against such rights? In particular, how do they relate to the underlying principles of liberal democracy, such as individual freedom, social equality, and democracy? The philosophical debate on these questions has changed dramatically, both in its scope and in its basic terminology. When I started working on these issues in the mid-1980s, there were very few other political philosophers or political theorists working in the area.[2] Indeed, for most of the twentieth century, issues of ethnicity were seen as marginal by political philosophers. (Much the same can be said about many other academic disciplines, from sociology to geography to history.)

Today, however, after decades of relative neglect, the question of minority rights has moved to the forefront of political theory. There are

---

[1] I use the term "rights of ethnocultural minorities" (or, for brevity's sake, "minority rights") in a loose way, to refer to a wide range of public policies, legal rights, and exemptions, and constitutional provisions from multiculturalism policies to language rights to constitutional protections of Aboriginal treaties. This is a heterogeneous category, but these measures have two important features in common: (a) they go beyond the familiar set of common civil and political rights of individual citizenship which are protected in all liberal democracies; (b) they are adopted with the intention of recognizing and accommodating the distinctive identities and needs of ethnocultural groups. For a helpful typology, see Jacob Levy, "Classifying Cultural Rights," in *Ethnicity and Group Rights*, ed. I. Shapiro and W. Kymlicka (New York: New York University Press, 1997), pp. 22–66.

[2] The most important of whom was Vernon Van Dyke, who published a handful of essays on this topic in the 1970s and early 1980s. There were also a few legal theorists who discussed the role of minority rights in international law, and their connection to human rights principles of non-discrimination.

several reasons for this. Most obviously, the collapse of communism unleashed a wave of ethnic nationalisms in Eastern Europe that dramatically affected the democratization process. Optimistic assumptions that liberal democracy would emerge smoothly from the ashes of communism were derailed by issues of ethnicity and nationalism. But there were many factors within long-established democracies which also pointed to the salience of ethnicity: the nativist backlash against immigrants and refugees in many Western countries; the resurgence and political mobilization of indigenous peoples, resulting in the draft declaration of the rights of indigenous peoples at the United Nations; and the ongoing, even growing, threat of secession within several Western democracies, from Canada (Quebec) to Britain (Scotland), Belgium (Flanders), and Spain (Catalonia).

All of these factors, which came to a head at the beginning of the 1990s, made it clear that Western democracies had not resolved or overcome the tensions raised by ethnocultural diversity. It is not surprising, therefore, that political theorists have increasingly turned their attention to this topic. For example, the last few years have witnessed the first philosophical books in English on the normative issues involved in secession, nationalism, immigration, group representation, multiculturalism, and indigenous rights.[3]

---

[3] Rainer Bauböck, *Transnational Citizenship* (Aldershot: Edward Elgar, 1994); Allen Buchanan, *Secession* (Boulder: Westview Press, 1991); Margaret Canovan, *Nationhood and Political Theory* (Cheltenham: Edward Elgar, 1996); Will Kymlicka, *Multicultural Citizenship* (Oxford: Oxford University Press, 1995); David Miller, *On Nationality* (Oxford: Oxford University Press, 1995); Anne Phillips, *The Politics of Presence* (Oxford: Oxford University Press, 1995); Jeff Spinner, *The Boundaries of Citizenship* (Baltimore: Johns Hopkins University Press, 1994); Yael Tamir, *Liberal Nationalism* (Princeton: Princeton University Press, 1993); Charles Taylor, "The Politics of Recognition," in *Multiculturalism and the Politics of Recognition*, ed. A. Gutmann (Princeton: Princeton University Press, 1992); James Tully, *Strange Multiplicity* (Cambridge: Cambridge University Press, 1995); Michael Walzer, *On Toleration* (New Haven: Yale University Press, 1997); Iris Young, *Justice and the Politics of Difference* (Princeton: Princeton University Press, 1990). I am not aware of full-length books written by philosophers in English on any of these topics pre-dating 1990, with the exception of John Plamenatz, *On Alien Rule and Self-Government* (Harlous: Longman, 1960). There have also been many edited collections of philosophical articles on these issues: Judith Baker (ed.), *On Group Rights* (Toronto: University of Toronto Press, 1994); Will Kymlicka (ed.), *The Rights of Minority Cultures* (Oxford: Oxford University Press, 1995); Percy Lehning (ed.), *Theories of Secession* (London: Routledge, 1998); Jocelyne Couture *et al.* (eds.), *Rethinking Nationalism* (Calgary: University of Calgary Press, 1989); Shapiro and Kymlicka (eds.), *Ethnicity and Group Rights*; Warren Schwartz (ed.), *Justice in Immigration* (Cambridge: Cambridge University Press, 1995); Juha Räikkä (ed.), *Do We Need Minority Rights?* (Dordrecht: Kluwer, 1996). For a comprehensive bibliography, see Will Kymlicka and Wayne Norman (eds.), *Citizenship in Diverse Societies* (Oxford: Oxford University Press, 2000).

But the debate has not only grown in size. The very terms of the debate have also dramatically changed, and this is what I would like to focus on. I will try to distinguish three distinct stages in the debate.

I.   The first stage: minority rights as communitarianism

The first stage was the pre-1989 debate. Those few theorists who discussed the issue in the 1970s and 1980s assumed that the debate over minority rights was essentially equivalent to the debate between "liberals" and "communitarians" (or between "individualists" and "collectivists"). Confronted with an unexplored topic, it was natural that political theorists would look for analogies with other more familiar topics, and the liberal-communitarian debate seemed the most relevant.

The liberal-communitarian debate is an old and venerable one within political philosophy, going back several centuries, albeit in different forms. So I won't try to rehearse the entire debate. But to dramatically over-simplify, the debate essentially revolves around the priority of individual freedom. Liberals insist that individuals should be free to decide on their own conception of the good life, and applaud the liberation of individuals from any ascribed or inherited status. Liberal individualists argue that the individual is morally prior to the community: the community matters only because it contributes to the well-being of the individuals who compose it. If those individuals no longer find it worthwhile to maintain existing cultural practices, then the community has no independent interest in preserving those practices, and no right to prevent individuals from modifying or rejecting them.

Communitarians dispute this conception of the "autonomous individual." They view people as "embedded" in particular social roles and relationships. Such embedded selves do not form and revise their own conception of the good life; instead, they inherit a way of life that defines their good for them. Rather than viewing group practices as the product of individual choices, communitarians view individuals as the product of social practices. Moreover, they often deny that the interests of communities can be reduced to the interests of their individual members. Privileging individual autonomy is therefore seen as destructive of communities. A healthy community maintains a balance between individual choice and protection of the communal way of life, and seeks to limit the extent to which the former can erode the latter.

In this first stage of the debate, the assumption was that one's position on minority rights was dependent on, and derivative of, one's position on the liberal-communitarian debate. If one is a liberal who cherishes individual autonomy, then one will oppose minority rights as an unnecessary and dangerous departure from the proper emphasis on the individual. Communitarians, by contrast, view minority rights as an appropriate way of protecting communities from the eroding effects of individual autonomy, and of affirming the value of community. Ethnocultural minorities in particular are worthy of such protection, partly because they are most at risk, but also because they still have a communal way of life to be protected. Unlike the majority, ethnocultural minorities have not yet succumbed to liberal individualism, and so have maintained a coherent collective way of life.

This debate over the relative priority and reducibility of individuals and groups dominated the early literature on minority rights.[4] Defenders of minority rights agreed that they were inconsistent with liberalism's commitment to moral individualism and individual autonomy, but argued that this just pointed out the inherent flaws of liberalism.

In short, defending minority rights involved endorsing the communitarian critique of liberalism, and viewing minority rights as defending cohesive and communally minded minority groups against the encroachment of liberal individualism.

II.   The second stage: minority rights within a liberal framework

It is increasingly recognized that this is an unhelpful way to conceptualize most minority rights claims in Western democracies. Assumptions about the "striking parallel between the communitarian attack of philosophical liberalism and the notion of [minority] rights" have been increasingly questioned.[5]

---

[4] For representatives of the "individualist" camp, see Jan Narveson "Collective Rights?," *Canadian Journal of Law and Jurisprudence*, 4 (2), 1991, pp. 329–345; Michael Hartney, "Some Confusions Concerning Collective Rights," *Canadian Journal of Law and Jurisprudence*, 4 (2), 1991, pp. 293–314. For the "communitarian" camp, see Ronald Garet, "Community and Existence," *Southern California Law Review*, 56 (5), 1983, pp. 1001–1075; Vernon Van Dyke, "The Individual, the State and Ethnic Communities in Political Theory," *World Politics*, 29 (3), 1977, pp. 343–369; Adeno Addis, "Individualism, Communitarianism and the Rights of Ethnic Minorities," *Notre Dame Law Review*, 67 (3), 1992, pp. 615–676; Darlene Johnston, "Native Rights as Collective Rights," *Canadian Journal of Law and Jurisprudence*, 2 (1), 1989, pp. 19–34; Michael McDonald, "Should Communities Have Rights?," *Canadian Journal of Law and Jurisprudence*, 4 (2), 1991, pp. 217–237; Frances Svensson, "Liberal Democracy and Group Rights," *Political Studies*, 27 (3), 1979, pp. 421–439; Dimitrios Karmis, "Cultures autochtones et liberalisme au Canada," *Canadian Journal of Political Science*, 26 (1), 1993, pp. 69–96.

[5] Marlies Galenkamp, *Individualism versus Collectivism: The Concept of Collective Rights* (Rotterdam: Rotterdam Filosofische Studies, 1993), pp. 20–25. The belief in such a

In reality, most ethnocultural groups within Western democracies do not want to be protected from the forces of modernity in liberal societies. On the contrary, they want to be full and equal participants in modern liberal societies. This is true of most immigrant groups, which seek inclusion and full participation in the mainstream of liberal-democratic societies, with access to its education, technology, literacy, mass communications, etc. It is equally true of most non-immigrant national minorities, like the Québécois, Flemish, or Catalans.[6] Some of their members may wish to secede from a liberal democracy, but if they do, it is not to create an illiberal communitarian society, but rather to create their own modern liberal-democratic society. The Québécois wish to create a "distinct society," but it is a modern, liberal society – with an urbanized, secular, pluralistic, industrialized, bureaucratized, consumerist mass culture.

Indeed, far from opposing liberal principles, public opinion polls show there are often no statistical differences between national minorities and majorities in their adherence to liberal principles. And immigrants also quickly absorb the basic liberal-democratic consensus, even when they come from countries with little or no experience of liberal democracy.[7] The commitment to individual autonomy is deep and wide in modern societies, crossing ethnic, linguistic, and religious lines.

"striking parallel" is partly the result of a linguistic sleight of hand. Because minority rights are claimed by groups, and tend to be group-specific, they are often described as "collective rights." The fact that the majority seeks only "individual" rights while the minority seeks "collective" rights is then taken as evidence that the minority is somehow more "collectivist" than the majority. This chain of reasoning contains several non-sequiturs. Not all group-specific minority rights are "collective" rights, and even those which are "collective" rights in one or other sense of that term are not necessarily evidence of "collectivism." See Kymlicka, *Multicultural Citizenship*, ch. 3, and "Human Rights and Ethnocultural Justice," in *Politics in the Vernacular* (Oxford: Oxford University Press, 2001), pp. 69–90.

[6] By national minorities, I mean groups that formed complete and functioning societies on their historic homeland prior to being incorporated into a larger state. The incorporation of such national minorities has typically been involuntary, due to colonization, conquest, or the ceding of territory from one imperial power to another, but may also arise voluntarily, as a result of federation. The category of national minorities includes both "stateless nations" (like the Québécois, Puerto Ricans, Catalans, Scots) and "indigenous peoples" (like the Indians, Inuit, Sami, Maori). For the similarities and differences between these two sorts of national minorities, see Kymlicka, "Theorizing Indigenous Rights," in *Politics in the Vernacular*, pp. 120–132.

[7] On Canadian immigrants, see James Frideres, "Edging into the Mainstream," in *Multiculturalism in North America and Europe*, ed. S. Isajiw (Toronto: Canadian Scholars Press, 1997), pp. 537–562; for American immigrants, see John Harles, *Politics in the Lifeboat* (Boulder: Westview Press, 1994). On the convergence in political values between Anglophones and Francophones in Canada, see Kymlicka, "Minority Nationalism and Immigrant Integration," in *Politics in the Vernacular*, pp. 275–289.

There are some important and visible exceptions to this rule. For example, there are a few ethnoreligious sects that voluntarily distance themselves from the larger world – the Hutterites, Amish, Hasidic Jews. And some of the more isolated or traditionalist indigenous communities fit this description as "communitarian" groups. The question of how liberal states should respond to such non-liberal groups is an important one, which I discuss elsewhere.[8]

But the overwhelming majority of debates about minority rights are not debates between a liberal majority and communitarian minorities, but debates amongst liberals about the meaning of liberalism. They are debates between individuals and groups who endorse the basic liberal-democratic consensus, but who disagree about the interpretation of these principles in multiethnic societies – in particular, they disagree about the proper role of language, nationality, and ethnic identities within liberal-democratic societies and institutions. Groups claiming minority rights insist that at least certain forms of public recognition and support for their language, practices, and identities are not only consistent with basic liberal-democratic principles, including the importance of individual autonomy, but may indeed be required by them.

This then has led to the second stage of the debate, in which the question becomes: what is the possible scope for minority rights within liberal theory? Framing the debate this way does not resolve the issues. On the contrary, the place of minority rights within liberal theory remains very controversial. But it changes the terms of the debate. The issue is no longer how to protect communitarian minorities from liberalism, but whether minorities that share basic liberal principles nonetheless need minority rights. If groups are indeed liberal, why do their members want minority rights? Why aren't they satisfied with the traditional common rights of citizenship?

This is the sort of question that Joseph Raz tries to answer in his recent work. Raz insists that the autonomy of individuals – their ability to make good choices amongst good lives – is intimately tied up with access to their culture, with the prosperity and flourishing of their culture, and with the respect accorded their culture by others. Minority rights help ensure this cultural flourishing and mutual respect.[9] Other liberal writers like David Miller, Yael Tamir, Jeff Spinner, and myself

---

[8] See Kymlicka, *Multicultural Citizenship*, ch. 8 and *Finding Our Way* (Oxford: Oxford University Press, 1998), ch. 4.

[9] Joseph Raz, "Multiculturalism: A Liberal Perspective," *Dissent*, Winter 1994, pp. 67–79; "Multiculturalism," *Ratio Juris*, 11 (3), 1998, pp. 193–205; Avishai Margalit and Joseph Raz, "National Self-Determination," *Journal of Philosophy*, 87 (9), 1990, pp. 439–461.

have made similar arguments about the importance of "cultural membership" or "national identity" to modern freedom-seeking citizens.[10] The details of the argument vary, but each of us, in our own way, argues that there are compelling interests related to culture and identity which are fully consistent with liberal principles of freedom and equality, and which justify granting special rights to minorities. We can call this the "liberal-culturalist" position.

Critics of liberal culturalism have raised many objections to this entire line of argument. Some deny that we can intelligibly distinguish or individuate "cultures" or "cultural groups"; others deny that we can make sense of the claim that individuals are "members" of cultures; yet others say that even if we can make sense of the claim that individuals are members of distinct cultures, we have no reason to assume that the well-being or freedom of the individual is tied in any way with the flourishing of the culture.[11] These are important objections, but I think they can be answered. In any event, they have not yet succeeded in dampening enthusiasm for liberal culturalism, which has quickly developed into the consensus position amongst liberals working in this field.[12]

However, even those sympathetic to liberal culturalism face an obvious problem. It is clear that some kinds of minority rights would undermine, rather then support, individual autonomy. A crucial task facing liberal defenders of minority rights, therefore, is to distinguish between the "bad" minority rights that involve restricting individual rights, from the "good" minority rights that can be seen as supplementing individual rights.

I have proposed distinguishing two kinds of rights that a minority group might claim. The first involves the right of a group against its own members, designed to protect the group from the destabilizing impact of internal dissent (e.g. the decision of individual members not to follow traditional practices or customs). The second kind involves the right of a group against the larger society, designed to protect the group from the impact of external pressures (e.g. the economic or political decisions of the larger society). I call the first "internal restrictions," and the

[10] Tamir, *Liberal Nationalism*; Miller, *On Nationality*; Spinner, *Boundaries of Citizenship*; Kymlicka, *Liberalism, Community and Culture* (Oxford: Oxford University Press, 1989).
[11] For a pithy statement of these three objections, see Jeremy Waldron, "Minority Cultures and the Cosmopolitan Alternative," in *The Rights of Minority Cultures*, ed. Kymlicka, pp. 93–121.
[12] It's an interesting question why this liberal-culturalist view – which is a clear departure from the dominant liberal view for several decades – has become so popular. I address this in "Liberal Culturalism: An Emerging Consensus?," in *Politics in the Vernacular*, pp. 39–48.

second "external protections." Given the commitment to individual autonomy, I argue that liberals should be skeptical of claims to internal restrictions. Liberal culturalism rejects the idea that groups can legitimately restrict the basic civil or political rights of their own members in the name of preserving the purity or authenticity of the group's culture and traditions. However, a liberal conception of multiculturalism can accord groups various rights against the larger society, in order to reduce the group's vulnerability to the economic or political power of the majority. Such "external protections" are consistent with liberal principles, although they too become illegitimate if, rather than reducing a minority's vulnerability to the power of the larger society, they instead enable a minority to exercise economic or political dominance over some other group. To over-simplify, we can say that minority rights are consistent with liberal culturalism if (a) they protect the freedom of individuals within the group; and (b) they promote relations of equality (non-dominance) between groups.[13] Other liberal culturalists, however, argue that some forms of internal restrictions can be accepted, so long as group members have an effective right of exit from the group.[14]

In the second stage of the debate, therefore, the question of minority rights is reformulated as a question within liberal theory, and the aim is to show that some (but not all) minority rights claims enhance liberal values. In my opinion, this second stage reflects genuine progress. We now have a more accurate description of the claims being made by ethnocultural groups, and a more accurate understanding of the normative issues they raise. We have gotten beyond the sterile and misleading debate about individualism and collectivism.

However, I think this second stage also needs to be challenged. While it has a better understanding of the nature of most ethnocultural groups, and the demands they place on the liberal state, it misinterprets the nature of the liberal state, and the demands it places on minorities.

---

[13] See Kymlicka, *Multicultural Citizenship*, ch. 3. I also argue that most of the minority rights sought by ethnocultural groups within Western democracies fall into the external protection category.

[14] This is likely to be the view of those who endorse a "political" conception of liberalism, rooted in the value of tolerance, rather than a "comprehensive" conception, rooted in the value of autonomy. See, for example, William Galston, "Two Concepts of Liberalism," *Ethics*, 105 (3), 1995, pp. 516–534; Chandran Kukathas, "Cultural Toleration," in *Ethnicity and Group Rights*, ed. Shapiro and Kymlicka, pp. 69–104. I discuss the differences between these approaches in Kymlicka, *Multicultural Citizenship*, ch. 8. For a discussion of the complications in determining what constitutes an "effective" right of exit, see Susan Okin, "Mistresses of their Own Destiny? Group Rights, Gender and Realistic Rights of Exit," paper presented to APSA, September 1998.

III. The third stage: minority rights as a response to nation-building

Let me explain. The assumption – generally shared by both defenders and critics of minority rights – is that the liberal state, in its normal operation, abides by a principle of ethnocultural neutrality. That is, the state is "neutral" with respect to the ethnocultural identities of its citizens, and indifferent to the ability of ethnocultural groups to reproduce themselves over time. On this view, liberal states treat culture in the same way as religion – i.e., as something which people should be free to pursue in their private life, but which is not the concern of the state (so long as they respect the rights of others). Just as liberalism precludes the establishment of an official religion, so too there cannot be official cultures that have preferred status over other possible cultural allegiances.

For example, Michael Walzer argues that liberalism involves a "sharp divorce of state and ethnicity." The liberal state stands above all the various ethnic and national groups in the country, "refusing to endorse or support their ways of life or to take an active interest in their social reproduction." Instead, the state is "neutral with reference to language, history, literature, calendar" of these groups. He says the clearest example of such a neutral liberal state is the United States, whose ethnocultural neutrality is reflected in the fact that it has no constitutionally recognized official language.[15] For immigrants to become Americans, therefore, is simply a matter of affirming their allegiance to the principles of democracy and individual freedom defined in the US Constitution.

Indeed, some theorists argue that this is precisely what distinguishes liberal "civic nations" from illiberal "ethnic nations."[16] Ethnic nations take the reproduction of a particular ethnonational culture and identity as one of their most important goals. Civic nations, by contrast, are "neutral" with respect to the ethnocultural identities of their citizens, and define national membership purely in terms of adherence to certain principles of democracy and justice. For minorities to seek special rights, on this view, is a radical departure from the traditional operation of the liberal state. Therefore, the burden of proof lies on anyone who would wish to endorse such minority rights.

This is the burden of proof which liberal culturalists try to meet with their account of the role of cultural membership in securing freedom

---

[15] Michael Walzer, "Comment," in *Multiculturalism*, ed. Gutman, pp. 100–110. See also Michael Walzer, *What it Means to be an American* (New York: Marsilio, 1992), p. 9.

[16] William Pfaff, *The Wrath of Nations* (New York: Simon and Schuster, 1993), p. 162; Michael Ignatieff, *Blood and Belonging* (New York: Farrar, Straus & Giroux, 1993).

and self-respect. They try to show that minority rights supplement, rather than diminish, individual freedom and equality, and help to meet needs which would otherwise go unmet in a state that clung rigidly to ethnocultural neutrality.

The presumption in the second stage of the debate, therefore, has been that advocates of minority rights must demonstrate compelling reasons to depart from the norm of ethnocultural neutrality. I would argue, however, that this idea that liberal-democratic states (or "civic nations") are ethnoculturally neutral is manifestly false. The religion model is altogether misleading as an account of the relationship between the liberal-democratic state and ethnocultural groups.

Consider the actual policies of the United States, which is the pro-totypically "neutral" state. Historically, decisions about the boundaries of state governments, and the timing of their admission into the fed-eration, were deliberately made to ensure that Anglophones would be a majority within each of the fifty states of the American federation. This helped establish the dominance of English throughout the territory of the United States.[17] And the continuing dominance of English is ensured by several ongoing policies. For example, it is a legal require-ment for children to learn the English language in schools; it is a legal requirement for immigrants (under the age of fifty) to learn English to acquire American citizenship; and it is a de facto requirement for employment in or for government that the applicant speak English.

These decisions are not isolated exceptions to some norm of ethno-cultural neutrality. On the contrary, they are tightly interrelated, and together they have shaped the very structure of the American state, and the way the state structures society. (Since governments account for 40–50 percent of GNP in most countries, the language of government is not negligible.)

These policies have all been pursued with the intention of promoting integration into what I call a "societal culture." By a societal culture, I mean a territorially concentrated culture, centered on a shared language which is used in a wide range of societal institutions, in both public and private life (schools, media, law, economy, government, etc.). I call it a societal culture to emphasize that it involves a common language and social institutions, rather than common religious beliefs, family customs, or personal lifestyles. Societal cultures within a modern liberal democ-racy are inevitably pluralistic, containing Christians as well as Muslims, Jews, and atheists; heterosexuals as well as gays; urban professionals as

---

[17] See Will Kymlicka, "Minority Nationalism and Multination Federalism," in *Politics in the Vernacular*, pp. 91–119.

well as rural farmers; conservatives as well as socialists. Such diversity is the inevitable result of the rights and freedoms guaranteed to liberal citizens, particularly when combined with an ethnically diverse population. This diversity, however, is balanced and constrained by linguistic and institutional cohesion; cohesion that has not emerged on its own, but rather is the result of deliberate state policies.

The American government has deliberately created such a societal culture, and promoted the integration of citizens into it. The government has encouraged citizens to view their life-chances as tied up with participation in common societal institutions that operate in the English language, and has nurtured a national identity defined in part by common membership in a societal culture. Nor is the United States unique in this respect. Promoting integration into a societal culture is part of a "nation-building" project that all liberal democracies have adopted.

Obviously, the sense in which English-speaking Americans share a common "culture" is a very thin one, since it does not preclude differences in religion, personal values, family relationships, or lifestyle choices.[18] While thin, it is far from trivial. On the contrary, as I discuss below, attempts to integrate people into such a common societal culture have often been met with serious resistance. Although integration in this sense leaves a great deal of room for both the public and private expression of individual and collective differences, some groups have nonetheless vehemently rejected the idea that they should view their life-chances as tied up with the societal institutions conducted in the majority's language.

So we need to replace the idea of an "ethnoculturally neutral" state with a new model of a liberal-democratic state – what I call the "nation-building" model. To say that states are nation-building is not to say that governments can only promote one societal culture. It is possible for government policies to encourage the sustaining of two or more societal cultures within a single country – indeed, as I discuss below, this is precisely what characterizes multination states like Canada, Switzerland, Belgium, or Spain.

However, historically, virtually all liberal democracies have, at one point or another, attempted to diffuse a single societal culture throughout

---

[18] Indeed, my use of the term "societal culture" is in conflict with the way the term "culture" is used in most academic disciplines, where it is defined in a very thick, ethnographic sense, referring to the sharing of specific folk-customs, habits, and rituals. Citizens of a modern liberal state do not share a common culture in such a thick, ethnographic sense – indeed, the lack of a common thick ethnographic culture is part of the very definition of a liberal society. But it is equally essential to modern liberal forms of governance that citizens share a common culture in a very different, and thinner, sense, focusing on a common language and societal institutions.

all of their territory.[19] Nor should this be seen purely as a matter of cultural imperialism or ethnocentric prejudice. This sort of nation-building serves a number of important goals. For example, standardized public education in a common language has often been seen as essential if all citizens are to have equal opportunity to work in this modern economy. Indeed, equal opportunity is defined precisely in terms of equal access to mainstream institutions operating in the dominant language. Also, participation in a common societal culture has often been seen as essential for generating the sort of solidarity required by a welfare state, since it promotes a sense of common identity and membership. Moreover, a common language has been seen as essential to democracy – how can "the people" govern together if they cannot understand one another? In short, promoting integration into a common societal culture has been seen as essential to social equality and political cohesion in modern states.[20]

So states have engaged in this process of "nation-building" – that is, a process of promoting a common language, and a sense of common membership in, and equal access to, the social institutions based on that language. Decisions regarding official languages, core curricula in education, and the requirements for acquiring citizenship, all have been made with the intention of diffusing a particular culture throughout society, and of promoting a particular national identity based on participation in that societal culture.

If I am right that this nation-building model provides a more accurate account of modern liberal-democratic states, how does this affect the

[19] For the ubiquity of the process, see Ernest Gellner, *Nations and Nationalism* (Oxford: Blackwell, 1983); Benedict Anderson, *Imagined Communities* (London: New Left Books, 1983). To my knowledge, Switzerland is the only exception: it never made any serious attempt to pressure its French and Italian minorities to integrate into the German majority. All of the other Western multination states have at one time or another made a concerted effort to assimilate their minorities, and only reluctantly gave up this ideal.

[20] For defenses of the importance and legitimacy of nation-building within liberal democracies, see Tamir, *Liberal Nationalism* and Miller, *On Nationality*. Of course, this sort of nation-building can also be used to promote illiberal goals. As Margaret Canovan puts it, nationhood is like a "battery" which makes states run – the existence of a common national identity motivates and mobilizes citizens to act for common political goals – and these goals can be liberal or illiberal (Canovan, *Nationhood*, p. 80). Liberal reformers invoke the battery of nationhood to mobilize citizens behind projects of democratization, economic development, and social justice; illiberal authoritarians invoke nationhood to mobilize citizens behind attacks on alleged enemies of the nation, be they foreign countries or internal dissidents. This is why nation-building is just as common in authoritarian regimes as in democracies (e.g., Spain under Franco, or Latin America under the military dictators). Authoritarian regimes also need a "battery" to help achieve public objectives in complex modern societies. What distinguishes liberal from illiberal states is not the presence or absence of nation-building, but rather the ends to which nation-building is put, and the means used to achieve them.

issue of minority rights? I believe it gives us a very different perspective on the debate. The question is no longer how to justify departure from a norm of neutrality, but rather do majority efforts at nation-building create injustices for minorities? And do minority rights help protect against these injustices?

This would be the third stage in the debate, which I am trying to explore in my own recent work. I cannot discuss all of its implications, but let me give two examples of how this new model may affect the debate over minority rights.

IV.   Two examples

How does nation-building affect minorities? As Taylor notes, the process of nation-building inescapably privileges members of the majority culture:

If a modern society has an "official" language, in the fullest sense of the term, that is, a

state-sponsored, -inculcated, and -defined language and culture, in which both economy and state function, then it is obviously an immense advantage to people if this language and culture are theirs. Speakers of other languages are at a distinct disadvantage.[21]

This means that minority cultures face a choice. If all public institutions are being run in another language, minorities face the danger of being marginalized from the major economic, academic, and political institutions of the society. Faced with this dilemma, minorities have (to over-simplify) three basic options:

(i)   they can accept integration into the majority culture, although perhaps attempt to renegotiate the terms of integration;
(ii)   they can seek the sorts of rights and powers of self-government needed to maintain their own societal culture – i.e., to create their own economic, political, and educational institutions in their own language. That is, they can engage in their own form of competing nation-building;
(iii) they can accept permanent marginalization.

We can find some ethnocultural groups that fit each of these categories (and other groups that are caught between them, such as

---

[21] Charles Taylor, "Nationalism and Modernity," in *The Morality of Nationalism*, ed. Jeff McMahan and Robert McKim (Oxford: Oxford University Press, 1997), p. 34.

African-Americans).[22] For example, some immigrant ethnoreligious sects choose permanent marginalization. This would seem to be true, for example, of the Hutterites in Canada, or the Amish in the United States. But the option of accepting marginalization is only likely to be attractive to religious sects whose theology requires them to avoid all contact with the modern world. The Hutterites and Amish are unconcerned about their marginalization from universities or legislatures, since they view such "worldly" institutions as corrupt.

Virtually all other ethnocultural minorities, however, seek to participate in the modern world, and to do so, they must either integrate or seek the self-government needed to create and sustain their own modern institutions. Faced with this choice, ethnocultural groups have responded in different ways.

National minorities: National minorities have typically responded to majority nation-building by fighting to maintain or rebuild their own societal culture, by engaging in their own competing nation-building. Indeed, they often use the same tools that the majority uses to promote this nation-building – e.g., control over the language and curriculum of schooling, the language of government employment, the requirements of immigration and naturalization, and the drawing of internal boundaries. We can see this clearly in the case of Québécois nationalism, which has largely been concerned with gaining and exercising these nation-building powers. But it is also increasingly true of the Aboriginal peoples in Canada, who have adopted the language of "nationhood," and who are engaged in a major campaign of "nation-building," which requires the exercise of much greater powers of self-government and the building of many new societal institutions.[23]

Intuitively, the adoption of such minority nation-building projects seems fair. If the majority can engage in legitimate nation-building, why not national minorities, particularly those which have been involuntarily incorporated into a larger state? To be sure, liberal principles set limits on how national groups go about nation-building. Liberal principles will preclude any attempts at ethnic cleansing, or stripping people of their citizenship, or the violation of human rights. These principles will also insist that any national group engaged in a project of nation-building must respect the right of other nations within its jurisdiction to protect and build their own national institutions. For example, the Québécois

---

[22] See Will Kymlicka, "A Crossroads in Race Relations," in *Politics in the Vernacular*, pp. 177–199 for a discussion of the complex demands of African-Americans.

[23] On the need (and justification for) Aboriginal "nation-building," see *Report of the Royal Commission on Aboriginal Peoples ii. Restructuring the Relationship*, 1996; Gerald Alfred, *Heeding the Voices of our Ancestors* (Toronto: Oxford University Press, 1995).

are entitled to assert national rights vis-à-vis the rest of Canada, but only if they respect the rights of Aboriginals within Quebec to assert national rights vis-à-vis the rest of Quebec.

These limits are important, but they still leave significant room, I believe, for legitimate forms of minority nationalism. Moreover, these limits are likely to be similar for both majority and minority nations. All else being equal, national minorities should have the same tools of nation-building available to them as the majority nation, subject to the same liberal limitations. What we need, in other words, is a consistent theory of permissible forms of nation-building within liberal democracies. I do not think that political theorists have yet developed such a theory. One of the many unfortunate side-effects of the dominance of the "ethnocultural neutrality" model is that liberal theorists have never explicitly confronted this question.[24]

My aim here is not to promote any particular theory of permissible nation-building,[25] but simply to insist that this is the relevant question we need to address. The question is not "have national minorities given us a compelling reason to abandon the norm of ethnocultural neutrality?," but rather "why should national minorities not have the same powers of nation-building as the majority?" This is the context within which minority nationalism must be evaluated – i.e., as a response to majority nation-building, using the same tools of nation-building. And the burden of proof surely rests on those who would deny national minorities the same powers of nation-building as those which the national majority takes for granted.

Immigrants: Historically, nation-building has been neither desirable nor feasible for immigrant groups. Instead, they have traditionally accepted the expectation that they will integrate into the larger societal culture. Few immigrant groups have objected to the requirement that they must learn an official language as a condition of citizenship, or that

---

[24] As Norman notes, these questions about the morality of nation-building have been ignored even by philosophers working on nationalism. They tend to ask about the morality of nation-states, not about the morality of *nation-building* states. In other words, philosophers of nationalism typically take the existence of nation-states as a given, and ask whether it is a good thing to have a world of nation-states. They do not explore the processes by which such nation-states are created in the first place (i.e., what methods of nation-building are permissible). Wayne Norman, "Theorizing Nationalism (Normatively): The First Steps," in *Theorizing Nationalism*, ed. Ronald Beiner (Albany: SUNY Press, 1999), p. 60.

[25] I made a preliminary attempt to develop criteria for distinguishing liberal from illiberal forms of nation-building in Kymlicka, "Ethnic Relations in Eastern Europe and Western Political Theory," in Will Kymlicka and Magda Opalski (eds.), *Can Liberal Pluralism be Exported? Western Political Theory and Ethnic Relations in Eastern Europe* (Oxford: Oxford University Press, 2001).

their children must learn the official language in school. They have accepted the assumption that their life-chances, and the life-chances of their children, will be bound up with participation in mainstream institutions operating in the majority language.

However, this is not to say that immigrants may not suffer injustices as a result of nation-building policies. After all, the state is clearly not neutral with respect to the language and culture of immigrants: it imposes a range of de jure and de facto requirements for immigrants to integrate in order to succeed. These requirements are often difficult and costly for immigrants to meet. Since immigrants cannot respond to this by adopting their own nation-building programs, but rather must attempt to integrate as best they can, it is only fair that the state minimize the costs involved in this state-demanded integration.

Put another way, immigrants can demand fairer terms of integration. To my mind, this demand has two basic elements: (a) we need to recognize that integration does not occur overnight, but is a difficult and long-term process that operates inter-generationally. This means that special accommodations (e.g., mother-tongue services) are often required for immigrants on a transitional basis; (b) we need to ensure that the common institutions into which immigrants are pressured to integrate provide the same degree of respect, recognition, and accommodation of the identities and practices of immigrants as they traditionally have of the identities and practices of the majority group. This requires a systematic exploration of our social institutions to see whether their rules and symbols disadvantage immigrants. For example, we need to examine dress codes, public holidays, even height and weight restrictions, to see whether they are biased against certain immigrant groups. We also need to examine the portrayal of minorities in school curricula or the media to see if they are stereotypical, or fail to recognize the contributions of immigrants to national history or world culture. These measures are needed to ensure that liberal states are offering immigrants fair terms of integration.

Others may disagree with the fairness of some of these policies. The requirements of fairness are not always obvious, particularly in the context of people who have chosen to enter a country, and political theorists have done little to date to illuminate the issue. My aim here is not to defend a particular theory of fair terms of integration (see chapter 8), but rather to insist that this is the relevant question we need to address. The question is not whether immigrants have given us a compelling reason to diverge from the norm of ethnocultural neutrality, but rather how can we ensure that state policies aimed at pressuring immigrants to integrate are fair.

The focus of this third stage of the debate, therefore, is to show how particular minority rights claims are related to, and a response to, state nation-building policies. And the logical outcome of this stage of the debate will be to develop theories of permissible nation-building and fair terms of immigrant integration.[26]

Of course, this is just a general trend, not a universal law. In some countries, immigrant groups have not been allowed or encouraged to integrate (e.g., Turks in Germany). Even in the United States, the usual tendencies towards immigrant integration have sometimes been deflected, particularly if the newcomers were expected to return quickly to their country of origin (as with the original Cuban exiles in Miami); or if the immigrants were illegal, and so had no right to employment or citizenship (as with illegal Mexican migrants in California). These groups were exempted, or precluded, from the usual state-imposed pressure to integrate.

The extent to which national minorities have been able to maintain a separate societal culture also varies considerably. In some countries, national minorities have been almost completely integrated (e.g., Bretons in France). Even in the United States, the extent (and success) of nationalist mobilization varies. For example, compare the Chicanos in the Southwest with the Puerto Ricans. The Chicanos were unable to preserve their own Spanish-speaking judicial, educational, or political institutions after being involuntarily incorporated into the United States in 1848, and they have not mobilized along nationalist lines to try to recreate these institutions. By contrast, Puerto Ricans mobilized very successfully to defend their Spanish-language institutions and self-government rights when they were involuntarily incorporated into the United States in 1898, and continue to exhibit a strong nationalist consciousness. The extent of nationalist mobilization also differs amongst the various Indian tribes in America. Moreover there are some groups which do not fit any of these categories – most obviously African-Americans – whose unique history has led to a very distinctive, and somewhat ambivalent, form of multiculturalism (see chapter 9 below).

There are many such complicated cases that do not fit neatly into the "ethnoreligious sect," "immigrant," or "national minority" patterns.

---

[26] I have discussed minority nationalism and immigrant multiculturalism in isolation from each other, but we also need to consider their interaction. Since both challenge the traditional model of a culturally homogeneous "nation-state," they are often treated as complementary but separate processes of deconstructing the nation-state. In reality, however, immigration is not only a challenge to traditional models of the nation-state; it is also a challenge to the self-conceptions and political aspirations of those groups which see themselves as distinct and self-governing nations within a larger state. This raises a host of interesting questions about whether minority nationalisms themselves must become more "multicultural." See Kymlicka, "American Multiculturalism in the International Arena," in *Politics in the Vernacular*, pp. 265–274.

I will return to some of these "in-between" cases later on. But we can best understand the complexities and ambiguities of these cases if we first have a clear picture of the more standard cases, since the demands of in-between groups are often a complex hybrid of different (and sometimes contradictory) elements drawn from the more familiar models of ethnoreligious marginalization, immigrant integration, and separatist nationalism.

I believe that we could extend this method to look at other types of ethnocultural groups which do not fit into the category of national minorities or immigrants, such as African-Americans, the Roma, guest-workers in Germany, or Russian settlers in the Baltics. In each case, I think it is possible – and indeed essential – to view their claims to minority rights as a response to perceived injustices that arise out of nation-building policies.[27] Each group's claims can be seen as specifying the injustices that majority nation-building has imposed on them, and as identifying the conditions under which majority nation-building would cease to be unjust.

The major task facing any liberal theory of minority rights is to better understand and articulate these conditions of ethnocultural justice. I expect that filling in these lacunae will form the main agenda for minority rights theorists over the next decade.

V.   A new front in the multiculturalism wars?

So far, I have focused on the significant shifts in the recent minority rights debate. However, there has been an important assumption that is common to all three stages of the debate: namely, that the goal is to assess the justice of minority claims. This focus on justice reflects the fact that opposition to minority rights has traditionally been stated in the language of justice. Critics of minority rights had long argued that justice required state institutions to be "color-blind." To ascribe rights on the basis of membership in ascriptive groups was seen as inherently morally arbitrary and discriminatory, necessarily creating first- and second-class citizens.

The first task confronting any defender of minority rights, therefore, was to try to overcome this presumption, and to show that deviations from difference-blind rules that are adopted in order to accommodate ethnocultural differences are not inherently unjust. As we have seen, this has been done in two main ways: (a) by identifying the many ways

---

[27] I discuss the claims of these other types of groups in Will Kymlicka and Magda Opalski (eds.), *Can Liberal Pluralism Be Exported?* (Oxford: Oxford University Press, 2001).

that mainstream institutions are not neutral, but rather are implicitly or explicitly tilted towards the interests and identities of the majority group. This bias creates a range of burdens, barriers, stigmatizations, and exclusions for members of minority groups which can only or best be remedied by minority rights; and (b) by emphasizing the importance of certain interests which have typically been ignored by liberal theories of justice – e.g., interests in recognition, identity, language, and cultural membership. If these interests are ignored or trivialized by the state, then people will feel harmed – and indeed will be harmed – even if their civil, political, and welfare rights are respected. If state institutions fail to recognize and respect people's culture and identity, the result can be serious damage to people's self-respect and sense of agency.

If we accept either or both of these points, then we can see minority rights not as unfair privileges or invidious forms of discrimination, but as compensation for unfair disadvantages, and so as consistent with, and even required by, justice.

In my view, this debate over justice is drawing to a close. As I noted earlier, much work remains to be done in assessing the justice of particular forms of immigrant multiculturalism or minority nationalism. But in terms of the more general question of whether minority rights are *inherently* unjust, the debate is over, and the defenders of minority rights have won the day. I don't mean that defenders of minority rights have been successful in getting their claims implemented, although there is a clear trend throughout the Western democracies towards the greater recognition of minority rights, both in the form of immigrant multiculturalism and of self-government for national minorities.[28] Rather I mean that defenders of minority rights have successfully redefined the terms of public debate in two profound ways: (a) few thoughtful people continue to think that justice can simply be *defined* in terms of

---

[28] There is also a trend towards codifying minority rights at the international level. It is now widely believed in the West that earlier attempts to suppress, coerce, or exclude minority groups were unjust, as well as unworkable, and that some minimal set of minority rights is needed to ensure ethnocultural justice. Many scholars and NGOs are therefore trying to institutionalize at the international level emerging Western models of minority rights, in the same way that Western liberals after the Second World War were able to secure a Universal Declaration of Human Rights. Such an international charter of minority rights seems unlikely in the foreseeable future. The trend towards greater recognition of minority rights is strong within Western democracies, but in many parts of Asia and Africa minority rights are still anathema. It is interesting to note that whereas minority rights were opposed in the West on the ground that they violated Western individualism, in East Asia they are often opposed on the grounds that they violate Asian communitarianism! See Boagang He, "Can Kymlicka's Liberal Theory of Minority Rights be Applied in East Asia?," in *New Developments in Asian Studies*, ed. Paul van der Velde and Alex McKay (London: Kegan Paul, 1998).

difference-blind rules or institutions. Instead, it is now recognized that difference-blind rules can cause disadvantages for particular groups. Whether justice requires common rules for all, or differential rules for diverse groups, is something to be assessed case-by-case in particular contexts, not assumed in advance; (b) as a result, the burden of proof has shifted. The burden of proof no longer falls solely on defenders of minority rights to show that their proposed reforms would not create injustices; the burden of proof equally falls on defenders of difference-blind institutions to show that the status quo does not create injustices for minority groups.

So the original justice-based grounds for blanket opposition to minority rights have faded. This has not meant that opposition to minority rights has disappeared. But it now takes a new form. Or rather it takes two forms: the first questions the justice of specific multiculturalism policies in particular contexts, focusing on the way particular policies may entail an unjust distribution of the benefits and burdens associated with identity and culture; the second shifts the focus away from justice towards issues of citizenship, focusing not on the justice or injustice of particular policies, but rather on the way that the general trend towards multiculturalism threatens to erode the sorts of civic virtues and citizenship practices which sustain a healthy democracy. I will say a few words about each of these lines of argument.

(a) *Justice in context*: Some critics accept that the justice of multicultural demands must be evaluated on a case-by-case basis, and so focus on the potential injustices of particular multicultural proposals in particular contexts, rather than making global claims about the inherent injustice of group-specific policies. These sorts of context-specific arguments are, I think, essential, and reflect real progress in the debate.

At the level of particular cases, the debate focuses, not on whether multiculturalism is right or wrong in principle, but rather on a range of more practical issues about the distribution of the benefits and burdens of specific policies – e.g., what exactly is the disadvantage which a minority faces within a particular institutional structure? Will the proposed multiculturalism reform actually remedy this disadvantage? Are the costs of a particular multiculturalism policy distributed fairly, or are some individuals or sub-groups inside or outside the group being asked to shoulder an unfair share of the costs?[29] Are there alternative

---

[29] As Shachar notes, there is a tendency within some schemes of minority rights for women to bear disproportionate costs of minority protection. She calls this the "paradox of multicultural vulnerability": i.e., some schemes for reducing the minority's vulnerability to the majority may increase minority women's vulnerability to discrimination within their own community. See Ayelet Shachar, "The Paradox of

policies which would remedy the disadvantage in a more effective and less costly way?

A good example of this sort of debate is the recent work on affirmative action in America. Whereas older debates focused almost entirely on whether race-based preferences in admissions or hiring were morally wrong in principle, there is increasing recognition that this is too simple. It is widely accepted that African-Americans and other minorities face real disadvantages in certain institutional contexts, despite the professed color-blind nature of these institutions, and that something needs to be done to remedy these disadvantages. The objection to affirmative action, therefore, is not that any deviation from color-blind rules is unjust in principle, but rather that current affirmative action policies do not actually benefit the people who are most in need (i.e., they help middle-class blacks, but not the inner-city poor), that the costs of affirmative action are borne disproportionately by one group (i.e., young white males, some of whom may themselves be disadvantaged), and that there are alternative policies which would be more effective (i.e., improved funding for inner-city schools). Others respond that affirmative action has been demonstrably successful, and that no alternative policy has been nearly as effective.[30]

This new debate on affirmative action in the US remains unresolved, to say the least, but at least it is the right *kind* of debate. It focuses, not on slogans about a color-blind constitution, but on how particular educational or employment institutions do or do not disadvantage the members of particular groups, and on how proposed group-specific policies would or would not remedy that problem. And while the result of the debate may be to trim or amend existing affirmative action programs, it is unlikely that the result will be to eliminate all forms of race-conscious policies. On the contrary, it may well be that the alternatives which replace or supplement affirmative action will be equally group-specific in their focus – e.g., support for black colleges, or state-sponsored mentoring programs for promising black students. That is,

Multicultural Vulnerability," in *Multicultural Questions*, ed. Christian Joppke and Steven Lukes (Oxford: Oxford University Press, 1999), pp. 87–111. But, unlike Okin, she doesn't view this as inherent to the very idea of minority rights, or as a blanket objection to the idea of minority rights, but rather as a crucial factor that needs to be kept in mind when examining the justice in context of particular policies. See Susan Okin, 'Is Multiculturalism Bad for Women?," in *Is Multiculturalism Bad for Women?*, ed. Joshua Cohen *et al.* (Princeton: Princeton University Press, 1999).

[30] Any plausible examination of this issue will show, I think, that affirmative action has worked well in some contexts, and less well in others. For an example of where it has been strikingly successful (the army), see Charles Moskos and John Sibley Butler, *All That We Can Be* (New York: Basic Books, 1996).

one form of multiculturalism policy will be replaced, or amended, or supplemented, with another form of multiculturalism policy (see chapter 9).

Indeed, we can generalize this point. Since mainstream institutions privilege the majority's culture and identity is so many ways, and since people's interests in culture and identity are so important, the question we face is not whether to adopt multiculturalism, but rather which kind of multiculturalism to adopt. Once we jettison the idea that group-specific rights are wrong in principle, and instead get down to brass-tacks and examine particular institutions, then the question becomes which sort of multiculturalism is most fair and effective, and how best to combine group-specific multiculturalism policies with difference-blind common rights. It is in this sense, as Nathan Glazer put it recently, that "we are all multiculturalists now," even though we profoundly disagree over the merits of particular multiculturalism policies.

(b) *Eroding citizenship*: Other commentators, however, still wish to make a more broad-ranging critique of minority rights and multiculturalism. Since it is no longer plausible to argue that all forms of multiculturalism are inherently unjust, critics have had to find another basis on which to condemn the very notion of minority rights. And the most common argument is one that focuses on stability rather than justice. Critics focus not on the justice or injustice of particular policies, but rather on the way that the general trend towards minority rights threatens to erode the sorts of civic virtues, identities, and practices that sustain a healthy democracy.

This focus on civic virtue and political stability represents the opening of a second front in the "multiculturalism wars." Many critics claim that minority rights are misguided, not because they are unjust in themselves, but because they are corrosive of long-term political unity and social stability. Why are they seen as destabilizing? The underlying worry is that minority rights involve the "politicization of ethnicity," and that any measures which heighten the salience of ethnicity in public life are divisive. Over time they create a spiral of competition, mistrust, and antagonism between ethnic groups. Policies that increase the salience of ethnic identities are said to act "like a corrosive on metal, eating away at the ties of connectedness that bind us together as a nation."[31]

This is a serious concern. The health and stability of a democracy depends, not only on the justice of its basic institutions, but also on the qualities and attitudes of its citizens: e.g., their ability to tolerate and

[31] Cynthia Ward, "The Limits of 'Liberal Republicanism': Why Group-Based Remedies and Republicanism Don't Mix," *Columbia Law Review*, 91 (3), 1991, p. 598.

work together with others who are different from themselves; their desire to participate in the political process in order to promote the public good and hold political authorities accountable; their willingness to show self-restraint and exercise personal responsibility; and their sense of justice and commitment to a fair distribution of resources. There is growing fear that this sort of public-spiritedness may be in decline, and if group-based claims would further erode the sense of shared civic purpose and solidarity, then that would be a powerful reason not to adopt minority rights policies.

But is it true? There has been much armchair speculation on this question, but remarkably little evidence. Reliable evidence is needed here, because one could quite plausibly argue the reverse: namely, that it is the absence of minority rights which erodes the bonds of civic solidarity. After all, if we accept the two central claims made by defenders of minority rights – namely, that mainstream institutions are biased in favor of the majority, and that the effect of this bias is to harm important interests related to personal agency and identity – then we might expect minorities to feel excluded from "difference-blind" mainstream institutions, and to feel alienated from, and distrustful of, the political process. We could predict, then, that recognizing minority rights would actually strengthen solidarity and promote political stability, by removing the barriers and exclusions which prevent minorities from wholeheartedly embracing political institutions. This hypothesis is surely at least as plausible as the contrary hypothesis that minority rights erode social unity.

We don't have the sort of systematic evidence needed to decisively confirm or refute these competing hypotheses. There is fragmentary evidence suggesting that minority rights often enhance, rather than erode, social unity. For example, the evidence from Canada and Australia – the two countries which first adopted official multiculturalism policies – strongly disputes the claim that immigrant multiculturalism promotes political apathy or instability, or the mutual hostility of ethnic groups. On the contrary, these two countries do a better job integrating immigrants into common civic and political institutions than any other country in the world. Moreover, both have witnessed dramatic reductions in the level of prejudice, and dramatic increases in the levels of inter-ethnic friendships and intermarriage. There is no evidence that the pursuit of fairer terms of integration for immigrants has eroded democratic stability.[32]

---

[32] Kymlicka, *Finding Our Way*, ch. 2.

The situation regarding the self-government claims of national minorities is more complicated, since these claims involve building separate institutions, and reinforcing a distinct national identity, and hence create the phenomenon of competing nationalisms within a single state. Learning how to manage this phenomenon is a profoundly difficult task for any state. However, even here there is significant evidence that recognizing self-government for national minorities assists, rather than threatens, political stability. Surveys of ethnic conflict around the world repeatedly confirm that "early, generous devolution is far more likely to avert than to abet ethnic separatism."[33] It is the refusal to grant autonomy to national minorities, or even worse, the decision to retract an already-existing autonomy (as in Kosovo), which leads to instability, not the recognizing of their minority rights.[34]

Much more work needs to be done concerning the impact of minority rights on social unity and political stability. This relationship will undoubtedly vary from case to case, and so requires fine-grained empirical investigation. It's not clear that philosophical speculation can contribute much here: we need to wait for more and better evidence.[35] But as with concerns about justice, it is clear that concerns about citizenship cannot provide any grounds for rejecting minority rights in general: there is no reason to assume in advance that there is any inherent contradiction between minority rights and democratic stability.

[33] D. L. Horowitz, *A Democratic South Africa: Constitutional Engineering in a Divided Society* (Berkeley: University of California Press, 1991), p. 224.

[34] Ted Gurr, *Minority at Risk* (Washington DC: Institute of Peace Press, 1993); Ruth Lapidoth, *Autonomy: Flexible Solutions to Ethnic Conflict* (Washington DC: Institute for Peace Press, 1996).

[35] Philosophers' claims about the relationship between minority rights and social unity are often doubly speculative: first we speculate about the sources of social unity (the "ties that bind"), and then we speculate about how minority rights affect these ties. Neither sort of speculation is grounded in reliable evidence. For example, some political philosophers have suggested (a) that it is shared values which form the bonds of social unity in modern liberal states, and (b) that immigrant multiculturalism and/or multination federalism reduce the level of shared values. There is no good evidence for either of these speculations. I seriously doubt that minority rights have reduced shared values, but I equally doubt that it is shared values that hold societies together. See Wayne Norman, "The Ideology of Shared Values," in *Is Quebec Nationalism Just?* ed. Joseph Carens (Montreal: McGill-Queen's University Press, 1995), pp. 137–159. Other philosophers suggest that it is shared experiences, shared identities, shared history, shared projects, or shared conversations that hold countries together. We have little evidence to support such claims about the source of social unity (and even less evidence about how minority rights affect these factors). We simply don't know what are the sources of social unity in multiethnic and multination states. To argue against minority rights on the grounds that they erode the bonds of social unity is therefore doubly conjectural.

VI.   Conclusion

I have tried to outline three stages in the ongoing philosophical debate about minority rights. The first stage viewed minority rights as a communitarian defense against the encroachment of liberalism. This has gradually given way to a more recent debate regarding the role of culture and identity within liberalism itself. In this second stage of the debate, the question is whether people's interests in their culture and identity are sufficient to justify departing from the norm of ethnocultural neutrality, by supplementing common individual rights with minority rights.

This second stage represents progress, I think, in that it asks the right question, but it starts from the wrong baseline, since liberal democracies do not in fact abide by any norm of ethnocultural neutrality. And so the next stage of the debate, I propose, is to view minority rights, not as a deviation from ethnocultural neutrality, but as a response to majority nation-building. And I have suggested that this will affect the way we think of the demands of both national minorities and immigrant groups. In particular, it raises two important questions: (a) what are permissible forms of nation-building?; and (b) what are fair terms of integration for immigrants?

Looking back over the development of this debate, I'm inclined to think that genuine progress has been made, although much remains to be done. It is progress, not in the sense of having come closer to resolving the disputes, but rather in the sense of getting clearer on the questions. The emerging debates about the role of language, culture, ethnicity, and nationality within liberal democracies are, I think, grappling in a fruitful way with the real issues facing ethnoculturally plural societies today. But getting clearer on the questions is no guarantee of getting clearer on the answers, and indeed I see no reason to expect that these debates will soon be resolved.

Postscript (December 2005)

This article was originally written in the late 1990s, and reflects the more confident mood of the times. My optimistic prediction about the trend towards liberal culturalism seems more difficult to sustain today. Indeed, some commentators argue that we are witnessing the very opposite trend: namely, an across-the-board "retreat from multiculturalism." On this view, multiculturalism will come to be seen as simply a passing fad of the 1980s and 1990s, replaced by a return to more traditional ideas of homogeneous and unitary republican citizenship, in which ethnocultural diversity is banished from the public realm.[36]

If my article was too rosily optimistic, these commentators are also too sweeping in their judgments. On closer inspection, what we actually see is a more complex set of trends. Ethnocultural diversity comes in many different forms, and with respect to several of them, the basic trends I identified in the direction of a liberal form of multiculturalism and minority rights remain firmly in place.

Consider, for example, the case of national minorities. In my article, I argued that there has been a trend towards greater recognition of sub-state national groups, often in the form of regional autonomy and official language status. That trend remains untouched: there has been no backlash against the rights of national minorities within the Western democracies. There is no case in the West of a country retreating from any of the accommodations it has accorded to its sub-state national groups. On the contrary, this trend has been reaffirmed and strengthened by the development of international norms, such as the Framework Convention for the Protection of National Minorities, adopted by the Council of Europe, and comparable declarations by the Organization for Security and Cooperation in Europe.[37]

Or consider the case of indigenous peoples. In my article, I argued that there has been a trend towards greater recognition of indigenous rights, often in the form of land claims and self-government rights. That trend remains fully in place, and it too has been reaffirmed and strengthened by the development of international norms, such as the UN's Draft Declaration on the Rights of Indigenous Peoples, or comparable declarations of indigenous rights by the Organization of American States, the International Labour Organization, or the World Bank.

So there is no across-the-board retreat from multiculturalism. For both sub-state national groups and indigenous peoples, the trend that I described towards the public recognition and accommodation of

---

[36] For representative discussions, see Hans Entzinger, "The Rise and Fall of Multi-culturalism in the Netherlands," in *Toward Assimilation and Citizenship: Immigrants in Liberal Nation-States*, ed. Christian Joppke and Ewa Morawska (Basingstoke: Palgrave Macmillan, 2003); Rogers Brubaker, "The Return of Assimilation?," *Ethnic and Racial Studies*, 24 (4), 2001, pp. 531–548; Christian Joppke, "The Retreat of Multiculturalism in the Liberal State: Theory and Policy," *British Journal of Sociology*, 55 (2), 2004, pp. 237–257.

[37] The Convention was adopted in 1995, but the monitoring bodies have adopted a norm of "progressive implementation" which means that the threshold countries are expected to meet continually rises. See Marc Weller (ed.), *The Rights of Minorities: A Commentary on the European Framework Convention for the Protection of National Minorities* (Oxford: Oxford University Press, 2004).

ethnocultural diversity remains intact, and indeed is now more firmly entrenched, rooted not only in domestic accommodations and negotiations, but also ratified and protected by international norms.

Moreover, these forms of minority rights and multiculturalism have taken the distinctly liberal form I described in my article. They have been codified within a larger framework of liberal-democratic constitutionalism and international human rights norms. They are not seen as a communitarian exception to the logic of liberal constitutionalism, or as a cultural relativist exception to the logic of universal human rights. On the contrary, as the 2001 UNESCO Universal Declaration on Cultural Diversity puts it, "cultural rights are an integral part of human rights, which are universal, indivisible and interdependent... No one may invoke cultural diversity to infringe upon human rights guaranteed by international law, nor to limit their scope." This principle – that minority rights supplement, rather than restrict, fundamental individual human rights – is clearly expressed throughout Western constitutions and international law.[38]

The retreat from liberal culturalism, therefore, is largely restricted to one domain of ethnocultural diversity – namely, immigration. Here, without question, there has been a backlash and retreat from multiculturalism policies relating to post-war migrants in several Western democracies.

It is an important question why immigrant multiculturalism in particular has come under such attack, and I will return to this below. But we can begin by dismissing one popular explanation. As I noted earlier, various commentators have suggested that the retreat from immigrant multiculturalism reflects a return to the traditional liberal belief that ethnicity belongs in the private sphere, that the public sphere should be neutral, and that citizenship should be undifferentiated. On this view, the retreat from immigrant multiculturalism reflects a rejection of the whole idea of liberal culturalism.

But this cannot be the explanation. If Western democracies were rejecting the very idea of liberal culturalism, they would have rejected the claims of sub-state national groups and indigenous peoples as well as immigrants. After all, the claims of national groups and indigenous peoples typically involve a much more dramatic insertion of ethnocultural diversity into the public sphere, and a more dramatic degree of differentiated citizenship, than is demanded by immigrant groups.

---

[38] I discuss the way minority rights are being codified at the international level in my book *Multicultural Odysseys: Navigating the New International Politics of Diversity* (Oxford: Oxford University Press, 2007).

Whereas immigrants typically seek modest variations or exemptions in the operation of mainstream institutions, historic national minorities and indigenous peoples typically seek a much wider level of recognition and accommodation, including such things as land claims, self-government powers, language rights, separate educational systems, and even separate legal systems. These claims involve a much more serious challenge to ideas of undifferentiated citizenship and the privatization of ethnicity than is involved in accommodating immigrant groups. Yet Western democracies have not retreated at all from their commitment to accommodating these historic minorities.

Western democracies are, in fact, increasingly comfortable with claims to differentiated citizenship and the public recognition of difference, when these claims are advanced by historic minorities. So it is not the very idea of liberal culturalism per se that has come under attack.[39] The problem, rather, is specific to immigration. What we need to sort out, therefore, is why liberal culturalism has proven so much more controversial in relation to this particular form of ethnocultural diversity.

But even that way of phrasing the question is too general. The retreat from immigrant multiculturalism is not universal – it has affected some countries more than others. Public support for immigrant multiculturalism in Canada, for example, remains at an all-time high. And even in countries that are considered the paradigm cases of a retreat from immigrant multiculturalism, such as the Netherlands or Australia, the story is more complicated. The Dutch military, for example, which in the 1990s had resisted ideas of accommodating diversity, has recently embraced the idea of multiculturalism, even as other public institutions are now shying away from it.[40] And in Australia, while the federal government has recently backed away from multiculturalism, the state governments have moved in to adopt their own new multiculturalism policies.[41] What we see, in short, is a lot of uneven advances and retreats in relation to immigrant multiculturalism, both within and across countries.

---

[39] Commentators who argue that Western democracies are rejecting liberal culturalism per se typically simply ignore the obvious counter-examples of national minorities and indigenous peoples – see, e.g., Joppke, "The Retreat of Multiculturalism," or Brian Barry, *Culture and Equality: An Egalitarian Critique of Multiculturalism* (Cambridge: Polity, 2001).

[40] See Rudy Richardson, "Multiculturalism in the Dutch Armed Forces" (presented at the International Seminar on "Leadership, Education and the Armed Forces: Challenges and Opportunities," La Paz, Bolivia, 13–15 September 2004).

[41] For example, the Principles of Multiculturalism Act adopted in 2000 by New South Wales.

What explains these variations? There are undoubtedly many factors at work, but let me mention three aspects of immigration that I suspect are particularly relevant.

(i) *Legal vs. illegal migration*: It is very difficult to gain public support for immigrant multiculturalism if the main beneficiaries are people who entered the country illegally. The presence of large numbers of illegal immigrants has several implications. First, it implies that the country is unable to control its borders, and this quickly generates fear about being "swamped" by unwanted migrants. By contrast, where illegal migration is minimal, the temperature of debates is lowered, and citizens feel secure that they are in control of their own destiny.

Second, in most Western countries there is a strong moralistic objection to rewarding migrants who enter the country illegally or under false pretenses (i.e., economic migrants making false claims about escaping persecution). Such migrants are seen as flouting the rule of law, both in the way they entered the country, and often in their subsequent activities (e.g., working illegally). Most citizens have a strong moral objection to rewarding such illegal or dishonest behavior. Moreover, they are often seen as "jumping the queue," taking the place of equally needy or equally deserving would-be migrants who seek entry through legal channels. There is also a prudential objection to providing multi-culturalism policies for illegal immigrants, since this may encourage yet more illegal migration.

If we put Western countries on a continuum in terms of the proportion of migration that is illegal, I suspect that this provides a fairly good pre-dictor of the level of public antagonism to immigrant multiculturalism. At one end of this continuum would be a country like Canada, which has probably the lowest level of illegal immigration amongst the Western democracies (primarily because of its geographical position) and the highest level of public support for multiculturalism (close to 80 percent according to recent surveys).[42] This is not a coincidence: I have no doubt that support for multiculturalism would rapidly and dramatically decline in Canada if it started confronting large numbers of illegal migrants. Consider the hysteria that accompanied the appearance off the Canadian shore of four boats containing just under 600 Chinese migrants in the summer of 1999. There was overwhelming support in the Canadian public for forcibly repatriating them to China, without allowing them to land and make asylum claims (which most Canadians assumed would be

---

[42] Andrew Parkin and Matthew Mendelsohn, *A New Canada: An Identity Shaped by Diversity* (Centre for Research and Information on Canada, CRIC paper No. 11, October 2003).

bogus).[43] I believe that Canadians are as opposed to illegal immigration as the citizens of any other Western country. If such boats appeared on Canadian shores every week, as happens in Italy or Spain or Florida, I have no doubt that there would quickly be a powerful anti-immigrant and anti-multiculturalism backlash.

(ii) *Liberal vs. illiberal practices*: A second important factor concerns the sort of "culture" that is being recognized and accommodated by multiculturalism policies. It is very difficult to get public support for multiculturalism policies if the groups that are the main beneficiaries of these policies are perceived as carriers of illiberal cultural practices that violate norms of human rights, and if they are seen as likely to invoke the idea of multiculturalism in order to maintain these practices (e.g., practices such as coerced arranged marriages of underage girls, female circumcision, or honor killings). From a legal or constitutional point of view, it is usually unambiguous that multiculturalism policies cannot be invoked to violate human rights. However, whatever the legal niceties, there is a fear in many Western democracies that certain immigrant groups might attempt to abuse the policy in this way, and many citizens are unwilling to accept this risk.

The extent to which immigrants are perceived as raising this risk varies considerably. White European immigrants to North America, such as the Italians or Poles, are not typically seen as carriers of illiberal practices. They are seen sharing a common "Western" and "Judeo-Christian" civilization. The same applies to immigrants from the Caribbean and Latin America, who are overwhelmingly Christian. Although they are seen as non-white, and are often subject to racial discrimination and stereotypes (e.g., about criminality, laziness, irresponsibility, lack of intelligence, and so on), they are not seen as bringing "barbaric" practices with them. And while Japanese and Chinese immigrants from East Asia are neither white nor Christian, they are not widely seen as having a religious or cultural commitment to offensive practices. In the West today, therefore, it is primarily Muslims who are seen as raising this risk. Muslims are not only seen as potentially bringing with them illiberal practices, but also as having a strong religious commitment to them, and hence as more likely to try to use the ideology of multiculturalism as a vehicle for maintaining these practices.

This perceived link between Islam and illiberalism has of course been strengthened by 9/11, and subsequent bombings in Madrid and

---

[43] Sean Hier and Joshua Greenberg, "Constructing a Discursive Crisis: Risk, Problematization and Illegal Chinese in Canada," *Ethnic and Racial Studies*, 25 (3), 2002, pp. 490–513.

London. Fears that Muslim immigrants will seek to use multiculturalism to perpetuate illiberal cultural practices within the country
are now combined with fears that multiculturalism will be used to
shelter the local nodes of militant international political movements that
seek to overthrow liberal democracy. Thus we see the "securitization"
of relations between Western states and their immigrant Muslim
communities.

As a result, the fear that multiculturalism is a vehicle for perpetuating
illiberal practices or movements is linked to the size or proportion of
Muslims. If we put Western democracies on a continuum in terms of the
proportion of immigrants who are Muslim, I think this would provide a
good predictor of public opposition to multiculturalism. Here again,
Canada is at one end of the continuum. In Canada, Muslims are a small
portion of the overall population (less than 2 percent), and form only a
small fraction of the recent non-white immigrant intake (90 percent of
Canada's recent immigrants are not Muslim). Moreover, the Canadian
multiculturalism policy was in fact adopted before the arrival of significant numbers of Muslims, and was initially designed in response to
the demands of older white ethnic groups, such as the Ukrainians and
Italians. In most of Western Europe, by contrast, the largest group of
non-European immigrants are Muslims – up to 80 or 90 percent in
countries like France, Spain, and Italy – and multiculturalism is
understood first and foremost as an issue of how to accommodate
Muslims. Moreover, many of these Muslim immigrants are from parts
of Africa or South Asia where traditions of female genital mutilation
(FGM) or arranged marriages persist, or where Islamic fundamentalism is
strong.[44] The numerical predominance of Muslims, combined with
racism and Islamophobia, generates a general perception of immigrants
as illiberal, and hence of multiculturalism as morally risky.

   (iii) *Economic contributors vs. burdens*: A third factor concerns perceptions of the economic impact of immigrants. It is difficult to sustain
popular support for multiculturalism where the immigrants who would
benefit from multiculturalism policies are seen as a burden on the
welfare state – i.e., as taking more out of the welfare state than they put
in. This is partly a matter of economic self-interest, but there is also a
moral component. The welfare state is seen as something that has been
built up by the sacrifices that each generation has made to protect the

---

[44] The popular view in the West that FGM is a "Muslim" practice is doubly incorrect:
FGM is practiced by Christians, Jews, and animists as well as Muslims in parts of sub-
Saharan Africa, and is strongly disavowed by many Muslim leaders. Yet this popular
perception is very strong.

next. If newcomers who have not contributed to the pool take away resources, that will leave less for our children.

By contrast, in some countries, like Canada, immigrants have been perceived as net contributors to the welfare state. Historically, this is due to the fact that immigrants to Canada have in fact put more in than they have taken out, and that historical pattern is today further strengthened by the perception that immigrants are needed to offset an aging population structure.[45] Without new working-age immigrants, Canada would have trouble sustaining healthcare spending or pensions as the population ages.

Whether immigrants are perceived as net contributors or net burdens depends on a number of factors. In the Canadian case, the perception that they are contributors is largely the result of the pro-active system of recruiting immigrants based on their education, skills, and experience. Since immigrants are chosen precisely for their employability, it is not surprising that they tend to have relatively high rates of employment. In many European countries, by contrast, most immigrants are not selected or recruited for their potential economic contributions. They may be ex-colonial populations who had the right to enter the imperial metropole, or refugee claimants, or illegal migrants. They often have low levels of education, and few job skills. As a result, they may suffer from high levels of unemployment, and depend on social benefits, and hence are seen as burdening the welfare state.

I believe that these three factors explain much (though not all) of the variation in public support for immigrant multiculturalism. To oversimplify, in countries where immigrants are seen as legally admitted, as complying with liberal norms, and as net economic contributors, then adopting multiculturalism is seen as low-risk, and will face the fewest obstacles. In countries where immigrants are perceived as primarily illegal, illiberal, and low-skilled, multiculturalism is seen as posing significant risks to both prudential self-interest and moral principles, and so will face the greatest obstacles.

No doubt there are other important factors at work in explaining resistance to immigrant multiculturalism in particular countries. But notice that we cannot start to identify these factors until we set aside the assumption that what is being rejected is liberal culturalism as such. What is happening here is not a general or principled rejection of the public recognition of ethnocultural diversity. On the contrary, many of

---

[45] Whether immigration in fact substantially changes the age structure is debated by experts: most working-age immigrants quickly sponsor their parents, thereby reproducing the same age structure as the native-born population.

the countries that are retreating from immigrant multiculturalism are actually strengthening the institutionalization of other ethnocultural differences. For example, while the Netherlands is retreating from immigrant multiculturalism, it is strengthening the rights of its historic Frisian minority; while the federal Australian government is retreating from immigrant multiculturalism, it is strengthening the institutionalization of Aboriginal rights; while France is retreating from immigrant multiculturalism, it is strengthening recognition of its historic minority languages; while Germany is retreating from immigrant multiculturalism, it is celebrating the fiftieth anniversary of the special status of its historic Danish minority; while Britain is retreating from immigrant multiculturalism, it has accorded new self-government powers to its historic nations in Scotland and Wales; and so on. None of this makes any sense if we explain the retreat from immigrant multiculturalism as somehow a return of orthodox liberal ideas of undifferentiated citizenship and neutral public spheres.

If this analysis is correct, it has important implications for the future of liberal culturalism in general, and of immigrant multiculturalism in particular. On the one hand, despite all the talk about the retreat from multiculturalism, it suggests that liberal culturalism in general has a bright future. There are powerful forces at work in modern Western societies pushing in the direction of the public recognition and accommodation of ethnocultural diversity. Public values and constitutional norms of tolerance, equality, and individual freedom all push in the direction of liberal culturalism, particularly when viewed against the backdrop of state nation-building. These factors explain the ongoing trend towards the recognition of the rights of sub-state national groups and indigenous peoples. Older ideas of undifferentiated citizenship and neutral public spheres have collapsed in the face of these trends, and no one today seriously proposes that these forms of minority rights and differentiated citizenship for historic minorities could be abandoned or reversed.[46] That minority rights, liberal democracy, and human rights can comfortably coexist is now a fixed point in both domestic constitutions and international law. There is no credible alternative to liberal culturalism in these contexts.

The situation with respect to immigrant groups is more complex. The same factors that push for liberal culturalism in relation to historic minorities have also generated a willingness to contemplate multiculturalism for immigrant groups, and indeed such policies seem to have

---

[46] Even a fierce critic of multiculturalism, like Brian Barry, makes no attempt to apply his ideas to the case of sub-state national groups and indigenous peoples.

worked well under "low-risk" conditions. However, immigrant multiculturalism has run into difficulties where it is perceived as carrying particularly high risks. Where immigrants are seen as predominantly illegal, as potential carriers of illiberal practices or movements, and/or as net burdens on the welfare state, then multiculturalism poses perceived risks to both prudential self-interest and moral principles, and this perception can override the forces that support liberal culturalism.

This suggests an uncertain future for immigrant multiculturalism. On the one hand, these basic risk factors are unlikely to change for most countries in the foreseeable future. In countries where the risk factors are low today, they are likely to remain so in the foreseeable future, and vice versa. There is no chance in the next ten or twenty years that Canada will suddenly be confronted with large numbers of illegal, unskilled Muslim immigrants. Conversely, it is virtually inevitable that Italy will continue to be confronted with large numbers of unskilled, illegal Muslim immigrants for the next few decades (North Africa is not likely to become a region of democracy and prosperity in the near future).

So the future of immigrant multiculturalism depends on whether citizens can be persuaded that the benefits of multiculturalism are worth the risks, and that the state has the capacity and determination to manage these risks. The experience to date suggests that this is a hard sell. In many countries, citizens are unconvinced that immigrant multiculturalism has significant benefits, and are also unconvinced that states have the capacity and commitment to tackle the prudential and moral hazards involved (e.g., to tackle issues of border control, to clamp down on illiberal practices, and to prevent abuse of the welfare state). Viewed this way, the future of immigrant multiculturalism in many countries looks rather bleak.

On the other hand, one could also argue that these very same factors also make the *rejection* of immigrant multiculturalism a high-risk move. It is precisely when immigrants are perceived as illegitimate, illiberal, and burdensome that multiculturalism may be most needed. Without some pro-active policies to promote mutual understanding and respect, and to make immigrants feel comfortable within mainstream institutions, these factors could quickly lead to a situation of a racialized underclass, standing in permanent opposition to the larger society.

Indeed, I would argue that, in the long term, the only viable response to the presence of large numbers of immigrants is some form of liberal multiculturalism, regardless of how these immigrants arrived, or from where. But we need to accept that the path to immigrant multiculturalism in many countries will not be smooth or linear. Moreover, we need to focus more on how to manage the risks involved. In the past, defenders of immigrant multiculturalism have typically focused on the perceived benefits of cultural diversity and inter-cultural understanding, and on condemning racism and xenophobia. Those arguments are sound, I believe, but they need to be supplemented with a fuller acknowledgment of the prudential and moral risks involved, and with some account of how those risks will be managed. That may be the next step in the evolution of the multiculturalism debate.

2   Structural injustice and the politics of difference

Iris Marion Young

It has become a truism that a politics of difference is equivalent to "identity politics," which is about claims of justice concerning cultural difference. In this chapter I take issue with this set of equivalences. There are at least two versions of a politics of difference, which I call a politics of positional difference and a politics of cultural difference. They share a critical attitude towards a difference-blind approach to politics and policy. They differ, however, in how they understand the constitution of social groups, and in the issues of justice that they emphasize. While both versions of a politics of difference appear in contemporary political debates, I perceive that over the last two decades both the attention of public discourse and that of political theorists has shifted from the politics of positional difference to a politics of cultural difference. I argue that this shift is unfortunate because it tends to obscure important issues of justice and because it tends to limit the framing of difference politics to a liberal paradigm. We should affirm both approaches, I argue, but also be clear on the conceptual and practical differences between them.

As a social movement tendency in the 1980s, the politics of difference involved the claims of feminist, anti-racist, and gay liberation activists that the structural inequalities of gender, race, and sexuality did not fit well with the dominant paradigm of equality and inclusion. In this dominant paradigm, the promotion of justice and equality requires non-discrimination: the application of the same principles of evaluation and distribution to all persons regardless of their particular social positions or backgrounds. In this ideal, which many understood as the liberal paradigm, social justice means ignoring gender, racial, or sexual differences among people. Social movements asserting a politics of difference, and the theorists following them, argued that this difference-blind ideal was part of the problem. Identifying equality with equal treatment ignores deep material differences in social position, division of labor, socialized capacities, normalized standards, and ways of living that continue to disadvantage members of historically excluded groups. Commitment to substantial equality thus requires attending to rather than ignoring such differences.

In the context of ethnic politics and resurgent nationalism, a second version of a politics of difference gained currency in the 1990s, which focused on differences of nationality, ethnicity, and religion. It emphasizes the value of cultural distinctness to individuals, as against a liberal individualism for which culture is accidental to the self or something adopted voluntarily. Most modern societies contain multiple cultural groups, some of which unjustly dominate the state or other important social institutions, thus inhibiting the ability of minority cultures to live fully meaningful lives in their own terms. Contrary to arguments for cultural neutrality which until recently have been the orthodox liberal stance, the politics of cultural difference argues that public accommodation to and support of cultural difference is compatible with and even required by just institutions.

I understand my own writing on the politics of difference as emphasizing the politics of positional difference in structural position. Both *Justice and the Politics of Difference* and *Inclusion and Democracy* critically assess the tendency of both public and private institutions in contemporary liberal democratic societies to reproduce sexual, racial, and class inequality by applying standards and rules in the same way to all who plausibly come under their purview. They consider how broad structures of the division of labor, hierarchical decision-making power, and processes of normalization inhibit the ability of some people to develop and exercise their capacities while offering wide opportunity to others. Each book, however, also contains elements that relate more to the politics of cultural difference. *Justice and the Politics of Difference* refers to cultural claims of indigenous people and speaks approvingly of movements of structurally oppressed groups to resist stigma by constructing positive group affinities, which I understand more as a means to the achievement of structural equality, rather than an end it itself.[1]

Justice and the Politics of Difference was published earlier than most work in recent political theory which focuses on a politics of cultural difference. That body of work might be said to begin with Charles Taylor's essay, "Multiculturalism and the Politics of Recognition," and to receive its first book-length treatment in Will Kymlicka's *Multicultural*

---

[1] Iris Marion Young, *Justice and the Politics of Difference* (Princeton: Princeton University Press, 1990).

Citizenship.[2] Published after I began to see that different theoretical approaches to a politics of difference were solidifying, *Inclusion and Democracy* tries more explicitly to distinguish focus on structural inequality from focus on injustice through cultural difference and conflict. While most of that book theorizes within the politics of positional difference, one chapter of *Inclusion and Democracy* articulates a relational concept of self-determination, to contrast with more rigid notions of sovereignty. I intend that chapter to contribute to discussions in the politics of cultural difference.[3] One motivation for the present essay is to sort out this distinction between two approaches to a politics of difference more thoroughly.[4]

In the two sections that follow, I first lay out and distinguish these two versions of a politics of difference. Both the politics of positional difference and the politics of cultural difference challenge commitments to political equality that tend to identify equality with sameness and which believe that the best way to pursue social and political equality is to ignore group differences in public policy and in how individuals are treated. They both argue that where group difference is socially significant for issues of conflict, domination, or advantage, equal respect may not imply treating everyone in the same way. Public and civic institutions may be either morally required or permitted to notice social group difference, and to treat members of different groups differently for the sake of promoting equality or freedom.

Despite these similarities, it is important to be clear on the differences between a politics of positional difference and a politics of cultural difference, for several reasons. In recent discussions of a politics of difference, I think that analysts sometimes either merge the two models or attribute to one features specific to the other. Such confusions can have the consequence that readers fail to notice important differences. For example, some critics aim objections at the wrong target.

In his recent book, *Culture and Equality*, for example, Brian Barry fails to distinguish any strands in the thick ball of theoretical writing that he

[2] Will Kymlicka, *Multicultural Citizenship* (Oxford: Oxford University Press, 1995); some of the ideas appeared in less developed form in Kymlicka's *Liberalism, Community and Culture* (Oxford: Oxford University Press, 1989).
[3] Iris Marion Young, *Inclusion and Democracy* (Oxford: Oxford University Press, 2000).
[4] Versions of this paper have been presented at the International Association of Feminist Philosophers, Gothenburg, Sweden, June 2004; a meeting of the Chicago area Conference for the Study of Political Thought at the University of Illinois at Chicago, November 2004; lecture at Duquesne University, November 2005; Mellon Seminar at Columbia University, November 2005. I have profited from discussions on those occasions. I am grateful to the following individuals for comments on earlier drafts: David Alexander, Joseph Carens, Jon Elster, Fred Evans, David Ingram, Anthony Laden, Patchen Markell, John McCormick, David Owen, and Jeremy Waldron.

winds together.[5] As a result, he levels criticisms at some writers that may be more apt for others, and he sometimes merges positions in a way that confuses the debate more than clarifies it. A second motive for this chapter, then, is to try to sort out some of this confusion that I find besets some recent discussions of the politics of difference.

A more important reason to elaborate the distinction between the two versions of a politics of difference, from my point of view, is to recover some issues of justice and ways of thinking about justice and difference that first motivated this line of thinking a quarter-century ago. As I will discuss below, a politics of positional difference concerns primarily issues of justice concerning structural inequality. Persons suffer injustice by virtue of structural inequality when their group social positioning means that the operation of diverse institutions and practices conspires to limit their opportunities to achieve well-being. Persons suffer specifically culture-based injustice when they are not free to express themselves as they wish, to associate with others with whom they share forms of expression and practices, or to socialize their children in the cultural ways they value, or when their group situation is such that they bear significant economic or political cost in trying to pursue a distinctive way of life. As I will discuss later, structural inequalities sometimes build on perceived cultural differences. To the extent that political thinking takes a politics of cultural difference as paradigmatic, however, thinking about justice and group difference tends to focus on issues of liberty and tends to obscure issues of inequality in opportunities structured by the division of labor, hierarchies of decision-making, and the norms and standards that institutions apply to reward achievement.

Thus the third section of this chapter discusses how the tendency which I detect in much recent political theory to narrow consideration of a politics of difference to a liberal paradigm has at least three unfortunate consequences. First, where structural injustices do build on perceived cultural differences, a politics of cultural differences and its emphasis on liberty does not make visible enough issues of structural inequalities. Second, because the politics and political theory of cultural differences tends to focus on what state policy properly should allow, forbid, or remain silent about, it tends to ignore civil society as a crucial site for working on injustice. Recent discussions of the politics of cultural difference, finally, especially regarding the status of women within cultural minorities, too often themselves tend to elevate particular group-based standards as normative for a whole polity without specifically noticing this normalizing move.

[5] Brian Barry, *Culture and Equality: An Egalitarian Critique of Multiculturalism* (Cambridge: Polity Press, 2001).

I.   Politics of positional difference

This approach defines social groups as constituted through structural social processes which differently position people along social axes that generate status, power, and opportunity for the development of capacities or the acquisition of goods. Important axes of structural social privilege and disadvantage concern the social division of labor, hierarchies of decision-making power, practices of sexuality and body aesthetic, and the arrangement of persons in physical and social space.

Persons in less advantaged positions suffer injustice in the form of structural inequality, or what Charles Tilly calls "durable inequality."[6] Some institutional rules and practices, the operation of hegemonic norms, the shape of economic or political incentives, the physical effects of past actions and policies, and people acting on stereotypical assumptions, all conspire to produce systematic and reinforcing inequalities between groups. People differently positioned in structural processes often have unequal opportunities for self-development, access to resources, to make decisions both about the conditions of their own action and that of others, or to be treated with respect or deference.

These structural inequalities do not determine that every member of a less privileged group suffers deprivation or domination. They do make most members of structurally disadvantaged groups more vulnerable to harm than others. They also put great obstacles to and constraints on the ability of group members to achieve well-being. It is these vulnerabilities and limitations that define structural injustice more than the amount of goods or power individuals may have at a particular time.[7]

The politics of positional difference argues that public and private institutional policies and practices that interpret equality as requiring being blind to group differences are not likely to undermine persistent structural group differences and often reinforce them. Even in the absence of explicitly discriminatory laws and rules, adherence to body aesthetic, struggle over power, and other dynamics of differentiation, will tend to reproduce given categorical inequalities unless institutions take explicit action to counteract such tendencies. Thus to remove unjust inequality it is necessary explicitly to recognize group difference and either compensate for disadvantage, revalue some attributes,

---

[6] Charles Tilly, *Durable Inequality* (Berkeley: University of California Press, 1998).
[7] I have elaborated a notion of structural group difference and structural inequality in several previous writings. See *Inclusion and Democracy*, pp. 92–102; "Equality of Whom? Social Groups and Judgments of Injustice," *Journal of Political Philosophy*, 9 (1), March 2001, pp. 1–18; "Taking the Basic Structure Seriously," *Perspectives on Politics*, 4 (1), 2006, pp. 91–97.

positions, or actions, or take special steps to meet needs and empower members of disadvantaged groups.

Socio-economic class is a paradigm of such structural grouping, where class does not refer simply to income level, but also to position in the social division of labor, decision-making structures, and group-segmented practices of fashion and taste. Here I will elaborate three additional forms of group difference which have motivated claims of a politics of difference: groups defined by disability, gender, and institutional racism.

Disability as structural inequality

Most theoretical writings on social justice either do not notice disability at all or bring it up in order to assert that disability is an outlier category, which theories of justice may deal with after addressing disadvantages which supposedly raise issues of justice in a more obvious way. John Rawls, for example, famously "puts aside" those disabilities "so severe as to prevent people from being cooperating members of society in the usual sense"[8] until the theory deals with the easier and more generally shared issues of justice. It is better to begin theorizing justice, he says, by assuming that "everyone has physical needs and psychological capacities within the normal range."[9]

Some philosophers recently have questioned this set of assumptions, and have begun to develop alternative analyses both of disability and justice.[10] Considering the large number of people who have impaired physical and mental capacities at some point in their lives, it is simply factually wrong to think of disability as a relatively uncommon condition not affecting how we should think about justice. I suggest that we can learn much about social justice generally as concerning issues of structural inequality, normalization, and stigmatization, if we decide to make disability *paradigmatic* of structural injustice, instead of considering it exceptional.

In his recent book attacking all versions of a politics of difference, Brian Barry devotes considerable space to defending a standard principle of merit in the allocation of positions. Merit involves equal

---

[8] John Rawls, *Political Liberalism* (New York: Columbia University Press, 1993), p. 20.

[9] John Rawls, *A Theory of Justice* (Cambridge, MA: Harvard University Press, 1971), p. 83.

[10] Eva Feder Kittay, *Love's Labor: Essays on Women, Equality, and Dependency* (New York: Routledge, 1999); Anita Silvers, "Formal Justice," in *Disability, Difference, Discrimination*, ed. Anita Silvers, David Wasserman, and Mary Mahowald (Lanham, MD: Rowman and Littlefield, 1998), pp. 13–146; Martha Nussbaum, *Boundaries of Justice* (Cambridge, MA: Harvard University Press, 2006), chs. 2 and 3.

opportunity in the following sense: it rejects a system that awards positions explicitly according to class, race, gender, family background, and so on. Under a merit principle, all who wish should have the opportunity to compete for positions of advantage, and those most qualified should win the competition. Positions of authority or expertise should be occupied by those persons who demonstrate excellence in particular skills and who best exhibit the demeanor expected of people in those positions. Everyone else is a loser in respect to those positions, and they suffer no injustice on that account.[11]

In this merit system, according to Barry, it is natural that people with disabilities will usually turn out to be losers.

Surely it is to be expected in the nature of the case that, across the group (disabled) as a whole, its members will be less qualified than average, even if the amount of money spent on their education is the average, or more than the average.[12]

Barry's is a common opinion. In our scheme of social cooperation, certain skills and abilities can and should be expected of average workers, and it is "in the nature of the case" that most people with disabilities do not meet these expectations. Thus they do not merit the jobs in which we expect these skills, and do not merit the income, autonomy, status, and other forms of privilege that come with those jobs. These people's deficiencies are not their fault, of course. So a decent society will support their needs and ensure them a dignified life, in spite of their inability to contribute significantly to social production.

One of the objectives of the disability rights movements has been to challenge this bit of liberal common sense. Most people who have not thought about the issues very much tend to regard being "disabled" as an attribute of persons: some people simply lack the functionings that enable normal people to live independently, compete in job markets, have a satisfying social life, and so on. Many in the disability rights movements, however, conceptualize the problem that people with

---

[11] I have argued that so-called merit standards often normalize attributes, comportments, or attainments associated with particular social groups, and thus often do not serve the impartial purpose they claim. *Justice and the Politics of Difference*, ch. 7. Brian Barry aims to refute this critique in *Culture and Equality*, pp. 90–102. For a good reply to Barry on these points, from the point of view of a politics of positional difference, see Paul Kelly, "Defending some Dodos: Equality and/or Liberty?," in *Multiculturalism Reconsidered*, ed. Paul Kelly (Cambridge: Polity Press, 2002), pp. 62–80. See also Clare Chambers, "All Must Have Prizes: The Liberal Case for Interference in Cultural Practices," in the same volume, pp. 151–173.

[12] Barry, *Culture and Equality*, p. 95.

disabilities face rather differently. The problem is not with the attributes that individual persons have or do not have. The problem, rather, is the *lack of fit* between the attributes of certain persons and structures, practices, norms, and aesthetic standards dominant in the society. The built environment is biased to support the capacities of people who can walk, climb, see, hear, within what is thought of as the "normal range" of functionings, and presents significant obstacles for people whose capacities are judged outside this range. Both interactive and technical ways of assessing the intelligence, skill, and adapatability of people in schools and workplaces assume ways of evaluating aptitude and achievement that unfairly exclude or disadvantage many people with disabilities from developing or exercising skills. The physical layout and equipment in workplaces and the organization of work processes too often make it impossible for a person with an impaired functioning to use the skills they have.[13] Hegemonic standards of charm, beauty, grace, wit, or attentiveness position some people with disabilities as monstrous or abject.

These and other aspects of the division of labor, hegemonic norms, and physical structures constitute structural injustice for people with disabilities. Many people with disabilities unfairly suffer limitation to their opportunities for developing capacities, earning a living through satisfying work, having a rewarding social life, and living as autonomous adults. A difference-blind liberalism can offer only very limited remedy for this injustice. It is no response to the person who moves in a wheelchair or who tries to enter a courtroom accessible only by stairs that the state treats all citizens in the same way. The blind engineer derives little solace from an employer who assures him that they make the same computer equipment available to all employees. The opportunities of people with disabilities can be made equal only if others specifically notice their differences, cease regarding them as unwanted deviance from accepted norms and unacceptable costs to efficient operations, and take affirmative measures to accommodate the specific capacities of individuals so that they can function, as all of us should be able to, at their best and with dignity.

The Americans with Disabilities Act recognizes this in principle, inasmuch as it requires employers, landlords, and public services to make "reasonable accommodation" to the specific needs of people with disabilities. It codifies a politics of positional difference. The law has

---

[13] I have discussed this issue in another essay, "Disability and the Definition of Work," in *Americans with Disabilities: Exploring Implications of the Law for Individuals and Institutions*, ed. Leslie Pickering Francis and Anita Silvers (New York: Routledge, 2000), pp. 169–173.

generated significant controversy, of course, concerning who counts as having a disability and about what kinds of accommodation are reasonable. As a group, people with disabilities continue to be unfairly excluded from or disadvantaged in education and occupational opportunities, and continue to have unfair difficulties in access to transportation, or in having simple pleasures like a restaurant meal or an evening at the theater. Only continued organized pressure on many institutions to conform with principles of fair accommodation will improve this structural situation.

I have begun with the example of injustice towards people with disabilities because, as I said earlier, I wish to suggest that it is paradigmatic of the general approach I am calling a politics of positional difference. It represents a clear case where difference-blind treatment or policy is more likely to perpetuate than correct injustice. The systematic disadvantage at which facially neutral standards put many people in this case, however, just as clearly does not derive from internal cultural attributes that constitute a group, "people with disabilities." It may be plausible to speak of a Deaf culture, to the extent that many Deaf people use a unique language and sometimes live together in Deaf communities. In a wider sense, however, there is no community or culture of people with disabilities. Instead, this category designates a structural group constituted from the outside by the deviation of its purported members from normalized institutional assumptions about the exhibition of skill, definition of tasks in a division of labor, ideals of beauty, built environment standards, comportments of sociability, and so on. The remedy for injustice to people with disabilities consists in challenging the norms and rules of the institutions that most condition the life options and the attainment of well-being of these persons structurally positioned as deviant.

Issues of justice raised by many group-based conflicts and social differences, I suggest, follow this paradigm. They concern the way structural social processes position individuals with similar physical attributes, socialized capacities, body habits and lifestyle, sexual orientations, family and neighborhood resources, and so on, in the social division of labor, relations of decision-making power, or hegemonic norms of achievement, beauty, respectability, and the like. The politics of positional difference focuses on these issues of inclusion and exclusion, and how they make available or limit the substantive opportunities for persons to develop capacities and achieve well-being. I will now all too briefly discuss racism and gender inequality as further examples of such structural inequality.

Racial inequality

Clearly this chapter's purpose is not to give an account of the structural inequalities of institutional racism. In this context, I want to make only a few points about racial inequality and the politics of difference. Although I will focus on racialized processes of structural inequality in the United States, I think that racial inequality structures many societies in the world. As I understand it, racism consists in structural processes that normalize body aesthetic, determine that physical, dirty, or servile work is most appropriate for members of certain groups, produces and reproduces segregation of members of these racialized groups, and renders deviant the comportments and habits of these segregated persons in relation to dominant norms of respectability.

What distinguishes "race" from ethnicity or nation, conceptually? The former naturalizes or "epidermalizes" the attributes of difference.[14] Racism attaches significance to bodily characteristics – skin color, hair type, facial features – and constructs hierarchies of standard or ideal body types against which others appear inferior, stigmatized, deviant, or abject. In Western structures of anti-black racism this hierarchy appears both as dichotomous and scalar. That is, racial categorization is organized around a black/white dichotomy, and this dichotomy organizes a grading of types according to how "close" they are to black (most inferior) or white (the superior).[15]

Processes of racialization stigmatize or devalue bodies, body types, or items closely attached to bodies, such as clothing; this stigmatization and stereotyping appear in public images and in the way some people react to some others. Racialization also involves understandings of the proper work of some and its hierarchical status in relation to others. The stigma of blackness in America, for example, has its origins in the division of labor, namely slavery.[16] The slave does hard labor under domination, from which owners accumulate profits; or the slave does

[14] I take the term "epidermalize" from Frantz Fanon, *Black Skins, White Masks* (New York: Grove Press, 1967), pp. 110–112; see also Thomas F. Slaughter Jr., "Epidermalizing the World: A Basic Mode of Being Black," in *Philosophy Born of Struggle*, ed. Leonard Harris (Dubuque, IA: Kendall Hunt Publishers, 1983), pp. 283–288.

[15] Lewis Gordon analyzes the logic of the dichotomy of anti-black racism according to an existentialist logic of absolute subject and the other; see *Bad Faith and Anti-Black Racism* (Atlantic Highlands, NJ: Humanities Press, 1995). I have brought a Foucauldian framework to articulate how racial dichotomy sets up norms that then organize bodies on a scale of better and worse; see *Justice and the Politics of Difference*, ch. 5, "The Scaling of Bodies and the Politics of Identity."

[16] See Glen Loury, *Anatomy of Racial Inequality* (Cambridge, MA: Harvard University Press, 2002), ch. 3.

servile labor to attend the needs and elevate the status of the ruling group. While chattel slavery was abolished a century and a half ago, racialized positions in the social division of labor remain. The least desirable work, the work with the lowest pay, least autonomy, and lowest status, is the hard physical work, the dirty work, and the servant work. In the United States these are racialized forms of work, that is, work thought to belong to black and brown people primarily, and these increasingly are also foreigners. A similar process of racialization has occurred in Europe, which positions persons of Turkish, North African, South Asian, sub-Saharan African, and Middle Eastern origin as other, and tends to restrict them to lower status positions in the social division of labor.

Segregation is a third common structure of racial inequality. It is not uncommon for migrants to choose to live near one another in neighborhood enclaves. I refer to this process as "clustering," and the urban residential patterning it produces might be considered a manifestation of cultural differentiation. While residential segregation often overlaps with or builds on such clustering processes, segregation is a different and more malignant process. Even when not enforced by law, segregation is a process of exclusion from residential neighborhood opportunity that leaves the relatively worse residential options for members of denigrated groups. The actions of local and national government, private developers and landlords, housing consumers, and others conspire – not necessarily by intention – to concentrate members of these denigrated groups. Dominant groups thereby derive privileges such as larger and more pleasant space, greater amenities, stable and often increasing property values, and so on.[17]

With segregation, the stigma of racialized bodies and denigrated labor marks space itself and the people who grow up and live in neighborhoods. People who live together in segregated neighborhoods tend to develop group-specific idioms, styles of comportment, interests, and artistic forms. These also are liable to be devalued and stigmatized by dominant norms. People who wish to appear respectable and professional, for example, had better shed the habits of walking, laughing, and talking in slang they have learned on the home block. If these are properly considered "cultural," they are better considered consequences of segregation and limitation of opportunity, rather than their causes. These structural relations of bodily affect,

---

[17] For a more thorough account of the distinction between segregation and clustering, and an account of the structural consequences of segregation, see Young, *Inclusion and Democracy*, ch. 6.

meanings, and interests in the social division of labor, segregation, and normalization of dominant habits operate to limit the opportunities of many to learn and use satisfying skills in socially recognized settings, to accumulate income or wealth, or to attain positions of power and prestige.

The main purpose of this brief account of racism here is to exhibit it as a set of structural relations in which processes of normalization have a large role. Being white is to occupy a social position, or set of social positions, that privileges some people according to at least the parameters I have outlined, and sets standards of respectability or achievement for the entire society. Being black, or "of color," means being perceived as not fitting the standards, being suited for particular kinds of work, or that one does not belong in certain places. An anti-racist politics of difference argues that such liabilities to disadvantage cannot be overcome by race-blind principles of formal equality in employment, political party competition, and so on. Where racialized structural inequality influences so many institutions and potentially stigmatizes and impoverishes so many people, a society that aims to redress such injustice must *notice* the processes of racial differentiation before it can correct them.

Even when overt discriminatory practices are illegal and widely condemned, racialized structures are produced and reproduced in many everyday interactions in civil society and workplaces. It is important that persons positioned similarly by racial structures be able to organize politically together to bring attention to these relations of privilege or disadvantage. While such organizing properly has some elements of the celebration of positive shared experience, or "identity politics," the primary purpose of such group-based organizing is, or ought to be, to confront and undermine the structural processes that perpetuate the limitation of opportunities.[18] Anti-racist movements are and ought to be directed at government policy to intervene in the structures. Government is not the only agent for institutional change, however, and I will return to this point.

---

[18] I have made a longer argument to this effect in ch. 3 of *Inclusion and Democracy*. See also Amy Gutmann, *Identity in Democracy* (Princeton: Princeton University Press, 2003). Gutmann's analysis would be even stronger if she theorized the social group as a product of structural processes of privilege rather than as a prejudicial ascription of denigrated status onto some people. Gutmann well articulates a distinction between an "identity politics" which might take pride in ascriptive identity as such, on the one hand, and a group-based politics in which "the appropriate object of pride is not the ascriptive identity in itself but rather the identity's manifestation of dignified, self-respecting personhood, the personhood of someone who has overcome social obstacles because of an ascriptive identity," on the other; p. 136.

Gender inequality

In the literature of political theory, the politics of positional difference and the politics of cultural difference conceive women's issues differently. As I will discuss below, some proponents of a politics of cultural difference implicitly invoke gender justice under norms of equal treatment. As discussed by much of the literature, the political struggle consists in getting women recognized as the *same* as men in respect to having rights to autonomy. In the politics of positional difference, by contrast, feminist politics are a species of the politics of difference; that is, on this approach, in order to promote gender equality it is necessary to notice existing structural processes that differently position men and women. On this account, gender injustice also involves processes of structuring the social division of labor and the fit or lack of fit of bodies and modes of life with hegemonic norms.

In the last quarter-century there have been many changes in gendered norms of behavior and comportment expected of men and women, with a great deal more freedom of choice in taste and self-presentation available to members of both sexes than in the past. Basic structures of gender comportment, assumptions that the normal body is implicitly male, the structures of heterosexual expectations, and the sexual division of labor nevertheless continue structurally to afford men more privilege and opportunity for access to resources, positions of power and authority, or the ability to pursue their own life plans.

People too often react to public evidence of female-specific conditions with aversion, ridicule, or denial. Public institutions which claim to include women equally too often fail to accommodate to the needs of menstruating, pregnant, and breastfeeding women, for example. This sometimes discourages them from participation in these institutions. Sometimes the costs to women of being positioned as deviant in relation to normal bodies are small inconveniences, like remembering to carry Tampax in anticipation that the women's room at work will not supply them. Sometimes, however, women suffer serious discomfort, threats to their health, harassment, job loss, or forgo benefits by withdrawing in order to avoid these consequences. Including women as equals in schools, workplaces, and other institutions entails accommodating to our bodily specificity to the extent that we can both be women and excel in or enjoy the activities of those institutions.

Aside from these stark examples of women's differences rendering us deviant in some settings, much contemporary feminist theory argues more broadly that the social imagination of this society projects onto women all the sense of vulnerability and chaotic desire attendant on being embodied and sexual beings. The norms of many public professional institutions, however, exclude or repress acknowledgment of bodily need and sexuality. The presence of women or womanliness in them, then, remains upsetting unless the women can present themselves like men.

The social differences produced by a gender division of labor constitute another access of gender difference that render women vulnerable to domination or exploitation or exclusion. Although large changes in attitudes have occurred about the capacities of men and women, and most formal barriers to women's pursuit of occupations and activities have been removed, in at least one respect change has been slow and minor. A structured social division of labor remains in which women do most of the unpaid care work in the family, and most people of both sexes assume that women will have primary responsibility for care of children, and other family members, and for housecleaning.

As Susan Okin theorized it more than fifteen years ago, this gender division of labor accounts in large measure for injustice to women, whether or not they themselves are wives or mothers. The socialization of girls continues to be oriented towards caring and helping. Occupational sex segregation continues to crowd women into a relatively few job categories, keeping women's wages low. Heterosexual couples sometimes find it rational to depend on a man's paycheck for their primary income, if it is larger enough. Thus women and their children are vulnerable to poverty if the husband/father ceases to support them.[19]

The structural positioning of women in the division of labor offers another instance of gender normalization. Most employers institutionalize an assumption that occupants of a good job – one that earns enough to support a family at a decent level of well-being and with a decent pension, vacation time, and job security – can devote himself or herself primarily to that job. Workers whose family responsibilities impinge on or conflict with employer expectations are deviants, and they find it difficult to combine real work and family responsibility.

Feminism construed as a politics of difference thus argues that real equality and freedom for women entail attending to both embodied, socialized, and institutional sex and gender differences in order to ensure that women – as well as men who find themselves positioned like many women in the division of labor in comportment or taste – do not bear unfair costs of institutional assumptions about what women and men are or ought to be doing, who they feel comfortable working with or voting for, and so on. For women to have equal opportunities with men

[19] Susan Moller Okin, *Justice, Gender and the Family* (New York: Basic Books, 1989).

to attain to positions of high status, power, or income, it is not enough that they prove that their strength, leadership capacities, or intelligence are as good as men's. This is relatively easy. It is more difficult to overcome the costs and disadvantages deriving from application of supposedly difference-blind norms of productivity, respectability, or personal authority, that in fact carry structural biases against many women.

The project of this section has been to explain what I call the politics of positional difference. The problems of injustice to which it responds arise from structural processes of the division of labor, social segregation, and lack of fit between hegemonic norms and interpreted bodies. I have dwelt on injustice to people with disabilities, racial injustice, and gender injustice in order to bring out social group difference not reducible to cultural difference, and in order to illustrate some diverse forms that these structural inequalities take. Each form of structural inequality concerns relations of privilege and disadvantage where some people's opportunities for the development and exercise of their capacities are limited and they are vulnerable to having the conditions of their lives and action determined by others without reciprocation. A politics of positional difference holds that equalizing these opportunities cannot rely on supposedly group-blind policies, because so many rules, norms, and practices of many institutions have group-differentiating implications. Promoting justice requires some efforts that attend to such structural differences and attempt to change them, not only within law and public policy, but also in many other social and economic institutions and practices.

II.   The politics of cultural difference

A politics of positional difference continues to have proponents among political theorists and those engaged in public discussion about the implications of group difference for values of freedom, equality, and justice. Indeed, I count myself as among them. What I am calling a politics of cultural difference has in recent years received more attention, both from political theorists, and in wider political debates.

I consider Will Kymlicka's book, *Multicultural Citizenship*, one of the earliest clear and thorough theoretical statements of this distinctive approach to a politics of difference. In that book Kymlicka explicitly distinguishes his approach to issues of group difference from one concerned with the situation of socially disadvantaged groups. "The marginalization of women, gays and lesbians, and the disabled," he says,

> cuts across ethnic and national lines – it is found in majority cultures and homogeneous nation-states as well as national minorities and ethnic groups – and it must be fought in all these places.[20]

Kymlicka does not elaborate this distinction between his approach to multiculturalism and that concerned with marginalized groups. It seems clear, however, that one basis of the distinction is that he thinks that groups defined by what he calls "societal culture" are different kinds of groups from the sort of group whose members face threats of marginalization or social disadvantage like that faced by women, sexual minorities, or people with disabilities. According to the terms I am using in this chapter the latter are *structural* social groups; what makes these groups *groups* is that their members are similarly positioned on axes of privileged and disadvantaged through structural social processes such as the organization of the division of labor or normalization.

The groups with which Kymlicka is concerned face distinctive issues, according to him, just because what defines them as groups is "societal culture." In his theory this term refers only to differences of nation and ethnicity. A "societal culture" is

> synonymous with "a nation" or "a people" – that is, an intergenerational community, more or less institutionally complete, occupying a given territory or homeland, sharing a distinct language and history. A state is multicultural if its members either belong to different nations (a multi-nation state), or have migrated from different nations (a polyethnic state), and if this fact is an important aspect of personal identity and political life.[21]

The societal culture to which a person relates is an important aspect of his or her personal identity; his or her personal autonomy depends in part on being able to engage in specific cultural practices with others who identify with one another as in the same cultural group; on being able to speak the language one finds most comfortable in the conduct of everyday affairs; on having the space and time to celebrate group specific holidays; and to display symbols important to the group. When the societal culture takes the form of nationality, this personal autonomy is tied to self-government autonomy for the group itself.

Kymlicka, along with most who theorize the politics of cultural difference, thinks that most political societies today consist of at least two cultural groups, and often more than two. The question the politics of cultural difference poses is this: Given that a political society consists of

---

[20] Kymlicka, *Multicultural Citizenship*, p. 19.   [21] Ibid., p. 18.

two or more societal cultures, what does justice require in the way of their mutual accommodation to one another's practices and forms of cultural expression, and to what extent can and should a liberal society give public recognition to these cultural diversities?

The politics of cultural difference assumes a situation of inequality common in contemporary polities in which members of multiple cultures dwell. It assumes that the state or polity is dominated by one of these cultural groups, which usually, but not always, constitutes a majority of the polity's members. The situation of political conflict, according to the politics of cultural difference, is one in which this dominant group can limit the ability of one or more of the cultural minorities to live out their forms of expression; or more benignly, the sheer ubiquity of the dominant culture threatens to swamp the minority culture to the extent that its survival as a culture may be endangered, even though the lives of the individual members of the group may be relatively comfortable in other ways. Under these circumstances of inequality of unfreedom, members of embattled cultural groups frequently demand special rights and protections to enable their culture to flourish, and/or claim rights to a political society of their own either within a federated relationship to that of the dominant culture(s) or, by way of secession, within a state of their own.

The politics of cultural difference explicitly rejects political principles and practices which assume that a single polity must coincide with a single common culture. This implies rejecting as well the assumption held by many liberals that for the state and law to treat all citizens with equal respect entails that all be treated in the same way. Kymlicka distinguishes two kinds of cultural groups existing within today's multicultural politics: ethnic groups and national groups. Much of the response to his theory has focused on whether this distinction is viable, whether Kymlicka has made it correctly, and whether he has correctly identified the requirements of justice appropriate for each. Neither this distinction nor the debates it generates concern the major argument of this chapter.

Kymlicka's theory has received wide attention because within it he has identified and clarified many of the major issues of conflict and potential accommodation that arise in the contemporary politics of cultural difference. Most subsequent theories take up these issues and add to them. What does freedom of cultural expression require? Does it entail forms of public recognition of and accommodation to practices, symbols, and ways of doing things, and not just allowing group members private freedom to engage in minority practices and forms of expression? Where the rules of public regulation, employers, or others come into conflict with what members of cultural minorities consider culturally obligatory or necessary for the survival of their culture, does justice require exemption from those sorts of rules? Can cultural groups make a legitimate claim on the wider polity for resources necessary to memorialize their cultural past and the means to preserve its main elements for future generations? Do some cultural groups have legitimate claims to national autonomy, and if so, what does this imply for forms of self-government and relations with other groups? Does justice require that state and society take special measures to try to prevent members of cultural minorities from suffering a loss of opportunity or other disadvantage because they are committed to maintaining their cultural identity? Since cultural minorities often suffer political disadvantage in getting members elected to office and in voicing their interests and perspectives in representative bodies, does justice call for installing forms of group representation? Kymlicka considers the question of whether liberal polities ought to go so far as to tolerate practices that members of a culture regard as important but which a wider societal judgment finds violate standards of liberal accommodation and individual human rights. He argues that such practices should not be tolerated.

I have dwelt on Kymlicka's text because he, more explicitly than others, distinguishes the politics of cultural difference from what I call a politics of positional difference. With one important exception, moreover, the issues and arguments he advances in *Multicultural Citizenship* have set an agenda of theorizing that subsequent texts have debated and debated. To the issues Kymlicka treats, theorists of a politics of cultural difference have added another: the extent to which religious difference should be accommodated and affirmed in a multicultural liberal polity.[22] No doubt partly because issues of religious difference and perceived freedom of religious practice have become more prominent in political debates within European and North American societies, as well as many other places, some theorists of politics and group difference have put religion alongside ethnicity and nationality as paramount forms of deep diversity.[23] The logic of religious difference and its implications for politics importantly diverges from ethnicity and nationality, at least because religious adherents often take doctrine and ceremony as not simply helping to define their identities, but also as obligatory for them.

---

[22] Jeff Spinner-Halev, *Surviving Diversity: Religion and Democratic Citizenship* (Baltimore: Johns Hopkins University Press, 2000).

[23] Texts that add a focus on religious difference, and separate it from but compare to issues of national and ethnic difference include Gutmann, *Identity in Democracy*; Bhikhu Parekh, *Rethinking Multiculturalism: Cultural Diversity and Political Theory* (Basingstoke: Palgrave Macmillan, 2000); Ayelet Shachar, *Multicultural Jurisdictions: Cultural Differences and Women's Rights* (Cambridge: Cambridge University Press, 2001); Seyla Benhabib, *The Claims of Culture: Equality and Diversity in the Global Era* (Princeton: Princeton University Press, 2002).

This raises the stakes in potential conflicts between majority commitments and the commitments of religious minorities.

Much recent theorizing about the politics of cultural difference takes issue with what writers charge is Kymlicka's overly homogeneous and overly bounded concept of societal culture. Joseph Carens, for example, argues that Kymlicka's concept of societal culture implicitly follows the logic of the concept of nation-state, even as the theory aims to challenge the singularity of one state for each nation.[24] Ethnic and national groups, on his model, are each bounded by a singular understanding of themselves, in which place, language, history, and practice line up, and are differentiated from other groups. The motive for Kymlicka's theory is precisely to challenge the singularity of the self-conception of the nation-state; but his logic of group difference may follow a similar logic. Many others theorizing a politics of cultural difference raise problems with what they fear is an "essentialism" of cultural difference, where either participants or observers take a culture to be a coherent whole, relatively unchanging, and fully separate from other cultures. Against this, theorists such as Bhikhu Parekh and Seyla Benhabib offer a politics of cultural difference which puts dialogue among cultures at the center.[25] On the dialogic view, members of different cultural groups within a society often influence one another and engage in productive cultural exchange, and this interaction ought to be mobilized to resolve intercultural conflict.

Since both the theoretical approaches I have reviewed in this chapter are versions of a politics of difference, it should not be surprising that they share some features. I find two major similarities in the analyses and arguments of the politics of positional difference and the politics of cultural difference. Both worry about the domination some groups are able to exercise over public meaning in ways that limit freedom or curtail opportunity. Second, both challenge difference-blind public principle. They question the position that equal citizenship in a common polity entails a commitment to a common public interest, a single national culture, a single set of rules that applies to everyone in the same way. They both argue that commitment to justice sometimes requires noticing social or cultural differences and sometimes treating individuals and groups differently.

While they are logically distinct, each approach is important. The politics of cultural difference is important because it offers vision and

---

[24] Joseph Carens, "Liberalism and Culture," in Joseph Carens, *Culture, Citizenship and Community: A Contextual Explication of Justice as Evenhandedness* (Oxford: Oxford University Press, 2000), pp. 52–87.
[25] Parekh, *Rethinking Multiculturalism*; Benhabib, *The Claims of Culture*.

principle to respond to dominative nationalist or other forms of absolutist impulses. We can live together in common political institutions
and still maintain institutions by which we distinguish ourselves as
peoples of cultures with distinct practices and traditions. Acting on such
a vision can and should reduce ethnic, nationalist, and religious violence. The politics of positional difference is important because it
highlights the depth and systematic basis of inequality, and shows that
inequality before the law is not sufficient to remedy this inequality. It
calls attention to relations and processes of exploitation, marginalization, and normalization that keep many people in subordinate
positions.

I am not here arguing that political actors and theorists ought to
accept one of these approaches and reject the other. Instead, my claim is
that it is important to notice the difference between them, a difference
sometimes missed in recent literatures. At the same time, I find that the
two forms of argument are compatible in practice. Indeed, for some
kinds of issues of group-based politics and conflict, both forms of analysis are necessary. As I have indicated above, and will discuss again in
the next section, for example, the oppression of minority cultures often
merges into structural inequalities of racism insofar as it entails the
limitation of opportunities for developing and exercising capacities.

Before turning to my worries that both theory and political discussion
pay too much attention to a politics of cultural difference at the expense
of a politics of positional difference, let me conclude this section by
addressing a question some readers may have. To what extent is this
distinction in theoretical approaches the same as or similar to the distinction that Nancy Fraser has drawn between a politics of redistribution
and politics of recognition? They are not in fact the same distinction at
all. As I understand Fraser's categorization, both forms of a politics of
difference I have articulated here fall under her category of a politics of
recognition. Indeed, in her most recent statement of her theory, Fraser
distinguishes what she calls a participatory parity approach – which
roughly corresponds to what I call the politics of positional difference –
and an identity politics approach – which roughly corresponds to what I
am calling the politics of cultural difference.[26] Insofar as there can be
any comparison, that is, I think Fraser would categorize both approaches to the politics of difference I have described as different forms of a
politics of recognition. Except for Charles Taylor, Fraser gives little

---

[26] See Fraser's contribution to her dialogue with Axel Honneth in Nancy Fraser and Axel
Honneth, *Redistribution or Recognition: A Philosophical Exchange* (London: Verso Books,
2003).

attention to theorists I associate with the politics of cultural difference, and she favors the approach she calls participatory parity as a response to structural inequalities of gender, race, and sexuality.

I find this distinction between different forms of recognition politics useful. I continue to think, however, that it is too polarizing to construct economic relations, or redistribution, and culture, or recognition, as mutually exclusive categories.[27] As I have tried to do in the first section of this chapter, it seems more useful to me to break out different aspects of the production of structural inequality such as normalization and the division of labor, each of which has both material effects on access to resources as well as the social meanings underlying status hierarchy.

III.   Critical limits to the politics of cultural difference

The politics of cultural difference exhibits a different logic from the politics of positional difference. I have argued that each highlights important issues of justice relevant to contemporary politics and the two approaches are often compatible in a particular political context. To the extent that recent political theory and public discourse focus on the politics of cultural difference, however, they inappropriately narrow debates about justice and difference. Some issues of justice retreat from view, and the discussion brings those that remain squarely under a liberal paradigm, which sometimes distorts their significance.

In this final section I will discuss three such worries with the ascendancy of issues of ethnic, national, and religious difference in debates about justice and social group difference. The paradigm of the politics of cultural difference tends to underplay important issues of group difference such as those I have discussed in giving an account of the politics of positional difference. Here I will take one example: the paradigm of cultural difference obscures racism as a specific form of structural injustice. Second, I will discuss how the liberal framework under which the politics of cultural differences brings its issues focuses too much on the state in relation to individuals and groups, and does not see relations in civil society either as enacting injustice or as a source of remedy. Because many theorists of the politics of cultural difference define their issues in terms of toleration, finally, I will argue that the politics of cultural difference easily slips into expressing and reinforcing a normalization exposed and criticized by a politics of positional difference.

---

[27] See Iris Marion Young, "Unruly Categories: A Critique of Fraser's Dual Systems Theory," *New Left Review*, 222, March/April 1997, pp. 147–160.

Tendency to obscure some issues of justice

As I discussed earlier, the politics of positional difference conceptualizes group difference primarily in structural terms. Social relations and processes put people in differing categorical social positions in relation to one another in ways that privilege those in one category in relation to another or others, both in the range of opportunities for self-development available to them, the resources they have or can access, the power they have over others or over the conditions of the lives of others, and the degree of status they have as indexed by others' willingness to treat them with deference or special respect. Class and gender are important structural axes in most societies. I have argued that physical and mental ability are functionally similar in our society that normalizes certain capacities. Race also names an important structural axis in most societies today.

The politics of cultural difference does not have a conceptual place for racial difference. To be sure, racialized social processes usually build on perceived differences in culture – language, religion, a sense of common lineage, specific cosmological beliefs, differing social practices, and so on. As I have discussed above, however, racialization and racism consist in a great deal more than that groups perceive themselves as distinct in relation to one another and refuse to recognize the equal legitimacy of the culture of others. It even consists in more than that groups that perceive themselves as ethnically or culturally different have conflicts or are hostile to one another. Such ethnic or cultural difference becomes racial hierarchy when the groups interact in a social system where one group is able to extract benefits by its hierarchical relation to the other. In the process of racialization, norms construct members of a sub-ordinate group as stereotyped and despised bodies, assign them to menial, dirty, or servile work, exclude them from high status positions, and tend to segregate the subordinate group from the dominant group.

The politics of cultural difference obscures this process. Many political claims and conflicts in contemporary multicultural societies involve both issues of cultural freedom *and* issues of structural inequality such as racism. Where there are problems of a lack of recognition of or accommodation to national, cultural, religious, or linguistic groups in liberal-democratic societies today (as well as others), these are often played out through dominant discourses that stereotype members of minority groups, find them technically inept or morally inferior, spatially segregate them, and limit their opportunities to develop skills and compete for high status positions.[28]

---

[28] See *Inclusion and Democracy*, pp. 102–107.

Issues of justice for Latinos in the United States, for example, concern not only cultural accommodation and acceptance, but also exposure and criticism of institutional racism. Many believe that the two are deeply intertwined. Demands for and implementation of policies that mandate English only in public institutions such as courts and schools limit the freedom of some Latinos to express themselves freely, stigmatize them, and often limit their ability to develop marketable skills. The position of many Latinos is racialized, moreover, in that their brown skin and facial features place them together as a group in the eyes of many Anglos, in spite of the fact that they or their parents hail from different parts of Latin America and experience differences of language and tradition among themselves. Within the dominant structures, "Hispanics" occupy particular positions in the social division of labor, and the benefits employers derive from this positioning are significant enough to limit the opportunities of members of this racialized group to move into other occupational positions.[29]

Everywhere that indigenous people make claims to freedom of cultural expression and political self-determination, to take another example, they do so in the context of racialized structural inequality. Indians in North America, Aboriginals in Australia, indigenous people in Latin America, are all victims of historically racist policies of murder, removal, spatial concentration, theft of their land and resources, and limitation of their opportunities to make a living. Structures of racialized inequality run deep in these societies, and discrimination and stereotyping persist.

Many conflicts over cultural toleration or accommodation in contemporary liberal democracies, in my observation, occur within a context of structural inequality between the dominant groups and cultural minorities. What is at stake in many of these conflicts is not simply freedom of expression and association, but substantively equal opportunity for individuals from marginalized groups to develop and exercise their capacities, and to have meaningful voice in the governance of the institutions whose roles and policies condition their lives. When the politics of cultural difference dominates political discourse on group difference, however, these positional issues are harder to raise and discuss. The weight of felt grievance about structural injustice then may load onto these cultural conflicts.

The example of political conflict between Latinos and Anglos in the United States that may focus on cultural difference, but still have roots

---

[29] See Iris Marion Young, "Structure, Difference, and Hispanic/Latino Claims of Justice," in *Hispanics/Latinos in the United States: Ethnicity, Race and Rights*, ed. Jorge J. E. Gracia and Pablo de Greiff (New York: Routledge, 2000), pp. 147–166.

in structural inequality is not unique. It seems to me that some group political conflict in multicultural European societies focuses on cultural difference in a context where structural inequality is a primary but understated issue. Many Muslim people dwelling in major European cities, for example, are victims of racial injustice. They are excluded from many opportunities for achieving status and income, they suffer stereotyping and objectification of their embodied presence, they lack recognized political voice, and they often live in segregated less desirable neighborhoods. The claims of such Muslims that they should have the freedom to wear headscarves or make their prayer calls in the public squares in the European cities where they live should not be divorced from this context of broad and entrenched structural privilege of majorities and social and economic disadvantage of minorities. Public debates seem to displace the structural problems onto issues of culture; the debates tend to ignore issues of poverty, unemployment, poor education, and segregation among Muslims, at the same time that they magnify issues related to religion and culture.

State and civil society

The paradigm situation assumed by the politics of cultural difference is that of a society in which there is a plurality of ethnic, national, and/or religious groups, but in the current moment one or some of them tends to wield dominant power through the state. These dominant groups tend to bias state action and policy in ways that favor members of their groups – for example, by declaring their language the official political language, or making only those religious holidays celebrated by members of their group holidays recognized by the state. Cultural minorities resist this dominative power, and make claims on the state and the other members of their society to recognize their right to freedom of expression and practice, to exempt them from certain regulations on religious or cultural grounds, to recognize their language as one among several constituting the political community, to allow and support their children being educated in their language, to take special measures to assure representation of minority groups in political decision-making, and many other claims for cultural recognition and freedom. Some minority groups claim to be distinct nations towards whom a right of self-determination should be recognized. An array of proposals and debates has arisen concerning what it can mean to accommodate such a right, not all of which involve creating a distinct sovereign state for the oppressed nationality, but most of which involve constitutional issues.

I cannot here catalogue all the claims made under a politics of cultural difference nor review the diverse positions people take in response to these claims. I have detailed this much in order to notice one thing: Most of the issues that arise both in theoretical writing and public discussion about the politics of cultural difference concern state policy, regulation, or the organization of state institutions.

In this respect the politics of cultural difference usually comes within a liberal framework. One of the features of a liberal framework, as distinct from other possible frameworks in political theory, such as critical theory, republicanism, or communitarianism, is that it often presumes that political struggle is primarily about state policy. This liberal framework assumes a simple model of society as consisting of the public – which coincides with what is under the administrative regulation of the state – and the private, which is everything else. Under this liberal model, the main question is, what shall the state permit, support, or require, and what shall it discourage or forbid? Framing questions of the politics of difference largely in terms of what the state should or should not do in relation to individuals and groups, however, ignores civil society as an arena both of institutional decision-making and political struggle, on the one hand, and processes of structural differentiation, on the other. It tends to ignore ways that non-governmental institutions often exercise exploitation, domination, and exclusion, as well as ways that private organizations and institutions can design remedies for these wrongs. The relations in which individuals and groups stand to one another within civil society, even apart from their relations to state policy, are very important both as causes of injustice and resources for remedying this injustice.[30]

The assumption that politics concerns primarily what the state allows, requires, or forbids, moreover, can generate serious misunderstanding about positions taken by proponents of a politics of difference, particularly with the politics of positional difference. Brian Barry is a case in point. He quotes disapprovingly my claim in *Justice and the Politics of Difference* that "no social practices or activities should be excluded as improper subjects for public discussion, expression and collective choice," and then cites Robert Fullinwider's interpretation of this statement to the effect that I advocate political intervention and modification into "private choices."[31]

The specter haunting Barry and Fullinwider is the limitation of individual liberty backed by state sanction. Apparently they envision no

---

[30] In ch. 5 of *Inclusion and Democracy* I further discuss the virtues and limits of action in civil society for remedying injustice.

[31] Barry, *Culture and Equality*, p. 270.

object of public discussion and collective choice other than state policies and laws. Certainly these are important objects of public discussion and choice in a democracy. A political theory concerned with the production and reproduction of structural inequalities even when laws guarantee formally equal rights, however, must shine its light on other corners as well. Movements of African-Americans, people with disabilities, feminists, gay men and lesbians, indigenous people, as well as many ethnic movements, realize that societal discrimination, processes of segregation and marginalization enacted through social networks and private institutions must be confronted in their non-state institutional sites. While law can provide a framework for equality, and some remedy for egregious violations of rights and respect, the state and law cannot and should not reach into every capillary of everyday life. A politics of positional difference thus recommends that churches, universities, production and marketing enterprises, clubs and associations all examine their policies, practices, and priorities to discover ways they contribute to unjust structures and recommends changing them when they do. Such a position is not tantamount to calling the culture Gestapo to police every joke or bathroom design. Numerous social changes brought about by these movements in the last thirty years have involved actions by many people that were voluntary, in the sense that the state neither required them nor sanctioned agents who did not perform them. Indeed, state policy as often follows behind action within civil society directed at undermining structural injustice as leads it.[32]

Seyla Benhabib distinguishes such a "dual track" approach to politics, which she associates with critical theory, and argues that liberal political theory typically ignores non-state dimensions of politics:

In deliberative democracy, as distinguished from political liberalism, the *official* public sphere of representative institutions, which includes the legislature, executive and public bureaucracies, the judiciary and political parties, is not the only site of political contestation and of opinion and will formation. Deliberative

---

[32] Brian Barry also blanches at the assertion I make in *Justice and the Politics of Difference* that the remedy for normalizing social processes is "cultural revolution." Barry, *Culture and Equality*, p. 15. In this phrase, which I borrowed from Julia Kristeva, "culture" refers to modes of comportment, gestures, speech styles, and other modes of communication and how people understand these in the everyday life-world. See Julia Kristeva, "Le Sujet en Proces," in *Polylogue* (Paris: Editions Seuil, 1977). "Revolution" may be a dramatic term. Eliminating ways that women, people with disabilities, or poor people are sometimes denigrated, however, among other things requires changing some symbolic meanings and interactive habits or some people. In her reaction to the phrase, "cultural revolution," Amy Gutmann also manifests an assumption that state and law are the primary motors of social change to undermine injustice. Processes that now I would call "denormalization," must involve change to interactive habits as well as institutional rule reform.

democracy focuses on social movements, and on the civil, cultural, religious, artistic, and political associations of the *unofficial* public sphere, as well.[33]

Barry, and others who consider issues of difference under a liberal paradigm, ignores this non-official public sphere of contestation and action, and thus "attempts to solve multicultural conflicts through a juridical calculus of liberal rights."[34] A conception of justice able to criticize relations of domination and limitation of opportunity suffered by gender, racialized, ethnic, or religious groups must consider relations within private activities and civil society and their interaction with state institutions.[35]

Normalizing culture

I said that the logic of most theorizing in the politics of cultural difference, as well as the logic of many political debates about multiculturalism, assumes the point of view of a power or authority which deliberates about what practices, forms of expression, forms of civic and political association, and so on, should be allowed, encouraged, or required, and which discouraged or forbidden. Both theoretical and political debates in the politics of cultural difference, that is, often take the traditionally liberal form of debates about what should and what should not be tolerated.

Framing issues of difference in terms of toleration, however, often introduces a normalizing logic in debates about multiculturalism. The political questions debated often have this form: shall we tolerate this expression or practice that we find of questionable value or morality, for the sake of mutual accommodation and civic peace? Should we allow methods of processing animals for food which require that the animals be conscious at the time of slaughter? I do not introduce this example to debate it, but rather as an example that this form is typical in multicultural debates. I think this form assumes the following. The primary participants in the debate are members of the "we," who argue among themselves for and against toleration. This "we" is the point of view of the dominant culture, which also assumes itself to have the power to influence the authorities who allow or forbid. While those holding the point of view debate among themselves whether toleration is the appropriate stance in this case, they all presume themselves to occupy a position as normal, which means not only in the statistical majority, but also holding values that lie within the range of acceptable and even good.

---

[33] Benhabib, *The Claims of Culture*, p. 21.   [34] Ibid., p. 21.   [35] See also ibid., pp. 118–121.

Those whose practices the normalized "we" debates have little or no voice in the public deliberations. They are the object of the discussion, but in it, if at all, only weakly as political subjects. The debate positions them as deviant in relation to the norm; as with all questions of toleration, the question is only, are these practices so deviant as to be beyond a line of permissibility? Those who find themselves positioned in this normalizing discourse often believe that the terms of the debate themselves are disrespectful, even before a resolution has been achieved. They also often believe that their being positioned as deviant makes them liable to other forms of denigration, exclusion, or disadvantage.

A funny inversion often happens to gender issues in this politics of cultural difference utilizing the normalizing logic implicit in many debates about toleration. I argued above that the politics of cultural difference obscures many issues concerning gender and justice that are matters of structural inequality. The politics of positional difference theorizes gender as a set of structural social positions. These structures operate in complex ways to render many women vulnerable to gender-based domination and deprivation in most societies of the world, including Western liberal democracies.

You might never know it, however, to listen to gendered debates among contemporary theorists of the politics of cultural difference. Many of the political debates currently taking place about multiculturalism focus on beliefs and practices of cultural minorities, especially Muslims, about women. These debates are especially salient in Europe, though George W. Bush used these issues to great rhetorical effect to legitimate the US-led invasion of Afghanistan in 2001.[36] A great deal of the recent political theoretical literature taking the approach of a politics of cultural difference devotes considerable attention to the treatment of women by cultural minorities.

In many theoretical writings on multiculturalism, gender issues serve as the test to the limits of toleration. Can we tolerate rules of a national minority that refuse to recognize the women who marry outside as group members? Can we allow Muslim women to accede to the pressure or expectation that they wear the hijab? Surely we cannot permit arranged marriages of teenage girls or female genital cutting under any circumstances.

My purpose in calling attention to the ubiquity of gender issues in contemporary political and theoretical debates on cultural difference is

---

[36] See Iris Marion Young, "The Logic of Masculinist Protection: Reflections on the Current Security State," *Signs: A Journal of Women in Culture and Society*, 29 (1), Fall 2003.

not to examine the arguments on various sides and take a position. I bring them up as instances of the normalizing discourse of toleration typical of the logic of the politics of cultural difference. The "we" in these questions occupies the position of the majority Western liberals. "We" can raise these questions about the extent to which the gender practices of the minority culture can be tolerated because among "us," women have the same freedom and autonomy as men. Our gender individualism is the norm against which the practices of many cultures come up deviant. Debates about gender in the politics of cultural difference thus serve the double function of positioning some cultural groups beyond the pale and encouraging a self-congratulatory arrogance on the part of the "we" who debate these issues. Gender has moved from being a difference to occupying the universal. In the process, the real issues of gendered structural inequality may be ignored.

IV.   Conclusion

The purpose of this chapter has been to clarify differences in approaches to political and theoretical debates about justice: whether and to what extent justice calls for attending to rather than ignoring social group differences. The fact that the politics of cultural difference has more occupied political theorists in recent years than a politics of positional difference is lamentable, I have suggested, for several reasons. It tends to narrow the groups of concern to ethnic, national, and religious groups, and to limit the issues of justice at stake to those concerned with freedom and autonomy more than equal opportunity of people to develop capacities and live a life of well-being. Its reliance on a liberal paradigm, moreover, tends to limit politics to shaping state policy and to reintroduce normalizing discourses into what began as denormalizing movements. My objective in making these distinctions and arguments has not been to reject the politics of cultural difference, but to encourage political theorists to refocus their attention to group differences generated from structural power, the division of labor, and constructions of the normal and the deviant, as they continue also to reflect on conflicts over national, ethnic, or religious difference.

3   Multiculturalism as/and/or anti-racism?

Charles W. Mills

Originally appearing in the 1970s in specific reference to Australian and
Canadian government policy towards national minority groups, the
term *multiculturalism* has now metamorphosed into an all-encompassing
political category centered around issues of culture, recognition, and
identity politics, a conceptual grab bag that sometimes seems to be
defined simply by negation – whatever does not fit into the "traditional"
political map of, say, the 1950s is stuffed in here. Given these elastic
boundaries, it has, unsurprisingly, suffered a corresponding dilution of
content: multiculturalism, suggests one writer, "is now often perceived
as an empty signifier onto which a range of groups project their fears and
hopes."[1] In the vast and ever increasing body of literature on the subject, numerous distinctions therefore need to be drawn. There is multiculturalism as state policy (itself varying from nation to nation) and
multiculturalism as minority activist demand, multiculturalism as applied
generally to the political theorization of society as a whole and multiculturalism as applied specifically to tertiary education and curriculum
reform, multiculturalism as including the politics of race, ethnicity, gender,
sexual orientation, and disability, and multiculturalism as excluding at least
some of these,[2] multiculturalism self-described, or hostilely described
by others, as weak, strong, liberal, conservative, corporate, "managed,"
critical, radical, insurgent...[3] And the list goes on.

---

[1] Sneja Gunew, *Haunted Nations: The Colonial Dimensions of Multiculturalisms* (New York: Routledge, 2004), p. 19.

[2] Contrast, for example, Cynthia Willett (ed.), *Theorizing Multiculturalism: A Guide to the Current Debate* (Malden, MA: Blackwell, 1998), which includes sections on feminism as well as critical race theory, post-colonialism, and pragmatism, with Susan Moller Okin's *Is Multiculturalism Bad for Women?*, with respondents, ed. Joshua Cohen, Matthew Howard, and Martha C. Nussbaum (Princeton: Princeton University Press, 1999), which, as the title implies, sees multiculturalism and feminism as opposed.

[3] See the sources cited above, and also David Theo Goldberg (ed.), *Multiculturalism: A Critical Reader* (Cambridge, MA: Blackwell, 1994); Tariq Modood and Pnina Werbner (eds.), *The Politics of Multiculturalism in the New Europe: Racism, Identity and Community* (New York: Zed Books, 1997); C. W. Watson, *Multiculturalism* (Philadephia: Open

In this chapter, as my title implies, I want to look narrowly at multi-culturalism and the issues of ethnicity and race with which the term was originally, and is still perhaps most tightly, associated. Multiculturalism in this context implies the recognition that the world is constituted of many peoples and cultures, of differing ethnicities and races, all of whom are deserving of respect. This global reality is, of course, not at all new; what has changed, at least in theory, is the prescribed normative attitude. While people of color are certainly entirely capable of discriminating against, and indeed massacring, other people of color, as an internationally comparativist perspective on multiculturalism reminds us,[4] the main debate has obviously historically been centered on the policies of Europe and the nations created through European expansionism to their various external and internal "others."

As such, multiculturalism is basically a post-Second World War phenomenon, a result of the confluence of several major historical developments: the (partial) discrediting of racism and the concept of race itself by the Holocaust, the global anti-colonial struggle and eventual success of decolonization, the civil rights movements of black Americans and indigenous peoples in the former white settler states, and the mass labor migrations of the last few decades from "South" to "North." Multiculturalism in this context can thus be seen as a back-handed, belated, and oblique (too oblique for some) acknowledgment that the modern world has in certain respects been a global polity shaped by the fact of transnational white European domination – invasion, expropriation, settlement, slavery, colonization, the color bar, segregation, restricted immigration and citizenship – and that a political correction for this history of general Euro-hegemony is called for.

The question then is how useful multiculturalism is as a vehicle for redressing this legacy of ethnic exclusion and racial subordination. Should it, most optimistically, be multiculturalism *as* anti-racism, implying that multiculturalism can on its own represent an adequate anti-racist politics? Should it, more cautiously, be multiculturalism *and* anti-racism, suggesting that multiculturalist reforms, though desirable and necessary, can only go so far and that the creation of a non-racist polity will require in addition more radical measures? Or should it, most negatively, be multiculturalism *or* anti-racism, a dichotomy indicating that in fact multiculturalism is of little use in such a project, and may indeed be a diversion from it? Or does the answer depend – to anticipate

University Press, 2000); Bruce Haddock and Peter Sutch (eds.), *Multiculturalism, Identity and Rights* (New York: Routledge, 2003).
[4] Watson, *Multiculturalism*, ch. 1.

the later discussion – on what specific social sphere and what particular ethnoracial group one is talking about? In what follows, I will try to investigate the extent to which a multiculturalist framework may be useful, or may be problematic, on both the descriptive and prescriptive levels, in understanding the origins of racial exclusion and in offering remedies to correct for it. My focus will be on the relationship between race and, respectively, culture, ethnicity, political economy, and liberalism.

I.   Race and culture

The worth of multiculturalism is seemingly most clear-cut and unequivocal in its commitment to the valorization of the cultures of the non-white other: the indigenous Third World peoples originally subordinated and expropriated by the expansionist European empires, the new immigrant populations of color arriving in the First World as, after the Second World War, the empire struck back. Originally, of course, these populations were all racialized in the processes of European conquest, settlement, and colonial rule, and their biological inferiority was taken to manifest itself in a corresponding cultural inferiority. Sociologists Howard Winant and Frank Füredi, contesting the standardly sanitized, ethnically cleansed, and whitewashed accounts of modernity prevalent in mainstream scholarship, remind us that colonialism created "a world racial system" that was originally "unabashedly white supremacist,"[5] in which "The domination of the world by the West was seen as proof of white racial superiority," so that "race was a central element in the composition of Western identity," "inextricably linked to the Western notion of 'civilisation'."[6] Similarly, historian Thomas Borstelmann refers to "the era of global white supremacy," marked by "the international character of white rule over people of color," and underwritten by "a common view of the world as divided between civilization and barbarism, with those possessing lighter skin in the former camp and those with darker skin in the latter."[7]

Contemporary multiculturalism thus challenges the older hegemonic norm of *monoculturalism*, the view that non-European cultures were to a greater or lesser extent clearly inferior to European ones, not deserving

---

[5] Howard Winant, *The New Politics of Race: Globalism, Difference, Justice* (Minneapolis: University of Minnesota Press, 2004), pp. x, xiv.

[6] Frank Füredi, *The Silent War: Imperialism and the Changing Perception of Race* (New Brunswick: Rutgers University Press, 1998), pp. 1, 5.

[7] Thomas Borstelmann, *The Cold War and the Color Line: American Race Relations in the Global Arena* (Cambridge, MA: Harvard University Press, 2001), p. 15.

of much or any respect, and (always assuming this option was even open) that they should be abandoned for assimilation to the superior "civilized" white European standard, whether in Europe itself or (what were originally) the "external Europes" of Euro-America, Euro-Canada, Euro-Australia, and elsewhere. (Though a further complication is that these various Europes and their respective "whitenesses" were themselves divided and contested: Anglo vs. Irish in Britain and Nordic vs. Mediterranean in continental Europe itself, WASP vs. non-WASP European in the United States, Anglo vs. French Canadian, Anglo-Celtic vs. NESB [Non-English Speaking Background] European immigrants in Australia.)

In conservative hard-line versions of racist theory, biology remained paramount: one's intrinsic and insuperable savagery was written on one's flesh. By contrast, more liberal versions allowed for the possibility of transformation through cultural assimilation: one was encouraged to become a colored European – *évolué, assimilado* – and, if only in the official ideology, promised the status of an equal. But in neither case, obviously, was the superiority of Europe in question. Cultural imperialism meant the suppression of languages, customs, traditions, religions, ways of seeing the world, all in the name of a higher European civilization.

A crucial dimension of any comprehensive anti-racist project must therefore be the repudiation of such a hierarchy, and the affirmation of a cultural pluralism. Canadian theorists James Tully and Will Kymlicka have been among the most prominent figures in the recent debates on multiculturalism and its relation to liberalism, group rights, and the self-government of native peoples.[8] Tully has argued that the accommodation of cultural diversity within a transformed constitutionalism requires the rejection of the "empire of uniformity" that has historically characterized modern European constitutional theory, which – "while masquerading as universal" – justified "European imperialism, imperial rule of former colonies over Indigenous peoples, and cultural imperialism" over a diverse citizenry.[9] Instead, what is called for is an acknowledgment of the validity of Aboriginal constitutions, and the commitment to an "intercultural dialogue" in which – within the framework of the perspectival metaphor provided by the Haida-Scottish artist Bill Reid's sculpture, *The Spirit of Haida Gwaii* – we are prepared to give up

---

[8] James Tully, *Strange Multiplicity: Constitutionalism in an Age of Diversity* (New York: Cambridge University Press, 1995); Will Kymlicka, *Liberalism, Community and Culture* (New York: Oxford University Press, 1989) and *Multicultural Citizenship: A Liberal Theory of Minority Rights* (New York: Oxford University Press, 1995).

[9] Tully, *Strange Multiplicity*, p. 96.

ethnocentric and racial self-privileging for a reciprocal "reversal of worldview" that makes a genuine conversation between equals possible. Kymlicka, whose work in this area has attracted perhaps the widest attention, has made the case that by its own presuppositions (though perhaps despite itself?), liberalism is required to recognize culture both as a good in itself and an instrumental good, insofar as people cannot exercise their autonomy without being enabled by a particular culture. Thus he has argued for group rights for Aboriginal peoples, claiming that for subordinated populations, it is necessary to guarantee their thriving.[10]

In this sphere, then, multiculturalism as state policy can clearly be plausibly represented as a necessary part of an anti-racist agenda, though many unresolved tensions remain around such issues as the equal rights of women.[11] Where the danger arises is in thinking that all aspects of racism can be handled on this level, which is dubious even for the clear-cut examples of the treatment of Aboriginal populations and voluntary immigrants, and becomes quite implausible for the particularly problematic situation of black Americans, descendants of a coerced slave population. In some cases we need, at the least, multiculturalism *and* anti-racism of additional kinds, while in the latter case, it can be argued that it really does become multiculturalism *or* anti-racism.

The problem hinges in part on how we should conceptualize race, culture, and their interrelation in a nominally post-racist world. For traditional racist theory, culture was thought of as a kind of emanation of race, generally conceived of biologically. Today, of course, not only would such alleged causal connections be seen as absurd but the putative cause, "race," is itself now taken to be non-existent. C. W. Watson points out that for many people today " 'race' ... has spurious biological connotations and is better avoided."[12] The discrediting of racism, though by no means complete, means that many whites now regard race as an illegitimate category, whose very retention perpetuates racial thinking and thus racism, insofar as it keeps alive the idea that races exist as biological entities. Hence the mainstream literature on multiculturalism often dispenses with it altogether. (It is noteworthy that neither of the two prominent theorists of multiculturalism mentioned, Tully and Kymlicka, make much use of the word, preferring to cast their accounts in terms of "peoples," "minorities," "ethnic groups," and so forth.) "Culture," on the other hand, is an eminently legitimate term, with "positive connotations": "If 'race' is now a suspect

[10] Kymlicka, *Liberalism, Community and Culture* and *Multicultural Citizenship.*
[11] See Okin, *Is Multiculturalism Bad for Women?*   [12] Watson, *Multiculturalism*, p. 2.

word, 'culture' by contrast is a vaunted, celebratory one, still strongly associated emotionally and nostalgically with a distinctive way of life."[13] Absent an alternative, non-biological conceptualization of race, then, a kind of semantic substitutionism is tempting that may seem innocent, even laudable, but which brings a certain unfortunate ideological baggage in its wake. A double displacement is likely. It is not merely that racial problems are dissolved into cultural problems, but that in effect culture in these discussions becomes a respectable proxy for race itself, self-congratulatorily free of biologism. Race as a category is culturalized, and racial oppression is diagnosed as a particular variety of cultural oppression. The result – to be discussed in greater detail in the next section – is an ethnicization of race.

Such an approach is multiply problematic. To begin with, it seems odd to represent the history of racism, with all its attendant atrocities, as a matter of mere cultural misunderstanding and deprecation. In his recent critique of James Sterba's discussion of the "challenge" posed by multiculturalism to traditional ethics, Gerald Doppelt underlines the peculiarity of such a framing:

> I find it difficult to understand the slaughter of American Indians, the carnage in Vietnam, or the legacy of slavery, segregation, and racial violence in the US, as the result of a simple failure to know or appreciate other cultures... Rather, such phenomena, in the past and in the present, embody powerful structures of racial fear, hatred, and violence – not simply ignorance of other cultures or ignorance of the obligations to them implied by traditional ethics... In sum, some of the challenges Sterba associates with multiculturalism are, in my view, better understood as issues of race.[14]

In other words, while it is not being denied that racism often has cultural dimensions, its multifold nature is reduced to one-dimensionality if we focus just on that aspect. In addition, its underlying dynamic is arguably misrepresented, and we are left with an inadequate conceptual framework to make sense of what have historically been its horrific consequences. The defining feature of racism, at least in its classic form, is not just the failure to recognize the equal worth of the culture of the racialized group but, more ominously, the failure to recognize their very humanity. As Anthony Appiah remarks: "It is not black culture that the racist [disdains], but blacks ... [N]o amount of knowledge of the architectural achievements of Nubia or Kush guarantees respect for

---

[13] Watson, *Multiculturalism*, p. 2.

[14] Gerald Doppelt, "Can Traditional Ethical Theory Meet the Challenges of Feminism, Multiculturalism, and Environmentalism?" (a review essay on James Sterba's *Three Challenges to Ethics* [New York: Oxford University Press, 2001]), *Journal of Ethics*, 6, 2002, pp. 393–394.

African-Americans ... [C]ulture is not the problem, and it is not the solution."[15] Native Americans, Africans, and Native Australians in particular have tended to be viewed as sub-persons rather than persons – indeed sometimes they were not regarded as human at all, but as an intermediate link between white humanity and the rest of the animal kingdom, or as fully-fledged members of that kingdom. "We look upon them with Scorn and Disdain and think them little better than Beasts in Human Shape," wrote one Englishman in early seventeenth-century Virginia about Native Americans.[16] *The Negro a Beast* was the title of one book published in the United States in 1900.[17] "There is no scientific evidence that the Aborigine is a human being at all," declared an Australian Member of Parliament as recently as 1902.[18] As numerous accounts in recent histories of racism make plain, the inferiority of non-whites as a particular kind of deficient humanoid being was taken for granted by scientific white opinion – as recorded in journal articles, scholarly treatises, and encyclopedias – as late as the 1930s, and by lay white opinion much longer.[19] And this has implications for how we should think of the corrective "politics of recognition," which, since Charles Taylor's classic essay on the subject, has been so closely tied to the subject of multiculturalism.[20]

Whatever Taylor's own intentions, his essay has assumed a canonical status in establishing the parameters and setting the agenda for subsequent work in this area, so that it has often been taken as an appropriate way of thinking about anti-racism. He begins by locating "the

[15] Appiah, "Multicultural Misunderstanding," p. 36; cited in Richard T. Ford, *Racial Culture: A Critique* (Princeton: Princeton University Press, 2005), p. 7.

[16] Cited in Richard Ashcraft, "Leviathan Triumphant: Thomas Hobbes and the Politics of Wild Men," in *The Wild Man Within: An Image in Western Thought from the Renaissance to Romanticism*, ed. Edward Dudley and Maximillian E. Novak (Pittsburgh: University of Pittsburgh Press, 1972), p. 151.

[17] *"The Negro a Beast"; or, "In the Image of God"* by Charles Carroll; cited in Lee D. Baker, *From Savage to Negro: Anthropology and the Construction of Race, 1896–1954* (Berkeley and Los Angeles: University of California Press, 1998), p. 79.

[18] Cited in Mark Cocker, *Rivers of Blood, Rivers of Gold: Europe's Conflict with Tribal Peoples* (London: Jonathan Cape, 1998), p. 13.

[19] See, for example, John S. Haller Jr., *Outcasts from Evolution: Scientific Attitudes of Racial Inferiority, 1859–1900* (1971; rpt. Carbondale and Edwardsville: Southern Illinois University Press, 1995); Stephen Jay Gould, *The Mismeasure of Man*, rev. and exp. edn. (New York: W. W. Norton, 1996), orig. edn. 1981; Elazar Barkan, *The Retreat of Scientific Racism: Changing Concepts of Race in Britain and the United States between the World Wars* (New York: Cambridge University Press, 1992); Baker, *From Savage to Negro*.

[20] Charles Taylor, "The Politics of Recognition," in *Multiculturalism and "The Politics of Recognition,"* ed. Amy Gutmann with commentary by Amy Gutmann, Steven C. Rockefeller, Michael Walzer, and Susan Wolf (Princeton: Princeton University Press, 1992).

modern preoccupation with identity and recognition" in the "collapse of social hierarchies," the displacement of honor by dignity, and the emergence in modernity of "an *individualized* identity, one that is particular to me," which is linked with the ideal of authenticity. Two politics – "a politics of universalism," based on equal dignity, and "a politics of difference," based on the uniqueness of identity – are the result. Multiculturalism for him is associated with the latter, and its underlying logic "seems to depend upon a premise that we owe equal respect to all cultures."[21] But obviously we can question whether this is the best way of thinking of the politics of anti-racism, which, though it will sometimes involve cultural valorization as a component, is far more a matter of the exposure of the *bogus character* of previous declarations of Western universalist humanism, and insistence on their genuine extension to non-whites. George Fredrickson's recent short history of racism also contextualizes its significance in the emergence of Western modernity's presumption of human equality. Unlike Taylor, though, he makes unequivocally clear that what is at stake is the (contested) claim to humanity itself:

What makes Western racism so autonomous and conspicuous in world history has been that it developed in a context that presumed human equality of some kind... If equality is the norm in the spiritual or temporal realms (or in both at the same time), and there are groups of people within the society who are so despised or disparaged that the upholders of the norms feel compelled to make them exceptions to the promise or realization of equality, they can be denied the prospect of equal status only if they allegedly possess some extraordinary deficiency that makes them less than fully human. It is uniquely in the West that we find [this] dialectical interaction.[22]

Lawrence Blum's critique of Taylor, with which I am in sympathy, is that Taylor's formulation ("everyone should be recognized for their unique identity") "conflates two distinct strands within 'recognition' – one, recognizing someone as an equal (a recognition involved in racial justice), and the other recognizing someone in her distinct (cultural or other) identity."[23] Blum suggests that the focus on the "equal worth" of

[21] Taylor, "Politics of Recognition," pp. 26–28, 37–38, 66.
[22] George Fredrickson, *Racism: A Short History* (Princeton: Princeton University Press, 2002), pp. 11–12.
[23] Lawrence Blum, "Multiculturalism, Racial Justice, and Community: Reflections on Charles Taylor's 'Politics of Recognition'," in *Defending Diversity: Contemporary Philosophical Perspectives on Pluralism and Multiculturalism*, ed. Lawrence Foster and Patricia Herzog (Amherst, MA: University of Massachusetts Press, 1994), p. 192. See also Lawrence Blum, "Recognition, Value, and Equality: A Critique of Charles Taylor's and Nancy Fraser's Accounts of Multiculturalism," in *Theorizing Multiculturalism*, ed. Willett, pp. 73–99.

cultures is mistaken (Blum doubts if it is even intelligible), that Taylor is in fact "little concerned directly with racism" in this essay, and that the real demand should be for equality "as a form of recognition directed toward human beings not in their distinctness but in their shared humanity and equal citizenship."

While Taylor initially credits this form of recognition, by the end of the essay, recognition has lost its link to the equality of common humanity and has gotten confined to the domain of distinctiveness. Thus Taylor both imports an equality where it does not belong (in respect to cultures), and also fails to recognize it where it does (in the arena of racism).[24]

To the extent that racism is intimately tied up with the denial of people's humanity, the denial of equal personhood, an anti-racist politics will need to be centered on issues of racial justice and the demanding of an end to the color-coding of nominally universalist, but in reality racialized, Western values of equality and inclusion. The "distinctiveness" cited will be not so much that of different cultures as that of systemically differential treatment, and what is now required to rethink conventional normative frameworks and accommodate the experience of people of color within their hitherto white terms of reference. If cultural distinctiveness were the sole or primary obstacle to white acceptance, then culturally assimilated people of color would not encounter racism, which has patently not been the case, from the 1830s removal to the west of the Mississippi of the "civilized" Cherokees in the United States to the contemptuous twentieth-century treatment in the mother countries of *les hommes de couleur* from the colonies, as famously attested to by such classic anti-colonial writers as Frantz Fanon.[25] The issue really has to do with non-white personhood itself, and the white refusal to recognize it.

In 1831, John Ridge, a Cherokee Indian educated at a Moravian mission school, appealed somewhat pathetically to a friendly white audience:

You asked us to throw off the hunter and warrior state: We did so – you asked us to form a republican government: We did so – adopting your own as a model. You asked us to cultivate the earth, and learn the mechanic arts: We did so. You asked us to learn to read: We did so. You asked us to cast away our idols, and worship your God: We did so.[26]

---

[24] Blum, "Recognition, Value, and Equality," pp. 73–75.
[25] Frantz Fanon, *Black Skin, White Masks*, trans. Charles Lam Markmann (New York: Grove Press, 1967).
[26] Cited in Scott L. Malcomson, *One Drop of Blood: The American Misadventure of Race* (New York: Farrar, Straus & Giroux, 2000), p. 83.

But their cultural imitation and assimilation were all in vain. In Scott Malcomson's sardonic summary:

The racialization of Indians and the taking of their land had become critical issues for the white people who were [US President Andrew] Jackson's professed constituency and who were in the majority ... For a variety of reasons, white people in this period felt an acute need to affirm their whiteness, and a correspondingly acute need to affirm the blackness of blacks and the Indianness of Indians ... Jackson singled out the Cherokees because they had imitated the United States too well ... Some Indians were becoming too much like whites, thereby threatening the coherence of the white United States – and so all Indians should go west, where they could continue being something they really weren't any longer, that is, real Indians ... except that, as the whites were themselves steadily going westward, it would again in the future be too late for the Indians. It would always be too late. The story of the Indians would always be like a suicide note written for them by whites.[27]

Whether culturally Cherokee or culturally white, then, whether unreconstructed Aborigines or assimilated red men in whiteface, the point is that they were still *racially* Indian, and as such a population marked out as legitimately excludable from the juridical guarantees of the racial polity. And in the end that was all that really mattered.

Similarly, a *New York Times* story on the November 2005 riots in the French *cités*, the segregated housing projects, cites one Semou Diof: "I was born in Senegal when it was part of France. I speak French, my wife is French and I was educated in France. [The problem] is the French don't think I'm French."[28] A Moroccan immigrant who came to France as a child of eight sums up the situation: "You're French on your identity card, French to pay taxes and to go into the army, but for the rest, you're an Arab."[29] The racial identity denied in the official ideology of French republicanism continues to silently determine who the real citizens of the polity are.

Moreover, even to the extent that cultural recognition *is* a legitimate goal, it has been questioned how apposite it is in connection with black Americans, whose struggles against racial subordination in the 1950s and 1960s inspired many other civil rights movements not merely nationally but globally, yet who, decades later, have yet to achieve racial equality. It is noteworthy that Will Kymlicka says explicitly that the situation of African-Americans is "virtually unique," and locates them

[27] Malcomson, *One Drop of Blood*, pp. 79–80, 81–82.
[28] Craig S. Smith, "France Faces a Colonial Legacy: What Makes Someone French?," *New York Times* (11 November 2005), A1.
[29] Craig S. Smith, "Inside French Housing Project, Feelings of Being the Outsiders," *New York Times* (9 November 2005), A11.

in a separate category in his multicultural taxonomy.[30] Even for the seemingly more clear-cut cases of voluntary immigrant groups, culture arguably needs to be thought of as more dynamic and open than in the reified and static versions of dominant multiculturalism. And for African-Americans in particular, whose very existence on US soil is a result of coercion and deracination, forced interaction with the dominant culture has obviously been a crucial factor in their cultural evolution from the start.

"Blackness" itself, of course (as in "black Americans"), is not an African concept but a white or New World one, a category in which people from many different ethnic groups and linguistic communities were originally subsumed against their will, and which they then tried to recreate in a more positive self-image. So there is no blackness without whiteness, and this intimately interrelational dynamic means that one cannot be studied in monadic isolation from the other. While African retentions undoubtedly exist, they were necessarily syncretically transformed by the experience of slavery and post-bellum Jim Crow.[31] Black culture has been shaped by, even when reacting in an oppositional way against, white culture. On the other hand, neither is there any whiteness without blackness. Cultural "purity" is as much a myth as racial purity: "incontestably mulatto" was the black theorist Albert Murray's famous characterization of American culture,[32] so that, in Eric Sundquist's seemingly paradoxical judgment, "the two traditions can be seen as both one and separate."[33] Thus, while the appreciation of black American culture is certainly a worthy goal, there is a sense in which the "cultural recognition" really called for is the demystified acknowledgment in the national white psyche of the *blackness at the heart of whiteness*, and what it says about the pervasiveness of cultural (and other kinds of) "miscegenation."

An additional concern is that the ghetto culture which – given the global success of hip-hop – is sometimes seen as "authentically" black (while, of course, being enthusiastically imitated by millions of suburban white kids) may require less an uncritical multiculturalist "respect" than an understanding of its sources in systemic social oppression. In their landmark text on what they call *American Apartheid*, Douglas

[30] Kymlicka, *Multicultural Citizenship*, p. 60.

[31] For an interesting essay and useful bibliography on the subject, see Tommy L. Lott, "African Retentions," in *A Companion to African-American Philosophy*, ed. Tommy L. Lott and John P. Pittman (Malden, MA: Blackwell, 2003), pp. 168–189.

[32] Albert Murray, *The Omni-Americans: Some Alternatives to the Folklore of White Supremacy* ([1970] Cambridge, MA: Da Capo Press, 1990).

[33] Eric J. Sundquist, *To Wake the Nations: Race in the Making of American Literature* (Cambridge, MA: Harvard University Press, 1993), p. 22.

Massey and Nancy Denton point out that as a result of the hyper-segregation of inner-city blacks – now "among the most isolated people on earth"[34] – many African-American youth live in what is virtually a world of their own, and have created an "oppositional culture" accordingly to affirm their humanity that is, in effect, a "culture of segregation," "defined *in opposition to* the basic ideals and values of American society."[35] The mass embrace of hip-hop in recent years by Muslim immigrants in the French *banlieues* is obviously best understood not in terms of any "natural" Afrocentrist commonalities between North African Arabs and the descendants in Babylon of those displaced Africans stolen from the home continent hundreds of years ago, but rather as a manifestation of a common alienation and exclusion from mainstream white society. So though it is a testimony to human beings' spiritual resilience that they have refused to let themselves be crushed by white racism, it would clearly be absurd to fetishize all aspects of this underclass "culture" instead of seeing it as a desperate reaction to terrible circumstances that themselves need to be changed. As Olivier Roy argues in a *New York Times* Op-Ed piece about the 2005 French riots:

[T]he reality is that there is nothing particularly Muslim, or even French, about the violence. Rather, we are witnessing the temporary rising up of one small part of a Western underclass culture that reaches from Paris to London to Los Angeles and beyond ... [T]he young men wear the same hooded sweatshirts, listen to similar music and use slang in the same way as their counterparts in Los Angeles or Washington ... [They] are not fighting to be recognized as a minority group, either ethnic or religious; they want to be accepted as full citizens. They have believed in the French model (individual integration through citizenship) but feel cheated because of their social and economic exclusion ... Contrary to the calls of many liberals, increased emphasis on multiculturalism and respect for other cultures in France is not the answer: this angry young population is highly deculturalized and individualized ... [T]he struggle to integrate an angry underclass is one shared across the Western world.[36]

Finally, replacing race by culture, or assuming that race and a particular culture are always linked, is problematic for the simple reason that there is no essentialist one-to-one correspondence between the two. Race has been historically created through discriminatory legislation and social custom, but this does not mean that people uniformly categorized across different regions, classes, and educational levels as members of

---

[34] Douglas S. Massey and Nancy A. Denton, *American Apartheid: Segregation and the Making of the Underclass* (Cambridge, MA: Harvard University Press, 1993), p. 22.
[35] Massey and Denton, *American Apartheid*, pp. 165–181.
[36] Olivier Roy, "Get French or Die Trying," *New York Times* (9 November 2005), A27.

one "race" are similarly uniform in their cultures, even if they are similarly structurally subordinated.

In sum, the displacement of race by culture, or fusion of race with culture, is methodologically dubious both in terms of socio-historical analysis and in what it leads to as public policy prescription. Race and racial injustice need to be theorized in much broader terms than simply culturalist ones even where cultural difference *is* the key factor. And in many cases it is not.

II.   Race and ethnicity

Let us turn now to the related subject of ethnicity. In the earlier literature on racial and ethnic relations, it would have been standard to draw a distinction between race and ethnicity, insofar as races were thought of as naturally *biologically* differentiated sections of the human race, identified as such by phenotype and genealogy, while what divided ethnic groups were primarily *cultural* traits like language, religion, dress, tastes in food, and so forth. (With the rise to prominence since the Second World War of "cultural racism," this original contrast has, of course, become somewhat muddied.) Thus race was thought of as permanent and unchanging in a way that ethnicity was not. Correspondingly, racism was demarcated from ethnocentrism by its presumption of ineluctable biological hierarchy, while ethnocentrism allowed for the acceptance of ethnic groups willing to give up their distinctive ways of life and acculturate to the majority. With the growing scientific consensus that biological race does not exist in the first place (and so cannot serve as a basis for hierarchy), ethnicity is now seen as real in a way that race (apparently) is not. Moreover, ethnicity, like culture, is a respectable term. As Sneja Gunew points out:

In an earlier era ethnicity was seen as a way of circumventing the racist history of "race" and was associated with apparently cultural choices; in other words, that one could choose the groups to which one belonged ... Ethnicity was also largely conceived in cultural terms as a matter of the rituals of daily life ... Race on the other hand has been associated with irreducible difference (akin to representations of sexual difference) often located in what have been termed "visible differences" (for example, skin colour) which gained their legitimation through association with so-called biological givens. This meant that choice was suspended in the face of racist projections emerging in response to ... visible differences.[37]

The elective affinity between multiculturalism and the discourse of ethnicity is therefore obvious: this is a respectable way of talking about

---

[37] Gunew, *Haunted Nations*, p. 21.

human difference, in culturalist rather than biologistic terms. But the danger of such an ethnicization of race is that by ignoring the *social* existence, past and present, of race, it runs the risk of conflating the histories of groups once thought of as (separate non-white) races with the histories of (white) groups not so regarded, thereby disastrously obfuscating the distinctive experience of the former. In other words, even if it is true that anthropologically only ethnicity exists, and in the end (in a future, post-racial world) talk of ethnicity should displace talk of race, in the interim we still need to draw a line of demarcation between those ethnicities so racialized historically as to dissolve into a larger (relatively privileged) "racial" whiteness and those ethnicities so racialized as to be antipodal to it. For racial categorization was not merely a (mistaken) inter-subjective consensus confined to the realm of ideas, but one that also manifested itself in public policy, first- and second-class citizenship, juridical prescription and proscription, discriminatory economic systems, state protection and its lack, and differential opportunity structures. So from the fact that race is not biologically real and that all human groups are really ethnic groups, it does not follow that the trajectory of those ethnics categorized as non-white can be simply represented as a minor variant on the white ethnic trajectory. Multiculturalism's explicit centering of what have traditionally been the markers of *ethnicity*, then, may end up assimilating the milder history of (usually temporary) white ethnic exclusion to the quite different and far more intransigent history of non-white racial subordination.

Native peoples in Australia and Canada, African and Asian immigrants to Europe, and black American activists have all, in different ways, challenged the ethnicity model. For example, Ellie Vasta writes about the Australian situation:

Aboriginal people's skepticism about multiculturalism is linked to their experience of a much more extreme form of racism than was the case of immigrants. In the colonial period, their communities, cultures and ways of life were systematically destroyed ... In terms of living conditions, health, life expectancy and education, Aboriginal people appear as a Third World population on the margins of a rich, white society ... The promise of integration and social mobility that Australia held out to post-war immigrants never applied to the oldest Australians ... Multiculturalism is rejected ... above all because its central concept of ethnicity is seen as unacceptable: Aboriginal people refuse to be seen as one ethnic group among others.[38]

---

[38] Ellie Vasta, "Dialectics of Domination: Racism and Multiculturalism," in *The Teeth Are Smiling: The Persistence of Racism in Multicultural Australia*, ed. Ellie Vasta and Stephen Castles (St. Leonards, Australia: Allen & Unwin, 1996), pp. 50–51.

Similarly, in the United States the white European voluntary immigrant experience has been radically different from the coerced experience of expropriated Native Americans, enslaved Africans, and annexed Mexicans – a difference crystallized in "race." But the delegitimization of race as a social category and tool of historical understanding has gone ideologically hand-in-hand with a conservative contemporary "color-blindness" which denies the reality and causal importance of race even while simultaneously refusing to give up (indeed refusing to see) the advantages of white privilege that race has brought about. What should have been, and obviously still is in significant measure, a tremendous moral and political advance – the discrediting of biological race as a concept – has been turned into a discrediting of racial analysis in general and corresponding public policy recommendations based on the need to redress racial injustice. To the extent that race is conceptualized through the categories of official multiculturalism, and thereby refracted into a culturalist discourse that is really more appropriate for ethnicity, its peculiar features and history will evade capture.

American legal theorist Richard Ford, for example, makes a provocative case that the 1978 *Bakke* US Supreme Court decision was crucial in motivating the shift from racial justice to "diversity" as a rationale for preferential treatment, and thus to the subsequent flourishing of multiculturalism in the United States. (Allan Bakke was the aspiring white medical student turned down by the University of California at Davis medical school, who then sued them on the grounds that the preferential admission of racial minorities with lower grades violated his constitutional rights. In a decision split several ways, Justice Lewis Powell's individual judgment that some consideration of race was permissible effectively became the court ruling. This shift has recently been re-affirmed in the 2003 *Grutter v. Bollinger* decision on the University of Michigan Law School's admission policy, which affirmed, 5 to 4, that race could be given some weight in admissions to promote educational diversity.[39]) The history of systemic discrimination and the need to make up for it vanishes in favor of the promotion of diverse cultures and perspectives:

The [Supreme Court Justice] Powell opinion silently institutionalized an ethnicity model of race that, by its very nature emphasizes the innocent "fact" of cultural difference over the politically imposed wrongs of status hierarchy. In the ethnicity paradigm, the position of blacks is analogous to that of, say, some Italian-Americans: both have distinctive cultural backgrounds and therefore may

---

[39] See Derrick Bell, *Silent Covenants: Brown v. Board of Education and the Unfulfilled Hopes for Racial Reform* (New York: Oxford University Press, 2004), pp. 142–145, 148–149.

contribute a unique perspective to the university environment. What is excluded by this paradigm is any acknowledgment that a very recent history of state-sponsored and institutional subordination distinguishes the two groups. Here the *cultural* identity of racial minority groups is emphasized at the expense of the history of racism ... In this light it would appear that a central function of "diversity" is to finesse, if not obscure the salience of contemporary racism.[40]

Contesting this theoretical vanishing-act has been one of the main reasons motivating the growing body of work mapping what could be termed the "metaphysics" of race: the attempt to delineate and demarcate the ways in which race is and is not real. Though there are variations in the details of the positions taken, the common theme for most writers is the socio-political reality of race. If race is not a "natural kind," it can at least be thought of as a "social kind," "constructed" by law, custom, and inter-subjective identification, and objectively signifying a particular location in a system of domination.[41] So it is a mistake to infer the socio-political non-existence of race from the biological non-existence of race. These authors would insist that – in a suitably glossed and hedged way – it is still perfectly legitimate to talk about "race," and to resist the racial "eliminativism" that has become the conventional wisdom in white American circles. In addition, the recognition of the dynamic of race-making – symbolized by the fact that "to race" and "to racialize" become verbs – and its contextualization in a setting of group conflict enables an understanding of why certain groups become "races" in the first place. Once we cease to regard race as natural, but as constructed, the question then becomes what motivates this construction. Instead of taking for granted as given the distinction between ethnic groups as cultural and races as biological, we are then conceptually oriented towards the crucial question of what made them so respectively depicted to begin with, and what this says about the link between race and political power. If some ethnicities are racialized while others are not, we need to investigate what interests that might serve.

III.   Race and political economy

And that brings us back to Charles Taylor's essay and its role in canonizing the "politics of recognition." If race exists – not merely (or at all)

---

[40] Ford, *Racial Culture*, pp. 45, 52.
[41] See, for example: Sally A. Haslanger, "Ontology and Social Construction," *Philosophical Topics*, 23 (2), 1995, pp. 95–125; Charles W. Mills, "'But What Are You Really?' The Metaphysics of Race," in Mills, *Blackness Visible: Essays on Philosophy and Race* (Ithaca, NY: Cornell University Press, 1998), pp. 41–66; Ronald R. Sundstrom, "'Racial' Nominalism," *Journal of Social Philosophy*, 33 (2), 2002, pp. 193–210.

as culture, not merely as ethnicity – but as enduring social construct historically linked with systems of domination and subordination, then an emancipatory politics cannot confine itself to "recognition," but must try to dismantle the structures of racial oppression themselves. Yet insofar as multicultural politics is primarily oriented towards the cultural, it will have difficulty in even seeing these structures. Until a few decades ago, radical oppositional political theory was, of course, dominated by Marxism, which made class the Archimedean point both for understanding and transforming the social order. Capitalism was the problem, and political economy was the appropriate tool of analysis. The rise of the "new social movements" of the 1960s onward, centered around gender, race, and sexual orientation, challenged the adequacy in both theory and practice of Marxist concepts and Marxist-inspired political parties. The later collapse of self-described socialist states signified a global defeat for the orthodox left, and seemed to confirm, as if any further proof were necessary, the intellectual bankruptcy of its theoretical methodology. In her well-known critique of a decade ago, Nancy Fraser warned that the new "'postsocialist' condition" had brought about an "apparent shift in the political imaginary" in which "the central problem of justice is recognition,"[42] whereas what was called for was "a political strategy for integrating recognition claims with redistribution claims," a need particularly urgent in the case of what she terms "paradigmatic bivalent collectivities," such as gender and race, where the group in question is subordinated *both* by "socioeconomic maldistribution and cultural misrecognition."[43]

But at least until comparatively recently, race has not, in respectable white academic circles, been recognized as a social structure in its own right.[44] To begin with, of course, race was for hundreds of years generally seen as natural and biological rather than social, so that such a conceptualization would have been ruled out a priori. But even when, by the mid-twentieth century, scientific racism was being refuted and biological race challenged, race tended either to be reduced to class (in the orthodox Marxist left, who were sympathetic to structural accounts) or reduced to individual prejudice incompatible with American ideals (in the liberal mainstream, who were not). In neither case, then, was race conceived of

---

[42] Nancy Fraser, "Introduction," in *Justice Interruptus: Critical Reflections on the "Postsocialist" Condition* (New York: Routledge, 1997), p. 2.

[43] Nancy Fraser, "From Redistribution to Recognition," in *Justice Interruptus*, pp. 12–13, 19.

[44] The qualification is necessary because there is a long oppositional black American intellectual tradition, either excluded from the academy altogether or ghettoized in an ignored and Jim-Crowed section of it, which – years before the "social construction of race" became a cliché in the radical white academy – argued for the essential artificiality of race.

as a social system in itself with an autonomy of its own. Thus a political economy of race was ruled out, either because it would turn out to be just a political economy of class (with race as a sub-proletarianized section of the white working class) or because racism was an anomaly in a basically egalitarian United States, and not to be conceived of in social-systemic terms.[45]

What has changed this situation is the emergence over the past decade in the United States of a growing body of work in "critical race theory" and "critical white studies," that – building on the pioneering insights of such black American thinkers as W. E. B. Du Bois and James Baldwin – has begun the systemic analysis of "race" and "whiteness" as artificial constructs central to the making not just of the United States but the modern world.[46] Meta-theoretical commitments vary among different writers, and it is not at all the case that all members of this movement – "school" would imply a unity that does not exist – would be sympathetic to the revival of political economy categories. But for some theorists, at least, it has seemed a fruitful strategy to think of white racial domination – what used to be called *white supremacy* – as a system in its own right, founded on racial exploitation. And just as classic Marxist political economy sought to link the typical functioning of the (ruling-class) state and the (bourgeois) legal system to the class dynamic of the capitalist economy, so theorists with these holistic commitments have drawn on work from political science, legal studies, sociology, cultural studies, and economics, to paint a global picture of the multiple interacting spheres in which white privilege and domination have manifested themselves. This theoretical body of work has been most extensively developed within the United States, but there is no reason why some of its key insights, suitably adjusted, may not be found useful elsewhere.

The legal system, for example, has generally not remotely been neutral, protecting the rights and freedoms of all, but has usually served as the political instrument of a white *Recht*, from the original judgments in international jurisprudence that legitimized European colonialism and

---

[45] See Rogers M. Smith, *Civic Ideals: Conflicting Visions of Citizenship in US History* (New Haven: Yale University Press, 1997), for an account of the framing of racism as an "anomaly" in a basically egalitarian American political culture by such canonical political theorists as Alexis de Tocqueville, Gunnar Myrdal, and Louis Hartz.

[46] See, for example, Kimberlé Crenshaw, Neil Gotanda, Gary Peller, and Kendall Thomas (eds.), *Critical Race Theory: The Key Writings That Formed the Movement* (New York: New Press, 1995); Richard Delgado and Jean Stefancic (eds.), *Critical White Studies: Looking Behind the Mirror* (Philadelphia: Temple University Press, 1997). An important recent contribution has been made by black philosophers: George Yancy (ed.), *What White Looks Like: African-American Philosophers on the Whiteness Question* (New York: Routledge, 2004).

settlement (the "Doctrine of Discovery," claims about *terra nullius*), through the codification of the norms governing slavery and the formal differentiation of the population into racialized categories with differing statuses, to laws restricting citizenship and immigration ("White American/Canadian/Australian" policies), and finally, in the present epoch of nominally repudiated white supremacy and some (weak) commitment to corrective measures, to anti-discrimination legislation tendentiously limiting the concept of discrimination to conscious discrete acts by specific perpetrators.[47] Similarly, the state has functioned as a racial state, whether through the overt creation of a white nation, as in the United States, South Africa, and Australia, where native peoples and blacks were originally formally excluded from full membership in the polity, or in Latin America and the Caribbean, where the white and light-skinned have been privileged at the expense of the darker mestizo and mulatto, indio and Negro, populations, in what have been called "pigmentocracies," or in the colonizing European mother countries themselves, where national identity was formed in part as a racial identity constituted in opposition to the non-white subject races abroad over which they ruled.[48]

The Marxist tradition of political economy is classically associated with the concept of exploitation, and in large part for that very reason liberals have not generally had much use for it. But if exploitation in the Marxist sense is discredited because of the demise of the labor theory of value, other conceptualizations of the notion are certainly easily and readily defensible within a mainstream liberal framework, needing no such dubious foundation. Recent books by Alan Wertheimer and Ruth Sample suggest that "exploitation" as a concept may be making a comeback, now predicated on standard liberal Kantian prohibitions against "using" others against their will for one's benefit.[49] Neither author has much to say about race, but I have argued elsewhere that we

[47] Crenshaw et al., *Critical Race Theory*; A. Leon Higginbotham Jr., *In the Matter of Color: Race and the American Legal Process – The Colonial Period* (New York: Oxford University Press, 1978) and *Shades of Freedom: Racial Politics and Presumptions of the American Legal Process* (New York: Oxford University Press, 1996); Ian F. Haney López, *White by Law: The Legal Construction of Race* (New York: New York University Press, 1996); Cheryl I. Harris, "Whiteness as Property," *Harvard Law Review*, 106 (8), 1993, pp. 1709–1791.

[48] Anthony Marx, *Making Race and Nation: A Comparison of the United States, South Africa, and Brazil* (New York: Cambridge University Press, 1998); Howard Winant, *The World is a Ghetto: Race and Democracy since World War II* (New York: Basic Books, 2001); David Theo Goldberg, *The Racial State* (Malden, MA: Blackwell, 2002).

[49] Alan Wertheimer, *Exploitation* (Princeton: Princeton University Press, 1996); Ruth J. Sample, *Exploitation: What It Is and Why It's Wrong* (Lanham, MD: Rowman & Littlefield, 2003).

need to develop a concept of *racial exploitation* to capture these realities of illicit white benefit, and that such a concept could help to illuminate the logic and motivational dynamic of the perpetuation of white domination, especially since attitudinal research in the United States shows that whites' perception of their group interests is the major causal factor in shaping their positions on public policy issues to do with race.[50] While in mainstream liberal theory racism is often represented as "irrational," there is a well-established and completely respectable economic sense in which it is indeed "rational" for the white population, tied to the reproduction of their group privilege. Reconceptualizing race in social-systemic rather than individual-attitudinal terms has had the theoretical virtue of bringing into focus white benefit as an explanatory factor. Various recent books have begun the documentation and analysis of the numerous ways in which black disadvantage in the United States has translated into cumulative, multiplying, self-perpetuating white advantage: not merely the obvious example of slavery itself, but also postbellum debt servitude, land theft, employment and promotion discrimination, racialized industry location, destruction of competing black businesses and the blocking of others' entry to the white market, differential educational funding, the color-coding of transfer payments by the state, selective urban renewal, and the federal role in sanctioning restrictive covenants for white homeowners, thereby guaranteeing that for decades blacks would be locked out of what has traditionally been the main way for the working and middle class to accumulate wealth, home ownership.[51] Certainly there should be no difficulty in extrapolating such approaches to other countries to understand Native Australian expropriation and continuing exclusion, or the denial of equal opportunities to non-white immigrants in Europe.

---

[50] Charles W. Mills, "Racial Exploitation and the Wages of Whiteness," in *The Changing Terrain of Race and Ethnicity*, ed. Maria Krysan and Amanda E. Lewis (New York: Russell Sage, 2004), pp. 235–262; Donald R. Kinder and Lynn M. Sanders, *Divided by Color: Racial Politics and Democratic Ideals* (Chicago: University of Chicago Press, 1996).

[51] See, for example: Richard F. America (ed.), *The Wealth of Races: The Present Value of Benefits from Past Injustices* (New York: Greenwood Press, 1990); Massey and Denton, *American Apartheid*; Melvin L. Oliver and Thomas M. Shapiro, *Black Wealth/White Wealth: A New Perspective on Racial Inequality* (New York: Routledge, 1995); George Lipsitz, *The Possessive Investment in Whiteness: How White People Profit from Identity Politics* (Philadelphia: Temple University Press, 1998); Dalton Conley, *Being Black, Living in the Red: Race, Wealth, and Social Policy in America* (Berkeley: University of California Press, 1999); Thomas M. Shapiro, *The Hidden Cost of Being African-American* (New York: Oxford University Press, 2004); Ira Katznelson, *When Affirmative Action Was White: An Untold History of Racial Inequality in Twentieth-Century America* (New York: W. W. Norton, 2005).

The point is, then, that a political economy of race, that explores the interrelation of economic subordination, juridical color-coding, racialized state policy, and white moral psychology, can be developed that does not rely on now-discredited Marxist shibboleths, nor seek imperialistically to encompass all social phenomena. While there are, as conceded, cultural aspects to race, a growing literature outside of political philosophy is making clear the extent to which traditional political economy categories – if not utilized on a traditional subject – can map racial subordination. A multicultural politics that confines itself to "recognition" without seeking to address these other dimensions will necessarily be a politics that changes very little.

IV.　　Race and Enlightenment liberalism

So finally we come to the question of the prescriptive: the relationship between race and liberalism, or more generally between race and normative Enlightenment theory. In these debates, for example as illustrated in the recent exchange between Brian Barry and his critics,[52] multiculturalism is standardly counterposed to Enlightenment liberalism, in a face-off between what is represented as a disingenuously abstract and *soi-disant* universalism, suppressing difference, versus a group-based particularism that insists on it. Universal prescriptions run aground on the reefs of local variation, capsizing the pretensions to an all-inclusive normativity; liberalism's atomic individualism, in abstracting away from cultural difference, proves inadequate to the task of politically representing the other.

Now I do not want to dismiss such a picture altogether. But as the line of argument of my discussion will have suggested, I do not at all see this as the main problem in the historic relation between Enlightenment liberalism and race. For me the problem with liberalism has not been its universalism, but its white exclusivism; the problem with the Enlightenment has not been its "totalitarian" illumination, but rather its white darkness. Thus the challenge that taking race seriously poses to the orthodox history of liberalism, and, more generally, modernity, arises from the failure to acknowledge the history of implicit hierarchy in its superficially egalitarian and inclusivist categories.

Desmond King argues that "illiberal elements appear to be part of liberalism itself. It is a defining but neglected feature of liberal

---

[52] Brian Barry, *Culture and Equality: An Egalitarian Critique of Multiculturalism* (Cambridge, MA: Harvard University Press, 2001); Paul Kelly (ed.), *Multiculturalism Reconsidered: Culture and Equality and its Critics* (Malden, MA: Polity/Blackwell, 2002).

democracy."[53] Three decades of feminist scholarship have made the truth of this claim with respect to gender obvious. But only recently has a comparable body of scholarship begun to emerge on colonialism and race.[54] Yet the implications will, I believe, turn out to be similarly far-reaching for our meta-philosophical narratives about the history of philosophy. A recent essay on Locke's *Second Treatise* begins with the matter-of-fact statement: "It is now a commonplace in the history of political thought that there has long been a mutually constitutive relationship between liberalism and colonialism," so that modern liberal theorists were "address[ing] contexts at once domestic and colonial."[55] The author, David Armitage, goes on to emphasize that "Not all liberals were complicit with colonialism."[56] But many were, and even when modern Western theorists have opposed colonialism they have often (as with opposition to slavery) continued to take white racial superiority for granted. Thus the theorists who define the modern political canon – David Hume, John Locke, Immanuel Kant, John Stuart Mill, Georg Hegel, Karl Marx – all reveal disparaging and contemptuous attitudes towards non-whites in their writing.

I suggest that – with some honorable exceptions[57] – liberalism has generally been "illiberal liberalism," "racial liberalism," in which whiteness has usually been a prerequisite for full personhood, and humans of color have for the most part been seen as sub-persons ("savages," "barbarians"). So the characterization of *actual* historic liberalism (as against a liberalism retroactively sanitized for a contemporary audience) in terms of race-neutral abstraction is misleading: it has generally rested on a white particularism, in which the famous "atomic" individuals are actually part of the "compound" of the white body. Rethinking the social ontology of this historic liberalism requires

---

[53] Desmond King, *In the Name of Liberalism: Illiberal Social Policy in the United States and Britain* (New York: Oxford University Press, 1999), p. 27.

[54] See, for example: David Theo Goldberg, *Racist Culture: Philosophy and the Politics of Meaning* (Cambridge, MA: Blackwell, 1993); Emmanuel Chukwudi Eze (ed.), *Race and the Enlightenment: A Reader* (Cambridge, MA: Blackwell, 1997); Charles W. Mills, *The Racial Contract* (Ithaca, NY: Cornell University Press, 1997); Uday Singh Mehta, *Liberalism and Empire: A Study in Nineteenth-Century British Liberal Thought* (Chicago: University of Chicago Press, 1999); Julie K. Ward and Tommy L. Lott (eds.), *Philosophers on Race: Critical Essays* (Malden, MA: Blackwell, 2002); Jennifer Pitts, *A Turn to Empire: The Rise of Imperial Liberalism in Britain and France* (Princeton: Princeton University Press, 2005); Andrew Valls (ed.), *Race and Racism in Modern Philosophy* (Ithaca, NY: Cornell University Press, 2005).

[55] David Armitage, "John Locke, Carolina, and the *Two Treatises of Government*," *Political Theory*, 32 (5), 2004, p. 602.

[56] Ibid., p. 603.

[57] For a discussion, see Tully, *Strange Multiplicity*, and, more recently, Sankar Muthu, *Enlightenment against Empire* (Princeton: Princeton University Press, 2003).

us to recognize the common ("communitarian"!) racial ontology that is the foundation of white individualism, and that denies the possibility of such individualism to others. If Hume thinks that non-whites may be the product of a separate creation, and that no race but whites is civilized; if Locke invests in African slavery, helps to write the Carolina slave constitution, and justifies Native American expropriation; if Kant regards blacks and Native Americans as natural slaves, and envisages an all-white future for the planet; if Mill, employee of the East India Company, justifies paternalism as appropriate in the case of barbarian nations like India, these are all political statements about the actual scope of their liberal principles, not anomalies to their non-racial thought. Liberalism is racialized and justifies a racialized world order ruled over by Europe and Europeans.

With only apparent paradox, then, a case can be made that contemporary theorists of race are not trying to *put race into* liberal political theory, but to *take it out* – in the sense that it has always been there, restricting the scope of normative principles, shaping the direction of their development – and that achieving a genuine race-neutrality requires us to *acknowledge* this history and its conceptual and material legacy, so that we can then work out what would be necessary both theoretically and practically for the realization of a truly non-racial liberal polity. It does not seem to me that, when it comes to race, the pontification on intrinsic multicultural "difference" and its ramifications ought to be the main task absorbing our energies, but rather, far more pressingly, the need to renew and relegitimize the struggle to correct for the inferior global condition of people of color resulting from their original categorization as "different" humans, less than full persons.

Moreover, the need for such a transformed, race-confronting rather than race-evading, liberalism is all the more urgent in light of the scandalous failure of mainstream white Anglo-American political philosophy to deal with race. The classic representative text here, of course, is John Rawls's by now canonized *A Theory of Justice*,[58] judged to be the most important twentieth-century work in political theory, the subject of a vast body of secondary literature numbering literally thousands of articles, discussed not merely in political theory but across numerous other disciplines, and, especially with the collapse of socialism and the global triumph of liberalism, a work of growing international influence, translated as of 2003 into twenty-seven languages – with next to nothing

[58] John Rawls, *A Theory of Justice*, rev. edn. (Cambridge, MA: Harvard University Press, 1999), p. 3; orig. edn. 1971.

to say about racism and its remediation. One would think that a book leading off with the inspiring statement that "Justice is the first virtue of social institutions" would promise to be the ideal framework to theorize what justice demands when the society's actual "basic structure" has been founded on racial oppression. But alas, John Rawls's "ideal theory" methodological orientation has proven to be disastrously *non*-ideal for addressing the racism that would not exist in his "well-ordered society," and which can therefore apparently be aprioristically excluded from his own consideration and that of his followers. Nor, of course, does his later – similarly idealized – *The Law of Peoples*, with its complete ignoring of the history of European colonialism and imperialism, African slavery, Amerindian and Native Australian expropriation, and non-white genocide (things one apparently does not know either behind or in front of the veil), offer any more favorable conceptual ground for the broaching of these matters.[59] Thus one gets the absurd situation – not just in Rawls's native United States, originally a white supremacist polity, but also in a post-colonial world still shaped by the legacy of global European domination – of a spectacular revival of political philosophy and a thriving corresponding discourse on justice in which issues of racial justice are barely mentioned by white philosophers. An edited five-volume collection of eighty-eight articles on Rawls from nearly three decades of writing has only one article on race, that by an African-American philosopher, while the *Cambridge Companion to Rawls* not only has none of its fourteen chapters dedicated to race, but not even a section or sub-section of any one of them on the subject.[60] As I said – racial liberalism.

---

[59] John Rawls, *The Law of Peoples with "The Idea of Public Reason Revisited"* (Cambridge, MA: Harvard University Press, 1999). Rawls does discuss the Holocaust (pp. 19–23) (and of course Jews were non-white in Nazi Germany), but he represents it as historically unique, with no mention of, say, the genocide of Native Americans on the two continents, or of the Congolese under Belgium's King Leopold II. See David E. Stannard, *American Holocaust: The Conquest of the New World* (New York: Oxford University Press, 1992) and Adam Hochschild, *King Leopold's Ghost: A Story of Greed, Terror, and Heroism in Colonial Africa* (New York: Houghton Mifflin Company, 1998). Thus his discussion of non-ideal theory is limited to the cases of contemporary "outlaw states" and "burdened" societies developing in unfavorable socio-economic circumstances.

[60] Henry Richardson and Paul Weithman (eds.), *The Philosophy of Rawls: A Collection of Essays*, 5 vols. (New York: Garland, 1999); Samuel Freeman (ed.), *The Cambridge Companion to Rawls* (New York: Cambridge University Press, 2003). For a review essay on the Richardson–Weithman collection, see Anthony Simon Laden, "The House that Jack Built: Thirty Years of Reading Rawls," *Ethics*, 113 (2), 2003, pp. 367–390. I am indebted to Laden for the information about the near-total absence of any discussion of race in this collection.

De-racializing liberalism would require an end to the idealizing abstractions that sabotage philosophy's pretensions to describe generally the human condition and prescribe generally for its improvement. The non-ideal needs to be theorized in its own right. Abstracting away from race (and likewise, of course, for class and gender) only guarantees philosophy's increasing marginality and irrelevance to the real world. To begin the redressing of racial injustice we must face the history of racial oppression, and its numerous manifestations not merely throughout the polity but, reflexively, on the meta-theoretical level, in our descriptive and normative characterizations of the polity. It would mean confronting the fact, with all its implications for rethinking political theory, that the societies created by modernity were certainly *not*, in Rawls's formulation, "cooperative venture[s] for mutual advantage," to be modeled by a hypothetical contract among "free and equal persons whose relations with respect to one another were fair."[61] Rather, this hegemonic political image is really an abstraction from the white (male) experience of modernity, in which Filmerian feudal hierarchy is overthrown in the name of white male equality. The United States, and other white settler states like Canada, Australia, New Zealand, and South Africa, were all established on the basis of the exploitation and expropriation of Aboriginal peoples not at all seen as equals, so that what seems like a neutral apparatus already begs crucial questions and obfuscates the non-ideal history. We would need to think through what corrective racial justice requires in polities either founded directly on white supremacy, as with the above, or molded by colonial white domination and the resultant privileging of white and light-skinned minorities, or affected by terms of trade and structures of global disadvantage originally established through European colonialism. It would mean confronting the fact that the modern world has been profoundly shaped by *global white supremacy*, that people of color have been exploited for white benefit, and the state, the legal system, the opportunity structure, and the dominant moral economy have all been biased towards facilitating this exploitation.

Above all, the implications of the original denial of full personhood to people of color need to be thought through in the reconstituting of liberalism on a genuinely inclusive basis. If native peoples have been denied Lockean property rights in their land, or, in the case of blacks, even Lockean self-ownership (so that, in a wonderful American phrase, running away from slavery was tantamount to "stealing oneself"), then what would a de-racialized Lockeanism prescribe to correct for, and

---

[61] Rawls, *A Theory of Justice*, pp. 4, 12.

return to their rightful owners, the illicit property distributions of a world where whiteness has been property? If non-whites in general have been regarded as less than full Kantian persons, so that their social "dissin"' was permissible not merely in the national moral economy, but by the Kantian *Rechtsstaat* itself, and this racial disrespect was embedded in schedules of rights, national narratives, and patterns of social (non-)recognition in general, then what juridical measures, what retellings of history, what public atonements, would now be justified to restore their dignity? If the social contract in the updated Rawlsian sense of a "device of representation" (rather than a literal historical account) is better conceptualized, given the non-ideal realities of racial subordination, as an exclusionary racial contract rather than a colorless one, then what rewriting of its terms and corresponding reparatory measures would be required for people of color to voluntarily sign on to it, and rebuild as a genuinely just "basic structure" the currently white-dominated social order? Not only in a full-blooded Lockean/ Kantian "comprehensive liberalism," but even in a more anemic "political liberalism," honestly acknowledging the history of non-white subordination would yield dramatic prescriptions for racial justice.

Such a liberalism cannot truly be said by multiculturalists to have failed – for the simple reason that such a liberalism has never been tried.

4 Feminism and multiculturalism: mapping the terrain

Ayelet Shachar

At the height of the first wave of literature on multiculturalism, between the late 1980s and mid-1990s, many political and legal theorists argued in favor of accommodating the distinct ways of life of minority communities.[1] While seeking to create a more just society through recommended accommodation policies, first-wave multiculturalists regrettably overlooked some of the potential risks and costs to more vulnerable group members. By the late 1990s, penetrating second-wave critiques of multiculturalism had become established in the literature.[2] A prominent place in this pantheon of critique is reserved for the burgeoning literature on women and multiculturalism – or the feminist critique of multiculturalism – which is the subject of this chapter.

The feminist critique of multiculturalism encompasses a rich array of theoretical approaches. Its key focus is twofold: first, it questions the basic assumption that "respect for difference" policies provide greater freedom and security for *all* group members (especially in those cases where persistent gender-based inequalities become entangled with struggles to consolidate communal identity). Second, it calls attention to in-group power relations and ongoing struggles over "authentic" interpretations of the group's tradition, which – when captured by more conservative or fundamental elements – disproportionately put women at risk.

Much of the early feminist scholarship was devoted to revealing the potential tension between accommodating religious (or other) self-identified groups and respecting women's hard-won citizenship and

---

[1] For an excellent summary of the core claims of this influential school in contemporary political theory, see Will Kymlicka, *Contemporary Political Theory: An Introduction*, 2nd edn. (Oxford: Oxford University Press, 2002).

[2] For a more detailed discussion of the first and second "waves" of the literature on multiculturalism, see Ayelet Shachar, "Two Critiques of Multiculturalism," *Cardozo Law Review*, 23, 2001, pp. 253–297.

equality rights. This initial critique highlighted the blindness of first-wave multiculturalism to a number of significant factors: intra-group rights violations, gendered power relations, and the central role that women play in many minority communities given their heightened gender responsibilities as "cultural" conduits of the group's distinct narrative of the world, that is, its *nomos*.[3]

To my mind, this formative stage of the feminism and multi-culturalism debate is largely over. Today, most stakeholders in the multicultural debate – academics, activists, group members, or law and policy-makers – acknowledge the potential tension between respecting cultural identities and protecting women's rights. In this respect, the early feminist critique has been extremely successful in asserting its main claims in contemporary multicultural and citizenship debates.

But harder questions remain unresolved. Specifically, what are the public policy implications of the feminist critique of multiculturalism? Do they require us to conclude that gender equality must always trump cultural diversity? Another key issue is defending qualified (or "weak") measures of accommodation: such measures may alleviate gender-related injustices, while at the same time respecting the fact that women may also be group members seeking recognition of their cultural or religious identity. Furthermore, what remedies may the legal system provide to vulnerable group members? And what precisely is the duty of the state vis-à-vis the group and the individual, in the face of internal diversity and struggles over who can speak for whom in representing collective identity claims? Finally, should the feminist critique of multiculturalism expand its horizons beyond national boundaries to take account of how global actors and transnational economic agents partake in constructing – and occasionally inflaming – ethnocultural tension, religious conflict, and gendered stratification (in particular, in ways that sustain unequal access to resources and opportunities) for the poorest of the poor, many of whom are women and children?

As it begins to address these complex issues, the debate over multi-culturalism and feminism is now entering its second stage, and includes contributions from a rich variety of disciplines: political science, law, philosophy, sociology, gender studies, women's studies, and cultural studies. This has led to the advancement of a lively debate over the normative and practical implications of the rise in claims for cultural and

---

[3] I devote considerable attention to these themes in my *Multicultural Jurisdictions: Cultural Differences and Women's Rights* (Cambridge: Cambridge University Press, 2001).

legal pluralism for women.[4] Focusing on the wide range of positions that adumbrate this terrain, we can identify at least three distinct variants of the feminist-multicultural critique. For the sake of clarity and simplicity, I have grouped these emergent theoretical positions into three broad categories: liberal feminism, post-colonial feminism, and multicultural feminism. In the following section, I consider the core arguments of each position. By discussing these variants, I hope to show that despite their shared commitment to advancing women's rights, they may diverge significantly in their normative assessments of, and policy responses to, real-life dilemmas of cultural or religious diversity. To illustrate this point, I turn to explore a debate that has recently emerged in Canada, which is of significant importance for constitutional democracies worldwide. This debate revolves around a proposal to use religious principles to resolve family law disputes through "private" dispute resolution processes. Viewed from the perspective of women's rights, this debate – which is still pending a final resolution – offers an excellent opportunity to explore the variations in the practical judgments and prescriptions offered by each of the feminist schools of thought identified here. In the concluding section, I step back to assess the comparative merits of the three variants on this fast-emerging terrain of scholarship on women and multiculturalism.

A word of caution is needed before we proceed. This chapter is written as a state-of-the-art review. It is not designed to provide an exhaustive account of each of the variants of the feminist critique. Rather, it offers a framework for thinking about the various dilemmas raised by the intersection of gender and culture in women's lives, and how these dilemmas play out through positive law and political theory.

I.   Three variants of the feminist critique of multiculturalism

Liberal feminism

The overarching goal of liberal feminism always has been, as Alison Jagger puts it, "the application of liberal principles to women as well as

---

[4] A parallel exploration of the relationship between gay and lesbian studies and multiculturalism has emerged more slowly, but it is coming to the fore in the work of authors such as Katherine Franke, "Sexual Tensions of Post-empire," *Studies in Law, Politics and Society*, 33, 2004. Another line of inquiry focuses on how children are likely to be affected by group-based accommodations. See, for example, Rob Reich, "Minors within Minorities: A Problem for Liberal Multiculturalists," in *Minorities within Minorities: Equality, Rights, and Diversity*, ed. Avigail Eisenberg and Jeff Spinner-Halev (Cambridge: Cambridge University Press, 2005), pp. 209–226.

men. Most obviously, this means that laws should not grant to women fewer rights than they allow to men."[5] The claim that women deserve equal rights as free and equal beings capable of self-determination and a sense of justice is far from trivial. It becomes truly radical, though, when it calls for the complete erasure of gender-biased norms and practices, especially in situations where women were never given a chance to define these norms and practices in the first place.[6]

The *liberal* component in this feminist position suggests a strong presumption in favor of depoliticizing group-based identities, a process that has been associated with the strict separation of law from religion, typically by guaranteeing the former's lexical priority over the latter (or any other potentially competing source of authority) within the state's territory.[7] In the debate over feminism and multiculturalism, the liberal feminist position has been most effectively articulated in Susan Okin's writings. Her work will therefore serve here as a representative of the liberal feminist approach in the multiculturalism debate.[8]

I believe that Okin's most significant contribution to the debate concerning the relationship between feminism and multiculturalism has been to provoke an extremely important and lively debate; like a true trailblazer, she put herself on the line in challenging what she viewed as an emerging orthodoxy of support for multiculturalism. To counter this view, Okin called our attention to the potentially gendered impacts of respecting cultural diversity. She emphasized in particular the need to be vigilant of extant patterns of discrimination towards women and girls in the "private" domain of family life. More provocatively, she asked whether group rights are part of the solution, or rather, as she saw it, an exacerbation of the problem of gender inequality within minority communities. The core themes advanced by Okin (perhaps excluding

---

[5] Alison M. Jagger, *Feminist Politics and Human Nature* (New Jersey: Rowman & Littlefield, 1988), p. 35.

[6] See Nancy L. Rosenblum, "Okin's Liberal Feminism as a Radical Political Theory," paper presented at Toward a Humanist Justice: A Conference Honoring and Examining the World of Susan Moller Okin, Stanford University, 3–5 February 2005.

[7] Brian Barry offers a comprehensive defense of the "depoliticization" strategy in *Culture and Equality: An Egalitarian Critique of Multiculturalism* (Cambridge, MA: Harvard University Press), pp. 19–54.

[8] This chapter was originally written before the untimely death of Susan Okin, an intellectual giant who belonged to a path-breaking "founding" generation of contemporary feminist scholarship. Despite our often spirited disagreements, I owe a great debt of gratitude to Okin and her fellow travelers for bringing to the fore the concerns of women in both law and political theory, in the process, opening the doors of academic discourse for scholars of my generation to continue to engage in similar questions while approaching them from differing angles.

the latter point) appear to fit squarely within the canons of liberal feminist theory. Why, then, have so many people responded so critically to the claims made by Okin in "Is Multiculturalism Bad for Women?"[9] I see three main reasons for these critical responses. The first deals with the over-simplified conception of culture and religion found in Okin's writing, which, when challenged, also sheds doubt on her conclusions regarding the incompatibility of multiculturalism and feminism. The second focuses on the perception of female group members as ultimately co-opted, if not downright "brainwashed," individuals, who cannot reasonably and genuinely wish to preserve their cultural or religious identity.[10] Within this perspective, it becomes normatively undesirable to even strive to promote both the value of gender equality and cultural/religious diversity.[11] The third reason for the strong reaction to Okin's "verbal 'grenade'" (as she herself later put it),[12] concerns the pattern of binary oppositions that underpins her analytical framework: these oppositions can be crudely summarized as a dichotomy between "us" (Western freedom-and-equality lovers) versus "them" (barbaric "others" who have no respect for women's rights or dignity).[13] This leaves Okin's framework of analysis open to the charge (made by post-colonial feminists) that she misguidedly places the blame for cross-cultural patterns of sexism and patriarchy on the already belligerent and marginalized "foreigner." Each of these ideas merits more detailed discussion.

In her original essay on this topic, Okin argued forcefully that "group rights are potentially, and in many cases actually, antifeminist."[14] She asserted that "most cultures have as one of their principal aims the control of women by men."[15] In support of this, Okin provided an

---

[9] Susan Moller Okin, "Is Multiculturalism Bad for Women?," *Boston Review*, reprinted in Joshua Cohen, Matthew Howard, and Martha C. Nussbaum (eds.), *Is Multiculturalism Bad for Women?* (Princeton: Princeton University Press, 1999).

[10] Ibid., p. 24.

[11] Okin significantly softened her position on this point in subsequent writings. See e.g., "Multiculturalism and Feminism: No Simple Question, No Simple Answers," in *Minorities within Minorities*, ed. Eisenberg and Spinner-Halev, pp. 67–89.

[12] Ibid., p. 69.

[13] See Okin, "Is Multiculturalism Bad for Women?," p. 15. This dichotomy takes many forms: "liberals" in contrast to "non-liberals," "those who consider ourselves politically progressive" versus "those that look to the past," "feminists" versus "multiculturalists." The contrast also appears to be between the "West and the Rest," as Homi Bhabha succinctly put it. See Homi K. Bhabha, "Liberalism's Sacred Cow," in *Is Multiculturalism Bad for Women?*, ed. Cohen, Howard, and Nussbaum, p. 82.

[14] Okin, "Is Multiculturalism Bad for Women?," p. 10. See also Susan Moller Okin, "Feminism and Multiculturalism: Some Tensions," *Ethics*, 108, 1998, pp. 661–684.

[15] Okin, "Is Multiculturalism Bad for Women?," p. 13.

eclectic collection of examples, drawn primarily from secondary sources, to reach the following ultimate conclusion:

[i]t is by no means clear, then, from a feminist point of view, that minority groups are "part of the solution." They may well exacerbate the problem. In the case of a more patriarchal minority culture in the context of a less patriarchal majority culture, no argument can be made on the basis of self-respect and freedom that the female members of the culture have a clear interest in its preservation. Indeed, they *might* be much better off if the culture into which they were born were either to become extinct (so that its members would become integrated into the less sexist surrounding culture) ...[16]

While I admire Okin's unflagging commitment to promoting women's rights, my main disagreement here concerns her secularist "outsider-looking-in" portrayal of culture and religion: this portrayal is characterized by a deep suspicion of the value of religion and culture for human flourishing.[17] Okin makes sweeping generalizations in this vein, such as the following: "much of most cultures is about controlling women."[18] She further contends that "virtually all cultures, past and present" display as one of their *principal* aims the control of women and the restriction of their freedom.[19] Such statements make the argument both descriptively inaccurate and normatively hard to swallow for anyone who attaches value to cultural membership and religious identity.

Equally important, this distorted conception leads to an overly simplistic allocation of blame. Tellingly, Okin attributes imbalances between men and women to "certain aspects of the *content* of the [minority] cultures,"[20] rather surprisingly de-emphasizing both context and history, as well as processes of internal contestation and cross-communal interaction. Similarly, she pays little attention to the macro-level factors, such as the division of powers between the state and the group, access to justice, and the structure of deliberation processes which may have dramatic impact on the type and scope of rights, protections, and opportunities that women can enjoy in practice.[21] Finally,

---

[16] Okin, "Is Multiculturalism Bad for Women?," p. 22.

[17] Okin is not alone in reaching this conclusion. See, for example, Frances Raday, "Culture, Religion, and Gender," *I.CON*, 1, 2003, pp. 663–715; Courtney W. Howland (ed.), *Religious Fundamentalism and the Human Rights of Women* (New York: St. Martin's Press, 1999).

[18] See Okin, "Feminism and Multiculturalism," p. 667.   [19] Ibid., p. 678.

[20] Ibid., p. 664 (emphasis in original).

[21] Much has been written on discursive and deliberative democracy in this context. See, for example, Seyla Benhabib, *The Claims of Culture: Equality and Diversity in the Global Era* (Princeton: Princeton University Press, 2002); Monique Deveaux, "A Deliberative Approach to Conflicts of Culture," *Political Theory*, 31, 2003, pp. 780–807; John S. Dryzek, "Deliberative Democracy in Divided Societies: Alternatives to Agonism and Analgesia," *Political Theory*, 33, 2005, pp. 218–242.

Okin apparently believes that while significant changes in the gender norms of the majority culture in Western societies have occurred as a result of human agency and resistance, no comparable potential for substantive egalitarian reform exists for the minority culture.[22]

This assessment must, however, be subject to a critical investigation. Growing numbers of female members of the more conservative branches of religious communities that have taken a "reactive" turn, such as Orthodox Judaism or Revivalist Islam, are challenging their tradition "from within."[23] This has been achieved by offering more gender egalitarian reinterpretations of sacred texts in Jewish orthodox law (*Halackha*), or by appealing to general principles of *Shari'a* (such as compassion and justice) in lieu of a technical reading of the tenets of Islamic law.[24] Indeed, most religious communities do recognize that at least part of their tradition is a construct of human or legal origin. It is this aspect of a religious tradition that women and other agents of reform can find conducive to amendment and reinterpretation.[25]

Clearly, feminist activists within conservative religious communities face towering obstacles. For instance, they must gain access to the tradition's centers of study and convince fellow group members that their voice is both valid and "authentic." Furthermore, in order to gain full legitimacy they must garner support from at least some respected authorities in the religious establishment. This is the case because *internal* reforms must by definition derive from revisionist readings and innovative methods of reinterpretation of the tradition, which nevertheless require some "anchoring" in existing jurisprudential texts or familiar methods of interpretation – the same is true for most secular

---

[22] Although Okin seems to acknowledge the possibility for change in the power balance within the minority community, she does not take seriously this possibility in her substantive analysis of the relations between feminism and multiculturalism. Instead, women who participate in minority group traditions appear as victims of such extreme socialization that they are represented as having little or no agency in Okin's account. As she puts it: "women living in minority cultures" are "socializ[ed] into inferior roles, resulting in lack of self-esteem or a sense of entitlement." See Okin, "Feminism and Multiculturalism," p. 675. She further contends that "older women often become co-opted into reinforcing gender inequality." Ibid., p. 680.

[23] For a concise elaboration on the conditions that may lead to such a "reactive" turn, see Shachar, *Multicultural Jurisdictions*, pp. 35–37.

[24] For more on this rich body of literature, see e.g., Susannah Heschel (ed.), *On Being a Jewish Feminist*, 2nd edn. (New York: Schocken Books, 1995); Amina Wadud, *Qur'an and Women: Rereading the Sacred Text from a Woman's Perspective* (New York: Oxford University Press, 1999; first published in Kuala Lumpur, Malaysia: Penerbit Bakati Sdn. Bhd., 1992); A. Barlas, *Believing Women in Islam: Unreading Patriarchal Interpretations of the Qur'an* (Austin: University of Texas Press, 2002).

[25] For a detailed discussion, see Khaled Abou El Fadl, *Speaking in God's Name: Islamic Law, Authority and Women* (Oxford: Oneworld, 2001).

legal systems as well, at least those following the common law tradition. To provide just one concrete illustration (in the context of religious law), there is an ongoing debate in Islamic jurisprudence over the methods of reinterpretation, which focuses on the question whether the "gates of *ijtihad*" have remained open. If this interpretive method is available (i.e., if *ijtihad* still permits the human endeavor of reaching conclusions about the *Shari'a*, the divine law), then internal change and reinterpretation, including feminist reinterpretation, more readily becomes a possibility. Add to this the fact that Islam is an institutionally decentralized religion, which has been influenced by different customary traditions in different parts of the world – and is further informed by four different schools of jurisprudence within the Sunni tradition and a separate Shi'i school of jurisprudence – leading to a multiplicity of authoritative sources that display divergent positions on basic issues of personal and family law.[26] This panoply of interpretive sources permits, at least in principle, an opening for invoking more progressive readings over less egalitarian ones. In practice, however, much depends here on *who* holds the power to make such juridical – if not outright political – determinations, and on the history of trust (or mistrust) between the minority community and the wider society or the state.[27]

This political dimension is extremely significant. Proposals for "alternative" readings of a religious tradition are often made in the face of resistance by representatives of the more established strands of interpretation, who, under extreme circumstances, seek to define any innovation as "corruptive." These hard-liners may genuinely fear the corruption of the identity, if not the very survival, of the minority culture. But reformers may also face opposition from established leaders within the group for more prosaic reasons: for instance, this may occur in situations where the call to adopt a more egalitarian interpretation of the tradition is seen as a threat to the existing structure of authority.

These are daunting challenges, which cannot be underestimated. Yet I mention them here because they clearly illustrate that the assertion that no argument can be made on the basis of self-respect and freedom that the female members of the culture have a clear interest in its preservation, fails to persuade unless one assumes that women who uphold their

---

[26] For a classic exposition of this internal diversity, see Noel J. Coulson, *Conflicts and Tensions in Islamic Jurisprudence* (Chicago: University of Chicago Press, 1969), especially ch. 2. I thank Anver Emon for sharing his wealth of knowledge of Islamic law with me.

[27] On this last point, see Gurpreet Mahajan, "Intra-group Equality and Cultural Diversity," in *Minorities within Minorities*, ed. Eisenberg and Spinner-Halev, pp. 90–112. See also Daniel Weinstock, "Building Trust in Divided Societies," *Journal of Political Philosophy*, 7, 1999, pp. 287–307.

cultural membership are akin to "blindfolk" who fail to see the light of reason.[28] When this is echoed by Okin's suggestion that cultural *extinction* might be a relevant "solution," it becomes clear that her view of the relations between culture and equality seriously discounts the potential value and meaning that women may attach to membership in a non-dominant identity community. Such value may exist even in those communities that systematically impose unfair moral and legal costs upon women, which ultimately make them more vulnerable.

Based on this analysis, the liberal feminist tradition maintains that women must be freed from the "shackles" of tradition, culture, and communal identity in order to flourish. This leads to an unnecessary conclusion: by valuing their communal membership, women have somehow implicitly lost the ability to understand the gendered power inequalities that they face, or surrendered the will to fight against such injustices. Neither of these claims is tenable, however, if we reject the notion that culture and equality stand in inherent opposition to one another. Unfortunately, this binary opposition seems to inform much of the liberal-feminist critique of multiculturalism. Taken to its ultimate logical conclusion, this position represents a *tout court* rejection of the very rationale for accommodating cultural diversity.

Post-colonial feminism

The second variation on the theme of feminism and multiculturalism draws upon the academic inquiry of post-colonial discourse, socio-legal scholarship, and critical race theory. The post-colonial feminist critique is generally associated with a rejection of simplistic and uncritical understandings of culture, providing instead a critical reading of mainstream depictions of racialized minority identities and practices.[29] But this critique goes deeper. Authors such as Uma Narayan argue that group leaders also contribute to the problem: although they claim to speak for the entire edifice of "our culture," these leaders actually actively exclude "the voices, concerns, and contributions of many who are members of the national and political community."[30] Post-colonial discourse also brings a number of unique elements to the contemporary debate about feminism and multiculturalism. One key element is that it

---

[28] A similar line of argument is advanced by Martha Nussbaum, "A Plea for Difficulty," in *Is Multiculturalism Bad for Women?*, ed. Cohen, Howard, and Nussbaum.

[29] See Leti Volpp, "Blaming Culture for Bad Behavior," *Yale Journal of Law and the Humanities*, 12, 2000, pp. 89–116.

[30] See Uma Narayan, *Dislocating Cultures: Identities, Traditions, and Third World Women* (New York: Routledge, 1997), p. 10.

challenges the juxtaposition of the "enlightened" West against the "barbaric" other. This juxtaposition, it is argued, reflects an orientalist-style perspective, with its degrading and stereotyping perception of non-white, non-Western cultures and peoples.[31]

The tendency to frame multicultural discussion in this way is particularly evident in the legal system. As one scholar notes, "[w]hen faced with cultural questions, the legal system often produces distorted and questionable versions of the content of non-mainstream cultures. At the same time, it paints an equally distorted, but often more flattering picture, of the mainstream."[32] Scholars like Lama Abu-Odeh have criticized this distortive tendency by comparing, for example, the legal treatment of "crimes of honour" in the Arab world with "crimes of passion" in the United States (both involve the killing of women by male partners or family members). For Abu-Odeh, there are deep similarities "between the internal tensions within each legal system as to what constitutes a killing of women is legally tolerated (either fully or partially)."[33] The argument here is that we cannot simply assume, in Abu-Odeh words, "the superiority of the American judicial system" in comparison to other parts of the world in addressing "the problem everywhere [of] men kill[ing] their wives."[34]

Other authors have similarly argued that the most successful claims for accommodation in the criminal law context – the "cultural defense," for example, where defendants have invoked the traditions of their culture to explain or mitigate their actions – have been those that have employed gendered stereotypes that are familiar to judges, precisely because they are prevalent in the majority society.[35] In other words, the

---

[31] By the term "orientalism" I am referring here to the charge that "Western power, especially the power to enter or examine other countries at will, enables the production of knowledge about other cultures." This production of knowledge, on balance, tends be negative: it is "stereotyping, Othering, dominatory." See Laura Chrisman and Patrick Williams, "Colonial Discourse and Post-colonial Theory: An Introduction," in *Colonial Discourse and Post-colonial Theory* (New York: Columbia University Press, 1994), p. 8.

[32] See Sonia N. Lawrence, "Cultural (In)Sensitivity: The Dangers of a Simplistic Approach to Culture in the Courtroom," *Canadian Journal of Women and the Law*, 13, 2001, p. 111.

[33] See Lama Abu-Odeh, "Comparatively Speaking: The 'Honor' of the 'East' and the 'Passion' of the 'West'," *Utah Law Review*, 1997, p. 290.

[34] Ibid., p. 307.

[35] See, for example, Daina C. Chiu, "The Cultural Defense: Beyond Exclusion, Assimilation, and Guilty Liberalism," *California Law Review*, 82, 1994, pp. 1053–1125; Leti Volpp, "(Mis)identifying Culture: Asian Women and the 'Cultural Defense'," *Harvard Women's Law Journal*, 17, 1994, pp. 54–101; Sarah Song, "Majority Norms, Multiculturalism, and Gender Equality," *American Political Science Review*, 2005, pp. 473–489.

claim is that courts are willing to recognize "cultural" factors for minority defendants only when they resonate with mainstream gendered norms. Anne Phillips eloquently summarizes the point: "in the end, it is the sameness, not the difference that matters."[36]

The general lesson to be drawn from this observation is that those who are engaged in the multiculturalism debate must be cautious in their assessment of the violations of women's rights within non-dominant communities (as compared with similar infringements in the majority society), lest they contribute to the broader cultural processes that tend to marginalize, judge, and relegate minority practices to the realm of the exotic, irrational, and "passionate." This line of argument leads the post-colonial feminist to policy conclusions that are not dissimilar from those of liberal feminists (this is perhaps surprising, considering that the latter are a favorite target for the former's sharp pens). This convergence occurs because the post-colonial feminist is ultimately hard-pressed to find any good reason to support the accommodation of cultural and religious diversity – the hallmark of multiculturalism – given her fear that such accommodation may turn into a double-edged sword, reconstituting anyone who is "different" as less-than-equal.

The irony is that by focusing almost exclusively on sexual violence, abuse, and murder committed by members of minority groups, post-colonial feminists are themselves unwitting participants in the production of an impoverished, not to mention pejorative, notion of cultural and legal pluralism. This leads to another issue: clearly, these scholars see the legal system as implicated in the abuse of culture. The opportunistic defense lawyer, for example, who will stop at nothing that is permissible within the bounds of zealous advocacy to get her client off the hook will often be complicit in reifying a damaging, degrading, and inaccurate description of minority cultures.

In this, the post-colonial theorists surely do have a point. However, no card-holding multicultural theorists (think of Will Kymlicka's work, for example) would defend a policy of accommodation if it failed to address the underlying causes of injustice that gave rise to the claims of group-differentiated rights in the first place. What is more, anyone who has ever read Catharine MacKinnon's work would balk at the suggestion that by merely adopting formal gender-equality laws, any Western (or other) country will miraculously see the deeply entrenched power

---

[36] See Anne Phillips, "When Culture Means Gender: Issues of Cultural Defense in the English Courts," *Modern Law Review*, 66, 2003, p. 529. A similar theme is advanced by Austin Sarat and Roger Berkowitz, "Disorderly Differences: Recognition, Accommodation, and American Law," *Yale Journal of Law and the Humanities*, 6, 1994, pp. 285–316.

hierarchies of gender subordination evaporate into thin air.[37] In other words, it is unlikely that most multiculturalists would defend the "abuses of culture" that post-colonial feminists rightly criticize. Furthermore, adamant feminists such as Okin hardly need a reminder that the majority of women have not yet achieved full equality in most, if not all, countries in the world; she and others of her generation have in fact devoted almost their entire professional lives to establishing this very claim.

Despite these critical observations, I believe that the post-colonial feminist critique of multiculturalism offers illuminating insights insofar as it flags the danger of over-generalizing about the inevitably complex relations of culture and gender. However, given this critique's almost exclusive focus on crimes of sexual violence, spousal abuse, and so-called "honor" or "passion" killings (in which the accused seeks individual exemption on the basis of culture), it remains to be seen how its core arguments hold up when applied to a broader range of requests for group-based accommodation in other contested arenas such as education, marriage and divorce, medical decisions concerning children, and so on.

Multicultural feminism

The third family of variants, multicultural feminism, is a more recent development. It has evolved as a response to the surge of the pro-identity-group literature over the last decade, and the liberal-feminist critique thereof. While rejecting the strong version of either of these discourses, it develops elements of both. Unlike the over-emphasis on group identity manifested by first-wave multiculturalism, or the liberal-feminist tendency to underestimate the value of such identity, multicultural feminism treats women as *both* culture-bearers and rights-bearers.

Also learning from the post-colonial critique, multicultural feminists reject simplistic definitions of "culture" that assume that minority communities offer unified, uncontested narratives of tradition, which are "pure," "authentic," or unaffected by their social context.[38] Instead they argue that identity groups, which today petition the state for special

[37] See, for example, Catharine A. MacKinnon, *Toward a Feminist Theory of the State* (Cambridge, MA: Harvard University Press, 1989), and the more recent collection of essays in *Women's Lives, Men's Laws* (Cambridge, MA: Belknap Press, 2005).

[38] This theme is marvelously explored by Benhabib in *The Claims of Culture*. For a related discussion in the context of Muslim societies, see Marie Aimee Helie-Lucas, "The Preferential Symbol for Islamic Identity: Women in Muslim Personal Laws," in *Identity Politics and Women: Cultural Reassertions and Feminisms in International Perspective*, ed. Valentine M. Moghadam (Boulder: Westview Press, 1994), pp. 391–407.

accommodation of their "difference," have in fact already been touched by the operation of that self-same state. Indeed, some of the most strict and so-called traditionalist or fundamentalist readings of religious texts can be interpreted as modern, revivalist responses to ongoing inter-communal interactions, which often occur under conditions that are unfavorable to the minority community.[39]

By adopting this more explicitly *political* conception of culture and identity, multicultural feminists dismantle the liberal-feminist notion that the only way to promote women's rights in a diverse society is to minimize the effect of religion (or other sources of communal identity) on their lives. Bluntly put, multicultural feminists do not believe in an ideal of a culture-blind society as a magic-bullet solution for the complex inter-sections of gender and group-based identities. However, they do share the liberal-feminist concerns about unequal power relations within minority communities, and the potential for encroaching on women's hard-fought citizenship entitlements that may occur if a state adopts "strong" accommodation measures.[40] But this leads them to different conclusions. For instance, the multicultural feminist believes that greater promise is found in freeing up a space for internal diversity to flourish within min-ority communities. This may be done, for example, by generating legal-institutional conditions that promote such openness; or by allowing women (and other historically at-risk members) access to, and voice in, decision-making processes that involve their cultural and religious com-munities.[41] Indeed, part of the optimism encapsulated in the multi-cultural feminist approach relies on granting more credence to minority women's agency, as well as a voice in navigating the complex intersection of gender and culture in their lived experience.[42] This perspective also delves deeper into the relationship between gender/sexuality and the construction of collective group (and national) identity.[43]

---

[39] I discuss this pattern of "reactive culturalism" in *Multicultural Jurisdiction*, pp. 25–44. For an empirical-oriented study of such interactions in contemporary Europe, see Paul Statham, Ruud Koopmans, Marco Giugni, and Florence Passy, "Resilient or Adaptable Islam? Multiculturalism, Religion and Migrants' Claim-making for Group Demands in Britain, the Netherlands and France," *Ethnicities*, 5, 2005, pp. 427–459.

[40] On "strong accommodation," see my discussion in "Group Identity and Women's Rights in Family Law: The Perils of Multicultural Accommodation," *Journal of Political Philosophy*, 6, 1998, pp. 285–305.

[41] See Deveaux, "A Deliberative Approach"; Madhavi Sunder, "Piercing the Veil," *Yale Law Journal*, 112, 2003, pp. 1399–1472.

[42] This theme is developed in the work of authors such as Uma Narayan, *Dislocating Cultures*; Patricia Jeffery and Amrita Basu, *Appropriating Gender: Women's Activism and Politicized Religion in South Asia* (New York: Routledge, 1997).

[43] For more on this growing body of literature, see the influential contribution of Nira Yuval-Davis and Floya Anthias (eds.), *Woman–Nation–State* (Basingstoke: Macmillan, 1989); Anne McClintock, *Imperial Leather: Race, Gender and Sexuality in the Colonial*

Because of their sensitivity to the political context in which the "claims of culture" are manifested, defenders of multicultural feminism treat with suspicion the liberal-feminist view of religion or tradition as internally static or irredeemably patriarchal. At the same time, they also reject the almost wholesale dismissal of culture by some post-colonial critics, who ultimately appear to believe that religion is no more than "the opium of the people," as Karl Marx famously exclaimed. In contrast, the multicultural feminist lends greater credence to women themselves in defining the value of religion and cultural membership for their sense of self, and in turn, their freedom and autonomy.

While retaining faith in the long-term promise of internal processes of contestation and reinterpretation, multicultural feminists also face an equally urgent task of investigating and highlighting the importance of *state* action (or inaction) in shaping, through law and institutional design, the context in which women can achieve their claims for equality vis-à-vis the group or fellow citizens outside their community.[44] For example, if the secular state relegates any expression of minority-cultural identity to the so-called private realm, devout women may well be asked to remove group- or religious-based markers of identity that *publicly* signify their "difference." The recent legislation in France that restricts the display of overt religious symbols in the public schools, which is widely interpreted as "interdicting" the *hijab* (the headscarf worn by some Muslim women), epitomizes this strict secular-absolutist approach.[45] A different aspect of "privatizing" identities, to which I return later, relates to the question of granting permission to use so-called private justice mechanisms (such as arbitration or mediation) to implement religious principles: does this represent a convenient way for the state to avoid taking responsibility for protecting women's rights precisely in those arenas of social life that are most crucial for realizing *both* sex equality *and* collective identity, such as the regulation of the family? Against these "privatizing" moves, we find other polities that have chosen an opposite path: granting *public* and *binding* authority to religious codes, often at the expense of implicitly curbing protections for women's rights to equality and full

---

Context (New York: Routledge, 1995). See also Deniz Kandiyoti (ed.), *Women, Islam and the State* (Basingstoke: Macmillan, 1991); Moghadam, *Identity Politics and Women.*

[44] See Lisa Hajjar, "Religion, State Power, and Domestic Violence in Muslim Societies: A Framework for Comparative Analysis," *Law and Social Inquiry*, 29, 2004, pp. 1–38.

[45] For a detailed analysis of this legislation, and citizenship theories informing it, see Ayelet Shachar, "Religion, State, and the Problem of Gender: New Modes of Governance and Citizenship in Diverse Societies," *McGill Law Journal*, 50, 2005, pp. 49–88.

citizenship. A dramatic example of this pattern at work is found in the recent "Islamization" of family law and criminal codes in the northern states of Nigeria. None of these institutional strategies is neutral in its effects on the status of women, as will be seen in the following section, which explores a pressing real-life controversy unfolding in Canada over the legal standing of religious arbitration tribunals in family law disputes.

In the debate over "differentiated" citizenship, multicultural feminists are thus deeply concerned about the possibility that the legal and sociological hardening of the borders of inclusion/exclusion between minorities and majorities may expose women to risk by twisting the logic of respect-for-difference into a license for intra-group subordination.[46] Militating against this unjust resolution, multicultural feminists are searching for new terms of engagement between the major players that have a stake in finding a viable path to accommodating diversity *with* equality, including the group, the state, and the individual, in ways that will acknowledge and benefit women as members of these intersecting (and potentially conflicting) identity- and law-creating jurisdictions.[47]

What multicultural feminists advocate, in short, is a shift in the focus on analysis from endless debates about "culture" (which are evident in the disagreements between liberal and post-colonial feminists) towards a more critical understanding of the *political* and *juridical* dimensions of multiculturalism and citizenship that may dramatically shape women's conditions. In this way, they propose that justice can be done to the multidimensional aspiration of achieving both equality and recognition as women, citizens, and minority-group members.

These core claims of multicultural feminism can be usefully contrasted to the three major flaws that we identified earlier: (1) an apolitical understanding of culture; (2) a conception of women as almost entirely without agency in terms of transforming their own community's tradition; and (3) a general disregard for the significance of macro-level legal-institutional conditions and group-based representation structures that may dramatically shape the scope and breadth of freedom and opportunity that women can realistically enjoy. Each of these conceptions has been challenged by the work of multicultural feminists.

---

[46] This represents a variant of what I have elsewhere labeled "the paradox of multicultural vulnerability." See Shachar, "On Citizenship and Multicultural Vulnerability," *Political Theory*, 28, 2000, pp. 64–89; Shachar, *Multicultural Jurisdictions*.

[47] For detailed analysis, see Shachar, *Multicultural Jurisdictions*, ch. 6 and appendix.

II.   Politics, female agency, and legal reform in multicultural feminism

Unveiling the political uses of culture

We have already discussed the rejection of a static vision of culture and identity. In recent years, multicultural feminists have identified not just the social invention of so-called "authentic" fundamentalism, but also the political use of "culture" by leaders who face opposition from within or without as a way to legitimize their hold on power. Under certain circumstances, respect-for-difference policies may also serve the interests of the *accommodating state*, particularly if it is seen as a less costly way to gain the support of established leaders who enjoy a hold on power in the minority communities.[48]

India provides an interesting example. In her detailed study of the history of Muslim personal law, Vrinda Narain argues that the introduction of British (colonial) legal structures facilitated an institutional framework allowing cooperation between elite members of the Hindu and Muslim communities and the colonial administration; this was done in part by setting up internally diverse religious communities as distinct, "unified," and separate juridical entities. Shaped by this history, personal law in India has assumed a crucial role as a marker of communal autonomy and as a legitimate route for the *Ulama* (religious scholars, literally "those who know") to stake a claim to political power. Although the autonomy granted to religious personal law in regulating the family was the result of legal-institutional choices made by the colonizers, "[i]n the imagination of the Ulama, the sphere of family and family law was recast as autonomous and uncolonized."[49] As such, gender and the family became the grounds on which culture and tradition were discursively created, by both the colonizers (and later the Indian state) and the Muslim community. Within the community itself, it was the religious leaders in particular who used their jurisdictional power under the Muslim Personal Law (Shari'a) Application Act and the Dissolution of Muslim Marriages Act to "strengthen their control over women of the community by subjecting them to narrow interpretations of women's

---

[48] Such accommodation (or "indirect rule" in the vocabulary of late colonialism) may be seen as a way to "appease" the established leaders of potentially "unruly" minority communities. For a rich analysis, see Mahmood Mamdani, *Citizen and Subject: Contemporary Africa and the Legacy of Late Colonialism* (Princeton: Princeton University Press, 1996).

[49] See Vrinda Narain, *Gender and Community: Muslim Women's Rights in India* (Toronto: University of Toronto Press, 2001), p. 18.

rights under high culture Islamic rules."[50] Such control, in turn, served to assert and galvanize the *Ulama*'s own authority within the group and to establish its status as the sole legitimate "representative" of the Muslim community in its various engagements with the Indian state and the Hindu majority.[51] It is precisely this astute *political* understanding of culture that is sorely lacking from the standard analysis of the relations between gender and culture. Such an understanding is also attentive to the manner in which gender inequality and claims for "authenticity" intersect under specific geo-political and legal-institutional structures.

Entering the temple: feminist theological study

In addition to these efforts to de-essentialize religion and culture, feminist scholars have taken a further step. They have now entered the "temple" of religion by undertaking the most revered of its internal mechanisms of cultural reproduction: theological study. Their strategy has been to highlight the potential within constitutive religious texts for alternate readings that are better able to mesh with women's freedom and equality. Feminist scholarship in Judaism, for example, is engaged with an extensive re-examination of the main *Halakhic* (Jewish law) sources: scholars are interpreting the Torah through a critical perspective that seeks to unmask hidden interests in traditional interpretations of religious texts, and to expose counter-traditions of resistance to patriarchy in biblical and rabbinical literature. As Susannah Heschel puts it, the former is important because "[w]e don't simply ask what the text seems to be saying, but whose interests are being served. We examine what the text reveals, but also explore what the text conceals."[52] The latter is significant because it demonstrates that rigid and inegalitarian interpretations, even if they gained authoritative power during particular historical periods, were always contested, representing "but only one element in a multitude of conflicting voices."[53] By infusing religious study with feminist perspectives, women are asserting not only their membership in the community, but also their contribution to it as full participants.[54]

This rejuvenation of tradition through textual interpretation also manifests itself in various Islamic schools of thought. For instance,

---

[50] Ibid., p. 19.
[51] For illuminating discussion, see Zoya Hasan, *Forging Identities: Gender, Communities and the State in India* (Boulder: Westview Press, 1994).
[52] Heschel, *On Being a Jewish Feminist*, p. xii.   [53] Ibid., p. xxiii.
[54] See Rachel Biale, *Women and Jewish Law: An Exploration of Women's Issues in Halakhic Sources* (New York: Schocken Books, 1984), p. 9.

female and progressive scholars have offered revisionist readings of the Qur'an, readings which are inclusive of women, and which treat women and men as equals before *Allah*. This "quiet revolution" has involved not only scriptural learning, but also prayer leading and marriage officiating by Muslim women.[55] These still represent controversial, yet increasingly negotiated, practices of updating the tradition to reflect contemporary realities.[56] Most important for our discussion is the recognition that entering the charged field of theological study and knowledge production has allowed women to demonstrate the importance of *their* agency and voice in the creation of more egalitarian cultural-religious norms and practices.[57] Contrary to the pessimistic outlook proposed by many critics, women who wish to uphold their religious membership in minority or orthodox communities can increasingly play an active role in shaping their own identities and social roles.

Institutional design and democratic deliberation

Having highlighted the political uses of culture, and considered how feminist theological study and revisionism is tackling potential tensions between religious accommodation and gender equality, multicultural feminists are now re-examining how law and governance – the pillars of institutional authority in the modern era – are engaged in shaping intercommunal and intra-group power relations. In this, they are following a well-regarded tradition of scholarship that treats institutional structures as variables which have a crucial effect on how behavior is shaped: it observes how individual and collective action is always influenced by the unique structures of authority under which it operates. For multicultural

---

[55] For a first-person account, see Kecia Ali, "Acting on a Frontier of Religious Ceremony: With Questions and Quiet Resolve, a Woman Officiates at a Muslim Wedding," *Harvard Divinity Bulletin*, 32, 2004, pp. 8–9.

[56] For more on these debates in recent works, see Kecia Ali, "Progressive Muslims and Islamic Jurisprudence: The Necessity for Critical Engagement with Marriage and Divorce Law," in *Progressive Muslims on Justice, Gender, and Pluralism*, ed. Omid Safi (Oxford: Oneworld Publications, 2003); Aziza Al-Hibri, "Islam, Law and Custom: Redefining Muslim Women's Rights," *American University Journal of International Law and Policy*, 12, 1997, pp. 1–44; Ziba Mir-Hosseini, *Islam and Gender: The Religious Debate in Contemporary Iran* (Princeton: Princeton University Press, 1999); Wadud, *Qur'an and Women*.

[57] This is not the place to analyze thoroughly these tectonic reverberations. Suffice it to say that women's growing participation in the reinterpretation of their own religious traditions clearly contradicts the picture of a singular and simplistic narrative of identity formation for Muslim women that is portrayed, ironically, by both Western popular media and Islamic resurgence movements. I discuss these mirror-image representations and their often troubling implications on the debate over women's rights and religious accommodation in Shachar, "Religion, State, and the Problem of Gender."

feminists, this observation opens up a space for innovation and creativity – as does the rich comparative evidence showing the wide variations in religious-code interpretation in different jurisdictions, at least theoretically allowing law and policy-makers to adopt the more gender egalitarian variants over those that impose disproportionate burdens on women as "conduits" of collective identity.[58]

One example of such creativity is found in Israel, which permits a form of "personal federalism" in its family law regime: there is no unified civil law that applies to all citizens in matters of marriage and divorce. Instead, for various political and historical reasons, the courts of the different religious communities hold exclusive jurisdiction over marriage and divorce regulation.[59] Despite the deeply "differentiated" character of this regulatory system, it has been dramatically transformed by *territorial* legislation that has, in effect, reshaped the legal-institutional context in which these semi-autonomous personal-law tribunals now operate.

Since the establishment of the state in 1948, the Israeli legislature has gradually enacted civil or "territorial" legislation, which applies equally to all Israelis, to some of the most contentious aspects of personal status regulation – including the core topics of property division, support, child custody, legitimacy, and inheritance, the very issues that have proved contentious in other polities, such as India, and more recently, in Canada with its debate over the religious arbitration tribunals. Following the 1992 "constitutional revolution," the Israeli Supreme Court has used its position as the apex of the legal system to limit the authority exercised by the religious courts.[60] In 1995, for example, the Supreme Court held in the *Bavli* decision that the adjudication of *all* religious tribunals (including the Great Rabbinical Court) is in principle subject to review by the Supreme Court. While the Court recognized the special

---

[58] Much of my own work in this field has followed this path. See e.g., Shachar, *Multicultural Jurisdictions*. See also Jean-François Gaudreault-DesBiens and Ayelet Shachar, "Thinking Through Faith-based Arbitration in a Free and Democratic State" (forthcoming).

[59] The roots of contemporary Israeli family law arrangements go back as far as the Ottoman Empire's ancient millet system. This diversity of personal status laws applicable to different communities was later cemented by the Palestine-Order-in-Council enacted by the British mandate administration in 1933. For further discussion of this complex system, see Ran Hirschl and Ayelet Shachar, "Constitutional Transformation, Gender Equality, and Religious/National Conflict in Israel: Tentative Progress through the Obstacle Course," in *The Gender of Constitutional Jurisprudence*, ed. Beverly Baines and Ruth Rubio-Marin (Cambridge: Cambridge University Press, 2005), pp. 205–229.

[60] On this "constitutional revolution," see Ran Hirschl, *Towards Juristocracy: The Origins and Consequences of the New Constitutionalism* (Cambridge, MA: Harvard University Press, 2004).

jurisdictional mandate awarded to Jewish, Muslim, Christian, and Druze courts by the legislature, it nevertheless asserted its power to impose constitutional norms upon their exercise of authority.[61] Based on its landmark decision in *Bavli*, the Court (in a majority opinion) held in the *Katz* case (1996) that since the rabbinical court system is a public organ that exists by force of law and draws its authority from the law, it could only exercise those prerogatives vested in it by law.[62] In 2001, the legislature again entered the fray, enacting the Family Court (Amendment No. 5) Law, which opened the doors of the civil courts to Muslim women, equalizing their family-law dispute resolution options to those that have become available to Jewish women in Israel with a prior legislative amendment introduced in 1995. In 2005, the Supreme Court further continued expanding its review mandate over the personal-law courts by holding that a Catholic tribunal could not deprive a wife of her secularly enacted statutory right to an equal share of the marital property, even after the religious tribunal had declared the marriage annulled according to Canon law.[63]

The Israeli experience over the last decades shows a steady attempt to enforce secular and gender egalitarian norms over the exercise of authority by religious tribunals, through a combined strategy of advancing national legislation and tightening judicial review. Yet perhaps the most illuminating legal-institutional lesson that can be drawn from the Israeli experience is found not in this state-centered assertion of the superiority of its norms over religious ones, but rather in the *internal* transformation and creative reinterpretation of *Shari'a* sources of personal status law that is found in the jurisprudence of the Muslim Shari'a Court of Appeals. As Moussa Abou Ramadan shows, this Shari'a Court has used the religious procedure of arbitration (incorporated into Israeli law through a provision originally enacted by the Ottoman Family Law statutory framework) to *facilitate* women's access to divorce, creating a legal option for both husband and wife to dissolve the marriage while maintaining the wife's right to a *maher* (the latter has in some cases been linked to the standard of living index, therefore increasing the value of the payment owed to the wife).[64] Based on a comprehensive study of the Shari'a Court of Appeal decisions, Abou

---

[61] *Bavli v. The Grand Rabbinical Court*, H.C. 1000/92, 48(2) P.D. 6 (1995). On *Shari'a* court jurisdiction, see also *Plonit ("Jane Doe") v. Ploni ("John Doe")*, C.A. 3077/90, 49 (2) P.D. 578 (1990).

[62] *Katz v. Jerusalem Regional Rabbinical Court*, H.C. 3269/95, 50(4) P.D. 590 (1996).

[63] See *Plonit v. Ploni*, C.A. 5794/03, decision given on 12 December 2005 (not yet published).

[64] See Moussa Abou Ramadan, "Divorce Reform in the Shari'a Court of Appeals in Israel (1992–2003)," *Islamic Law and Society*, 3, 2005, pp. 2–33.

Ramadan concludes that these internal reforms represent a "process of hybridization of Islamic law: the Shari'a Court applies elements of Israeli secular law, such as the theory of inherent jurisdiction, to the [Islamic] institution of *niaz wa-shiqaq* [quarrel and disagreement as the basis for divorce]."[65] This development is potentially far-reaching: it shows that at least under certain circumstances, engaging state *and* religious norms in the governance of a minority community's family-law jurisprudence leads to internal *reinterpretations* of the religious tradition in ways that better respect and protect the interests of women.

Obviously, such innovation must be studied carefully and con-textually, understanding the dynamics and factors that have led to a path that better protects (rather than mitigates) women's rights through the intersection of religious and secular sources of authority. Advocates of deliberative procedures, for their part, call for discursive processes designed specifically to enhance the voices of historically vulnerable segments of the group population by facilitating specific conditions for dialogue within the minority community, within the wider society, and between the two.[66] Theorists such as Benhabib and Monique Deveaux take as their starting point the need to acknowledge intra-group inequalities rather than lay trust in representation and dialogue con-ducted through group official "spokesmen."[67] Similarly, advocates of institutional reform seek to include women in any processes of legal renegotiation so as to ensure that their voices have direct representation in any mega- or semi-constitutional bargaining situation that is likely to affect them. The value of generating such deliberative venues and understanding the "optimal" institutional and juridical conditions for accommodating diversity *with* equality cannot be over-stated. To return to the Israeli example, the methods of interpretation and the content of the decisions issued by the Shari'a Court of Appeal represent develop-ments that must be contrasted with the type of radicalization of Islam that we have seen in other non-Muslim democracies with a significant Muslim population that have resisted permitting such "hybrid" or joint-governance interaction to take place. A case in point is Britain, where an unofficial *parallel* system of marriage and divorce according to

---

[65] Ibid., p. 29.

[66] On the deliberative approach, see Seyla Benhabib, *The Claims of Culture*; on the dialogical approach, see Bhikhu Parekh, *Rethinking Multiculturalism: Cultural Diversity and Political Theory* (Cambridge, MA: Harvard University Press, 2000). See also Duncan Ivison, *Postcolonial Liberalism* (Cambridge: Cambridge University Press, 2002).

[67] One example of such inclusive processes is nicely described by Deveaux in her account of the pre-legislative consultation processes that took place in South Africa before the adoption of the new Recognition of Customary Marriage Act of 1998. See Deveaux, "A Deliberative Approach."

Islamic law has emerged *outside* the regulatory boundaries of the civil justice system, generally endorsing a less favorable interpretation to women regarding their access to religious divorce and its material implications.[68]

To better understand these complex patterns, we must pay careful attention to specific case studies as well as comparative examples that may support, refute, or modify theoretical arguments about how different legal-institutional relations between "state and religion" are likely to affect women's rights. This more nuanced approach is important for another reason. It permits expanding the pool of observations available to decision-makers whenever members of minority cultures (claiming to "represent" the group) raise vocal claims that juridical and governance structures are in need of re-negotiation. These concerns are far from merely hypothetical. One concrete example, which I consider next, is the framework that has permitted the rise of a passionate debate in Canada over the proposed use of religious principles to resolve family law disputes.

III.   The *Shari'a* tribunal example

The previous sections have elaborated the core themes advanced by each of the leading schools of thoughts in the contemporary literature on the intersection of culture and gender – liberal, post-colonial, and multicultural feminism. In the following pages, I put these approaches to the test of responding to a real-life controversy that has recently erupted in Canada, and which represents challenges that are likely to emerge in other diverse societies in the future. A concise presentation of the pertinent facts behind the controversy is required.

In 2003, the Canadian Society of Muslims, a private association, publicized a proposal to establish a *private* (i.e., non-state) tribunal offering arbitration – including *family* arbitration – based on Islamic principles. This announcement followed little dialogue within the large and diverse Muslim community in Canada, and virtually no consultation with any representative of the legislature or the government. The advocates of the tribunal never clarified which "Islamic principles"

---

[68] In 1982, a group of Muslim scholars established "The Islamic Shari'a Council," which offers services for the termination of Islamic marriage. As the Council acknowledges, their divorce certificate "nullifies the Islamic marriage only and has nothing to do with the civil contract." The latter must be terminated by the civil court system. The ISC allows women to initiate the divorce, but often at the expense of "buying" their way out of the religious marriage, e.g., by returning the *maher*. The ISC is not legally recognized by the official civil justice system in the UK. See: online: www.islamic-sharia.co.uk. For analysis, see S. N. Shah-Kazemi, *Untying the Knot: Muslim Women, Divorce and the Sharia* (London: Nuffield Foundation, 2001).

would be used to resolve family disputes, and how they would be interpreted if they substantively conflicted with Canada's civil legislation on family law matters. No similar ambiguity was found in reference to a source of authority that the advocates of this tribunal saw as legitimizing their effort to create, as they put it, a "private Islamic Court of Justice."[69] Here, the proponents of the tribunal referred to an existing provincial statute, the Arbitration Act, as the legal source for their authority to arbitrate family-related or personal status-related disputes.[70] They further held the view that any arbitral awards rendered by the *Shari'a* tribunal (as this proposal came to be known in the public debate) would be enforceable by the *secular* court system.[71]

This proposal raises a host of concerns and uncertainties. To begin, it has yet to be established which interpretation of *Shari'a* norms the religious arbitration tribunal will enforce: there are four major Sunni schools of Islamic legal interpretation, with considerable differences among them, and the Shi'a have their own school of jurisprudence. It is also unclear how dissent will be registered and whether a woman will be free to reject the tribunal's authority if she comes to believe that, despite her initial consent to arbitration, her rights and interests would be better served by a state court applying secular law.[72] With this background in mind, let us consider how each of the theoretical frameworks identified above might address the real-life dilemmas raised by the proposal.

From a liberal-secular feminist perspective, the main concern with this initiative is its break with the monopoly and universality of state law, which is seen as a better protector of women's rights that any potential competitor, be it a faith-based arbitration forum or any other alternative dispute resolution (ADR) mechanism. This assumption may prove correct in many circumstances (though it needs to be substantiated by hard core and context-specific facts, rather than by anecdotal evidence and fear-mongering rhetoric about how religious principles per se will inevitably and intrinsically lead to an erosion of women's equality rights). An illustration of this thinking is found in a public statement released by a coalition of organizations opposed to the use of religious arbitration: "METRAC joins other organizations in our opposition to

---

[69] Syed Mumtaz Ali, "Establishing an Institute for Islamic Justice (Darul Qada)," *Canadian Society of Muslims News Bulletin* (October 2002), online: http://muslim-canada.org.

[70] *Arbitration Act, 1991*, S.O. 1991, c. 17.

[71] For a comprehensive discussion of the legal and normative challenges raised by this proposal, see Marion Boyd, "Dispute Resolution in Family Law: Protecting Choice, Promoting Inclusion" (2004, available at: http://www.attorneygeneral.jus.gov.on.ca/english/about/pubs/boyd/fullreport.pdf).

[72] For a detailed analysis, see Shachar, "Religion, State, and the Problem of Gender."

the use of any religious laws in family matters using the Arbitration Act in Ontario. We are *shocked* by the possibility of the erosion of equality rights."[73] The coalition opposes the use of "religious arbitration and/or any other principles, which would undermine the equality guarantees of the Charter."[74] What is puzzling about this statement is that it is made without any concrete evidence to show that various dispute resolution processes, which already occur informally in many mosques in Toronto, have either violated the Charter or left women with less than what they would have received through a secular settlement.[75]

But this brings us to an ironic coincidence: while the debate over the *Shari'a* tribunal was unfolding (and without any connection to it), the Supreme Court of Canada recently upheld, in the 2004 *Hartshorne* decision, the use of *secular* contractual mechanisms to evade the basic equitable provisions that protect women's entitlements in divorce, as encoded in various provincial and federal statutes governing the breakdown of family relations.[76] In that decision, a wife entered a marriage agreement that was identified by independent legal advice as "grossly unfair": pursuant to the agreement, the wife was entitled to property valued at $280,000 on separation, while the husband was entitled to property worth $1.2 million. Such domestic contracts, as they are known in the legal jargon, are permitted by the governing family law statutes.[77] In this case, it was clear that the wife received far *less* than what she would have been entitled to under the default statutory regime. The trial judge who heard the evidence in the *Hartshorne* case concluded that the domestic agreement was unfair and ordered a more balanced distribution in favor of the wife. The trial judge's decision was then challenged by the husband, but it was approved by the Court of Appeal. The case ultimately reached the Supreme Court of Canada, which *over-turned* the ruling of the trial judge. Instead of aiding the wife, the country's top justices ruled that "courts should be reluctant to second-guess the

---

[73] See Ontario Women's Justice Network, "URGENT: Declaration on Religious Arbitration in Family Law," 1 June 2005 (emphasis added).

[74] Ibid.

[75] See, for instance, the dispute resolution examples described by the Canadian Council on American-Islamic Relations (CAIR-CAN), "Appendix to Review of Ontario's Arbitration Process and Arbitration Act: Supplementary Survey" (September 2004). Obviously, more research is required in order to provide more comprehensive and systemic evidence regarding the impact of these informal dispute resolution processes on the rights of women and children.

[76] See *Hartshorne v. Hartshorne* [2004] 1 S.C.R. 550.

[77] See *Family Law Act*, R.S.B.C. 1996, c. 128, Part 5, ss. 56, 58, 59, 61, 65, 68, 89. See also *Divorce Act*, R.S.C. 1985, c.3 (2nd Supp), ss. 15.2 [amended 1997, c.1, s.2], 15.2 (4) [formerly s.15(5)]. The *Family Law Act* permits such "domestic contracts," but they are subject to judicial reapportionment of property.

arrangements on which [private parties, here the husband and wife] reasonably expected to rely. Individuals may choose to structure their affairs in a number of ways, and it is their prerogative to do so."[78]

The *Hartshorne* case represents a classic example of a court deciding to privilege notions of contractual freedom over the statutory default rules of gender equality. But because there was no "culture" or religion or a threatening minority to blame, the Court's controversial decision has not raised the same ire as has the idea of using religious sources to resolve family law disputes. A post-colonial feminist would surely militate against this different response, labeling it as a double standard.[79] Indeed, she might wish to challenge the very representation of secular and religious family law norms as posing dramatically different alternatives for women in terms of protection of their interests.

The argument might proceed as follows: it is true that religious tribunals may (ab)use tradition to curb the promise of gender equality. Still, what matters – according to this line of argument – is that the secular system too has failed women. As we have just seen in the *Hartshorne* decision, this is a critique that finds support in positive law. It shows that, even without adding the complexities of the religious tribunal into the mix, the current regulation of the family is not as uniform as it may, at first blush, appear. This is a powerful argument. However, the post-colonial feminist is arguably over-extending the logic of her claim: it surely requires a great deal of over-simplification to suggest that religious pressures are no different in kind than economic (or related) pressures imposed on women in our society, although these different sources of pressure may unfortunately lead to the same result of *limiting* a woman's freedom and infringing on statutory provisions designed to protect her interests. This slippage occurs in part because by making an equation between the secular and the religious, the post-colonial theorist is drastically discounting the communal pressures that may be imposed on a devout believer to comply with what is presented as a *religious* duty. In other words, a woman's perception of the spectrum of options or course of actions available to her is restricted not only by familiar factors such as economic or informational asymmetry, but also by distinctive identity-based pressures.

Paradoxically, then, it appears that the post-colonial feminist's zeal to demystify "community" and "identity" has led her to turn a blind eye to

---

[78] *Hartshorne*, para. 36.

[79] It is implausible to assume that inter-communal tensions in the post 9/11 era have had no influence on the heightened alert with which the quest for private religious arbitration, which is specifically raised by *Muslim* clerics, was met. This observation fits with the broader themes of post-colonial feminism.

what makes religion – and its exercise in concert with others – both important and distinct for its beholders. Despite adopting a highly critical position with respect to cultural and gender essentialism, the post-colonial feminist appears trapped in a rigid framework of old orientalist hierarchies. This leaves little room, in John Strawson's words, for "both sides of the former imperial divide . . . [to] construct a new jurisprudential discourse on an inclusive basis."[80] Without the prospect of such new jurisprudential discourse, we risk having little to offer minority women but despair.

What troubles me most with the liberal-feminist and post-colonial responses is not so much the bottom-line conclusion that the proposed arbitration tribunals ought to be treated with suspicion, but rather the justification process. Both positions do not allow for any serious discussion of whether there are any valid reasons for devout women to turn to a religious arbitration tribunal in the first place. Instead, we find towering resistance to even entertaining the possibility that the official court system, with its adversarial and impersonal features, may not be the most welcoming and accommodating place for women from marginalized communities. Under such conditions, no real dialogue and deliberation is possible. In addition, the voices of the women who are voting with their feet, those who are already turning to religious dispute-resolution processes, are silenced. Add to this the fact that female members of minority communities tend to under-utilize – rather than embrace – the civil justice system, and it becomes prudent to pause before jumping to a policy conclusion that *this* system provides sufficient resources to address minority women's specific gender and communal concerns.

This call for nuance does not necessarily endorse the legal claim for setting up an arbitration tribunal by members of a given minority community. In fact, the tribunal proposal is likely to disturb a multicultural feminist because it raises the familiar specter of using family law as a tool for forcing a homogenizing and often conservative interpretation of what "loyalty" to the group requires, which is here defined in deeply gendered terms that revolve around women's roles as wives and mothers. Another curious aspect of this debate is that the proponents of the *Shari'a* tribunal have never fully clarified the reasons why the state *ought* to justify the adoption of what is, in effect, a measure of "strong" accommodation of a minority group's tradition through the back door of

---

[80] See John Strawson, "Islamic Law and English Texts," in *Laws of the Postcolonial*, ed. Eve Darian-Smith and Peter Fitzpatrick (Ann Arbor: University of Michigan Press, 1999), p. 123.

private yet *binding* arbitration. This is a crucial aspect of the debate, which received surprisingly little attention, but must be addressed head-on: what is at stake here is no less than an attempt to use a technique of "privatizing justice" to redefine the relationship between state and religion in regulating family law.[81]

Investigating the foreseeable consequences of such changes, which is coupled with a critical analysis of the motivations of both state and group representatives in their struggles over jurisdictional authority, is at the core of multicultural feminist analysis. It leads to skepticism that the absolutist-type solution of legally prohibiting the operation of religious tribunals by decree can take the place of a more pluralistic solution. For one, it will probably fail to protect the most vulnerable women, those who may lack the knowledge or resources to turn to a secular institution in lieu of a community-based network or tribunal. The state's anti-religious arbitration "crackdown" may do little to motivate their established group leaders (in this particular example, religious arbitrators) to adopt a more egalitarian and reformist interpretation of the tradition.[82] As a solution that relies on external imposition by state fiat, it may well lead to a "reactive culturalism" backlash, strengthening the more conservative spokespersons of the group (who may feel "under siege" by the state) instead of encouraging the already existing processes of reformist internal reinterpretation.

As a stop-gap measure, a plausible decision-maker informed by the feminist-multicultural perspective may hold that "alternative" dispute resolution forums may operate, but add a condition that they can do so if and only if they voluntarily agree to comply with the default rules defined in general family legislation. These rules typically establish a "floor" of protection, beyond which significant room for variation is permitted. These basic protections were designed in the first place to address concerns about power and gender inequities in family relations, concerns that do not typically stop at the doorsteps of religious communities. If anything, they probably apply with equal force in the communal context as in the individualized, secular case. On this account, if a resolution by a religious tribunal falls within the margin of discretion that any secular family law judge or arbitrator would have been permitted to employ, there is no reason to discriminate against that tribunal solely for the reason that the decision-maker used a different

---

[81] This point is addressed at length in Shachar, *Multicultural Jurisdictions*.

[82] Certain aspects of family law are barred from reaching mediation or arbitration, whether secular or religious. This includes circumstances of domestic violence, for example. This prohibition should continue to exist, and has not been challenged by any of the parties to this debate.

tradition to a reach a permissible resolution. Put differently, the multi-cultural feminist finds no threat in the idea that, in a diverse society, at least some individuals might prefer to turn to their "communal" institutions, assuming that they are assured that basic state-backed rights are protected by these alternative forums. Putting aside cases of duress, coercion, or violence, which by law invalidate *any* dispute-resolution process, the permission to turn to a faith-based tribunal may in fact hold the promise of encouraging moderate interpretations of the tradition by the religious arbitrators. The reason for this is simple: the decision of the tribunal will not become legally binding and enforceable if it breaches the basic protections to which each woman is entitled by virtue of her equal citizenship status. In short, this resolution may eventually prove to offer effective, non-coercive measures to encourage a process of "change from within" the religious tradition.

In this particular debate, rather than following the almost automatic rejection of the idea of a religious tribunal (as has been the predominant secular-liberal and post-colonial response), a multicultural feminist would try to reframe the debate. Instead of treating it as an either-your-culture-or-your rights dilemma – in which either the state or the group must gain absolute authority to resolve all aspects of a family-law dispute – we can think of the religious-tribunal initiative as an invitation for a public dialogue. After all, this proposal was made public by the more conservative members of the Muslim Canadian community *without* any practical reason for them to do so. Legally, they could have simply gone ahead and established their tribunal under the original provisions of the Arbitration Act.[83] By reframing the situation as a renegotiation, we are inevitably altering the terms of the debate, distancing it away from the potentially "isolationist" intention of the early advocates of the *Shari'a* tribunal. Deliberative democrats, for their part, would emphasize the importance of allowing women from various sects to participate in any negotiations or consultations that may result from the religious tribunal initiative.

To some extent, this process has already begun. By making the issue public, the advocates of the *Shari'a* tribunal generated an unprecedented debate within the Muslim community in Canada (and beyond, as well) to national and international audiences. Interestingly, issues of voice and representation soon became central to the debate. Although the proponents of the tribunal claimed to have the moral and legal authority to arbitrate family law disputes according to *Shari'a*-based principles, their assertion of power was flatly rejected by many of their opponents *within* the Muslim community. Indeed, this debate provided plentiful evidence

[83] S.O. 1991 c. 17.

to the sociological account that religious groups are internally diverse and, in this case, the debate also revealed deep fractures over who can "speak" in the name of the community. These internal divisions were amplified by different visions of the state's role, and the intersection of citizenship and communal identification in the lives of group members.

Legal-institutionalists would likely highlight the need to ensure that if the religious tribunals are recognized by the state, they could not under any condition gain a monopoly.[84] The justification for this position is that even if these tribunals arbitrated according to religious principles, the enforceability of their awards involves state action. As such, we cannot pretend that these tribunals are in some way operating "outside" the realm of public authority. If they operate, directly or indirectly, under the color of state law, these institutions are at minimum subject to regulation by general principles of procedural fairness and administrative justice.[85] The "no monopoly" requirement is also supported by the very conceptualization of these mixed-jurisdictional bodies as providing services for women who find value and meaning in following their community's religious tradition, yet without revoking the basic protections and entitlements granted to them as citizens of the state.

A related option is to hold arbitrators liable for breach of their professional responsibility if they fail to protect the basic interests of the more vulnerable party in the arbitration conducted before them. As such, arbitrators may be subject to professional discipline or repudiation as well as civil liability charges.[86] In this way, the burden is shifted from vulnerable group members (who have their "loyalty" to demonstrate) to the arbitrators themselves. These arbitrators would have an incentive to find balanced solutions or risk losing their constituents to competing religious tribunals or alternative dispute-resolution centers (let alone the possibility of turning to the standard family-law courts system). We have already seen that such processes of internal transformation by authorized power holders are possible in our discussion of the Israeli example.

At the same time, what makes this a complex situation for a multicultural feminist is that we may face a situation where the use of strict and rigid interpretations of religious law is justified internally in the name

---

[84] For justification of the "no monopoly" requirement, see Shachar, *Multicultural Jurisdictions*, ch. 6.

[85] These requirements already apply under the current *Arbitration Act*, ss. 6, 9. See also *Hercus v. Hercus* [2001] O.J. No. 534.

[86] The idea of enforcing professional liability responsibilities as a "reversal point" derived out of conversation with my colleague Lorne Sossin of the University of Toronto. I thank him for this insight.

of upholding the autonomy and "authenticity" of the minority community vis-à-vis a hostile majority in situations of deep inter-communal tension. In this scenario, immense pressure is likely to be imposed on women to turn to community-based tribunals, even at the risk of eroding their state-guaranteed rights and entitlements. For a complex set of reasons, which I have explored elsewhere and cannot reiterate here, women and the family often serve a crucial symbolic role in constructing group solidarity vis-à-vis the wider society.[87] Under such conditions, women's indispensable contribution in transmitting and manifesting a group's "culture" is coded as both an instrument and a symbol of group integrity. As a result, idealized and gendered images of women as mothers, caregivers, educators, and moral guardians of the home come to represent the ultimate and inviolable repository of "authentic" group identity. These carefully crafted gendered images of devout religiosity then become cultural markers that help erase internal diversity and disagreement, while at the same time allowing both minority and majority leaders to politicize selective and often invented boundaries between the "self" and the "other."[88]

Such hardening of the borders of inclusion and exclusion may unfortunately serve as a ready-made rationale for conservative group leaders to impose further restrictions on women; this may occur in the name of the collective effort to preserve the group's distinct identity in the face of (real or imagined) external threats. It may also motivate aggressive responses by the majority community, which may feel threatened by the resurgence and radicalization of religious minority-group identity. In this way, the conflation of increasingly "revivalist" claims of culture with gendered images of idealized womanhood becomes a focal point for an unprecedented spate of "state and religion" conflicts over foundational collective identity and basic citizenship questions. Even if legally banned, as currently proposed by the government, these faith-based institutions could unofficially operate as providers of mediated solutions, which may never be subject to regulation by

---

[87] See e.g., Shachar, *Multicultural Jurisdictions*, ch. 3; Shachar, "Religion, State, and the Problem of Gender." My work is part of an emerging interdisciplinary body of literature now exploring the relationship between gender/sexuality and the construction of collective identity. See Yuval-Davis and Anthias, *Woman–Nation–State*; Hélie-Lucas, "The Preferential Symbol for Islamic Identity"; Kandiyoti, *Women, Islam and the State*; Inderpal Grewal and Caren Kaplan (eds.), *Scattered Hegemonies: Postmodernity and Transnational Feminist Practices* (Minneapolis: University of Minnesota Press, 1994); Narain, *Gender and Community*; Franke, "Sexual Tensions of Post-empire."

[88] Ironically, such gendered constructions of group identity may be shared by representatives of both minority and majority communities, as is demonstrated by the current debate over the *hijab* in France. See Shachar, "Religion, State, and the Problem of Gender."

state norms if they remain unchallenged by the parties. This may leave extremely vulnerable precisely those women who may be most in need of joint-governance resolutions in the regulation of family affairs – namely women, who for either economic or cultural reasons might feel obliged to have at least some aspects of their marriage and divorce regulated by religious principles.

The government response currently being proposed is to close down any constructive dialogue, a response that is based on the classic liberal divide between the public realm of citizenship and the private realm of group membership. This may appear as a magic-bullet at first blush by virtue of removing the state "out of the business" of engaging directly with competing and/or overlapping sources of normative authority. But this has never been the feminist inclination on these matters; the three schools of thought that I have identified here share the concern that the most penetrating violations, if not outright abuses, of women's rights will occur precisely in this artificially shielded "private" domain of family and community. A resolution of the tribunal debate that merely brushes under the rug the problem of intersectionist identities may satisfy some as a "neat" solution. But beneath the surface, for the most vulnerable group members, the re-crowning of the civil justice system as the sole regulator of family law – coupled with the relegation of group-based dispute resolution processes to a no-man's land of a shadowy, unofficial system – may prove to be of little assistance in blocking communal pressures to turn to "their" community's (now unrecognized) authorities, which will remain free of any regulatory oversight. The real concern here is that those most in need of the benefits of inter-cultural dialogue and pluralistic legal regimes – those whose lives genuinely manifest overlapping and potentially conflicting belongings – will become the "collateral" of a more rigid divide between citizenship and group membership, rights and tradition, gender and culture.

IV. Judgment calls: assessing the contributions of the three variants of the feminist critique of multiculturalism

The preceding discussion articulated the three main strands of the feminist critique of multiculturalism and exposed the potential practical applications of each. The question that remains to be addressed concerns how the comparative merits of these approaches are to be assessed. Obviously, much will depend on the standard chosen for such assessment. For instance, if one is looking for an unambiguous answer, then the liberal-feminist approach offers an attractive solution. As we have already seen, according to this approach, women's rights must trump cultural diversity whenever the two stand in ostensible conflict.[89] If, on the other hand, one is looking for reasons to reject multicultural citizenship because of the belief that any act of ascribing "difference" (no matter what the motivation) will inevitably lead to the perpetuation of existing patterns of racial, economic, gendered, and cultural domination, then the post-colonial feminist approach clearly prevails. While offering immensely valuable contributions to the scholarly debate, I find both these alternatives ultimately unsatisfying. They force us to choose between despair (by the post-colonial position), or the false comfort of imposing secular and state norms on those deemed too "different" (the liberal-feminist position).

In moving to the world of applied political and legal theory, however, the multicultural feminist position may prove to have an unparalleled advantage. This jurisprudential discourse begins by acknowledging the complexities that are inevitably found in those experiences of individuals, communities, and states that have tried – however imperfectly – to use deliberative democratic methods and innovative legal-institutional designs to directly tackle the tension between respecting cultural diversity and promoting gender equality. In the *Shari'a*–tribunal debate, this leads to a search for workable and realistic solutions to problems that women face in practice, such as that of the "dual status" of marriage and divorce that must be terminated by both state and religious authorities to fully release a woman from an unwanted or soured marital relationship. The idea of creating some form of regulated interaction between different sources of law and jurisdiction takes away the "sting" from the original proposal to establish the religious tribunal as a wholesale *alternative* to the state's regulatory framework, with its built-in protections of women's rights, as was envisioned by the Canadian Society of Muslims. But neither they, nor any other authority, have a monopoly over interpreting the intersection of Islam, citizenship, and gender equality rights in Canada.

In anything, bringing the informal practices of dispute resolution more closely in line with the secular legislation governing the dissolution of family relations allows significant room for reinterpretation of the

---

[89] The qualification of the existence of conflict is significant here. We can interpret many of the critical responses to the liberal-feminist position as challenging its over-extension of the definition of what counts as legitimate accommodation in the first place. For instance, circumstances that involve violations of women's rights to bodily integrity, such as domestic violence, spousal murder, abuse, rape, psychological threats, and so forth, have *not* been defended on the grounds of cultural or religious freedom even by the most staunchest proponents of multiculturalism. However, they regularly appear in the liberal-feminist (as well as the post-colonial) critique.

tradition. Admittedly, the combined effects of these formal-juridical and informal-deliberative solutions cannot offer a panacea to the difficult challenges raised in the new era of diversity: such challenges often manifest themselves in gendered terms of reasserting "authentic" identity in the context of deep inter-communal struggles. They do, however, put female members of minority communities, especially those who have been historically vulnerable, at the center of debate. This is accomplished by allowing them, perhaps for the first time, the potential to become promising agents of renewal of their own cultural traditions. This is surely a celebrated moral achievement, which further represents the most practical hope for ensuring that women and other at-risk members do not become the primary casualties of the renewed struggles between state and religion the world over; it is this core goal which is shared by all three variants of the feminist critique.

Part II

Approaches

5 Egalitarian liberalism and universalism

Simon Caney

Those who maintain that there are universal liberal principles of political morality have come in for much sustained criticism. The critics make a variety of different complaints. For many the problem with a universal theory is that it is guilty of arrogance: of thinking "we" have the right answers, that other unfortunate cultures are less wise and that we know what it is better for them. For others the problem is that principles of justice should fit the specific historical conditions of a society and they charge that a universalistic account is insensitive to the different historical contexts: it just stipulates some ideals. In the light of these, and other, concerns some have been tempted to reject the idea of universal moral ideals and have embraced *anti-universalism*. Others have been tempted to conclude that the only universal moral ideals are very basic and minimal ones: they have embraced, that is, *minimal universalism* (or *minimalism* for short).[1]

My aim in this chapter is to motivate some support for a specific kind of universalism, namely an egalitarian liberal brand of universalism, and to argue that anti-universalism and minimalism are more problematic than is frequently recognized. In order to do so the chapter begins by introducing and defending two formal, and hopefully uncontentious, features of a sound theory of global justice. It then argues that these call into question the tenability of anti-universalist and minimalist political moralities. In particular I suggest that if there are powerful arguments for applying egalitarian liberal principles in the domestic realm (by which I mean "within a state") then these principles should be adopted at the global level. It is, so I argue, incoherent to affirm liberalism at home, on the one hand, and yet abandon it abroad, on the other. Furthermore, I suggest that to claim that the only universal rights are

---

[1] For two illuminating treatments of minimalism and human rights see Charles Beitz, "Human Rights as a Common Concern," *American Political Science Review*, 95 (2), 2001, pp. 269–282; Joshua Cohen, "Minimalism about Human Rights: The Most We Can Hope For?," *Journal of Political Philosophy*, 12 (2), 2004, pp. 190–213.

minimal ones overlooks the extent to which minimal rights often entail the whole liberal package of rights.

I.

Prior to examining the argument for egalitarian liberal universalism, it is necessary to explain what is meant by "egalitarian liberal universalism" and to elaborate more fully on what anti-universalism and minimal universalism state. A good account of universalism is provided by Onora O'Neill. She characterizes it using the notions of universal "scope" and "form." Universalism avers that some values have universal scope.[2] So if we maintain that "X-ing is immoral" is a universally valid claim then we are maintaining that a principle with the same form "do not do X" should apply everywhere (it has universal scope). If we turn now to anti-universalism we can use the same terminology. Anti-universalism avers that no moral value has universal scope: it denies the claim that some values apply universally. There are no principles with universal jurisdiction. As we have noted above, many people ostensibly embrace anti-universalism, arguing that a universalist approach is a form of imperialism or is hostile to diversity or is simply without warrant. A paradigmatic anti-universalist position is cultural relativism, where this claims that the right values for persons are those that correspond to the values of their culture.

Having characterized "universalism" and "anti-universalism" it is necessary to explain what I mean by an egalitarian liberal universalism. I shall take egalitarian liberalism to refer to the doctrine that persons should enjoy the complete set of liberal civil and political rights (such as rights to democratic government, freedom of association, freedom of conscience, and, more generally, the freedom to choose what conception of the good one pursues so long as it does not violate the rights of others); and, moreover, there should be a set of broadly egalitarian distributive principles in place. Egalitarian liberal universalism, thus, maintains that all persons are entitled to these liberal rights. Proponents include Brian Barry whose robust *Culture and Equality*, as well as earlier works such as *Justice as Impartiality*, affirms an emphatic and uncompromising defense of liberal principles of justice.[3]

---

[2] Onora O'Neill, *Towards Justice and Virtue: A Constructive Account of Practical Reasoning* (Cambridge: Cambridge University Press, 1996), pp. 11, 74.

[3] See Brian Barry, *Culture and Equality: An Egalitarian Critique of Multiculturalism* (Cambridge: Polity, 2001); *Justice as Impartiality: A Treatise on Social Justice*, Volume II (Oxford: Clarendon Press, 1995). For my own defense of an egalitarian liberal theory of

Not all who are skeptical of egalitarian liberal universalism embrace anti-universalism. Some adopt what I have termed minimal universalism. They contend that the only values which apply universally are very minimal and basic ones. This position can be found in the work of Michael Walzer who posits a "minimal and universal moral code" (whose content is comprised of prohibitions on "murder, deception, betrayal, gross cruelty") in *Interpretation and Social Criticism*.[4] A similar position is defended by John Rawls in *The Law of Peoples*.[5] In this work Rawls explicitly rejects an egalitarian liberal universalism. Liberals, in their foreign policy, he insists, should subscribe only to some very basic human rights – ones that decent non-liberal peoples also find acceptable. These include the following:

> Among the human rights are the right to life (to the means of subsistence and security); to liberty (to freedom from slavery, serfdom, and forced occupation, and to a sufficient measure of liberty of conscience to ensure freedom of religion and thought); to property (personal property); and to formal equality as expressed by the rules of natural justice (that is, that similar cases be treated similarly).[6]

My aim in this chapter is, in part, to draw attention to some difficulties that this kind of minimal universalism faces.

II.

To do so let me begin the argument by introducing and defending one formal feature that I believe should apply to any defensible theory of global justice. (I shall then introduce a second formal feature in section III.) To do so it is useful to introduce a terminological point. The discussion in this section and the following one concerns the principles of justice that should apply to those who are not members of one's society. We might term these principles "just principles of foreign policy." To give some examples, someone's just principles of foreign policy might include the principle that all persons' fundamental needs should be satisfied. Or they might include the principle that torture is wrong. "Just principles of foreign policy" can be contrasted with "just principles of

---

global justice see my *Justice Beyond Borders: A Global Political Theory* (Oxford: Oxford University Press, 2005).

[4] See Michael Walzer, *Interpretation and Social Criticism* (Cambridge, MA: Harvard University Press, 1987), p. 24.

[5] John Rawls, *The Law of Peoples with "The Idea of Public Reason Revisited"* (Cambridge, MA: Harvard University Press, 1999), pp. 65, 79, 80 (footnote 23).

[6] Ibid., p. 65. I have omitted three footnote references from this passage.

domestic policy" where the latter phrase refers to the principles that should apply to those who are members of one's society.

Let us now introduce the first thesis. This reads as follows:

> **Thesis 1: the "Domestic Policy Coherence" Constraint (DPCC).**
> This stipulates that one's account of "just principles of foreign policy" must be consistent with one's "just principles of domestic policy."

The "domestic policy coherence" constraint states, then, that one's account of "global" justice must cohere with one's account of "domestic" justice. One's arguments for the latter should be consistent with one's account of the former.[7]

Before proceeding further, it is worth making two clarificatory comments about the DPC constraint. First, we should record that it should not be confused with the view that the principles to be adopted in the global realm should be identical to the principles that should be adopted in the domestic realm. The DPC constraint allows that different principles may apply in the two different contexts *but* it insists that, in such circumstances, there must be a persuasive argument showing that the two realms are disanalogous in a morally significant way which entails that it is appropriate to apply different ideals to the different realms. The DPC constraint calls, that is, for consistency and not identity. So to elaborate further: one could argue that a principle P applies to some countries but that it is inapplicable to others. And in such a case one would be saying that a reason when conjoined with various other assumptions, provides support for P but also that where those other assumptions do not obtain, P is not appropriate. To give a practical example, one might think that there is a good consequentialist case for democratic government. However, one might also think that democratic government will flourish only when certain socio-economic conditions obtain. With these in mind, one can quite consistently argue for democratic government in certain countries but deny that it should be applied universally. One's affirmation of democracy in countries *a*, *b*, and *c* and denial of democracy in countries *d*, *e*, and *f* can be perfectly consistent if democracy requires certain socio-economic conditions and they exist in *a*, *b*, and *c* but not in *d*, *e*, and *f*.

Let us turn now to a second point. It is worth distinguishing between a theory's fundamental principles, on the one hand, and its more specific principles on the other. By the former is meant a theory's most basic

---

[7] A similar point has been made by Lea Brilmayer. As she puts it, there is a "consistency requirement between domestic and international norms," *Justifying International Acts* (Ithaca and London: Cornell University Press, 1989), p. 28. See further *Justifying International Acts*, esp. pp. 23, 24, 28–29, 48, 81, 161.

principles, and by the latter is meant its specific prescriptions. To illustrate, consider utilitarianism. Its fundamental principle is its claim that utility should be maximized. Once we take into account political and economic circumstances we can see that utilitarianism might recommend one kind of specific prescription in some circumstances and other specific prescriptions in others. The key point is that where there are different circumstances utilitarianism recommends different principles. Now with this distinction in mind, we can further clarify the DPC constraint. For the latter is a claim about a theory of justice's fundamental principles. Its contention is that the fundamental principles that apply in the global realm should be consistent with the fundamental principles that apply in the domestic realm.

Now that we have clarified the nature of the DPC constraint it seems to me hard to reject. To embrace values in one realm and deny them in another when the same reasoning supports their application in both is obviously incoherent and inconsistent. There are, of course, cases where we might think that it is acceptable to embrace conflicting principles. Following thinkers like Bernard Williams and Sir Isaiah Berlin we might affirm a number of principles which conflict with each other – values such as mercy and justice.[8] But to accept this kind of pluralism gives us no reason to reject the DPC constraint. In these cases of moral conflict one is not treating two groups of people according to different principles: rather, one is treating all people the same but saying that when treating those same people we should balance different competing principles. To violate the DPC constraint is to act according to double standards – it is to treat people differently for no reason – and this is not what Berlin and Williams are arguing for.

III.

Having identified one formal property that I believe that any global political theory must satisfy, I wish now to introduce a second. This second property is introduced in the following claim:

> **Thesis 2: the "Foreign Policy Coherence" Constraint (FPCC).**
> This stipulates that one's account of which principles should be accepted as "just principles of foreign policy" should cohere with one's

---

[8] See Sir Isaiah Berlin, "The Pursuit of the Ideal" and "Alleged Relativism in Eighteenth-Century European Thought," in *The Crooked Timber of Humanity: Chapters in the History of Ideas*, ed. Henry Hardy (London: Fontana, 1991); and Bernard Williams, "Conflicts of Values," in *Moral Luck: Philosophical Papers 1973–1980* (Cambridge: Cambridge University Press, 1981), pp. 71–82.

account of which proposed principles of justice should not be accepted as "just principles of foreign policy."

The FPC constraint forbids cases where one affirms one principle P and rejects another Q when a commitment to P entails a commitment to Q.[9] To give an example: there is an incoherence in someone's foreign policy if they affirm a human right to freedom of action (P) but reject the claim that there should be private property (Q) if it is the case that private property is necessary to secure the human right to freedom of action. A foreign policy, then, that advocates freedom of action but repudiates one of its preconditions is empty. One must be able to give a consistent and persuasive account as to why some values are universally applicable whereas other values are not. Without this we are again faced by incoherence and ad hoc-ery.

Given the FPC constraint it is natural to ask when and why a commitment to one kind of global principle entails a commitment to a second distinct kind. To answer this question we might distinguish between four distinct kinds of interconnection – what one might term "logical," "empirical," "normative," and "mutual dependence" interconnections.[10]

#1. The first refers to a "logical" relation between two rights. As some have observed, a commitment to one right entails as a matter of logic that one commits oneself to another right. To give an example provided by Cécile Fabre, the right to privacy logically requires the right to housing.[11] Another possible example given by Henry Shue maintains that subsistence rights are a necessary component of other rights. The claim, as Shue presents it, is not that one right facilitates another: it is that it is constitutive of one right that the other right obtains.[12] This kind

---

[9] See relatedly what James Nickel terms a "consistency test," *Making Sense of Human Rights: Philosophical Reflections on the Universal Declaration of Human Rights* (Berkeley: University of California Press, 1987), p. 101. Nickel, note, is not discussing what rights a foreign policy should endorse. His focus is broader and is concerned with the connections between different rights regardless of whether we are talking about domestic policy or foreign policy.

[10] The distinction between "logical" and "empirical" relations has been noted by Cécile Fabre, *Social Rights under the Constitution: Government and the Decent Life* (Oxford: Clarendon Press, 2000), p. 123, cf. pp. 123–124. The same distinction is made by Nickel, *Making Sense of Human Rights*, p. 101. Nickel points out that affirmations of one right and repudiations of another may suffer from either "logical inconsistency" or "practical inconsistency," ibid.

[11] Fabre, *Social Rights under the Constitution*, pp. 123–124.

[12] See Henry Shue, *Basic Rights: Subsistence, Affluence, and US Foreign Policy*, 2nd edn. with a new afterword (Princeton: Princeton University Press, 1996), pp. 22–27 esp. pp. 26–27. For a good critical discussion see Nickel, *Making Sense of Human Rights*, pp. 102–104.

of relation seems to me a rather rare one but it is nonetheless worth noting.

#2. A second kind of interconnection is empirical in nature. It is sometimes argued that implementing one right is, in practice, the only means of ensuring that another right is honored. For example, if someone thought that democratic government was empirically the only effective system for protecting civil and political liberties then, *ceteris paribus*, a commitment to the latter provides us with a commitment to the former. It would be incoherent to commit oneself to protecting civil and political liberties but eschew a commitment to democracy. For another example of an empirical link one might consider some remarks made by Hannah Arendt in *The Origins of Totalitarianism*. In the latter she suggests that persons' "human rights" would not receive adequate protection unless those persons were not stateless but had the right to be a citizen of a state.[13] As she puts it, "[t]he Rights of Man, supposedly inalienable, proved to be unenforceable ... whenever people appeared who were no longer citizens of any sovereign state."[14] The realization of human rights thus requires, as a prerequisite, "a right to belong to some kind of organized community."[15]

Three further points should be observed. First, although this second kind of relationship between two rights is an empirical, as opposed to a logical, relationship it ideally involves more than just an empirical correlation between establishing one right and achieving another. The best situation would be one in which one is able to draw attention to a mechanism whereby one right has the effect of protecting another. One wants, that is, to be able to show the process by which establishing one right leads in practice to the protection of the other. For this reason it might, perhaps, be better to talk of two rights being "causally" related. A second point: we should note that the empirical connection that the FPCC requires is a strong one. To establish that one cannot coherently affirm one right (right A) and yet also reject another right (right B) because the two are empirically related one has to show more than that right A leads to right B. For the latter is compatible with it being the case that right C (and D or whatever) also leads to right B. What one needs to violate the FPCC are instances in which (i) a foreign policy affirms

---

[13] See Hannah Arendt, *The Origins of Totalitarianism* (San Diego: Harcourt, 1994 [1951]), ch. 9 esp. section II on "the perplexities of the rights of man." See too p. 279.

[14] Ibid., p. 293.

[15] Ibid., p. 297. For a further statement of this position see her contention that "[n]ot only did loss of national rights in all instances entail the loss of human rights; the restoration of human rights, as the recent example of the State of Israel proves, has been achieved so far only through the restoration or the establishment of national rights," ibid., p. 299.

A, (ii) it repudiates B, and (iii) B is a *necessary* means for achieving A. So it is not good to enough show that B is *a* means towards achieving A. If it is only *a* means and there are other means then one could quite consistently affirm A and repudiate B. To use logical terminology, to establish that "A will be the case if B is the case" is not good enough: the FPCC requires cases where "A will be the case only if B is the case." An example may help to illustrate the point. Amartya Sen is well known for having argued that famines never occur in democratic political systems.[16] Suppose that this claim is correct. We should note that it is perfectly possible (i) to affirm a right not to suffer from famine whilst also (ii) repudiating democratic government. (i) and (ii) do not violate the FPCC. For them to do so it must be true not simply that "famines never occur in democratic political systems" but also that a "democratic political system is necessary if people are to enjoy the right not to suffer from famine."[17] Only if the latter is true is it the case that one cannot affirm (i) and (ii).

A third, and final, point is worth observing about "empirical" (or "causal") links between two (or more) rights. To see this point we need to distinguish between the two following kinds of statements:

(i) an individualistic statement: persons can, in all particular instances, enjoy right A only if they also possess right B;
(ii) a systemic statement: persons can, in general, enjoy right A only if they also possess right B.[18]

Now the point of this distinction is to enable us to allow for the possibility of a scenario in which one right (right A) in general requires the prior implementation of another right (right B) and yet there are some exceptions (cases where right A does not require right B). In this state of affairs (ii) holds but (i) does not. What bearing does this have for the FPCC? The reason it matters is that it affects how we formulate the empirical links between rights. Must it be true *in every instance* that right A can be secured only if right B is protected for the FPCC to show that

---

[16] Amartya Sen, *Development as Freedom* (New York: Anchor Books, 1999), pp. 16, 51–53, 152–154.

[17] Sen's view, as I interpret it, is indeed that democracy is necessary for the avoidance of famine. He writes, for example, that "achievement of development is thoroughly dependent on the free agency of people," *Development as Freedom*, p. 4. See, further, ibid., pp. 4, 10, 51–53, 152–154.

[18] Note that one might, speaking very loosely, observe that this distinction is similar in spirit to the distinction between act and rule utilitarianism: (a) focuses on an individual instance (is right A needed in this particular instance to achieve right B?) in a way similar to act utilitarianism; (b) focuses on the general rules (is right A in general needed to achieve right B?) in a way similar to rule utilitarianism.

one cannot affirm A and yet reject B? At first glance this might seem right and indeed obviously right. We might think that it is not enough to show that right A, in general, requires right B. However, this would be mistaken. Suppose, for example, that we have good reason to think that one right is *in general* required to achieve a second right, although there are some exceptions (so (ii) holds but (i) does not). However, suppose, further, that we are unable to work out in advance when there will be exceptions to this correlation. In this kind of situation it would seem entirely reasonable to say that the FPCC forbids affirming right A and rejecting right B when a systemic link of the kind affirmed by (ii) holds. It would, that is, be incoherent to affirm right A but not right B if right B is, in general, a prerequisite of right A *and if we cannot work out the exceptions to this general correlation*. To express it slightly differently: if right B is the maximally reliable mechanism for ensuring the protection of right A then it would, other things being equal, surely be an act of bad faith to affirm right A but to reject B and select another less reliable mechanism for achieving A.[19]

#3. Let us turn now to a third kind of link between rights. The kind of link between two (or more) rights that I have in mind is what might be termed a "normative" link. A normative link obtains when the normative grounding for one right also provides support for another right. Suppose, for example, that one prizes one right (such as freedom of action) because it furthers people's capacity to flourish. Now suppose further that another right (such as material support) would, if adopted,

---

[19] Two other complications in any "empirical" link are noted by James Nickel in a short but illuminating discussion. First, as he observes, one should distinguish between, on the one hand, cases where one right makes the realization of a second right more likely (it is, as he puts it, "helpful to the successful implementation") and, on the other hand, cases where one right is "essential to the effective implementation" of another right (*Making Sense of Human Rights*, p. 101). Second, Nickel points out that when discussing whether one right is necessary (or useful) to the realization of a second right we should note that it is unduly simplistic to talk of the realization of a right. As Nickel writes:

> [s]uccess in implementing a right – in employing people and institutions to prevent violations – is always a matter of degree. The answers to the question of whether implementation of R1 is consistent in practice with the nonimplementation of R2 will sometimes depend on the degree of implementation we have in mind. Very rudimentary protections for R1 may be consistent with the absence of R2. But full or elaborate implementation of R1 may be inconsistent with the absence of R2 (ibid., p. 102).

Elsewhere Nickel provides a full account of the kinds of empirical links between various kinds of rights, noting in particular how various civil and political rights protect the right not to suffer from starvation. See James Nickel, "A Human Rights Approach to World Hunger," in *World Hunger and Morality*, ed. William Aiken and Hugh LaFollette, 2nd edn. (Upper Saddle River, NJ: Prentice Hall, 1996), pp. 171–185, esp. pp. 179–184.

also further people's capacity to flourish. In this situation the normative rationale that grounds the first right (it enables people to lead fulfilling lives) also grounds the second right (it too furthers this goal). And, assuming all other things to be equal, it would hence be incoherent to affirm the first right but not the second when the reasoning for the first also gives us reason to embrace the second. So where two rights have normative links then affirming one but denying the other would violate the FPC constraint.

#4. Let us now consider a fourth kind of relationship between rights. This fourth kind of relationship might be described as involving "complementarity" links.[20] I use this term to refer to instances where a commitment to a right A also needs a commitment to a right B. The claim is neither that A logically entails B nor that B is an empirical precondition of A, nor that the rationale for A is also a rationale for B. Rather the thought is that right A stands in need of being complemented by right B. Complementary links may take different forms. Consider three possibilities.

(a) First, consider a case where a right X will achieve its (beneficial) outcomes (which are its rationale) only if right Y is also adopted. Suppose, for example, that democracy will reach sound decisions only if freedom of expression is also affirmed. In such cases right X needs right Y and it would violate the FPCC to affirm the former but deny the latter. Another illustration of the kind of reasoning again starts with a commitment to democratic decision-making. It then maintains that the benefits that democracy is supposed to produce can be realized only if citizens in a democracy have certain socio-economic needs realized, such as the right to health, the right to education, and the right to a basic standard of living.[21]

---

[20] What I term "complementarity" links should not be equated with what Fabre calls "the complementarity thesis" in *Social Rights under the Constitution*, p. 45, and also pp. 45–49. She employs that term to refer to the thesis that an interest may generate both negative rights and positive rights. In her words, the "complementarity thesis" applies where rights " 'complement one another, in that they each protect interests in certain ways, and taken together afford full protection to these interests'," *Social Rights under the Constitution*, p. 47. I have omitted a footnote (footnote 14) at the end of this quotation. Scenario (a) would, I think, conform to Fabre's "complementarity thesis" but scenarios (b) and (c) do not.

[21] An example of this kind of reasoning can be found in the work of David Held. Held lists seven clusters of rights which, so he claims, are required for a cosmopolitan democracy to function, *Democracy and the Global Order: From the Modern State to Cosmopolitan Governance* (Cambridge: Polity, 1995), pp. 192–194. These include rights to medical care, education, and childcare and a minimum income (pp. 192–198). As Held puts it: "Each bundle of rights represents a fundamental enabling condition for political participation and, therefore, for legitimate rule. Unless people enjoy liberty in these

(b) Consider now a second possibility. Suppose that there is a reasonable case for right X but that that right also has malign side-effects. Suppose, further, that right Y would counteract those malign side-effects. Then we might say that a commitment to right X also needs right Y.

(c) Consider now a third possibility that is prompted by an argument developed by Jürgen Habermas. In *Between Facts and Norms*, Habermas argues that liberal rights and democracy are in need of each other. On the one hand, liberal rights need to be specified in concrete detail and they also need to be legitimized. Democratic procedures can do both of these: the people can use democratic processes to decide exactly what vague concepts like freedom of expression should look like in practice. Furthermore, democratic procedures can confer legitimacy on these principles. Liberal rights thus need to be supplemented by democratic processes. The relationship also holds the other way around. Democratic processes need liberal rights of freedom of belief, association, and speech in order to be able to function.[22]

This taxonomy is not necessarily exhaustive but it does hopefully show a number of distinct ways in which rights can be interrelated. And where two or more rights are linked in any of the above four ways – logical, empirical, normative, or complementarity – then, it would be incoherent to affirm one of the rights but repudiate the other. These kinds of links are of critical importance because if we find that minimal rights are

---

seven spheres, they cannot participate fully in the 'government' of state and civil affairs. To repeat an earlier argument, the seven categories of rights do not articulate an endless list of goods; rather, they articulate necessary conditions for free and equal participation," *Democracy and the Global Order*, p. 199. See, further, ibid., pp. 187, 190, 199–200, 208, 210–212, 223–224, 250, 252–253, 271. Similar reasoning is advanced by Michael Saward. He derives rights to freedom of speech and association ("basic freedoms"), rights to medical support and education ("social rights"), and a right to a "minimum income" ("basic income") from a commitment to democratic self-rule. See Michael Saward, *The Terms of Democracy* (Cambridge: Polity, 1998), p. 64 and, more fully, pp. 87–103.

[22] See Jürgen Habermas, *Between Facts and Norms: Contributions to a Discourse Theory of Law and Democracy*, trans. William Rehg (Cambridge: Polity, 1997), esp. pp. 118–131, 454–457. For a succinct statement of Habermas's argument see Thomas McCarthy, "Two Conceptions of Cosmopolitan Justice," in *Reconstituting Social Criticism: Political Morality in an Age of Scepticism*, ed. Iain MacKenzie and Shane O'Neill (Basingstoke: Palgrave Macmillan, 1999), pp. 200–201. Finally, we might also note that Allen Buchanan has argued that liberal civil and economic rights are indeterminate in a number of ways and he plausibly suggests that democratic procedures are the appropriate mechanisms for producing more specific interpretations of these rights. See Allen Buchanan, *Justice, Legitimacy, and Self-Determination: Moral Foundations for International Law* (Oxford: Oxford University Press, 2004), pp. 180–190.

dependent in any of the ways detailed above on more expansive non-minimal rights it follows that we should reject a minimalist position. The formal property of foreign policy coherence would rule out a minimalist position.

Before turning to consider the implications of the DPCC and the FPCC for egalitarian liberalism, it is worth considering four points. First, although the above analysis outlines four separate ways in which two or more rights might be interrelated, I am not claiming that each is of equal significance. It might, for example, be the case that the normative or the empirical links are more fruitful as ways of establishing links than, say, the logical.

Second, we should note that two rights might be linked in more than one way. Right A and right B might be both normatively linked and also empirically linked. That is to say, it might be that the case for right A also grounds right B and, furthermore, that right B is a necessary precondition for securing right A. Put less abstractly, one might argue that the case for freedom of action and for democratic government is that they, separately, best enable people to flourish (a normative link). And one might, further, argue that democratic government is required if people are to enjoy freedom of action (an empirical link).

Third, we should record that some of the types of links between rights are more watertight than other types of links. To explain: if a logical relationship holds then right A entails right B in all circumstances. Consider, however, normative links between two rights. These are, perhaps, less watertight than logical links because one can imagine situations in which the rationale for one right also provides support for a second right and yet it is possible to affirm one right but not the other. Suppose, for example, that it is important for persons to reach a certain standard of living. Suppose now that right A serves this goal and that right B also does to the same extent. Must we necessarily affirm both rights? Not necessarily: for if one's goal is simply to attain a certain threshold level and two rights both serve this ideal then one can quite reasonably embrace one but not the other. To examine how much this qualifies the strength of a "normative" link it is useful to compare different kinds of ways of grounding rights. Let us examine two. (i) Consider, for example, a deontological approach. Suppose that someone defends persons' human rights not to be tortured and they do so on the grounds that torture fails to treat persons as ends in themselves. Let us suppose now that we find that another type of action, enslavement, also fails to treat persons as ends in themselves. In such a situation there is what I have termed earlier a normative link between the two rights: the reasoning that grounds the one (a right not to be tortured) also grounds the other (a right not to be enslaved). A deontological argument could not, *ceteris paribus*, support just the one right. So if one's reasons for embracing a right are deontological in character then any normative links between rights will be strong. (ii) The same is true if one takes a maximizing consequentialist viewpoint. If the reason underpinning right A is that it promotes well-being and if right B would also promote well-being and if one has a goal to maximize well-being then, one cannot coherently affirm right A but not B (or vice versa). So, a maximizing consequentialist approach is not vulnerable to the qualification introduced earlier in this paragraph. In the light of the above observations let me make then the following suggestion: if the normative grounding for right A also applies to right B then there is a normative link and, from the point of view of a maximizing consequentialism and from the point of view of a deontological approach, it is incoherent to affirm right A but not B. However, it might be coherent to affirm one right but not the other if one adopts, for example, a satisficing kind of consequentialism for in such a case the fact that the reason for A is also a reason for B does not logically entail that one must affirm both A and B.[23] One right on its own may be sufficient to attain the "satisficing" level.

Fourth, we should recognize the possibility of links between more than two rights. To explain: it might be the case that right A entails right B and furthermore that right B entails right C. The relevant point is that there might be knock-on effects of affirming one right. Not only might it lead to a commitment to a second right. It might also entail committing ourselves to a third or even fourth right. And this lends further support to my general position that rights are highly interlinked: the more that individual rights have multiple entailments to other rights, the more it is difficult to pursue a minimalist strategy.

IV.

The DPC constraint and the FPC constraint are formal constraints that, I am claiming, any sound global political theory must honor. As formal constraints, of course, they do not say what the content of any global principles should be. For example, as has been stressed above, the DPCC is concerned only with ensuring consistency between one's domestic political theory, on the one hand, and one's global political

---

[23] For the concept of "satisficing" see Herbert A. Simon, *Administrative Behavior: A Study of Decision-Making Processes in Administrative Organization*, 3rd edn. expanded with a new Introduction (New York: Free Press, 1976 [1945]), pp. xxviii–xxxi, 38–41, 80–84. For its application to moral philosophy see Michael Slote, *Common-sense Morality and Consequentialism* (London: Routledge & Kegan Paul, 1985).

theory, on the other, *whatever the content of one's domestic or global political theory happens to be.*

In this section, I want to turn to matters of content. I want, in particular, to introduce some key egalitarian liberal tenets and to conjoin these with the DPCC and FPCC. Doing so can enable us to ascertain whether egalitarian liberal values must be universalized or whether we can coherently take a minimalist or anti-universalist position.

Let us begin by combining the DPCC with some of the orthodox defenses of egalitarian liberal values. In the space available it is possible only to provide the bare bones of some of the main liberal theories. Consider, first, consequentialist approaches. Suppose, for example, that we think that individual rights best enable persons to flourish and to live rich and rewarding lives because individuals (above the age of maturity) are best at discerning and furthering their own good. If this is a good argument then, Mill's own reservations notwithstanding, it entails that all adult persons should possess this right.[24] Consider now more deontological arguments. If one thinks, as Thomas Nagel and Frances Kamm have argued, that persons possess an inviolable "status" that should be respected and one further thinks that this grounds the complete set of liberal civil and political rights then it would be incoherent to restrict this right to members of some countries alone.[25] Or consider Hillel Steiner's defense of liberal rights in his celebrated *An Essay on Rights.* In the latter, Steiner maintains that persons own themselves: they own their bodies and, as such, possess the complete set of liberal rights. Given the rationale for holding these rights (the premise of self-ownership) it clearly follows, as Steiner himself emphasizes, that all persons should possess this same extensive set of liberal rights.[26] The analysis so far then lends support to the conclusion that the logic of standard egalitarian liberal theories of justice entails that their principles apply universally. Given the above consequentialist and deontological rationales for rights, to adopt such rights only within one's own state would violate the DPCC. Accordingly, it would be incoherent to affirm any of these

[24] See J. S. Mill, "On Liberty," in *Essays on Politics and Society: Collected Works of John Stuart Mill,* Volume XVIII, ed. J. M. Robson, with an introduction by Alexander Brady (Toronto: University of Toronto Press, 1977 [1859]), pp. 213–310.
[25] See F. M. Kamm, "Non-consequentialism, the Person as an End-in-Itself, and the Significance of Status," *Philosophy and Public Affairs,* 21 (4), 1992, pp. 354–389 and Thomas Nagel, "Personal Rights and Public Space," *Philosophy and Public Affairs,* 24 (2), 1995, pp. 83–107.
[26] See Hillel Steiner, *An Essay on Rights* (Oxford: Blackwell, 1994); see, in particular, pp. 262, 265.

egalitarian liberal theories and yet take an anti-universalist or minimal universalist position.[27]

Several objections to this line of reasoning might be raised.

#1. First, it might be objected that the best justification of liberal values is simply that they cohere with our own traditions and norms. The most persuasive defense of egalitarian liberal principles, then, on this account, refers not to some universalist principle whose logic entails that it applies everywhere. It invokes a purely parochial (or as Richard Rorty would put it, an "ethnocentric") defense of liberal values.[28] The argument invokes a culturally specific (that is, non-universal) reason and hence the conclusions it defends are similarly culturally specific. Now, if this is the rationale for egalitarian liberal values then there would be no incoherence, so the argument goes, in affirming these values at home (because they mesh with our traditions) but not in all other societies (because they do not mesh with their traditions).

This challenge has the right kind of structure since it gives a reason for liberal egalitarian rights that, on the one hand, has force in some societies and, yet, on the other hand, does not commit us to claiming that these liberal egalitarian ideals should be adopted universally. It is, however, not, in my view, a plausible line of argument. In the first place, the meta-ethical assumption on which this argument is based is in itself not a convincing line of reasoning for egalitarian liberal values. Establishing that egalitarian liberal ideals are justified on the grounds that they cohere with our traditions could be a promising approach only if we had reason to think that our traditions are constitutive of what is just. But this assumption is fraught with problems. For one, it is not an accurate account of why we think that liberal values are correct: when defending liberal values, liberals tend to give reasons. They do not think it enough to say "this is our custom" but try to adduce considerations in support of those beliefs. Furthermore, we recognize that our common values can be mistaken and flawed.[29] The "ethnocentric" approach that Rorty

---

[27] This paragraph has concentrated on liberal arguments for civil and political liberties. The same points could, I believe, be made about liberal arguments for distributive justice. For an excellent discussion of this see Samuel Black, "Individualism at an Impasse," *Canadian Journal of Philosophy*, 21 (3), 1991, pp. 347–377, especially his discussion of what he terms "the fallacy of *restricted universalism*" (p. 357). For a further extended argument to this effect see Caney, *Justice Beyond Borders*, ch. 4, and "Cosmopolitan Justice and Equalizing Opportunities," *Metaphilosophy*, 32 (1/2), 2001, pp. 113–134.

[28] See Richard Rorty, "Solidarity or Objectivity?" (esp. pp. 29–30) and "On Ethnocentrism: A Reply to Clifford Geertz," both in *Objectivity, Relativism, and Truth: Philosophical Papers*, Volume I (Cambridge: Cambridge University Press, 1991).

[29] For persuasive arguments see: William A. Galston, *Liberal Purposes: Goods, Virtues, and Diversity in the Liberal State* (Cambridge: Cambridge University Press, 1991), p. 158;

celebrates is then false to people's understanding of their own moral beliefs and ideals.

#2. A second challenge to the claim that egalitarian liberal rights must be adopted universally if they are not to violate the DPCC might draw on the concept of special rights. As H. L. A. Hart famously pointed out, we can distinguish between "special rights" and "general rights." Special rights are rights that persons have in virtue of some kind of social relationship – such as a promise or contract. General rights, on the other hand, are rights that persons have simply as persons.[30] Now using this distinction someone might argue that we have a strong moral conviction that there are special rights: some rights, we think, are possessed only by some persons. We can make perfect sense, that is, of the notion that some rights should not be held universally. Employees of a firm have (special) rights that non-employees lack; students at a university have (special) rights that non-members lack. And so on. Now drawing on this, a critic might argue that we can respond to the preceding analysis that the sorts of rights that I have been discussing (liberal civil, political, and economic rights) are in fact special rights not general ones. As such they are not rights that all persons hold. The challenge then is that my argument against minimalism and anti-universalism ignores the existence of special rights and the fact that standard liberal rights are special rights: they are rights held qua citizens and not general rights.

In reply: I accept of course that there are special rights but I deny that all the economic, civil, and political rights that have been discussed so far fall into this category. The reason why they cannot be classified as special, as opposed to general, rights can be seen by examining the arguments adduced for these rights. For in each case, the arguments justifying those rights appeal to universal attributes and hence, inescapably, entail general rights. Steiner's argument, for example, appeals to the rights of *persons* as self-owners: what grounds the right to equal freedom is a universal property and it cannot establish a non-universal, that is special, right. The same point comes out by examining Kantian arguments that invoke Kant's categorical imperative: if one grounds persons' rights by appealing to their "humanity" then, of course, the conclusion must be that the rights are held by all humans, not by all

Amy Gutmann, "The Challenge of Multiculturalism in Political Ethics," *Philosophy and Public Affairs*, 22 (3), 1993, pp. 176–177; Will Kymlicka, *Liberalism, Community and Culture* (Oxford: Clarendon Press, 1989), pp. 65–66; Jeremy Waldron, "Particular Values and Critical Morality," *California Law Review*, 77 (3), 1989, pp. 575–578; and Jeremy Waldron, "What is Cosmopolitan?," *Journal of Political Philosophy*, 8 (2), 2000, pp. 234–236.

[30] See H. L. A. Hart, "Are There Any Natural Rights?," in *Theories of Rights*, ed. Jeremy Waldron (Oxford: Oxford University Press, 1985), pp. 84–88.

one's citizens. So it is true that there is an important distinction between special and general rights but this does not undermine my argument for the *justifications* of liberal egalitarian rights entail that these rights are general, and not special, rights.

We have seen, then, that two challenges to the contention that the rationales for liberal values entail that they should be adopted universally fail. When we conjoin, (i), the standard rationales for liberal civil, political, and economic rights with, (ii), the Domestic Policy Coherence Constraint we are driven to the conclusion, (iii), that liberal civil, political, and economic rights should be held by *all*.[31] Those who hold liberal values for their own society cannot coherently adopt a minimalist or anti-universalist position.

V.

Let us move our attention from the DPCC and apply the FPCC to minimal accounts of human rights. Is it coherent to posit just some minimal rights and not subscribe to a more expansive package? Let me propose several kinds of links between "minimal rights" and "more-than-minimal rights," links which, if true, make a minimalist position hard to sustain.

We might consider, first, five "empirical" links between minimal rights and more expansive rights. These can be formulated as follows:

[1] Subsistence rights require, in general, democratic rights.

The rationale for this is well known and has already been cited earlier in this chapter. The thought is simply that democratic governments have the incentive to prevent famine for if they were to allow it they would almost certainly lose office. We lack a reason for endorsing any other system for no other has the same incentive to eliminate poverty.

Consider now a second suggestion:

[2] Basic civil rights (rights not to be enslaved, say) require, in general, democratic rights.

---

[31] It is important to emphasize that the DPCC alone does not necessarily entail universalizing liberal values. It depends on what one's domestic theory holds. This point can be illustrated with the example of abortion. Consider in particular those who think that abortion should be illegal because it is murder. What should be their attitude to a person in their state who plans to leave the country in order to have an abortion? If one thinks that abortion is murder it would seem highly problematic to think that, as a matter of principle (as opposed to a phenomenon one could not in reality prevent), it is acceptable for pregnant women to leave to have an abortion (that is, commit a murder). To ban it because it is murder at home but to grant persons a right to go abroad to have an abortion would seem to violate the DPCC.

Again, the rationale for this is familiar. Democratic institutions provide their leaders with an incentive for not visiting egregious injustices on their people. Of course, democratic political procedures do not guarantee that there will not be violations of basic civil rights but, in comparison with other kinds of political order, it would seem reasonable to suggest that they are less prone to inflict injustice on the people. Minorities are, of course, vulnerable in majoritarian democracies but this gives us no reason to prefer a non-democratic system to a democratic one because a non-democratic system will also have no incentive to treat minorities fairly that is not possessed by a democratic system. In the light of this [2] seems a reasonable hypothesis.[32]

A third, less well-known, hypothesis maintains that:

[3] Rights to physical security require, in general, rights to a sustainable environment.

The thought underlying this is that environmental scarcity and degradation lead to social tensions which, in turn, lead to violent conflict. This general hypothesis has been extensively discussed, notably by Thomas Homer-Dixon. As Homer-Dixon notes, there are a number of different mechanisms by which environmental degradation and scarcity cause violent conflict. Sometimes they lead to migration which, in turn, generates social conflict. On other occasions they lead to competition for scarce resources and hence to the intensification of rivalry and hostility between the advantaged and disadvantaged. Either way, though, these threats to the environment contribute to violent conflict and, as such, jeopardize persons' rights to their physical security.[33]

Another empirical connection worth considering contends that:

[4] Rights to fair treatment (such as a fair trial), in general, require transparent government and hence rights to freedom of information.

The administration of justice requires, in general, a transparent decision-making procedure – one governed by a norm of "publicity." We can discern two separate mechanisms here. First, publicity enables people to detect injustice. Hence it makes it more difficult for people to get away with perpetrating an injustice. Rights to information and open decision-making enable people to scrutinize public policy and as such

---

[32] See, further, Robert Dahl's discussion of what he terms "Madisonian democracy" in *A Preface to Democratic Theory* (Chicago: University of Chicago Press, 1956), esp. ch. 1.

[33] See Thomas F. Homer-Dixon, "On the Threshold: Environmental Changes as Causes of Acute Conflict," *International Security*, 16 (2), 1991, pp. 76–116 and "Environmental Scarcities and Violent Conflict: Evidence from Cases," *International Security*, 19 (1), 1994, pp. 5–40.

identify injustice and then campaign to change them. Second, it is reasonable to hypothesize that publicity changes the motivations of state officials. In a political order where decision-making is transparent state officials will be self-censoring. Given transparency they will not consider policies that they might have considered in a non-transparent order for fear of the criticism that they will get and the cost to their reputation. Rights to fair treatment generally require, then, a system in which persons have rights to know what decisions have been taken and for what reasons.[34]

To the above, we might also add the following empirical link:

[5] Rights not to suffer from life-threatening environmental harms require equal civil, economic, and political rights.

This claim is grounded in the observation that many environmental harms fall disproportionately on the poor and least powerful.[35] There is, for example, considerable evidence that environmental pollution emitted from industrial plants is distributed primarily among the poor. Furthermore, and slightly separately, there have been a number of well-documented cases which found that pollution has been located in areas inhabited by racial minorities. A well-known case of this is Love Canal in the United States. The reasons for [5] are not hard to find. Poor families are less able to move to other areas. In addition to this they have less (financial) ability to represent their views in the political process and are under-represented. The only way to ensure that one group of people is not disproportionately exposed to such hazards is to have equal civil, political, and economic rights.

These five "empirical" links between basic and minimal rights, on the one hand, and more expansive rights, on the other, can also be buttressed by noting a "normative" link, namely

[6] Rights to basic civil and political rights also entail rights to economic resources.

---

[34] For good discussions of "publicity" see Robert E. Goodin, *Motivating Political Morality* (Oxford: Blackwell, 1992), pp. 124–146; Amy Gutmann and Dennis Thompson, *Democracy and Disagreement: Why Moral Conflict Cannot be Avoided in Politics, and What Should be Done about It* (Cambridge, MA: The Belknap Press of Harvard University Press, 1996), pp. 95–127; David Luban, "The Publicity Principle," in *The Theory of Institutional Design*, ed. Robert E. Goodin (Cambridge: Cambridge University Press, 1996), pp. 154–198. For a seminal discussion of the relationship between publicity, on the one hand, and justice and injustice, on the other, see Immanuel Kant, "Perpetual Peace: A Philosophical Sketch," in *Kant's Political Writings*, ed. Hans Reiss, trans H. B. Nisbet (Cambridge: Cambridge University Press, 1989 [1795]), pp. 125–130.

[35] For pertinent discussion see Robert D. Bullard, "Anatomy of Environmental Racism and the Environmental Justice Movement," in *Debating the Earth: The Environmental Politics Reader*, ed. John S. Dryzek and David Schlosberg (Oxford: Oxford University Press, 1998), pp. 471–492; Kristin Shrader-Frechette, *Environmental Justice: Creating Equality, Reclaiming Democracy* (New York: Oxford University Press, 2002), pp. 6–18.

The rationale for this claim is, again, a familiar one. The line of reasoning underlying [5] goes as follows: a compelling argument for thinking that there are rights to basic civil and political rights is that they protect people's fundamental interests (interests in attaining a certain quality of life). But then, the argument runs, these very same interests also, and equally, justify rights to economic resources (by which is meant rights to the material resources needed to support oneself). For these too are needed if people are to attain a certain standard of living. One cannot then coherently affirm civil and political rights only and eschew rights to economic support.[36]

One further link might be advanced. Consider a "complementarity" link between minimal rights and more than minimal rights. The hypothesis in question maintains that

[7] Liberal civil and economic rights require the validation by democratic rights and democratic rights require the existence of civil and economic rights.

The Habermasian reasoning for this was set out above (p. 161) and so need only be restated briefly. The key thought is that liberal rights will enjoy "legitimacy" only if they are authorized by the people and this requires democracy. (Other ways of making these rights part of the law [such as by the common law] lack this legitimizing effect.) And, at the same time, democracy requires the same civil and economic rights that it is legitimizing.[37]

In light of the preceding analysis, then, we can see that a minimalist position is problematic. The logical, empirical, normative, and complementarity-related links between rights call into question a political morality that affirms minimal universal rights and eschews more-than-minimal rights. As such it undermines those who maintain that liberal values are applicable in the domestic realm but adopt only a minimal set of human rights.

VI.

It is time to conclude. Our conclusions can be summed up using figure 6.1. Consider now each of the positions, starting with [1]. [1] is the most problematic position for it refers to political moralities that fall

[36] This point is well made by Buchanan, *Justice, Legitimacy, and Self-Determination*, p. 197.
[37] See, ibid., pp. 118–131, 454–457; Habermas, *Between Facts and Norms*, pp. 200–201; McCarthy, "Two Conceptions of Cosmopolitan Justice," pp. 180–190.

	Violates the Domestic Policy Coherence Constraint	Honors the Domestic Policy Coherence Constraint
Violates the Foreign Policy Coherence Constraint	[1] e.g. minimalist liberalism	[2] e.g. universal minimalism
Honors the Foreign Policy Coherence Constraint	[3] e.g. anti-universalist liberalism	[4] e.g. universalist liberalism

Figure 1

afoul of both the DPCC and the FPCC. One political theory that fits in this quadrant is the view that liberal values apply at home but that only minimal rights should be adopted at the global level ("minimalist liberalism"). This doctrine violates the DPCC because the arguments establishing the validity of liberal rights at home also establish that these rights hold universally. Furthermore, it violates the FPCC because, so I have suggested above, minimal rights require the acceptance of the entire liberal package.

Consider now position [2]. It is not easy to think of a political morality that falls into this category. One possibility is a thoroughgoing minimalism: this claims that there is a set of minimal rights that applies everywhere and it denies that more-than-minimal rights should be applied anywhere. Now this position honors the DPCC: the reasons for its domestic commitments (the arguments for some minimal rights) are quite consistent with its foreign policy principles (which also comprise simply those same minimal rights). It quite consistently denies liberalism both at home and abroad. If, however, this chapter is right in arguing that minimal rights require more-than-minimal rights then this position violates the FPCC. It affirms some rights (the minimal ones) and repudiates others (more-than-minimal ones) and yet the former rights require the latter ones.[38]

Let us consider now position [3]. This refers to those political moralities that honor the FPCC but fail the DPCC. As we have seen above, one position that falls into this category is anti-universalism. It affirms

---

[38] This, obviously, entails that this doctrine not only fails the FPCC but it also has an incoherent domestic policy. The reason is, of course, the same. If minimal rights entail (for logical, empirical, normative, or whatever reasons) a complete liberal package then it would be incoherent to affirm a *domestic* theory of justice that affirms minimal rights and reject any more expansive rights.

no universal values and so cannot fail the FPCC: since it denies that there are any universal values it cannot be accused of affirming an inconsistent set of universal values. However, the fact that anti-universalism affirms no universal values entails that it violates the DPCC for, as we have seen, there are numerous powerful arguments for liberal economic, civil, and political rights and the logic of those arguments entails that these rights should apply universally.

Let us turn now finally to position [4]: this, of course, is the only satisfactory position of the four options available. One theory that passes it is, I have argued, a universalist theory of liberal rights.

What, then, has been established? Using figure 6.1, and drawing on the analysis of this chapter, we can draw attention to four important conclusions. These are as follows:

(1) the Foreign Policy Coherence Constraint undermines "minimalist liberalism" (position [1]) but does not tell against "anti-universalist liberalism"; and

(2) the Domestic Policy Coherence Constraint undermines both "minimalist liberalism" and "anti-universalist liberalism." This is represented by positions [1] and [3]. It delivers an immanent critique of all those who maintain that liberal principles of justice are applicable in the "domestic" realm but do not apply those same values in the "global" realm.

Or to put matters slightly differently, we might say that

(3) a minimalist liberalism is doubly flawed for it violates both the Foreign Policy Coherence Constraint and the Domestic Policy Coherence Constraint; and

(4) anti-universalist liberalism is also flawed for it is undermined by the Domestic Policy Coherence Constraint.

In short: the commonly expressed view that egalitarian liberal values should inform "domestic" policies but should not inform "foreign policy" is much more problematic than is generally recognized.

Contextualism, constitutionalism,
     and *modus vivendi* approaches

     Jacob T. Levy[1]

> For political philosophy's habitual, and it seems, ineliminable,
> dependence on the urgency of political questions which are not in the
> first place philosophical is of a piece with its insistence, when at all
> interesting, on being both normative and impure. It is … impure in the
> sense that materials from non-philosophical sources – an involvement
> with history or the social sciences, for example, are likely to play a more
> than illustrative part in the argument.[2]

In the last decade's body of work on the political theory of multiculturalism, ethnic pluralism, and nationalism, increasing attention has
been paid to issues of context and to the particularities of institutional
design in multiethnic states. The "first wave" of work on these questions
was largely devoted to establishing that topics such as the rights of
indigenous peoples, language policy, secession and irredentism, and
exemptions for religious minorities belonged on the agenda of Anglo-
American political theory at all – that nations and nationalism, for
example, raised genuine questions in political philosophy, rather than
being (as had commonly been assumed) pre-philosophical prejudices of
no theoretical interest. The "second wave" has often been concerned
with bridging the gap between first-wave philosophy and concrete cases.
While discussions of real cases have often been present in political
theory and philosophy, many have suggested that there is some particular affinity between theorizing about *multiculturalism* and context.

  Contextualism in multicultural theory has been raised to the level of
a methodological commitment by some, most prominently Joseph

---

[1] I thank Emily Nacol for valuable research assistance, Victor Muniz-Fraticelli for
  discussion of political liberalism, David Owen for detailed and thoughtful comments,
  and Daniel Weinstock for inadvertently stimulating some of what follows, with his
  presentation on a roundtable on the thirtieth anniversary of the publication of *A Theory
  of Justice* at the 2001 Annual Meeting of the American Political Science Association.
[2] Bernard Williams, "Political Philosophy and the Analytical Tradition," in *Philosophy as a
  Humanistic Discipline* (Princeton: Princeton University Press, 2006), p. 156.

173

Carens.[3] But I think it is fair to say that Carens has made explicit something that goes beyond his own work. Second-wave multiculturalist work – dating roughly from the publication of Will Kymlicka's *Multicultural Citizenship* – simply doesn't *look* like, for example, most work on distributive justice from the 1970s, or for that matter like work on distributive justice or contractarianism from the past ten to fifteen years,[4] or like first-wave multicultural theory. As a genre, it seems set apart by a proliferation of proper nouns, a noticeable scaling down of the level of philosophical abstraction. Jeff Spinner-Halev[5] has forcefully argued that first-wave multicultural theory was marked by a tendency to over-generalize from particular but unexamined cases, in the pursuit of a universal theory of cultural rights or nationalism. This suggests the remedy of laying one's cases on the table and examining what they do or do not share with other cases. And he has affirmatively promoted (and practiced) such work himself, maintaining[6] that locally particular histories of injustice are of greater importance in justifying cultural rights claims than is any universal right of cultural or communal preservation. As Chandran Kukathas has summarized matters, "much of the political theory of multiculturalism seems to be of the contextual variety."[7]

That there is some particular affinity between multiculturalism and context in political theory is further suggested by the curious case of Brian Barry.[8] In Barry's broadside against multiculturalism, he often lays down a universal principle that has the virtues of clarity and simplicity, e.g., that laws either ought to be enforced across the board or repealed across the board, with no regimes of "rule-plus-exemption" for cultural minorities particularly burdened by a law. But, in spite of himself, he constantly ends up discussing contextual details and acknowledging that local circumstance may make some multicultural

---

[3] Joseph H. Carens, *Culture, Citizenship, and Community: A Contextual Exploration of Justice as Evenhandedness* (Oxford: Oxford University Press, 2000); "A Contextual Approach to Political Theory," *Ethical Theory and Moral Practice*, 7, 2004, pp. 117–132.

[4] For example, Philippe Van Parijs, *Real Freedom for All* (Oxford: Oxford University Press, 1993); Brian Barry, *Justice as Impartiality* (Oxford: Oxford University Press, 1995); John Roemer, *Theories of Distributive Justice* (Cambridge, MA: Harvard University Press, 1996); T. M. Scanlon, *What We Owe to Each Other* (Cambridge, MA: Harvard University Press, 1999); G. A. Cohen, *If You're an Egalitarian How Come You're So Rich?* (Cambridge: Harvard University Press, 2001); Stuart White, *The Civic Minimum* (Oxford: Oxford University Press, 2003).

[5] Jeff Spinner-Halev, "The Universal Pretensions of Cultural Rights Arguments," *Critical Review of International Social and Political Philosophy*, 4 (2), 2001, pp. 1–25.

[6] Jeff Spinner-Halev, "Land, Culture, and Justice: A Framework for Group Rights and Recognition," *Journal of Political Philosophy*, 8 (3), 2000, pp. 319–342.

[7] Chandran Kukathas, "Contextualism Reconsidered: Some Skeptical Reflections," *Ethical Theory and Moral Practice*, 7, 2004, p. 215.

[8] Brian Barry, *Culture and Equality* (Cambridge, MA: Harvard University Press, 2001).

accommodations prudent, wise all-things-considered, or reasonable compromises given the intensity of minorities' (*ex hypothesi* illegitimate) attachment to a given policy.[9]

There is one obvious reason why there might be such an affinity, and it is probably no less true for being obvious. In liberal and democratic theory, abstraction has often been used (and often rightly been used) in the service of universalism. But the premise of most political theory work about multiculturalism is that formal legal uniformity and political quality are in some sense deficient or insufficient, that there is some morally weighty need to which they do not respond. (Even critiques of multiculturalism, if they are to be longer than a sentence or two, have to proceed on the thought that this at least *might* be true, or else there is no more of philosophical interest to say about cultural difference than there is to say about the difference between brown- and green-eyed people.) It is not especially surprising that complaints about what is omitted by abstraction and universalization generate detailed attention to some set or another of particulars. Whether there are, or might be, other reasons for contextualist approaches to be especially appropriate for considerations of multiculturalism will be considered below.

But it is not always clear what is meant by invocations of context. To take the simplest dichotomy: when a political theorist invokes a particular social and political context, is it for the purpose of *illustrating the application* of an already in-hand theory? Or is that context somehow relevant for *determining the content* of the theory? In this essay I attempt to disentangle some of the meanings and uses of context. I then dwell on a few of them at greater length, suggesting that they may represent especially promising directions for research.

Before proceeding I want to note that sensitivity to context is far from an unalloyed virtue. "Context" is the sort of thing that it is too easy to be "for," in some general way; it sounds nice. But abstraction has real intellectual uses, and it is easy for context to become a substitute for and then a rejection of principle. As Kukathas puts it,

> One important way of proceeding when matters are in dispute, and when the disputants come from different perspectives or have different interests, is to try to find some principles or perspectives that abstract from particular attachments and have more general, or possibly universal, applicability. When we disagree about concrete issues we seek a little critical distance ... We try to abstract from our own concerns and put forward arguments or theories, or simply accounts that we think might appeal to others more generally. In doing this we in effect

---

[9] See my review essay of *Culture and Equality*, "Liberal Jacobinism," *Ethics* 114 (2), 2004, pp. 318–336.

say to others: we need to take matters out of context, at least for a while, because what characterizes the context is disagreement.[10]

In other words, there are very good reasons for attempting to import the virtues of the rule of law and the blindfolded image of justice into political philosophy, and for thought experiments that abstract away from our particular prejudices and attachments and loyalties.[11] The balance of this chapter will largely be about the uses of context in multicultural political theory, but I do not mean for it to be a wholesale endorsement of contextualism or a rejection of abstraction.

Throughout I will assume the priority of justice, or at least treat it as a point of departure. That is, I assume that it makes sense to talk about normative political principles that are binding and generate valid claims of right and rights; and that such principles at least could be true and binding cross-culturally. I am considering the uses (and sometimes abuses) of context against the background of this sort of justice-theorizing. I suppose that in wholly utilitarian or consequentialist theories, or in theories based on agonistic political choice,[12] or perhaps in communicative democratic theories in which principles of justice are constituted by deliberate collective decision,[13] context would be more obviously relevant but also relevant in different ways. And in theories that rely on an Aristotelian conception of justice rather than the rules-and-rights conception we see in Grotius, Hume, and Kant as in Hayek, Nozick, and Rawls, it would be strange to even imagine an *absence* of context from justice-theorizing.[14] In casuistry as in common-law reasoning and its philosophical analogues, there is no *problem* of context to consider at all. But contextualism does appear anomalous, or at least novel and distinctively characteristic of work on multiculturalism, against the background of post-1971 Anglo-American political theory I am generally

---

[10] Kukathas, "Contextualism Reconsidered," p. 221

[11] While the state-of-nature theorizing of classical social contract theory and the veil of ignorance modeling in John Rawls's *Theory of Justice* are not simply exercises in this kind of abstraction, they are most centrally that.

[12] For agonistic democratic theory, see, for example, Bonnie Honig, *Political Theory and the Displacement of Politics* (Ithaca: Cornell University Press, 1993); William Connolly, *Identity/Difference* (Ithaca: Cornell University Press, 1991).

[13] For communicative democratic theory brought to bear on questions of nationalism and multiculturalism, see Jürgen Habermas, *The Inclusion of the Other*, trans. Ciaran Cronin and Pablo De Greiff (Cambridge, MA: MIT Press, 2000); Jürgen Habermas, *The Postnational Constellation*, trans. Max Pensky (Cambridge, MA: MIT Press, 2001); Seyla Benhabib, *The Claims of Culture: Equality and Diversity in the Global Era* (Princeton: Princeton University Press, 2002).

[14] For neo-Aristotelian theories, see John Finnis, *Natural Law and Natural Rights* (Oxford: Clarendon Press, 1980); Martha Nussbaum and Amartya Sen (eds.), *The Quality of Life* (Oxford: Oxford University Press, 1993).

concerned with. For the remainder of this chapter I concern myself primarily with contextualism in Rawlsian and post-Rawlsian liberal and justice-centered theory, though justice may be of the Rawlsian (social) or Humean (rules of conduct) sort.[15]

I.   Cases and illustration

The first use of context is simply to illustrate the application of an already-settled theory. I take it that this is familiar enough and easy enough to understand not to require much elaboration. At its most minimal it is a kind of stylistic choice made by moral or political philosophers: in order to show what a particular principle or theory means, one uses a real-world example rather than one involving baby spores being crushed by runaway trolleys or famous basketball players' brains being suspended in vats.

"Cases" in this context needn't mean *court* cases, though American political theory in particular often proceeds with reference to judicial opinions. While there are tight connections between jurisprudence and political theory, and in particular between common law and Anglo-American liberal theory, there is much to be said for *not* using court cases as our illustrative cases as often as we do. First of all, those of us primarily interested in illustrating some key normative principle at stake are very likely to simplify away much that is legally relevant. We endorse or reject a decision of the US Supreme Court the way the *New York Times* does, when its outcome comports or fails to comport with our normative preferences – regardless of, and often even failing to acknowledge, procedural issues, precedent, and constitutional or statutory text. This is likely to be misleading to some readers who *do* understand that court cases are more than just exercises in applied moral theory, and who therefore take us to be making claims about the law that we are not, in fact, making. *If* we think that real cases are valuable, it ought to be for their variety and complexity. If we are going to abstract from details and stylize facts so that one normative question is isolated and highlighted, we might be better served sticking with thought experiments. Otherwise we invite rejoinders from those pointing out that the actual case involved more than that one question.

Second, especially when we rely on the judicial summary of the facts of a case, we get stuck in a kind of intellectual inbreeding from too small

---

[15] But one possibility to bear in mind is that the introduction of contextualism at least suggests a turning away from this kind of justice-theorizing, away from the legacy of Hume, Kant, and Rawls and towards something more Aristotelian or Hegelian or Benthamite.

a gene-pool of empirical knowledge. When studying the possibility of exit from Amish society, it is better to get out and read a book or two about the Amish than to endlessly rehash the few facts about Amish communities and social mobility that happened to get mentioned in an opinion in *Wisconsin* v. *Yoder* thirty years ago.

Another danger in the illustrative use of cases (judicial or otherwise) in the elaboration of a theory derived without reference to the cases is that of overlooking the gap between outcomes that a theory permits and outcomes that it compels. It's all too easy to over-estimate the specificity of one's own arguments, to imagine that they dictate particular outcomes that happen to correspond to one's prereflective judgments on particular disputes. Perhaps one can notice an actual *contradiction*, a theory that requires that one *reject* such an initial judgment. But it is hard to notice the difference between a moral argument that is *compatible with* a particular conclusion and one that *compels* that conclusion. And I suspect that the danger on this count is greatest where the case is the most familiar. The illustrative use[16] of cases can thus sometimes mislead readers as well as authors into thinking that a given theory has greater determinacy than it actually does. It can disguise the possibility of disagreeing with the author's judgment of a case while still endorsing the theory.

On the other hand, familiar cases – judicial or otherwise – can serve a useful signposting function, and this is why they continue to be used. After reading an abstract philosophical statement about the rights of women in minority cultures, it can help to know whether the author thinks the rule at stake in *Santa Clara Pueblo* v. *Martinez* was morally acceptable or not.[17] It's a bad habit to jump from "morally unacceptable" to "the case was decided wrongly," without presenting a theory of decision-making authority and accountability, delineating the boundaries of both tribal authority and judicial power, and recognizing

---

[16] *Wisconsin* v. *Yoder*, 406 US 205 (1972), a US Supreme Court case that ruled that members of the Old Order Amish had a constitutional right, under the Free Exercise Clause of the First Amendment, to a partial exemption from Wisconsin's compulsory schooling law, such that their children could leave school at age 14 rather than age 16.

[17] *Santa Clara Pueblo* v. *Martinez*, 436 US 49 (1978), a US Supreme Court case adjudicating a Santa Clara Pueblo tribal rule that denied membership in the tribe to children of a tribal mother and a non-tribal father, though not the reverse. This is often treated as a synecdoche for the right of gender equality in minority cultures, or as a case about the directly constitutional rights of members of Indian tribes, but the case actually turned on jurisdictional questions – the interaction of tribal sovereign immunity with the interpretation of a Congressional statute, the Indian Civil Rights Act, that constitutionally could have but did not authorize an individual cause of action against tribes. So a view about whether the rule is morally acceptable does not amount to a view about whether the case was rightly decided as a matter of law.

that the case involved a choice between decision-makers (any one of which would sometimes make wrong decisions), not a choice between different systems of moral principle. But, if one exercises suitable restraint in their use, well-known cases can help a theorist mark out his or her sense of the meaning and application of his or her theory.

The illustrative use of cases is indeed so common that I doubt it marks out any particularly distinctive subset of moral or political theory at all, even though some literatures during some periods have preferred thought experiments. If "contextualism" is to identify something unusual, it must mean more than just this.

II.   Test cases

A second use of context and cases – slightly more controversial as well as according the context and cases slightly more weight in formulating a theory – is the checking and testing of a theory against hard cases. This does not have the same meaning as the testing of an *explanatory* theory against hard cases and uncomfortable facts. An empirical claim can (at least sometimes) be straightforwardly falsified by a fact in the world that contradicts it. A normative claim, in this approach, is tested against a moral intuition or a pre-reflective judgment or a conclusion drawn from other normative arguments. But every normative argument should, at least sometimes, push those persuaded by it away from their preconceptions and intuitions; the latter cannot simply falsify the former. On the other hand, often we are more confident in our intuition about at least some, important, cases than we are about the soundness of our moral arguments. We know that a moral argument that dictates the conclusion that chattel slavery or genocide is morally acceptable is deficient as a moral theory.

As I said, this is controversial. Some would insist that the only thing that can show the invalidity of an argument is actually to show its invalidity, not to point to some conclusion we don't like. If that's so, then this use of context collapses into the one discussed above. Hard cases are just signposts, too; they show what bullets need to be bitten. Others, prominently including Rawls, maintain that we must sometimes revise our theoretical formulations in light of our fixed moral judgments. Once the move has been made from Benthamite or Kantian purism to reflective equilibrium, then I doubt much can be said a priori about how to proceed or where to stop. How confident must we be in a judgment – how fixed does it have to be – to justify revising a theory that conflicts with it rather than conflicting with the judgment? How *many* fixed moral intuitions should we bring to the process of theory-testing and revising? Should we look for unfamiliar cases about which to have intuitive responses, and test the theory against those responses? Should we be more sure of a moral intuition if it corresponds with very longstanding social norms – or should that make us suspect the autonomy of our moral judgment? These questions hardly seem even sensible to ask in any general way, and I certainly do not mean to answer them here. I only mean to note that cases are sometimes introduced in a way that pushes against the general direction of a theory, and that they are sometimes allowed to push hard enough to suggest faults in the theory itself.

III.   Conditions and circumstances

Another kind of use of context is to identify circumstances, conditions, and situations in which an already-developed theory's application takes on importantly new, unusual, or surprising turns. Here the theory precedes the context; but, unlike when cases are merely illustrative, it does not emerge unchanged from its encounter with the context. This is the approach taken by the most influential work on liberal multicultural theory, Will Kymlicka's *Liberalism, Community and Culture*. Kymlicka endorses the liberal theory, including the methodology, of Dworkin and (early) Rawls. Reasoning behind a veil of ignorance about what primary goods all persons need and want regardless of their particular conceptions of the good, and opting for a principle of justice that demands maximin distribution of those primary goods; or a hypothetical insurance market in which persons with an equal initial distribution of resources differentially insure themselves against a variety of unchosen risks and disadvantages – Kymlicka has no dispute with these approaches to formulating principles of justice in distribution. He proceeds, however, to argue that the existence of a stable and secure cultural framework, and the context of choice that it creates, meets the characteristics of a Rawlsian primary good, that the loss of such a framework is a disadvantage against which Dworkinian persons would insure themselves. One couldn't realize this without appreciating some facts and social circumstances. Fish don't notice that they need water, and Anglophone Americans don't notice that they need – and that one might not have – a secure cultural-linguistic framework in which to make choices. But, Kymlicka suggests, attention to the kinds of disadvantages faced by, e.g., Canadian First Nations, demonstrates the possibility of losing that framework, and thereby throws the framework's existence and necessity into relief.

Once that existence and necessity have been noticed, Rawls's and Dworkin's theories must be adjusted accordingly, on their own terms. Those theorists happen not to have noticed this set of circumstances to which their theories applied; and that application has some non-trivial consequences. (The distribution of a secure and stable context of choice seems to require quite different policies and institutions from the distribution of income or of voting rights; it may be a good that is similar in moral kind to those on Rawls's list of primary goods, but it is different in practical kind – as, indeed, many of the goods on the original list differ from one another.) But *Liberalism, Community and Culture (LCC)* embraces rather than challenges the justificatory approach of, e.g., *Theory of Justice*.

One can easily think of or imagine other examples of this sort. A fully developed theory of justice in property holdings in land, a theory with principles of restitution and rectification for past wrongful dispossessions, will be incomplete if the theorist thinks only of individual landowners and of dispossessions that occurred under a legal system and titling regime with which the present system and regime are continuous. An examination of the dispossession of indigenous peoples need not disrupt the core principles of the theory of just property. But it is likely to demonstrate the need for those principles to be significantly adapted to the distinctive circumstances of restitution to collective landowners whose property rights were never founded on, and may never have been recognized by, the current system of positive law or its continuous forebears. (Robert Nozick famously worried that, in this case, the adaptation would be so extensive as to swallow the original theory.) Here again, the *application* of a theory to novel or previously unconsidered circumstances requires developing new principles and altering our sense of the theory's implications. The foundation of the underlying theory is not challenged or changed by the examination of context; but our sense of its meaning in practice is modified, sometimes dramatically. One wouldn't know to *have* principles of justice in rectification of long-since dispossessed tribal land if one didn't know there *were* such cases. The knowledge shows that the theory as originally stated was incomplete, and that completing it requires revising it.

Thus, the use of context here differs markedly from the use of cases discussed above, where they are examples used to illustrate and signpost the boundaries of a particular theory, not occasions for revising it. On the other hand, here as above, *the normative theory comes first, and does not depend on context or circumstances for its content*. The range of cases in the real social world has *epistemic value for showing the range of questions a theory of justice must answer*. But those cases do not themselves shape the answers. At most, the context provides a kind of scaffolding. We need to look at the circumstances of indigenous peoples to understand the primary good of a secure context of cultural choice, or the need for a particular kind of theory of restitution. But once we have such understanding, the cases could be removed, leaving the theory standing. And what is left is a theory *of justice*. That is, the stage at which the context is relevant is that of generating binding principles of right. Members of minority cultures have a right to public action to shore up their endangered cultural frameworks, just as those who are poor through no deserved fault of their own have a right to the public provision of material primary goods. Indigenous peoples whose tribes were rightful owners and then wrongfully dispossessed have a right to restitution or compensation, like the fair buyer of a justly owned piece of property has a right to it.

It is noteworthy that this approach goes beyond the use of *cases*, and moves towards the consideration of whole *sets of circumstances*. Both the illustrative and the testing use of cases rely on the comprehensibility, and usually the familiarity, of some easily isolable choice. Should the Yoder parents be compelled to send their children to school, or not? The idea of a cultural or linguistic context of choice as a primary good is not like that; it is an unfamiliar idea that can't be particularly well illustrated by discussing one person or one policy decision, though there are particular persons and policies at stake. It can only be well understood by considering a general set of social, political, and economic circumstances – here, the circumstances faced by a minority that must bid out of its own resources for the perpetuation of a context of choice which members of the majority are provided automatically, for free.

It seems to me that this is a particularly important kind of use of context in political theory, and often one with very high intellectual returns for the first theorists to engage in it with respect to a particular topic. But it also seems not to be, in any particularly strong sense, contextual theory. Again, this is only a matter of semantics and definition. So long as we understand how context is used in *LCC* nothing serious rides on simply classifying it as contextual or non-contextual. But I do think it is worth noting that, once the particular case of, e.g., Canadian Inuits has done its epistemic work of illustrating a kind of theoretical dilemma, the case is free to fall away from the theory. The relationship of the circumstances of an imperiled cultural context of choice to Kymlicka's eventual theory is not different in kind from the circumstances of the Reformation and the Wars of Religion to Rawls's eventual political liberalism. Without the history of the sixteenth and seventeenth centuries the problem to which liberal toleration was the solution might not have been confronted by Western philosophy. But, that solution having been developed, it no longer depends for its explication on any discussion of Luther, Calvin, the Apostolic Succession, or the Treaty of Westphalia.

Carens has repeatedly identified Kymlicka and Michael Walzer as the leading examples of contextualist political theory. Walzer's *Spheres of Justice*[18] certainly stands out as the best-known and most important work of political theory in the past three decades to argue for the central importance of context. When it was first published, when the established level of abstraction for political philosophy had been set by Rawls, Nozick, and Sandel, it marked an extraordinary break and shift in direction – a change from veils of ignorance and experience machines to discussions of the union of political and commercial power in Pullman, Illinois; distributive justice in medieval Jewish communities; the draft and buyouts from it during the American Civil War; the White Australia policy; and Israeli *kibbutzim*. But I doubt that it is helpful to think about Walzer and Kymlicka in quite the same light here. Walzer's understanding of distributive justice is contextual all the way down; the proper nouns never fall away. Justice just is a matter of respecting the shared communal understandings of this or that society. To push the architectural metaphor another step (probably one step too far), if context is scaffolding for *LCC*, it makes up all the load-bearing walls of a Walzerian theory of complex equality.

Given the centrality of Kymlicka's work to the entire field of study under consideration in this chapter, I think it appropriate to devote some particular attention to that work's trajectory. One striking fact is that his work has become, in some sense, more concerned with context over time, and the pre-context philosophy has thinned out. *Multicultural Citizenship (MC)* concerns itself with a broader range of cases than *Liberalism, Community and Culture*, and a major argumentative pillar of *MC* is that, *in fact*, immigrant "ethnic groups" make claims for multicultural accommodation that are different in kind from those made by indigenous and (other) "national" minorities. Philosophical foundations are almost nowhere to be seen, and it is very unclear whether Kymlicka can successfully ground a *normative* distinction between the rights that ethnic and national minorities *ought to be able* to claim, a problem that has been the focus of much criticism. But that apparent failing hasn't diminished the book's agenda-setting power; and its greater attention to a greater range of cases has made it more widely read

---

[18] Michael Walzer, *Spheres of Justice* (New York: Basic Books, 1983).

among policy-makers and people interested in actual ethnic politics than the more-philosophical *LCC*.

But more contextual still has been Kymlicka's series of essays on minority rights in Eastern and Central Europe,[19] in which he has seriously questioned the applicability of his own theories to that region, and has suggested that the analyses of *LCC* and *MC* are themselves more context-dependent than he had previously realized. National minorities, he now thinks, are relevantly differently situated in North America and Western Europe than they are in Central Europe and the Soviet Union's successor states, where they are often local remnants of former imperial majorities and share national identities with neighboring states. This seems much less like scaffolding than did the analysis of indigenous peoples in *LCC*; we seem to now have different normative theories for different regions of the world, different security contexts, and so on. But in principle this, too, could fall away, leaving behind a theory that now incorporates the categories of revanchism, imperial-national minorities, and so on. The range of relevant circumstances Kymlicka considers continues to expand; his work seems to become more sensitive to the complexities of the world and the particularity of any particular set of socio-political circumstances of pluralism. But I think that most of his use of circumstances continues to be epistemic. His work continues to have the *telos* of a general theory of liberal justice and minority rights from which the proper nouns have been or could be removed.

Spinner-Halev has suggested that Kymlicka, as well as David Miller, Charles Taylor, and Yael Tamir, illegitimately generalizes from particular cases. "When theorists write about cultural rights, they typically write with a few cases in mind. This makes sense; it is hard to imagine how to argue about cultural rights without referring to any cultures. Still, problems arise when theorists use cases. Since these theorists want to claim that their arguments are universal, they do not note how cases limit the applicability of their arguments."[20] But the arc of Kymlicka's work seems to have been to note this more and more. The critique is accurate as against *LCC*, but it has become progressively less so.

---

[19] Will Kymlicka, "Multiculturalism and Minority Rights: West and East," *Journal of Ethnopolitics and Minority Issues in Europe*, 4, 2002, pp. 1–25; "Western Political Theory and Ethnic Relations in Eastern Europe," in *Can Liberal Pluralism be Exported? Western Political Theory and Ethnic Relations in Eastern Europe*, ed. Will Kymlicka and Magda Opalski (Oxford: Oxford University Press, 2002); "Justice and Security in the Accommodation of Minority Nationalism," in *The Politics of Belonging: Nationalism, Liberalism and Pluralism*, ed. Alain Dieckhoff (New York: Lexington, 2004), pp. 127–154.

[20] Spinner-Halev, "The Universal Pretensions of Cultural Rights Arguments," pp. 12–13.

IV.   Stability

A quite different configuration of justice and context is suggested by the work of John Rawls. On the face of things, of course, Rawls was a strikingly uncontextual theorist; indeed, for Carens, Rawls is the archetypal non-contextualist. There are few real-world cases discussed in his work, and these discussions are far from the most interesting or edifying parts of his writings. The original position and veil of ignorance are paradigmatic cases of a-contextual intellectual devices, indeed devices the *purpose* of which is to abstract from context. It has been usual to think that contextual considerations enter the Rawlsian structure only at the level of application to, and undesirable compromise with, the messy social world – in Rawlsian terms, at the level of non-ideal theory.

And yet Rawls's theory – as it stands, at the level of ideal theory – demands a kind of attention to context. Consider the Rawlsian concept of the "well-ordered society" and the concern with social stability that was evident in *Theory of Justice* but became a major theme in *Political Liberalism*, along with such related concepts as the "overlapping consensus."[21] Rawls of course insists that these are not to be understood in any empirical way. In *developing* the idea and the content of an over-lapping consensus among reasonable comprehensive doctrines, "[w]e leave aside comprehensive doctrines that now exist, or that have existed, or that might exist" (*Political Liberalism*, p. 40). But this leaves a lingering place for context: the inquiry into whether there are any well-ordered societies, whether there are any reasonable comprehensive doctrines, and whether there really is or can be adequate overlap among these to provide stability to a social concept of justice. Rawls himself engages in some relatively perfunctory examinations along these lines. But more robustly contextual work, trying to put empirical flesh onto the bones of political liberalism in a multicultural society, is done by Stephen Macedo.[22] And George Klosko[23] has offered a sustained critique of the political liberal understanding of stability and overlapping consensus, arguing for the priority of democratic procedures and norms of reciprocity and fair play over substantive liberal rights, drawing on (and arguing for the relevance of) attitudinal and survey research. At a minimum, Klosko has given us some reason to doubt the empirical

---

[21] John Rawls, *A Theory of Justice* (Cambridge, MA: Harvard University Press, 1971); John Rawls, *Political Liberalism* (New York: Columbia University Press, 1993).

[22] Stephen Macedo, *Diversity and Distrust: Civic Education in a Multicultural Democracy* (Cambridge, MA: Harvard University Press, 2000).

[23] George Klosko, *Democratic Procedures and Liberal Consensus* (Oxford: Oxford University Press, 2000); George Klosko, *Political Obligation* (Oxford: Oxford University Press, 2005).

plausibility of the well-ordered society under a Rawlsian overlapping consensus, and has illustrated that the Rawlsian categories that refer to the substance of citizens' beliefs cannot forever remain innocent of inquiry into what those beliefs actually are.

I do not mean to discuss this kind of use of context at length. For one thing, there has not been much written along these lines. For another, I am unsympathetic to the distinction between ideal and non-ideal theory that it presupposes, as well as to the idea that justice operates primarily at the level of a unified basic structure of a unified, but isolated from the rest of the world, closed and well-ordered society. Moreover, I doubt that I can add much to most readers' understanding of Rawls or Rawlsian theory. But the need for contextual analysis of Rawlsian stability theory points in the direction of what I take to be particularly interesting uses of context in multicultural theory: the analysis of the stability of (at least moderately) just arrangements, theoretical inquiries into how institutions should be designed so as to generate (at least moderately) just outcomes, and just terms of coexistence among a plurality of cultural and religious groups.

We thus turn to some alternatives to ideal-theory stability analysis, and to what I take to be less familiar uses of cases and context, further afield from Rawls's or Kymlicka's methods. In the approaches considered up until now, cases or context illustrate what a theory of right political action means in practice; or they provide the mechanism for introducing countervailing moral intuitions and so demanding that the theory be made more limited or nuanced; or they bring to light new sets of circumstances in which we need to know what is the right thing to do. None of these approaches need to answer the very question "what is the right thing to do?" with "it depends on the context." In the remainder of the chapter I consider approaches in which context is admitted into a theory itself, ways in which one might think that the right thing to do *does* depend on the context.

V.   The limits of justice

Most theories of justice, of course, acknowledge that a theory of justice is not the whole of a theory about what ought to be done in politics and law. Justice is the language of that which is morally prohibited and that which is morally mandatory, not that which is morally more-or-less, preferable or dispreferable, or of that which requires balancing considerations. On any but the most extraordinarily demanding theory of justice, there remain innumerable political and legal decisions that are neither demanded nor prohibited as a matter of right.

Before the first wave of multicultural theorizing, the tacit assumption or explicit conclusion of most liberal theory was that *any differentiations of legal rights or privileges based on ethnic or other ascriptive group identities are prohibited as a matter of right*.[24] This is the position that Barry has tried to revitalize; policies of multicultural accommodation are ruled out as a matter of first principle. The response of the first wave was to argue that *the protection of minority cultures, or of societal or encompassing cultures more generally, is* demanded *as a matter of right*. Both approaches aspire to bring multiculturalism within the rubric of justice claims, and thereby to settle them once and for all.

I think that a general characteristic of the second wave has been to suspect that many possible policies of multicultural accommodation lie in the realm of legitimate choice, that they are neither universally prohibited nor universally required as a matter of justice. This is of course itself a particular claim about justice; it is not somehow agnostic about the demands of justice, though it may often appear that way because a theory about how to make choices in the range between the prohibited and the mandatory does not spend much time discussing the prohibited or the mandatory.[25] On the other hand, it is not necessary to specify the *whole* of a theory of justice in order to argue that a particular policy domain lies within the space of the permissible-but-not-required. Consider state symbolism – the policy domain of designing flags, naming streets and cities and provinces, commissioning statues and memorials on public property, designating public holidays and national anthems. Decisions about state symbolism do not affect the legal rights or resource holdings of any person. This leaves them outside the boundaries of (at least) most Anglo-American liberal theories of justice. If I say that the adoption or removal of the Confederate battle flag from US state flags is neither prohibited nor mandated by justice, but must be decided with respect to other moral and normative categories, that is a particular claim about the boundaries of justice. But it is not a claim that depends on a highly specified theory of justice; it does not require choosing between Rawls and Nozick, much less choosing between

---

[24] Here I elide the 1970s debates about affirmative action or preferential hiring and admissions policies. See Kymlicka's commentary on these debates in *Liberalism, Community and Culture* (Oxford: Oxford University Press, 1989).

[25] A theory that denied that *any* part of law or politics is properly governed by a deontological concept such as justice, or by its rule-consequentialist cognates, would maintain that *all* of law and politics lies in this range of neither-prohibited-nor-mandatory, this range of it-depends. That, of course, is itself a particular, non-agnostic claim about justice.

Jacob T. Levy

early and late Rawls or between rival conceptions of the Difference Principle.[26]

Across a significant range of options, the same is true for questions of the institutional design of governing institutions: first-past-the-post voting systems versus proportional representation party lists, alternate voting, cumulative voting, or instant runoff voting; presidentialism versus parliamentarism; bicameralism versus unicameralism, and the principle of representation or selection in the second chamber. Some theories of justice probably make claims that some of these options are mandatory or prohibited. But, for the most part, one can discuss the reasons for preferring one or another institutional choice of this kind without specifying a theory of justice, because for the most part theories of justice are agnostic about this sort of thing. Different institutional choices may affect the probability of rights being respected and just policies being adopted, a point to which I return below. But that is rather different from claiming that justice mandates a particular institutional design, that persons have a right to bicameralism in the way that they have a right to freedom of religion or to due process of criminal law.

In both symbolic politics and the design of governing institutions, then, one should expect to see normative analysis proceed with reference to consequences, balancing, and better-or-worse considerations. These are, in general, the sort of considerations that require sustained attention to context. Consequences vary according to a wide range of circumstances. Balancing proceeds differently when different sets of claims are in play.

Moreover, both symbolic politics and the design of governing institutions are major topics in the politics of ethnocultural pluralism. Disputes about symbols are very often, even usually, instances of identity politics of one sort or another. In many countries federalism and/or guaranteed representation in governing bodies are central demands of ethnic minorities. And so, for instance, Margaret Moore,[27] in a work that casts doubt on many of the standard attempts at abstract justice-based arguments for national self-determination or minority-national self-government, offers careful normative evaluation of rules of elections and representation that are neither required nor prohibited by justice, and identifies some of the local facts that are relevant for such

---

[26] It does, however, require rejecting a Rawlsian theory that has such a robust account of the right to the social bases of self-respect that African-Americans could claim that the Confederate flag's presence violated that right. Some theories of justice, and some conceptions of some theories of justice, take up more of the space of politics than others.

[27] Margaret Moore, *The Ethics of Nationalism* (Oxford: Oxford University Press, 2002).

evaluations. Similarly, Wayne Norman[28] offers wide-ranging normative analyses and considerations of federalism, noting many of the social and political facts that affect the fairness and suitability of various federalist institutions in multiethnic and multinational societies. And Daniel Weinstock[29] has argued that, in the case of both language rights and civic education for nation-building, the constraints placed by justice on policy choices are real but not very narrow, and that more competing and fact-sensitive normative considerations must be used for the evaluation of the policies within these constraints. Examples can, I think, be multiplied. The subject matter of multiculturalism often does not allow for a single outcome uniquely determined by logic and justice. It calls for the analysis of better and worse, not just and unjust.

It is important not to slip from this insight into an abandonment of the enterprise of normative evaluation. David Laitin and Rob Reich[30] note, "the fundamental indeterminacy of liberal principles of justice in coming to grips with competing language claims." But they seem to suggest that what follows from this is normative agnosticism, with theorists saying nothing more about "competing language claims" than "let the democratic process sort it out." This is a non-sequitur, albeit one that is partly explicable in terms of the tendency to run together normative and judicial arguments. It is simply not the case that a normative argument about which language rights regimes are morally better than which others is the same as a call for judicial intervention to override democratic decision-making on the question. But, by the same token, identifying democratic procedures as the proper ones for resolving a question *in practice* does not impugn normative evaluation and criticism of the procedures' outcomes.

I have not said anything in this section about what normative considerations *are* relevant to these policy domains that lie mostly in the range of legitimate choice and disagreement. I will give some examples below. Here I mean only to suggest that this is where much of the political theory work on multiculturalism is being done in the second wave: at the level of normative principles that fall short of bindingness, with a sense that policies of multicultural accommodation are neither prohibited nor (at least in their particular details) required. Kymlicka himself may, as suggested above, be an exception. He still seems to aim

---

[28] Wayne Norman, *Negotiating Nationalism: Nation-Building, Federalism, and Secession in the Multinational State* (Oxford and New York: Oxford University Press, 2006).

[29] Daniel Weinstock, "The Antinomies of Language Policy," in *Language Rights and Political Theory*, ed. Will Kymlicka and Alan Patten (Oxford: Oxford University Press, 2003); Daniel Weinstock, "The Problem of Civic Education in Multicultural Societies," in *The Politics of Belonging*, ed. Dieckhoff.

[30] David D. Laitin and Rob Reich, "A Liberal Democratic Approach to Language Justice," in *Language Rights and Political Theory*, ed. Kymlicka and Patten, p. 81.

at binding principles of right with respect to multiculturalism, albeit binding principles that are increasingly aware of the complexity of the circumstances to which they must apply. But even he has sometimes turned to work at this level – for example, in his discussions of guaranteed representation and of social unity in *MC*.

VI.   Constitutionalism and *modus vivendi* approaches

Constitutionalism is a sub-set of the category discussed in the previous section. It begins with the introduction of context at the stage of institutional design, attempting to generate procedures, mechanisms, and constellations of interests that will generally tend to produce just outcomes – where the meaning of "just" is not itself given by context or the outcomes of particular procedures. Constitutionalist thought of this sort relies on a prior theory of justice. But it need not rely on a particularly fine-grained account of such a theory; the tools of institutional design are typically blunter than those of moral philosophical analysis. It operates in the morally discretionary range of institutional design; and constitutionalist theories typically assume that this range is considerable. This sets it at odds with at least some variants of democratic theory, in which it is morally required to opt for, for example, systems of representation that weight each enfranchised voter's votes as equally as possible – and it is therefore morally prohibited to permit any institutions such as the United States Senate, in which states of wildly different populations are represented with two votes apiece. Constitutionalism approaches questions of institutional design in consequentialist fashion, but the consequences to be measured are typically more overtly moralized than "utility," and may be given by the prior theory of justice.

In the circumstances of multiculturalism in modern, democratic, mass-literate states, I have argued[31] that the primary concern of constitutionalism should be to build in institutional counterbalances to the tendency of such states to centralize and to engage in projects of unjust and coercive assimilation. Such counterbalances are likely to involve an element of over-correction, vesting greater-than-equal governing authority, representation, or legal autonomy in cultural minorities, especially indigenous peoples, territorially concentrated national minorities, and linguistic minorities. My arguments have centered on ethnic

---

[31] Jacob T. Levy, "Indigenous Self-government," in *NOMOS XLV: Secession and Self-Determination*, ed. Stephen Macedo and Allen Buchanan (New York: New York University Press, 2003); "Literacy, Language Rights, and the Modern State," in *Language Rights and Political Theory*, ed. Kymlicka and Patten; "National Minorities Without Nationalism," in *The Politics of Belonging*, ed. Deickhoff.

federalism and on the incorporation of indigenous and religious minorities' legal codes,[32] which counterbalance against the *combination* of
majority-cultural dominance and state centralization characteristic of
modern states. But others, emphasizing different risks, might emphasize
guarantees of group representation in the institutions of the central
government.

This kind of constitutionalist reasoning is quite overtly of the second-
best variety. If state officials both reliably intended to promote justice and
reliably knew what justice demanded, there would be no point in
designing institutions to over-correct for their predictable errors. ("If
angels were to govern men," of course, "no internal or external controls
on government would be necessary.") There is no reason for *anyone* to
view a constitutionalist settlement as a first-best institutional arrangement, either as a freestanding matter or from within their particular
worldviews. This, I take it, makes it ineligible for inclusion in a Rawlsian
overlapping consensus.[33] Rawls famously insisted that the overlapping
consensus is not a "mere *modus vivendi*," which would fail to offer
"stability for the right reasons." At the stage of ideal theory and of
understanding the concept of a well-ordered society, the overlapping
consensus must be (1) a consensus of *reasonable* comprehensive views,
which may or may not correspond with the comprehensive views that
large numbers of a society's citizens happen to hold; (2) a consensus
around an account of justice that persons are committed to *both* as a
freestanding political theory and from within their own comprehensive
doctrines; and therefore (3) a consensus around an account of justice that
persons would continue to be committed to even if the balance of power
in a society changed, e.g., even if the adherents of one's own comprehensive doctrine were to become an overwhelming electoral majority.

This distinction, or at least the distinction drawn this sharply, has
been the object of sustained criticism. Hershovitz[34] is representative in
claiming that "Rawls grossly underestimates the power of a *modus
vivendi*."[35] And, unsurprisingly, much of this criticism has emphasized

---

[32] See also, Jacob T. Levy, *The Multiculturalism of Fear* (Oxford: Oxford University Press, 2000).
[33] Perhaps Rawls would say that the *details* of political institutions, unlike the basic principle of democratic government, aren't properly part of the basic structure, and so aren't part of the subject matter that must come under the overlapping consensus in a well-ordered society.
[34] Scott Hershovitz, "A Mere Modus Vivendi?," in *The Idea of a Political Liberalism*, ed. Victoria Davion and Clark Wolf (New York: Rowman and Littlefield, 2000), p. 221.
[35] Claudia Mills, " 'Not a Mere Modus Vivendi': The Bases for Allegiance to the Just State," in *The Idea of a Political Liberalism*, ed. Davion and Wolf, pp. 190–203; Robert B. Talisse, "Rawls on Pluralism and Stability," *Critical Review*, 15 (2), 2003,

the management of ethnic, cultural, and religious pluralism. That is, those who advocate the relevance and usefulness of *modus vivendi* theorizing are typically *not* talking about a *modus vivendi* between utilitarians and Kantians but rather between members of different religious or ethnic groups. Rawls, however, typically assimilates the case of religious pluralism to the case of the utilitarian–Kantian divide. A *modus vivendi* approach seems potentially useful and fruitful in the former kind of case.

A *modus vivendi* settlement need not be derivable from within each of the reasonable comprehensive doctrines; and it need not be willed as a first-best arrangement that makes sense independent of the pluralism and divisions within a society. Indeed it would be very odd if policies of multicultural accommodation *were* willed as a first-best solution, or advocated regardless of the actual degree of pluralism in society. Multicultural *modus vivendi* solutions are institutions and policies that would not be advocated if a particular kind of pluralism or a particular cleavage were not present in society. In a linguistically homogeneous society (as Rawls stipulates at the level of ideal theory; religious pluralism is admitted as a permanent social fact, but ethnic, cultural, and linguistic pluralism are not), an elaborate regime of official multilingualism would be pointlessly complex and expensive. A system of language rights is a "mere *modus vivendi*," which no one would advocate if society were genuinely linguistically homogeneous. That is *not* to say, as Rawls supposes the concept of *modus vivendi* to entail, that the parties in a really existing pluralistic society governed by such a system constantly hope for the chance to overturn the settlement. It can be genuinely supported as a freestanding matter, *given* the fact that society is pluralistic.

Indeed I would suggest that the same is true of Rawls's central case of religious liberty. One need not believe in the absolute moral worth of freedom of conscience to believe, really believe, in religious freedom as a constitutional fundamental for a religiously divided society. One could sincerely wish for religious homogeneity, and think that a homogeneous society would have no need for such freedom, and still think that one's really existing heterogeneous society demanded religious freedom even when one's co-believers were in the majority. A *modus vivendi* can give rise to principles that garner support that is more than merely tactical or temporary, *even though* those principles would not be willed as first-best ones for a more homogeneous society, or be generated from within even reasonable comprehensive doctrines.

pp. 219–246; Bernard P. Dauenhauer, "A Good Word for a Modus Vivendi," in *The Idea of a Political Liberalism*, ed. Davion and Wolf, pp. 204–220.

Modus vivendi theorizing has, in an odd and roundabout way, come to seem more credible in the light of G. A. Cohen's criticisms of Rawls in *If You're An Egalitarian, How Come You're So Rich?* Cohen draws attention to the motivational asymmetry at work in Rawls's vision. It is important that persons sincerely will the basic principles of justice, and not merely accept it as an institutional second-best that they would change if only they had enough power. But persons' sincere willing of, e.g., the Difference Principle as a principle of justice is apparently compatible with their not acting *as persons* to maximize the positions of the worst off, and indeed compatible with the (according to Cohen, exploitative) threat on the part of the talented to withhold labor that would benefit the worst off unless they (the talented) receive disproportionate rewards. An instability appears to result. Rawls insists that a well-ordered society is made up of persons with a certain motivational structure and acceptance of the principles of justice as one's own, while at the same time he maintains that it is unacceptably demanding to internalize the principles of justice as reasons for action. Cohen resolves this instability in the direction of an egalitarian ethos all the way down. But Cohen's critique also opens some intellectual space for, and may stimulate, theorizing that resolves the instability in the other direction: rejecting the personal obligation to will the principles of justice, and accepting a *modus vivendi*-level acceptance of liberal democratic institutions.

VII.   Relativism

Finally, we have theories that are contextual all the way down. Theorizing circumstances helps us to understand what justice demands; middle-range theorizing analyzes policies and institutions within the permissive range set by constraints of a more-or-less given theory of justice; constitutionalism attempts to maximize the generation of just policies, where justice is defined more-or-less non-contextually; and a *modus vivendi* scales back the claims of justice. But in a theory like Michael Walzer's,[36] justice is in part or wholly *constituted* by context. In Walzer's case, this means that justice is a matter of respecting a certain understanding of a society's shared social understandings about the meaning and distribution of goods.

Justice itself can be partly or substantially contextual without a theory traveling quite as far as Walzer does into cultural relativism (and, in his more recent work, Walzer himself has moderated the deep contextualism of *Spheres of Justice*). Say that persons have a right, a claim in

---

[36] Walzer, *Spheres of Justice*.

justice, to due process of law, to the rule of law defined in a fairly robust way to include requirements that rules be promulgated, comprehensible, compossible, non-retroactive, and so on.[37] What will count as promulgation or comprehensibility will vary so widely depending on context that almost-identical cases could generate opposite outcomes in justice in two different settings. If a law creates a new legal right vested in A, that law is published, and B violates the law and A's right, should B be punished? At first blush we would say: justice demands that he should; we are out of the moral middle range, and back into the domain of the right. But if the society in question is a largely non-literate one and the local meaning of "promulgation" requires a lengthy period of oral communication, then B *must not* be punished. B has not pushed the question out of the domain of justice and invoked consequentialist or perfectionist considerations; he has a claim of right, a claim in justice, to set against A's claim of right.

Something similar happens whenever a theory of justice makes reference to categories such as intent, settled expectations, custom, reasonableness, or even shared understandings, all of which become meaningful only in particular cultural frameworks. In a negligence case, governed by the standard of customary prudence, either one party or the other has a right to a judgment in his or her favor; but who has the right will depend on whether the precautions taken do or do not meet the locally relevant standard of customary prudence. If they do not, the plaintiff's rights are violated by a judgment for the defendant. If they do not, the defendant's rights are violated by a judgment for the plaintiff. Different cultural contexts flip the correct answer to the question "who has a right?," but in neither case is the correct answer "this isn't a matter of right and justice but of better or worse." Moreover, this kind of contextual meaning of justice isn't relativist in the strong sense. The rule "there is a duty to enforce as law those rules, and only those rules, that are duly enacted and promulgated," or the rule "failure to exercise customary and reasonable prudence to prevent an accident generates liability for that accident, while exercising such prudence immunizes against such liability," is operating cross-culturally, even though the content of those formal rules is varying.

---

[37] Lon Fuller, *The Morality of Law* (New Haven: Yale University Press, 1969); Michael Oakeshott, "On the Rule of Law," in *On History and Other Essays* (Indianapolis: Liberty Fund, 2000); Joseph Raz, "The Rule of Law and Its Virtue," in *The Authority of Law* (Oxford: Oxford University Press, 1979); Judith Shklar, "Political Theory and the Rule of Law," in *Political Thought and Political Thinkers*, ed. Stanley Hoffmann (Chicago: University of Chicago Press, 1998).

Invocations of full-blown cultural relativism are actually fairly rare in the political philosophical debates about multiculturalism – both because of relativism's well-known weaknesses as an intellectual position, and because multiculturalism is so often about how (members of) one culture will treat (members of) another, about how to find terms of coexistence. When Hindu nationalists claim that all Indians are part of a Hindu-derived cultural civilization and Indian Muslims reply that they have a distinct cultural tradition and the right to practice it, it simply won't do to say "the Hindu nationalists are right on their terms and the Muslims are right on their terms." It can't be that Indian Muslims both do and do not have the right to perpetuate their cultural separateness from the Hindu majority. Full-blown cultural relativism is of no use in demarcating or navigating the boundaries between cultural groups; it depends on the groups being easily identifiable and separate to begin with. More moderate versions of relativism suffer these problems to a more moderate degree; but, insofar as they are relativist, they still suffer them. We know that the content of cultural disputes often involves competing culturally distinctive claims about morality or justice. A normative political theory of multiculturalism needs to attempt to *resolve* such disputes, not merely to report on their terms. I have suggested that most of the more-modest uses of context and circumstances are particularly well suited to the analysis of multiculturalism. But theories that are contextual all the way down are particularly *badly* suited to that enterprise.

VIII. Concluding remarks

How does the preceding compare with other methodological statements about contextualism and multicultural political theory? Carens has said that

A contextual approach to political theory has five interrelated elements. First, it involves the use of examples to illustrate theoretical formulations. Second, it entails the normative exploration of actual cases where the fundamental concerns addressed by the theory are in play. Third, it leads theorists to pay attention to the question of whether their theoretical formulations are actually compatible with the normative positions they themselves take on particular issues. Fourth, it includes a search for cases that are especially challenging to the theorist's own theoretical position. Fifth, it promotes consideration of a wide range of cases, and especially a search for cases that are unfamiliar and illuminating because of their complexity.[38]

---

[38] Carens, "A Contextual Approach to Political Theory," p. 118.

Carens's first "element" corresponds to the first, illustrative, use of context I have described. His third and fourth correspond to the second, testing, use. I am not sure whether the second corresponds to my description of the epistemic use of circumstances (as in *LCC*), or whether it is just an injunction to choose *relevant* illustrative cases and then allow them to be complex rather than simple. And the fifth is not a *use* of context at all; it precedes any such use. One has to learn some facts about the world before considering their relevance to a normative theory, after all.

This list of elements seems curiously modest to me. It presupposes the priority of the theory to the context. It mainly describes a way to engage in illustrative and testing uses of cases in an intellectually open and honest way. It does not mention revision, much less formulation or reformulation, of a theory in response to the encounter with cases or context; it does not allow for the building of context into the theory itself. This surely does not describe the strong contextualism of *Spheres of Justice*. It does not describe the methodological ambition or novelty of Carens's own *Culture, Citizenship, and Community*.[39] I even doubt that it conveys a sense of the use of circumstances in a work like *Liberalism, Community and Culture*. With the reach of contextualism scaled back so far, Kukathas can credibly retort that:

> the contextual approach is not a particularly distinctive approach in political theory ... If we consider the history of modern political theory, there is no shortage of thinkers, from Vitoria and Grotius to David Hume and John Stuart Mill to F. A. Hayek and Ronald Dworkin, who draw on real examples to illustrate or clarify philosophical points.[40]

But both Carens's scaling back, and Kukathas's rejoinder about distinctiveness and novelty, are misleading. Certainly, none of the uses of contextualism I describe here is wholly novel or without pedigree. Modern political thought received a great deal of its impetus from the consideration of novel sets of circumstances: the European encounter with the Americas, the Reformation and subsequent development of intra-Christian pluralism within states, the commercial and financial and, later, industrial revolutions, mass literacy, and so on. What I refer

---

[39] Regarding "novelty": it is true that by the time Carens's *Culture, Citizenship, and Community* was published, the second wave, with its contextualist turn, was well underway. But that book mainly consisted of articles and chapters published as early as 1990; and the chapter that probably did the most to establish Carens's brand of contextualism, that on Fiji, was published in 1992. Carens was among the earliest, perhaps *the* earliest, to clearly link multiculturalism with contextualism in political theory.

[40] Kukathas, "Contextualism Reconsidered," p. 218.

to as "constitutionalism" is not characteristic of all the projects of constitutional design that dot modern political thought; Condorcet, Turgot, and (oddly enough) Hume abstracted from context rather than making use of it. But *The Federalist Papers*, Rousseau's *Government of Poland*, and Constant's *Réflexions sur les Constitutions*, among many others, suggested institutional designs that made use of particular and local social facts and conditions in order to generate just outcomes. Montesquieu and Tocqueville do rather more than "draw on real examples to illustrate or clarify philosophical points." And their use of context, their arguments about the interplay between normative and particular empirical claims, mark their approaches as quite distinct from, say, Kant's.

Contextual and non-contextual approaches both have their pedigrees; but I cannot see how this leads to the denial that they are meaningfully distinguishable. That contextualism is not new over the course of the history of political thought does not impugn the claim that it is relatively novel in the post-1971 intellectual landscape. To the degree that we have lost sight of contextualism's pedigree, this may simply be because of the primacy of neo-Kantianism and, later, neo-Hegelianism in the revitalization of political theory brought about by the publication of *A Theory of Justice*. To the degree that attention to multiculturalism has increased the prominence of contextualism and constitutionalism in liberal thought, it has been a restoration rather than a revolution.

7   Negotiation, deliberation, and the claims of politics

Anthony Simon Laden

On 30 April 1987, Brian Mulroney, the Canadian prime minister, and the premiers of Canada's ten provinces emerged from hours of negotiation held at a conference center on Meech Lake to announce that they had reached agreement on a set of constitutional changes that were designed to satisfy the demands of Quebec. This final round of negotiations was the culmination of five years of constitutional negotiations stemming from Quebec's refusal to ratify the 1982 Constitution Act. The accord and agreement, involving a complex set of compromises and the bracketing of other contentious issues, was short-lived, however, failing to win ratification in some provincial legislatures. By the time it met its legal death, it was widely unpopular, and the two sides (Quebec and the Rest of Canada) were further apart than they had been prior to the negotiations. A similar set of negotiations on a broader range of constitutional issues and involving a broader range of parties yielded a new agreement, the Charlottetown Accord, in 1992, which also failed to be ratified, this time as a result of a nationwide referendum. Once again, the breakdown of the agreement led the various parties to harden their demands, leaving them further apart than before the talks began.[1]

In 1993, Yitzhak Rabin, prime minister of the State of Israel, and Yasser Arafat, chairman of the Palestinian Liberation Organization, signed the Oslo Peace Accords. The fruit of months of secret peace talks between Israelis and the PLO, the Oslo Accords did not lay out a final peace settlement, but rather set the stage for future talks on the way to an envisioned final settlement to be worked out in the future. They nevertheless represented an historic agreement between parties who had

---

[1] For a detailed history of the Canadian constitutional negotiations, see Peter Russell, *Constitutional Odyssey*, 2nd edn. (Toronto: University of Toronto Press, 1993). For discussion of the implications of the breakdown of the negotiations and a variety of interpretations of them, see Curtis Cook (ed.), *Constitutional Predicament* (Montreal: McGill-Queen's University Press, 1994).

been long-time enemies. Somewhere between 1993 and 2001, however, the Oslo "peace process" broke down. As with the Canadian Accords, though with much more tragic consequences, the breakdown of the agreements left the two sides in many ways further apart and more hostile than they had been prior to 1993.[2]

The many crucial differences between these two cases make the similarities between them all the more striking. In each case, a dominant interpretation of the talks saw them as negotiations aimed at reaching a conclusive settlement of competing claims. The settlement would take the form of a compromise, whereby each side would give up some of its claims in order to satisfy others. If successful, these negotiations would result in a binding agreement that would resolve and thus end the struggles, both hostile and political, between the parties. This agreement would then herald the dawn of a period of peace and stability in which all sides could turn their energy to "normal" politics: things like tax policy, trade, and water rights.

Contrast this interpretation with an alternative one that could also be found among participants and observers: these talks were part of an ongoing process that served two primary purposes. First, they, along with the policies that they aimed to implement and foster, were to build trust between and among the parties, trust that was a necessary condition for continued peaceful coexistence. Second, they served, quite independently of any final agreements reached, as themselves a manifestation of an agreement among the parties to work out their problems together through dialogue, rather than through violence (as in the Israeli-Palestinian case) or through legal fiat (as in the Canadian case). Seen in this light, the talks were themselves part of a larger political process, not a means to solving a problem.

In this chapter, I make three claims. First, one of the factors contributing to the dominance of the dominant interpretation of these and similar cases is the prevalence of what I call a theoretical approach to questions of cultural pluralism. Second, one of the consequences of adopting a theoretical approach is that it obscures the difference between the two interpretations by obscuring the difference between two forms of political dialogue: what I will call negotiation and

---

[2] For detailed histories of the Oslo process from a number of different perspectives, see Yossi Bellin, *Touching Peace* (London: Weidenfeld & Nicolson, 1999); Benny Morris, *Righteous Victims* (New York: Knopf, 1999); Dennis Ross, *The Missing Peace* (New York: Farrar, Straus & Giroux, 2004); Avi Shalim, *The Iron Wall* (New York: Norton, 2000); Edward Said, *The End of the Peace Process* (New York: Pantheon, 2000). I do not think that the Israeli-Palestinian conflict and the attempts to end it are best thought of under the heading of cultural accommodation or multiculturalism. I use it here and throughout the chapter as an example of a negotiation that failed.

deliberation. In contrast, adopting what I call a political approach to questions of cultural pluralism allows us to distinguish between negotiation and deliberation and thus to think about political dialogue in terms of deliberation. Finally, in many instances, thinking about political interaction across differences only in terms of negotiation has some unfortunate consequences, such as those found in the examples above. If we can approach these interactions as deliberations, however, a more hopeful array of possibilities opens up.

I.   Approaching politics

As I am using the term here, an "approach" is neither a particular theory nor a subject matter for a theory. It is, rather, something like a prior theoretical orientation that guides how we conceptualize a subject matter and shapes the kinds of questions we develop our theories to answer. Because an approach to political philosophy is a prior orientation, it is rarely the subject of explicit examination and reflection. Rather, it sets the terms under which much of our examination and reflection proceeds. And yet, insofar as it orients reflection, the particular approach we adopt can have an enormous influence on that reflection. For instance, it can draw our attention to some issues rather than others, highlight certain phenomena and obscure others. It can help make certain conclusions or observations seem intuitive or obvious, and make others particularly hard to see or take seriously.

Much of the recent work on cultural pluralism by political theorists and philosophers takes up a theoretical approach, and this approach stands behind a great deal of the more concrete political analysis and action surrounding issues of pluralism as well. The hallmark of the theoretical approach is that it takes the fact of cultural pluralism as a problem to be solved, a problem that admits of a theoretical solution. It thus begins from the thought that in the ideal case, at least, one could work out all the details of a just or legitimate accommodation of cultural pluralism and then straightforwardly apply it to plural societies. To the extent that political processes play a role in working out such accommodations, their role is either instrumental or justified by the overwhelming complexity of the theoretical problem.

Taking a theoretical approach thus involves seeing politics as, essentially, an unfortunate concession to the limits of our theoretical abilities, and seeing cultural pluralism as first and foremost a problem for political theories. It is a sign of the dominance of the theoretical approach in discussions of cultural pluralism that the current wave of interest in questions of cultural pluralism and multiculturalism takes the form of debates over whether and how universalist political theories like liberalism can accommodate cultural diversity.

Political approaches, in contrast, start from the thought that what justifies political action and political principles is not the correctness of a theory, but the actual endorsement (in a suitably defined sense) of actual people acting politically in actual societies.[3] Cultural pluralism thus raises issues for this approach in political philosophy when it affects citizens' ability to individually or collectively endorse various political principles. Where a theoretical approach raises the question of whether and how a universal theory can accommodate difference, a political approach raises the question of whether and how citizens who do not share a set of cultural practices, beliefs, and attitudes can nevertheless develop shared political policies and principles. Notice that on this approach, politics is not relegated to a back seat. Understanding how citizens might come to share policies and principles across cultural differences is in no way a substitute for citizens actually coming to do so, nor does it necessarily tell us what, in any precise sense, those principles will be. Unlike the theoretical approach, the political approach takes politics to be necessary, not as instrumental or a concession to the limits of our calculating abilities, but rather because politics is seen as a set of practices through which citizens can exchange reasons and thus come to share them.[4] Political philosophy that takes a political approach thus need not displace democratic politics.[5] Rather, it can give us hope that democratic politics can reconcile our differences without erasing them.

II.   Political theory and the logic of negotiation

Theoretical approaches implicitly assume that the problems that cultural pluralism generates admit, at least in principle, of a theoretical solution if they are solvable at all. This assumption, in turn, helps to

---

[3] The best-known recent work of political philosophy to take a political approach is John Rawls's *Political Liberalism*, paperback edition (New York: Columbia University Press, 1996), though the interpretation of Rawls's work as adopting a political approach is perhaps controversial. Other works that more uncontroversially adopt this approach are James Tully's *Strange Multiplicity* (Cambridge: Cambridge University Press, 1995) and my *Reasonably Radical* (Ithaca: Cornell University Press, 2001).

[4] In describing politics as a set of practices through which citizens can exchange reasons, I do not mean to dismiss a view of politics as about power, but to assert a fact about politics that is compatible with it being about power. To say that citizens can exchange reasons through politics does not imply that they always do so, or that that exchange is not ever fatally distorted by imbalances of power.

[5] For a clear articulation of the worry that political theory will serve to displace politics, see Bonnie Honig, *Political Theory and the Displacement of Politics* (Ithaca: Cornell University Press, 1993). See also Chantal Mouffe, *The Democratic Paradox* (London: Verso, 2000).

entrench a certain picture of politics and political conflicts: that politics is centrally about the distribution of the satisfaction of competing claims in a more or less peaceful manner.[6] The assumption entrenches this picture because the picture makes it appear that the assumption is uncontroversial: if politics is, as the picture suggests, centrally about the distribution of the satisfaction of competing claims, then it is quite plausible that there is a theory that can tell us what a proper distribution looks like. Applying this picture to issues of cultural pluralism yields an analysis of cultural pluralism in terms of competing cultural claims.

On this analysis, the importance of membership in a particular cultural group is that it generates needs that are not shared with other members of the pluralist society. Members of a minority linguistic community may need official documents and state support for public education in their language, and members of a religious minority may need different days off to observe religious holidays, or exemptions from requirements of dress or behavior in order to follow the dictates of their religion in a society whose official holidays and codes of behavior are designed with members of the majority religion in mind.[7] Cultural pluralism thus generates a set of competing claims in a manner analogous to that of scarce resources or different personal preferences, and the aim of politics here, as with those other competing claims, is to distribute the satisfaction of those claims in a rational and fair manner.

Within the theoretical approach to cultural diversity, there is room for a wide variety of positions, depending, for instance, on whether the claims of cultural membership are given a great deal of weight or treated as mere tastes, whether they are seen as threatening to political unity or their suppression as threatening to political legitimacy. There is also, importantly, room for difference on just how much of a solution to these problems political theory can provide ahead of time. Thus, some theorists have defended comprehensive theories of individual and cultural

---

[6] The entrenchment of a picture of politics as concerned with conflicts of interests rather than, say, recognition and freedom is generally traced to the work of Thomas Hobbes. It is often contrasted with a republican tradition resuscitated by Machiavelli that develops into a politics of freedom and recognition in Hegel. For a reading of the history of modern philosophy along such lines along with an attempt to develop the Hegelian branch more fully, see Axel Honneth, *Struggles for Recognition*, trans. Joel Anderson (Cambridge, MA: MIT Press, 1996).

[7] To cite some of the more common examples: in Western societies where Christmas and Good Friday are national holidays, Jews but not Christians will have to use personal days to observe their most important religious holidays. Sikh men wear turbans, and this can conflict with the requirements of official uniforms (the broad-brimmed hat of the RCMP in Canada, the wig of the barrister in the UK) or safety laws requiring motorcyclists to wear helmets. Muslims and Jews who follow the dietary laws of their religions only eat animals killed in a manner that may violate anti-cruelty laws.

rights, offering what amounts to a prior theoretical account of which claims deserve satisfaction, whereas others have been wary of such one-size-fits-all approaches, and have suggested that the most political theory can do is to offer some general concerns that must be heeded by any political system faced with such claims.[8] Nonetheless, even such a hands-off approach sees the basic problem that cultural pluralism raises for political society as one of competing claims, and the ultimate aim of political theory to provide at least steps towards a solution of that problem.

Claims as vectors

If the problems generated by competing claims are to admit of a theoretical solution then it must be the case that everything that is essential to those claims can be understood from a theoretical perspective, one external to the practices in which the claims are raised and answered. From such a perspective we can grasp the content of a claim – what is being demanded – and perhaps its strength – how many people make the demand, with what urgency, etc. Other features of a political claim may be obscured from this perspective, however. In particular, it will be hard to grasp the relevance of more particular connections between claims and claimants, such as the complex ways that raising a political claim can serve to express an identity as politically relevant, or publicly bear witness to one's commitments in addition to or even instead of raising a demand to be satisfied. It may also obscure the difference between a claim that is raised because it is what a group ideally wants and a claim that is raised because it is what a group has been manipulated or subjected into thinking is all they can demand. Finally, an external perspective can obscure distinctions between the response a claim elicits, and thus fail to take seriously the difference between a dismissive rejection of a claim and its rejection for reasons the claimant takes seriously.

Adopting a theoretical approach thus leads to a conception of political claims that I will call claims as vectors. To view the claims we make on one another and our common institutions as vectors is to see them as demands that pull in a certain direction (more funding for this, more liberty to do that) and with a certain force. Moreover, it is to assume that all that ultimately matters with regard to a claim is the degree of its

---

[8] For an example of the latter, with discussions of the former, see Jacob Levy, *The Multiculturalism of Fear* (Oxford: Oxford University Press, 2000) as well as his contribution to this volume.

204 *Anthony Simon Laden*

satisfaction. In other words, if I make a claim on a social institution, I attempt to pull it in a certain direction. Understood this way, the only question of importance is whether and to what extent the institution moves in that direction. Since, by hypothesis, different members of the society pull in different directions and with different forces, the problem of politics thus becomes the problem of figuring out how to properly balance all these pulls, and we assess how well certain institutions succeed in balancing those pulls by, as it were, measuring where they are in relation to those pulls. If Sikh men demand exemptions from motorcycle helmet laws, then according to this logic, all that matters at the end of the day is whether or not they get such exemptions, or perhaps what level of exemption they receive. It does not matter, for instance, whether or not the refusal to grant such exemptions is the result of a failure to even consider the demand, an outright rejection of the possibility of making religious exemptions for safety laws, or the result of public political discussion in which the Sikhs themselves feel that their case got a fair hearing.

The logic of negotiation

The analysis and interpretation of political claims as vectors reduces politics to what I will call negotiation, and leads political theories and the political debates and actions those theories inform to work within the logic of negotiation.[9] We can thus understand the consequences of adopting a theoretical approach by unpacking the logic of negotiation and its implications.

Negotiated agreements are compromises amongst parties who have different pre-existing interests. They engage in negotiation in order to maximize the satisfaction of these interests because they realize that the presence of others with different interests places an obstacle in their way. The point here is not that parties engaged in negotiation treat each other purely instrumentally, and negotiation as merely more cost-effective

---

[9] I use the term "negotiation" and its contrasting term "deliberation" in this chapter as somewhat technical terms, whose meaning is given by the features of their respective logics, as described below. The contrast I draw here is meant to capture at least some senses of these words as they are used in ordinary English, though in ordinary language their meanings overlap and so are not as clearly distinct as I make them out to be here. As a result, it is sometimes the case that what I call "deliberation" others will call "negotiation." For example, some forms of peace and constitutional negotiation will count as "deliberation" in my terminology. Similarly, a number of thinkers who have advocated political negotiation as a response to pluralism in recent years also count, in my terms, as offering theories of deliberation rather than negotiation. See, for instance, Tully, *Strange Multiplicity*, and Richard Bellamy, *Liberalism and Pluralism* (New York and London: Routledge, 1999).

than outright domination. We can see someone as an obstacle to our plans without seeing them as an object. In fact, many of the ways that people can stand in our way depend on our seeing them as persons. The student who shows up to talk to me as my office hours are ending stands in the way of my going home in a very different manner than my office door does. Nevertheless, there is an important difference between seeing others as obstacles and seeing them as partners with whom we disagree, and it is this difference that I mean to highlight here. Negotiation involves seeing others as obstacles and thus the need to deal with them as an unfortunate fact. So, if we approach politics as embodying a logic of negotiation, we will be led to a view of politics as a kind of concession to the unfortunate plurality of our social world. When, for instance, a religious minority is granted an exemption from a requirement of dress or conduct as a result of negotiation, this may result in the majority culture taking the need for this concession as yet a further sign that the minority group is truly foreign, and a lingering "problem."

Seeing politics in terms of negotiation has several related consequences. First, negotiated agreements always require further compliance mechanisms. Negotiators do not enter negotiation with the thought it will transform their interests. Negotiation is a procedure by which the satisfaction of interests can be distributed, but it takes and leaves those interests as given. Negotiated compromises thus necessarily leave some pre-existing claims unsatisfied. Considered as a vector, however, all that matters about a claim is the degree to which it is satisfied. So some claims linger even after the compromise is reached. As a result, each side in a negotiation has a motivation to break the agreement when doing so will serve their interests better than keeping the agreement will. Negotiated agreements thus always come with problems of compliance. Since nothing internal to the process of negotiation fosters trust or a sense of a shared project, even if negotiations can end or forestall open conflict, they may not lead to a true cessation of hostility. One sign of the dominance of the theoretical approach is the centrality of issues of compliance in political theory. Second, negotiation leads each side to exaggerate its claims and thus paradoxically drives parties apart as they try to reach agreement. The basic idea is that the less I am willing to give up, the better deal I can make, and so I have an incentive to exaggerate my interests and their importance to me. Linguistic communities, for instance, may develop an overstated sense of the vulnerability of their language or the degree to which a bilingual population would destroy what they are trying to preserve. National or religious groups may overstate their need for purity in order to survive, or the depth of the source of their demands in religious obligations or national identity as a means of giving greater force to the claims they make.

It is important to be clear about the force of this claim. I mean to say more than that sometimes people enter negotiation in bad faith and thus violate accepted practices to get a better deal. Clearly that happens. My point here is that the structure of negotiation itself can push even those who enter negotiation in good faith to exaggerate their claims. The process may be complex and need not involve outright intentional deception. Rather, each side may respond to resistance to their claims from the other side by, as it were, pulling harder and digging in its heels. The rejection of a claim may serve to make its satisfaction seem more important, giving it new symbolic value as a question of respect or recognition. Insofar as negotiation involves not only interaction between the groups but the separation of those groups into separate sides, it may have the effect over time of solidifying intra-group ties and emphasizing inter-group differences. All of these dynamics, then, have the effect of exaggerating the claims of the negotiating groups even in the absence of bad faith and an initial intention to deceive.

Third, when negotiations fail to reach agreement, or that agreement breaks down, this can leave the conflict more intense than before, the failure of negotiations taken by both sides as a sign that their differences really are irreconcilable, and that the only full solution to the problem will come from one side overcoming the obstacles that the other side represents. This is one of the factors, I contend, that helps to explain the rhetoric and behavior of the Israelis and the Palestinians in the wake of the breakdown of the Oslo process, and in the rhetoric of many Canadians and Quebeckers in the aftermath of Meech Lake and Charlottetown. In each case, the effect of seeing the issues under discussion as about the distribution of the satisfaction of demands and the forum where solutions were discussed as negotiations had the effect of hardening each side's demands. It also contributed to the sense on both sides that when full settlements were not reached, there was no legitimate political route out of the conflict.

Fourth, the logic of negotiation leads to a conception of political stability that turns out to be hostile to pluralism. Though a negotiated agreement may leave the original competing claims in place, it nevertheless represents a kind of lining up of the demands of the various groups. Negotiated agreements, if honored, thus yield a kind of political stability. Such stability rests on unity, and is conceived as the absence of struggle. That is, on this model, stability is achieved when struggles between competing groups give way to negotiation, and negotiation yields agreement. Since stability, so conceived, just is the absence of struggle, when some parties continue to raise objections to an agreement and struggle to change its terms, they are likely to be seen as a threat to the stability of the society, rather than as participating in legitimate politics.[10] The dangers of such an attitude are most clearly on display when government officials and other guardians of public order condemn and dismiss the demands and tactics of various movements for social justice as disloyal or dangerous to the continued functioning of political society.[11] There is thus a danger that the very theoretical structures used to address issues of cultural pluralism lend support to arguments that preserve a hegemonic status quo that excludes or assimilates cultural pluralism in the name of political stability.[12]

Finally, the theoretical approach can obscure the place of inequality and oppression in questions of pluralism. The model of claims as vectors obscures the connection between demands made and the status of those who make them. In particular, it fails to distinguish between either the force or the importance of the claims of those with power and those without.[13] As a result, political theorists who follow this logic have generally adopted either of two unsatisfactory strategies for addressing issues of oppression and inequality. The first assimilates inequality to mere difference. It has thus been common to reconceptualize race or gender as a matter of difference rather than oppression, so that racial and gender politics can be easily brought under the banner of multiculturalism.[14] The second approach acknowledges that issues of inequality cannot be treated with the tools developed to handle issues of mere difference but then says nothing about the relationship between pluralism and inequality. This leaves us asking, "recognition or

[10] See, for example, Arthur Schlesinger, *The Disuniting of America* (New York: W. W. Norton, 1998) and Samuel Huntington, *Who Are We? America's Great Debate* (New York: Simon & Schuster, 2004).

[11] Examples abound, from those who argued against the legitimacy of civil disobedience in the 1960s to members of the Administration of US President George W. Bush claiming that dissent from the US government position after the terrorist attacks on 9/11/01 amounted to aiding the terrorists.

[12] The concern that political stability serves the interests of hegemony is clearly articulated by radical and agonistic democratic theorists. See for instance, Mouffe, *Democratic Paradox*. It is also the crux of the argument in favor of a politics of difference. See Iris Young, *Justice and the Politics of Difference* (Princeton: Princeton University Press, 1990).

[13] As we saw, this is a direct result of the external standpoint the theoretical approach adopts. It is notoriously difficult to appreciate the subtle dynamics of power within relationships when they are seen from outside. See, for instance, Catharine MacKinnon, "Consciousness Raising" and "Method and Politics" in *Towards a Feminist Theory of the State* (Cambridge, MA: Harvard University Press, 1989), pp. 83–125, see esp. pp. 100–101.

[14] For discussions of this dynamic and its dangers, see the contributions by Iris Young and Charles Mills in this volume.

redistribution?'' as if this was a choice between not only separate problems but separate political theories.[15] The difficulty that many thinkers who address questions of cultural diversity have had in also addressing structural inequality can thus be taken as further evidence of the prevalence that the logic of negotiation and theoretical approaches more generally have had in academic discussions of cultural diversity.

III.   The logic of deliberation and the claims of politics

According to the argument of the last section, the theoretical approach runs into certain problems because it sees all politics through the lens of a logic of negotiation. The logic of negotiation was, in turn, claimed to be a natural outgrowth of the analysis of the competing claims of members of diverse cultures as vectors, and the role of politics as working out a reasonable distribution of the satisfaction of those claims, an analysis that the adoption of a theoretical approach supports. Political approaches avoid these problems because they allow for a different interpretation of competing claims.[16]

Claims as proto-reasons

In treating political claims as vectors, the theoretical approach focuses on what those claims say rather than on what those making the claims aim to do. This leads us to conflate people's interests or needs with their claims. But, neither individuals nor particular groups within a society raise the satisfaction of all of their needs and interests as political demands. Some needs and interests seem ill-suited to generate claims. Other needs and interests may generate claims, but not in any important sense on all other members of a society. It is thus a mistake to think of the political claims that people make on one another as simply the expression of their interests and needs.

Because a political approach looks at political struggles over cultural pluralism from the perspective of engaged participants, those who are

---

[15] This phrasing comes from Nancy Fraser. For a discussion of debates on this question, see Nancy Fraser and Axel Honneth, *Recognition or Redistribution?* (London: Verso, 2003) and David Owen and James Tully's contribution to this volume.

[16] There may very well be ways of avoiding the problems that I catalogued in the last section either within the logic of negotiation or by avoiding or altering the logic of negotiation while holding on to the basic tenets of the theoretical approach. I do not take the arguments in this chapter to rule out such possibilities. The central reason I offer for not investigating those options is what I take to be the attractiveness of the approach I describe in the rest of the chapter. Those who are less attracted to it than I am will have reasons to explore different options.

making claims and evaluating the claims made on them, the question of what claims do, and why people make them, comes to the fore. When I make a claim on others, I do not merely express an interest. I make a demand. Furthermore, I make a demand that I think deserves a reasonable response. In other words, when I make a claim on someone, I take myself to have made a demand that is backed by an appropriate authority. We can thus think of the kinds of political claims that individuals and groups make as proto-reasons. They are proto-reasons because they may ultimately lack the authority they purport to have. In cases where a given claim has the appropriate authority it is a full-blown reason.

Taking up a political approach, then, opens up a rather different way to understand the role of cultural claims in politics, and of the role of political philosophy in the face of competing claims. Perhaps most importantly, it allows a more fine-grained distinction among responses to a claim that do not differ along the axis of degrees of satisfaction. For instance, I can acknowledge the importance of the interest that generates the claim, but nevertheless dispute that the claim has the authority it purports to have. I might dispute the authority of the claimant over me, or her authority to make this particular kind of claim. In other cases, I can accept that the claim has authority over me, but reject it because it is overridden by other concerns, concerns that the original claimant may or may not regard as authoritative over her. In a third set of cases, I can accept the reason as one that must be answered but not fully satisfied, or urge the original claimant to reconsider her claim in the light of other considerations she has failed to heed. In all of these cases when the original claim runs into obstacles, I can also re-evaluate the status of the obstacles in light of the claim.[17]

The logic of deliberation

When different groups of citizens urge competing proto-reasons on one another, what is needed is not a formula or procedure for finding a political center of gravity, but a way of understanding and evaluating the subsequent activity of reasoning together that such claims initiate. That activity then need not be analyzed through the logic of negotiation. Rather, we can see it in terms of what I will call the logic of deliberation. Whereas negotiation involves the search for a compromise that balances

---

[17] I discuss the variety of ways deliberators can respond to the claims of others in more detail in my "Outline of a Theory of Reasonable Deliberation," *Canadian Journal of Philosophy*, 30 (4), December 2000, pp. 551–580 and "Evaluating Social Reasons: Hobbes vs. Hegel," *Journal of Philosophy*, 102 (7), July 2005, pp. 327–356.

a set of competing pre-existing interests of parties who view themselves as competitors, deliberation involves an exchange of claims among people who regard themselves as partners working out a shared solution to a shared problem.[18]

The aim of deliberation is not merely a mutually acceptable compromise, but rather a shared solution that each of the parties can regard as expressing their investment in the issue under discussion. Despite this common aim, deliberators come to deliberation with different perspectives, and urging claims that compete with one another. What is distinctive about deliberation is that despite their differences, all parties attempt to work out a set of shared reasons. They do not merely hold out for the best deal they can get, but rather try to figure out what authority the various competing claims they each urge actually have, and how they can, together, respond appropriately to the complex terrain of reasons that their competing claims generate. Part of their task in deliberation, then, is to find a way to understand their divergent claims in terms of shared reasons.

In deliberation, parties treat reasons as inter-subjective.[19] To treat reasons as inter-subjective is to act as if their authority derives from the relationships between and among people, and in particular, from the practical identities they share.[20] In other words, when I urge a claim on you, I take myself to be placing you under an authoritative demand. I claim that the demand has authority for you because of something in our relationship that supports the demand. As a fellow member of this committee, I can rightfully expect that you will do your share of the work, and thus any demand I make on you that asks you to do your share of the work derives its authority from our relationship as fellow members of the committee. Thus, if we are engaged in an attempt to figure out what reasons we can share, we will be led to an investigation of our relationships to one another and the reasons they generate.

---

[18] Much, though not all, work in "deliberative democracy" works with a logic of deliberation. See, for example, James Bohman and William Rehg (eds.), *Deliberative Democracy* (Cambridge, MA: MIT Press, 1997); Tully, *Strange Multiplicity*, and my *Reasonably Radical.*

[19] For a more thorough discussion of reasons as inter-subjective see Christine Korsgaard, "The Reasons We Can Share," reprinted in her *Creating the Kingdom of Ends* (Cambridge: Cambridge University Press, 1996), pp. 275–310, and my "Outline of a Theory of Reasonable Deliberation."

[20] The term "practical identity" is from Christine Korsgaard. See her *The Sources of Normativity* (Cambridge: Cambridge University Press, 1996). I use the term as a way of characterizing the relationships that ground the authority of reasons in deliberation in "Outline of a Theory of Reasonable Deliberation," and more fully with regard to political deliberation in *Reasonably Radical.*

Since we may come to the deliberation with different understandings of just what relationship we bear to one another or what sorts of claims that relationship authorizes, the very process of deliberation may involve one or both of us changing our understanding of these matters and thus what claims have authority for us. If deliberating together moves us from an unarticulated disagreement about our relationship to a new understanding of that relationship, we may resolve our competing claims by understanding them in a new and common light. When we reach agreement in this fashion, our agreement will not have the features I highlighted in the compromise that results from negotiation. Because the agreement rests on a shared understanding of the merit of the various claims, it need not be regarded by either side as merely a second-best. Through deliberation, each party genuinely refines her understanding of herself, her relationship to others, and the claims they generate. If a shared understanding is reached in this manner, the original claims that go unsatisfied do not continue to exert their pull because they are seen to have insufficient authority. The final agreement expresses where each side now stands.

The very fact that each side in a deliberation can be changed, and must be open to being changed, by the deliberative encounter means that deliberation in good faith requires a certain level of trust on behalf of all parties. Note two consequences of this fact. First, when the politics of cultural pluralism embodies a logic of deliberation, questions of trust come to the fore. These questions have not been front and center, however, in a lot of theoretical discussions of multiculturalism.[21] Second, there will be situations where straightforward engagement in deliberation is not a feasible alternative because one or both sides lack sufficient trust to accept the vulnerability that good faith deliberation entails. There is a large difference, however, between an analysis that concludes that deliberation is not a live option in a particular situation and one which lacks the conceptual resources to see it as a distinct alternative to begin with. For one, if deliberation holds out attractive possibilities for reconciliation and yet circumstances (such as a lack of trust between the parties) make deliberation impossible, we have reasons to think about how to change those circumstances to make true deliberation possible, and a further reason to try to implement such policies beyond whatever direct good they do. This, I take it, is the reasoning that supported the alternative reading of Meech Lake, and especially Oslo.[22]

---

[21] See Melissa Williams, *Voice Trust and Memory* (Princeton: Princeton University Press, 2000) for an interesting exception.

[22] For such an interpretation of the Canadian case, see James Tully, "Diversity's Gambit Declined," in *Constitutional Predicament*, ed. Cook. Dennis Ross sums up this reading of

Even when there is sufficient trust to engage in good faith deliberation, it can fail to reach an accord. Nothing guarantees that parties to
deliberation will find sufficient common ground on which to stand
together. Nevertheless, the dynamics of deliberation can generate some
level of solidarity even in the absence of a final agreement. Unlike
negotiation, deliberation does not generate incentives for exaggeration.
In deliberation, each party is motivated not solely or primarily by getting
as many of its own claims as possible satisfied, but in coming to a set of
shared understandings. In order for such shared understandings to be
reached, each side must come to understand the demands under which
the other side finds itself. Deliberative partners are thus led to think
more about their relationships to one another, and not to dwell solely on
intra-group commonalities. Moves in a deliberation thus do not function as tugs on a rope, provoking stronger counter-tugs from the other
side. Rather, even when rejected, good faith suggestions of what the
sides share draws the other side into thinking together. Thus, rather
than having the effect of hardening initial differences, deliberation can
serve to bring different sides towards mutual acknowledgment and
understanding even when it fails to bring them to embrace a fully shared
identity.[23] The internal dynamic of good faith deliberation serves to
increase rather than erode what trust exists. As a result, deliberation that
does not arrive at a final agreement is less likely to generate an even
more divisive conflict.

As a result of this and other features, deliberation can be ongoing
without this being a sign that it has failed.[24] The very act of deliberation
reflects a kind of agreement among the parties to resolve their differences cooperatively and on mutually acceptable terms, to find and
develop shared identities that can support mutually acceptable claims.
Participation in deliberation thus involves each party showing respect

Oslo and its failure: "Transformation defined the meaning of Oslo for both sides.
However, neither side succeeded in transforming itself" (Ross, *The Missing Peace*,
p. 764). For a less hopeful reading of Oslo that is compatible with the points made here,
see Said, *End of the Peace Process*. From the beginning, Said maintained that the
imbalance in power between the two sides meant that no real deliberation went on, and
no real trust could be generated until issues of inequality were acknowledged and
addressed.

[23] Of course, the mere fact that deliberation encourages good faith participation is no
insurance against the possibility that some parties will enter deliberation in bad faith.
My claim is merely that the logic of deliberation does nothing itself to pervert the
incentives of those who enter such deliberations in good faith, whereas the logic of
negotiation can itself have the effect of pushing those who enter negotiation in good
faith further apart.

[24] Tully stresses this aspect of deliberation (though he calls it negotiation) in *Strange
Multiplicity*, pp. 135–136. See also *Reasonably Radical*, p. 127.

towards and recognition of the status of the other parties as parties whose claims matter. Contrast this with what is required to engage in negotiation: recognizing the other party as an obstacle to the unimpeded pursuit of one's ends that must be dealt with, and cannot be merely ignored or overrun.[25]

In addition, since deliberation involves an attempt to determine jointly the authority of various competing claims, it provides parties who disagree with one another a wider array of responses to the claims of others short of fully satisfying them. Thus, in the course of deliberation, it is possible for one side to acknowledge the legitimacy of the other side's claim without thereby fully giving in to it, by acknowledging that it gives rise to a reason, but urging that it is a reason that is overridden in this context. Such recognition of legitimacy can, in certain cases, go a long way towards resolving issues generated by cultural pluralism by making those whose claims are overridden at least feel that they are heard, and belong as full members to the polity.

The continual recognition of one another as engaging together in a shared project then serves to hold a political society together, to create a kind of political stability that does not rely on a lining up of more particular interests. The result is a different conception of political stability, one that John Rawls calls "stability for the right reasons," and which he describes as resting on "the deepest and most reasonable basis of social unity available to us in a modern society."[26]

Note that stability so conceived is not an end that can be pursued through illegitimate means, but is, rather, a by-product of pursuing other ends legitimately. Stability for the right reasons is generated by citizens acting in good faith with one another, and recognizing this fact. What leads citizens to feel allegiance to their shared political society is precisely the way in which that society leaves room for them and their particular demands, and recognizes those demands even when it does not satisfy them. The allegiance that generates stability for the right reasons relies on the ongoing commitment to reasonable deliberation.

---

[25] This recognition is neither trivial nor empty as it includes the rejection of domination as a means to satisfy one's claims, whether because it is not practically feasible or not morally acceptable. Nevertheless, it is minimal compared to the recognition afforded in deliberation, and, within negotiation, it is merely considered a necessary condition for something else rather than one of the points of the activity itself.

[26] John Rawls, "Reply to Habermas," reprinted in the paperback edition of *Political Liberalism*, p. 391. Rawls says that the basis of such unity is a reasonable overlapping consensus, but I think it is clear from the preceding passages and other parts of his work that this consensus is best thought of not on the model of a negotiated agreement, but as the sort of joint commitment to address differences through reasonable deliberation of the sort discussed above.

Any attempt to achieve such stability through coercive or manipulative tactics, or by excluding certain voices in the name of unity and agreement, is bound to fail, as precisely such tactics are what will undermine the very features of the deliberation that command the allegiance that generates stability for the right reasons in the first place.

A political society in which pluralism is approached through deliberation can thus be stable in a way that is compatible with, and that in fact requires, the recognition and acceptance of the demands for the accommodation of diversity. When particular cultural groups press particular demands through political deliberation, it is precisely the willingness of others to hear and take seriously those demands that serves to support their continued identification with the political society they share. Seen in this manner, pluralism is not a threat to political stability. Instead, what ultimately secures the stability of such a society is its continual openness to challenge and disagreement, its willingness not to shut its eyes to diversity for fear that diversity will erode unity. In identifying with such a political society, one need not foreclose the possibility of identifying with more particular attachments, be they religious, cultural, or ethnic. The stability that can thus result from the varying diverse groups within a plural society taking part in political deliberation is a stability that can take hold amid ongoing deliberative struggles.

Finally, let me turn to the question of inequality. The theoretical approach sees only a logic of negotiation because it treats claims without regard for the position of those who raise them. It is this lack of connection between claim and claimant that I argued places an obstacle in the way of a theoretical approach addressing questions of structural inequality together with questions raised by cultural pluralism. As I have described them, neither the political approach nor the logic of deliberation need accept the separation of claim from claimant. In fact, insofar as deliberation proceeds in large part through the parties trying to figure out whether various claims have authority, and that authority is taken to rest on the relationships among the deliberating parties, it will be important within deliberation to pay attention not only to what claims are raised, but to who raises them and the nature of their relation to other groups and the state.

In addition, on at least some theories of deliberation, for deliberation to yield agreements that have a claim to political legitimacy, certain background conditions must hold. I have already alluded to the need for mutual trust. In addition, one of the most frequently mentioned and discussed conditions is some form of equality or reciprocity. Deliberation can yield the kind of shared resolution that all can accept, only if it does not proceed through coercion or manipulation, but really represents a true exchange of reasons. If deliberation takes place within a context of systematic and widespread inequality, it may be impossible to distinguish a resolution that is genuinely shared from one in which the subordinate party acquiesces as a result of its subordinate position. Furthermore, in many cases of systematic inequality, the grounds of trust will be lacking. Since inequality can serve to undermine the possibility that deliberation can confer legitimacy on the decisions it yields, an approach that analyzes politics within the logic of deliberation will have to address issues of inequality alongside issues of mere pluralism. If inequality undermines the possibility that deliberation will yield truly shared reasons, then the presence of systematic inequality or oppression provides a claim one party can raise in the context of political discussion. Such a claim would hold that until something is done to address the structural inequality, neither side can achieve its aim of finding a deliberative solution to the problems raised by their differences. This need not mean that until there is justice, there can be no politics. Rather, it can point to the types of measures that politics should address first in oppressive contexts.[27] The logic of deliberation thus suggests reasons to dismantle forms of structural inequality in part as a way of enabling a political society to reconcile its pluralism within a non-hegemonic form of stability. Note that this approach neither conflates inequality with mere difference nor takes them to be two fundamentally different problems between which we have to choose. Rather, it argues that inequality and difference each have a distinct effect on the possibility of legitimacy-conferring deliberation, and as such any account of what makes deliberation legitimacy-conferring will need to address both issues of inequality and issues of mere difference within a single conceptual framework while still acknowledging that they raise different sorts of problems.

IV.   Conclusion

I have argued that taking a political approach rather than a theoretical approach to issues of cultural pluralism allows us to draw a distinction between negotiation and deliberation and thus both to see some political activity as deliberation and perhaps to see how to undertake deliberative politics. I have suggested that looking at these issues from within a logic

---

[27] It may also provide reasons why here and now parties should engage in negotiation rather than deliberation. In such a situation, where negotiation is entered in this way some of its problems highlighted above may be mitigated.

of deliberation makes those issues seem less intractable, and less of a threat to the possibility of political stability. I have not suggested anything by way of a theory of how to resolve such issues. That is because taking up a political approach changes not only how we see issues of cultural pluralism, but also what role philosophy can play in their resolution.

Political theorists who take a theoretical approach have been guided by the logic of negotiation to try to work out appropriate agreements, or appropriate methods for reaching agreements, among competing claims. In contrast, philosophers who adopt a political approach, and work within the logic of deliberation have not developed theoretical solutions. They claim that resolution and accommodation must come through deliberation, and that is our task as citizens, not as philosophers and theorists. To paraphrase Rawls, in political deliberation, there are no philosophical experts.[28] What, then, can philosophy and political theory do? Philosophers are left either setting out criteria for judging the reasonableness of deliberation,[29] highlighting the conditions (like the need for mutual trust) necessary for good faith deliberation, or in trying to engage directly in that deliberation by offering particular suggestions about how to conceive the issues at stake. Thus, for instance, rather than generating or applying a particular theory of group rights in order to determine the proper balance of competing claims, we might take the role of the philosopher of deliberation to involve offering a conception of the parties' shared identity that would allow deliberation to move forward, or providing an analysis of the reasonableness of the arguments of both sides, or of the structural background against which deliberation takes place.[30]

If that seems to be an overly modest understanding of what political philosophy can do, then it may help to note that it is a view of the point and role of political philosophy shared by no less an ambitious philosopher than Hegel. When it takes a political approach, political philosophy can help to reconcile us to the fact of pluralism, to come to see it not as a threat to political unity, as a set of problems that "they" pose for "us," or a theoretical problem to be solved by experts, but as an outgrowth of something we value, and as offering us the possibility

---

[28] Rawls, *Political Liberalism*, p. 427.

[29] I have tried to lay out the conditions for what I have called "reasonable" deliberation in "Outline of a Theory of Reasonable Deliberation" and *Reasonably Radical*. See also Tully, *Strange Multiplicity*; James Bohman, *Public Deliberation* (Cambridge, MA: MIT Press, 2000).

[30] For a fuller discussion of the role of political philosophy within a political approach, see my "Taking the Distinction Between People Seriously," *Journal of Moral Philosophy*, 1 November 2004, pp. 277–292.

of a more open and legitimate politics. If we learn to see the cultural pluralism of our various political societies through the lens of the logic of deliberation, we can learn to see that pluralism as an opportunity rather than a threat, as the product of reason, not chaos. So conceived, political philosophy need not replace or displace democratic politics; rather, political philosophy can give us reason to engage in democratic politics.

Part III

Critical issues

8 Multiculturalism and the critique of essentialism*

Andrew Mason

Whatever else it is, multiculturalism is an approach to cultural diversity. As such, any fully worked out version of it must involve some conception of what a culture is. A number of critics have maintained that multiculturalism is wedded to a problematic way of understanding culture which they term "essentialist." Indeed multiculturalists have sometimes been accused of peddling an essentialism with regard to culture even when they have taken the trouble to repudiate views of this kind.[1] The ensuing debate has shown few signs of progress: multiculturalists accuse critics of failing to read their work with due scholarly care, whilst their critics respond that multiculturalist arguments must rest upon an essentialist conception of culture whatever view of culture is officially espoused.[2] I hope to advance this debate by clarifying precisely what it means to hold an essentialist view of culture, by asking why essentialism about culture is supposed to be bad, and by exploring how essentialist assumptions are supposed to figure in some of the key arguments that have been developed by multiculturalists. I shall maintain that most of these arguments either do not involve problematic essentialist assumptions or can be reconstructed in order to avoid relying upon them. Once the charge of essentialism has been properly addressed, we are left with some questions about the adaptability of individuals in the face of cultural change or cultural disintegration which in turn raise the important normative issue which has preoccupied many political philosophers over the past decade or so, namely, what burdens is it fair to require a person to bear when a culture to which he or she belongs is forced to change or the very existence of which is under threat?

* I would like to thank Anthony Laden, Sune Laegaard, David Macdonald, Jocelyn Maclure, David Owen, and Julie Reeves for helpful comments.

[1] See B. Barry, *Culture and Equality* (Cambridge: Polity, 2001), p. 11; A. Jaggar, "Multicultural Democracy," *Journal of Political Philosophy*, 7, 1999, p. 314.
[2] See the chapters by Brian Barry and James Tully in Paul Kelly (ed.), *Multiculturalism Reconsidered* (Cambridge: Polity, 2002), pp. 104–105, 210–211.

I.   Essentialism about culture

Essentialism in the strict philosophical sense is best understood as an approach that imputes essential properties to an object of study, where its essential properties are those that it must have to be an object of the kind that it is and which make it the particular kind of object that it is. Essentialism is not uncommon as an approach to the natural world; for example, some have argued that water has the essential property of being made up of two hydrogen atoms and one oxygen atom bonded together. But the term "essentialism" is not always used in this way. Amongst social and political theorists in particular, "essentialism" is a slippery notion, meaning different things to different theorists, although there is something of a consensus that it is a bad thing when it comes to the study of culture and identity. Before we can determine whether this consensus is well founded, however, we need to delve more deeply into the various ways in which the charge of essentialism has been understood in this context.

What, then, do political theorists mean when they say that a conception of culture is essentialist? According to the usage which bears most resemblance to the strict philosophical sense of essentialism, a conception of culture is essentialist if it assumes that when the members of a group share a culture, they do so in virtue of sharing some characteristic, or set of characteristics, and that the particular characteristics they share make it the particular culture that it is.[3] On this account, any view which has it that when people share a culture they do so because they share a language or a history, and that the particular language or history that they share makes that culture the particular culture it is, would be essentialist. (So, for example, it might be said that French nationals share a culture because they each speak French, and that this language they share makes their culture the particular culture it is.) If essentialism of this general sort is to be regarded as problematic, we need to be given reasons why. These reasons cannot consist solely in showing that particular essentialist conclusions are mistaken, since that might be simply because they have misidentified the characteristics which make a culture a culture, or the characteristics which make a particular culture the culture it is.

Although Wittgenstein's remarks on family resemblance are relevant here, they do not settle the case against an essentialism of this kind.[4] For

---

[3] R. Keesing, "Theories of Culture Revisited," in R. Borofsky (ed.), *Assessing Cultural Anthropology* (New York: McGraw-Hill, 1994), p. 303.

[4] See L. Wittgenstein, *Philosophical Investigations* (Oxford: Blackwell, 1958), ss. 66–67.

Wittgenstein's point is that we should not suppose that the objects which fall under general terms must share some set of properties which justify the use of that term to refer to these objects. As John O'Neill points out, "[T]he legitimate conclusion to draw from Wittgenstein's discussion is that one cannot assume in advance that there must be a set of essential properties shared by all entities that fall under some concept, not that there are no essential properties of objects."[5]

Although the interpretation I have considered is the most straight-forward way of understanding what it means to say that a conception of culture is essentialist, it is not the only way. For example, the charge that a conception of culture is essentialist is sometimes made to rest upon the contention that it involves either or both of the following assumptions. First, the assumption that cultures are clearly demarcated, rather than overlapping and with blurred boundaries, and separate, both in the sense that membership of one excludes membership of any other (so that, for example, one cannot be a member of both the French nation and the German nation, conceived as cultural groups) and in the sense that the same practice can't be a constitutive element of more than one culture (so that, for example, a practice that is partially constitutive of French culture cannot also be a constituent of German culture). Second, the assumption that cultures are internally uniform, that is, that the members of cultural groups are alike in terms of their values or interests, or that the practices in which they participate are homogeneous in the sense that they do not vary significantly across the culture. An account of culture that makes both of these assumptions is sometimes referred to as the billiard ball model.[6] It is allied to a particular conception of a person's cultural identity as singular rather than plural (so, for example, a person cannot have an Anglo-French cultural identity) and as unaffected by other features of their identity such as their gender or race (so it cannot be the case that the way in which people are French, culturally speaking, varies with their gender or race).

In case there are doubts, let me explain why this second view is genuinely different from the first one. Nothing in the idea that when a group shares a culture, they do so in virtue of sharing a number of characteristics, and that the particular characteristics they share make it the particular culture it is, entails the idea that cultures must be separate and clearly bounded or internally uniform. In order to see this, consider an account that is essentialist according to the first view, namely, that

---

[5] J. O'Neill, *The Market: Ethics, Knowledge and Politics* (London: Routledge, 1998), p. 14.
[6] J. Tully, *Strange Multiplicity: Constitutionalism in an Age of Diversity* (Cambridge: Cambridge University Press, 1995), p. 10.

when a group shares a culture, they share a way of life and the way of life they share makes it the particular culture that it is. For a variety of reasons this does not entail that cultures must be separate and bounded or internally uniform. The notion of a way of life is vague but at the most abstract level, a way of life is merely a set of rule-governed practices that are at least loosely woven together and structured in some way, and which constitute at least some central areas of social, political, or economic activity. People share a way of life because they participate together in these practices, which involves coordinating their actions in the light of their understanding of the norms that govern the practices. So it might be said that a group of people share a rural way of life, constituted by various farming practices that are characterized by the use of particular farming techniques and a particular division of labor, and structured by particular hierarchical relations between landowners and farm laborers. But if we understand what it is to share a way of life in these terms, the boundaries between ways of life may be blurred, for it may be hard to discern where practices begin and end. A person may also be a participant in more than one way of life because ways of life may overlap or be nested inside another in such a way that a particular practice may be a component of more than one way of life. For example, farming practices might be partially constitutive of a larger economy that links the rural villages around which these practices are centered to manufacturing industries in cities, and these economic relations and activities might themselves have a particular character that allows us to identify them as constitutive of a particular way of life. As a result, if sharing a culture is defined in terms of sharing a way of life, cultures may overlap and have blurred boundaries, and an individual may belong to more than one in virtue of how ways of life may overlap or be nested inside one another.

Of course, the mere fact that a practice is a component of more than one way of life does not entail that a participant in that practice must therefore take part in each of the ways of life in which it figures. Even if it was true that the same practice of monogamous heterosexual marriage is a component of a British way of life and a German way of life, it would not follow that someone who participates in that practice takes part in both of these ways of life. To be a participant in a way of life one must take part in a range of the practices that constitute it. As I have suggested, this allows the possibility of participating in more than one way of life. (But does it also allow the possibility that the same way of life might exist in different geographical areas such that participants in that way of life might be divided into two groups with no interaction between them? We need to distinguish between type and token here. Two groups who are geographically separated in this way might be participants in the same type of way of life, but they could not participate in the same token of it. Compare the way in which two people may own different cars that are exactly similar. In order for people to participate in exactly the same way of life, it is not enough that they follow the same rules; there must also be some interaction between them, or between them and others, such that we can say that they genuinely cooperate together in following those rules.)

Not only does this understanding of what it is to share a culture give reason to reject the idea that cultures must be separate and clearly bounded, it also stands against the idea that cultures must be internally homogeneous, for a shared way of life may allow for considerable diversity and tolerate, even celebrate, difference; for example a particular way of life might be characterized in part by its willingness to allow different religions to coexist or by its encouragement of inter-faith dialogue. (But this does raise an issue that will become important below, namely, how much commonality of interests and values, if any, can a conception of culture assume must obtain amongst the members of a culture before that conception becomes problematic?)

There is also a third view, or set of views, about what makes a conception of culture essentialist, which has an overtly normative character. The very presence of one or more of the following ideas, which each appeal to some ideal of authenticity, is often taken to be grounds for holding that an essentialist conception of culture is at work: the idea that we can distinguish a group's authentic culture; the idea that a culture can change and develop in authentic and inauthentic directions; the idea that a culture can be corrupted or "stolen." It may be that these ideas are regarded as essentialist because they are thought to presuppose a conception of culture which would count as such according to the first view I have distinguished: a group's authentic culture, it might be said, has to be understood as that part of its culture which exhibits the particular set of characteristics which make it what it is. But sometimes talk of authenticity in the context of culture is taken to be essentialist in its own right, thus invoking a distinctive account of what it is for a conception of culture to be essentialist.[7]

Of course, these normative claims about authenticity do not, by themselves, provide us with an account of what it is to share a culture. At best, they provide us with a means of distinguishing authentic and inauthentic cultures, or authentic and inauthentic practices, and make various

---

[7] See, for example, J. Squires, "Culture, Equality and Diversity," in *Multiculturalism Reconsidered*, ed. Kelly, p. 115.

normative claims about authenticity and inauthenticity. Nevertheless, according to the view I am considering, a conception of culture can count as essentialist simply in virtue of making these claims, independently of the account it is also obliged to give of what it is to share a culture.

When claims about the authenticity of a tradition or practice are made, they are generally understood in such a way that they license a number of evaluative judgments, for example, the judgment that there is always a reason to preserve a group's authentic culture, or that there is always a reason to prevent a group's culture from changing in an inauthentic direction, or that a group has a right to its authentic culture. But claims of this sort go well beyond either of the views I have so far considered. Consider the first view of what it is for a conception of culture to be essentialist. The idea that when a group of people share a culture, they share a set of characteristics, and that the particular characteristics they share make it the particular culture that it is, does not imply that there is always a reason to preserve a culture, and does not imply that the group has a right to its culture of a kind that could make sense of the idea that its culture can be stolen by others.[8] Nor does an account of culture which meets the criteria laid down by the second view, that is, any account which holds that cultures are separate, clearly bounded, or internally uniform, have normative implications of this kind.

If a group's authentic culture is simply that part of its culture which exhibits the particular set of characteristics which make it what it is, then claims about authenticity do appear to involve a commitment to essentialism when it is understood in terms of the first view. But claims about authenticity do not seem to incur any necessary commitment to essentialism on the second view of what this means, and indeed may be in tension with it. These claims have no implications for the issue of whether cultures must be discrete and may have implications that cut against the idea that cultures are necessarily internally uniform. For someone who opposes a cultural change on the grounds that it is inauthentic may lament the fact that the group's culture is no longer internally homogeneous because it consists of new practices that coexist alongside its traditional ones.

II.   What's wrong with essentialism?

Let me begin by assessing the second view I distinguished concerning what it is for a conception of culture to be essentialist, namely, that it

---

[8] See Walter Benn Michaels, *Our America: Nativism, Modernism, and Pluralism* (Durham and London: Duke University Press, 1995), p. 128.

regards cultures as separate, clearly bounded, and internally uniform, for here I think we can be brief. A conception of culture that views cultures in this way faces obvious problems. Although it is internally consistent, it is virtually useless for understanding actual groups, for almost none of them possess any of these features. The concept of a culture, so understood, would lack empirical application.[9] The "billiard ball" conception of culture is objectionable insofar as it seeks to impose a model that does not fit social reality.

It is not just that the billiard ball conception fails to match reality, however. One of the assumptions made by this conception, that cultures are internally uniform, with members sharing values and interests, may also mask the way in which policies aimed at accommodating or recognizing a cultural minority can affect different members of that minority in different ways, fostering conformity by setting up perverse incentives for them to adopt certain traditions and practices, and providing tools for some to dominate others.[10] A culture may contain subgroups whose interests diverge and there may also be divergence of interests within such groups between its ordinary members and its elite.[11] Once we acknowledge that cultures are internally diverse, the evaluation of a policy that aims to recognize or accommodate a cultural minority must take into account its effects on different groups within them, and the way in which that policy may affect the power relations between those groups.

When cultural essentialism is understood instead as the view that when a group shares a culture, they do so in virtue of sharing a number of characteristics, and the particular characteristics they share make it the particular culture that it is, then it is not clear why this should necessarily be regarded as problematic. Consider the most plausible variant of this view, namely, that when a group of people share a culture, they share a way of life, and this way of life makes that culture the particular culture it is. According to this view, if a culture's way of life were to change to such an extent that we were no longer able to regard it as the same way of life, then we would have to say that their culture had changed and, indeed, that they no longer had the same culture they once did. This view would also have to allow that a culture might disintegrate

[9] See Keesing, "Theories of Culture Revisited" and A. Vayda, "Actions, Variations, and Change: The Emerging Anti-Essentialist View in Anthropology," in *Assessing Cultural Anthropology*, ed. Borofsky, pp. 301–302.
[10] See C. Kukathas, "Are There Any Cultural Rights?," *Political Theory*, 20, 1992, pp. 105–139; N. Fraser, "Rethinking Recognition," *New Left Review*, 3, 2000, pp. 107–120; A. Rorty, "The Hidden Politics of Cultural Identification," *Political Theory*, 22, 1994, pp. 152–166.
[11] See Kukathas, "Are There Any Cultural Rights?," pp. 110–115.

altogether with nothing replacing it, so that a group of people no longer shared anything that could plausibly be regarded as a way of life. But neither of these possibilities that are allowed by the view appears to raise any real difficulties for it.

But does the view I am evaluating require groups to be internally homogeneous in a way that effectively commits it to essentialism in the second sense I distinguished, and which I have already agreed is problematic? In addressing this issue it is important to appreciate just how unrestrictive is the idea that people share a culture when they share a way of life. It would allow considerable internal variations to exist within a culture, for people may share a way of life without necessarily sharing the same interpretations of the rules that govern their practices, without living their lives in the same manner and also, more importantly, without sharing values or interests. Let me explain.

The rules that govern a practice may be open to different interpretations that generate divergent patterns of behavior, with the different participants nevertheless supposing that they are following the same rules, perhaps even contesting the proper interpretation of those rules. For example, members of a culture may disagree about whether its practices require property to be passed on to the first-born son or whether they allow it to be distributed equally between all the sons and daughters. Indeed a practice may itself be partially constituted by disagreement over the proper interpretation of the rules that govern it. For example, artistic activity might be partially constituted by disagreement over what constitutes a work of art.

The rules of a practice may also be interpreted in such a way that they specify different patterns of behavior for different groups of participants; for example, they may require men and women to act in very different ways. In consequence, a theorist might maintain that sharing a culture requires sharing a way of life but acknowledge that the identities of different participants in the same culture may vary depending on other significant facts about them and their experience. (A person might be regarded as French, culturally speaking, but what it means for her to be French might be affected by her sex and her ethnicity.)

Sharing a way of life also permits considerable divergences in values. To participate in the practices that make up a way of life, one must have some understanding of the rules that govern them and of the different interpretations these rules are given, and hence of the behavior that is expected of participants. But this is consistent with holding very different values and as a result having divergent attitudes and responses to these rules. Indeed, some may be dissidents, refusing to comply with conventional norms or conventional interpretations of them. Although they would not be following these norms in the sense of conforming to them, they might still be participants in the same practice and way of life because their behavior is a critical response to the norms, and hence in that sense involves acknowledging these norms and displays an understanding of them. So, for example, a farm laborer might refuse to show deference to a landowner by not touching his cap when he passed him, but we could still regard him as participating in a practice and way of life which involved a norm that required him to do so, or which was widely interpreted in those terms.

Still, however, the worry may persist that it is too restrictive to maintain that members of a culture must share a way of life. Can't differences within a culture go "all the way down," so that members of a culture lead such divergent lives, behave in such different ways, interpret norms so differently, or perhaps not even acknowledge the same norms, that it makes no sense to say that they share practices or a way of life? If differences were to go all the way down in this way, it is hard to see why we should say that the people concerned shared a culture. For what could justify our claim that they shared the same culture? (And if we are going to distinguish between, say, Japanese culture and Chinese culture, how could we do so unless we make reference to differences in ways of life or something similar?)

Questions such as these have led some cultural anthropologists to wonder whether we should abandon the idea of culture altogether, on the grounds that it must demand more uniformity or homogeneity than we will find if we observe human behavior rather than approach it with preconceptions about how it must be.[12] However, not all of those who think that the dominant conceptions of culture presuppose too much homogeneity to be of any explanatory value recommend abandoning the notion altogether. Some, such as Brian Street, propose that we should think of culture as "an active process of meaning making and contest."[13] But it is not clear that this genuinely provides us with a different view of culture. Suppose we were to interrogate this view with the question: what is it for people to share a culture? (If the idea of culture is to have any point at all, surely we need to be able to judge, sometimes at least, that two people share a culture or lack a shared culture.) On this

---

[12] See, for example, L. Abu-Lughod, "Writing Against Culture," in *Recapturing Anthropology: Working in the Present*, ed. R. Fox (Santa Fe: School of American Research Press, 1991).

[13] B. Street, "Culture is a Verb: Anthropological Aspects of Language and Cultural Process," in *Language and Culture*, ed. D. Graddol, L. Thompson, and M. Byram (British Association of Applied Linguistics in association with Multilingual Matters, 1993), p. 25.

view sharing a culture must presumably amount to participating together in an activity of meaning-making. Yet isn't this simply to participate in a shared practice or set of practices of some sort? And if a group of people participate together in an encompassing shared practice of this kind, why can't we say that they share a way of life?

We seem to have come full circle, back to the view that if people share a culture, then this consists, at least in part, in sharing a way of life. This may seem like a hollow victory, however, since it leaves open the possibility of abandoning altogether the idea that a group shares a culture, on the grounds that it is unrealistic to suppose they ever share something called "a way of life." But this option is not one most critics of essentialism would favor. In any case I would urge that abandoning the notion is unnecessary since sharing a way of life does not require a degree of uniformity that it is unrealistic to expect.

In response it might be said that sharing a way of life allows for diversity precisely because the idea of "a way of life" is so vague. The abstract characterization of a way of life that I have given places some constraints on what can count as one, but these are so minimal that (it might be claimed) it is hard to see how, for example, one might distinguish one way of life from another, especially when they overlap or one is supposedly nested in another. But I have already acknowledged that boundaries between ways of life, and therefore cultures, may be blurred. Furthermore, how we distinguish one practice from another, and also one way of life from another, depends in part upon the purposes of doing so. For some purposes, it may be defensible to talk about the manner in which hospitality is given and received in a particular region, and to suppose that there is a practice of hospitality in that region that is to some degree discontinuous with practices outside that region, whereas for other purposes there may be reason to emphasize the continuity between the practices in that region and the wider area of which that region is a part. This also means that whether we regard two people as sharing a culture may depend partly upon our purposes: for some purposes, we may regard people as sharing a culture, for example, European culture, whereas for others we regard them as inhabiting different cultures, for example, French culture and German culture. (Of course, these purposes may be partly or wholly normative. We may distinguish one way of life from another partly in order to capture the way in which a set of practices may be of fundamental importance to the well-being of those who participate in them: see pp. 237–240 below.)

The final set of views associated with essentialism, namely that we can distinguish a cultural group's authentic culture, or that a culture can be corrupted or stolen, or that it may develop in authentic or inauthentic directions, faces some deep difficulties – though I shall suggest that there are versions of these views that may be defensible. Describing a culture as authentic, or characterizing a change to it as inauthentic, or maintaining that a culture has been corrupted or that it has been stolen, is to make an evaluative judgment. Consider the idea that a culture can be stolen. In order to make sense of that idea, it seems that we would need to believe that a group owns its culture.[14] It is hard to see what could justify that idea (though, of course, members of a culture, or even in some cases the cultural group itself, may create artefacts or develop ideas which they can rightfully be said to own).

What of the idea that cultures may be authentic or inauthentic, or develop in authentic or inauthentic directions? Of course cultures and cultural change can be assessed from a normative perspective; we can always ask whether a culture (or elements of it) is good or bad, or whether a given change to it is good or bad. If the claim that a culture has changed in an inauthentic way simply registers the thought that it has changed for the worse for some reason or another, then it is unobjectionable in principle. But the charge that a culture has undergone an inauthentic change sometimes seems to rest on the specific idea that any change to a traditional practice marks a change in an inauthentic direction, that it corrupts the practice in some way or other, and that this is always bad in one respect. As such it would imply that any change to a traditional practice, for whatever reason, has something to be said against it simply because it marks a failure to preserve that tradition in its current form. Again, such a view is highly implausible. (We should not confuse it with a view that will be considered in the next section, that there is a reason to preserve a traditional practice when its collapse would place unreasonable or unfair burdens on its current participants.)

Are there any other ways of characterizing what makes a change in a practice inauthentic which might support the conclusion that inauthentic change is bad, in some respect at least? Consider one possibility: that a change is authentic only if it arises as a result of reasons that come from "within the culture," that is, which come from members of that culture or which are in some sense internal to its practices. If any change that arises as a result of reasons that originate from outside the way of life that constitutes the culture is inauthentic, it is hard to see why inauthentic change should always be regarded as bad, even in one respect. What matters, it might be said, is not where the reasons come from, but whether they are good or bad.

[14] See Michaels, *Our America*, p. 129.

Perhaps instead the thought is that a change in a traditional practice counts as inauthentic if it comes about as a result of costs that are in effect imposed on that practice by outsiders (suppose, for example, that the wider society levies a tax on the activities) or as a result of incentives that the wider society creates, either accidentally or in order to persuade them to give it up (suppose, for example, that the wider society subsidizes the setting up of small businesses to produce souvenirs for the tourist industry in order to persuade members of the cultural minority to give up their traditional fishing practices). In the most extreme cases, the costs imposed on a practice might amount to a form of coercion.

It is not clear why change that results from outsiders influencing the structure of costs and benefits attached to participating in a traditional practice should necessarily be regarded as objectionable. But in the extreme case where this amounts to coercion, and the change is in effect imposed, then we might agree that it is bad in one important respect. Different reasons are possible here. It may be that what makes it bad is that the coercion involved constitutes a violation of individual rights. But in that case the language of authenticity is not particularly helpful, since the fact that it is outsiders who have violated the rights is irrelevant to the argument. It would be better to speak simply of injustice to individuals. The language of authenticity would be more appropriate, however, if the idea is that imposition by outsiders violates a culture's right of self-determination. I shall not evaluate this argument here. It is not obviously flawed and there are different ways in which the idea that cultures have a right of self-determination might be defended. (There is the possibility, however, that the most promising defenses of it might be objectionably essentialist in some other way, for instance, by assuming that members of the culture share vital interests in its survival or its flourishing whereas in fact some do not. I shall return to this issue on pp. 237–240.)

III.   Multiculturalist arguments

Like the cultures with which they are concerned, the arguments of multiculturalists are diverse. In this section I propose to consider a range of these arguments to determine the extent to which they rest upon objectionable essentialist assumptions. I shall classify these arguments either by reference to their premises or by reference to their conclusions. (Because I classify them in this way, there is no reason to think that the different categories are mutually exclusive; one set of arguments distinguished in terms of their conclusions may overlap with another set of arguments distinguished in terms of their premises.)

Arguments for group representation

Arguments which defend the idea of group representation for cultural minorities might seem to be straightforwardly guilty of an objectionable form of essentialism.[15] For how could one defend group representation without at some point appealing to the objectionable "essentialist" idea that members of the group in question share the same interests? This requires a degree of internal uniformity that there is no reason to expect – indeed it might be said that there is more reason to expect conflicts of interest within groups – and seems committed to the second account of what it is for a conception of culture to be essentialist that I argued in section II made essentialism problematic. If we are to suppose that, say, an individual Sikh can represent Sikhs as a group, must not we be assuming that all Sikhs share the same interests? In what sense could a Sikh represent the interests of Sikhs unless there was some set of interests shared by Sikhs in general?[16] This may in turn have damaging political effects: group representation itself may become a device by which elite members of these groups pursue their own interests and agenda, in effect using group representation as a tool to dominate other members.

There is no doubt that group representation can be abused. Individuals who represent groups can use their power to pursue their own interests, or the interests of some elite to which they belong. But that is true of any form of representation. The more difficult question is: must a defense of group representation in the case of cultural minorities be founded on some assumption of uniformity that is false and which means that group representation in this case lends itself more readily to the abuse of power?

Although I think it is right to approach arguments for group representation with worries about essentialism at the front of our minds, a number of these arguments appear to avoid the pitfalls of essentialism, on any reasonable account of what this involves. For example, we might appeal to the idea that group representation has symbolic significance: that it symbolizes inclusion within the polity and thereby promotes a sense of belonging to the polity, which is especially important for members of groups that have been discriminated against or marginalized

---

[15] Of course not all arguments for group representation presuppose that members of the relevant group share a culture. Some feminists argue for the representation of women but they need not claim that all women share a culture.

[16] See Barry, *Culture and Equality*, p. 11, p. 330 n. 16; Barry, "Second Thoughts – and Some First Thoughts Revived," in *Multiculturalism Reconsidered*, ed. Kelly, p. 211; Jaggar, "Multicultural Democracy," p. 314.

in various other ways.[17] Of course, some radical members of disadvantaged groups might think that promoting such a sense of belonging would be a bad thing (perhaps because it would defuse effective resistance to unjust policies) but that would not make this argument essentialist: it need not suppose that all members of such a group will regard the promotion of a sense of belonging as beneficial.

It might be claimed, however, that once we move beyond this kind of argument to one which appeals to the idea that the content of law and policy would be different, more just perhaps, were disadvantaged groups to receive direct representation in legislatures, we must be invoking some essentialist claim about the convergence of interests amongst members of these groups. In response, however, it needs to be emphasized that these arguments might suppose some degree of convergence of interests, without assuming unanimity.[18] The claim that the shared experience of members of some group has led to some degree of convergence of interests amongst them would stand in need of defense, including empirical evidence, but it is not obviously flawed. We may also think that, in some cases, members of a cultural group may share experiences in a way that, even though it does not generate shared interests, nevertheless justifies policies of group representation on the grounds that members of the group are in a better position to provide well-informed comment or argument on issues that relate to this shared experience. Iris Young makes the point in this way: "People in different groups often know about somewhat different institutions, events, practices, and social relations, and often have different perceptions of the same institutions, relations, or events. For this reason members of some groups are sometimes in a better position than members of others to understand and anticipate the probable consequences of implementing particular social policies."[19]

Still it might be thought that none of this justifies the idea that, say, an individual Sikh can represent Sikhs as a group, even if it justifies, for example, reserving some seats in a legislature specifically for Sikhs. Even if the inclusion of Sikhs within the legislative has symbolic significance, promotes a sense of belonging, and in some cases provides knowledge of a kind that is less readily available to non-Sikhs, why should we say that

---

[17] See A. Phillips, *The Politics of Presence* (Oxford: Oxford University Press, 1995), p. 45; David Macdonald, "Difference and Belonging: Liberal Citizenship and Modern Multiplicity," doctoral dissertation, London School of Economics and Political Science, 2002, Part 3.

[18] See Phillips, *The Politics of Presence*, p. 158.

[19] I. Young, *Justice and the Politics of Difference* (Princeton: Princeton University Press, 1990), p. 186.

those Sikhs who serve on the legislative represent Sikhs in general? This is a genuine challenge but note that if it rests upon the idea that a person can represent a group only if he or she shares the same interests as all members of that group, then this raises quite general practical difficulties for the view that an individual may represent a group. Those who believe that a Member of Parliament can represent his constituents could hardly claim that he shares the same interests as all of those constituents on any important issue, not even in relation to issues that bear directly upon the constituency, for example whether a motorway should be built through it.

The idea of political representation is a complex one, but if it did require that all those who are being represented share the same interests, then for all practical purposes we should simply have to abandon it. It would be premature to think of abandoning it, however. We can make sense of the idea of an individual representing a group without invoking the idea that they all share the same interests (and indeed we can allow that an individual may represent a group which contains conflicting interests), provided that we can properly think of him as acting on behalf of, and accountable to, those he is supposed to be representing. This is at least part of what we ordinarily mean when we talk about representation. For example, when we say that a Member of Parliament represents his constituents, we sometimes mean no more than that he speaks on their behalf, that his authority to do so comes from the fact that he is elected by his constituents, and that he can be held to account for his actions by those constituents.[20] More generally, we might say that the idea of group representation is intelligible in this way provided those who are said to represent the group are elected by the members of the group and only the members of the group.[21] It follows, however, that on this conception men may in principle represent women, for a man could in principle be elected by women as a group to speak on their behalf. If proposals for including members of previously disadvantaged groups in assemblies are unwilling to countenance this idea even in principle, they should give up the language of representation. (This would not of course require abandoning the proposal itself, for that can be defended without invoking the idea of representation, as we saw above.)

---

[20] In her classic study, Hannah Pitkin acknowledges that these are central uses of the term "representation": see H. Pitkin, *The Concept of Representation* (Berkeley: University of California Press, 1967), especially chs. 2–3.

[21] This is one of the arguments developed by David Macdonald, "Difference and Belonging," ch. 4.

Arguments based upon the idea that recognition of cultural identities is a human need

It is sometimes held that members of minority cultural groups have a need for due recognition of their cultural identities. Charles Taylor, for example, argues that due recognition of cultural identities is not just a courtesy that we owe people but is a vital human need.[22] But is this idea in some way or other founded upon an objectionable essentialist view of culture? The short answer is that it may be but it does not have to be. We can recognize a cultural identity without supposing that cultures are discrete entities or internally uniform. We can also give due recognition to a cultural identity without having to suppose that this means recognizing some "authentic identity" that has to be distinguished from any false or inauthentic identity that has been adopted by some members of the group. (And even if we do distinguish between authentic and inauthentic identity we might do so in an unproblematic way, for example by appealing to the idea that an identity is fully authentic only if it is freely negotiated and not imposed by outsiders or by some sub-set of the group.)

But does the very idea of "recognizing an identity" presuppose that there is an uncontested identity that is in some way independent of whatever social, political, and economic institutions might be put in place, thus ignoring the way in which identities are, in general, partly a product of the interaction between individuals and some set of these institutions? The idea that cultural identities should be given due recognition in the design and operation of democratic procedures, and in the content of law and policy, need not deny that these identities are themselves the product of a complex process that is inherently "dialogical" in character, involving contest and conflict, and deeply affected by existing social, political, and economic institutions.[23] But once we acknowledge the complex processes of identity formation, we will need to accept that what constitutes "giving due recognition" will itself vary over time, be affected by changes in the wider social, political, and economic context, and be a matter of contest. (This is so even if we suppose that it is a person's authentic identity that requires recognition, and that his identity is authentic when it is freely negotiated with other members of the groups to which he belongs, for this position still maintains that his authentic identity is a product of his social interactions.)

---

[22] See C. Taylor, "The Politics of Recognition," in *Multiculturalism and the "Politics of Recognition,"* ed. A. Gutmann (Princeton: Princeton University Press, 1992), p. 26.
[23] See Taylor, "The Politics of Recognition."

Indeed we might begin to wonder whether the relevant human need has been specified inaccurately: perhaps it is a need to struggle for recognition, to be involved in constantly renegotiating the terms of citizenship as forms of misrecognition are challenged, and contest arises over whether there has been a failure to give due recognition, rather than a need to achieve some end-state.[24]

Arguments that appeal to the way in which the flourishing of members of cultural groups depends upon the prosperity of those groups

Avishai Margalit and Joseph Raz attempt to establish the conclusion that cultural groups, or some sub-set of them, have a right to self-determination by appealing to the way in which individual flourishing can depend upon the flourishing of cultural groups to which they belong.[25] In particular they focus on membership of what they call encompassing groups, which are defined, in part, in terms of possessing a wide-ranging shared culture. They argue that the flourishing of members of these groups is deeply dependent upon the flourishing of the groups, and that under some conditions (for example, when these groups are being persecuted or neglected) the best way of securing the prosperity of encompassing groups is to grant them some degree of self-determination.

Does Raz and Margalit's argument rest upon objectionable essentialist assumptions? They don't regard encompassing groups (or the culture that members of these groups share) as separate and clearly bounded, but do they suppose that these groups are internally homogeneous? They do seem to assume that almost all members of these groups share at least one vital interest, namely, an interest in the prosperity of the group. For they suppose that the well-being of members of an encompassing group is intimately connected with the flourishing of that group. This needn't amount to an assumption of complete internal uniformity, however, for people may share an interest in the prosperity of a group despite having very different values. Nor, indeed, are Raz and Margalit assuming that there is one authentic culture which binds together an encompassing group and that merits protection.

---

[24] See J. Tully, "Citizenship, Democracy and Diversity: Rethinking Identity Politics and Struggles for Recognition," The Hannah Arendt Memorial Lecture, delivered at the University of Southampton on 9 June 1998, p. 13; J. Maclure, "Disenchantment and Democracy: Public Reason under Conditions of Pluralism," doctoral dissertation, University of Southampton, 2003, ch. 6.

[25] See A. Margalit and J. Raz, "National Self-Determination," *Journal of Philosophy*, 87, 1990, pp. 439–461.

Nevertheless, the idea that almost all members of an encompassing group share a vital interest in its survival is a demanding assumption. Might it not be the case that a significant number of members of the group cannot flourish within it and that their best hope of flourishing lies outside of it? The idea that the members of an encompassing group have a vital interest in its survival also seems to entail that they do not belong to any other cultural groups that have real significance for them, the membership of which would allow them to continue to flourish if the encompassing group they belong to were to decline. (Note, however, that Raz and Margalit are not claiming that all cultural groups are encompassing groups. In order for a cultural group to be encompassing in the relevant sense, its common culture must be pervasive, covering a whole range of areas that are of great importance for the well-being of individuals. They can leave it an open question how many cultural groups fall into this category.)

Will Kymlicka has developed perhaps the most influential argument that attempts to forge a link between cultural preservation and individual well-being. In broad outline it maintains that a culture, or more strictly, what Kymlicka calls "a societal culture," provides the structure within which we make our choices. Were this structure to disintegrate, the individuals left behind would be "at sea," unable to lead lives or make choices that they could find meaningful.[26] Some have objected to this argument on the grounds that it appeals to a controversial value, the value of autonomy, that some cultures may not accept, or indeed that some members of a particular culture may contest, and hence that it presupposes a degree of uniformity that is absent. There is one strand of Kymlicka's argument that appears vulnerable to this objection, but there are other strands which are left unscathed by it; for Kymlicka appeals to the importance of being able to lead a life that one finds meaningful, something which presumably anyone, whatever their cultural membership, will value.

Does Kymlicka's argument rest upon essentialist assumptions? Clearly he is not distinguishing between authentic and inauthentic cultures then arguing for the preservation of only authentic cultures, so he is not committed to the objectionable kind of essentialism that this move might involve. Indeed he distinguishes between the structure and character of a cultural community in a way that clearly separates his approach from one that appeals to an ideal of authenticity.[27] He

---

[26] See W. Kymlicka, *Liberalism, Community and Culture* (Oxford: Oxford University Press, 1991), esp. chs. 8–9; W. Kymlicka, *Multicultural Citizenship* (Oxford: Oxford University Press, 1995), esp. chs. 5–6.

[27] See Kymlicka, *Liberalism, Community and Culture*, pp. 166–169.

maintains that changes in the character of a cultural community do not provide any grounds for intervening to protect its original character nor for enabling its members to do so. But he argues that when the very structure of a cultural community is under threat, then intervention to protect it, perhaps by providing its members with group differentiated rights which enable them to sustain it, may be justified because individual members of that community through no fault of their own will find it hard, perhaps impossible, to flourish without it.

Some critics of Kymlicka, such as Jeremy Waldron, have claimed that his argument rests on the assumption that each of us belongs to a single culture which has a particular structure.[28] Waldron argues that this misrepresents the truth, that instead we are faced with an array of cultural materials, but no single cultural structure that gives meaning to our lives. Does this amount to the charge that Kymlicka holds an essentialist view of culture? Waldron's argument does connect up with concerns about essentialism. It raises the question of whether Kymlicka is exaggerating the extent to which individuals are reliant on the persistence of a single societal culture for their prosperity. If individuals are members of more than one overlapping cultural group, their interests in the survival of a particular one of these cultural groups may vary. In other words, Kymlicka may again seem to be presupposing an unrealistic degree of internal uniformity in terms of the interests of members of cultural groups, one way in which an approach may be objectionably essentialist.

But note that Kymlicka's argument can be adapted so that it need not presuppose that all the members of a cultural community, or all those who share a societal culture, must share the same vital interest in its preservation. Alan Patten, for example, points out that one reason for saying that people may be so deeply affected by the destruction of a particular cultural community that they are unable to lead a life they can find meaningful might be that they are unable to acquire the language, or languages, required to be able to participate to any significant extent in the wider society.[29] This argument will apply at best to only some members of the disintegrating community, for many are likely to know already the language used by the wider society or at least to possess the capacity needed to acquire it. But then we can see Kymlicka's argument as applying only to those individuals whose vital interests are damaged in this way by cultural disintegration. This might make it hard to justify providing all members of the culture with a group-differentiated right as

---

[28] See J. Waldron, "Minority Cultures and the Cosmopolitan Alternative," in *The Rights of Minority Cultures*, ed. W. Kymlicka (Oxford: Oxford University Press, 1995).

[29] See A. Patten, "Liberal Egalitarianism and the Case for Supporting National Cultures," *The Monist*, 82, 1999, pp. 387–410.

a means of protecting the interests of this sub-group, but it would nevertheless support the conclusion that ignoring the effects of cultural disintegration on this sub-group would be to allow an injustice to take place.

Arguments for providing exemptions for cultural groups from laws and policies

There is also a range of arguments in the multiculturalist literature for providing exemptions from law and policy on the grounds that these are necessary to protect a traditional cultural practice even though the way of life as a whole is not under threat.[30] These arguments sometimes suppose that when a practice has been a central part of a group's way of life, then this provides a reason, often a sufficient reason, to take steps to preserve that practice. Some versions of this argument appeal to an idea of authenticity of a kind that I have argued is problematic because they invoke the idea that there is always a reason for preserving a culture's traditional practices. In general, however, we should not suppose that arguments for protecting a cultural practice must rely on objectionable essentialist assumptions. They may rely instead on the idea that the demise of a practice would place unfair burdens on its participants, together with an appeal to a general principle that when law or policy has this effect on members of a cultural group there is a case for exempting them from its requirements. One much-discussed example of this is the exemption in English law that allows Sikhs to ride motorbikes without a crash helmet provided that they wear their turbans. Requiring everyone, including Sikhs, to wear a crash helmet on a motorbike would, it is argued, place an unfair burden on Sikhs for they would be faced with a choice between not riding a motorbike or violating a requirement that is part of their religion.

This sort of approach might, in principle, allow us to justify a range of exemptions from laws and policies, though it would require some account of how we are to determine whether a burden is unfair or not. As Brian Barry points out, the mere fact that a law or policy imposes greater burdens on some rather than others is not sufficient to show that that the greater burden is unfair on those who suffer it.[31] A defender of

---

[30] See Tully, *Strange Multiplicity*, pp. 169–172. Tully has subsequently made it clear he does not think that the centrality of a traditional practice to a way of life provides any reason, on its own, to protect it: see J. Tully, "The Illiberal Liberal: Brian Barry's Polemical Attack on Multiculturalism," in *Multiculturalism Reconsidered*, ed. Kelly, esp. p. 107.

[31] See Barry, *Culture and Equality*, p. 34.

this style of argument would also need to address the contention that members of a minority culture can legitimately be required to bear the costs of their commitment to that culture, in much the same way those with expensive tastes, such as an expensive taste for champagne, should bear the costs of those tastes.[32] My purpose is not to defend a practice of making exemptions on cultural grounds, but merely to show that it need not rest upon problematic essentialist assumptions.

It might be argued that arguments of this sort are always guilty of one kind of objectionable essentialism, however. They must always make assumptions about the centrality of a practice to a group, whilst in truth its centrality will always be a matter of contest within that group. Even if that is so as a matter of empirical fact, it is not clear that it is fatal to the "rule plus exemption" approach. In principle at least, members of a group could be given an equal say in the formulation of any proposal for an exemption from a general law. Of course the law may still end up serving the interests of some members – those who regard the exemption as necessary to facilitate a practice they regard as central to their identity – without promoting the interests of others. This is not necessarily objectionable, however, provided the interests of the other members are not damaged by the exemption. The more difficult case, which does raise issues of fairness, is when some gain the benefit of being exempted from a rule even though they would not have to suffer the relevant extra burden were they to be required to obey it. For example, Sikhs who do not care whether they wear a turban or not will be able to enjoy the freedom of riding a bike without a helmet provided that they nevertheless wear a turban.

What about arguments for providing exemptions from policy in order to permit the *resurrection* of a practice that was once traditional for a particular cultural group but has since faded away? Must these arguments rest on essentialist assumptions? For example, the Makah Indians requested an exemption (in the form of a quota) from the International Whaling Commission's ban on whaling, partly on the grounds that although none of them had whaled for seventy years, they nevertheless had a cultural right to resurrect the practice.[33] This argument might seem to make an objectionable appeal to authenticity, for it might seem to involve the idea that there is always a reason to preserve or sustain traditional practices. That would be so if the argument is simply that

---

[32] Ibid., pp. 34–35.
[33] See www.makah.com/whales.htm. (I am grateful to Julie Reeves for this reference. She discusses these issues further in her doctoral dissertation, "The Historical Development of 'Culture' in IR: Word and Concepts," University of Southampton, 2001, pp. 84–86.) See also Barry, *Culture and Equality*, pp. 254–255.

whaling is one of the Makah's traditional practices (even though they are no longer involved in it) and that therefore they have a right to resurrect it.

But is this the only way of interpreting their argument? Of course the Makah may have a variety of different reasons for wanting to return to whaling that are not wedded to an objectionable notion of authenticity. But the crucial question for the purpose of this chapter is whether it is possible to reconstruct the argument that they have a cultural right to kill whales in a way that does not presuppose such a notion. On certain assumptions, it may be possible to do so. For example, if the practice had died out as a result of the oppressive intervention of outsiders, then it might be argued that the group should be granted a right to resurrect it. (Indeed it might be said that the change in practices was inauthentic precisely because it was in effect imposed from outside the culture: see section II.) It might be contended that compensation is merited because members of the cultural group would be better off today if that oppressive intervention had not happened, and that the best way in practice to compensate them is to allow them, perhaps even help them, to resurrect the practice. Again, my purpose is not fully to assess this line of argument, but merely to determine whether it must rest upon some objectionable kind of essentialism. If it could plausibly be reconstructed in the way I have suggested, it would seem that it does not need to do so. For it need not suppose that all members of the relevant cultural group possess a vital interest in the survival of the practice, nor that all were adversely affected by its demise. The idea would be that the best practical means to provide compensation for past injustice would be to allow the practice to be resurrected, even if this would mean that some would benefit who had not suffered the consequences of injustice and that some would not receive compensation even though they had suffered the consequences of injustice.

IV.   Conclusion

Essentialism can be objectionable, but it is not always so. Its objectionable forms do sometimes infect the arguments of multiculturalists, but not in a way that ultimately defeats many of their arguments. The main ones that I have considered either do not invoke a flawed essentialist view of culture, or if they do so, they can be reconstructed in order to avoid relying upon one. When these arguments are considered in the light of the critique of essentialism, however, it becomes apparent that they often rely on empirically sensitive claims about the adverse effects on members of cultural groups that can be caused by a failure to give due recognition to them, or by the destruction or neglect of their traditional practices or way of life, or by the implementation of culture-blind laws and policies. The claim is often that members of a cultural group have a vital interest in the preservation of their traditional practices or way of life, or a vital interest in being exempted from a given law or policy, or a vital interest in due recognition. Even when these claims take into account the differences between members of a cultural group and the way in which their interests may vary, there is still the question of whether members of these groups, and their cultures, may be more adaptable than the claims allow.

Indeed in a related context Brian Barry argues that it is "profoundly patronizing" to suppose that Aboriginal cultures are so fragile that they are incapable of adapting to change.[34] This accusation is likely to be met by the counter-charge that Barry underestimates the burdens associated with change in a way that belittles the achievement of those who succeed in adapting and ignores the plight of those who genuinely cannot. The truth, no doubt, lies somewhere between the extreme view that adapting to cultural change is always either impossible or unfairly burdensome, and the view that the burdens associated with such change are never any greater than those borne by, say, a middle-aged worker who needs to retrain because the industry in which he has been employed is no longer economically viable. What follows from this, in terms of the justice of providing cultural groups with exemptions from law or policy, or the justice of intervening in some other way to protect (or enable them to protect) their traditional practices, is a further question that goes beyond the scope of the present chapter, for it would require a more comprehensive evaluation of the arguments I described in the previous section. This in turn would require some account of when minorities may justly be asked to bear burdens that members of the dominant group escape. The aim of this chapter was simply to assess the charge of essentialism against multiculturalism in order to clear the way for a proper consideration of these arguments.

[34] See Barry, *Culture and Equality*, p. 256.

Liberalism, multiculturalism, and the
problem of internal minorities

Daniel M. Weinstock

I attempt to do two things in this chapter. First, I provide the reader
with an overview of debates surrounding the responsibilities of the liberal state towards "internal minorities" – those citizens whose rights
might be threatened by the authority vested in minority communities by
theories and practices of multicultural accommodation. I suggest that it
may be much harder than some liberal theorists of multicultural
accommodation seem to think it is to square the liberal's traditional
commitment to individual rights with the granting of cultural autonomy,
at least if we accept the terms in which the debate has been set in recent
years. Second, I suggest some avenues that might be explored by theorists wanting to break out of the impasse in which debates over minority rights have become mired.

A word about the scope restriction of this chapter. It situates itself
squarely within the liberal tradition. Thus, I ask whether liberalism can
both hold to its traditional commitment to individual rights and welfare,
and accommodate group autonomy. I do not ask whether group
autonomy is good *simpliciter*.

There are two principal reasons for this. First, I am convinced that the
forms of political association that will prove over time to best conduce to
human happiness and flourishing will be recognizably liberal democratic. In the context of this chapter, I must allow this to stand as an
unargued starting point. Second, I do not think that there is anything
like a single theory called "liberalism." As we shall see, liberalism should
rather be thought of as a family of concepts, values, institutional
arrangements, and practices that do not cohere into anything quite so
neat as a *theory*. As Kwame Anthony Appiah has aptly put it, the liberal
tradition "is not so much a body of doctrine as a set of debates."[1]
So to ask whether group autonomy can find its place within the

---

[1] Kwame Anthony Appiah, *The Ethics of Identity* (Princeton: Princeton University Press,
2005), p. ix.

liberal-democratic framework should not shoehorn the discussion to too great a degree.

This chapter also deliberately sets aside what might be termed *deliberative democratic* approaches to the problems raised by multi-culturalism. Some theorists have in recent years defended the view that in order to face up to the problems raised by deep diversity, liberal democracies should become more *democratic*. They hold that as liberal norms and institutions might legitimately be seen by some members of a pluralist social order as reflecting the traditions and values of particular groups within that society, the weight traditionally afforded to such norms and institutions ought to be given over to democratic *practices*. The deliberative democratic approach thus circumvents some of the problems that liberal theories have in meeting the challenges of diversity, while raising others. Considerations of space prevent me from discussing such approaches here. A full consideration of their promise and limitations will have to await another occasion.[2]

I.

Many political philosophers working within the liberal framework have come to believe that liberal justice not only permits, but actually *requires* that liberal states provide cultural minorities with a certain degree of collective autonomy. Many liberal values seem to converge on this general conclusion. A principled concern with individual *autonomy*, combined with the recognition of the fact that autonomy cannot be exercised in a vacuum, has led some to the conclusion that liberal states must protect certain kinds of cultural groups because they provide their members with "contexts of choice."[3] A commitment to value pluralism has led some to the conclusion that cultural groups should be allowed to organize their internal affairs as they see fit, because the plurality of ways of life reflects the plurality of legitimate values and value orderings.[4] The imposition of the values of the majority as they are enshrined through the laws and institutions of the state would, according to this view, amount to a denial of pluralism.

---

[2] Simone Chambers, *Reasonable Democracy: Jürgen Habermas and the Politics of Discourse* (Ithaca: Cornell University Press, 1996); Monique Deveaux, *Cultural Pluralism and Dilemmas of Justice* (Ithaca: Cornell University Press, 2000); and Anthony Simon Laden, *Reasonably Radical: Deliberative Liberalism and the Politics of Identity* (Ithaca: Cornell University Press, 2001), are leading exponents of the deliberative democratic approach.

[3] Will Kymlicka, *Multicultural Citizenship* (Oxford: Oxford University Press, 1995).

[4] William A. Galston, *Liberal Pluralism* (Cambridge: Cambridge University Press, 2002); John Gray, *Two Faces of Liberalism* (New York: New Press, 2000).

Toleration and freedom of association are also values close to the core of liberal theory and practice that have been taken by some as grounding an argument for group autonomy.[5]

Let us call the family of theories that are grounded in arguments that start from some recognizably liberal value and end up on the basis of that value arguing for some degree of group autonomy *liberal theories of multicultural accommodation*, or LTMAs for short. These theories are quite diverse both in the types of groups that they see as appropriate holders of group rights and in the kinds of rights that they deem it appropriate to ascribe, but they are united in thinking that many groups ought to be able to run some aspect of their internal affairs without interference of the political and legal institutions representing the broader society.[6]

The worry has been voiced by many in recent years that LTMAs, grounded though they might be in values that seem impeccably liberal on their face, actually represent a grave danger for the theory and the practice of liberal democracy. The reason is this: liberalism is above all a theory of individual rights. Liberal democracies, if they do anything at all, must ensure that the rights of their members are realized. There is obviously great debate among liberals about what the scope of these rights should be. Do they encompass social and economic rights, or does the sanctity of rights depend upon their being limited to a relatively short list of civil and political rights? But the critics of LTMAs have argued that multicultural accommodations risk cutting at the very heart of liberalism: by granting groups powers to organize their internal affairs as they see fit, power would in effect be vested in the most powerful elites within these groups to lord it over their members without the kinds of constitutional constraints and dispersals of power that are part and parcel of the organization of liberal states. This places individual members of these groups at risk. They are subjected to the decision-making power of their elites, but do not possess the recourse that other citizens do. Other citizens are indeed protected by laws enacted democratically and by charters of rights. But what the claims of groups against the state often amount to is precisely to be exempted from the reach of such laws and charters. In practice, this has created particular

---

[5] Chandran Kukathas, *The Liberal Archipelago* (Oxford: Oxford University Press, 2003).

[6] For a thorough account of the kinds of rights that might be claimed by groups, see Jacob Levy, "Classifying Culture Rights," in *Ethnicity and Group Rights*, ed. I. Shapiro and W. Kymlicka (New York: New York University Press, 2000). For an interesting recent account of the full range of types of groups to which group rights can apply, see Robert Sparrow, "Defending Deaf Culture: The Case of Cochlear Implants," *Journal of Political Philosophy*, 13 (2), 2005.

vulnerability for the most powerless members of these groups, most often women[7] and children.[8]

Various ripostes are available to those theorists who want to continue to affirm the rights of collectivities to govern their affairs according to their own norms without thereby countenancing illiberal practices within these collectivities. One of them, again due to Will Kymlicka,[9] states that liberal regimes should allow groups to put up external protections in order to protect themselves from assimilation, but should frown upon internal restrictions. As Kymlicka himself acknowledges, however, the distinction is hard to make out in practice. Are educational provisions aimed at ensuring that the children of members will continue to speak an embattled language best thought of as an external protection (it is after all aimed at protecting the language from something "outside," namely another language) or as an internal restriction (since it curtails the educational choices of members)? Are rules that religious groups enact in order to define who counts as one of the faithful best seen as demarcating with clean lines the faithful from those who lie outside the faith, or as targeting internal dissidents (gays and lesbians for example) who by their espousal of practices or beliefs viewed by the elites as "external" to the faith have placed themselves outside? It turns out that most measures that groups will promulgate in order to protect themselves have both an internal and an external dimension.

Partisans of some version or other of LTMAs have in recent years argued that the best way to reconcile group autonomy and support for individual rights is to ensure that *exit rights* are in place for internal dissidents and for other internal minorities.[10] The argument runs as follows: if an individual is subject to illiberal treatment as a member of a group, and yet decides to maintain her membership in it, though she possesses the right to exit, then her continued adherence can be taken as a sign of consent. The liberal state has on this view no place getting in the way of individuals accepting subordinate positions within their personal relations, or agreeing that as women, or as members of a certain caste, they and people like them can never aspire to positions of

---

[7] Susan M. Okin, *Is Multiculturalism Bad for Women?* (Princeton: Princeton University Press, 1999); Susan M. Okin, "'Mistresses of Their Own Destiny': Group Rights, Gender, and Realistic Rights of Exit," *Ethics*, 112 (2), 2002; Ayelet Shachar, *Multicultural Jurisdictions* (Cambridge: Cambridge University Press, 2001).

[8] Robert Reich, "Minors within Minorities," in *Minorities within Minorities*, ed. Avigail Eisenberg and Jeff Spinner-Halev (Cambridge: Cambridge University Press, 2005).

[9] Kymlicka, *Multicultural Citizenship*.

[10] Kukathas, *The Liberal Archipelago*; Galston, *Liberal Pluralism*; Jeff Spinner-Halev, "Autonomy, Association and Pluralism," in *Minorities within Minorities*, ed. Eisenberg and Spinner-Halev.

authority and decision-making, so long as the consent condition is in place. So the role of the state is not to tell collectivities what they can and cannot do to their members, but rather to ensure that members of the collectivities have a secure right of exit.

Opponents of LTMA have argued that the exit rights strategy is inadequate, because it makes the dissident or the member of an oppressed internal minority pay an inordinately high price for the illiberality and repressiveness of her group.[11] Many people may identify quite strongly with the very groups that oppress them. A religious person may be extremely devout and unable to conceive of leaving her faith community, even if she is extremely badly treated within it. Though exit may be a theoretical option for her, she might have great difficulty imagining her life on the "outside," and in any case be quite psychologically and materially ill-equipped for it. The price exacted by exit is thus extremely high for such a person. It seems unfair that the state should tolerate that such individuals be forced to choose between continued harsh treatment within their communities and the high cost of exit, all on the pretext of tolerating groups that do not ascribe the same value as do liberal democracies to autonomy and equality.

The riposte given by defenders of advocates of LTMAs (as well as by some skeptics)[12] is that there are some costs that states simply cannot compensate, as they are intrinsically related to ceasing membership in a group with which one has long identified. The state can enact rules designed to ensure that groups are unable to place prohibitive material costs upon members who decide to leave (say by preventing them from removing any private property from the community), but it cannot do anything about what it will cost the individual personally no longer to belong to the group, and no longer to be able to associate with friends and family that may decide to shun her.[13] As Jacob Levy points out, "to have a culture whose exit is costless ... is to have no culture at all."[14] Some of the relations that contribute most to the value of our lives are the ones that place us in a position of heightened vulnerability to loss. They are so valuable that to lose them would be unimaginably painful, and yet the anticipation of pain is no reason to abstain from them. And it

---

[11] Okin, "'Mistresses of Their Own Destiny'"; Shachar, *Multicultural Jurisdictions*; Daniel Weinstock, "Beyond Exit Rights: Reframing the Debate," in *Minorities within Minorities*, ed. Eisenberg and Spinner-Halev.

[12] Brian Barry, *Culture and Equality* (Cambridge, MA: Harvard University Press, 2001), pp. 150–152.

[13] Ibid., pp. 150–154.

[14] Jacob Levy, *The Multiculturalism of Fear* (Oxford: Oxford University Press, 2000), p. 112; Jeff Spinner-Halev, *Surviving Diversity* (Baltimore: Johns Hopkins University Press, 2000), p. 72.

is none of the state's business to regulate relationships that risk exacting this kind of cost.

This response cannot fully vindicate the exit rights strategy. For there is all the difference in the world between the costs one incurs by leaving an association with which one greatly identifies, simply in virtue of the centrality of the beliefs and practices of the association to one's identity and conception of the good life, and those that are imposed by other people's intentional manipulation of the costs. No harm has been done to me if I experience tremendous suffering in leaving my religious community of my own accord, because of the continued hold that its rituals, practices, and personal relations have upon me. But I am harmed if others knowingly manipulate the costs that exit will entail, precisely so as to make it less likely that I will exercise my exit right even though I endure hardships and discrimination at the hands of other members of the community.

It should also be pointed out that the coherence of the exit rights strategy very much depends on how the notion of an effective exit right is cashed out. Defenders of LTMAs who rely on exit rights in order to secure the compatibility of group autonomy with the liberal protection of individual rights face a dilemma: Either they defend exit rights in a minimal manner, so that any person who does not literally face physical obstacles to leaving is considered to possess adequate exit rights,[15] or they impose conditions that have to be fulfilled in order for a "bare" right of exit to become "real."[16] In the former case, problems emerge for the defender of LTMAs' claim that the failure to avail oneself of exit rights can stand proxy for consent. Indeed, physical accessibility is compatible with all manner of brainwashing, psychological bullying, and cultivated ignorance of options. We wouldn't normally say of someone who failed to satisfy minimal psychological and epistemic conditions, and who found herself in circumstances of intimidation and fear, that her continued participation in a practice in any way signified consent. To see this, think of what we would say to someone who in a clinical context attempted to persuade us of a person unaware of her options and in any case unable to access them psychologically, and/or subjected to pressure amounting to coercion, that she met the standards of informed consent to a medical act.

In the latter case, however, what is imperiled is the defender of LTMAs' commitment to cultural autonomy. Consider William Galston's account of the conditions that in his view must be in place in

---

[15] Kukathas, *The Liberal Archipelago*, pp. 103–114.
[16] Galston, *Liberal Pluralism*, p. 123.

order for exit rights to be "meaningful." In Galston's view,[17] four sets of conditions have to be satisfied. In order to have exit rights worthy of the name, an individual must be *aware* of options open to her outside the association to which she belongs; she must be able to *assess* them and to view them as real options *for her*; she must be free from coercion; and finally, she must have aptitudes and abilities that enable her to take part in the practices of other associations.

There can be no doubt that where these four sets of conditions are in place to a tolerable degree, individuals who belong to groups and associations of various kinds will be secure in their possession of exit rights. But it is worth reflecting on the breadth and extent of state action that will be required to ensure that these conditions *are* in fact in place. Now, we can assume that the knowledge conditions of which Galston writes will almost automatically be in place for all but the most isolated minority groups living in the context of modern societies. Orthodox Jews, Mennonites, Amish, and others, live cheek by jowl with people leading all kinds of lives and pursuing myriad conceptions of the good. For example, Nomi, the heroine of Miriam Toews's *A Complicated Kindness*, about life in a Mennonite community in rural Manitoba, lives in frustrated awareness of ways of life that she fears she will never be able to participate in.[18]

But the other conditions will doubtless require substantial intervention. Precisely because they cannot shelter their young from an *awareness* of the options that lie close at hand within the broader society, minority communities often enact all kinds of material, epistemic, and psychological barriers designed to prevent them from being able to *access* them. They sometimes attempt to present these options as debased and immoral (think of many communities' strictures against intermarriage, or against women entering the workplace), thus contravening the condition that Galston sees as central to exit rights, according to which individuals must be able to assess options on their merits.

My principal claim in this context is this: were the state systematically to see to it that all citizens had secure rights of exit from whatever groups and associations they happen to belong to, it would have to counteract the epistemic and motivational obstacles that groups routinely, and quite rationally, put in place to retain membership. This would involve intrusions much more far-reaching than the disallowing of legal and financial obstacles that many other theorists have seen as marking the limits of the state's reach with respect to associational life. It would have to put in place a compulsory educational program with an avowedly

---

[17] Galston, *Liberal Pluralism*, p. 123.
[18] Miriam Toews, *A Complicated Kindness* (Toronto: Knopf, 2004).

perfectionist agenda, aimed at counterbalancing many of the teachings and ethical dispositions inculcated by teachers and parents within the community in question.

Imagine a community whose norms were structured around a clear division of gender roles between men and women. According to this community's norms, the role of women is to raise children and to take care of the household. In order to reinforce these gender roles, this division of labor is sanctioned by an ethical code that ascribes great value to the virtues of domesticity and childrearing, and that shrouds any departure by women from these virtues in the aura of vice. It also tailors the education of girls to their taking on of these roles. Capacities and aptitudes that might be of service in the economic and professional arenas are simply not inculcated, as they are seen as useless for the roles that women will be called upon to perform. Through a variety of subtle and not-so-subtle mechanisms, moreover, the identities of members are "policed" in ways that make it unlikely that they will defect even if they come to perceive the norms and practices of the community as painful and oppressive.

According to the conception of exit rights that Galston affirms, the liberal-democratic state would have to observe that the community in question fails to provide its members with meaningful exit rights. It would be duty-bound to counteract this failure. The most obvious lever that the state disposes of to do so is the educational system.[19] In order to ensure that members of the community possessed full exit rights, it would have to require attendance by the children of the community in public schools, or impose a curriculum on the community's private schools. That curriculum would have to go further than simply juxtaposing the conception of gender roles put forward by the community with one that does not constrain the prospects of women as severely. It would have to present the community's vision of the proper role of women as false. And it would have to put in place mechanisms whereby the psychological and motivational hold of the community upon children is lessened, else the psychological conditions that Galston sees as central to exit rights not be satisfied. Guaranteeing exit rights would thus require much more on the part of the state than simply ensuring that the doors connecting minority communities and the broader society be kept physically open. It would require quite massive incursions into those very spheres of life that these communities typically claim sovereignty over.

[19] Daniel Weinstock, "The Problem of Civic Education in Multicultural Societies," in *The Politics of Belonging*, ed. A. Dieckhoff (Lanham, MD: Lexington Books, 2004).

Jeff Spinner-Halev[20] has attempted to strike a compromise between Kukathas's libertarian minimalism with respect to exit rights and Galston's more demanding liberal position. He argues that as long as members of groups receive basic education, are not subjected to physical coercion, and have access to a diverse society, then they are possessed of exit rights which, while perhaps not optimal, are sufficient from the point of view of liberalism's concern with voluntariness and consent.

His position has the attractiveness of moderation, but it suffers from difficulties similar to those that afflict Kukathas's. To begin with, Spinner-Halev only focuses on the capacities that individuals have to resist the rights-denying actions of others, but does not place any real limits on the lengths to which others can go in order to prevent internal minorities from possessing real exit rights. But we do not ordinarily think that a person's rights are adequately protected just because those who would thwart them are only imperfectly capable of doing so. That is, we tend to prohibit rights-negating actions, whether or not they are successful. Liberal society aims at making people's enjoyment of their fundamental rights robust. A liberal society aims at removing obstacles to the satisfaction of rights, rather than satisfying itself with the ineptness of those that would deny others their rights. Spinner-Halev's proposal would consider that the exit rights of internal minorities are adequate if they are able to exercise them. A liberal position would go further in looking askance at intentional attempts at negating them.

There is also a problem with any position that merely points to the existence in the broader society of a wide range of options theoretically available to members of conservative communities as providing us with guarantees of individual members' exit rights. As we have seen, options that are theoretically available can in practice be emotionally and epistemically unavailable. A group member's entire upbringing can be tailored towards making the ways of life present in the broader society inaccessible to members. It is one thing for options to exist in the individual's environment; it is quite another for individuals to be able to consider them as options *for them*.

To reiterate a point made above, the liberal state cannot compensate for individuals' psychological and emotional weaknesses when they are, as it were, native to the individual. If an individual voluntarily joins a group and then finds that, though she is mistreated in various ways as a member, she is unable to exercise her exit rights because of the emotional dependence that she comes to form with the practices of the group and the individuals with whom she comes to associate, then that is

---

[20] Spinner-Halev, "Autonomy, Association and Pluralism."

regrettable, though not something with which the liberal state need concern itself. But if the actions of others are systematically geared towards preventing her from exercising these rights, then that is another matter altogether.

Liberal hackles ought to be particularly raised when those who are subjected to such pressures are children. Children do not consent to the beliefs and practices of the communities to which their parents belong. Though parents cannot, and indeed ought not to, raise their children without any beliefs and convictions,[21] the liberal state has a legitimate concern that the education that they receive prepares them to become agents who can give meaningful consent.[22] Surely, that is the idea at the core of Joel Feinberg's much-cited slogan to the effect that children have a "right to an open future."[23] If an adult member's inability to divest herself of an identity is causally related to burdens and obstacles designed to limit her autonomy, and imposed upon her when she was a child, we have additional reason to deny that she enjoys adequate exit rights. It is one thing to manipulate an adult's psychology so as to make it less likely that she will be able to leave a group in which she is mistreated. It is quite another to begin to do this when the individuals in question are still children.

The exit rights strategy is therefore bedeviled by a dilemma that cannot be easily avoided. If exit rights are looked to as providing liberals with the reassurance that granting some measure of collective autonomy to groups that do not share the values of the broader liberal society will not compromise the liberal commitment to consent, then they must avoid the empty formalism of the conception of exit defended by Kukathas, while not giving rise to the massive interventions that Galston's liberal conception would inevitably involve. Spinner-Halev's middle road does not successfully avoid this dilemma, as it does not address the fact that rights are not adequately secured when agents are contingently *unable* to deny individuals their rights. The security of rights also requires that they be *prevented* from doing so, especially when the main obstacles to their being able to enjoy these rights are imposed upon them as children.

---

[21] Eamon Callan, "Autonomy, Child-rearing, and Good Lives," in *The Moral and Political Status of Children*, ed. David Archard and Colin Macleod (Oxford: Oxford University Press, 2002).

[22] For a bracing critique of the threat that religious schooling can come to pose for children's rights, see James G. Dwyer, *Religious Schools v. Children's Rights* (Ithaca: Cornell University Press, 1998).

[23] Joel Feinberg, "The Child's Right to an Open Future," in *Freedom and Fulfillment: Philosophical Essays* (Princeton: Princeton University Press, 1992), pp. 76–97.

A number of responses are available at this point to the defender of LTMAs. Some argue that the strictures that we appropriately impose upon the state should not apply to groups within the state. After all, the latter are voluntary associations that do not, as does the state, possess ultimate legal authority over their members.[24] Others question the assumption that seems to be written into much liberal writing about the problems posed by conservative or otherwise non-liberal minorities, to the effect that while the state is an altogether benign, benevolent force, minorities are under a constant cloud of suspicion as potential abusers of their members' rights and fundamental interests. In fact, many minorities view the state with suspicion and fear, as they have often suffered at its hands. More, they often turn to supposedly "illiberal" minority associations in order to find a haven from a state that is perceived by them as transparently promoting the interests and conceptions of the good of the majority.

Let me begin by addressing the latter set of concerns. It would be disingenuous to deny that states claiming to be liberal have visited great harm upon their minorities. In many societies, majority/minority relations have been built upon the shaky foundations of colonialism and slavery. It is not surprising, therefore, that minorities in many countries today view the claims made on behalf of a wholly benevolent liberal state with skepticism and trepidation.

Despite the undeniable failure of the liberal state to live up to its ideals, something can be said of the liberal state that cannot be said of the groups that have emerged in many societies in some degree to contest liberalism's dominion, namely, that when they treat their minorities badly, they are acting *wrongly*, that is, they are failing to live up to standards that are internal to liberalism itself. Liberalism recognizes in a way that other forms of social organization do not that those who exercise political power cannot be the ultimate arbiters of the values that underpin the political order. Power is exercised by fallible individuals, and so mechanisms designed to offset the fallibility of humans must be built deeply into the political order. Thus the panoply of features of the institutional design of liberal democracies aimed at ensuring that laws, rather than individual agents, wield ultimate authority, and that the enforcement of these laws is distributed among a number of agencies rather than concentrated in a small number of hands, and the (admittedly imperfect) legal mechanisms that aim to give individuals

[24] Jeff Spinner-Halev, "Feminism, Multiculturalism, Oppression, and the State," *Ethics*, 112 (1), 2001; Nancy Rosenblum, *Membership & Morals* (Princeton: Princeton University Press, 1998).

recourse when they are badly treated by authorities, or when laws discriminate against them as members of a minority group.

The illiberality of illiberal groups that poses problems from the point of view of liberal justice is not so much a *doctrinal* as it is an *institutional* matter. Many religious associations for example vest ultimate interpretive authority of the group's religious doctrine in an individual or a small set of individuals that also holds ultimate decision-making authority. There are no mechanisms distributing power over diverse hands, or providing members with recourse against their leaders. Though the debate about whether the liberal state is a better protector of individual rights and interests than associations within the state is often couched as a *psychological* (who of liberal or community leaders are better *disposed* towards their members?) or as a *doctrinal* (which set of beliefs best conduces to the protection of these rights and interests?) question, it is best thought of as an institutional one. And here there can be no doubt that liberalism provides a more robust set of institutional bulwarks for the protection of individual rights.

This brings us to the first of the defenses cited above. The claim that it can be said of all voluntary associations that, since they do not wield ultimate authority over their members, they need not be held to the liberal and democratic standards that we justly impose upon the state, is untenable. First, as we have seen, the political claim of many such groups, especially religious ones, is precisely to be able to wield ultimate authority over members at least on a narrow range of issues perceived to be particularly important to a group's survival. This is what is at stake in the debate currently underway in many Western countries over whether courts applying *Shari'a* law ought to be able to settle family law disputes. And second, though it may be true that even "totalizing" religious groups, such as the Amish, cannot pretend to govern *every* aspect of their members' lives, the way in which they are able to govern that limited range of issues over which they should have jurisdiction according to defenders of LTMA poses problems. As we have seen, the conferral of rights to minority groups is not accompanied by the requirement that the power that these rights create be exercised in accordance with the kinds of constitutional constraints that we are familiar with in the case of liberal-democratic constitutionalism. Power is often concentrated, and mechanisms for contestation do not exist. Combine these two points, and you get elites within minority groups wielding ultimate authority over a limited range of issues on group members.

Where does this discussion leave us? It leaves us with a version of what Christopher Heath Wellman has recently called "The Paradox of

Group Autonomy.''[25] There are impeccable liberal reasons to permit people to associate in groups organized along all kinds of different lines, including illiberal ones. Tolerance, freedom of association, and value pluralism all conduce to recognizing the right for individuals to join together as consenting adults free from interference from the state. Even a liberal-perfectionist value such as autonomy can be marshaled in the defense of group autonomy. As Kwame Anthony Appiah has recently argued, one can very well exercise one's autonomy by taking up a role of servility and submission.[26] There is no paradox in using one's capacity for autonomous choice in order to join a group in which one subjects oneself to an unquestioned authority. And so, it seems, a host of liberal values converge upon the need to recognize group autonomy.

At the same time, group autonomy threatens some core liberal values as well. When sovereignty is ceded to groups even over a small range of issues, individual rights are threatened, especially when the groups in question claim autonomy in order to be able to implement a set of norms more conservative or traditional than those obtaining in the broader society. The compatibility of group autonomy with the liberal commitment to individual rights thus comes crucially to depend upon the degree to which members actually consent to the strictures that are visited upon them as group members. Liberals must attempt on this issue to straddle the line between two unattractive positions. They must avoid the complacent position, associated with the exit rights strategy as propounded by Kukathas and Spinner-Halev, according to which we can infer consent from the fact that members do not exercise their (minimalistically conceived) exit rights, and a liberal-perfectionist position, that would in effect place conditions upon exit rights so stringent that they would in effect negate group autonomy, or that would assume that no reasonable person could consent to subjugation, and that would justify intervention into a group's affairs on that basis. It is difficult to see exactly where that middle ground lies.

Is there any way out of this apparent paradox? In the second section of this chapter, I want to subject a pair of assumptions that underpin the debate as it has been characterized thus far to critical scrutiny. Relaxing these assumptions will, I will argue, make the internal minorities debate seem less intractable.

---

[25] Christopher Heath Wellman, "The Paradox of Group Autonomy," *Social Philosophy & Policy*, 20 (2), 2003.
[26] Appiah, *The Ethics of Identity*.

II.

The assumptions I want to interrogate have to do with the sociology implicit in the debate over group rights. They are moreover largely shared by both sets of protagonists to the debate. Borrowing a telling image from Chandran Kukathas's work,[27] I will refer in this context to the "archipelago" view of society. According to this view, people belong, primitively as it were, to communities that embody convictions, ways of conceiving of the good life, and shared practices. Now since these groups tend to share geographic space, they come into interaction with one another, and a settlement emerges organically as to the terms upon which the ensuing public space will be governed. Such a public realm is fragile, contested, always open to renegotiation. "[I]t is the product of a convergence which produces a stability and social unity that falls short of the permanence or durability many thinkers seek."[28] But the important point for our purposes is that the public realm is a creation of several pre-existing "communities of conviction." It is an artifice that serves an instrumental purpose in the lives of these communities. Thus the archipelago image: political society is thought of as formed by discrete, insular communities that happen to share space, and that willy-nilly must come to an understanding of how to govern the commons. Though Kukathas is the most extreme and forthright of contemporary political theorists affirming the archipelago vision, it is shared in important respects by other important contributors to the debate. For example, John Gray has written that we should think of democracy "as a means whereby *disparate communities* can reach common decisions."[29] Joseph Raz suggests that "we should learn to think of our societies as consisting not of a majority and minorities, but of a *plurality of cultural groups*."[30] And in what may be the most telling example of all, Jeff Spinner-Halev[31] has gone so far as to analogize the relationship of the liberal state to its minorities to that which obtains between states in the international arena, arguing that the conditions under which a state is morally permitted to intervene in the internal life of a group are analogous to those in which humanitarian intervention is justified. Here communities are thought of as analogous to sovereign states, and the state is thought of as having no more substance than does the international arena encompassing those states.

---

[27] Kukathas, *The Liberal Archipelago*.   [28] Ibid., p. 133.
[29] Gray, *Two Faces of Liberalism*, p. 127. Emphasis added.
[30] Joseph Raz, "Multiculturalism," in *Ethics in the Public Domain* (Oxford: Oxford University Press, 1994). Emphasis added.
[31] Spinner-Halev, "Feminism, Multiculturalism, Oppression, and the State," pp. 105–106.

I want to contest two underlying assumptions of the archipelago view. The first is what I shall term the *independence assumption*. It claims that people's cultural identities are formed independently of the broader social and political structures of which they are a part. The second will be referred to as the *completeness assumption*. It claims that membership in a group accounts completely for members' identities. Both of these assumptions are entailed by the archipelago view. People are thought of as relating to the public sphere and to other communities exclusively *as* members of a particular community (the completeness assumption), and as forming their identities within those communities independently of their contact with those communities (the independence assumption). They are both deeply implausible, in ways that make the archipelago view impossible to defend.

Let's begin with the completeness assumption. The assumption is crucial to the archipelago view because, as we have seen, it sees individuals entering the public sphere *as* members of already-formed communities. The public sphere comprises a set of norms and rules that make up the negotiated settlement that different groups have come to in order to manage their common affairs. But according to this assumption, individuals relate to this sphere instrumentally. It is a necessary artifice with which members of communities provide themselves in order, as it were, to direct traffic among themselves. All individuals must therefore ask themselves something like the following question: "What set of rules best allow me to live with members of my group according to our beliefs/convictions/practices while minimizing the interference with this way of life that living cheek by jowl with members of other groups occasions?" The public sphere results from negotiations among members of groups that have all come to somewhat different answers to this question.

A moment's reflection suffices to observe that the completeness assumption is mistaken. Typically, individuals belong to a plurality of groups, none of which claims to exhaust individuals' membership-based identities. People who pray devoutly in the same churches, synagogues, or mosques typically belong to different political parties, practice different professions, speak different languages, and often belong to different ethnocultural groups. It is a mistake to use the extreme case of the Old-Order Amish or the Mennonites as a paradigm case for all manner of group affiliation. There are groups in modern societies that do attempt to live in quasi-autarky from other groups, often distancing themselves physically from others in order to achieve this goal, and that try to provide their members with a "total" environment, one that precludes them from becoming members of any other kind of group in any strong sense.[32] But they are few and far between. Most people are members of a variety of groups, and the way in which this diversity of memberships informs individual identities is a profoundly individual matter. The image of a set of totalizing, Amish-like communities warily defining their relations so as to arrive at an uneasy truce with one another as to the way to manage the waters that separate one insular group from another just fails to make sense of the way that the majority of people in modern societies lead their lives.

Why does it matter that the picture of communities as discrete insular entities completely accounting for their members' identities is wrong? It matters because it shows that the debate over "internal minorities" has tended to mischaracterize the relationship between the state and the public sphere on the one hand, and the associations to which individuals belong on the other. Unless they belong to one of the very few groups that have managed to achieve almost complete autarky from the broader society, citizens' identities cannot be accounted for completely by any one particular membership. For all of us, the delineation of our identities is an individual achievement, the result of complex, highly individual negotiations by which we attempt to bring some order to our variegated affiliations. It is therefore an unhelpful idealization to claim that citizens encounter one another principally *as* members of this or that group. To the extent that their identities are complex, their affiliations are correspondingly overlapping rather than mutually exclusive.

This means that it is also a mistake to see the moral individualism at the heart of the principles and institutions of the liberal state as somehow foreign to the allegedly more "real," lived identities that individuals achieve through their memberships in discrete groups. Rather, individualism *is* the lived reality of citizens with different, complex affiliations, attempting to construct an identity (and a life) without having to sacrifice any one affiliation at the altar of one of the others. To the extent that the public sphere embodies individualist values, modern citizens are always already there.

The principles and institutions at the heart of the liberal-democratic dispensation are therefore not best thought of as an uneasy compromise among totalizing communities each one of which completely accounts for the identities and interests of their members. Rather, they encompass

---

[32] One example of these are the communities that are the subject of Lucas Swaine's recent work on "theocratic communities." Lucas Swaine, "How Ought Liberal Democracies to Treat Theocratic Communities," *Ethics*, 111 (2), 2001; Lucas Swaine, "A Liberalism of Conscience," in *Minorities within Minorities*, ed. Eisenberg and Spinner-Halev.

the conditions required for each individual to be able to concoct a life-plan out of a welter of affiliations and memberships.

It may be argued that this account badly misrepresents the situation of the citizens of modern societies. We may agree that individuals who have plural and complex affiliations are necessarily involved in negotiating these attachments in forming their identity and consequently that the completeness assumption is mistaken, but it does not obviously follow from this that such persons must be committed to moral individualism or individualist values since the fact that one has to negotiate different memberships/identities says nothing in and of itself about *how* one does this. It may be the case, for example, that I affirm a belief in the moral priority of the group over the individual and that I understand all my attachments in this light and organize them in terms of a particular ranking.[33]

This objection mislocates my claim that individualism is the lived experience of modern individuals with complex overlapping identities. The claim is, as it were, ontological rather than ethical. An individual who, surveying the landscape of his multiple attachments and identities, decides to organize them in a certain manner, and in so doing to ascribe priority to communal values, differs in crucial respects from an individual who is so enmeshed in a particular community that she cannot see it as an object of choice, and can certainly not see it as coexisting with other memberships in a highly individual concoction. The latter does not in any relevant sense *identify* with her community, as identification involves a kind of reflectiveness and voluntariness that is out of reach for a person whose identity is entirely constituted by membership in an insular and totalizing community. The former is engaged in an activity of self-making that is entirely individualistic in its workings, even if its result might end up affirming values that are not. It is in this sense that I am claiming that individualism is an inescapable part of the condition of citizens of modern pluralist societies.

The archipelago view is not only inadequate as an empirical description of the way in which communities relate to each other, to their individual members, and to the public sphere. It is also normatively inadequate. As we have seen, very few groups have managed to achieve complete autarky with respect to the broader society. Even the groups that we tend to think of as most insular live in cities, share neighborhoods with people from different walks of life, consume services, and in myriad ways benefit from the goods that modern societies offer. Their

---

[33] I thank David Owen for pressing me on this point. Its formulation borrows liberally from his incisive editorial comments.

proximity and their participation in society means that they are not to be thought of solely as formulating claims against the state and the broader society within which they live. They must also be thought of as having obligations towards the state and the broader society. To revert to the archipelago image, since citizens of modern societies actually spend quite a bit of time in the waters separating groups from one another, they all have a responsibility to make sure that they are suitable to the needs of all. Unless they manage to take themselves out of contact with society and its institutions, members of even the most conservative and traditional associations are also citizens, whether they like it or not.

Thus, it is wrong to think of the moral individualism at the heart of liberal democracies as alien to the members of associations whose identities are claimed to be completely swallowed up by a particular membership. Rather, individualism is the natural condition of individuals with complex attachments. Moreover, it is wrong to think of the claims that the public sphere makes upon associations as intolerant intrusions into the lives of insular communities that ask nothing more than to be left alone. Rather, they are the natural implications of a basic principle of reciprocity.

How does the rejection of the completeness assumption change the terms of the debate between defenders of LTMAs and their opponents? On the one hand (*pace* defenders of LTMAs), it blunts the objection that when the liberal state (for example) imposes an educational curriculum upon members of a conservative group, it intolerantly subjects them to alien values. It allows us to see what should have been plain from the outset, but that tends to get obscured by the archipelago view, namely that when the state imposes a curriculum upon members of minority associations, it is also in so doing educating its *citizens*.

On the other hand (*pace* LTMAs' opponents), the complexity of most individuals' attachments means that the cost of exercising exit rights will not ordinarily be as high as the arguments of some make it out to be. For most of us, the decision to sunder one group affiliation does not leave us bereft. Those who leave an orthodox religious community because they are poorly treated there, or because they disagree with some of the community's stances, can join a more liberal group. And they will in the normal run of things have other stable group affiliations that will soften the disorientation and pain brought about by the decision to leave a particular community. Now, there are to be sure individuals in modern societies who despite their multiple affiliations choose to identify most deeply with a particular group, and who will suffer correspondingly if they ever decide to leave. But in their case the argument can be made that their identity is a matter of decision rather than of fate. A liberal democracy will justly not place as much importance on rectifying harms resulting from individuals' choices as they will those that stem from their unchosen circumstances.

But doesn't this last remark fly in the face of much casual observation of the facts on the ground? Modern multicultural societies include many people who seem to fit the model I have been expounding here: their identities are fluid, impossible to account for in terms of any one orthodox set of beliefs. They are Jeremy Waldron's cosmopolitans, or something very much like them.[34] But there also seem to be many people living in religious or ethnic communities that seem to flee (as much as is possible in large modern urban contexts) contact with others, and to cleave to a very traditional, conservative understanding of what it means to be a member of that community. How does my critique of the completeness assumption square with the apparent proliferation of such conservative identities?

Answering this question requires that I address the second assumption which I stated above to be central to the archipelago view. I have termed it the "independence assumption." On this assumption, the beliefs, practices, and authority structures that groups adopt are as they are because of properties endogenous to the group in question. They emanate for example from a group's sacred texts, or from its ancestral traditions. The independence assumption is an integral part of the archipelago view. For on this view, the working out by a group of how they are to structure their internal affairs, what rites to adopt, what beliefs to make central, and the like, is conceptually prior to interaction with other groups, and to the delineation of the terms of the public sphere. Were processes of group identity formation not endogenous, it would not make as much sense to talk of discrete groups.

Why is the independence assumption mistaken? Because orthodoxy and insularity are not the natural states of cultures, be they religious, cultural, linguistic, or otherwise. Cultures learn and evolve, and they do so by being syncretic and opportunistic, by taking advantage of the resources available in neighboring cultures so as to increase their overall fitness. As Jeremy Waldron has recently put it, "for human cultures, it is the rule, not the exception, that ideas and ways of doing things are propagated and transmitted, noticed and adapted."[35]

Insularity of the kind required by the archipelago view is thus not the default position for cultures. Rather, it is a *decision*. And like all

[34] Jeremy Waldron, "Minority Cultures and the Cosmopolitan Alternative," *University of Michigan Journal of Law Reform*, 25, 1992.

[35] Jeremy Waldron, "What is Cosmopolitan?," *Journal of Political Philosophy*, 8 (2), (2000), p. 232.

decisions, it gets made in a context in which alternatives are weighed and assessed as to their costs and benefits.

What are the contextual features that might push a culture in the direction of what Ayelet Shachar has neatly called "reactive culturalism,"[36] that is, the tendency to enact an orthodox, insular, and "traditionalist" reading of one's culture, and a fairly rigid authority structure? In previous writing,[37] I have argued that majority/minority relations are often marked by fear on the part of the minority of the assimilative pressure that even well-disposed majorities can exercise, and, when such relations follow on from a colonial past, by suspicion of the majority's motives. The combination of these two properties of minority/majority relations creates an incentive on the part of the minority as it were to "circle the wagons" and cleave to a fairly rigid characterization of its culture, lest syncretism and *mélange* give rise to outright assimilation.

Other features of the context within which minority groups find themselves can also create incentives for "reactive culturalism." Paradoxically, certain generous provisions of multicultural societies can have this effect. If a state lets it be known that it will provide resources and spheres of autonomy to its constituent cultural groups, pressures are created for a group to offer up an exaggeratedly "distinct" picture of itself, as it is less likely that the state will extend such largesse to groups that are not clearly demarcated from the cultural majority. Multicultural policies can also lead to the adoption of hierarchical authority structures. If the state is going to extend rights to groups, it will want to be able to identify a clear right-holder, and this is more difficult when decision-making and authority are fluid. If there are cultural rights, moreover, these will have to be operationalizable in a judicial setting, and as Richard T. Ford has shown, "[c]ourts and judges will most likely protect cultural styles that can be easily framed in terms of fixed categories, bright-line rules, and quasi-scientific evidence."[38] Thus, multicultural policies may encourage reactive culturalism, as the state requires for the enactment of such policies that cultural groups be easily identifiable, and that they possess clear authority structures.

Why does the fact that the independence assumption is wrong matter? For two principal reasons. First, as has been suggested by the foregoing discussion, it broadens the palette of policy options that states can draw from in order to protect internal minorities. Rather than being limited to

---

[36] Shachar, *Multicultural Jurisdictions*.
[37] Weinstock, "Beyond Exit Rights: Reframing the Debate."
[38] Richard T. Ford, *Racial Culture: A Critique* (Princeton: Princeton University Press, 2005), p. 71.

the intervention/tolerance-and-exit-rights option which, as we have seen, leads to an impasse, states can attempt to impact on group members' decisions context so as to lessen the likelihood that they will opt for "reactive culturalism." Cultures are not genetically programmed to oppress their internal minorities. They choose to do so for reasons that are often rational from a strategic standpoint. The state can thus act on the incentives that groups have to organize themselves in this way, rather than asking itself how to deal with groups that are destined by their "natures" to deny internal minorities their rights.

Second, and perhaps more controversially, the fact that insularity and orthodoxy are decisions rather than fate changes how liberal theories of justice need to address cultural claims. If liberal justice requires that people take responsibility for their choices, then it could be that the decision to enact an orthodox "script" precludes minority groups from being able to claim autonomy as a matter of justice.

Thus, interrogating the archipelago view, with its constituent completeness and independence assumptions, has the potential to take us out of the impasse that the debate over internal minorities threatened to lead us into. Further work will have to be done to determine exactly where the reframing of the problem of internal minorities suggested here might lead.

10 Redistribution and recognition: two approaches

David Owen and James Tully

The past twenty years have seen theoretical and practical arguments for the rights of minority cultures and for multicultural policies advance on a broad range of fronts and, as they advance, encounter skeptical arguments concerning both justifications for, and the practical effects of, multiculturalism, particularly with regard to the socio-political bases of redistributive politics. Such skeptical concerns have arisen not least since, first, significant theoretical and practical attention has been paid to issues of multiculturalism at a time when the political ascendancy of neo-liberalism has resulted in a scaling back of redistributive policies and an apparent "crisis" of the welfare state and, second, multicultural policies can easily appear as claims to special (i.e., unequal) treatment against an inherited background picture of citizenship as a relatively uniform bundle of rights and duties. In this context, it is relatively easy to slide to the thoughts that the defense of redistribution could have been more politically robust if people's attention had not been diverted onto issues of multiculturalism and, even, that multicultural policies are somehow inadvertently complicit with the neo-liberal critique of, and policies towards, the welfare state by emphasizing differences at the expense of commonalities and hence undermining the basis of social solidarity. Thus, for example, Brian Barry remarks: "Pursuit of the multiculturalist agenda makes the achievement of broadly based egalitarian policies more difficult in two ways. At a minimum it diverts political effort away from universalistic goals. But a more serious problem is that multiculturalism may very well destroy the conditions for putting together a coalition in favour of across-the-board equalisation of opportunities and resources."[1]

Much depends in considering claims such as Barry's on whether multicultural policies can be understood to be grounded in the recognition

---

[1] Brian Barry, *Culture and Equality: An Egalitarian Critique of Multiculturalism* (Cambridge: Polity Press, 2001), p. 325.

of citizens as free and equal persons or members of a polity, and addressing this issue will be a central task of this chapter. We'll consider this issue in the context of two distinct approaches to, or modes of, liberal political theory which we'll describe, following Laden,[2] as adopting "theoretical" and "political" perspectives respectively. In respect of the "theoretical" approach, the task of the political philosopher is to work out a theory of justice in virtue of which judgments concerning the degree of justice or injustice exhibited by institutions, policies, and, perhaps, forms of personal conduct can be articulated: "Those who take a theoretical approach to political philosophy hold that it is the reasoning of the theorist that ultimately determines the shape of just political principles, and so their justification depends entirely on the soundness of the theorist's reasoning."[3] By contrast, the "political" approach holds that politically legitimate principles of justice are to be determined by citizens reasoning together under conditions of fair deliberation and, consequently, that the role of the political philosopher is to offer public reason arguments concerning both the principles that might be endorsed and the conditions of fair deliberation.[4] Perhaps unsurprisingly, while those committed to a "theoretical" approach have sought to spell out a full account of the idea of the recognition of persons as moral equals in terms of the principles of justice that they endorse, advocates of a "political" approach have focused more (although not exclusively) on the idea of struggles over recognition in relation to citizens as political equals deliberating over the terms of their political relation to one another. In setting these approaches, we will also offer arguments for the priority of the political over the theoretical approach.

A word before we move onto the substance of this chapter on the general understanding of recognition that it assumes. In general, we take "recognition" in evaluative contexts to denote *acknowledging an object of value in a way that is appropriately responsive to its value*[5] and, given the subject of this chapter, we will take political recognition to mean *acknowledging citizens in ways that are appropriately responsive to their status as free and equal persons or members of the polity*. Such members may have cultural differences that are worthy of recognition and respect. However, it is important to mark a difference between theoretical and

---

[2] See his *Reasonably Radical: Deliberative Liberalism and the Politics of Identity* (Ithaca: Cornell University Press, 2001), esp. pp. 15–17 and his "Taking the Distinction between Persons Seriously," *Journal of Moral Philosophy*, 1, November 2004, pp. 277–299 as well as his essay in this volume.

[3] Laden, "Taking the Distinction," p. 288.   [4] Ibid., pp. 290–292.

[5] We adapt this from Joseph Raz's essay "Respecting People" in his *Value, Respect and Attachment* (Cambridge: Cambridge University Press, 2001), pp. 124–175.

political approaches with respect to the working out of the form and content of political recognition. For advocates of a theoretical approach, struggles by minority groups are seen as struggles *for* recognition in which the form and content of political recognition is spelt out in terms of a theory of justice or, for critics of liberalism such as Taylor and Honneth, a theory of ethical life – and such theories will include some accounts of how the goods specified by the favored metric of equality (e.g., primary and secondary goods, resources, opportunity for welfare, etc.) are to be distributed. For proponents of a political approach, struggles by minority groups are seen as struggles *over* recognition in which the form and content of political recognition is governed by the conditions of public reasoning (i.e., compatibility with acknowledging each other as free and equal members of the polity) and the actual processes of deliberation and contestation in which citizens engage. Anticipating somewhat, we can say that theoretical approaches focus on a claim for recognition advanced by an agent and go on to evaluate it in abstraction from the field in which it is raised, whether the claim is advanced in terms of rights, identities, or culture, whereas we believe that we should focus on the field of interaction in which the conflict arises and needs to be resolved, since a conflict is not a struggle of one minority for recognition in relation to other actors who are independent of, unaffected by, and neutral with respect to the form of recognition that the minority seeks; rather, a struggle for recognition of a "minority" always calls into question and (if successful) modifies, often in complex ways, the *existing* forms of reciprocal recognition of the other members of the larger system of government of which the minority is a member. The most perspicuous way of putting this is to say that struggles over recognition are struggles over the inter-subjective "norms" (laws, rules, conventions, or customs) under which the members of any system of government recognize each other *as* members and coordinate their interaction. Hence, struggles over recognition are always struggles over the prevailing inter-subjective norms of mutual recognition through which the members (individuals and groups under various descriptions) of any system of action coordination (or practice of governance) are recognized and governed.

Note that this conceptualization of these approaches to the issue of redistribution and recognition is oriented to warding off a confusion which may follow from the fact that "the politics of recognition" and "the politics of redistribution" are often rhetorically opposed to one another or treated as analytically distinct. Typically such uses of the notion of recognition reduce the general concept of recognition to the idea of cultural recognition and hence obscure the crucial point that struggles for, or over, recognition always have a redistributive dimension and struggles for, or over, redistribution are always already struggles for, or over, recognition.[6]

I.

Following the publication of Will Kymlicka's *Liberalism, Community and Culture*, debates within the "theoretical" mode of political philosophy concerning egalitarian views of distributive justice and their relationship to issues of cultural rights and policies have tended to be conducted within the framework of "luck-egalitarianism" and, more specifically, of debates concerning equality of resources and equality of opportunity of welfare in relation to (a) the analogy or lack of analogy between culture and expensive tastes, and (b) the justifiability of compensation for expensive tastes. Consequently, we will begin by sketching this philosophical context before turning to consider the salient arguments.

Luck-egalitarians are opposed to the influence on distribution of *exploitation* (i.e., unfair advantage being taken of a person) and bad *brute luck* (i.e., bad luck that is not the product of a risk that could have reasonably been avoided or not chosen).[7] Indeed, luck-egalitarians are concerned to *extinguish*, rather than simply mitigate, the effects of exploitation and bad brute luck in seeking to ensure the equality of

---

[6] An illustration of how things can easily go wrong in the context of these different uses is provided by the recent exchange between Nancy Fraser and Axel Honneth published under the title *Recognition or Redistribution: A Political-Philosophical Exchange* (London: Verso, 2003). In this work, Fraser argues that issues of recognition and of redistribution refer to analytically distinct dimensions of justice, the former being exemplified by status inequalities and the latter by class inequalities, whereas Honneth argues that issues of redistribution are to be understood in terms of a more basic framework of recognition. The problem with this "exchange" is that Fraser uses "recognition" in a restricted sense to refer only to issues relating to cultural status, whereas Honneth uses "recognition" in a general sense to refer to the acknowledgment of the value of others (for example, as objects of love, respect, and esteem). Consequently, the "debate" between them becomes an engagement in talking past each other in which Honneth's insistence that issues of redistribution are only intelligible in terms of an account of recognition (in the general sense) is "opposed" to Fraser's insistence that issues of redistribution bear no necessary relationship to an account of recognition (in the restricted sense). It is worth noting that although the motivation for the restriction of the concept of recognition to issues of cultural status or identity, at least in Fraser's work, is to avoid the dangers of reductionism by specifying the distinct *causes* of forms of structural inequality, this restriction actually encourages at least two forms of reductionism. First, it offers the view that, given formal legal and political equality, inequalities can be analytically sorted out in terms of two basic types of cause – economic and cultural – and, second, it thereby supports the view that redistribution is merely concerned with material goods and recognition merely with symbolic goods.

[7] G. A. Cohen, "On the Currency of Egalitarian Justice," *Ethics*, 99 (4), July 1989, p. 908.

citizens.[8] However, despite this basic common commitment, luck-egalitarians have adopted different answers to the question of what dimension of persons counts fundamentally for egalitarians and hence what metric should be used for judging the degree to which the just recognition of citizens as equal persons is realized in any given society. For the purposes of this chapter, two candidates for this role are important: equality of resources and equality of opportunity for welfare. We will begin by briefly sketching the main features of equality of resources before considering two opposed arguments concerning cultural rights that both endorse this position. We will then turn to sketch equality of opportunity for welfare as offering an important criticism of equality of resources which has significant implications for these arguments concerning cultural rights.

The thesis of equality of resources is developed by Ronald Dworkin and has been adopted, in the context of the cultural rights debate, by such opposed figures as Kymlicka and Barry. We can situate this proposed metric as developing from two criticisms of equality of welfare proposed by Rawls and taken up by Dworkin. The first criticism concerns *offensive tastes* which argues that "the pleasure a person takes in discriminating against other people or subjecting others to lesser liberty should not count equally with other satisfactions in the calculus of justice"; on the contrary, from the standpoint of justice such pleasures and their corresponding preferences have no claim to be satisfied "even if they would have to be satisfied for welfare equality."[9] This criticism is not fundamental with respect to equality of welfare in that it can be accommodated by a shift to equality of *non-offensive* welfare; however, the second criticism which concerns *expensive tastes* is thought to be fundamental. The criticism here is that equality of welfare would require granting a higher level of income to a person with expensive tastes than to a person with inexpensive tastes to ensure they are equally satisfied but, as Rawls argues, to adopt this position is to treat people's preferences as propensities or craving beyond their control, that is, to deny the plain truth that people are, to some extent, responsible for the shaping and development of their preferences and so, to that extent, should bear the costs of their expensive tastes.[10] Reflecting on, and developing, Rawls's criticism, Dworkin proposes equality of resources as the relevant metric on the grounds that it offers compensation with respect to inequalities that result from the uneven distribution of

---

[8] For a critical discussion of this issue, see Samuel Scheffler, "What is Egalitarianism?," *Philosophy and Public Affairs*, 31 (1), 2003, pp. 5–39.
[9] Cohen, "On the Currency," p. 912.   [10] Ibid., p. 913.

material resources to, and mental and physical capacities of, an agent but not with respect to inequalities that result from tastes and preferences that are chosen or endorsed by the agent (hence Dworkin does allow for compensation in the case of "cravings" that the agent regrets having which are treated as handicaps).[11] Thus, at the heart of the thesis of equality of resources is a distinction between *choice* and *circumstances*, where inequalities arising from the former do not require compensation (except in the special case of cravings) and inequalities arising from the latter do require compensation.

This thesis plays a central role in Will Kymlicka's argument for rights for cultural minorities, but to see how its plays this role, we need to situate it in relation to Kymlicka's Rawlsian argument concerning self-respect. Kymlicka's starting point is Rawls's claim that liberals see the freedom to form, revise, and reject our beliefs about value as a precondition of pursuing our fundamental interest in leading a good life and, more specifically, Rawls's argument that seeing the value of our activities is crucial to the most important primary good, *self-respect*, insofar as self-respect is a precondition of carrying out our plan of life yet such self-respect is dependent on seeing our goals as worthwhile.[12] Given this starting point, Kymlicka's next crucial step is to argue that (a) we do not, in determining how to live our lives, start *de novo* but are situated within a context of choice in which a range of options is presented to us as possible ways of life and, hence also, as objects for reflection with which we can identify, and (b), taking up a suggestion of Dworkin's,[13] that this context of choice is provided by our culture or, more precisely, our culture considered as a *cultural structure*, that is, a set of processes based on a shared societal language through which cultural meanings are generated. Kymlicka contends that it is only in virtue of a secure (which does not mean static) cultural structure that people can come to see, vividly, the options available to them and reflect on these options. Hence he concludes that cultural membership is a primary good.

The second part of the argument puts Dworkin's equality of resources thesis to work by noting that members of subordinate/minority cultures within a multicultural or multinational polity will typically require

---

[11] See Ronald Dworkin, "What is Equality? Part II: Equality of Resources," *Philosophy and Public Affairs*, 10 (4), 1981, pp. 283–345.

[12] See John Rawls, *A Theory of Justice* (Oxford: Oxford University Press, 1972), pp. 440–441 and Will Kymlicka, *Liberalism, Community and Culture* (Oxford: Oxford University Press, 1989), pp. 164–165.

[13] Will Kymlicka, "Dworkin on Freedom and Culture," in *Dworkin and His Critics*, ed. J. Burley (Oxford: Blackwell, 2004) pp. 117–119.

resources to support access to (i.e., maintain) a secure cultural structure that members of the dominant/majority culture get for free. Since, Kymlicka claims, being born into a given culture is an unchosen circumstance rather than a choice for which one can be held responsible (and hence cannot be treated as, or on a par with, an expensive taste), it follows that the fact that members of a minority culture will need to use up resources maintaining a secure cultural structure that others get for free is an inequality that ought to be rectified. He concludes by pointing out that this inequality can be rectified through mechanisms such as the provision of certain rights and resources for minority cultures.[14]

This argument has been attacked in a considerable variety of ways.[15] Here we will restrict ourselves to discussion of one crucial issue for Kymlicka, namely, the claim that cultural membership is not relevantly analogous to an expensive taste. This is a particularly pertinent issue on which to focus since the core claim of an important critical polemic against multiculturalism advanced by Brian Barry, who also endorses the equality of resources thesis, hangs on making the argument that cultural beliefs *are* analogous to expensive tastes. We can, therefore, helpfully develop this issue by considering Barry's argument.

The core claim of Barry's argument is straightforward: "From an egalitarian liberal standpoint, what matters are equal opportunities. If uniform rules create identical choice sets, then opportunities are equal."[16] The fact that people will make different choices based on divergent preferences, and that some of these preferences may be derived from culture, "is irrelevant to any claims based on justice, since justice is guaranteed by equal opportunities."[17] So: "The crucial distinction is between limits on the range of opportunities open to people and limits on the choices that they make from within a certain range of opportunities."[18] Central to the defense of this argument are the claims that cultural beliefs are analogous to expensive tastes and the concept of opportunity refers to an objective state of affairs independent of the beliefs of subjects.

The argument that Barry provides for the expensive tastes analogy is that beliefs are, in all relevant respects, like preferences and, hence, that

---

[14] Kymlicka, *Liberalism, Community and Culture*, chs. 8 and 9 and *Multicultural Citizenship* (Oxford: Oxford University Press, 1995), chs. 5 and 6.
[15] See, for example, J. Danley, "Liberalism, Aboriginal Rights and Cultural Minorities," *Philosophy and Public Affairs*, 20 (2), 1991, pp. 168–185; J. Tomasi, "Kymlicka, Liberalism and Respect for Aboriginal Cultures," *Ethics*, 105 (3), 1995, pp. 580–603; T. Modood, "Kymlicka on British Muslims," *Analyse und Kritik*, 15 (1), 1993, pp. 87–91.
[16] Barry, *Culture and Equality*, p. 32.   [17] Ibid.   [18] Ibid.

we should bear the costs of our beliefs in the same way that justice requires that we bear the costs of our preferences:

> The usual reaction to the idea that those with expensive tastes should get extra resources is that it is absurd, and such a reaction is perfectly sound . . . The error lies in thinking that, even as a matter of principle, fair treatment requires compensation for expensive tastes . . . Suppose that you and I have an equal claim on society's resources, for whatever reason. Then it is simply not relevant that you will gain more satisfaction from using those resources than I will. What is fair is that our equal claim translates into equal purchasing power: what we do with it is our own business.[19]

Against the objection that we cannot choose what to believe, Barry points out that we cannot necessarily choose our preferences either. Consequently, he concludes:

> The upshot is, then, that beliefs and preferences are in the same boat: we cannot change our beliefs by an act of will but the same can be said equally well of our preferences. It is false that the changeability of preferences is what makes it not unfair for them to give rise to unequal impact. It is therefore not true that the unchangeability of beliefs makes it unfair for them to give rise to unequal impacts.[20]

Barry's argument for his next key claim, namely, that opportunity is an objective, and not a subject-dependent, concept, is presented by way of example. He offers this argument initially in terms of a rejection of the claim he takes Parekh to make that beliefs are an encumbrance in a way directly analogous to physical disability:

> The position of somebody who is unable to drive a car as a result of some physical disability is totally different from that of somebody who is unable to drive a car because doing so would be contrary to the tenets of his of her religion. To suggest that they are similarly situated is in fact offensive to both parties.[21]

Barry rather helps himself here by picking an extreme contrast between the religious believer and the wheelchair-bound agent but consider two intermediate cases. First, consider an agent who suffers from an allergy which ensures that engaging in a particular activity is physically distressing to them. It is not that they cannot engage in the activity (in the strong sense of "cannot" invoked by Barry) but that to do so imposes certain costs of (at least) physical suffering on them. Second, consider an agent who suffers from a phobia which ensures that engaging in a particular activity – say, flying – is mentally distressing to them. Again it is not that they cannot engage in the activity in the relevant sense but that doing so imposes certain costs of (at least) mental suffering on

---

[19] Barry, *Culture and Equality*, p. 35.   [20] Ibid., p. 36.   [21] Ibid., p. 37.

them. Since in neither case does the affliction "limit the opportunity" in Barry's strong sense, we are forced to conclude that Barry would deny that justice in any way requires that agents suffering from allergies or phobias be compensated for their condition. But this conclusion is surely overly harsh. Why should people who are disadvantaged by allergies and phobias (for which they are not responsible) not have a claim in justice to compensation or special treatment? We are not, of course, saying that religious or cultural beliefs are like allergies or phobias,[22] merely that Barry's "crucial distinction" is overly rigid. The obvious way to differentiate religious or cultural beliefs from allergies or phobias in terms of Dworkin's resource-based view of equality would be to distinguish between having a phobia of flying and belonging to a culture that, say, regards flying as against the will of God on the grounds that the former presumably would not want to have the phobia, would be willing to be treated for it, and merits compensation if treatment is either too expensive or unavailable, whereas the latter would not wish to fly come-what-may, would regard the idea that they might be treated as offensive, and have no proper grounds for compensation just because they happen to have and identify with that set of beliefs. Indeed, this is just the argument that Barry has made elsewhere.[23] However, to make this argument, Barry would have to drop the "crucial distinction" which he insists on and introduce a distinction between beliefs or preferences that we regret having and beliefs or preferences with which we identify. So let us make this change on Barry's behalf and draw the relevant conclusion, namely, that insofar as people identify with (or reflectively endorse) their cultural beliefs, such beliefs are relevantly akin to expensive tastes and so do not entitle them to compensation.

At this stage, a defender of Kymlicka's position could legitimately point out that Barry does not address Kymlicka's argument for the importance of access to a cultural structure as a context of choice, that is, as "an unchosen *framework* within which tastes are formed and choices are made."[24] However, G. A. Cohen helpfully supplies the missing argument in two parts, claiming "first, that the cultural framework is not the only relevant one, that there is also a larger one to the detriment of Kymlicka's attempt to represent support for culture as

---

[22] Thanks to Alan Ware for the example and to Susan Mendus for pressing this point.

[23] It is this latter distinction which Barry defended in an earlier essay "Chance, Choice and Justice," in his *Liberty and Justice: Essays in Political Theory* (Oxford: Clarendon Press, 1991), vol. II, pp. 142–158.

[24] G. A. Cohen, "Expensive Tastes and Multiculturalism," in *Multiculturalism, Liberalism and Democracy*, ed. R. Bhargava *et al.* (New Delhi: Oxford University Press, 1999), pp. 92–93.

special, and, in particular, as different from support for (other) expensive tastes; and, second, that the framework/practice distinction is relative rather than absolute, and therefore cannot bear the weight that Kymlicka places on it."[25]

The first argument has two steps. The opening move is to note that while we can distinguish culture as a context of choice from particular preferences, "we may also distinguish, contrariwise, between a particular culturally phrased preference and a set of possible lifestyles not all of which are in all pertinent respects coloured by a particular culture."[26] The second move is to concatenate all the lifestyles possible within a given society to get "what can be called its *lifestyle space*," where this space is not synonymous with Kymlicka's notion of societal culture, and to note (i) that "lifestyle space is no less a context of choice than culture is" and (ii) it may be no less expensive to sustain threatened lifeways (regions of lifestyle space) that do not have a cultural character in Kymlicka's sense than to secure threatened cultures. So, for example:

Think of English rural lifeways. The hunt, forest to walk in, country buses, protection against overdevelopment of villages: these are not particularly cheap, and they bear no particular cultural stamp ... but they represent an unchosen and not specially cultural (in the relevant narrow sense) context of choice for those who are reared in their ambit, and who identify with those lifeways and gain a sense of self from them.[27]

Cohen's second argument is that the distinction between framework of choice and choice is variable:

For frameworks of choice may themselves be chosen, and particular choices may enfold sub-choices. Thus one may distinguish between different frameworks of consumer choice (e.g., within food, between vegetarian and carnelian ...) and particular choices within each (asparagus vs. lettuce, and so on). The contrast between frameworks and particular choices is a relative distinction, along a continuum of more and less specific choices. Strongly contrastive distributive conclusions cannot be grounded in so shifting a distinction.[28]

Taken together, these arguments appear to undermine Kymlicka's claim that (expensive) culture is distinct from expensive tastes (e.g., an expensive taste for rural lifeways) since Kymlicka's claim that we should treat access to a secure cultural structure as something people would want independent of more particular conceptions of the good is equally true of lifeways.

So should we conclude that, although he doesn't supply all the arguments needed, Barry is right and that the fact that maintaining one's

[25] Cohen, "Expensive Tastes and Multiculturalism," p. 93.   [26] Ibid., p. 93.
[27] Ibid., p. 94.   [28] Ibid., pp. 94–5.

culture or cultural commitments may be expensive for members of minority cultures does not imply that they should be compensated since maintaining such commitments is, in the relevant respect, an expensive taste? Before reaching such a judgment, we should note that Cohen himself does not endorse Barry's conclusion; on the contrary, Cohen argues for the claims (a) that those who, like Barry, Dworkin, and Kymlicka, reject compensation for expensive tastes as a matter of *principle* are mistaken to do so and (b) that Kymlicka's view that we should support cultural minorities is justified.

Cohen's starting point involves rejecting equality of resources in favour of (something akin to) equality of opportunity for welfare. The rationale for this rejection is provided by reference to Dworkin's famous example of egalitarians shipwrecked on an island who use the worthless item of clamshells as currency to bid in an auction for the island's resources which, if the auction is properly conducted, gives rise to an "envy-free" distribution of resources (on the assumption that there is no inequality in people's talents). Addressing the typical situation in which people are disadvantaged by handicaps or differential talents is accommodated by Dworkin through some form of post-auction redistribution to rectify for these disadvantages. Cohen's objection runs as follows:

suppose that there are two things to eat on the island, eggs and fish. Fish are abundant and eggs are scarce. Consequently, fish are cheap and eggs are very expensive. Most people love fish, but Harry hates them. Most people mostly eat fish, reserving eggs for special occasions, and finding themselves consequently with plenty of clamshells to pay for other things, such as shelter, clothing, recreation, and so forth. Unlike them, Harry has a tough choice, which is between regularly eating eggs and therefore having little of anything else, and eating lots of fish, at the cost of gagging whenever he nourishes himself. Although the example is stylized and peculiar, it stands for the unpeculiar phenomenon of different people finding the same commodities differentially satisfying, and therefore being differentially placed with respect to what they get out of life with a given income. And, in my view, that phenomenon explodes the pretension of Dworkin's auction to being an engine of distributive justice. It shows that equality of resources should give way to equality of opportunity for welfare, because identical quantities of resources are capable of satisfying people to different degrees, since people are made differently, both naturally and socially, not only (a fact to which Dworkin is sensitive) in their capacities to produce but also (a fact to which he is insensitive) in their capacities to obtain fulfilments.[29]

Given this argument, Cohen takes expensive tastes to refer to "a dispositional characteristic" in that a "person's tastes are expensive in the

---

[29] Ibid., pp. 83–4.

required sense if and only if . . . they are such that it costs more to provide that person than to provide others with given levels of satisfaction or fulfillment."[30]

To see Cohen's argument, we can distinguish among expensive tastes according to whether or not their bearer can reasonably be held responsible for the fact that her tastes are expensive. With respect to *brute* (non-valuational) tastes we can distinguish those she could not have helped forming and, hence, for which she cannot be held responsible (i.e., is entitled to compensation) and those she could have forestalled or could unlearn and, hence, can be held responsible (i.e., is not entitled to compensation). With respect to tastes informed by valuational judgment, Cohen argues:

we can still ask whether their bearers could have avoided developing them or could be asked to rid themselves of them, and the answers will be variously relevant, but I no longer think that the mere fact that people choose to develop and/or could now school themselves out of an expensive judgmental taste means that they should pick up the tab for it, and that is *precisely* because they *did* and *do* identify with it, and therefore cannot *reasonably* be expected to have not developed it or to rid themselves of it.[31]

We should note two points at this juncture. First, for members of subordinate or minority cultures, their cultural commitments are expensive *judgmental* tastes in that they identify with these commitments and, further, they cannot reasonably be held responsible for the fact these commitments are expensive. Second, Cohen's argument runs exactly counter to the point endorsed by Barry, Dworkin, and Kymlicka that you are entitled to compensation only if you don't identify with the expensive taste (e.g., the case of phobias):

So what Dworkin gives as a reason for *withholding* compensation – the subjects' approving identification with their expensive tastes – is something that I regard as a reason for offering it, since, where identification *is* present, it is, standardly, the agents' very bad luck that a preference with which they strongly identify happens to be expensive, and to expect them to forgo or to restrict satisfaction of that preference (because it is expensive) is, therefore, to ask them to accept an alienation from what is deep in them.[32]

The argument is thus that expensive preferences may be relevantly unchosen bad luck, where this does not require (as Dworkin insists) that "although it is unchosen, the agents cannot regard it as a piece of bad luck for which they should be compensated, on pain of incoherently

---

[30] G. A. Cohen, "Expensive Taste Rides Again," in *Dworkin and His Critics*, ed. Burley, p. 6.
[31] Ibid., p. 7.   [32] Ibid.

repudiating their own personality" since the relevant bad luck does not consist of the mere *having* of the expensive taste but in the fact that the taste is *expensive* and "people can certainly without any self-misrepresentation or incoherence ask for compensation for (what might be, in every relevant sense) the *circumstance* that their taste is expensive."[33] This argument justifies support for cultural minorities on the grounds that it is simply bad luck that they are situated in circumstances in which acting according to their cultural commitments or maintaining their culture is expensive (since if they were the cultural majority, these preferences would not be expensive).

Cohen's argument is, we think, persuasive in that it makes clear that where the expensiveness of my reflectively endorsed taste is a product of the preferences or commitments of others, I cannot justly be required to bear the full burden of the costs of my taste unless I endorse this taste solely because it is expensive (e.g., for snobbish reasons). In this respect, we can conclude that recognition of citizens as free and equal persons is compatible with, and in all culturally diverse polities requires, acknowledging their cultural identities and that this cultural recognition has significant implications for the equal distribution of opportunity for welfare.

However, although we think that Cohen's argument is persuasive within the context of luck-egalitarianism, there are three increasingly general considerations that we take to be compelling with regard to the case against the luck-egalitarian approach. The first is that we doubt that the choice/circumstance distinction can bear the theoretical weight that is being placed on it. The second is that the emphasis on correcting for unchosen bad luck can conflict with other egalitarian values that need to be acknowledged in any account of the recognition of citizens as equals. The third is that luck-egalitarianism fails to take the distinction between persons seriously enough and hence commits itself to a monological approach oriented to the presumption of finality. We will describe this "theoretical" approach as an "administrative" perspective in contrast to a "political" or "civic" perspective.

With regard to the choice/circumstance distinction, luck-egalitarianism confronts a dilemma. On the one hand, if luck-egalitarianism leaves us up to our necks in debates about free will, as Cohen at one point suggests,[34] this seems indicative of a need for the kind of moralistic "deepening" of the essentially superficial notion of the voluntary against which Bernard Williams has cogently protested.[35] If, however, luck-egalitarianism

---

[33] Ibid., p. 11.   [34] Cohen, "On the Currency," p. 934.
[35] See Bernard Williams, *Shame and Necessity* (Berkeley: University of California Press, 1994).

appeals solely to the notion of the voluntary as it is elaborated in ordinary moral and legal contexts, then its implicit claim that responsibility is to be cashed out solely in terms of what is chosen runs against powerful intuitions that go in the contrary direction and do not align responsibility with fault. Thus, for example, as Williams has noted, we find intelligible Ajax's suicide following his deranged slaughter of the sheep because even though the Homeric Greeks (and Ajax himself) do not regard him as having chosen to act in this way and, hence, not at fault, the fact that *he* has acted in this way and the consequent contrast between this action and his conception of himself are unbearable to him. A more contemporary example is provided by the legal doctrine of strict liability that makes some persons responsible for damages their actions or products cause, regardless of any "fault" on their part. A further and independent point with regard to the weight-bearing potential of the choice/circumstance distinction is that it requires a pre-political conception of agency that can command universal assent yet we have no good reason to suppose in the light of contrasting cultural conceptions of agency that any such conception is available; on the contrary, as Judith Shklar notes with respect to the related distinction between injustice and misfortune, the line of separation is "a political choice, not a simple rule that can be taken as given."[36]

Independent of the force of this first objection, a second objection is that fully implementing a luck-egalitarian view of justice would require not merely considerable invasion of privacy (as Cohen has it: "intolerably intrusive state surveillance"[37]) but also, as Jonathan Wolff has pointed out, that, under certain (unchosen) circumstances, individuals would be required to engage in practices of self-disclosure that undermine their self-respect, e.g., explaining why, in circumstances of near full employment when jobs are readily available, they have not chosen to be unemployed but can't get a job because they lack even basic abilities such as literacy and/or numeracy. This objection is telling because there is an important sense in which luck-egalitarianism is an attempt to spell out what recognition-respect for persons as equals would require and, consequently, to the extent that the rigorous implementation of its principles involves conflict with our basic intuitions concerning recognition-respect, it cannot be expected that citizens could reasonably endorse these principles.

The issue of recognition-respect raised by the second objection can be pressed further, becoming a third objection that applies not simply to

---

[36] Judith Shklar, *The Faces of Injustice* (New Haven: Yale University Press, 1990), p. 5.
[37] Cohen, "On the Currency," p. 910.

luck-egalitarianism but to theoretical approaches more generally. Thus, Anthony Laden offers the following argument. First, Rawls's characterization of the utilitarian theorist as taking up an *administrative* rather than *civic* point of view can be generalized across "theoretical" approaches, that is, approaches that conceive of political philosophy in terms of the task of working out a correct theory and how to apply it rather than in terms of participating in the process of working out terms of reasonable agreement with fellow citizens. Second, taking up the administrative standpoint, rather than the perspective of a citizen, fails to treat the distinction between persons seriously enough because occupying this standpoint involves failing to take seriously the diverse grounds which citizens might have for objecting not merely to the theory but also to the theorist's implicit presumption that it is the extent to which the theory is correct that governs the legitimacy of its implementation. Third, within a democratic society, the authority to determine principles of justice lies in the hands of citizens and, thus, "doing political philosophy within and for a democratic society requires abandoning the perspective of the theorist favored by utilitarians and many other political philosophers and adopting the perspective of the citizen."[38] The upshot of Laden's argument is that luck-egalitarian political philosophy fails to be sufficiently egalitarian at the level of its conception of political philosophy because in failing to take the distinction between persons seriously enough at this level, it fails to acknowledge that its commitment to the recognition of persons as equals needs to extend to the form and not merely the content of its philosophical practice. If this argument is cogent, it implies that egalitarians should be led by their own normative commitments to adopt a political rather than theoretical approach to issues of recognition and redistribution.

That said, it is not immediately clear that Laden's argument is cogent since it is not obvious that those engaged in the theoretical approach *must* be committed to the "implicit presumption" that the legitimacy of implementation is governed by the correctness of the theory; on the contrary, such theorists may agree with Jeremy Waldron that working out what one takes to be the best possible account of justice has no direct relevance for politics. Waldron's position constructs a distinction between two activities: the theoretical task of developing the best possible account of justice and the political task of addressing how we can fairly make jointly binding decisions about how to conduct our common affairs and political relationship with one another under conditions of disagreement that may extend to the fundamentals of our

---

[38] Laden, "Taking the Distinction," p. 23.

understandings of justice.[39] In response to this objection, however, it might be argued that the very enterprise of presenting a theoretical view of justice as articulating an ideal set of arrangements for political society is held captive by an implicit commitment to the picture (or fantasy) of the political philosopher as the *lawgiver* who does not engage in politics but lays down the definitively just constitutional conditions of possibility of political activity. However, such a picture of founding is problematic in that it draws too sharp a distinction between the constitutional (foundational politics) and democratic (everyday politics) dimensions of modern politics, and hence too "foundational" an image of founding. This presents just conditions of practical democratic dialogue, disagreement and contestation as only possible within, and as definitively fixed by, the limits imposed by the theoretical determination of justice; by contrast, a political approach redirects attention from a theoretical determination of the political relationship of citizens to the political conditions of being able to work out the terms of this relationship as free and equal members of the political community in an ongoing political contest and, in doing so, takes the distinction between persons seriously.

Of course this does not do away with the theoretical orientation. If we are going to grant priority to democratic practice, and thus work towards democratizing actual existing democracies, then the theoretical perspective will have an indispensable yet less lofty and transcendental role to play. Instead of determining the limits of democracy and the forms of representation under which members are recognized and resources distributed from on high, the role will be to make presentations for consideration to their fellow citizens of possible theories of justice with respect to recognition and redistribution, to clarify the strengths and weaknesses of the procedures, proposals, and agreements of actual democratic deliberations, and thus to enter into a dialogical relationship with democratic practice, as in fact many deliberative democratic theorists are doing.

II.

To adopt the political mode of political philosophy in relation to issues of distributive justice and cultural diversity is to acknowledge, first, that the reasons offered to citizens must be such that they could be reasonably endorsed by citizens as consistent with their freedom and equality and, second, that the authority of such *public* reasons is grounded in

---

[39] See his *Law and Disagreement* (Oxford: Oxford University Press, 1999), for an extended effort to argue for this distinction and address its implications.

their endorsement by citizens, where such endorsement is given in virtue of their shared identity as citizens. More specifically, the political turn can be grasped in terms of a commitment to a dialogical and processual orientation to struggles over recognition in which political philosophy is not viewed as a distinct, higher-order activity of theoretical reflection on historically (and culturally) situated practices of practical political reasoning but, rather, as the methodical extension of the self-reflective character of these historically situated practices of practical political reasoning. In this section, we will focus on explaining why we take a political approach to be dialogical and processual; in the following section, we will develop an account of such an approach in terms of democratic civic freedom.

What are the main reasons for the claim that an acceptable norm of mutual recognition should be worked out by those subject to it through some form of the exchange of reasons in negotiation, deliberation, bargaining, and other forms of dialogue? We can note, first, that the legitimacy of contemporary political associations is oriented around two critical and abstract norms, namely, the principles of constitutionalism and democracy. The principle of constitutionalism requires that the exercise of political power in the whole and in every part of any *constitutionally* legitimate system of political, social, and economic cooperation should be exercised in accordance with and through a global system of principles, rules, and procedures, including procedures for amending any principle, rule, or procedure. The principle of democracy requires that, although the people or peoples who comprise a political association are subject to the global constitutional system, they, or their entrusted representatives, must also impose the global system on themselves in order to be sovereign, and thus for the association to be *democratically* legitimate. The people or peoples "impose" the constitutional system on themselves by means of having a say through exchanging reasons in democratic practices of deliberation, either directly or indirectly through their representatives, usually in a piecemeal fashion by taking up some sub-set of the principles, rules, and procedures of the system. These democratic practices of deliberation are themselves rule governed (to be constitutionally legitimate), but the rules must also be open to democratic amendment if they are to be democratically legitimate.[40]

The second consideration is a condition of the acceptability of a norm of mutual recognition. The identities under which individuals and

---

[40] James Tully, "The Unfreedom of the Moderns in Relation to Their Ideals of Constitutionalism and Democracy," *Modern Law Review*, 65 (2), 2002, pp. 204–228.

groups are reciprocally recognized in any form of cooperation actually count as *their* identities only if they can accept them from a first-person perspective: that is, acknowledge them as their own. If an elite determines them they are experienced as imposed and alien. It follows that the persons who bear them need to have some sort of say over their formulation, or over the selection and accountability of trusted representatives who negotiate for them, as individuals or groups, if they are not to be alienated from the outcome.[41] Due to the relational character of recognition this consideration holds not only for the members of the minority seeking recognition, but also for the other members of the system of governance, whose present form of recognition *and corresponding rights to resources* will be affected by any alteration in the prevailing norms of mutual recognition of the members.[42] Thus, to ensure that a new norm of mutual recognition is acceptable by all, it needs to pass through an inclusive dialogue or what we should call a "multilogue." If all affected are not in on the exchange of reasons they will not understand why the agreement was reached, what were the reasons for the demands of others that helped to shape the agreement, why their own negotiators seemed to moderate their demands, and so on. The agreed-upon norm of mutual recognition would thus seem like a sell-out or an unnecessary compromise, and thus as imposed and unacceptable.[43]

The third reason relates to an important characteristic of the identities recognized under any norm. Identities, and thus acceptable forms of recognition and modes of cooperation with others, are partly dependent upon and constituted by the dialogical exchange of reasons and rhetoric over them. The forms of recognition that individuals and groups struggle for are articulated, discussed, altered, reinterpreted, and renegotiated in the course of the struggle. They do not pre-exist their articulation and negotiation in some unmediated or ascriptive pre-dialogue realm. For example, the self-understanding of men and women, Muslim and Christian, French and English, and indigenous and non-indigenous has changed enormously over the last decades of conflict, negotiation, and discussion. The reason is that engagement in the give and take of reasons for and against different proposed norms of mutual

---

[41] We are assuming that in cases where public deliberation is performed by representatives, the systems of representation are themselves systems of dialogical relations between members and representatives.

[42] For a more detailed analysis of the interrelation between forms of recognition and entitlement to resources, and thus between recognition and redistribution in practice, from our "political" perspective, see James Tully, "Struggles over Recognition and Distribution," *Constellations*, 7 (4), 2000, pp. 469–482.

[43] Laden, *Reasonably Radical*, pp. 99–185.

recognition from the various perspectives of the participants changes (and often transforms) the self-understandings and background comprehensive doctrines and worldviews of the interlocutors, breaking down unexamined group prejudices, stereotypes, and blind spots that they bring to the dialogue. Free dialogue does not rest on and shield background assumptions from discussion. It subjects them to critical discussion. Thus, our understanding of who we are, of the partners with whom we are constrained to cooperate, and hence the acceptable norms of mutual recognition changes in the course of the dialogue. Accordingly, the members need to be in on the webs of interlocution of the struggle in order to go through these changes in self-understanding and other-understanding or they will literally not be able to identify with the norm of recognition that others, who have gone through the negotiations, find acceptable.[44]

A fourth, pragmatic consideration is that the only fairly reliable and effective way to work up a norm of mutual recognition that does justice to the diversity and changeability of the members of contemporary political associations is to ensure that all affected have an open and effective say in the deliberations and formulations. A lone theorist, an elite court, and a distant ministry are in contrast probably least able to meet this requirement and more likely to universalize their own partial and *administrative* perspective or to work with unexamined stereotypes. For example, struggles over recognition were initially simply taken to be conflicts between particular cultural, religious, linguistic, indigenous and other forms of "minority diversity" and the impartial and universal "equality" of individuals. But this was based on a lack of understanding of many of the claims classified under "diversity." Many of the claims that indigenous peoples are actually making around the world are not claims for minority status nor are they primarily based on culture or diversity. They are claims to be recognized as "peoples" with the "universal" right of self-determination, based on prior occupancy and sovereignty, and thus to be recognized as "equal" in status to other "peoples" under international law and federal constitutional law. As a result, the monological orientation, with its pre-set categories, misconstrued the nature of the demands.[45]

If we listen to what people are trying to say in actual cases, the demands of minorities are often made in the face of the majority having the power to suppress or misrecognize minorities, to assimilate them to

---

[44] Ibid., pp. 194–199.
[45] James Tully, "The Struggles of Indigenous Peoples for and of Freedom," in *Political Theory and the Rights of Indigenous Peoples*, ed. Duncan Ivison, Paul Patton, and Will Sanders (Cambridge: Cambridge University Press, 2000), pp. 36–59.

the majority's cultural norms, and to present this as if it were universal. These cases are not conflicts between "cultural diversity" and "equality," as the theoretical approach tends to presuppose, but among groups with tremendous inequalities in power and resources (legitimated by the prevailing norms of mutual recognition), and corresponding inequalities in the power to construct the identities of themselves and others through the day-to-day exercise of the prevailing norms of governance and cooperation.[46] Yet this is precisely what the theoretical approach claims to address. The actual struggles are often about these sorts of underlying inequalities, not some hypothetical conflict between cultural diversity or special treatment on one side and the defenders of the universal equality of the status quo on the other, as the monological approach tends to structure the debate. Therefore, the point is not to start with some general thesis about cultural diversity versus equality, as we saw in Part I, but to examine actual cases to see what the conflict is about. This entails *listening* to the people engaged in the struggles over the prevailing norms of recognition in their own terms, taking the dialogical step, and accepting the maxim of *audi alteram partem* (always listen to the other side) as integral to a political approach to issues of recognition.[47]

Alongside this commitment to dialogue is an equally basic rejection of the presumption of finality, that is, the presumption that monological or dialogical approaches should be oriented to a just, definitive, and final resolution of the struggle over recognition. This rejection of the presumption of, and orientation to, finality is based on acknowledging that no matter what procedures for the exchange of reasons are applied to proposed norms of mutual recognition, in either theory or practice, an element of "reasonable disagreement" or "reasonable dissent" will usually remain. That is, an agreement on a norm reached through dialogue can be reasonable (i.e., there are good but not decisive reasons for accepting it) even though some interlocutors will have good but not decisive reasons for not accepting it. What are some of the main reasons for advocating this step from consensus to accepting the reasonableness of those who dissent and can give good reasons for their disagreement?

First, John Rawls argued that there are several reasons for thinking that even in "ideal theory" practical reasoning of this general and complex kind is inherently indeterminate and disagreement ineliminable, thus leaving a plurality of contestable conceptions of the just norms

[46] Laden, *Reasonably Radical*, pp. 133–185.
[47] David Owen, "Cultural Diversity and the Conversation of Justice," *Political Theory*, 27 (5), 1999, pp. 579–596.

of mutual recognition in any case.[48] This insight has brought about the profound reconceptualization of the law as a field of norms over which there is always ongoing reasonable disagreement, and thus must be understood in terms of the norms of democracy and constitutionalism laid out above.[49] In practice, reasonable disagreement may seem an obvious point to anyone familiar with negotiations. First, there are always asymmetries in power, knowledge, influence, and argumentative skills that block the most oppressed from getting to negotiations in the first place and then structure the negotiations if they do. Time is always limited; a decision has to be taken before all affected have had their say and so usually the powerful have an inordinate say; future generations have no say yet are often the most affected; limitations in the agreement are often exposed only after it is implemented and experimented with; and so on. Second, as we have seen, the identities of those involved in the multilogue are modified in the course of the negotiations in complex and unpredictable ways. Given these features, non-consensus and reasonable disagreement seem inevitable. Moreover, and third, there is always a certain "room for maneuver" (*Spielraum*) or field of possible comportments in interpreting and acting in accord with a norm of mutual recognition (whether it is a norm of argumentation in the dialogue or a norm of mutual recognition that has been implemented in practice after negotiations). Even in the most routine activity of acting in accord with a norm of mutual recognition, the members of an association subtly alter it in unpredictable ways through interpretation, application, and negotiation. They can often appear to agree while thinking and acting differently. In other cases, overt agreement, or a manufactured consensus, can mask the vast terrain of hidden scripts and arts of resistance by which subjects act out their reasonable disagreement to oppressive norms in day-to-day life. This field of existential possibilities renders any "agreement" on a norm subject to the "uncertainty, the suspense, the possibility of irreversible change, which surrounds all significant action, however 'rule-guided'."[50]

One response to this argument is to claim that even though agreements would always be liable and likely to be subject to reasonable dissent, there still could be a consensus on a definitive theory of the just procedures of dialogue. This could be worked up in theory and

---

[48] J. Rawls, *Political Liberalism* (New York: Columbia University Press, 1993), pp. 54–58, 2005: 129–180.

[49] Neil Walker, "The Idea of Constitutional Pluralism," *Modern Law Review*, 65 (3), 2002, pp. 317–359.

[50] Charles Taylor, "To Follow a Rule," in *Philosophical Arguments* (Cambridge, MA: Harvard University Press, 1997), p. 177.

employed as a transcendental standard to judge any existing negotiation and to specify what counts as a reasonable and unreasonable claim.[51] However, there is no reason why the considerations of "reasonable disagreement" should not apply to the procedures of negotiation, and thus to the concept of a "reasonable" claim as well.[52] For it is the most common thing in both the ideal world of theoretical debate and the real world of negotiation for theorists and negotiators to move backwards to challenge the procedural rules with which they began. So we now have the view that the procedures of negotiation must be open to question in the course of negotiations, reasonable disagreement over them will persist, and there will be an indeterminate plurality of reasonable procedures. This should be unsurprising, for procedures of negotiation are themselves norms of mutual recognition. Consequently, the modes of acceptable argumentation have expanded from the initial ideal of consensus on what counts as a "public reason," "claim of validity," or "procedure of argumentation," to the view that criteria and procedures of argumentation and "reasonable" are plural and open to question in the course of the negotiations.[53]

For these reasons, we adopt the presumption that any agreement will be less than perfect. It will rest to some extent on unjust exclusion and assimilation and thus be confronted with ineliminable reasonable disagreement (overt or covert). A norm of mutual recognition is thus never final, but questionable – a thing of this world. It follows that, in a free and open society, existing norms of mutual recognition should be open to public questioning so that the reasons *pro* and *contra* can be heard and considered. They should be open to review and potential renegotiation. Reconciliation is thus not a final end-state but an experiential and experimental activity that inevitably will be reactivated from time to time.

III.

If the preceding argument is cogent, what implications follow? Our suggestion is that if the route to resolving conflicts over norms of mutual recognition is to turn to inclusive and dialogical practices of negotiation and if, in the best of circumstances, there will be reasonable disagreement

---

[51] Jürgen Habermas, *Moral Consciousness and Communicative Action* (Cambridge, MA: MIT Press, 1995), pp. 43–116, and *Between Facts and Norms* (Cambridge, MA: MIT Press, 1996).

[52] Waldron, *Law and Disagreement*, makes an extended case for this claim.

[53] For the theoretical and practical aspects of this feature, see Alain-G. Gagnon and James Tully (eds.), *Multinational Democracies* (Cambridge: Cambridge University Press, 2001).

over the imperfect procedures and particular resolution, it follows that the primary orientation of reconciliation should not be the search for definitive and final procedures and solutions, but, rather, the institutionalization and protection of a specific kind of democratic *or civic* freedom. The primary aim will be to ensure that those subject to and affected by any system of governance are always free to call its prevailing norms of recognition and action coordination into question, to present reasons for and against modifying it, to enter into dialogue with those who govern and have a positive duty to listen and respond, to be able to challenge the prevailing procedures of negotiation in the course of the discussions, to reach or fail to reach an imperfect agreement to amend (or overthrow) the norm in question, to implement the amendment; and then to ensure that the implementation is open to review and possible renegotiation in the future. This is the fundamental democratic or civic freedom of citizens – of having an effective say in a dialogue over the norms through which they are governed.

We can specify the nature of this dialogical civic freedom in terms of the idea that conditions of reasonable political deliberation should be such not only that all citizens have an equal opportunity to advance public reasons concerning the character of their civic relationship to one another, and to their trusted and accountable representatives all the way up or down, but also that the reasonable acceptance or rejection of a claim expressed as a public reason makes a difference to the course of the deliberation through which we shape and reshape the content of our shared identity as citizens. If this latter condition is not met, then the person accepting or rejecting the public reason in question is not being treated as an equal and a variety of forms of civic protest and disobedience will be justified. As Laden argues "the reasonableness of deliberation depends on the relevance of uptake of proffered reasons" and further:

Two central ways in which uptake can be rendered irrelevant are by ignoring it or assuming it. Ignoring uptake requires having the power to render rejection of a reason irrelevant. In such cases, we exclude others from our deliberations. Their uptake of our reasons has no effect because their rejection could have no effect. Assuming uptake requires being blind to the fact of deep diversity and how it shapes the plurality of political deliberation. In such cases, we assimilate others to our own perspective. We take for granted that because we find a reason authoritative, they will too.[54]

Consider in this respect two types of social exclusion: the first involves the imposition of a demeaning identity and the second simply the imposition of an identity.[55] The former type straightforwardly

---

[54] Laden, *Reasonably Radical*, p. 129.   [55] Ibid., p. 136.

undermines the possibility of reasonable political deliberation. Such deliberation requires not only that we enjoy sufficient self-respect to regard ourselves as *political equals* (which may be undermined by the internalization of demeaning stereotypical views of oneself as, say, a black person) but also that we see our fellow citizens as political equals: "If whites in the United States regard blacks in the United States as conforming to racist stereotypes, then these attitudes will be sufficient to undermine the preconditions for reasonable political deliberation. Here the problem will be not one of lack of black self-respect, but of white disrespect for blacks."[56] However, even the latter type of social exclusion undermines the conditions of reasonable political deliberation in that imposing an identity on someone is a way of determining which claims have normative authority for them independent of their own view of these claims and thus involves a denial of their status as political equals, that is, "as coauthors with us of the nature of our political relationship" irrespective of whether the imposed upon would endorse the identity in question.[57]

When we turn from exclusion to assimilation, the issue is slightly different in that attention is now focused not on what Laden refers to as the "form" features of citizenship as such, for example, freedom and equality, but on the "content" features of that civic identity. The issue can be brought into focus by returning briefly to the implications of Brian Barry's critique of multiculturalism. We can reconstruct the debate between Barry and Bikhu Parekh in terms of an analogy with moral dilemmas of the form: "I cannot do X or Y and yet I must do X or Y." The contrast between Parekh and Barry is that Parekh takes "can" in the sense of the initial "I cannot do X or Y" and Barry takes it in the later sense of "since I must do X or Y, it follows that I can do X or Y." So one way of construing the difference would be that between:

I cannot do X or Y (hence I don't have an opportunity) since doing X or Y would involve significant damage to my soul or, more prosaically, loss of integrity with respect to my reasonable non-political identity (Parekh)

I can do X or Y (hence I do have an opportunity) since doing X or Y is practically possible for me (Barry)

Now, without endorsing Parekh's position concerning opportunity, we can draw out an important implication of Barry's argument. It is this: an egalitarian politics which resulted in members of a certain cultural community being more or less systematically exposed to tragic conflicts, that is, an inability to maintain their reasonable religious or cultural

---

[56] Laden, *Reasonably Radical*, p. 145.   [57] Ibid., p. 149.

identities with integrity without incurring very significant costs, gives them no grounds in justice for complaint. A liberal polity is not concerned as a matter of justice with the fact that its laws and policies concerning employment, for example, may result in the burdens of citizenship being significantly greater for members of one cultural community than another. Approached from a standpoint of concern with reasonable public deliberation about the content of their shared identity as citizens in which they recognize that citizens are already characterized by reasonable non-political identities that make authoritative claims on how they live their lives (where "reasonable non-political identities" are identities compatible with a commitment to democratic citizenship), it seems unlikely that rational and reasonable citizens would be so reckless as to embrace principles that pay no attention to the degree to which citizenship might be differentially burdensome in respect of their ability to rule themselves in accordance with their cultural or religious self-understandings, where such burdens are not a *necessary* consequence of maintaining the freedom and equality of citizens. As Jeremy Waldron points out, in relation to the proposed introduction of state law regulating some aspect of our lives as citizens and, thus, shaping the nature of our political relationship to one another, the existence of a cultural practice among some members of the polity may figure in two ways. First, it may figure "as the experiential basis of a view about how the wider society should organize itself":

For example, Native American users of peyote may oppose a blanket ban on the use of this hallucinogen, arguing on the basis of their experience with it that the substance has valuable psychological and spiritual properties when used moderately in a properly supervised environment.[58]

Second, it may figure as the basis of a proposal for an exemption from the general application of the regulation in question on the grounds that, to stick with the same example, a ban on the use of peyote creates a special burden with respect to North American Indians that does not apply to other citizens. In respect of this second role, citizens confront two questions: (1) is there room for an exemption? And (2) is it fair to distribute that room to this cultural or religious group?[59] In cases where the policy is not integral, directly or indirectly, to maintaining conditions of reasonable political deliberation, it will often be the case that there is room for an exemption, and where the policy creates significantly differential burdens on citizens in virtue of their religious or cultural

[58] Jeremy Waldron, "One Law for All? The Logic of Cultural Accommodation," *Washington and Lee Law Review*, 59, 2002, p. 33.
[59] Ibid.

identities, it is reasonable that the room for exemption is granted to those subject to extra burdens as a result of the adoption of the policy in question.

Moreover, it is not only the case that the protection of dialogical civic freedom provides a basis for reasonable political deliberation concerning struggles over recognition; we may also note that the experience of direct or indirect participation in these kinds of dialogical struggles helps to generate a new kind of second-order citizen identity appropriate to free, open, and pluralistic forms of association. One comes to acquire an identity *as* a citizen through participation in the practices and institutions of one's society, through having a say in them and over the ways one is governed. In complex contemporary political, legal, cultural, and economic associations, one of the fundamental ways that this process of citizenization occurs is through participation in the very activities in which the norms of mutual recognition in any sub-system are discussed, negotiated, modified, reviewed, and questioned again. The partners involved, while struggling for recognition of their group, nevertheless come to develop an attachment to the larger association, precisely because it allows them to engage in this, second-order free and democratic activity from time to time. These activities of struggling over recognition also allow citizens to dispel *ressentiment* that might otherwise be discharged in violent forms of protest and terrorism if this openness is suppressed and a norm of mutual recognition is imposed unilaterally. On this hypothesis, the turn to violence and terrorism increases as the openness to dialogical civic freedom decreases.[60]

Note that even those who do not win the latest struggle have good reasons to develop a sense of belonging to a political association that is free and open in this contestatory sense. Because they were in on the discussions they learn that there were good reasons on the other side and vice versa, they probably gained some degree of recognition in the compromise agreement, and, given reasonable disagreement, they can continue to believe that their cause is reasonable and worth fighting for again. Most importantly, they know that they have the freedom to challenge the latest hegemonic norm of mutual recognition in the future if they can generate the reasons to support it. And, in fact, this kind of identification is a common feature of most contestatory games: the players competing in them generate a form of identification with the game itself above their team loyalties and their particular victories and losses. So, perhaps it is appropriate that the Greek term for the arts of

---

[60] Compare Benjamin Barber, *Jihad v. McWorld: How Globalism and Tribalism are Reshaping the World* (New York: Ballantine Books, 2003), p. 292.

contestation, "agonistics," is now widely used to characterize these struggles, the complex set of civic virtues the participants acquire and exercise, and the conflicting goods they pursue.[61] This approach thus provides a genuinely democratic solution to the problem of generating a sense of solidarity and conviviality (and thus peace) in any kind of association composed of non-homogeneous members.

IV.

This chapter has sought to provide an overview of both theoretical and political approaches to the topic of redistribution and recognition, and to argue for the priority of the political approach over the theoretical approach. We have argued that both approaches favor the acknowledgment of cultural identities and the burdens that these may generate for citizens – and hence entail redistributive effects. However, our main concern has been to show how the turn to a political approach to this issue produces a fundamental focus on what we have called "dialogical civic freedom," arguing that the protection of such freedom is both a necessary condition of a just polity and a way of generating (as a "by-product," in Elster's phrase) a sense of belonging to this polity on the part of citizens that will support the dispositions required for the reciprocal acknowledgment of each other as culturally diverse political equals. As we have also shown, the theoretical approach will have the indispensable role of clarifying and criticizing procedures and proposals in practice, and, rather than legislating from above, of putting their own theories of recognition and redistribution to the reciprocal test of democratic discussion.

---

[61] Russell Bentley and David Owen, "Ethical Loyalties, Civic Virtue, and the Circumstances of Politics," *Philosophical Explorations*, 4 (3), 2001, pp. 223–239.

11   A critical theory of multicultural toleration

Rainer Forst

I.   The contested concept of toleration

In times of accelerated social change and intense political conflicts, there is a growing need to hold onto traditional concepts that appear to show ways towards a peaceful mode of coexistence. Yet at the same time, we recognize that the closer we look at such concepts, we find them deeply ambivalent and to be more an expression of social conflict than a means to overcome it. In the current debates about multiculturalism, within as well as beyond nation-states, the concept of toleration is a case in point. It is a heavily contested concept, such that for some, toleration is a word that signifies a peaceful way of social life in difference, while for others it stands for relations of domination and repression.

A few examples show the deep disagreements about what toleration means in the context of contemporary debates: Is a law that says that crucifixes should be hung up in public classrooms a sign of intolerance, or is, rather, the opposition against it intolerant? Is it intolerant to demand that teachers or students should refrain from wearing a head-scarf in school, or is, rather, wearing it a sign of intolerance? Is it intolerant to deny homosexual couples the right to marry, or is such a right much more than toleration of homosexuality would require? And generally, is it a good thing to be "merely tolerated" in such a way? Finally, is publishing caricatures of the prophet Muhammad an act of intolerance, or is the negative reaction against it such an act? And is tolerating such reactions a sign of "false tolerance"?[1]

Before, however, in view of such debates we come to the conclusion that toleration is an arbitrary concept that can be used for just any purpose, we should hold onto a clear definition of its conceptual core, for that core needs to be explained by the three components of *objection*,

---

[1] I will come back to these examples in sections VII and VIII. Many more cases could be added, such as the one that concerns the question whether disallowing "creationism" to be taught on an equal footing with evolutionary theory is a case of secularist intolerance.

acceptance, and *rejection*.[2] First, a tolerated belief or practice has to be seen as false or bad in order to be a candidate for toleration; otherwise, we would not speak of toleration but of either indifference or affirmation. Second, apart from these reasons of objection there have to be reasons why it would still be wrong not to tolerate these false or bad beliefs or practices, i.e., reasons of acceptance. Such reasons do not eliminate the objections, they only trump them in a given case. Third, there have to be reasons of rejection which mark the limits of toleration, i.e., reasons that specify which beliefs or practices cannot or must not be tolerated. All three of those reasons can be of one and the same kind – religious, for example – yet they can also be of different kinds (moral, religious, or pragmatic, to mention a few possibilities).

While this conceptual core is (or rather, should be) generally agreed upon, the disagreement begins once these components are fleshed out: What can or should be tolerated, for what reasons, and where are the limits of toleration? Since toleration is what I call a *normatively dependent concept*, i.e., a concept that is in need of other, independent normative resources in order to gain a certain content and substance, there have been and there still are many debates about how to fill in the three components in an appropriate way. And because toleration is not an independent value, there are not just debates about how to ground and how to limit toleration but also debates about whether toleration is something *good at all*, like the ones just mentioned. And this is no recent phenomenon; just contrast, if we look at the debates in the eighteenth century, the arguments of Voltaire and Lessing for tolerance as a sign of reasonableness and true humanity with Kant's remark about the "presumptuous title of tolerant," or with Goethe's famous saying that "to tolerate means to insult."[3]

---

[2] With respect to the first two components I follow Preston King, *Toleration* (New York: St. Martin's Press, 1976), ch. 1. Glen Newey, *Virtue, Reason and Toleration* (Edinburgh: Edinburgh University Press, 1999), ch. 1, also distinguishes between three kinds of reasons in his structural analysis of toleration (which, however, differs from mine in the way these reasons are interpreted). For a more extensive discussion, see my "Toleration, Justice and Reason," in *The Culture of Toleration in Diverse Societies: Reasonable Tolerance*, ed. Catriona McKinnon and Dario Castiglione (Manchester: Manchester University Press, 2003), pp. 71–85. Since I believe that there is such a core concept, I do not regard toleration to be an "essentially contested concept" in the sense of W. B. Gallie, "Essentially Contested Concepts," *Proceedings of the Aristotelian Society*, 56, 1956, pp. 167–198; since it is a normatively dependent concept, it does, however, share some of Gallie's characterizations.

[3] Immanuel Kant, "An Answer to the Question: 'What is Enlightenment?'," in Kant, *Political Writings*, ed. H. Reiss, trans. H. B. Nisbet (Cambridge: Cambridge University Press, 1991), p. 58; Johann Wolfgang Goethe, "Maximen und Reflexionen," *Werke*, 6 (Frankfurt am Main: Insel, 1981), p. 507: "Toleranz sollte nur eine vorübergehende Gesinnung sein: sie muss zur Anerkennung führen. Dulden heißt beleidigen."

Such conflicts about the concept of toleration result from the fact that historically a number of rival *conceptions* of toleration have evolved, the two most prominent of which are in constant struggle.[4] From a historical perspective, therefore, one should not just speak of conflicts between the party of "toleration" and various forms of "intolerance"; apart from that, we find important struggles between parties which held different accounts of toleration. What is more, as I will try to show, these debates still determine contemporary conflicts about toleration to a large extent. To analyze such conflicts and their inherent "grammars" of justice as well as of power is the main task of a *critical* theory of toleration, as I see it.

II.   The permission conception

The first prominent conception of toleration I call the *permission conception*. According to it, toleration is a relation between an authority or a majority and a dissenting, "different" minority (or various minorities). Toleration then means that the authority (or majority) gives qualified permission to the members of the minority to live according to their beliefs on the condition that the minority accepts the dominant position of the authority (or majority). As long as their expression of their differences remains within limits, that is, is a "private" matter, and as long as they do not claim equal public and political status, they can be tolerated on both pragmatic and principled grounds – on pragmatic grounds because this form of toleration is regarded as the least costly of all possible alternatives and does not disturb civil peace and order as the dominant party defines it (but rather contributes to it); and on principled grounds because the members of the majority may find it wrong (and in any case fruitless) to force people to give up their deep-seated beliefs or practices.

We find the permission conception in many historical documents and precedents illustrating a politics of toleration such as the Edict of Nantes in 1598, the Toleration Act after the "Glorious Revolution" in England in 1689, or the "Toleration Patents" of Joseph II in the Habsburg Monarchy in 1781. Toleration here means that the authority or majority which has the power to interfere with the practices of a minority

---

[4] I discuss two other conceptions, the "coexistence conception" and the "esteem conception," in my "Toleration, Justice, and Reason," section 2. The following argument is an extremely condensed version of my comprehensive reconstruction of the development of the various conceptions of toleration and of the justifications for toleration from ancient times to the present in my *Toleranz im Konflikt. Geschichte, Gehalt und Gegenwart eines umstrittenen Begriffs* (Frankfurt am Main: Suhrkamp, 2003).

nevertheless tolerates it, while the minority accepts its dependent position. The situation or the "terms of toleration" are non-reciprocal: one party allows another party certain things on conditions specified by the former. The values of the majority – a certain religion or confession, traditionally – define all three components mentioned above: objection, acceptance, and rejection (the limits of the "tolerable").

It is this conception that Kant and Goethe had in mind in their critique of toleration, a critique which shows the ambivalence that is characteristic of that conception. For on the one hand, the mentioned acts and policies clearly did protect certain endangered minorities and granted them certain liberties they did not have before. Yet on the other hand, it is precisely this act of "granting" which renders this hierarchical conception of toleration problematic. For such policies were (mostly) strategically motivated acts of limited liberation which did not grant rights but certain permissions which could also be revoked at any time and therefore forced the minorities into a precarious position of second-class citizens dependent upon the good-will of the authorities. Thus those forms of toleration had liberating as well as repressive and disciplining effects: *repressive* because to be tolerated meant to accept one's weak and underprivileged position, and *disciplining* because those policies of toleration "produced" stigmatized and "non-normal" identities that were at the same time socially included and excluded.[5] The toleration of the Jews from the Middle Ages to modern times is an especially obvious example of such complex forms of excluding inclusion; loyalty and subservience was the price demanded for some protection. Toleration quite often proved to be an extremely effective form of exercising and preserving one's power.[6]

III.   The respect conception and the ambivalence of liberalism

As opposed to this, the alternative conception of toleration that evolved historically and still is present in contemporary discourse – the *respect conception* – is one in which the tolerating parties recognize each other in a reciprocal, "horizontal" way: Even though they differ strongly in their ethical beliefs about the good and true way of life and in their cultural practices, they respect each other as moral and political equals in the sense that their common basic framework of social life should be guided

---

[5] For a contemporary analysis of such effects of toleration see Wendy Brown, "Reflections on Tolerance in the Age of Identity," in *Democracy and Vision*, ed. A. Botwinick and W. E. Connolly (Princeton: Princeton University Press, 2001), pp. 99–117.

[6] See Amy Chua, *Day of Empire* (Doubleday, forthcoming).

by norms that all parties can equally accept and that do not favor one specific cultural or "ethical community," so to speak. The basis for that is the respect for others as autonomous and equal citizens, which presupposes the capacity and willingness to differentiate between (a) the realm of those values and practices which one fully affirms, (b) the realm of beliefs and practices one judges to be ethically bad but which one still tolerates because one cannot judge them to be morally wrong in a generally justifiable sense, and (c) the realm of what cannot be tolerated, judged on the basis of norms and principles that are justifiable to all citizens and not determined by only one party.

This conception of toleration is the result of a complex history of struggles against various forms of intolerance as well as against forms of one-sided toleration based on the permission conception. The connection between *toleration* and *justice* that is essential here constitutes the core of the claim for *mutual* toleration (among citizens) and for a general *right* to religious liberty – a claim that was seen as undeniable given basic demands of political justice and equal respect. Hence, the discourses of "toleration" and of "individual rights" are, seen from the perspective of the respect conception, not mutually exclusive (as it seems from the perspective of the permission conception).

Traditionally, the right to religious liberty was seen to be a "natural" right that God had given to men and that could not be handed over to a worldly authority. The political "freedom of conscience" was based on the idea that conscience is exactly *not free* from a religious perspective: faith is "divine work" (as Luther had called it).[7] Conscience was to be free because it was bound to and led by God. But this thought only constituted the core of the revolutionary claim for religious liberty – in the Revolution of the Netherlands for the first time, then the English Revolutions (where in the 1640s the Levellers claimed religious liberty as a "birthright"), and finally the American and French Revolutions – in connection with the further thought that the state was created by men in order to secure their rights (and duties). It was in the light of these liberties that the "business of civil government" (Locke) was to be defined. Thus, historically speaking, liberalism was a latecomer in the discourse of toleration, but a powerful one, because it provided some of the resources for an alternative understanding of toleration: one that followed a logic of emancipation rather than domination.

---

[7] Martin Luther, "Secular Authority: To What Extent it Should be Obeyed" (1523), in Luther, *Selections from His Writings*, ed. J. Dillenberger (New York: Anchor, 1962), p. 385.

But, again, there are a number of ambivalences in that cluster of ideas we today call "early liberalism." On the one hand, there was the idea of individual rights that human beings had "by nature," as moral rights, which gave them a certain dignity that every other human being or human authority had to respect. On the other hand, the religious grounding of such rights, especially the right to religious liberty, meant that there could be no liberty *not* to believe in God, and also that certain forms of religion which questioned the stress on individual conscience and were bound by other, innerworldly religious authorities could not be tolerated. Hence, in his *Letter Concerning Toleration* (1689), Locke (like many others) excluded atheists and Catholics from the realm of the tolerable.[8] The ambivalence here was that certain individual rights were claimed that separated political from religious authority while the basis of morality as well as of the state still was seen to consist in the right kind of religious beliefs: "The taking away of God, tho but even in thought, dissolves all."[9] The fear that without a common religious basis – without the fear of God (in whatever form he was worshiped) – there could be no morality and no functioning state one could call *Locke's fear*, because he expressed it in such a clear way; it is, however, not just Locke who had this fear, for it is also shared by Enlightenment thinkers such as Montesquieu, Rousseau, and Voltaire. And if we look at contemporary debates about the basis of social and political integration in a multicultural society, this fear is still present (as I will discuss below).

IV.   Bayle's justification of toleration

Historically speaking, there is a very important, original, and extremely underestimated voice in the history of toleration that questioned Locke's fear (though not as a direct reaction to Locke): Pierre Bayle. In his *Pensées diverses sur la comète* (1683), he introduced what was later called "Bayle's paradox" by saying that religion was not necessary to support morality which rested on other motives (such as the desire for social recognition) and insights (of "natural reason"), and that religious fanaticism was the main danger to morality and the state. He even ventured the idea that a society of atheists would be possible – and possibly would be more peaceful than religious societies.[10]

---

[8] John Locke, *A Letter Concerning Toleration*, ed. J. Tully (Indianapolis: Hackett, 1983), pp. 49–51.

[9] Ibid., p. 51. For a contemporary discussion and elaboration of that view, see Jeremy Waldron, *God, Locke, and Equality* (Cambridge: Cambridge University Press, 2002).

[10] See Pierre Bayle, *Various Thoughts on the Occasion of a Comet*, trans. and ed. R. C. Bartlett (New York: State University of New York Press, 2000), esp. section 129ff.

What is more, one of Bayle's decisive insights was that mutual toleration among persons with different religious beliefs could only be
possible if there was a generally shared moral basis of respect among
human beings that would rule out the exercise of religious force and that
would be independent from the religious beliefs that separated persons.
In his *Commentaire philosophique sur ces paroles de Jésus-Christ "Contrain-
les d'entrer"* (1686),[11] he provides such a justification of toleration which
avoids the problems that Locke's defense of religious liberty faced. For
from studying Augustine's arguments about the possibility and productivity of *terror* in freeing men from religious error and enabling them
to see the truth, if properly informed,[12] Bayle already knew what Locke
had to acknowledge after being confronted with Jonas Proast's critique:
that even though authentic beliefs could not be directly produced by
external force, there were many other – "indirect" – ways to block men
on a road of error and to make them turn around so that they could see
the truth.[13] Only in his *Second Letter* (1690) did Locke see the force of

[11] Pierre Bayle, *Philosophical Commentary*, trans. and ed. A. Godman Tannenbaum (New
York: Peter Lang, 1987).
[12] See especially, Augustine's famous letter to Vincentius, written in 408, published in
Saint Augustine, *Letters*, vol. II, ed. Sister W. Parsons (New York: Fathers of the
Church, 1953), # 93.
[13] "I readily grant that Reason and Arguments are the only proper Means, whereby to
induce the Mind to assent to any Truth, which is not evident by its own Light: and that
Force is very improper to be used to that end *instead* of Reason and Arguments ... But
notwithstanding this, if Force be used, not instead of Reason and Arguments, i.e. not to
convince by its own proper Efficacy (which it cannot do,) but onely to bring men to
consider those Reasons and Arguments which are proper and sufficient to convince
them, but which, without being forced, they would not consider: who can deny, but that
indirectly and *at a distance*, it does some service toward the bringing men to embrace that
Truth, which otherwise, either through Carelesness and Negligence they would never
acquaint themselves with, or through Prejudice they would reject and condemn
unheard, under the notion of Errour?" Jonas Proast, *The Argument of the Letter
Concerning Toleration, Briefly Consider'd and Answer'd*, reprint of the edition of 1690
(New York: Garland, 1984), p. 4f. For a convincing critique of Locke on the basis of
Proastian considerations, see especially Jeremy Waldron, "Locke, Toleration, and the
Rationality of Persecution," in *Liberal Rights: Collected Papers 1981–1991* (Cambridge:
Cambridge University Press, 1993), ch. 4. Where I disagree with Waldron, however, is
about his claim that Locke did not find a plausible counter-argument to Proast. For
that, however, he had to change his position and move towards the epistemological-
normative argument that we find in Bayle (in superior form). In his later letters on
toleration, Locke argues that the use of religious-political force is in need of mutual
justification, and that Proast's main assumption of the undeniable truth of the Church
of England is unfounded. See especially Locke, *A Second Letter Concerning Toleration*, in
The Works of John Locke, vol. VI (Aalen: Scientia, 1963), p. 111, where he asks Proast to
put forth a mutually justifiable argument "without supposing all along your church in
the right, and your religion the true; which can no more be allowed to you in this case,
whatever your church or religion be, than it can to a papist or a Lutheran, a presbyterian
or anabaptist; nay, no more to you, than it can be allowed to a Jew or a Mahometan." I
discuss these questions in more detail in my "Pierre Bayle's Reflexive Theory of

this counter-argument against his main point for toleration, so the argument against religious force had to be changed and could no longer rest on the empirical-psychological assumption of the "unforceability" of conscience and sincere faith. Bayle had already taken this into account in his critique of the "convertists" of his time. Hence he argued that every person had a general duty to justify any exercise of force, and that in a case in which there was a stand-off of one religious reason versus another, there was *no* sufficient justification on either side. And this not because Bayle was a religious skeptic (as many have thought), but because Bayle insisted on faith being *faith* and not knowledge: as long as there was no undisputable proof as to the truth of one religion or confession, the duty of mutual justification called for tolerance (but not for skepticism). From that perspective, the claim of people like (his contemporary) Bishop Bossuet who believed that they were in possession of the truth and therefore could legitimately exercise force – for which Bossuet, following Augustine, referred to the famous parable of the Lord who asks his servants to force those who do not want to accept the invitation to the prepared dinner to come in (Luke 14, 15ff.) – would turn into nothing but a pure and illegitimate act of violence.

In his writings, Bayle carefully explained the distinction between knowledge and faith and the possibility of a form of "natural" practical reason that would lead to an insight into the duty of mutual justification.[14] Faith was not seen, in a fideist sense, as being *against* reason but as being *beyond reason*: faith was not irrational, but at the same time reason could not prove the true faith.[15] Human reason had to accept its own boundaries and finitude. Hence in a conflict in which the truth of one religion or confession was disputed by others, those who believed in such truth were not required to doubt it, yet they were required to see that mutual toleration was called for: a form of living together where each side accepts that it must not force its own views on the other.

Toleration," in *Toleration and Its Limits, Nomos*, 48, ed. J. Waldron and M. Williams (New York: New York University Press, forthcoming).

[14] See Bayle, *Philosophical Commentary*, p. 30: "[B]ut if it's possible to have certain limitations with respect to speculative truths, I don't believe there ought to be any with regard to those practical and general principles which concern morals. I mean that all moral laws without exception, must submit to that idea of natural equity, which, as well as metaphysical light, *enlightens every man coming into the world* ... I would like whoever aims at knowing distinctly this natural light with respect to morality to raise himself above his own private interest or the custom of his country, and to ask himself in general: '*Is such a practice just in itself? If it were a question of introducing it in a country where it would not be in use and where he would be free to take it up or not, would one see, upon examining it impartially, that it is reasonable enough to merit being adopted?*'" (Emphasis in original.)

[15] See especially Bayle, *Historical and Critical Dictionary*, Selections, trans. R. Popkin (Indianapolis: Hackett, 1991), Second and Third Clarification, pp. 409–435.

What this little historical digression shows is the following. A justification of toleration such as Bayle's avoids the pitfalls of a traditional argument for the liberty of conscience, which are (to repeat): (a) that the claim *credere non potest nisi volens* (Augustine)[16] – there can be no faith without voluntary acceptance – does not provide an argument against the suppression of religious "errors" or against religious "guidance" because it seems quite possible that "mild" force can bring about sincere beliefs, and (b) that such toleration could only extend to *authentic* religious beliefs (whereas a criterion for such beliefs seems to be lacking), and of course only to *religious* beliefs (and not to atheists).

V.   Autonomy and respect

A Baylean justification for toleration also avoids, if we look at contemporary liberal thought in the Lockean (and, we should add, Millian) tradition, the problems of the view that religious liberty is justified because personal autonomy is a precondition for the good life, for only the life lived "from the inside," on the basis of autonomously chosen ethical options, could be good, as Will Kymlicka argues.[17] In his theory of multicultural justice – the (by now already) classic reference point for these debates – he argues that rather than seeing different cultures and traditions as threats to individual liberty and autonomy, liberals should see them as important "contexts of choice," providing their members with meaningful possibilities for leading their lives. Thus, for immigrant groups certain "polyethnic" rights are called for, and for national minorities rights to self-determination. Yet since these cultural rights are justified as enabling conditions for the exercise of personal autonomy, the cultural groups can only claim "external protections"; they cannot impose "internal restrictions" on the basic liberties of their members. More than that, these groups not only have to respect the priority of individual liberties as a political imperative; they also have to accept a Millian notion of autonomy implying that a prerequisite for living a good life is having the capacity to question or revise one's ethical convictions and "choices." According to Kymlicka, one cannot "accept the ideal

---

[16] Augustine, *In Joannis Evangelium*, 26, 2, in *Patrologiae cursus completus*, ed. P. G. Migne, vol. 35 (Turnhout: Brepols, 1981), p. 1607.

[17] Will Kymlicka, *Multicultural Citizenship* (Oxford: Clarendon, 1995), pp. 80–84. For a detailed critique, see my "Foundations of a Theory of Multicultural Justice," *Constellations* 4 (1), 1997, pp. 63–71, and Kymlicka's reply in "Do We Need a Liberal Theory of Minority Rights? A Reply to Carens, Young, Parekh and Forst," in the same volume, pp. 72–87 (reprinted in Kymlicka, *Politics in the Vernacular* [Oxford: Oxford University Press, 2001], pp. 49–68).

of autonomy in political contexts without also accepting it more generally."[18]

From a (neo-)Baylean (and, I should add, Kantian) perspective, however, such a notion of autonomy cannot provide the foundation of a theory of multicultural justice, for it seems to be a matter of reasonable disagreement whether a life lived according to traditional values that are taken over in a conventional way or accepted because of a certain "calling" would be *worse* – i.e., of lesser subjective or objective value – than one that is autonomously "chosen" (whatever that could mean in practice). We must instead accept that the politically *free*, the personally *autonomous*, and the ethically *good* life may be three separate and independent things – and that a different normative argument for the protection of autonomy is needed. To base a scheme of multicultural justice and toleration on a reasonably contestable liberal notion of the good not only draws too close a connection between the three concepts of liberty, autonomy, and the good, it also leads to the (familiar) problem that according to an ethical-liberal, "comprehensive" justification for tolerance, those conceptions of life that do not exhibit the right kind of autonomy would not deserve to be fully tolerated. Rather, the liberal state might then have the perfectionist duty to "make" people autonomous, the interpretation and exercise of which could interfere with justified claims to political liberty and social equality. And if the liberal state refrained from doing so, "non-autonomous" groups could only be tolerated according to the permission conception.[19]

The alternative view I propose obviously also calls for a certain kind of respect for the autonomy of persons.[20] Yet this notion of autonomy is not based on a particular conception of the good, but on a moral notion of the person as a reasonable being with (what I call) a *right to justification*. This right to justification is based on the recursive principle that every use of force, or (more generally) any morally relevant interference with others' actions, needs to be justified by reciprocally and generally non-rejectable reasons in order to be seen as legitimate.[21] Reciprocity

---

[18] Will Kymlicka, "Two Models of Pluralism and Tolerance," in *Toleration: An Elusive Virtue*, ed. D. Heyd (Princeton: Princeton University Press, 1996), p. 91.

[19] Depending on the arrangement, this could constitute a new form of a liberal "Millet system," the traditional form of which Kymlicka discusses in "Two Models of Pluralism and Tolerance," pp. 83–87.

[20] See my discussion of various conceptions of autonomy in "Political Liberty: Integrating Five Conceptions of Autonomy," in *Autonomy and the Challenges to Liberalism: New Essays*, ed. J. Christman and J. Anderson (Cambridge: Cambridge University Press, 2005), pp. 226–242.

[21] I explain this principle and its moral and political implications more fully in my *Contexts of Justice: Political Philosophy beyond Liberalism and Communitarianism*, trans. J. M. M. Farrell (Los Angeles and Berkeley: University of California Press, 2002).

here means that one party must not make any claim to certain rights or resources that are denied to others, and that one party does not project its own reasons (values, interests, needs) onto others in arguing for its claims. One must be willing to argue for basic norms that are to be reciprocally and generally valid and binding with reasons that are not based on contested "higher" truths or on conceptions of the good which can reasonably be questioned and rejected. Generality, then, means that the reasons for such norms need to be shareable among all persons affected, not just dominant parties.

The respect for each individual's right to justification is not based on the idea that this is demanded as a necessary precondition of the good life; rather, it is a moral demand to respect each other's moral autonomy as reason-giving and reason-receiving beings, in the Kantian sense of "morality," apart from any notion of "happiness" (*Glückseligkeit*). Whether those who are respected in that way will eventually lead a better life can therefore be the object of disagreement; no disagreement, however, must exist about the duty of justification and the criteria of reciprocity and generality. The important difference between those who reject a liberal notion of autonomy concerning the good and those who reject the moral autonomy of persons having a right to justification, then, is that the first rejection can (and should) be based on the latter notion of autonomy, arguing against an unjustifiable imposition of a notion of the good, whereas the rejection of moral autonomy is either reciprocally unjustifiable, for one denies to others what one claims for oneself, i.e., to be respected as a person whose reasons and claims are taken seriously, or it is self-contradictory, for one would argue (with reasons) that one does not want to be respected as someone whose reasons and claims need to be respected. Again, think of the above-mentioned difference between the free, the autonomous, and the good life. The central argument against "internal restrictions" (imposed by a cultural group, for example, or by the state) limiting personal autonomy is not that this will destroy the possibility of a person leading a good life (though this may be true, too); rather, the argument is that this denies a person's basic right to justification and violates his or her dignity as an equal moral person (and citizen) endowed with reason.

Hence, even if there were "no evidence that groups which reject personal autonomy are likely to adopt a definition of morality that privileges moral autonomy," as Kymlicka argues against my view,[22] it makes an essential difference whether a democratic state asks a cultural

---

[22] See his reply to me in "Do We Need a Liberal Theory of Minority Rights?," p. 85.

group to respect "personal autonomy" because of a notion of the good that they might not and need not share, or whether they are asked to respect a form of autonomy to which they themselves need to take recourse when they demand a justification for a political or legal norm and reject ethical "colonization." If the democratic state argues on the basis of a principle of reciprocal justification which gives equal chances to raise claims to all involved, members of majorities, minorities, and minorities *within* minorities, it can justifiably claim to establish a system of multicultural justice. In the eyes of some groups, this may in the end just seem to be another form of (pseudo-)liberal destruction of their ways of life, yet what matters is whether this critique is mutually justifiable or itself based on a denial of the principle of justification. The acceptance of that principle defines the limits of the tolerable, for those who deny it deny basic norms of impartiality and public justification that lie at the core of what a just multicultural society needs to be based on if it wants to "do justice" to the claims of minorities.[23]

VI.   Ethics and morality

The *normative* component of the justification of toleration, then, lies in the principle of justification itself, while the *epistemological* component consists of an insight into the finitude of reason: reason is not sufficient to provide us with the one and only, ultimate answer about the truth of the good life which would show that all other ethical beliefs are false. There is a parallel to Rawls's conception of toleration and of the need to accept the "burdens of reason" (or of "judgment") here,[24] the crucial normative difference with Rawls's view being that the conception I propose is based on a deontological view of moral rights and duties in the political realm, not on a "political" conception of justice. From an epistemological perspective, what is most important is that such an insight into the finitude of reason does not imply religious or ethical skepticism, as for example Brian Barry argues, for contrary to his view it is quite plausible that "certainty from the inside about some view can coherently be combined with the line that it is reasonable for others to reject that same view."[25] All one needs to accept in order for that to make sense is a distinction between religious faith and knowledge based on reason alone, accepting that faith is not necessarily a system of beliefs

---

[23] On this, see my "The Limits of Toleration," *Constellations*, 11 (3), 2004, pp. 312–325.

[24] John Rawls, *Political Liberalism* (New York: Columbia University Press, 1993), pp. 54–58.

[25] Brian Barry, *Justice as Impartiality* (Oxford: Oxford University Press, 1995), p. 179.

"against" but still (at least in part) "beyond" reason, as Bayle argued.[26] As he phrased it, the believer "who allows himself to be disconcerted by the objections of the unbelievers, and to be scandalized by them, has one foot in the same grave as they do."[27] In that respect, a Rawlsian notion of toleration is much more Baylean than Lockean.

Most important in this context is the insight that to be tolerant in this way implies the willingness and the capacity to distinguish between one's *ethical* beliefs about the true and good life, on the one hand, and the *moral* norms and principles one thinks every person, regardless of his or her view of the good, has to accept, on the other.[28] Bayle's theory clearly implies such a distinction, and looking at the history of toleration one may say that the working out of such a differentiation, in theory as well as in practice, may be the greatest achievement within the discourse of toleration. It comes, however, at a certain cost, which makes tolerance (according to the respect conception) into a demanding *moral and political virtue*: the cost is that in the case in which you cannot present reciprocally and generally non-rejectable arguments for your ethical judgments, you have to accept that there is no justification for forcing them upon others or for making them the basis for generally binding legal norms.[29]

Referring back to the three components of toleration (see section I above), the main difference between the permission conception and the respect conception is that according to the former all three components are determined by the ethical views of the dominant majority or authority, while in the respect conception things look different. The *objection* is based on one's particular ethical (or religious) views; the *acceptance*, however, is based on a moral consideration of whether the reasons of objection are good enough to be reasons of *rejection*, i.e., whether they qualify for being generally enforceable. If they turn out to be sufficient for a negative *ethical* judgment, but not for a negative *moral* judgment of certain practices or beliefs, the case for toleration arises: for then one has to see that one's ethical judgment does not justify a generally shareable

---

[26] Bayle, *Historical and Critical Dictionary*, p. 410. This distinction also explains why "creationism" should not be part of the school curriculum as an alternative to evolutionary theory.

[27] Ibid., p. 429.

[28] Here I follow Jürgen Habermas's idea of a "discourse ethics," especially in his *Moral Consciousness and Communicative Action*, trans. C. Lenhardt and S. W. Nicholsen (Cambridge, MA: MIT Press, 1990).

[29] As far as "public justification" within a democratic regime is concerned, however, one must add that Bayle – due to his political experiences – stood in the tradition of the *politiques* who thought that only a strong sovereign (like Henri Quatre) would be powerful enough to protect minorities like the Huguenots. Thus there is no strong argument for democracy – or for a political, democratic version of the respect conception.

moral condemnation and a rejection. This is the insight of toleration. The decisive difference, then, lies in the way the *limits of toleration* are being drawn: on the basis of particular ethical values or on the basis of considerations based on the principle of justification itself.

My main claim thus is that the neo-Baylean justification for toleration I suggest is superior to others precisely by being a *reflexive* one: rather than being based on a particular idea of (traditionally speaking) salvation or (more generally) the good, it rests upon the very principle of justification, a higher-order principle of the demand to give adequate reasons for claims in the political realm. This is also why it serves as the basis for a *critical* theory of toleration: it contains the principle of the critique of false forms of toleration or justification in its very core.

VII.   Applications

Let me briefly come back to the examples mentioned in section I to explain the implications of such a view, highlighting the way in which the permission conception of toleration and the respect conception are at odds in contemporary conflicts. In a much-debated decision (in 1995), the German Federal Constitutional Court declared unconstitutional the law that ordered crosses or crucifixes to hang in classrooms of Bavarian public schools.[30] In the debate that followed, many argued that to be tolerant of non-Christian (or non-religious) minorities simply meant to refrain from religious pressure and indoctrination, but that it did not require a "neutral" school devoid of traditional Christian symbols. At the same time, they stressed that these minorities also have the duty to be tolerant and not to force the majority to refrain from expressing their religious beliefs. In their view, the minority plaintiffs were to be charged with intolerance. Others, like the Court, argued that toleration means not to prefer particular religious symbols by law, even if they stand for the religious beliefs of the dominant majority of citizens. The first understanding of toleration followed a logic of preference for a majority that only "permits" others to be different – thus here the permission conception reappears in a democratic version, not, of course, in the older absolutist form. The second conception followed a logic of equal respect. On the basis of the principle of reciprocal and general justification, the minorities who argued against the crucifixes thus had a reciprocally non-rejectable point: they argued for equal recognition, while the other side argued for the preservation of its dominant position.

---

[30] For a detailed analysis of that decision, see my "A Tolerant Republic?," in *German Ideologies Since 1945*, ed. Jan-Werner Müller (New York: Palgrave, 2003), pp. 209–220.

Hence according to the first conception, toleration meant that the majority tolerates persons with "different" beliefs as long as they do not claim equal public or legal status, whereas according to the second conception, toleration required the majority to refrain from having the symbols of their faith be supported by law. To be sure, both conceptions are conceptions of toleration, yet the second one is preferable for normative reasons of *justice* most adequate for a multicultural society. In such a society, the normatively dependent concept of toleration should be substantiated with the help of the principle of reciprocal and general justification.

A similar situation arises with respect to the question of homosexual marriage. The German Federal Constitutional Court recently affirmed a law that establishes such a possibility (though not on fully equal footing with heterosexual marriage) as constitutional.[31] In the debate about the case, some argued against that law and found that to tolerate homosexuality was one thing, but to grant equal rights was quite another and not justified, for the traditional institution of marriage should be preserved in its meaning and priority (a slogan of a conservative political party said "Tolerance yes, marriage no!"). Those who held the opposed view found that position to be deeply intolerant. Again, the question was whether toleration is mere permission to be different, but not fully equal, or whether toleration requires equal respect of differences and therefore also equal rights. And again the notion of toleration itself does *not* settle this dispute. Seen through the lens of the principle of justification, however, it seems that the argument for equal rights in questions of marriage is a claim that is hard to reject, if one-sided ethical and religious views are ruled out as a basis for decision. Then toleration means more than "putting up" with minority practices that are stigmatized as "non-normal" and remain in a situation of legal discrimination (toleration being, in Goethe's words, an "insult"); it means accepting that certain ethical objections are insufficient for a general rejection and that therefore such practices have to be granted equal rights.

A final example. In many liberal-democratic societies, we find debates about the *hijab* of Muslim women and girls; in the German context, teachers' headscarves are an especially contested issue.[32] Whereas some argue that the *hijab* is a sign of intolerance, especially of the oppression

[31] Decision of 17 July 2002 (1 BvR 1/01).
[32] In a decision of 24 September 2003 (2 BvR 1436/02), the Federal Constitutional Court found that the state of Baden-Württemberg must not deny a Muslim teacher the right to wear a *hijab* in school since there is no sufficient legal ground within the laws of the state for such infringements of basic rights to religious freedom and an equal chance to

of women and of an explicit distance from liberal society, others argue that it is intolerant to use such a one-sided interpretation to determine what the practice of wearing a *hijab* means. For the first party, toleration means to accept Muslim teachers in school, yet it does not mean to accept them wearing a headscarf; for the second party, it means exactly this as long as one cannot prove individually that a teacher fails in performing her duties and does actually try to influence students in a problematic way. No general exclusion is justified, then, on the basis of controversial interpretations of a symbol. This is what the respect conception implies: equal rights for identities even though some of them are not just "different" but also objected to by social majorities – as long as such an objection is insufficient to justify a rejection by law.[33]

Examples like these (and many others could be added) show that contemporary discourses of toleration are over-determined by the conflicts between different understandings of toleration – and they show especially how strong the permission conception still is in liberal-democratic societies, holding the political imagination captive.

VIII. A critical theory of toleration

For an analysis of such conflicts, the conception of multicultural toleration I have suggested has two major advantages. First, it provides a recursive, reflexive justification of toleration: since the question of toleration in political contexts always *is* the question of the justification of the rejection component especially, the superior justification of toleration as an attitude as well as a practice is the one that rests on the principle of impartial and public justification itself as the core of democratic justice. Its criteria for determining the limits of toleration are discursive and open, demanding that no voices in the social and political struggles involved will be ignored – a critical idea which has important institutional implications for establishing at least a minimally just political structure of justification.

The second advantage, then, is that this approach does provide conceptual resources for what I call a critical theory of toleration. Based on a (historically informed) understanding of the complex matrix of power that corresponds to the permission conception, one can see that such forms of toleration at the same time include and exclude

gain public office. It is a matter of debate, however, how much room that decision leaves for the state to provide such a basis.

[33] I find myself in agreement here with Joseph Carens's notion of justice as "evenhandedness." See his *Culture, Citizenship, and Community* (Oxford: Oxford University Press, 2000).

minorities. They include them and give them some recognition and protection, yet at the same time they stigmatize them as citizens of second class. Such forms of toleration are liberating and at the same time repressive and disciplining, as pointed out above (section II); liberating because they are an advantage as compared to more oppressive policies, repressive because to be tolerated means to accept one's underprivileged status, and disciplining because such policies "produce" different "non-normal" identities that are marked as such.[34] A critical political theory consists not only of a normative theory of justification that rests on the principle of public criticism, it also implies an analysis of existing asymmetrical and biased "relations of justification" among members of a social and political basic structure – in terms of substance as well as of procedure. Furthermore, it contains conceptual space for a reconstructed notion of ideology, meaning "false" forms of justification which cannot withstand a test of reciprocity and generality; and connected with that it implies, as I mentioned above, the task of finding possibilities for institutionalizing adequate forms of critique and of political justification.[35] Seen in that way, a critical political theory of toleration contains the following components:

(1) a genealogical, historical component, reconstructing the many different conceptions and justifications for toleration that have developed in past contexts and conflicts and that still inform our contemporary use of the term;

(2) a normative theory of justification, critique, and toleration (and its epistemological implications);

[34] For a more detailed analysis, see my *Toleranz im Konflikt*, ch. 12. I should note here that I use the term "repressive tolerance" in a way that differs from Herbert Marcuse's classic essay "Repressive Tolerance," in Robert P. Wolff, Barrington Moore, and Herbert Marcuse, *A Critique of Pure Tolerance* (Boston: Beacon Press, 1965), pp. 81–118. Whereas he calls a system of toleration "repressive" that veils unjust relations of power in an ideological way by neutralizing real opposition (in ideas and practice), I call forms of toleration "repressive" when they help to uphold unjustifiable relations of power by forcing those who are dominated to accept their inferior position.

[35] Hence I agree with James Tully, "Political Philosophy as a Critical Activity," *Political Theory*, 30 (4), 2002, pp. 551f., that the main critical question is "what are the possible practices of freedom in which free and equal subjects could speak and exchange reasons more freely over how to criticise, negotiate, and modify their always imperfect practices," yet neither do I see that this would put the question of "freedom before justice," nor do I think that such a practice-oriented and genealogical account of our practices of governance can do without a critical and normative theory of public justification. For an important suggestion of a theory of political justification that focuses on issues of power and exclusion, see Anthony Simon Laden, *Reasonably Radical: Deliberative Liberalism and the Politics of Identity* (Ithaca: Cornell University Press, 2001).

(3) a critical analysis of existing forms of power and justification in connection with toleration issues, i.e., forms of intolerance as well as of "disciplining" toleration according to the permission conception;

(4) a wider social, political, and cultural analysis of the contexts in which religious or cultural antagonisms arise and the factors that can turn them into violent conflicts; and

(5) perspectives on possibilities of establishing a minimally just basic structure of justification, with the task of institutionalizing reflexive forms of questioning the terms and limits of toleration.[36]

I cannot spell out these components in any detail here,[37] just indicate some of the ways in which such an approach might contribute to an understanding of the current "clashes of culture" to be witnessed in many parts of the world – nationally and internationally. A genealogical account, to start with that, will most of all avoid reified and essentialist, dichotomous views of the current situation as being one of a "tolerant West" standing opposed to a "fundamentalist Islam."

In what sense, for example, is it true that toleration is the achievement of a "Christian culture"? To begin with, it is undeniable that in the course of Western history, especially after the Reformation, Christian faith has been reinterpreted in many ways and that, as I argued above, many arguments for toleration did have a religious character. Yet these reinterpretations were caused by movements that questioned and fought against the intolerance of religious authorities, first against the Catholic church but later also against the intolerance of other, Protestant confessions. Hence Christian institutions and doctrines were *forced* to change given such opposition, and this force sometimes resulted from a different reading of religious sources, but often also from other demands for political freedom or social equality – up to the point where a language of respect, freedom, or equality developed which did not ground normative concepts in particular religious beliefs, as Bayle already argued. Toleration in the West is to a considerable extent a product of struggles *against* as well as *within* Christianity, but that does not make it a product *of* Christianity.[38]

---

[36] This is an idea to be found in a number of critical political theories, see especially James Bohman, "Reflexive Toleration in a Deliberative Democracy," in *The Culture of Toleration*, ed. McKinnon and Castiglione, pp. 111–131; Nancy Fraser, "Recognition Without Ethics?," ibid., pp. 86–108; Seyla Benhabib, *The Rights of Others: Aliens, Residents and Citizens* (Cambridge: Cambridge University Press, 2004), esp. ch. 5 on "democratic iterations."

[37] For a fuller account, see my *Toleranz im Konflikt*.

[38] One should not forget, for example, that it was only in the Second Vatican Council that the Catholic church made its peace with the right to religious liberty.

A component of a one-sided view of the normative genesis of toleration is the social presence of what I called *Locke's fear.* If a specific ethical-religious background is necessary for understanding "values" like human dignity or toleration, then religious communities that do not share that background are by definition seen as less trustworthy citizens in a democratic state (or in international society). Just as the Catholics in Locke's time, they are suspected of being intolerant (and intolerable) by nature of their beliefs. In fact, Locke's argument against Catholics, couched in terms directed against the Muslims, still rings familiar:

> It is ridiculous for any one to profess himself to be a *Mahumetan* only in his Religion, but in every thing else a faithful Subject to a Christian Magistrate, whilst at the same time he acknowledges himself bound to yield blind obedience to the *Mufti* of *Constantinople*; who himself is intirely obedient to the *Ottoman* Emperor, and frames the feigned Oracles of that Religion according to his pleasure.[39]

Today, examples of violent fanaticism by Muslims – like the killing of the film director van Gogh in Amsterdam in 2004 – are seen to support that general suspicion. And the result is all too often that the Muslim population is generally viewed as a community of strangers who do not belong to liberal-democratic states (say, in Europe) because they adhere to other, hostile authorities and values. A critical theory of toleration has the task of analyzing the complex character of such situations and their deeper social, religious, cultural, and political roots. Understanding intolerance – on all sides – is the first step towards understanding the conditions for toleration; and again a relation between justice and toleration appears, though now in social-theoretical terms: the social exclusion of minorities (and feelings of cultural humiliation) is connected with and leads to further intolerance.

Problematic reifications of "culture blocks" or "ethical worlds" can be found not only in Western discourses but also, in a reverse form, in similar discourses in the Muslim world.[40] In both cases a general identity is imposed upon complex social and cultural constellations, sometimes with ideological implications. And even those who call for a "dialogue" between ethical-religious worlds to establish peaceful relations of toleration may perpetuate such constructions, for some ideas of "cultural conversation" again presuppose the dichotomy of closed

---

[39] Locke, *Letter Concerning Toleration*, p. 50.

[40] See, for example, the letter "What We're Fighting For" (12 February 2002) by American intellectuals, and the response by Saudi intellectuals "How We Can Coexist" (7 May 2002), to be found at www.americanvalues.org/html/what_we_re_fighting_for. html and www.americanvalues.org/html/saudi_statement.html.

cultural wholes. The rhetoric of toleration once more proves to be deeply ambivalent, reifying identities.

In such a situation, a critical genealogy of the long struggles for toleration has the task of emphasizing the normative difference between the values of particular, historically developed forms of life, on the one hand, and norms or principles on the basis of which such forms of life have been criticized and forced to change, on the other. Claims for social equality and recognition, in whatever particular language they have been expressed (and they always come in a "thick" form), did and do follow a dynamic that can be analyzed on the basis of the principle of justification: in social and political conflicts, people questioned the reasons that in their eyes could no longer legitimate existing relations of power and domination – just as some do today in Muslim (or Western) societies, women especially, without thereby favoring a particular "Western" (or traditional "Muslim") form of life. The development of toleration is the result of such conflicts: the given reasons for religious force or political-spiritual domination increasingly come under attack and no longer hold. Thus in the light of the principle of justification, the possibility and the normative force of the distinction between particular values and general norms becomes visible – not, again, as a fixed distinction but as a dynamic one. It is this very principle of justice which should be the basis of justifying as well as limiting toleration, if the basic right to justification is violated. It is always justified to reject such violations, regardless of whether its addressee is a majority or a minority.

Multicultural toleration, within as well as beyond states, stands for a problem rather than a single solution; but if there is an answer to that problem, it needs to be based on reflexive principles and practices of equal respect – reflexive in the sense of conceptually allowing for the critique of hierarchical and exclusionary social arrangements and identity constructions. It is the task of critical political theory to point to ways to institutionalize what we can call – following and modifying Habermas – the "force towards the better argument," to give minorities a voice in political debates and to avoid it being only in courts (as my examples show) that minorities can have sufficient power to contest political norms.[41] The virtue of toleration is both an important precondition for such discursive arrangements as well as their product, provided that a society is committed to the idea of multicultural justice.[42]

---

[41] See especially Jürgen Habermas, *Between Facts and Norms: Contributions to a Discourse Theory of Law and Democracy*, trans. W. Rehg (Cambridge, MA: MIT Press), chs. 7 and 8.
[42] Thanks to David Owen and Benjamin Grazzini for helpful editorial advice.

Part IV

New directions

12 Law's necessary forcefulness: Ralph Ellison vs. Hannah Arendt on the Battle of Little Rock

Danielle Allen

I.   Introduction

The men who wrote the Constitution of the United States aimed to make the legislature the central power. They thus installed a paradox at the heart of the politics of modern liberal democracies. The legislature, in this case composed of the House of Representatives and Senate, is charged with both representing the citizenry and law-making. As representative, the legislature is, in accord with long tradition in liberal theory, meant to make visible the diverse interests of all the citizens.[1] But law-making turns about and once again renders some citizens, and their interests, invisible insofar as the legislative bodies produce general rules as the basis for collective action and so explicitly fail to respond to the diversity of citizens' experiences and circumstances. Although laws aim at the common good, they invariably harm some citizens. Indeed, the legal system is, in an important way, a method of managing the variable distribution of harms and benefits throughout a citizenry. But the phrase "the common good" generally ignores the differential distribution of losses and benefits throughout a citizenry that result from

---

[1] For instance, the Swiss legal theorist J. C. Bluntschli wrote: "Truly, as the map represents mountains and valleys, lakes and rivers, forests and meadows, cities and villages, the legislative body, too, is to form again a condensation of the component parts of the People, as well as of the People as a whole, according to their actual relationships. The more noble parts may not be crushed by the more massive ones, but the latter may not be excluded either. The value of each part is determined by its significance in the whole and for the whole. The relationships are organic, the scale is national." J. C. Bluntschli, *Lehre vom modernen Stat* (Stuttgart, 1876), p. 60 translated in Hanna Fenichel Pitkin, *The Concept of Representation* (Berkeley: University of California Press, 1967), p. 62. As Melissa Williams puts it, "here is something so compelling about the view that representation means accurate reflection, once it has been articulated that the critics have accepted it unchallenged." Melissa S. Williams, *Voice, Trust, and Memory: Marginalized Groups and the Failings of Liberal Representation* (Princeton: Princeton University Press, 1998), p. 65.

collective action, and manages the problem of loss in politics (or, the defeat of a citizen's interests in the public sphere) simply by asking citizens to bear up in moments of disappointment. Like the phrase "the common good," political theory has by and large not directly attended to the problem of loss in politics.

The purpose of this chapter is to analyze what becomes of the concept of "law" if one recovers its connection to the production of loss. What becomes of the concept if one attends to the necessary forcefulness even of laws directed at the common good? The analysis herein proceeds by way of case study: I will examine the debate between the mid-twentieth-century novelist and democratic theorist Ralph Ellison and his contemporary, the philosopher Hannah Arendt, over how to think about and describe the "Battle of Little Rock." The standoff in Little Rock between citizen and citizen marked a turning point for the politics of school desegregation. Clearly, the events surrounding the desegregation of public schools handed out losses in spades to a dizzying array of interested parties. In this chapter, I will focus not on all aspects of the events in Little Rock, nor on all the facets of citizenship involved in those tumultuous days, but only on the subject that Arendt and Ellison debate: the nature of the actions and experiences of African-American citizens during the sequence of events around the effort to integrate (or to prevent the integration of) Central High in Little Rock, Arkansas. Here is a subject in respect to which law's forcefulness can be analyzed.

Let me say upfront that Ralph Ellison is the right thinker from whom to begin an investigation of the place of loss in politics, and of the relationship between loss and law. He makes political disappointment a central theme of his writing, both in the 1952 novel *Invisible Man* and in his many essays. In the novel, especially, Ellison recuperates the term "sacrifice" as critical to understanding how politics works and what law is in a democratic society. *Invisible Man* is fundamentally concerned with the nature of democratic political action, and in it Ellison argues, through the movement of the narrative, that a legitimate account of collective democratic action must begin by acknowledging that communal decisions inevitably benefit some members of a community at the expense of others, even in cases where the whole community generally benefits.[2] Since democracy claims to secure the good of all citizens, it is the people who benefit less than others from particular political decisions, but nonetheless accede to those decisions, who preserve the

---

[2] For the full argument on this point, see D. Allen, *Talking to Strangers* (Chicago: University of Chicago Press, 2004).

stability of political institutions. Their sacrifice makes collective democratic action possible.[3]

Ellison also establishes ethical parameters for democratic sacrifice.
When sacrifices are not voluntary but demanded, those who give
something up for the common good have been treated as scapegoats and
are not sacrificers. And when a sacrifice is accepted without the honor
due to the benefactor and without eventually being reciprocated, those
who gain from their fellow citizens' losses also abuse them. In his texts,
democracy is not a static end-state that achieves the common good by
assuring the same benefits or the same level of benefits to everyone, but
rather a political practice by which the diverse negative effects of collective political action, and even of just decisions, must be distributed
equally, and constantly redistributed over time, on the basis of consensual interactions. If Ellison's direct attempt to address the problem of
loss in politics makes him the right person from whom to start this
investigation, his debate with Arendt over Little Rock is also the right
case to investigate. Although they argue about practical political issues,
their differences of opinion rest, finally, on their divergent understandings of the relationship between law and the defeat of a citizen's
interests in the public sphere.

II.   The case: uncovering the place of sacrifice in politics

It is fairly well known that Hannah Arendt wrote a controversial article
against school desegregation in the wake of the September 1957
struggles in Little Rock, Arkansas. The city exploded over whether nine

---

[3] This point comes out in Ellison's essays: Ralph Ellison, *The Collected Essays of Ralph
Ellison*, ed. John F. Callahan (New York: Viking, 1995), and interviews: Robert Penn
Warren, *Who Speaks for the Negro?* (New York: Random House, 1965), as well as in
Ralph Ellison, *Invisible Man*, 2nd edn. (New York: Vintage, International edn., 1995).
For instance, the point arises in his interview with Robert Penn Warren:

> *Warren*: ... Here in the midst of what has been an expanding economy you have
> a contracting economy for the unprepared, for the Negro.
> *Ellison*: That's the paradox. And this particularly explains something new which
> has come into the picture; that is, a determination by the Negro no longer to be
> the scapegoat, no longer to pay, to be sacrificed to – the inadequacies of other
> Americans. We want to socialize the cost. A cost has been exacted in terms of
> character, in terms of courage, and determination, and in terms of self-
> knowledge and self-discovery. Worse, it has led to social, economic, political,
> and intellectual disadvantages and to a contempt even for our lives. And one
> motive for our rejection of the old traditional role of national scapegoat is an
> intensified awareness that not only are we being destroyed by the sacrifice, but
> that the nation has been rotting at its moral core. (Warren, *Who Speaks for the
> Negro?*, p. 339)

African-American students who had recently been admitted to the previously whites-only Central High would in fact be able to attend. Arendt's article, "Reflections on Little Rock,"[4] criticized the NAACP and the parents of the children for using the public sphere and political institutions such as the courts to effect what she considered to be not a political program but self-interested social advancement.[5] Much affected by the news photographs of fifteen-year-old Elizabeth Eckford being attacked by a nasty mob as she tried to enter the high school unaccompanied, Arendt argued furthermore that the parents were abusing their children to achieve that social advancement. "The girl, obviously, was asked to be a hero," Arendt wrote, "which is ... something neither her absent father nor the equally absent representatives of the NAACP felt called upon to be."[6] The article shocked the literary establishment in which Arendt enjoyed a great deal of prestige and provoked countless responses from the decade's public intellectuals. It also won the "1959 Longview Foundation award for the year's outstanding little-magazine article"[7] and contributed to making Arendt's firm social/political distinction common currency.

It is less well known that novelist Ralph Ellison twice responded publicly to Arendt's article, the second time in an interview with Robert Penn Warren, published in *Who Speaks for the Negro?*, where he explicitly invoked his ideas about sacrifice, remarking: "I believe that one of the important clues to the meaning of [American Negro] experience lies in the idea, the ideal of sacrifice. Hannah Arendt's failure to grasp the importance of this ideal among Southern Negroes caused her to fly way off into left field in her 'Reflections on Little Rock'."[8] He continues:

But she has absolutely no conception of what goes on in the minds of Negro parents when they send their kids through those lines of hostile people. Yet they are aware of the overtones of a rite of initiation which such events actually constitute for the child, a confrontation of the terrors of social life with all the mysteries stripped away. And in the outlook of many of these parents (who wish that the problem didn't exist), the child is expected to face the terror and contain his fear and anger precisely because he is a Negro American. Thus he's required to master the inner tensions created by his racial situation, and if he gets hurt – then his is one more sacrifice.[9]

---

[4] Hannah Arendt, "Reflections on Little Rock," *Dissent*, 6, 1959, pp. 45–56.
[5] See Elisabeth Young-Bruehl, *Hannah Arendt: For Love of the World* (New Haven: Yale University Press, 1982), pp. 308–318.
[6] Arendt, "Reflections on Little Rock," p. 50.   [7] Young-Bruehl, *Hannah Arendt*, p. 315.
[8] Warren, *Who Speaks for the Negro?*, p. 343. The article was "The World and the Jug," in *The New Leader* (9 December 1963).
[9] Warren, *Who Speaks for the Negro?*, p. 344.

Ellison invokes the term "sacrifice" to explain the actions of the parents of the Little Rock nine but also and more importantly to make the case for the political status of their actions.[10]

Here we need to lay out more fully the content of Arendt's distinction between social and political spheres, between political and social action. For Arendt, the political world consists of the voting booth and the campaign trail; indeed, she considered the right to vote and the right to be eligible for public office as our only two political rights. In the exercise of these we constitute a "common world" or "political realm" with our fellow citizens. Otherwise, when we leave the confines of our homes, the private world, we enter most immediately not the political sphere but the social interactions through which we pursue our vocation, earn a living, and find the pleasures of company. Like associates with like, Arendt says, which divides the social world along lines of class, profession, and ethnicity. As members of the body politic we are equal; as members of the social world, the world of discrimination, we are not.[11]

Arendt is adamant that the law and democratic political structures should leave to citizens the right to control their private life and household, including their choice of whom to marry, and also their social spaces. Arendt had argued in *The Human Condition*, published in 1958, that participating in the world consists of the ability to construct a common world, the ability to speak qua men and not qua members of society.[12] It also depends on a citizen's ability to "fight a full-fledged political battle,"[13] to articulate one's "own ideas about the possibilities of democratic government under modern conditions,"[14] and to propose "a transformation of the political institutions."[15] In contrast, advocacy of interest positions and participation in "interest parties" is work we do as members of society.[16] For Arendt, the parents of the Little Rock nine were acting as members of society and not as political agents.

For Ellison, however, the African-American parents were indeed acting politically. They had involved themselves in democratic ideals by struggling over school desegregation. They were articulating positive visions about new political forms. Moreover, in Ellison's view, a citizen's participation in public life introduces her to pains and disappointments

---

[10] Hanna Fenichel Pitkin has recently provided thorough analysis of Arendt's category "the social." See Hanna Fenichel Pitkin, *The Attack of the Blob: Hannah Arendt's Concept of the Social* (Chicago: University of Chicago Press, 1998).

[11] Arendt, "Reflections on Little Rock," p. 51.

[12] See Hannah Arendt, *The Human Condition* (Chicago: Chicago University Press, 1958), p. 219.

[13] Ibid.   [14] Ibid., p. 216.   [15] Ibid.   [16] See ibid., p. 218.

that, though generated in the public sphere, will be experienced in the social and personal realms. For Ellison, learning how to negotiate the losses one experiences at the hands of the public is therefore central to becoming a political actor, not only for minorities or those suffering political abuses, but for all citizens. Ellison says to Warren of the African-American parents involved in the events at Little Rock: "We learned about forbearance and forgiveness in that same school, and about hope too. So today we sacrifice, as we sacrificed yesterday, the pleasure of personal retaliation in the interest of the common good."[17] All citizens must, as a part of their political education, learn how to negotiate the experience of political loss, which is felt personally and socially.

African-American parents therefore feel obliged, according to Ellison, to teach their children the lesson that the political and legal worlds are imbricated in a social context (sometimes of terror) that constrains the possibilities for action supposedly protected by law. These African-American parents simultaneously taught their children that they would have to pay a social price for exercising the democratic political instrument provided to them by legal institutions and that both the use of the democratic political instrument and its preservation were worth that price. The concept of sacrifice pinpoints the relation between the social world – the realm of custom and citizenly interaction in which one suffers mental, physical, and economic harm from other citizens – and the political world, the institutions and practices for the sake of which one may be able to master that harm. Moreover, the ability to make such a sacrifice constitutes, for Ellison, "the basic, implicit heroism of people who must live within a society without recognition, real status, but who are involved in the ideals of that society and who are trying to make their way, trying to determine their true position and their rightful position within it."[18] As Ellison describes them, the African-American parents were, over the course of their struggle, articulating and acting on ideas about how a democratic community might best organize itself. Moreover, they were giving rich lessons in citizenship.[19] They were therefore, on Arendt's own terms, pursuing in the public sphere a properly political battle.

Notably, Ellison's reliance on "the ideal of sacrifice" to explain what was political about what Arendt had called the "social" actions of the African-Americans involved in Little Rock accurately captures the nature of the citizenly action and interaction involved in the struggle over

---

[17] Warren, *Who Speaks for the Negro?*, p. 342.   [18] Ibid.
[19] See Allen, *Talking to Strangers*, chs. 4–5.

Little Rock. The story of Little Rock, briefly, is this. In the spring of 1957 the Little Rock school board formulated, and was required by courts to abide by, a policy for integration that would begin with Central High School the following September. Over the summer, many African-American students applied for admission to Central, very often against their parents' wishes, and nine students were finally selected by school authorities. As the NAACP was readying the students with extra academic training to enter Central, Governor Faubus worked to pass new legislation reinstating segregation in the state's schools, and citizen groups organized against the projected opening of an integrated Central High. (Strangely, several other schools in Arkansas had been integrated in preceding years without incident.) On 2 September, the day before school was to start, 250 national guardsmen, under the supervision of the State of Arkansas, surrounded Central on Faubus's orders. Faubus announced on television that this was his response to warnings that carloads of white supremacists were headed to Little Rock; he also announced that on the next day Central High School would be off-limits to black students and Horace Mann, the black school, would be off-limits to white students.[20]

Central High sat empty on 3 September, but the Little Rock school superintendent reasserted his local authority and rescheduled the opening for the 4th. He also authorized going ahead with integration. As the morning of the 4th arrived, so did large crowds, watching and waiting as the guardsmen began to let a few white students through their ranks to the school. Then Elizabeth Eckford, the first black student, arrived. As the crowd surged around her with curses and cries that she be lynched, and radios reported, "A Negro girl is being mobbed at Central High,"[21] she walked the length of the mob to reach the school entrance. She had seen the white students enter between the ranks of guardsmen but, when she also tried to pass through, the soldiers thrust their bayonets at her chest. She tried twice before turning and returning, passing again along the whole length of the crowd, to the bus stop where she sat. There, Benjamin Fine, a white reporter for the *New York Times*, sat down with her, putting his arm around her. With a white woman he tried to help Elizabeth escape, first by cab (the mob prevented this) and then at last by bus. This was the first event in what has come to be called "The Battle of Little Rock," where victory was determined, though the fighting not ended, by the arrival of federal troops (as distinct from the guardsmen) on 24 September. "Sure we're in Central ... But how did

---

[20] Daisy Bates, *The Long Shadow of Little Rock* (New York: David McKay Company, 1962), p. 61.
[21] Ibid., p. 66 (quoting radio reports).

we get in?"[22] one of the students said, on the 25th. "We got in, finally, because we were protected by paratroops. Some victory!"[23] This student regretted that the law had needed military enforcement and could not be enforced simply through the ordinary interactions of citizens.

Ellison's suggestion that Arendt had failed to recognize that the actions undertaken in Little Rock involved sacrifice rather than ambition for social advancement married to cowardice opens up another interpretation of Elizabeth Eckford's lonely, awful walk. Her parents and those of the other children were enduring social abuse – the taunts and threats addressed to their children – and asking their children, many of whom had wanted to attend Central High over their objections, to endure that abuse too, in order to secure democratic law and render functional a legal system that, albeit only recently, had banned the legal imposition of segregation on schools. They suffered the abuse of their children, a problem "they wished didn't exist,"[24] to help assure that the law worked. The political sphere demands sacrifice not merely in search of stability but more regularly in its effort to secure the rule of law.

Daisy Bates, president of the Arkansas State Conference of NAACP branches, gives an account of the events at Little Rock and some of the negotiations of legal authority involved in them that confirms Ellison's analysis of both the centrality of sacrifice to democratic politics and also of the close relationship between sacrifice and democratic legal authority.[25] On the afternoon of the 3rd, the school superintendent called a meeting of leading African-American citizens in Little Rock along with the children's parents and "instructed the parents not to accompany their children the next morning when they were scheduled to enter Central. 'If violence breaks out,' the superintendent told them, 'it will be easier to protect the children if the adults aren't there.' "[26] The parents were extremely troubled by this – Superintendent Blossom had not explained how the children would be protected – but they agreed. Bates was also worried by the instructions and, doing what she could to provide protection for the children while also following the superintendent's orders, she spent the night making phone calls: first, to a white minister to ask if he could round up colleagues to accompany the children in place of the parents; second, to the police to ask that they accompany the children as close to the school as Faubus's national guardsmen would permit; third, to the parents to tell them not to send their children straight to school but rather to the ministers and police.

[22] Bates, *The Long Shadow of Little Rock*, p. 106.   [23] Ibid.
[24] See Warren, *Who Speaks for the Negro?*, p. 344.
[25] See Bates, *The Long Shadow of Little Rock*.   [26] Ibid., p. 63.

Accidentally, she missed the Eckfords because they had no phone.[27] In the morning, not knowing of the new arrangements, the Eckfords simply followed the superintendent's instructions and sent Elizabeth directly to school alone.

After being mobbed, Elizabeth slipped inside herself, remaining there wordless during all of the news reports in the following days, screaming at night in her dreams.[28] When she began to talk again, she described the morning of 4 September. Her focus is on her parents:

While I was pressing my black and white dress – I had made it to wear on the first day of school – my little brother turned on the TV set. They started telling about a large crowd gathered at the school. The man on TV said he wondered if we were going to show up that morning. Mother called from the kitchen, where she was fixing breakfast, "Turn that TV off!" She was so upset and worried. I wanted to comfort her, so I said, "Mother, don't worry." Dad was walking back and forth, from room to room, with a sad expression. He was chewing on his pipe and he had a cigar in his hand, but he didn't light either one. It would have been funny, only he was so nervous.

Before I left home Mother called us into the living room. She said we should have a word of prayer. Then I caught the bus and got off a block from the school.

. . . .

...Someone shouted, "Here she comes, get ready!" I moved away from the crowd on the sidewalk and into the street. If the mob came at me I could then cross back over so the guards could protect me. The crowd moved in closer and then began to follow me ...

. . . .

They moved closer and closer. Somebody started yelling, "Lynch her! Lynch her!"

...Someone hollered, "Drag her over to this tree! Let's take care of the nigger."[29]

Then Elizabeth walked to the school, could not get in, and returned to the bus stop where she was helped onto a bus:[30]

I can't remember much about the bus ride, but the next thing I remember I was standing in front of the School for the Blind, where Mother works...

. . . .

...Mother was standing at the window with her head bowed, but she must have sensed I was there because she turned around. She looked as if she had been

---

[27] Ibid., pp. 65–66.   [28] See ibid., p. 72.   [29] Ibid., pp. 73–75.   [30] See ibid., p. 75.

crying, and I wanted to tell her I was all right. But I couldn't speak. She put her arms around me and I cried.[31]

Elizabeth's parents obeyed Superintendent Blossom's instructions not to accompany their daughter, and they did so in order to support the rule of law and the institutions that were purportedly available to all citizens to obtain their democratic rights, and which claimed to offer all citizens equal protection. The result was psychological terror for them and for their daughter, which was endured for a future good; this constitutes sacrifice.

Those involved in events on the ground knew they were negotiating the sacrifices demanded by the rule of law, as their own words reveal. Indeed, an interesting exchange between Daisy Bates and the father of one of the children indicates the degree to which the superintendent's orders were being equated with the law of the land. On 24 September, the night before the students were to re-enter the school with the protection of the 101st Airborne Division, Daisy Bates went to the home of one of the students. She found an angry father, unwilling to let his daughter face the mobs again. When she, "in her most pleasant, friendliest voice, and trying to look at him instead of the gun ... said that the children were to be at her house by eight-thirty the next morning, and that those were the instructions of Superintendent Blossom," the father answered, "I don't care if the President of the United States gave you those instructions! ... I won't let Gloria go. She's faced two mobs and that's enough."[32] Here was a father who explicitly viewed the sacrifices demanded of him and his daughter as originating from the demands of legal authority.[33]

These are the sacrifices Arendt did not see – one father pacing with pipe in mouth and cigar in hand; another father ready and wishing to throw the legal system to the winds – when she chastised Elizabeth Eckford's parents and the "absent representatives of the NAACP"[34] for allowing Elizabeth to go to Central High alone and when she insisted that they were not acting politically. The invisibility of their sacrifice made the representatives seem "absent" when they were not. Their invisibility in turn ensured the invisibility of those whom they represented. The representatives of the NAACP, rushing around at midnight to find white ministers to accompany the children to school instead of

---

[31] Bates, *The Long Shadow of Little Rock*, pp. 75–76.   [32] Ibid., p. 102.

[33] Bates concluded the story thus: "[The next morning, however,] Mr. Ray, shy and smiling, led Gloria into the house. He looked down at his daughter with pride. 'Here, Daisy, she's yours. She's determined to go.'" Ibid., p. 103.

[34] Arendt, "Reflections on Little Rock," p. 50.

their parents, were, at the time, unable to shed light on their situation or on that of the children and parents they represented. Indeed, in *Invisible Man*, invisibility is regularly used to describe the experience of sacrifice without recognition or honor.[35] And Ellison, by invoking the idea of sacrifice in the context of a discussion of Little Rock in his Robert Penn Warren interview, suggests that the source of this invisibility was not merely the failure of one theorist to see individual sacrifice, but rather and more broadly, the general absence from democratic practice of a language to comprehend sacrifice, or the losses and disappointments people accept for the sake of maintaining the communal agreements that constitute legality. The cause of invisibility, Ellison suggests, is our unwillingness to acknowledge law's forcefulness.

As we have seen, such a language of sacrifice existed on the ground; indeed citizens of Little Rock could remark:

We've had the Constitution since 1789 ... Last night they came into our neighborhood and rocked our homes, breaking windows, and all that. We've taken a lot because we didn't want to hurt the chances of Negro kids, but I doubt whether the Negroes are going to take much more without fighting back. I think I'll take the rest of the day off and check my shotgun and make sure it's in working condition.[36]

But the public language of political theory, which can directly interact with policy, did not reflect such a precise awareness of the particular sacrifices involved in the production of democratic agreement and laws. As a result, political theory was not in a position to offer a full account of democratic citizenship or of the full range of potential citizenly action. It could not responsibly engage the subject of law.

III.   Sacrifice and the rule of law

No doubt it seems naive to introduce the topic of responsibility in the midst of an effort to recuperate, or at least to draw attention to a recuperation of, the term "sacrifice." After all, sacrifice is a notoriously dangerous word when introduced to political discussion, and those who use it are often charged with irresponsibility. Abraham's total allegiance to God and the near sacrifice of Isaac leaps to mind; and Agamemnon's sacrifice of Iphigenia for the sake of winning Troy is also immediately conjured up. A recuperation of the idea of sacrifice for political discourse, however tentative, must spawn a bevy of anxious questions: do we not ask too much of people when we turn to the language of sacrifice;

---

[35] See Allen, *Talking to Strangers*, ch. 4.
[36] Bates, *The Long Shadow of Little Rock*, p. 99.

isn't the language of sacrifice one of the most easily wielded tools of political abuse; don't we encourage blind allegiance when we pay too much attention to the sacrifices and losses involved in communal endeavor? And finally, doesn't sacrifice encourage violence? The term arrives accompanied by alarm bells.

Indeed, our understanding of law changes radically when we conceive of it as resting to some degree on sacrifices that are made freely, but are nonetheless still sacrifices. The relation of law to sacrifice brings to the fore the fact of *law's necessary forcefulness*. In a democratic context, where full consent is the guiding aspiration, acknowledgment of this forcefulness is troubling. Indeed, the project of many recent democratic theorists (e.g., writers in the deliberative democracy tradition) has been to seek methods of pursuing full and enthusiastic consent, and such efforts might be seen in part as pushing against the necessary fact of law's forcefulness in order to allay our worries about it.[37] Our discomfort at the idea of sacrifice perhaps simply reflects our unease about what will happen to democratic aspirations if we do concede law's necessary forcefulness.[38] But is it indeed dangerous to acknowledge law's forcefulness?

Or is it more dangerous to leave this aspect of democratic politics unacknowledged? Although Arendt neither sees the political sacrifice of citizens nor frankly acknowledges its place in politics, and the connection, through sacrifice, of social to political action, her essay is in fact constructed around a request for sacrifice. In the first page of the essay, she asks whether political institutions might one day be able to achieve social equality.[39] She decides that "ironing out" inequalities of economic and educational condition may eventually be possible, but warns that "the principle of equality ... cannot equalize natural, physical characteristics."[40] She continues:

At that juncture [where all differences have been equalized but for those that cannot be] a danger point, well known to students of history, invariably

---

[37] Seyla Benhabib argues, in writing on Hegel, that utopian politics is associated with a lack of sacrifice: "The utopia of a non-sacrificial non-identity of the subject is intimated in that non-compulsory relation to otherness which forces the subject to forget him or herself and to catch a glimpse of the moment of reconciliation." Seyla Benhabib, *Critique, Norm, and Utopia: A Study of the Foundations of Critical Theory* (New York: Columbia University Press, 1986), p. 212.

[38] E. A. Goerner and W. J. Thompson provide a useful overview of different approaches to consent and coercion. They write: "The liberal state is a paradox: a coercive public order to guarantee individualistic liberty." E. A. Goerner and W. J. Thompson, "Politics and Coercion," *Political Theory*, 24, 1996, pp. 620–621. Deliberative democracy theories are trying to get away from the idea that the liberal state is in fact a "coercive public order." Ibid.; see also Hannah Arendt, *Crises of the Republic* (New York: Harcourt and Brace, 1972).

[39] Cf. Arendt, "Reflections on Little Rock," pp. 46–47.   [40] Ibid., p. 48.

emerges: the more equal people have become in every respect, and the more equality permeates the whole texture of society, the more will differences be resented, the more conspicuous will those become who are visibly and by nature unlike the others.

It is therefore quite possible that the achievement of social, economic, and educational equality for the Negro may sharpen the color problem in this country instead of assuaging it.[41]

Arendt's sensitivity to history recalls the Holocaust – abuse of sacrifice in its most extreme form (it is scapegoating in Ellison's terms though not in Arendt's).[42] And this memory leads her to advise African-Americans to accept social inequality lest the price for equality be the breakdown of the rule of law:

We have not yet reached the danger point, but we shall reach it in the foreseeable future ... Awareness of future trouble does not commit one to advocating a reversal of the trend which happily for more than fifteen years now has been greatly in favor of the Negroes. But it does commit one to advocating that government intervention be guided by caution and moderation rather than by impatience and ill-advised measures.[43]

What worries Arendt about desegregation is that in a poll of Virginians only 21 percent said that they would feel bound to obey the laws on the point of integrated schooling; what she sees in Little Rock is "the sorry fact ... that the town's lawabiding citizens left the streets to the mob, that neither white nor black citizens felt it their duty to see the Negro children safely to school."[44] The essay's penultimate paragraph forecasts similarly that "as for the children, forced integration means a

---

[41] Ibid.

[42] Arendt begins *The Origins of Totalitarianism* by arguing against the use of the term "scapegoat" in discussions of the Holocaust. See Hannah Arendt, *The Origins of Totalitarianism* (San Diego: Harcourt Brace & Co., 1964). On the problems of comparing different types of horror, for instance slavery and the Holocaust, see Emily Miller Budick, *Blacks and Jews in Literary Conversation* (Cambridge: Cambridge University Press, 1998), p. 73.

[43] Arendt, "Reflections on Little Rock," p. 48. Unfortunately, there are a number of points in Arendt's essay that read rather like Ellison's satirical presentations of similar arguments. For instance, I.M. receives a letter that reads:

This is advice from a friend who has been watching you closely. Do not go too fast. Keep working for the people but remember that you are one of us and do not forget if you get too big they will cut you down. You are from the South and you know that this is a white man's world. So take a friendly advice and go easy so that you can keep on helping the colored people. They do not want you to go too fast and will cut you down if you do. Be smart. (Ellison, *Invisible Man*, p. 383)

[44] Arendt, "Reflections on Little Rock," p. 49.

very serious conflict between home and school, between their private and their social life ... The result can only be a rise of mob and gang rule, as the news photograph we mentioned above so eloquently demonstrates."[45] Arendt fears that what she sees as a struggle for social equality will jeopardize the political instrument that has made the struggle possible. Although she does not use a language of sacrifice, she nonetheless proposes that democracy needs a social sacrifice for the political end of maintaining the rule of law. She asks for sacrifice, but slyly, and here her distinctions between social and political are all-important.

The distinction is primarily ethical. That is, Arendt's arguments outline how those who wish to gain honor in the polity can best do so: They must refuse to allow their social interests to affect their political choices. They must, in other words, make sacrifices. Her strong opposition between social and political is, among other things, an exhortation for citizens to give up some things (pursuing economic interests in the public realm) for others (glory and the greater wholeness of the whole). Where Ellison uncovers sacrifices and asks that democratic theorists attend to the way in which citizens negotiate their losses, Arendt simply insists that citizens sacrifice the social to the political. But sacrifice is not something to be insisted upon, Ellison argues; it is something to be negotiated, discussed, recorded, and reciprocated. Rather than insisting on sacrifices, citizens should work to develop practices of and conversations about equity that will surround the polity's political institutions and provide a backdrop to its decisions. Because Arendt does not acknowledge the importance of requests for sacrifice to her own argument, she leaves herself without conceptual resources and analytical grounds to address the full ethical implications of collective public decisions.

Ellison was a tactical writer whose art was governed, in Ken Warren's words, "by his assessment of ... the measures necessary to counter what he believed to be those ideas that could be instrumentalized to sanction the nation's administration of its race problem."[46] Ellison had thus already in 1952 prepared the ground of his critique of Arendt when in *Invisible Man* he called attention to the unreflective use of the language of sacrifice so prevalent in discourse about "the Negro problem."[47]

---

[45] Arendt, "Reflections on Little Rock," pp. 55–56.

[46] Kenneth W. Warren, "Ralph Ellison and the Reconfiguration of Black Cultural Politics," *REAL: The Yearbook of Research in English and American Literature*, 11, 1995, pp. 139, 154.

[47] To quote Budick: "As in so many things, Ellison anticipated the issues that came to dominate the scene in the following decades." Budick, *Blacks and Jews in Literary*

By drawing attention in his Robert Penn Warren interview to the topic of sacrifice, he forces readers to ask two questions: First, what enables political analysts to ask for sacrifices to support the law without acknowledging the nature of their requests? And second, what are the practical effects of such blind requests?

To answer the second question first, those who ask for sacrifices without acknowledging the nature of their requests generate invisibility. Not only are particular sacrifices and sacrificers rendered invisible but so too is the basic logic of democratic decision-making: if democratic decisions are to rest on full consent, then those citizens who lose political arguments, whose interests are defeated in the public forum, must consent to their losses; democratic consent and legitimacy, in other words, depend on sacrifice. To ignore sacrifice, to avoid talking about it directly, is to turn away from a fundamental feature of democracy.

We are left, then, with the first question: what causes invisibility? Or rather, what allows political analysts to ignore or occlude the inevitable presence of requests for sacrifice in democratic politics? To answer this question, it is necessary to analyze the conceptual moves that protect democratic theorists from acknowledging the difficult, even alarming, nature of democratic law-making. Here I would like to turn to the trope of invisibility itself, for not only Ellison, but Arendt also uses it in her writing. A close examination of how each writer uses the figure of invisibility, and how each describes the causes of invisibility, will allow us to draw out, and elucidate the stakes of, their different approaches to law's forcefulness.

IV.   Invisibility and law

Contrary to what many think of the friendly exchange between Arendt and Ellison – and their exchange was friendly, unlike some of Arendt's conversations on the subject – the point at issue between them does not involve political contingencies but a deep theoretical dispute about how to conceptualize disagreement, law, and political action. Their conflicting positions about desegregation actually arise from what each has to say in other texts about the effects of radical disagreement on politics. Extraordinarily enough, both thematize such effects in terms of invisibility and darkness, as though they were thinking together, in the same

Conversation, p. 81 (speaking of the shift from the "damage" theory of slavery to the "resistance" theory, for which Ellison was a spokesperson). There is no question, however, that Ellison was right to notice that the term "sacrifice" comes up frequently in political theory and political discussions, but is always disavowed when addressed directly.

figure, Ellison in *Invisible Man* and Arendt in her *Men in Dark Times*, written between 1952 and 1968.

It seems jarring at first to claim that *Invisible Man*, which is about racism, segregation, and the reign of violence in the South in the first half of the twentieth century, and *Men in Dark Times*, which is about anti-Semitism and the approach of the Holocaust, are about disagreement, but both texts support my claim. Arendt's conviction that "human plurality" is "the basic condition of both action and speech,"[48] and therefore of politics, reappears in the final paragraph of the opening essay of *Men in Dark Times* when she warns against modernity's fascination with the possibility of finding "one will" or perfect agreement for a people:

It might have the result that all men would suddenly unite in a single opinion, so that out of many opinions one would emerge, as though not men in their infinite plurality but man in the singular, one species and its exemplars, were to inhabit the earth. Should that happen, the world, which can form only in the interspaces between men in all their variety, would vanish altogether.[49]

Similarly, Ellison's most explicit conclusion in *Invisible Man* is:

Whence all this passion toward conformity anyway? – diversity is the word. Let man keep his many parts and you'll have no tyrant states ... America is woven of many strands; I would recognize them and let it so remain. It's "winner take nothing" that is the great truth of our country or of any country. Life is to be lived, not controlled; and humanity is won by continuing to play in the face of certain defeat. Our fate is to become one, and yet many – This is not prophecy, but description.[50]

But, as Ellison often points out, as different perspectives fill the public sphere, we always choose among them, by making laws and installing politicians who enact before us representations of who we are as a citizenry. Our speech and action in the public sphere, fraught as they are with difference and disagreement, therefore return to us as laws and decisions that make us feel the force of our disagreements. The question, then, is how a politics of plurality and diversity or, as I would prefer, of intricacy can ensure that the winner of an argument "takes nothing," even when some people remain unconvinced by the outcome of debate.

Like Ellison, Arendt believes that collective decisions, including laws, produce our realities, our shared world. In *The Human Condition* Arendt argues that "the presence of others who see what we see and hear what

[48] Arendt, *The Human Condition*, p. 175.
[49] Hannah Arendt, "On Humanity in Dark Times," in *Men in Dark Times* (New York: Harcourt, 1968), p. 31.
[50] Ellison, *Invisible Man*, p. 577.

we hear assures us of the reality of the world and ourselves."[51] Again, like Ellison, she believes that collective agreements inevitably entail loss; in their most extreme form, they bring dark times and invisibility by hiding from view, more or less violently, that which threatens the collectively chosen "reality." In "On Humanity in Dark Times," Arendt insists that the expulsion of Jews from the German political arena in the first half of the twentieth century, as well as the retreat of some non-Jewish non-communist Germans from it, should be seen precisely as the result of that communicative power to establish reality:

> Flight from the world in dark times of impotence can always be justified as long as reality is not ignored, but is constantly acknowledged as the thing that must be escaped ... [People who flee] must remember that they are constantly on the run, and that the world's reality is actually expressed by their escape.[52]

It is Arendt's and Ellison's conviction that, after any political debate, some people will always remain unconvinced, and that there should always be some who remain unconvinced, that draws me to them as theorists of disagreement. The difficult question of democratic practice is in handling the experience of being unconvinced democratically. Both Arendt and Ellison answer that winners in a debate "take nothing" when they leave behind no more disagreement than is compatible with friendship.[53] Thus Arendt, again in *Men in Dark Times*, admires Lessing because "any doctrine that in principle barred the possibility of friendship between two human beings would have been rejected by his untrammeled and unerring conscience."[54] Collective decisions that deal with disagreement in ways that undo the possibility of friendship hurtle the world into "dark times" and cast some of its inhabitants into invisibility.[55] And what is this invisibility?

---

[51] Arendt, *The Human Condition*, p. 50.
[52] Arendt, "On Humanity in Dark Times," p. 22.
[53] See Allen, *Talking to Strangers*.
[54] Arendt, "On Humanity in Dark Times," p. 29. For the role of friendship in Ellison's ethics of citizenship, see Allen, *Talking to Strangers*, ch. 4.
[55] In *The Human Condition*, Arendt writes:

> Yet what love is in its own, narrowly circumscribed sphere, respect is in the larger domain of human affairs. Respect, not unlike the Aristotelian philia politike, is a kind of 'friendship' without intimacy and without closeness; it is a regard for the person from the distance which the space of the world puts between us, and this regard is independent of qualities which we may admire or of achievements which we may highly esteem. (Arendt, *The Human Condition*, p. 243)

See also the final pages of Arendt, "On Humanity in Dark Times," and L. J. Disch, "On Friendship in 'Dark Times'," in *Feminist Interpretations of Hannah Arendt*, ed. B. Honig (Pennsylvania: Pennsylvania State University Press, 1995), pp. 285–311.

Here I want to examine the texts of each writer to establish the similarities in Arendt's and Ellison's answers. It is worth hearing from them at length. In *Men in Dark Times* Arendt writes:

(1) Everywhere...the public realm has lost the power of illumination which was originally part of its very nature.[56]

(2) For what was wrong, and what no dialogue and no independent thinking ever could right, was the world – namely, the thing that arises between people and in which everything that individuals carry with them innately can become visible and audible.[57]

(3) History knows many periods of dark times in which the public realm has been obscured and the world become so dubious that people have ceased to ask any more of politics than that it show due consideration for their vital interests and personal liberty.[58]

(4) Then a brotherly attachment to other human beings...springs from hatred of the world in which men are treated "inhumanly." For our purposes...it is important that humanity manifests itself in such brotherhood most frequently in "dark times." This kind of humanity actually becomes inevitable when the times become so extremely dark for certain groups of people that it is no longer up to them, their insight or choice, to withdraw from the world.[59]

(5) But it is true that in "dark times" the warmth which is the pariahs' substitute for light exerts a great fascination upon all those who are so ashamed of the world as it is that they would like to take refuge in invisibility. And in invisibility, in that obscurity in which a man who is himself hidden need no longer see the visible world either, only the warmth and fraternity of closely packed human beings can compensate for the weird irreality that human relationships assume wherever they develop in absolute worldlessness, unrelated to a world common to all people.[60]

(6) Wherever such a friendship succeeded at that time...a bit of humanness in a world become inhuman was achieved.[61]

When people are expelled from or withdraw from politics, they settle into conditions of weird irreality. Without a place to be seen and to be heard and to act, pariahs and also those people who are fascinated with escaping from a polity they abhor, turn to fraternity, says Arendt, and forsake politics. In dark times what is wrong is the world, understood as that which is between people and allows for political action.

---

[56] Arendt, "On Humanity in Dark Times," p. 4.   [57] Ibid., p. 10.   [58] Ibid., p. 11.
[59] Ibid, pp. 12–13.   [60] Ibid., p. 16.   [61] Ibid., p. 23.

Ellison too engages the themes of the loss of reality and of the world, the turn to fraternity, the need for action, and the absurdity of invisibility. The protagonist of *Invisible Man* – who is never named, so let's call him I.M. – says this:

(1) I am an invisible man... I learned in time though that it is possible to carry on a fight against them without their realizing it... My hole is warm and full of light. Yes, full of light... And I love light. Perhaps you'll think it strange that an invisible man should need light, desire light, love light. But maybe it is exactly because I am invisible. Light confirms my reality, gives birth to my form... To be unaware of one's form is to live a death.[62]

(2) I could feel the words forming themselves, slowly falling into place... [I said to the crowd:] "I feel your eyes upon me. I hear the pulse of your breathing. And now, at this moment, with your black and white eyes upon me, I feel... I feel... I feel suddenly that I have become more human... Not that I have become a man, for I was born a man. But that I am more human. I feel strong, I feel able to get things done!... My true family! My true people! My true country! I am a new citizen of the country of your vision, a native of your fraternal land. I feel that here tonight, in this old arena, the new is being born and the vital old revived."[63]

(3) Now... I was painfully aware of other men dressed like the boys, and of girls in dark exotic colored stockings, their costumes surreal variations of downtown styles.[64]

(4) All life seen from the hole of invisibility is absurd.[65]

One sees in these quotations that the objects of Arendt's and Ellison's investigations are the same. But one also already begins to sense a difference between their two approaches to invisibility. The two titles of the books themselves suggest a mirror inversion of perspective: Compare *Invisible Man* to *Men in Dark Times*. In one case people are unseeable, even in times of full light; in the other case, seeable men have retreated or been pushed into the dark. In the first case, there are patches of darkness within a world otherwise full of light – the political realm is a dappled space; in the other case, a stark line separates the world of light from the world of darkness. What is at stake for law, sacrifice, and citizenly agency in this inversion?

The key difference between Arendt's and Ellison's account of invisibility lies in what they think becomes of the invisible. Arendt treats

---

[62] Ellison, *Invisible Man*, pp. 3, 5, 6–7.   [63] Ibid., pp. 345–346.
[64] Ibid., p. 443.   [65] Ibid., p. 579.

invisibility as a condition that arises within politics, yet she nonetheless then sets those who become invisible outside of politics, or the common world that produced their invisibility, regardless of whether they have ended up outside politics because they were pushed out or because they left. Thus, for her, "inner emigration" signified

on the one hand that there were persons inside Germany who behaved as if they no longer belonged to the country, who felt like emigrants; and on the other hand ... that they had not in reality emigrated, but had withdrawn to an interior realm, into the invisibility of thinking and feeling.[66]

The text of this essay was originally a speech given at Arendt's acceptance, in Germany, of the Lessing Prize. And here, in accepting "inner emigration" as a real form of invisibility, she is holding out an offer of reconciliation to those non-Jewish Germans who had retreated from politics and claimed not to be involved in their country's doings. She is taking their withdrawal seriously and with it their claim to have been outside politics. Thus, the "inner emigration" can be treated analogously to the invisibility of the enslaved and disfranchised.

But it is these latter groups, whom in *Men in Dark Times* and also in *The Human Condition*, Arendt most regularly describes as invisible.[67] In *On Revolution*, she is explicit about setting "invisible people" outside of politics when she deals with John Adams's discussion of the political experience of the poor. As we have seen, she quotes the following passage from him:

The poor man's conscience is clear; yet he is ashamed ... He feels himself out of the sight of others, groping in the dark. Mankind takes no notice of him ... He is in as much obscurity as he would be in a garret or a cellar ... To be wholly overlooked, and to know it, are intolerable.[68]

For Adams, as for Ellison, citizens experience invisibility within the political body; they live within the patches of darkness in a polity otherwise bright. The condition of invisibility indicates that the rights to vote and hold office do not ensure access to the political realm, where opinions are consequential and action, possible. Arendt acknowledges the problem of obscurity or invisibility but dismisses it as irrelevant to the democratic tradition:

I have quoted these words [of Adams] at some length because the feeling of injustice they express, the conviction that darkness rather than want is the curse of poverty, is extremely rare in the literature of the modern age ... [Adams's]

[66] Arendt, "On Humanity in Dark Times," p. 19.
[67] See Arendt, *The Human Condition*, p. 55.
[68] Hannah Arendt, *On Revolution* (New York: Faber, 1963), p. 69.

insight into the crippling consequences of obscurity... could hardly be shared by the poor themselves; and since it remained a privileged knowledge it had hardly any influence upon the history of revolutions or the revolutionary tradition... Moreover, modern sensibility is not touched by obscurity, not even by the frustration of "natural talent" and of the "desire of superiority" which goes with it.[69]

She uses the opportunity provided by Adams's remarks to argue for a very different formulation of invisibility's significance to theories of democratic founding:

The fact that John Adams was so deeply moved by obscurity, more deeply than he or anyone else of the Founding Fathers was ever moved by sheer misery, must strike us as very strange indeed when we remind ourselves that the absence of the social question from the American scene was, after all, quite deceptive, and that abject and degrading misery was present everywhere in the form of slavery and Negro labour... From this, we can only conclude that the institution of slavery carries an obscurity even blacker than the obscurity of poverty; the slave, not the poor man, was "wholly overlooked."[70]

For Adams, law's forcefulness permeates even relatively successful forms of democratic life. Rights to vote and hold office did not ensure access to the political sphere. Statutory or everyday law, and not just constitutional law, will need to be aware of and responsible to invisibility.

But in responding to Adams's argument, Arendt shifts the condition of obscurity and political poverty from the citizen to the slave. In so doing, she moves the analysis of invisibility beyond the political realm. Mundane, everyday disagreements and legal structures are no longer at issue, only those that explicitly disfranchise. She is surely correct to argue that slavery and disfranchisement constitute an extreme violation of the recognition due members of a polity from one another, but her transfer of the language of invisibility from poverty to slavery deprives democrats of an important tool to assess the degree to which democracies are fulfilling their promise. In her use of the trope of invisibility, analysis of law's forcefulness is limited to the most extreme case. More importantly, when Arendt banishes the problem of law's forcefulness from everyday politics and from squabbles over statutory (as opposed to constitutional) law, she also diminishes the project of citizenship. Citizens with full political rights are no longer expected to have to negotiate law's forcefulness, loss, and sacrifice. Citizenship comes to be seen as something free of "all that," and those people who are too obvious in trying to renegotiate the pattern of sacrifice that obtains in a polity fail in her view to attain political agency.

[69] Ibid., pp. 69–70.   [70] Ibid., pp. 70-71.

Once Arendt has argued that a condition, invisibility, which arises from politics, actually removes people from the political arena, it is no surprise that she argues that invisible people lose not only the context but also the ability for political action. Thus, she argues that although

the world's reality is actually expressed by [people's] escape [into invisibility] ... we cannot fail to see the limited political relevance of such an existence, even if it is sustained in purity. Its limits are inherent in the fact that strength and power are not the same; that power arises only where people act together, but not where people grow stronger as individuals.[71]

This alone, she argues, are they able to do in conditions of invisibility. Thus, in conditions of invisibility, Arendt argues, political skills atrophy:

Humanity in the form of fraternity invariably appears historically among persecuted peoples and enslaved groups ... This kind of humanity is the great privilege of pariah peoples; it is the advantage that the pariahs of this world always and in all circumstances can have over others. The privilege is dearly bought; it is often accompanied by so radical a loss of the world, so fearful an atrophy of all the organs with which we respond to it – starting with the common sense with which we orient ourselves in a world common to ourselves and others and going on to the sense of beauty, or taste, with which we love the world – that in extreme cases, in which pariahdom has persisted for centuries, we can speak of real worldlessness. And worldlessness, alas, is always a form of barbarism.[72]

This account depends heavily on her arguments in *The Human Condition*. There, as we have seen, participating in the world consists of the ability to construct a common world and to articulate one's "own ideas about the possibilities of democratic government under modern conditions."[73] Political action is the opposite of what we do as members of society, which is merely to defend "economic interests,"[74] and ask for "due consideration of vital interests."[75] Finally, worldlessness is a condition in which men have become entirely private, that is, they have been deprived of seeing and hearing others, of being seen and being heard by them. They are all imprisoned in the subjectivity of their own singular experience, which does not cease to be singular if the same experience is multiplied innumerable times.[76]

People trapped in worldlessness, she argues, are unable to move from articulating subjective social desires to articulating visions of the future that will be relevant to a whole society. Nor are they capable of an "openness" to worldly discussions that is necessary for political action.

[71] Arendt, "On Humanity in Dark Times," pp. 22–23.   [72] Ibid., p. 13.
[73] Arendt, *The Human Condition*, p. 216.   [74] Ibid., p. 219.
[75] Arendt, "On Humanity in Dark Times," p. 11.
[76] Arendt, *The Human Condition*, p. 58.

Arendt thus draws out of her account of invisibility a theoretical justification for distinguishing people who know well how to act politically from those who know only, because of political oppression, how to act socially. This theoretical sub-structure underlies her argument in "Reflections on Little Rock": "Oppressed minorities were never the best judges on the order of priorities in such matters and there are many instances when they preferred to fight for social opportunity rather than for basic human or political rights."[77] Citizenship is diminished by the idea that it should avoid the difficult negotiation over how collective decisions are experienced by citizens in the social realm.

Against Arendt's view of political action, Ellison argues that citizens interact with the law not only when negotiating sacrifices in the public sphere but also when acting socially. Even when acting in response to social experiences, they engage the possibility for democratic government under modern conditions. Let us return to Ellison's protagonist so as to have a better understanding of how the invisible can act politically, both in the political and in the social sphere.

I.M. opens his narration of his life story by pondering on what he, as a boy, overheard of his grandfather's deathbed words:

Son, after I'm gone I want you to keep up the good fight. I never told you, but our life is a war and I have been a traitor all my born days, a spy in the enemy's country ever since I give up my gun back in the Reconstruction. Live with your head in the lion's mouth. I want you to overcome 'em with yeses, undermine 'em with grins, agree 'em to death and destruction, let 'em swoller you till they vomit or bust wide open...Learn it to the younguns.[78]

I.M.'s grandfather is insistent: even the invisible never leave politics; they can remain always actively engaged in their polities even if no one is noticing. But what does it mean to "agree 'em to death and destruction"? Or to be swallowed in such a way that the swallowers "bust wide open"? Here is an approach to agreement that is strange indeed, focusing on agreement with force rather than simply on the force of agreement.

His grandfather's words torment I.M. throughout the whole of his odyssey. Only in the epilogue does he think he is finally beginning to understand them:

I'm still plagued by his deathbed advice...Could he have meant – hell, he must have meant the principle, that we were to affirm the principle on which the country was built and not the men, or at least not the men who did the violence. Did he mean say "yes" because he knew that the principle was greater than the

---

[77] Arendt, "Reflections on Little Rock," p. 46.   [78] Ellison, *Invisible Man*, p. 16.

men...? Or did he mean that we had to take the responsibility for all of it, for the men as well as the principle, because we were the heirs who must use the principle because no other fitted our needs?...Or was it, did he mean that we should affirm the principle because we, through no fault of our own, were linked to all the others in the loud, clamoring, semivisible world...?

"Agree 'em to death and destruction," grandfather had advised. Hell, weren't they their own death and their own destruction except as the principle lived in them and in us? And here's the cream of the joke: Weren't we part of them as well as apart from them and subject to die when they died?[79]

I.M. has come to realize that the old slave's advice is the following: Insist, by agreeing, that you are part of those who speak and agree and construct reality. Insist that, although you are invisible, you are invisible within the political realm and not outside it; you may have lost a particular argument but you are still part of the body that concluded the agreement. With such invisible people included in it, agreement must be admitted to be imperfect. The invisible represent the fact of loss and disappointment in politics and the forcefulness of law. Part and apart, the invisible prove that the whole cannot add up to one. The question, then, is how the processes of representation that produce collective agreements can also acknowledge the invisible and find ways to relate them, and law's forcefulness, to collective agreement, thereby undoing their invisibility and preserving the legitimacy of democratic law.

I.M. comes to the conclusion that "the part," both a part and apart from the whole, has political work to do: "I learned in time though that it is possible to carry on a fight against them without their realizing it."[80] Lodged within Ellison's remarks about fighting from within are the two points of difference between Ellison's account of invisibility and Arendt's: for Ellison, even the invisible never leave the political world; and because of this, they need not forget, although they may, how to act politically. Adams speaks of the poor man as having a clear conscience and yet being ashamed. He means the shame of being free and yet unfree. This is the shame of Daisy Bates and parents who are called absent, cowardly, and grasping despite their work, activism, and sacrifice. I.M. puts it thus: "Discover[ing your invisibility and]...that [you also have] yourself to blame...that is the real soul-sickness...the drag by the neck through the mob-angry town...but you continue stupidly to live."[81] The discrepancy between democratic rights and social violence can bring even citizens to doubt their own humanity; invisibility captures the falseness of freedom rather than its absence. I.M. thus eventually comes to realize that his grandfather, a slave emancipated at

---

[79] Ellison, *Invisible Man*, pp. 574–575.   [80] Ibid., p. 5.   [81] Ibid., pp. 575–576.

the end of the Civil War, "never had any doubts about his humanity," for "that was left to his 'free' offspring."[82] Similarly, he laments: "Outside the Brotherhood we were outside history; but inside of it they didn't see us. It was a hell of a state of affairs."[83] The rights to vote and hold office are fundamental features of citizenship, but analysis cannot stop here. These rights get one into the "brotherhood" of democracy, but do not get one "seen" or represented. Although law is the sovereign source of power in democracy, it is not the sovereign source of democracy. Its power must always be supplemented by practices that negotiate and allow for the assimilation of the experience of law's forcefulness. And these practices can be employed in any number of places, not merely in the assembly or courtroom but also, for instance, in the streets of Little Rock.

From the moment when the parents and children had received the superintendent's instructions to the moment when the federal troops arrived, citizens were regularly reconfiguring democratic agreements as they went. During the course of the events in Little Rock, many citizens had to learn for the first time that any encounter with the law can give rise to political action; any such encounter is also an opportunity for further "making" of the law. One citizen who learned this was Benjamin Fine, the reporter who helped Elizabeth Eckford, and who was especially astonished to find that the national guardsmen would not guard either her or him. He later said to Daisy Bates: "The irony of it all, Daisy, is that during all this time [while the mob was threatening us] the national guardsmen made no effort to protect Elizabeth or to help me. Instead, they threatened to have me arrested – for inciting to riot."[84] But the real irony lies in the upending of his expectations that institutions and paper outlines of procedure secure the rule of law.

The result, for Fine, is a moment of recognition: to work, legal institutions depend on "the 'thick' context of interpersonal relations, habits, and customs that determine the meanings and associated

---

[82] Ibid., p. 580. Kenneth Warren makes a similar point:

> First, *Invisible Man* specifically uncouples the problem of slavery and the problem of emancipation. Speaking about his grandfather, the novel's protagonist observes that his formerly enslaved ancestor 'never had any doubts about his humanity – that was left to his "free" offspring.' The problems of the enslaved and the problems of their free descendants, though related, were different. In fact the problematic that the novel worries is not the problem of slavery but that of emancipation. (Warren, "Ralph Ellison and the Reconfiguration of Black Cultural Politics," p. 150 [citation omitted])

[83] Ellison, *Invisible Man*, p. 499.
[84] Bates, *The Long Shadow of Little Rock*, p. 71.

expectations of formal rules."[85] Fine's trust in his fellow citizens had formerly blinded him to this aspect of the rule of law. Similarly, democratic theorists also too often conceive of the realm of law and political institutions as consisting of procedures that guarantee themselves, not as a set of practices secured only through social interaction. Fine could afford his blindness because his relations with his fellow citizens were generally good. "Our beliefs about, as well as our affective and social relations to, the personnel account for standing in a trust relation to the institution they staff."[86] Citizens of the post-reconstruction American South, habituated to poor standards of citizenly interaction, understood something that Fine and political theorists often have not: the politico-juridical world comes to exist out of the social world, which sets limits on and also facilitates the operations of the political world.[87] Conditions of trust secure the politico-juridical world; one comes to be most aware of the importance of trust cultivation, achieved in part by paying direct attention to losses, only when it is functioning at its worst. The social is linked to the political not only because it is affected by political actions but because it secures the political realm.

Whereas Arendt tries to hold the social and the political firmly separate, Ellison refers regularly to the "sociopolitical."[88] He acknowledges that laws, although they are an artefact of political institutions, both affect the social realm and are also constantly renegotiated in the social realm. In our encounters with law, we feel the forcefulness of our disagreements, for even legitimate laws cannot exist without imposing on some citizens. And we feel that forcefulness in the social realm. This forcefulness must at least be acknowledged, and should also be weighed, assimilated, and, where necessary, redressed. As Mansbridge puts it:

The injustices we commit as we act collectively – for not to act coercively would in many cases create a greater injustice than to act and coerce some unfairly – should not be forgotten and put behind us. Our collective deliberations should find ways to recognize, store, and rethink our understandings of these actions, so that we do not foreclose the opportunity of making reparation, or of someday

---

[85] Mark E. Warren, "Introduction," in *Democracy and Trust*, ed. Mark E. Warren (Cambridge: Cambridge University Press, 1999), p. 15.

[86] Rom Harré, "Trust and Its Surrogates: Psychological Foundations of Political Process," in *Democracy and Trust*, ed. Warren, pp. 249, 260.

[87] This is not the (Edmund) Burkean point that policy cannot too far outrun social opinion and custom. It is rather the point that even once policies are in place their effects dramatically depend on social contexts.

[88] See, e.g., Warren, *Who Speaks for the Negro?*, p. 327.

understanding how to make the coercion we must use more procedurally fair and its outcomes more substantively just.[89]

The attempt to redress law's forcefulness leads directly to political engagement. Thus, our experience of particular laws in the social realm can lead to larger discussions about how the polity's laws distribute harms and benefits. If, in a democratic polity, we cannot understand law without a language for both acknowledging and recuperating its forcefulness, we cannot fully understand the political status of law in a democracy without a language of sacrifice, or some term like it, for it is through the negotiation of sacrifice, the negotiation of losses, that citizens are able to preserve, on the basis of imperfect consent, the rule of law. Finally, law must be understood as linking the social and political if we are to avoid making the structure of democratic decision-making invisible and if political analysts are to understand the richly political nature even of those legal squabbles that do not rise to constitutional levels.

V.   The relatedness of the social and political

I have argued thus far that Ellison took advantage of the Little Rock events to challenge a dominant treatment of law's forcefulness within political theory of his day. The argument of Arendt's essay in fact confirms Ellison's suggestion that democratic theory was not, in his time, ready to grapple with the complexities of law's necessary forcefulness. Indeed, the greatest logical problems in Arendt's essay occur when she is obliged to grapple with the forcefulness of law.

As we have seen, she was a theorist who accepted and placed her hopes in perpetual disagreement. But argument and disagreement also result in policy, momentary pauses in the constant debate of politics. What then are we to do, according to Arendt, with the practical results of disagreement, and the force of policy? Arendt and Ellison's dispute is exemplary of the problem, for they are ideal Arendtian interlocutors. Arendt argues that the survival of a common world depends on "the fact that, differences of position and the resulting variety of perspectives notwithstanding, everybody is always concerned with the same object."[90] And she and Ellison surely were focused on the same object but from different perspectives. But their inversion of each other's

[89] Jane Mansbridge, "Using Power/Fighting Power: The Polity," in *Democracy and Difference,* ed. Seyla Benhabib (Princeton: Princeton University Press, 1996), pp. 46, 60.
[90] Arendt, *The Human Condition,* pp. 57–58.

perspectives ultimately led not just to argument in the public sphere but also to incompatible policy proposals for Little Rock.

Quite tellingly, Arendt argues that public space "is constituted by [men's] acting together and it then fills of its own accord with the events and stories that develop into history."[91] In her account, differences of perspective somehow on their own develop and resolve themselves into a single history. In *The Human Condition*, she was boldly unconcerned for statutory, or everyday law, as distinct from constitutional law, and adopted what she wrongly considered the position of the Greeks. They, she says, "did not count legislating among the political activities."[92] Instead, it was a form of poiesis, or making, and so alien to the sphere of action proper to politics.[93] James Bohman argues that for Arendt "law is quite limited in its function: It guarantees the equal freedom of all citizens and nothing else."[94] Law does this by providing the franchise and eligibility for political office.[95] But protection of the two political rights is insufficient to preserve the rule of law, for laws must be drawn up about other matters (otherwise there would be no point to the right to vote for law-makers or to be a law-maker) and must then be enforced within social contexts. In Arendt's refusal to take statutory law seriously lies a corresponding refusal to take loss in the deliberative forum seriously.

This is most obvious in "Reflections on Little Rock" when Arendt does try to talk about the "enforcedness" of the desegregation policies that resulted from arguments like Ellison's. She contrasts the voting rights policies that she supports and the desegregation policies that she opposes in these terms: "The present massive resistance throughout the South is an outcome of enforced desegregation, and not of legal enforcement of the Negroes' right to vote."[96] The distinction between "legal enforcement of the right to vote" and "enforced desegregation"

---

[91] Arendt, "On Humanity in Dark Times," p. 9.

[92] Arendt, *The Human Condition*, p. 194.

[93] In fact, just the opposite was the case. The Greek word politeia could mean "policy," as well as "constitution." The daily work of legislation was always a practice of constituting, for the Athenians. Danielle S. Allen, *The World of Prometheus: The Politics of Punishing in Democratic Athens* (Cambridge: Cambridge University Press, 2000), ch. 8.

[94] James Bohman, "The Moral Costs of Political Pluralism: The Dilemmas of Difference and Equality in Arendt's 'Reflections on Little Rock'," in *Hannah Arendt: Twenty Years Later*, ed. Larry May and Jerome Kohn (Cambridge, MA: MIT Press, 1997), pp. 53, 63.

[95] Ellison was sensitive to the importance of the second of these two political rights: "Yet I recalled that during the early, more optimistic days of this republic it was assumed that each individual citizen could become (and should prepare to become) President." Ellison, *Invisible Man*, p. xxi.

[96] Arendt, "Reflections on Little Rock," p. 48.

suggests that pursuit of voting rights and desegregation entailed distinguishable, and in the case of desegregation, illegitimate, uses of law.[97] But in fact the legal basis of both efforts was the same. The Civil Rights Act of 1957 began the abolishment of laws that effectively restricted the franchise in terms of race, and federal officers began enforcing these abolishments across the South. Similarly, the 1954 Supreme Court decision in *Brown* v. *Board of Education*[98] made null and void all federal, state, and local laws mandating or permitting discrimination in schools, an abolishment that federal officers enforced. "Until 1968, federal district courts and the Supreme Court required no more than the elimination of de jure segregation and freedom of choice in school attendance in southern school districts."[99]

Why then does Arendt treat these issues differently? She had no objection to the abolition of segregationist laws. In fact, she argued: "For the crucial point to remember is that it is not the social custom of segregation that is unconstitutional, but its legal enforcement. To abolish this legislation is of great and obvious importance."[100] Both the protections of voting rights and the fight against segregation therefore rested on, in her own account, the legitimate abolishment of unconstitutional laws. And once one disavows, as she does, the use of law to maintain segregation, one must support government protection for anyone wishing to enter a space open to her by law; Arendt must agree that if a student should, albeit against Arendt's advice, choose to attend a school that is legally open to her but from which custom mandates she stay away, legal institutions should protect her in that choice in order that the law be enforced.

Lyman Abbott, a school official in North Carolina, acknowledged as much in the 1860s: "There should be no attempt to prohibit children from attending institutions of their preference; each might choose to attend school with companions of his own race, but no pupil could be barred from any commission school if he chose otherwise."[101] Desegregation, like voting rights, would entail "legal enforcement" as Americans had known since the mid-nineteenth century.

[97] See Bohman, "The Moral Costs of Political Pluralism."
[98] 347 US 483 (1954).
[99] J. Hochschild, *Thirty Years After Brown* (Washington DC: Joint Center for Political Studies, 1985), p. 18.
[100] Arendt, "Reflections on Little Rock," p. 49. Arendt also argues: "Segregation is discrimination enforced by law, and desegregation can do no more than abolish the laws enforcing discrimination." Ibid., p. 50.
[101] Robert C. Morris, "Reading, 'Riting, and Reconstruction: Freedmen's Education in the South, 1861–1870," p. 226 (1976), Ph.D. dissertation, University of Chicago Press (on file at the University of Chicago).

It seems, then, that Arendt's distinction between "enforcedness" and "legal enforcement" supports an argument that is not about law but just about the children's parents. They should not have "forced" their children upon people who did not want them; they should not have, out of respect for customary restrictions on their choices about schools, exercised their legal rights.[102] This argument contains an implicit wish that laws might be changed without affecting social possibilities.[103] But, as we have seen, law always affects the social world. In fact, it is ultimately law's ability to make a polity whole (the laws touch everyone), while having particular and diverse impacts throughout the polity, that ensures the permanent and inevitable permeability of the social and the political. In a law-oriented politics, citizens grant their representatives the power to make decisions that have widely ramifying effects; decisions are not made person-by-person. It is precisely because law's effects

---

[102] Governor Faubus's argument, as presented by Daisy Bates, was similar:

> That evening Governor Faubus went on television and announced that he had withdrawn the national guardsmen in compliance with the Federal Court order. Having created the mob, he now tried to shift the responsibility onto the Negro community. He said he hoped the Negro pupils, of their own volition, would refrain from exercising their rights under the court order by staying away from Central High until such time as school integration could be accomplished without violence. (Bates, *The Long Shadow of Little Rock*, pp. 83–84)

[103] There are blank spaces and evasion in those moments when the nature of the democratic political project forces Arendt to consider necessary interconnectedness of the social and the political. That distinction left Arendt's theoretical apparatus tongue-tied when she wished to distinguish between legitimate and illegitimate forms of social discrimination. She accepted the fact that vacation hotels and resorts determine what sort of clientele they wish to serve, but argued:

> It is however, another matter altogether when we come to "the right to sit where one pleases in a bus" or a railroad car or station, as well as the right to enter hotels and restaurants in business districts – in short, when we are dealing with services which, whether privately or publicly owned, are in fact public services that everyone needs in order to pursue his business and lead his life. Though not strictly in the political realm, such services are clearly in the public domain where all men are equal. (Arendt, "Reflections on Little Rock," p. 52)

Elsewhere in the article, restaurants, businesses, and so forth are considered part of the social realm, but here they fall into the "public domain." Insofar as she designates such business services within the jurisdiction of the realm where "all men are equal," elsewhere called the political realm, she presumably expects the rule of law to protect citizens' access to such services. By acknowledging the proximity of buses, restaurants, and hotels to the public realm, she undermines her own sharp distinction between the social and the political; the phrase "public domain" confesses the inadequacy of those categories. Although she condemns the use of political instruments to improve social opportunities in the case of desegregation, she paradoxically acknowledges that within the social realm citizens may be harmed by segregation to a degree that damages their livelihood and ability to participate in the public sphere; she thereby accepts the Hobbesian idea that the political has a role in securing social interests.

outstrip its intended consequences that our private and social worlds are so thoroughly tied to the political.[104]

Indeed, Arendt maintains her strange distinction between legal enforcement and enforcedness primarily by relying on her distinctions among the private and intimate world of the household, the social world of discrimination, and the political world of equality. She analyzes desegregation in schools by arguing that education is an unusual institution in coming under the purview of all three realms: parents have a private right to educate their children as they see fit; the child's social world is oriented towards school relationships; and the polity's pursuit of the "common good" quite reasonably involves attention to the education of citizens. But she decides that the governmental power over schooling should be limited to making education compulsory. Control over the child's education and social world should, in all other respects, be left to parents. "To force parents to send their children to an integrated school against their will," she held, "means to deprive them of rights which clearly belong to them in all free societies – the private right over their children and the social right to free association."[105] But her request to African-American parents to go slow demands that they give up precisely the right she defends for white parents. It is clear that the private right that parents have over how to educate their children could not be equally protected for all citizens in conditions such as those that obtained in Little Rock in 1957.[106] Her argument against allowing politics to affect the social and private realms is therefore constantly shadowed by a worry that for some portion of the citizenry the political realm will indeed, despite Arendt's protestations, affect the social realm.

Arendt senses this problem and tries to solve it by drawing on sociological observations. She interprets the desire of many white Southern parents for segregated schools as arising from long-standing social custom and as enforceable by custom, while interpreting the

---

[104] And at an even greater rate than the doer's deeds outstrip hers, to use Arendtian terms.

[105] Arendt, "Reflections on Little Rock," p. 55.

[106] I.M. dwells on the truism that "there's always an element of crime in freedom," Ellison, *Invisible Man*, p. 155, and by this he means that one person's freedom restricts someone else's. In his first brotherhood speech, he urges a crowd to cease being blind to that fact:

> Up to now we've been like a couple of one-eyed men...Someone starts throwing bricks and we start blaming each other...But we're mistaken! Because there's a third party present. There's a smooth, oily scoundrel running down the middle of the wide grey street throwing stones...He claims he needs the space – he calls it his freedom. And he knows he's got us on our blind side and he's been popping away till he's got us silly...In fact, his freedom has got us damn-nigh blind! (Ibid., p. 344)

desire of many African-American parents for an end to segregated schools as without customary base and with no means of realization other than through political imposition on social spaces. Accordingly, she assesses the relative value of the rights according to the means being used to secure them.

But had she looked more closely she might have learned that the system of segregated schooling had relied heavily on the political instruments of law to bring itself into existence. Prior to 1877 the South had a small number of integrated schools as well as segregated ones; the question of expanding the number of integrated schools was under debate between 1865 and the mid-1870s.[107] The Catholic church was integrating schools and churches, with a reported 170,000 African-American students attending parochial schools by 1869, many of those in the South, and this spurred the Methodists, who were losing in the competition to recruit new members from the newly freed, to consider doing the same.[108] It was possible for an African-American to hold the position of Superintendent of Schools in the newly formed public school system.[109] During reconstruction, laws were even enacted in the deep South making it illegal for railroads, hotels, and other institutions to discriminate on the basis of race;[110] Congress confirmed these laws for places of public accommodation in the 1875 Civil Rights Act.[111] But then in 1877, thanks to the Hayes-Tilden agreement, control of law enforcement in the South was handed over to Southern Democrats, and everything changed in the state legislatures. Laws were passed installing a fully segregated regime. Private money that would have supported integrated schools was disbursed by public school officials who were against integration.[112]

Much of Arendt's criticism of policies of desegregation, that they used political institutions to secure social benefits, applied equally well to segregation. Thus, her conviction that the success of segregationist practices depended wholly on social custom, an erroneous historical and sociological observation, is finally what allows her to ignore the forcefulness of law in some contexts. But it takes not only mistakes about history but also the elaborate conceptual apparatus of her social-political

---

[107] See Morris, "Reading, 'Riting, and Reconstruction," pp. 224–229.

[108] Ibid., p. 227. Ultimately, the Methodists decided against integration, but the point is that the issue was handled with some degree of fluidity during reconstruction, despite the undisputed tendency of black and white Southerners to remain aloof from one another.

[109] See Eric Foner, "Reconstruction," in *Encyclopedia of African-American Culture and History*, vol. IV (Basingstoke: Macmillan, 1996), pp. 2274, 2282.

[110] See ibid.   [111] See ibid., p. 2284.

[112] See Morris, "Reading, 'Riting, and Reconstruction," p. 345.

distinction to maintain an approach to politics that can avoid direct consideration of law's ubiquitous and necessary forcefulness.[113] In short, Arendt must build an elaborate conceptual structure to avoid directly addressing the fact of law's forcefulness, and then this elaborate conceptual framework leads to misjudgments of citizenship and the actions of particular citizens. A more fruitful approach to citizenship, capable of developing ethical criteria for addressing law's forcefulness would, in contrast, look the problem of loss squarely in the face.

VI.   Where to?

Let me conclude, then, by returning to the theme of invisibility and the resources this figure makes available for thinking about both law and citizenship. As it turns out, Arendt's "Reflections on Little Rock" also employs the trope of visibility. Thus Arendt remarks:

The Negroes stand out because of their "visibility." They are not the only "visible minority," but they are the most visible one. In this respect, they somewhat resemble new immigrants, who invariably constitute the most "audible" of all minorities and therefore are always the most likely to arouse xenophobic sentiments. But while audibility is a temporary phenomenon, rarely persisting beyond one generation, the Negroes' visibility is unalterable and permanent. This is not a trivial matter. In the public realm, where nothing counts that cannot make itself seen and heard, visibility and audibility are of prime importance.[114]

"Visibility" and "audibility" are, of course, concepts that are of prime importance to Arendt, not only in *Men in Dark Times* but also in *The Human Condition*, where they are the goals of political participation and indicators of full involvement in the public world.[115] In the above passage, Arendt does not explain precisely how "the visibility of Negroes" relates to their political rights, but the last sentence implies that, at the time of her writing, African-Americans were fully in and of the common world and were having no trouble being heard since "in the public

---

[113] Arendt's argument produces a paradox in which abridgment of the right to control where one's children go to school should be simply "sufferable" for one group of parents (the African-American parents) while being an indefensible violation of legal right for another set (white parents). I owe the term "sufferable" to Debbie Nelson. Benhabib writes in a similar vein: "For those who feel that the reconciliation in social life has been achieved at their expense, it might be morally justified to refuse participating. This does not imply resorting to violence or to force, but simply the refusal to engage in dialogue before the realization has been reached that the mutuality of shared existence is indeed endangered by the existing constellation of power." Benhabib, *Critique, Norm, and Utopia*, p. 321.

[114] Arendt, "Reflections on Little Rock," p. 47.

[115] Her arguments about visibility presume direct democracy.

realm ... nothing counts that cannot make itself seen and heard."[116] As citizens and not slaves, African-Americans had on paper, in 1957, the political rights that she suggests ensure access to the common world. But Ellison's development of the theme of invisibility starts precisely from a rejection of this treatment of citizenship.

He writes in the introduction to *Invisible Man*: "Thus despite the bland assertions of sociologists, 'high visibility' actually rendered one un-visible – whether at high noon in Macy's window or illuminated by flaming torches and flashbulbs while undergoing the ritual sacrifice that was dedicated to the ideal of white supremacy."[117] His figure (invisibility) and the idea of sacrifice provide conceptual resources for assessing the modes of participation that any particular form of democracy has achieved; analysis of invisibility and the sacrifices within politics also force us to see that law is most political precisely as a mediator of the social and the political. Citizens make law together through their political institutions; those laws regularly structure and restructure their social and private worlds. Law promises that we are all better off as "a whole" than apart, and the terms "invisibility" and "sacrifice" test that promise. Democratic law needs this testing, and it needs to be able to respond to it, if it is to ensure its continued legitimacy, for if we cannot aim for a set of laws that is based on the glad consent of all citizens, we should aim for laws that do keep in mind the question of whether, under their auspices and made into a "whole" by them, we are indeed all better off.

Arendt responded to Ellison's criticism by letter, admitting precisely that she had not "grasped the element of stark violence, of elementary, bodily fear in the [Little Rock] situation."[118] Her admission that she had not grasped the violence that obtained in the South did not, however, prompt her to revise her theoretical framework for understanding democratic politics and the rule of law, because for her the violence of the South made it a place where democracy had to be constituted from scratch and out of tyranny, not a place where democracy had rather to be reconstituted from within itself. The former task, she continued to insist, required no more than voting rights, eligibility for office, and good laws. The latter task, Ellison insists, requires both that we rethink our

[116] Arendt, "Reflections on Little Rock," p. 47.
[117] Introduction to Ellison, *Invisible Man*, p. xv. On the relation between lynching, sacrificing, and scapegoating, see B. Eddy, "The Rites of Identity: The Religious Naturalism and Cultural Criticism of Kenneth Burke" (unpublished dissertation, Department of Religion, Princeton University) and Ralph Ellison (1998) (unpublished dissertation) (on file at the Department of Religion, Princeton University).
[118] Young-Bruehl, *Hannah Arendt*, p. 316. On the response, see also Bohman, "The Moral Costs of Political Pluralism," pp. 57–59.

modes of law-making and representation to account for the sacrifices we make for each other, and that we generate the social contexts and practices of recognition that can bring the democratic rule of law into existence. Once the importance of building trust to assimilate loss is reintroduced to politics, we see clearly that both representation and law-making draw on the resources provided by the cultivation of trust. Representatives and law-makers are responsible for replenishing that trust by keeping alive the discourse that acknowledges and addresses loss and law's forcefulness. We cannot bring about the rule of law, which Arendt so treasured, without also acknowledging its necessary and inevitable forcefulness. In the final analysis, citizens will themselves be responsible for making law democratic, and for democratizing its forcefulness, as they interact over the enforcement of law. The institutions of democratic law-making must be understood as being situated in a much wider context of public speech that aims at the negotiation of loss and the constant redistribution of loss within the citizenry. And theorists of democracy are responsible for assessing what can make law's necessary forcefulness justly assimilable.

13 Imagining civic relations in the moment of their breakdown: a crisis of civic integrity in the Netherlands[1]

Bert van den Brink

I.

On the morning of 2 November 2004, Dutch film director and columnist Theo van Gogh was murdered in a street in Amsterdam, the Netherlands. Only minutes later, after a shoot-out with the police, a Moroccan-Dutch young man, Mohammed Bouyeri, who many witnesses identified as the killer, was arrested. A letter found on van Gogh's body and another letter Bouyeri had on him strongly suggested that he had committed the murder and had been motivated by extremist-Islamist ideas.[2] Although, remarkably, van Gogh was not mentioned in Bouyeri's letters, it was not hard to guess why he had been targeted. Pricked on a knife that had been stabbed into van Gogh's breast, one of the letters was addressed to Ayaan Hirsi Ali, Member of Parliament for the liberal party and the most influential critic of traditional and political Islam in the Netherlands.[3] With Hirsi Ali, van Gogh had released a film, *Submission*, in which the treatment of women in Islam was severely criticized. The film had been first shown on public television just a few months before the murder. It had been quite controversial and was still on many people's minds. So the public's first reaction was that van Gogh had been killed because of the film. The killer was also targeting

---

[1] For helpful comments on earlier versions of this article, I should like to thank the editors of this volume, Anthony Laden and David Owen, Marcus Düwell of Utrecht University, and members of Rainer Forst's political theory colloquium at Goethe University, Frankfurt am Main, especially Rainer Forst, Peter Kraus, Regina Kreide, Peter Niesen, and Martin Saar.

[2] In July 2005, Bouyeri was found guilty of the murder. He admitted having killed van Gogh and he stressed that he had done so for religious reasons. During his trial, he declared that he would kill again, for the same reasons, if he were ever released from prison. He serves a life sentence.

[3] See Ayaan Hirsi Ali, *De Zoontjesfabriek* (Amsterdam: Augustus, 2002); *De Maagdenkooi* (Amsterdam: Augustus, 2004); *Submission* (Amsterdam: Augustus, 2004).

Hirsi Ali, who had written the script for the film. The letter that was left on van Gogh's body contained a direct threat against her: "Since your fall in with the political arena in the Netherlands, you have been constantly terrorizing Muslims and Islam with your statements ... With all these hostilities you have thrown a boomerang and you know that it is only a matter of time before this boomerang will settle your fate."[4]

This horrific murder and death threat led to a crisis of civic relations in the Netherlands. But what kind of political crisis was this? The main political and social institutions of this liberal-democratic society were firmly standing, yet a worrying breakdown of civic competence among politicians, intellectuals, journalists, columnists, and "ordinary" citizens acting within these institutions was witnessed. This became most clear in a considerable part of the contributions to public debate over the issue. I will claim that, from a standpoint interested in competent citizenship, a serious lack of political judgment of several opinion leaders drove this debate in an entirely false direction from the start. Mohammed Bouyeri's horrific deed did not so much spark a debate about the very real dangers of Islamist terrorism. Rather, it gave rise to a debate about the question as to whether Muslim immigrants can be good citizens at all. As we will see, some argued that Bouyeri's deed made it necessary for all Muslim immigrants to take a stand with regard to their appreciation of liberal-democratic citizenship. I aim to show that the form and content of these critics' contributions to the debate, which were meant as defenses of the liberal-democratic order, actually fell short of one of the most basic requirements of liberal-democratic citizenship: that each individual citizen be addressed as a free and equal member of the political community, not as a member of other communities, such as religious, cultural, or ethnic ones.

The crisis in civic relations initially became visible in the dialogical etiquette and rhetorical style of contributions to public debate. Later, the use of violence against mosques, churches, and Islamic schools took over. Eventually, on the late evening of the day that Theo van Gogh was cremated, seven days after the murder, three young boys set fire to an Islamic school in the provincial town of Uden, which burned down to the ground. The words "Theo R.I.P." and a "white power" symbol were painted on one of the school's windows.[5] I will argue that not only in the latter, but also in the former case, the limits set by an ideal of decent *civic* interaction in a time of crisis were not observed. By

---

[4] Bouyeri's letters can be read on the website of Dutch public television: www.nos.nl/nosjournaal (last consulted on 12 July 2005).
[5] The boys (14 and 15 years of age) were arrested and found guilty of the attack.

choosing a rhetorical style of head-on confrontation of the supposedly clearly identifiable group of "Muslim immigrants," leading politicians and intellectuals dominated public debate in a manner that was not respectful of the normative status of free and equal membership of the political community of all those captured under this general term. Indeed, by addressing Muslim immigrants in this way, they addressed them not *as* citizens, but *as* Muslims. I will show that the way in which these critics constructed the relation between native and Muslim immigrant citizens tells us much about the informal patterns of expectation and evaluation with regard to citizenship in culturally diverse Dutch society. The dominant tone in public debate was that Muslim immigrants should either largely *assimilate* (make harmless) their religious-ethnic identity to that of majority culture, or *exclude* themselves (as different and dangerous) from the political community in the case of a refusal to assimilate themselves (see section III).

Interestingly, a brief look into the history of cultural pluralism and social and political integration of different cultural-religious groups in the Netherlands shows that Dutch authorities and the native population carry at least as much responsibility for the failed social and political integration of a considerable number of Muslim immigrants as these immigrants themselves. Remarkably, this circumstance – which was widely known through a report of a parliamentary committee published in early 2004[6] – did not prevent dominant voices in public debate constructing an image of the Muslim immigrant as someone who, for his or her own cultural-religious reasons, tends to refuse social and political integration into larger society. In short: the generalized Muslim immigrant and his cultural-religious identity were made into a scapegoat for the failed social and political integration of part of the Muslim immigrants (see section IV).

Ultimately, by looking into some of the more ugly details of what happened to civic interaction after a horrible murder, I aim to bolster the theoretical position that our normative status as free and equal citizens is not to be understood solely as a legal status. It also depends, both in theory and in practice, on concrete forms of acknowledgment of the freedom and equality that citizens, each individually, receive in more informal social and political relations. Ultimately, I will argue that the forms of civic competence that citizens need in order to shape their informal political relations are best accounted for as requirements of *civic* integrity; most importantly a requirement of *justice* with regard to

---

[6] See the committee's report, *Bruggen Bouwen* (Den Haag: Sdu, 2004). An English summary can be downloaded from the site of the Dutch Parliament: www.tweedekamer.nl.

the acknowledgment of each and every citizen's normative status as a free and equal member of the political community, and *truthfulness* with regard to the quality of one's civic performance in light of that status. I will argue that the crisis of civic relations in the Netherlands can best be understood as a crisis of civic integrity among those opinion leaders and "ordinary" citizens who did not exercise these virtues in their reactions to the murder. As a contribution to political theory, I will show that civic integrity presupposes that citizens acknowledge at least three circumstances of politics in culturally diverse liberal-democratic societies: the facts of ethical and political pluralism and disagreement, the need for concerted political action despite this pluralism, and the role of often unspoken but still influential informal power relations (see sections V and VI).

II.

In the days that followed van Gogh's murder, the citizens of the Netherlands were obviously in a state of shock. One might want to say that they were confronted with the task of imagining their citizenship anew. I realized this after having read, in the weeks following van Gogh's murder, Danielle Allen's interesting book, *Talking to Strangers*.[7] The book starts with an interpretation of photos of the exclusion of African-American student Elizabeth Eckford by white fellow students and their parents from Central High School, Little Rock, Arkansas, on 4 September 1957. On that day, Allen claims, "US democracy was reconstituted."[8] Allen can make that claim because she thinks of a constitution as consisting of written laws *and* customs, including the ways in which "democratic citizens imagine 'the people' of which they are a part."[9] In moments of crisis, citizens can reconstitute their democracy because what they experience makes them question their laws, their customs, and the ways in which they imagine themselves as a democratic people. This is why Allen says about the picture of Eckford being cursed by white student Hazel Brown: "Much as a violent wound reveals bone, sinew, blood, and muscle, the picture stripped away idealized conceptions of democratic life and directed the eyes of the citizenry to the ordinary habits that in 1957 constituted citizenship despite the standing law ... [H]abits of citizenship begin with how citizens imagine their political world."[10]

---

[7] Danielle S. Allen, *Talking to Strangers: Anxieties of Citizenship since Brown v. Board of Education* (Chicago: University of Chicago Press, 2004).
[8] Ibid., p. 3.   [9] Ibid., p. 17.   [10] Ibid., p. 3.

Perhaps the day of the murder of van Gogh and the week that followed it can be understood in a similar way. After the first week, the increasing radicalization gradually came to a halt after the realization sunk in that, not somewhere in a nasty foreign place, but in the Netherlands, a school had been burned down after a religiously motivated murder and a week of ethnic tensions. This was indeed a time to call idealized conceptions of democratic life and habits of citizenship into question. Most importantly, the hard to root out idea that citizens of the Netherlands are remarkably tolerant of cultural and religious diversity was buried at last. In the Netherlands, citizens' capacities to deal with explosive issues of cultural difference, multiculturalism, and ethnic-religious extremism are limited. There are citizens like Mohammed Bouyeri, who are prepared to kill for their extremist ideas, and there are citizens like the radical youths in the provincial town of Uden, who burned down an Islamic school in an extremist reaction to Bouyeri's extremism. But, perhaps more importantly, apart from these extremists, many citizens and professional politicians and opinion leaders had been without a clear *civic* orientation in the crisis that unfolded itself. There was remarkably little orientation inspired by a principled idea as to how fellow citizens are to treat each other *as fellow citizens* when confronted with circumstances that test the quality of their bonds. As we shall see, the important call for restraint and dialogue, especially with regard to the dangers of conceptualizing the murder in terms of the suspect's generalized ethnic and religious identity, was not taken seriously by all in positions of political responsibility and influence. Indeed, the exercise in public scapegoating in the wake of the murder made it clear that something was fundamentally wrong with civic relations in the Netherlands.

In the following I will argue that the *integrity* of these relations was affected, especially with respect to the quality of the civic dispositions of certain politicians and opinion leaders. Following Danielle Allen, I will focus on the quality of the informal "conceptions of democratic life" that speak from these opinion leaders' contributions to public debate.[11] Such informal conceptions tell us how citizens interpret their civic bonds in practice, who they regard as competent citizens, who they regard as incompetent, how much unity and how much diversity they think a democratic polity needs or can endure, and so on. Informal conceptions of citizenship tend to draw a different picture of what it means to regard each other as free and equal members of the political community than the legal framework of citizenship does. But although the legal framework has more formal power than informal conceptions of citizenship, it would be a

---

[11] Allen, *Talking to Strangers*, p. 5.

mistake to think that it alone determines what citizenship consists in. Informal conceptions influence laws and policy and, perhaps even more importantly, they contribute to what James Tully, further developing Michel Foucault's concept of "subjectivation,"[12] has called practices of "citizenization."[13] Both in formal and informal social and political relations, citizens are subject to "the languages and powers" of forms of governance that determine "the diverse kinds of relational subjectivity [they] internalize and negotiate through participation over time, with their range of possible conduct and individual variation."[14] In other words, informal conceptions of citizenship and the social power relations they represent co-determine the ways in which citizens who are differently situated within the informal power relations of society think of themselves and act as citizens. Some citizens will think of themselves as representing a widely acknowledged and rightly praised type of citizenship, others will think of themselves as representing hardly acknowledged and unjustly ridiculed alternative standards of citizenship, still others will think of themselves as not being taken seriously at all, etc. I will assume that it is a requirement of civic integrity that citizens recognize the formative influence of informal conceptions of citizenship on the political subjectivity of citizens and that they are willing to exercise restraint, change their beliefs and behavior, and so on, when the informal "citizenization" of some citizens results in their effective exclusion from the political community of free and equal citizens. This will happen, for instance, when the political claims of members of certain democratic minorities are almost by definition not taken seriously in political debate. Where this is the case, democratic institutions and procedures may all be in place. Still, informal conceptions of citizenship can make effective democratic association impossible. Where citizens do not show the kind of civic integrity that criticizes such a state of affairs in a community all members of which are to be seen as free and equal, the civic integrity of these citizens individually and of the form of political cooperation as such is in danger. This conception of civic integrity, which I will develop further in the course of this chapter, presupposes *truthfulness* with respect to our influence on the effective "citizenization" of our fellow citizens and *justice* with regard to our disposition to treat our fellow citizens as free and equal members of the political community. Democratic cooperation is a demanding game in

---

[12] See for instance, Michel Foucault, "The Subject and Power," in *Power: Essential Works of Michel Foucault 1954–1984*, vol. III, ed. Paul Rabinow (New York: New Press, 2000), pp. 326–348.
[13] James Tully, "Political Philosophy as a Critical Activity," *Political Theory*, 30 (4), 2002, p. 540.
[14] Ibid.

which we constantly have to test the truthfulness and justice of our own and our fellow citizens' civic performance with regard to the power relations in which we stand.[15]

III.

In the chaotic public debate that followed the murder of van Gogh, dominant patterns of expectation and evaluation became visible with regard to the citizenship of both powerful and less powerful groups in society. I will study the two most dominant informal conceptions of democratic life from that week, which are both critical of the ideal of multiculturalism. The first of these is perhaps best understood as an aggressive form of secular humanism. Here, the informal conception of democratic life is that unless citizens share in a largely secularized and modern constitutional-democratic culture, they cannot be competent members of the liberal-democratic political community. As a consequence, it sets patterns of expectation and evaluation that openly declare the moral superiority of post-traditionalist, modern, and individualistic lifestyles.[16] The second informal conception of democratic life rejects the secular-humanist aspect, but agrees that consent to the substantive norms and values of liberal-democratic citizenship is a requirement of competent citizenship. Yet, it seeks these norms and values not just in the institutions and founding documents of the state, but also – to put it with John Rawls – in reasonable comprehensive conceptions of the good,[17] which may be Christian, Islamic, liberal, etc. Yet, going beyond a politically liberal view, it claims that only comprehensive conceptions of the good that embrace values such as personal autonomy and religious pluralism qualify as reasonable.

Without any doubt, the secular-humanist conception, which is closest to Ayaan Hirsi Ali and Theo van Gogh's vision of the requirements of competent citizenship, was most dominant in the debate. It almost seemed as if secular humanists took the murder of van Gogh as proof for

[15] I have benefited from David Owen, *Nietzsche, Politics, Modernity* (Thousand Oaks and London: Sage, 1995), pp. 132–170.
[16] Here, the work of the right-wing populist politician Pim Fortuyn, who was murdered in May 2002, has been very influential. See his books *Tegen de Islamisering van Nederland: Nederlandse identiteit als fundament* (Utrecht: Bruna, 1997); *De puinhopen van acht jaar paars* (Uithoorn: Karakter Uitgevers, 2002). The best study on Fortuyn's political ideas and successes is Dick Pels, *De geest van Pim: Het gedachtegoed van een politieke dandy* (Amsterdam: Anthos, 2003). An influential theorist of the presumed superiority of Western culture is the philosopher of law, Paul Cliteur. See his *Tegen de decadentie: De democratische rechtsstaat in verval* (Amsterdam: Arbeiderspers, 2004).
[17] John Rawls, *Political Liberalism* (New York: Columbia University Press, 1993).

one of their core assumptions: that loyalty to constitutional-democratic principles cannot be combined with strong, traditionalist religious convictions. With regard to the convictions that seem to have motivated Bouyeri's murder of van Gogh, this may be true. Yet, as seen from the ideal of civic interaction among free and equal members of the political community, Bouyeri's deed does not in any way justify the categorizations of Islamic immigrants as falling mainly under the category of traditionalist believers on the one hand and native Dutch citizens as falling under the category of enlightened secular humanists on the other. Yet, this construction of the personal beliefs and dispositions of citizens was without any doubt central to the contributions to public debate of secular humanists in this eventful week.

This rhetoric of extremes probably explains why in the heated public debates they engaged in, defenders of secular humanism spoke *about* rather than *with* those they criticized. Using a politically "realist" rhetorical strategy, secular humanists claimed to tell the presumably clear truth about certain "facts" about society; "facts" that certain intellectual and political elites – sympathizers of multiculturalism mostly – are said to hide by turning them into taboos.[18] With this political realism, Dutch Muslims' presumed approval of the murder of van Gogh, their presumed unwillingness to integrate into larger society, and the presumed incompatibility of Islamic religious beliefs and democratic-constitutional citizenship were addressed.

The fact that the rhetorical approach used here is not reciprocal or dialogical in orientation does not discredit it as such. There are many rhetorical techniques that are not dialogical and that do not presuppose deliberative reciprocity between speaker and listener or addressee. However, the approach becomes potentially undemocratic when it is not just one rhetorical register among many, but claims to have privileged access to criteria of political truth and rightness in situations of a crisis. As we will see, that was exactly the case here. Let us look at some examples.

Jozias van Aartsen, leader of Ayaan Hirsi Ali's liberal party in Parliament, declared, one day after the murder, that the *jihad* had reached the Netherlands. "[W]e should be beyond a state of denial by now . . . [t]hese people do not want to change our society, but destroy it. We are their enemy. And we have not seen that since 1940."[19] The problem

---

[18] See Baukje Prins, *Voorbij de onschuld: Het debat over integratie in Nederland* (Amsterdam: Van Gennep, 2004), pp. 23–44. My discussion of the rhetorical aspects of the debate is indebted to Prins's analysis of rhetorical strategies in the debate on multiculturalism in the Netherlands.

[19] Jeroen van der Kris and Gretha Pama, "Tien dagen crisis," *NRC Handelsblad*, 13 November 2004.

with these words, which when restricted to a small group of extremists are undoubtedly true, was that van Aartsen did not make it sufficiently clear who he was talking about. He could not, since all that was known at this point was that one suspect who looked like an Arab had been arrested, that the intelligence services knew of 150 potential Islamist extremists in the Netherlands, and that the suspect of van Gogh's murder was not among them. This alarmed van Aartsen greatly and gave him the opportunity to suggest that the problem was much bigger than everyone had thought and that political elites had been extremely naive about this. Van Aartsen now tried to awaken the masses, to make people face the "real facts" before them: that the country was confronted with the greatest danger since the Second World War. The subtext was that the country had gradually been occupied by a foreign power.

The day after the murder the sociologist and journalist, Herman Vuijsje, stated in an interview with a daily newspaper, *de Volkskrant,* that "what has now happened shows what we have allowed to develop, which people we have allowed into our country and have given all the room they need, how we have let it rot for too long."[20] Again we see that the country is said to be in great danger because of its foreign occupation by uncivilized hordes. Again we see the suggestion that the belief in the goodness of all newcomers was naive.

The same charge, mixed with the suggestion that every Muslim may be an Islamist extremist, speaks from an attack by Joost Zwagerman, well-known novelist and columnist, on the social-democratic mayor of Amsterdam, Job Cohen. From the day of the murder, Cohen (who had been addressed with anti-Semitic slander in Mohammed Bouyeri's letter to Hirsi Ali) had tried to keep up dialogue and mutual respect between ethnic groups in his city. With regard to Cohen's warnings against generalizing judgments about Muslims (who make up 11 percent of the population of Amsterdam[21]), and gatherings between Muslims and non-Muslims he had organized, Zwagerman wrote: "There is a real chance that a much bigger percentage than we assume is of the opinion that the hand reached out to them may be one of a perverse blasphemer who, in the name of Allah, may and can be ignored, despised, and, since November 2, killed."[22]

[20] *De Volkskrant,* 3 November 2004.
[21] *De Amsterdamse Burgermonitor 2004,* Amsterdam: Gemeente Amsterdam, Dienst Onderzoek en Statistiek (www.os.amsterdam.nl, 16 January 2005).
[22] Joost Zwagerman, "Toon nu burgerschap, geen slachtofferschap," *de Volkskrant,* 6 November 2004.

These reactions to the murder of van Gogh were not about the possibility that a grip of radical Islam on *one* Moroccan-Dutch man had led to a horrific murder. Or, as would have been perfectly understandable and justified, they were not about the likelihood that there are more men such as Mohammed Bouyeri and that they form a serious threat to public safety and social order. Rather, they were about irrational, never substantiated fears that the majority of Dutch Muslims silently approved of the murder; even that hundreds of thousands of religious fanatics had been let into the country. Secular-humanist "truth telling" became highly speculative here and, given the way in which it strengthened pre-existing irrational fears, itself a danger to public safety and social order.[23] In this time of crisis, it neatly divided up the social world into two basic categories: those who can be trusted to have decent civic dispositions and those who, because of their ethnicity and religious beliefs, most probably do not. By this logic the murder became a political "wedge issue."[24] Van Gogh, Hirsi Ali, and all their sympathizers were now presented as martyrs of the freedom of expression, which was presented as a typically Western, even Dutch value, rather than as a fundamental human right. Decent, modern, secularized citizens respect this freedom, so the claim went, but Muslims are in danger of opposing it because of their religious and ethnic practices and beliefs. Of course, such suggestions were often accompanied by the reassurance that there are also *good* Muslims. But whether good or bad, in the eyes of secular-humanists, all Dutch Muslims now had to show where their real loyalties were. They were said to have the civic duty to prove that they were good citizens by publicly denouncing the use of violence and by publicly accepting liberal-democratic values.

The considerable appeal of this secular-humanist conception of democratic life in those days of crisis revealed that in the Netherlands, there is a huge potential for thinking about citizenship as a practice that is *mastered* by a particular group of people, i.e., the already socially and politically dominant, largely modernized and largely secular native population. Besides this group, there are those who do not master citizenship in practice, i.e. religious immigrants, Muslims especially. Note that this informal conception of democratic life does not deny that Muslim immigrants can *learn* to master the game of democratic citizenship. But it does not leave room for critical questions as to the basic assumption of the model of secular humanism: either you *assimilate* and

---

[23] See for this thesis, Geert Mak's controversial but I think correct analysis of the "trade in fear" in Geert Mak, *Gedoemd tot Kwetsbaarheid* (Amsterdam: Atlas, 2005).

[24] Maarten Hajer and Marcel Maussen, "Betekenisgeving aan de moord: een reconstructie," *Socialisme en Democratie*, 12, 2004, pp. 10–19, here: p. 12.

are with us, or you belong to a backward culture and thus *exclude yourself* from participation in our democratic game.[25]

There was another dominant voice in public debate that week. It was a typically Dutch voice that called for orientation towards social harmony and a foundational consensus on core norms and values that would unite all citizens in a common cultural practice. The prime minister, Christian-Democrat Jan-Peter Balkenende, was the main representative of this position, as he has been since he first became prime minister in 2002. Balkenende is a schoolbook *liberal* communitarian; that is, a principled defender of the constitutional-democratic state and of individual rights who at the same time stresses that citizens will not be able to make the most of the opportunities that constitutional-democratic association has to offer so long as they are not united by a foundational consensus about the core norms and values that hold society, as made up of different societal cultures, together.

Balkenende was clearly worried about the consequences of the near-total dominance of secular humanism in the debate. His opportunity for gaining back some power for his religion-friendly communitarian vision in the midst of a civic crisis came when the Islamic school burned down in the provincial town of Uden. The day after this happened Balkenende visited the site. There, a mother of children who attended the school articulated to Balkenende her worries about the generalizing judgments about, and now the violence against, Muslims. Live on television, she attacked the most famous and among Muslims most controversial secular humanist in the Netherlands: "The clear cause of all this is Hirsi Ali. Is it not important that she understand that she should have respect for Islam? That she is the one who causes all this? Or should we just accept this and let her talk like that? . . . If people from the government [*sic*[26]] continue with statements like hers, then society will continue to be confronted with these kinds of actions."[27]

---

[25] For an example of a Dutch intellectual who presents the issue straightforwardly in these terms, see Annette van der Elst, "Ze hoeven niet allemaal hutspot te eten: interview met Herman Philipse" ("They do not all have to eat stew"), *Filosofie Magazine*, 14 (2), 2005 pp. 10–13. For a thorough analysis of exclusion and assimilation as endangering deliberative equality between citizens, see Anthony Laden, *Reasonably Radical: Deliberative Liberalism and the Politics of Identity* (Ithaca, NY: Cornell University Press, 2001), pp. 131–185.

[26] Hirsi Ali does not have a position in the acting government. She is a Member of Parliament for the VVD, the liberal party in the coalition government under Christian-Democrat Balkenende. Note that, in the Netherlands, the term "liberalism" is not necessarily associated with a left-wing position on socio-economic justice. There is a liberal right that combines a progressive take on ethical issues with a neo-liberal position on socio-economic issues.

[27] Van der Kris and Pama, "Tien dagen crisis."

Of course, the woman could not expect the prime minister to silence Hirsi Ali. Hirsi Ali, who understandably went into hiding for more than two months after the murder, was clearly a victim in this crisis. Still, the woman's remarks were not pushed aside entirely. Balkenende, a devout Protestant, seemed to recognize something in what the woman had said. Especially her deep grievance at being criticized and now – by extremist youths – attacked simply for holding certain religious ideas could clearly count on the prime minister's sympathy. In an evasive move by which he aimed to remain respectful both to Hirsi Ali and to the woman standing next to him, he answered, "Let us recognize each other. Let us realize that we are one country, one people. That is the point."[28]

As he has done on many other occasions, the prime minister was looking for harmony through a plea for both political and cultural unity, for consensus as to the fundamental norms and values that could make the divided nation *one again*. A day later, in a similar context, he claimed that "[p]eople are not interested in intensified political oppositions right now. People wonder how the media sometimes tear issues from their context or stir up controversial issues."[29] Balkenende's informal conception of democratic life is that of a diverse democratic society in which a substantive consensus with regard to constitutional-democratic values is nonetheless supported by various reasonable and dialogically disposed societal cultures. To this image of citizenship and the call for overcoming opposition, the reaction of the perhaps most unrelenting secular-humanist truth-teller in political debate was, "Yes, dialogue is fundamental, we think so too. But don't start talking about solidarity, mutual respect, and responsibility now. Everyone, us included, rejects strongly the excesses in the schools, the mosques and the churches that were set on fire. Dialogue is important, but it is not the first concern."[30] The first concern, he might have added, was the safety of the constitutional-democratic state and the war against those who want to destroy it.

IV.

Note that both informal conceptions of citizenship that I have analyzed focus strongly on *unity* and *substantive consensus* on quite comprehensive cultural norms and values as prerequisites of a healthy political community. And note that the way in which these conceptions of citizenship

[28] Ibid.   [29] Ibid.

[30] Ibid. The Islamic school in Uden was the most widely published attack on a religious site, but there were more attacks on such objects – Islamic and Christian – during the week after the murder.

present themselves is very self-assured and hardly self-critical: we, competent citizens of the Netherlands, know how you, incompetent Muslim immigrants, can become competent citizens. The answer is: assimilate to our way of doing things, for we don't trust your way. It is true that the secular-humanist contribution to the debate comes closest to this assimilationist answer. But the liberal-communitarian view is not all that far removed from it either. It is more pluralistic and leaves more room for reasonable religious conceptions of the good. But it too presents itself as a keeper of the true Dutch civic and cultural identity that newcomers have to assimilate to.

This is, of course, the point at which the question about civic integrity becomes acute. For it seems that both informal conceptions of citizenship actively foster two very different forms of citizenization as addressed to well-integrated citizens on the one hand and presumably not-so-well-integrated citizens on the other. In the next section, I will argue that both political conceptions' unwillingness to question the quality of the civic bonds they have to offer reveals serious blind spots with respect to their capacity to acknowledge basic circumstances of democratic politics. But before I develop that argument, let me first look into the question as to where, in the Dutch situation, the strong stress on unity, oneness, and consensus is coming from in the first place, and whether it might be related to a lack of truthfulness with respect to the responsibilities of the dominant political culture as to the civic and social integration of immigrants. By showing that this is indeed the case, I will substantiate my claim that a crisis of civic integrity that concerns much more than questions of multiculturalism and social integration is at the heart of this problematic.

Between roughly the last quarter of the nineteenth century and the 1960s, Dutch Protestants, Roman Catholics, socialists, and liberals were immersed in cultural "pillars" of their own. Members of these societal cultures went to their own schools and had their own recreational clubs. There was not much intermarriage between members of the pillars; even small businesses and healthcare institutions sometimes seemed to have their "own" denominations; pillars had their own newspapers and later radio and television stations, their own labor and employers' unions, and knew at least one, sometimes (with the Protestants especially) two or three political parties. What resulted was a landscape in which the pillars largely defined themselves in opposition to other pillars and the state.[31] The political parties played a crucial role.

---

[31] Remieg Aerts, "Living Apart Together? Verdraagzaamheid in Nederland sinds de zeventiende eeuw," in *De lege toleratie: Over vrijheid en vrijblijvendheid in Nederland*, ed.

They were able to work out between them a remarkably pragmatic democratic cooperation through which they set the terms for a pluralistic societal life. Despite their, at times grotesque, rivalry, the pillars built a nation together. After a sustainable balance of power had been reached around 1920, the pillars started to understand the *modus vivendi* between the pillars as an *inherent* common good that served the *intrinsic* good of upholding their own societal cultures. Representative democracy and the rule of law were nearly universally accepted as setting the rules of the game. But what they implied for institutional design, the exact rights of citizens, and the specific interests and political conceptions of the pillars, remained contested until the end of the pillar system. Government by pacified conflict, coalitions, and compromises, not government by substantive consensus, characterized the pillar system.

Under the pillar system, from generation to generation, members of different pillars had the time to gradually grow accustomed to the changes that occurred in society. They were introduced to the rule of law, battled together or with each other for certain civil rights, were introduced to democratic politics, to universal political rights for men, later for women, social rights against child labor, to education and healthcare, and finally to the attractions of the welfare state and of individualism that eventually led to the demise of the pillars, etc.[32] These layers of familiarity with a developing liberal-democratic state and society made the *different* societal cultures *similar* in the sense that they went through and cooperated in processes of modernization, emancipation, and political empowerment at more-or-less the same pace. As one historian puts it, "Despite all cultural differences between the pillars, the gradual emergence of a dominant social-cultural norm was undeniable. Education, increased mobility, the increased influence of state institutions and social workers contributed to the establishment of 'high' Dutch language, social disciplining and the spread of *bourgeois* living patterns."[33] To be sure, the pillars had their downsides, their internal intolerances, and forms of exclusion – issues related to the politics of the family and to sexual morality are the obvious examples. But they gave individuals social-cultural institutions through which they

Marcel ten Hooven (Amsterdam: Boom, 2001), pp. 74–75. See also J. C. H. Blom and J. Talsma (eds.), *De verzuiling voorbij: Godsdienst, stand, en natie in de lange negentiende eeuw* (Amsterdam: Het spinhuis, 2000); Arendt Lijphart, *The Politics of Accommodation: Pluralism and Democracy in the Netherlands* (Berkeley: University of California Press, 1968).

[32] Gabriël van den Brink, *Mondiger of moeilijker: Een studie naar de politieke habitus van hedendaagse burgers* (The Hague: Sdu, 2002).

[33] Aerts, "Living Apart Together?," p. 76.

learned to be productive, informed, emancipated members of society; they were "citizenized" in similar ways.

The many immigrants who came to the Netherlands as "guest-workers" from the 1960s until the 1980s and in family reunion plans since then, from rural and hardly modernized areas in Morocco and Turkey mostly, have not gone through a similar process of citizenization. One obvious reason for this is that when they started arriving, Dutch society was just about to leave the pillar system behind. Second, the quite individualistic and libertarian culture of the 1960s and 1970s, in which rebellion against the more repressive and disciplinary aspects of the societal pillars was widespread, was hardly an ideal context for enculturation. Third, and for our discussion most importantly, Dutch authorities could have done much more to be sufficiently responsive to the specific need for enculturation of immigrants than they have. Initially, Dutch authorities did not think of labor migrants in terms of new citizens at all. Until the end of the 1970s, they expected them to return to their countries of origin. So they refrained from taking coordinated action towards the new and future citizens' successful social, economic, and political integration through, for instance, education, employment, and housing policies. As a parliamentary research committee concluded in early 2004,[34] it was not until the 1990s, when considerable numbers of political asylum seekers applied for citizenship, that coordinated programs for enculturation and social-economic integration were introduced. Fortunately, the same committee could conclude that despite the failures of the authorities, most new immigrants, often through their own initiatives, had at least reached considerable socio-economic integration. As for cultural integration, however, things look more worrying. For the first and second generation of immigrants especially, attempts of the Dutch authorities to reach them often came too late. Here, informal discrimination against Muslim citizens especially plays its part. The committee concluded "that unfortunately, discrimination in public life is a fact. Many immigrants feel integrated into Dutch society, but not accepted."[35] Perhaps as a result of these (and many other) factors, in the larger cities especially, a considerable underclass of immigrants has developed that, in all statistics, shows the familiar rates in political estrangement, crime, illiteracy, and domestic violence.

Now, I want to claim that these insights into the failures of integration policy and the lack of stable social institutions for immigrants *and* native citizens since the demise of the pillar system can help us make sense of

[34] *Bruggen Bouwen.*   [35] Ibid.

the strong call for unity, consensus, and assimilation we have seen in recent public debate. Where social institutions that are transparently linked to political culture are not (or no longer) given, other institutions such as ethnic nationalism and religion are likely to gain ground. And it is true that in immigrant communities such social practices tend to play a significant and often problematic role.[36] If immigrants were to assimilate to secular and modernized majority culture and whole-heartedly consent to a canon of core values and norms characteristic of Dutch social and political culture, then many social and political problems would indeed vanish into thin air. But as we have seen, immigrant citizens do not have much reason to feel welcome in the Netherlands. On the contrary, after the events that followed upon the murder of van Gogh, the informal conception of democratic life of a good willing Dutch government and enlightened native citizenry that had met with the religiously motivated unwillingness of immigrants – Muslim immigrants especially – to integrate into society could no longer be kept up. A call for consensus and unity as a basis for citizenship must remain infertile as long as it is (a) not accompanied by social institutions through which integration can be achieved and (b) not accompanied by an informal conception of democratic life with the help of which immigrant citizens can be represented *as* citizens rather than as representatives of an ethnic, cultural, or religious group.

To the extent that they are valid civic ideas at all, unity and consensus will not be reached so long as the government and the native citizenry do not acknowledge their responsibility for part of the felt gap between immigrants and other citizens. This would be a sign of truthfulness with regard to the causes of the huge lack of civic trust that became visible in the days after van Gogh's murder. And it would be a sign of justice with regard to those members of society who, after having been victims of failed integration policies and even discrimination in Dutch society, are now being depicted as less than competent citizens – not because they have misused their status as free and equal citizens, but because they fit into dominant conceptions of citizenship mainly under ethnic and religious categories and not under civic ones.

V.

Now that informal conceptions of citizenship that oppose competent native citizens to incompetent immigrant citizens have been deconstructed

---

[36] See Margalith Kleijwegt, *Onzichtbare ouders: De buurt van Mohammed B.* (Zutphen: Plataan, 2005).

through an analysis of their historical truthfulness, it seems in order to reconceptualize the breakdown of civic relations in the days after the murder as a crisis of *civic integrity*, i.e., of truly *civic* reactions to a *decisively non-civic* event. In this section, I will switch to a more theoretical vocabulary in order to prepare that reconceptualization. My account starts from an investigation into three inevitable circumstances of democratic politics that the informal conceptions of citizenship we have analyzed do not sufficiently acknowledge. They are: (1) the facts of ethical and political pluralism and disagreement, (2) the need for concerted political action despite this pluralism, and (3) the role of often unspoken but still influential informal power relations.

Let us start with the need for concerted action and the existence of deep political disagreement taken together. Jeremy Waldron has claimed that they make up the "circumstances of politics."[37] They make democratic politics as we know it both possible and necessary. We can only successfully deal with what we call our political disagreements by looking for a common framework or course of action. But in their turn, common frameworks and courses of action tend to arouse disagreements because they often claim to represent a unity of purpose and ideas that the partial and temporary agreements underlying them often do not warrant. By this logic, a political cycle emerges that will not come to an end as long as democratic association exists.

This understanding of circumstances of politics enables us to see that, often, it is better to accept a rule, a principle, or a law that one agrees with only halfheartedly or merely strategically, than to have no basis for concerted action at all. Indeed, in our complex and pluralistic societies, this is a common situation. Because citizens disagree about so many political issues, political theories that start from the assumption that an ideal democratic society would be founded on a firm political, moral, or cultural consensus as to shared values and norms must either argue against political pluralism per se, or accept a serious problem of fit with political practice.[38]

Some may want to claim that such theories can deal with pluralism because they recognize, with John Rawls, the "fact of pluralism."[39] But this discussion is not about Rawls's important conception of

---

[37] Jeremy Waldron, *Law and Disagreement* (Oxford: Clarendon Press, 1999), pp. 102ff.; cf. John Rawls, *A Theory of Justice* (Cambridge, MA: Harvard University Press, 1971), pp. 126–130.

[38] See for similar arguments, James Tully, "The Agonic Freedom of Citizens," *Economy and Society*, 28 (2), 1999, pp. 161–182; Herman van Gunsteren, *A Theory of Citizenship: Organizing Plurality in Contemporary Democracies* (Boulder: Westview Press, 1998).

[39] Rawls, *Political Liberalism*, p. xxiv.

pre-political pluralism. In the democratic practices we stand in, there is a circumstance of *political* pluralism that cannot be transcended by means of a meta-political, politically neutral judgment.[40] Consider that some people are conservatives and some are liberals. This implies that they may well hold very different ideas as to the meaning of rights and duties, principles of desert and distributive justice, the goals of civic association, standards of civic excellence, the moral soundness of specific laws, policies, legal decisions, and so on. We tend to find that a normal aspect of political cooperation on democratic terms. But even if one day almost all citizens would become liberals, or alternatively conservatives, the dominant group would still have to find an acceptable way of respecting the rights and opinions of the few who hold other political views. They have to recognize and acknowledge these dissidents' (and their own) *normative status as free and equal democratic citizens*, who have a right to dissent and who have their own reasons for accepting or rejecting common courses of action. Members of constitutional-democratic societies are expected to ascribe this normative status of citizenship to one another reciprocally. It serves as a guarantee against common frameworks or courses of action that overcome disagreement by excluding dissidents or minority members from an equal chance at participation, or by forcing them to assimilate their deeply held beliefs to, for instance, majority opinion. Civic cooperation is about finding common frameworks and courses of action *despite* the frequent occurrence of deep political disagreements.[41] What citizens need to agree on is not the acceptability of this or that arrangement, but rather that they engage in civic interaction from a mutual acknowledgment of each other's normative status *as* free and equal members of the political community.

Now, these circumstances of politics become still more complex if we realize that in democratic societies some members have more *effective power* over their fellow citizens than others do. The common frameworks and courses of action that a political community accepts will favor the interests and beliefs of democratic majorities. This is not necessarily bad and the burdens for dissidents and minorities flowing from this circumstance can partly be repaired. The rule of law and the freedoms of religion, of expression, of association, and special political and cultural

---

[40] Bert van den Brink, *The Tragedy of Liberalism: An Alternative Defense of a Political Tradition* (Albany, NY: State University of New York Press, 2000), pp. 41–61.

[41] Good and much more detailed accounts as to why a foundational political agreement is not a circumstance of democratic politics can be found in Herman van Gunsteren, *A Theory of Citizenship*; James Tully, "The Agonic Freedom of Citizens."

rights have proven to be good instruments for the protection of political dissidents and democratic minorities. The important point is that, in a respectable constitutional-democratic society, with the exercise of power come responsibilities in light of which *agents of power can be held accountable*. At a minimum, such accounting practices have to include a test as to whether the normative status of citizenship has not been harmed by the misuse of power. In legal courts and in parliament, this happens all the time. Because procedures in such institutions are meticulously structured in terms of the rights of the parties involved, agents of power such as, for instance, criminal suspects, civil law offenders, the government, the opposition, the state, house majorities, and house minorities can be held accountable for their possible harming of citizens' rights. Practices in which, through the reciprocal exchange of reasons, citizens hold each other accountable for the consequences of their actions for the rights and legitimate interests of their fellow citizens are at the very heart of the practice of citizenship.

In what Thomas Scanlon has called the "informal politics of social life,"[42] such accounting practices tend to be less well organized than they are in institutions of the state. With this term, Scanlon refers to dominant ethical-political attitudes, beliefs, and practices in society. They set powerful standards of expectation and evaluation that define what it means to be acknowledged as a "good" citizen, who holds "respectable" beliefs, and who engages in social and political action in a "respectable way." Here, of course, the ironic quotation marks identify a problem: in the informal politics of social life, what *counts* as "good" and "respectable" modes of civic interaction is not necessarily good and respectable as seen from the normative ideal of citizenship as civic cooperation between free and equal members of the political community. The dominance of such – often unspoken – standards is one of the main issues in theoretical and practical debates over multiculturalism. Political theories that account for citizenship in terms of a common institutional framework for association tend to neglect these powerful standards and the informal conceptions of democratic life (Allen) that underlie them.

Following Scanlon and Danielle Allen, we have to accept that there is a difference between the normative status that standing law grants us on the one hand, and what that status is worth in the informal practical politics of social life on the other. One important difference between the two is that our status in the first sense is usually tied to much more solid,

---

[42] Thomas Scanlon, "The Difficulty of Tolerance," in *Toleration: An Elusive Virtue*, ed. David Heyd (Princeton: Princeton University Press, 1996), pp. 226–239, here p. 229.

more formally organized accounting practices than our status in the second sense is. In the informal politics of social life, we are especially vulnerable to the misuse of power because the accounting practices such misuse calls for either have to be constructed in face-to-face communication with those who do not respect their fellows' normative status as citizens, or have to be sought in institutions external to the practice in which the misuse of power occurs, such as a legal court. For both reasons, there is a real chance that the actual misuse of power will never be adequately accounted for because the less powerful party does not succeed in putting one of the possibilities to work. This will happen, for instance, when the dominated party is largely unfamiliar with both the official and the more informal civic accounting practices that do exist in society, as is the case with many Muslim immigrants in the Netherlands who are unfamiliar with the layers of civic knowledge presupposed by competent citizenship.

Now, I would claim that both the vision of democratic cooperation as expressed by secular humanism and the communitarian vision fail to take these circumstances of politics in diverse societies seriously. In different ways, both start from the assumption that we need substantive agreements on cultural values and legal and political arrangements *before* decent politics can begin. For the communitarian vision, this is clear. For secular humanism, it may be less so. Yet, the realism characteristic of this approach is founded on the assumption that there is one single best description of the reality of a political situation. We need agreement on that description, such as an agreement that Muslim immigrants have a problem accepting principles of constitutional-democratic cooperation, *before* decent politics can begin. That is, the realism characteristic of this position represents a vision of democracy according to which one party is cognitively privileged over the other and will remain so unless the other party accepts the special knowledge that the privileged party possesses. Where the communitarian vision is too utopian to be convincing, we at least have to acknowledge that it starts from an idea of reciprocity between free and equal political fellows. Were it not for its unlikely ideal of a substantive consensus on – in John Rawls's terms – partly comprehensive values and norms as a *starting point* for democratic politics, it could be used as a model for understanding how citizens reach agreements, and how accounting practices between citizens work. The rhetorical strategy through which secular humanism dominated the debate in the Netherlands, however, is not a reciprocal vision of politics at all. It can neither be used as a model for understanding the way in which citizens arrive at common frameworks, nor for understanding accounting practices between such citizens in face of power relations. Indeed, because this position is so convinced of the truth of its own account of problems of multiculturalism in Dutch society, it is largely blind with regard to its own exercise of power through which it constructs a highly generalized image of the civic competences of native and immigrant citizens.

VI.

Recognition of the circumstances of politics in diverse societies constitutes a specific type of civic integrity. Let me conclude my argument by looking in some detail at the two most important building blocks of civic integrity that I have distinguished: *truthfulness* and *justice*.

Truthfulness requires that citizens do not deceive themselves about their own civic performance.[43] We have seen that we can only act from our normative status as free and equal members of a democratic citizenry if we take account of several fundamental circumstances of politics. In order to ask whether we do, we need to be *truthful* about our attitudes towards disagreement, commonality, and power in our past and present contributions to the political community. Provided that we are sufficiently powerful, we can suppress disagreement, misrepresent fragile commonality as based in firm agreement, and choose not to account for our – past and present – exercise of power in formal and informal interactions with our fellow citizens. Where this is the case, we do not live up to our own and our fellow citizens' status *as* citizens, which can be acknowledged only reciprocally. As with so many things of value, citizenship as a practice is vulnerable in face of the many reasons persons may have not to engage in it. There is no knock-down argument that can show why we should take the normative status of the democratic citizen seriously. Here, it is best to take the constructivist route that says that *if we do, then* we have to show integrity as truthfulness with regard to our own civic performance in light of the ideal of free and equal members of the political community who reciprocally account for their uses of power over each other.

Civic integrity as truthfulness can be judged only in combination with a sense of *justice* in light of the normative status of the citizen. If justice is the virtue of giving to each and every individual what they deserve in light of a specific kind of membership, we learn about the limits of our own civic performance by testing its consequences in light of the legitimate needs, as citizens, of members of society. First and foremost among these is their need to be recognized as free and equal members of society in the circumstances of politics. Where the perspective of justice

---

[43] Owen, *Nietzsche*, p. 143.

shows that because of our own civic conduct, disagreement is being suppressed by way of stifling our fellow citizens' voices, an only seeming agreement is reached by way of not acknowledging such voices. Arbitrary power relations that cannot be reconciled with respect for the normative status of citizenship are then being kept in place by our refusal to account for our formal and informal uses of power. Where this is the case, our civic actions are both untruthful and unjust. As such, they no longer qualify as signs of competent citizenship. Where we harm the normative status of citizenship of others, we show what is wrong with our own conception of citizenship.

In the Netherlands, a lack of civic integrity understood in this double way of not wanting to account for both the truthfulness and justice of informal interactions with Islamic immigrants has characterized civic relations for quite some time. Ministers of government, Members of Parliament, and citizens on the dominant side of the informal politics of social life have been both less than truthful and less than just with regard to their role in integration policies. As we have seen, a report by an official committee of Parliament identified this. The generalizations in terms of which they dominated the debate after the murder of van Gogh are not only refuted by statistical material that points in the direction of relatively successful social and economic integration of the majority of immigrants.[44] These generalizations also cannot be reconciled with political judgment from the status of citizenship. Furthermore, the wishing away by a rhetoric of assimilation not just of cultural and religious, but of fundamental *political* pluralism and disagreement shows that secular humanists especially simply do not want to acknowledge the circumstances of politics in modern, complex society. I do not in any way mean to suggest that there are no social and political problems with a considerable group of Muslim immigrants in the Netherlands. But I do believe that given the untruthful self-assessments with regard to the causes of these problems we have identified and the unjust generalizations with regard to the citizenship of Muslim immigrants that were used in public debate, the lack of *civic integrity* on behalf of dominant voices in public debate deserves much more attention in the analysis of what happened than has been the case so far.

VII.

By taking a close look at what happened during a recent crisis in informal civic relations in the Netherlands, I have tried to arrive at an

---

[44] *Bruggen Bouwen.*

insight as to which civic virtues at the heart of such relations count most when such a crisis occurs. I have found reason to assume that, in the particular case I discussed, a lack of civic integrity in the informal political interaction in public debate played a role. Where there is no *truthfulness* with regard to our own civic performance and no *justice* with regard to our assessment of others' civic needs and performance, the integrity of civic relations is in danger. This is the case because without these virtues, we cannot take seriously our own and our fellow citizens' normative status as free and equal members of the political community, who can hold each other accountable for their respective social and political actions. Furthermore, without these virtues, citizens cannot shape their relations in light of a fair assessment of the dangers and possibilities of three circumstances of politics that I have distinguished: disagreement, commonality, and power relations.

14 Democracy and foreignness: democratic cosmopolitanism and the myth of an immigrant America[1]

Bonnie Honig

"A hero is missing from the revolutionary literature of America," says Louis Hartz in *The Liberal Tradition in America*. "He is the legislator, the classical giant who almost invariably turns up at revolutionary moments to be given authority to lay the foundations of the free society."[2] Hartz may be right about the absence of the legislator from America's revolutionary literature. But in American democratic theory and political culture, the legislator's place is occupied by a different classical figure – the foreign founder. The classical foreign founder is refigured by American exceptionalists, from Tocqueville to Hartz to Walzer, who treat immigrants as the agents of founding and renewal for a regime in which membership is supposed to be uniquely consent-based, individualist, rational, and voluntarist rather than inherited and organic.[3] For these and many other thinkers, the future of American democracy depends not on the native born but on the recent arrival, not on someone with a past to build on but rather on someone who left his past behind. In short, exceptionalist accounts of American democracy are inextricably intertwined with the myth of an immigrant America.

The myth of an immigrant America depicts the foreigner as a supplement to the nation, an agent of national re-enchantment that

[1] This is an abbreviated version of "The Foreigner as Citizen," chapter 4 of *Democracy and the Foreigner* (Princeton: Princeton University Press, 2001). Thanks to Princeton University Press for permitting its appearance in this volume. My thanks also to the editors of this volume and to Diego Rosello for assistance in the preparation of this chapter for publication here.
[2] Louis Hartz, *The Liberal Tradition in America* (New York: Thomson Learning, 1991), p. 46.
[3] I do not discuss Tocqueville in detail here, but see vol. I, ch. 2, and later pp. 280–281ff. of *Democracy in America* for his views on how immigration and especially "the double movement of immigration" (p. 281) are fundamental to the shape, character, and success of the unique phenomenon of American democracy. *Democracy in America*, ed. J. P. Mayer, trans. George Lawrence (Garden City, NY: Doubleday, 1969).

might rescue the regime from corruption and return it to its first principles. Those first principles may be capitalist, communal, familial, or liberal.[4] In the capitalist version of the myth, the immigrant functions to reassure workers of the possibility of upward mobility in an economy that rarely delivers on that promise, while also disciplining native-born poor, domestic minorities, and unsuccessful foreign laborers into believing that the economy fairly rewards dedication and hard work.[5]

The communitarian immigrant responds to the dissolution of family and community ties, or the prevention of community formation that results in large part from a capitalist economy's unresisted need for a mobile labor force. Periodic infusions of community by way of immigration are said to soften the alienating effects of capitalism's mobilities and of the American liberal individualism that eases their way.

Still others position immigrants as the saviors of traditional patriarchal family arrangements that have been variously attenuated by capitalist mobility and materialism, liberal individualism and feminism. The patriarchal immigrant models proper gender roles and relations for a nation that has lost its sexual bearings. New World American families depend upon Old World masculinities and femininities – family values – that need to be imported periodically from elsewhere.

Finally, liberal consent theorists look to immigrants to solve the problem that Rousseau addressed in the *Social Contract*. Recall that for Rousseau, a legitimate regime is one in which the law, which is always alien, can be made our own by our willing it. Rousseau understood that merely periodic practices such as voting do not position citizens to experience the law as their own. Hence, he argued, the law must be willed frequently, and this was possible under certain, elusive circumstances (by relatively homogeneous citizenries in small polities, and so on). Those circumstances do not exist in the mass, heterogeneous democracy of the United States. While some liberals have argued that American democracy legitimates itself through tacit consent, there is also another mechanism of legitimation at work here, one that operates through the agency of foreignness. The regime's legitimacy is shored up by way of the explicit consent of those celebrated

---

[4] Thomas Sowell, *Migrations and Cultures: A World View* (New York: Penguin, 1984); Michael Walzer, *What it Means to be an American* (New York: Marsilio, 1992); and Peter Schuck and Rogers Smith, *Citizenship without Consent: Illegal Aliens in the American Polity* (New Haven: Yale University Press, 1985).

[5] The American dream performs similar functions, as Jennifer Hochschild points out in *Facing Up to the American Dream: Race, Class and the Soul of the Nation* (Princeton: Princeton University Press, 1995). My argument here is analogous in some ways to Hochschild's. She and I are both trying to find progressive possibilities in apparently conservative myths, rather than reject those myths outright.

foreigners – immigrants – who are regularly sworn into citizenship in the nation's naturalization ceremonies. The liberal consenting immigrant addresses the need of a disaffected citizenry to experience its regime as choiceworthy, to see it through the eyes of still-enchanted newcomers whose choice to come here also just happens to re-enact liberalism's own cleaned-up Sinai scene: its fictive foundation in individual acts of uncoerced consent. Simultaneously, the immigrant's decision to come here is seen as living proof of the would-be universality of America's liberal democratic principles.

In all four versions, the myth of an immigrant America recuperates foreignness, en masse, for a national project. It does so by drawing on and shoring up the popular exceptionalist belief that America is a distinctively consent-based regime, based on choice, not on inheritance, on civic not ethnic ties. The exceptionalist's America is anchored by rational, voluntarist faith in a creed, not ascriptive bloodlines, individualism, not organicism, mobility, not landedness.[6] The people who live here are people who once chose to come here, and, in this, America is supposedly unique. In short, the exceptionalist account normatively privileges one particular trajectory to citizenship: from immigrant (to ethnic, as in Walzer but not in Tocqueville) to citizen.

The exceptionalist account captures something about American democracy while also missing a great deal. American democracy is founded not only on immigration but also on conquest (Native Americans) and slavery (the forced importation of African slave labor), and, in the post-founding era, on expansion (Hawaii, Alaska, Puerto Rico, etc.), annexation (French settlements in Illinois, St. Louis, and New Orleans as well as a significant Spanish-speaking population in the southwest as a result of the war with Mexico). This complexity is obscured by the hegemonic myth of an immigrant America. In Charleston, South Carolina, for example, a tourist pamphlet announces that Sullivan Island, off the coast of the city, "might well be viewed as the Ellis Island of black Americans."[7]

---

[6] Sacvan Bercovitch redeploys the exceptionalist interpretation of American identity even while subjecting it to greater critical scrutiny than is customary among exceptionalists: "Of all symbols of identity, only *America* has united nationality and universality, civic and spiritual selfhood, secular and redemptive history, the country's past and paradise to be, in a single synthetic ideal." *The American Jeremiad* (Madison: University of Wisconsin Press, 1978), p. 176. My aim in this chapter is not to assay the historical success of this nationalist project, but to attend to some of its political and cultural costs.
[7] The phrase is taken from Peter H. Wood, *Black Majority: Negroes in Colonial South Carolina*, p. xiv, itself cited in R. N. Rosen, *A Short History of Charleston* (Charleston: Peninsula Press, 1992), p. 63. Thanks to Paul Pierson for calling the South Carolina quote to my attention and to Michaele Ferguson for tracking it down. See also Roger Daniels,

In its favor, we might say that at least the myth generates an open and inclusive tolerance of diverse immigrants. But things are not so simple. In fact, the myth generates a sense of *anxious* dependence upon the kindness of strangers. The foreigners whose immigrations to the United States daily reinstall the regime's most beloved self-images are also looked on as threats to the regime. And this is no accident.

American political culture is marked by a play of xenophobia and xenophilia that is not simply caused by periodic power changes from nativists to inclusionists, as Michael Walzer and Rogers Smith both suggest.[8] Nor is it merely a sign of changing economic "realities," from expanding to shrinking labor needs.[9] These may be parts of the story, but there is a deeper logic at work here.

In the various versions of the myth of an immigrant America, it is the immigrant's *foreignness* that positions him to reinvigorate the national democracy, and that foreignness is undecidable: our faith in a just economy, our sense of community or family, our consent-based sense of legitimacy, or our voluntarist vigor are so moribund that only a foreigner could reinvigorate them. But the dream of a national home, helped along by the symbolic foreigner, in turn animates a suspicion of immigrant foreignness at the same time. "Their" admirable hard work and boundless acquisition puts "us" out of jobs. "Their" good, reinvigorative communities also look like fragmentary ethnic enclaves. "Their" traditional family values threaten to overturn our still new and fragile gains in gender equality. "Their" voluntarist embrace of America,

Coming to America: A History of Immigration and Ethnicity in American Life (New York: HarperCollins, 1990), p. 54, emphasis added: "The slave trade was one of the major means of bringing *immigrants* to the New World in general and to the United States in particular." Thanks to Kunal M. Parker for calling my attention to Daniels's work. For a thoughtful analysis of how the politics of race was mapped, historically, as an immigration politics by towns seeking to refuse financial responsibility for destitute former slaves, see Kunal Parker, "Making Blacks Foreigners" (paper on file with author).

[8] See Walzer, *What it Means to be an American*, and Rogers Smith, "Beyond Tocqueville, Myrdal and Hartz: The Multiple Traditions Thesis in America," *American Political Science Review*, 87 (3), September 1993, pp. 549–566.

[9] The economistic explanation is also judged to be limited by Ali Behdad, whose work on immigration politics I discuss below. "The conventional liberal wisdom about the public reaction to immigration is this. 'When things are going well and there's a shortage of labor, people either look the other way or are actively supportive of bringing cheaper labor into the United States. But when jobs are tight, and the cost of supporting people goes up, then we suddenly redo the calculus'" (political scientist Bruce Cain, quoted in Ronald Brownstein and Richard Simon, "Hospitality Turns into Hostility," *Los Angeles Times*, 14 November 1993, A6). Behdad argues that "such an economic view of anti-immigration consensus ... fails to address the role of immigration as both a necessary mechanism of social control in the formation of the state apparatus and an essential cultural contribution to the formation of national identity." Ali Behdad, "Nationalism and Immigration to the United States," *Diaspora*, 6 (2), 1997, pp. 155–178, p. 155.

effective only to the extent that they come from elsewhere, works to reaffirm but also endangers "our" way of life. The foreigner who shores up and reinvigorates the regime also unsettles it at the same time. Since the presumed test of both a good and a bad foreigner is the measure of her contribution to the restoration of the nation rather than, say, to the nation's transformation, nationalist xenophilia tends to feed and (re)produce nationalist xenophobia as its partner.

Ali Behdad is the only critic who comes close to seeing this undecidability of foreignness. He describes the "nation's mode of identification" as always "ambivalent: on the one hand, we are a nation of immigrants; on the other hand, we identify ourselves against our immigrants as we try to control them." That ambivalence is worth attending to, Behdad astutely argues, because it is a productive site for the state's development of myriad "strategies of discipline, normalization, and regulation."[10] In other words, rather than strive to undo that ambivalence – by attributing it to different parties (as Walzer does) or to different traditions (as Smith does) or to different time periods (as many historians do) – Behdad asks about the performative effects of that ambivalence. What productive energies are unleashed at its site? How does that site serve as "a space of contestation where concepts of nationality as citizenship and state as sovereignty can be re-articulated and re-affirmed"?[11]

Behdad's account and mine work these issues through different texts, and we use different analytic lenses, but we form an obvious and, I hope, productive alliance that calls for the re-examination of some staple assumptions in the study of American nationalism and democracy. However, we differ on one crucial point: when Behdad traces out American ambivalences about immigrants, he misses the pole that is, to my mind, most important. Pointing out that both pro-and anti-immigration movements in the United States are marked by an "us" and "them" mentality, he argues that even those who favor immigration tend to cast immigrants in "symbolically violent" terms.[12] He illustrates

---

[10] Behdad, "Nationalism and Immigration to the United States," p. 175.
[11] Ibid., pp. 165–166.
[12] Ibid., p. 166. Although Behdad thinks I miss the most important pole, too:

> The different functions of the immigrant, I would add, are the effect of an ambivalent mode of national identity in the United States, which simultaneously acknowledges the nation's immigrant formation and disavows it. When I say an ambivalent mode of national identity, I have in mind not only the general split between hospitality and hostility, xenophilia and xenophobia, that Honig convincingly discusses in her article, but also the particular ways in which the competing myths of American identity themselves are ambivalently articulated. As I will show in the cases of Crevecoeur's valorization of immigrant America (xenophilia) and the Know-Nothings in the mid-nineteenth century (xenophobia),

the American ambivalence regarding foreigners with the following list of "contradictory stereotypes: on the one hand, the immigrant is weak and wretched [and therefore possessed of a claim on our 'humanitarian' sentiments], and, on the other, powerful and dangerous [and therefore a threat to our nation]; on the one hand an opportunist who steals our jobs, and, on the other, a lazy parasite who abuses our social welfare funds." In sum, Behdad concludes, "these stereotypes point to the ambivalence of the nation toward its immigrants, an ambivalence marked by both knowledge and disavowal, control and defense, exclusion and amnesty, acceptance and rejection."[13]

But one stereotype is missing here: the supercitizen immigrant.[14] Neither needy nor threatening, as such, but always mirrored by and partnered with those others, the supercitizen immigrant is the object of neither American hostility nor charity but of outright adoration. The stereotypically weak immigrant and the stereotypically powerful one both elicit disavowal. But the supercitizen immigrant is an object of identification. He is the screen onto which we project our idealized selves. He works harder than we do, he values his family and community more actively than we do, and he also fulfills our unfulfillable liberal fantasy of membership by way of consent. Somehow, this iconic good immigrant manages to have it all – work, family, community, and a consensual relation to a largely non-consensual democracy – even though these very goods are experienced by the rest of us as contradictory or elusive: work in late modern capitalist economies often demands hours and mobilities that are in tension with family and community commitments; meaningful consent eludes the native born for reasons I discuss below.

> every discourse of immigration espouses opposite notions of what constitutes an American identity. Forgetting in each instance allows for an ideologically divided response to the question of "Who is an American?" The idyllic and heterogeneous America presented in Crevecoeur, for example, is also revealed as a racially segregated community that excludes both Native Americans and enslaved Africans. Similarly, the reactionary attitude of Know-Nothings toward immigrants is also a progressive response to the industrialists' exploitative uses of immigrants." (Ali Behdad, "Forgetful Nation: Reflections on Immigration and Cultural Identity in the United States" [manuscript])
>   Although often significantly reformulated, similar arguments can be found in Behdad's book *A Forgetful Nation: On Immigration and Cultural Identity in the United States* (Durham: Duke University Press, 2005), pp. 18–31.

[13] Behdad, "Forgetful Nation" (manuscript). Similar arguments can be found in Behdad, *A Forgetful Nation*, pp. 4, 32, 174.

[14] Actually, more than one stereotype is missing here. Also absent is the leftist internationalist foreigner by way of whom public passions were inflamed during the trial of Sacco and Vanzetti as well as during the McCarthy era.

The immigrant as supercitizen is a staple of the exceptionalist literature and is worth attending to now because the figure is still very much alive as a political-cultural resource today. Throughout the 1990s, Americans on both the right and the left sought to counter xenophobic initiatives in the US by redeploying the iconic good immigrant who once helped build this nation and whose heirs might contribute to the national future. Both political theorists and activists have responded to renewed anti-immigrant sentiment by stressing the gifts that foreigners have to offer receiving regimes. But what if their xenophilia is intimately connected with the xenophobia they seek to combat? Deploying the supercitizen immigrant on behalf of a national ideal, do these xenophiles feed the fire they mean to fight?

Another perhaps useful way of exploring the potentially intimate connections between xenophobia and xenophilia might be to recast what I am calling the undecidability of foreignness in terms of the politics of friendship elucidated by Jacques Derrida. Derrida recalls Aristotle's distinction among three kinds of friendship – virtue, pleasure, and use – and claims, contra Aristotle, that politics is not confined to the register of use but arises instead when mistakes are made among the different kinds of friendship. Aristotle's three kinds of friendship correspond to the varieties of immigrant supplement traced here. Friendship as use is represented by the capitalist immigrant who comes here to make money. Friendship as virtue is represented by the communitarian and familial immigrants who model proper community and family devotion. And friendship as pleasure is represented by the consenting immigrant who exhibits an exemplary love for the law. The lines of demarcation are not perfectly clear; there are traces of all three kinds of friendship in each of the four supplements of foreignness mapped out here. For example, there is virtue in loving the law and pleasure in capitalist success. Nonetheless, the trichotomy works well enough to enable us to map out the patterns of misunderstanding and disappointment that generate a politics among would-be friends (and not, *pace* Behdad, between an us and a them, per se).

I.   Class mobility as American citizenship

It is by now commonplace to hear the capitalist success of (a small minority of) immigrant and ethnic groups explained in terms of their immigrant drive (often said to be lacking in domestic minorities) and in terms of their large extended families and communities who provide cheap labor and pool their resources. What is valued here are the resources available to be sacrificed for financial success, not the affective family or community relations themselves, nor their potential to serve as sites of associational political power.[15]

The capitalist immigrant helps keep the American dream alive, upholding popular beliefs in a meritocratic economy in good times and bad. If he can do it, starting with nothing and not knowing the language, surely anyone can. At the same time, however, the use of foreignness to supplement the national economy and discipline the domestic poor engenders resentment of foreigners for competing with the native born for scarce resources. Because the capitalist foreigner is depicted as someone who is interested only in material things, he quickly turns from someone who has something to offer us into someone who only wants to take things from us.[16] His virtuosic acquisitiveness slides easily into a less admirable, crass, and self-serving materialism. The nationalist, xenophilic deployment of the foreigner to model the American dream does not just offset these xenophobic reactions, it itself helps to generate them.

The effects of the capitalist version of the myth of an immigrant America on American democracy are particularly unwelcome. The resources of democratic citizenship are diminished, not enhanced, by a supplement of foreignness that is made to stand for privatization, the accumulation of extreme wealth, and a complete disinterest in civic and political life. The myth undermines potential inter-ethnic and transnational coalitions of labor, and it celebrates radical inequalities that are in deep tension with democratic citizenship. The new model minorities do not just "make it"; they become outlandishly wealthy. This version of the myth identifies citizenship with materialism, capitalism, and

---

[15] See, for example, Lewis Winnick, "America's 'Model Minority,'" *Commentary*, 90 (2), August 1990, pp. 22–29. Arthur Schlesinger, too, makes stereotypical note of the strong family relations of Jews and Asians, remarking the power of those relations as a resource for individuals in *The Disuniting of America* (New York: Norton, 1993). A recent, less stereotypical and more sustained empirical effort in this direction is Sowell, *Migrations and Cultures*.

Celebrants of model minorities highlight the ways in which extended families (and their cheap labor) are necessary for capitalist success, but they say nothing about how capitalist economies also attenuate such ties. Symptomatic was a front-page *New York Times* story (Judith H. Dobrzynski, "For More and More Job Seekers, an Aging Parent is a Big Factor," *New York Times*, 1 January 1996) on the increasing reluctance of middle-income labor to move for employment, given their desire to remain close to aging parents. In the second paragraph, the language of the story switches. The phenomenon is now called a "problem," and the perspective adopted for the rest of the report is that of the companies who have to deal with this resistance. The same story could, of course, have been written (also problematically) in a celebratory way with a headline such as: "The Return of Family Ties."

[16] For a psychoanalytic account of the foreigner as someone who only wants to take "our thing," see Slavoj Žižek, *Tarrying with the Negative: Kant, Hegel, and the Critique of Ideology* (Durham: Duke University Press), pp. 201ff.

consumption. The foreigners depicted here are not politically engaged. They are too busy living the American dream.

Hence the tone of surprise governing a typical *New York Times* article reporting on the politicization of Asian Americans: "Marty Shih is the kind of person who has earned Asian Americans the widespread characterization as the model minority," writes Steven A. Holmes, perversely assigning to Mr. Shih the responsibility for the media's label. In just eighteen years, Mr. Shih, "through grit and hard work," turned the $500 with which he arrived in America into a $40 million business. "But Mr. Shih's rags-to-riches story *took an unusual path* last month when he established the Asian American Association to, among other things, campaign against legislation that would drastically reduce the levels of legal immigration, an issue that has galvanized Asian Americans like no other in recent times."

The "usual" trajectory of Asian American incorporation is commercial, not political.[17] Immigrants, especially America's model minorities, stay away from politics. But do they? Completely absent from this now conventional picture are non-citizen or new citizen political actors as diverse as the Haymarket activists (imprisoned or deported), Sacco and Vanzetti (executed), Harry Bridges (leader of the 1934 San Francisco general strike who fought deportation efforts in the courts and won),[18] Emma Goldman (expelled), Harry Wu, and a whole slew of others involved in contemporary labor, local, and school politics, from undocumented workers in Southern California active in unionization politics

---

[17] Steven Holmes, "Anti-Immigrant Mood Moves Asians to Organize," *New York Times*, 3 January 1996, A1, emphasis added. An example of the more usual story about immigrants is "Hospitality is Their Business," an account of Indian-American involvement in the hotel industry (popularized in the film *Mississippi Masala*). The role of these immigrants as supplements to the American dream is made quite clear by Joel Kotkin, quoted in the *New York Times* story as follows: "These Indians are modern Horatio Algers. They're willing to start in marginal and sometimes risky areas that native-born Americans are not interested in going into, and working [*sic*] incredibly hard hours" ("Hospitality is Their Business," D1 and D9). Success is here measured by the move in one to two generations from hands-on labor to office management and serious wealth.

The story does not note a small irony: these immigrants are in the *hospitality* business at a time when the country is particularly inhospitable towards immigrants. Nor does it make much of one complication of the Horatio Alger comparison: some of these immigrants seem to have arrived with rather substantial reserves of capital. Mr. Patel, who "attributes the Indians' success to 'the way we were brought up' " – (whole families put their shoulder to the wheel and community members lend each other money without interest or collateral) – immigrated after "a 20-year career with Barclays Bank in Kenya" (D9).

[18] The US Supreme Court opinion claimed to have seldom seen "such a concentrated and relentless campaign to deport an individual." Harry Bernstein, "Harry Bridges: Marxist Founder of West's Longshoremen Union," *Los Angeles Times*, 31 March 1990.

to Cambodians agitating for decent public schooling for their children in Lowell, Massachusetts, to Chinese locals involved in "educational struggle" in San Francisco, to aliens stumping for local candidates in New York.[19]

Contemporary depictions of immigrants as concerned only with material acquisition and not with empowered democratic agency are not only misleading. Worse yet, they are often *enforced* in response to immigrants who become politicized enough to trouble this dominant normative image of quiescence. Efforts to control, diminish, or stop immigration – efforts such as California's Proposition 187, passed by voters in 1994 – have complicated effects. They may hope to deter new immigrants from entering the state but, given the local economy's dependence upon foreign labor, it is likely that something other than deterrence is also hoped for: the recriminalization of the alien population and heightened costs of alien visibility. Restrictionist policies do not just reduce illegal immigration; they quash the potential power of the undocumented as political actors, labor organizers, and community activists.[20]

II.   Ethnic bases of social democracy: Michael Walzer's immigrant America

Michael Walzer's communitarian version of the myth of an immigrant America is tailored to respond to the private realm withdrawalism wrongly valorized by the capitalist version of the myth. Given the success of the capitalist economy and America's liberal ideology in

---

[19] On undocumented worker involvement in unionization activities, see the cases of construction workers in Richard Rothstein, "Immigration Dilemmas," in *Arguing Immigration*, ed. N. Mills (New York: Simon & Schuster, 1994); and mattress manufacturing workers in Héctor L. Delgardo, *New Immigrants, Old Unions: Organizing Undocumented Workers in Los Angeles* (Philadelphia: Temple University Press, 1993). On workplace activism earlier in the century, see Victor Greene, *The Slavic Community on Strike* (Notre Dame: University of Notre Dame Press, 1968); and John H. M. Laslett, "Labor Party, Labor Lobbying, or Direct Action?," in *The Politics of Immigrant Workers*, ed. Camille Guerin-Gonzales and Carl Strikwerda (New York: Holmes and Meier, 1993). On school politics in Lowell, Massachusetts, see Camilo Peréz-Bustillo, "What Happens When English-Only Comes to Town?," in *Language Loyalties: A Source Book on the Official English Controversy*, ed. James Crawford (Chicago: University of Chicago Press, 1992). On Chinese political involvements, see Victor Low, *The Unimpressible Race* (San Francisco: East/West Publishing, 1982). On current alien political activism, see Barry Newman, "Foreign Legions: Lots of Noncitizens Feel Right at Home in U.S. Political Races," *Wall Street Journal*, 31 October 1997, A1.

[20] On this point, and others related to the arguments developed here, see Michael Shapiro, *Cinematic Political Thought: Narrating Race, Nation and Gender* (New York: New York University Press, 1999).

individuating, uprooting, and alienating most of the regime's members, Walzer argues, only newcomers can be counted upon to have and to foster the social, civic, and familial ties that social democracy presupposes. For Walzer, then, the model immigrant is not the capitalist over-achiever but the family member who cares for his own and builds community institutions. The communitarian immigrant imports a form of citizenship that liberal capitalist America is always in danger of losing or consuming. Walzer's iconic immigrant reinvigorates civil society and the mediating institutions upon which social democracy depends.

In *What it Means to be an American*, Walzer observes that "citizens are not effective one by one but only when they are bound together in states or freely associated in parties, interest groups, or social movements. And culture is not sustained by private men and women but by families, nations, and communities of faith."[21] The health and vigor of social democratic pluralism depends upon new waves of immigration because the newest hyphenates are the most zealous in their community-sustaining activities.[22] But activists get battle fatigue. Community members get distracted by private concerns and withdraw their energies from one another and from public concerns over time. The black feminist activist, Bernice Johnson Reagon, responds to these inevitabilities with the instruction to keep our eyes on the oldest activists whose commitments have somehow endured.[23] Walzer's counsel is to focus on the newest comers: "Continued large-scale immigration . . . create[s] new groups of hyphenate Americans and encourag[es] revivalism among activists and believers in the old groups."[24]

Walzer's immigrants import the family and community ties that life in capitalist America destroys. They tend to their own and – with federal government help in the way of funding and support for continued immigration – they are empowered to build and run much-needed institutions.[25] Walzer's America is dotted by Jewish hospitals, Muslim schools, and Swedish old-age homes. If ethnic communities are allowed

[21] Walzer, *What it Means to be an American*, p. 11.

[22] Walzer provides no empirical evidence for this. But the claim fits well with Irving Howe's account of Jewish immigrants of an earlier generation in New York (*The World of Our Fathers* [New York: Schocken Books, 1990]) as well as with Ronald Takaki's account of Chinese and Japanese immigrants on the American West Coast in *In a Different Mirror* (Boston: Little, Brown, 1993).

[23] Bernice Johnson Reagon, "Coalition Politics: Turning the Century," in *Home Girls: A Black Feminist Anthology*, ed. Barbara Smith (New York: Kitchen Table – Women of Color Press, 1983).

[24] Walzer, *What it Means to be an American*, p. 48. See Holmes, "Anti-Immigrant Mood Moves Asians to Organize": "They want relatives to join them from overseas. They want their culture replenished with new arrivals" (A11).

[25] Walzer, *What it Means to be an American*, p. 66. Cf. p. 18.

to deteriorate, or if they are prevented from forming (by way of enforced assimilation, lack of funds, or the elimination of immigration), then, Walzer worries, the basic institutions of American social democracy will vanish as well. For Walzer, America's immigrants and ethnics moderate the excesses of American individualism (the form of corruption that attaches to liberalism) while also refusing the fragmentation of sub-nationalism and separatism (the forms of corruption that attach to communitarianism).

Walzer's image of the immigrant as, effectively, a refounder of American civil society is powerful, and its worthy aim is to generate a tolerance and magnanimity towards newcomers that is all too often absent from the American political landscape. But, positioned as the bearers of a "communitarian corrective" to American liberal capitalism, Walzer's immigrant communities attract not only gratitude but also, inevitably, suspicion.[26] These much-lauded organic communities of virtue, positioned as so contributive to the national democracy, are also seen as threatening enclaves that reject American values even while living in our midst.[27] The communitarian xenophilic deployment of foreignness on behalf of a national project itself plays into the hands of and, indeed, helps to feed this xenophobic response.

That xenophobic response may in fact be amplified by the other gift borne by Walzer's immigrants. For Walzer, the supplement of immigrant foreignness perpetually resecures the character of American liberal democracy as thinly patriotic rather than zealously so. American national affect consists in little more than "the flag and the pledge" *because* it is a nation of immigrants, Walzer says. "However grateful they are for this new place, [immigrants] still remember the old places."[28] But what is the significance of their memory? Does Walzer mean to say

---

[26] Walzer develops the idea of a "communitarian corrective" in "The Communitarian Critique of Liberalism," *Political Theory*, 18 (1), February 1990, pp. 6–23.

[27] Arthur Schlesinger gives voice to the fragmentation concern (*The Disuniting of America*). Others, like Randolph Bourne, see the fragmentary potential of immigrants and ethnics but differ from Schlesinger in their evaluation of that potential. Rather than decry fragmentation as a threat to citizenship, Bourne celebrates it as a healthy check on American nationalism. "The Jew and Trans-National America," in *War and the Intellectuals: Collected Essays, 1915–1919* (New York: Harper & Row, 1964), pp. 124–133.

Although I am relying on two different figures to give voice to it, I nonetheless insist that we see this play of xenophilia and xenophobia as a national ambivalence, rather than as a difference of opinion between two discrete parties. This will continue to be the case in the sections that follow, as well, in which we shall see again and again how two supposedly opposing, xenophilic and xenophobic, assessments not only mirror each other but also both feed the nationalism that is a necessary condition of their respective opponent's position.

[28] Walzer, *What it Means to be an American*, p. 24.

that it stands in the way of immigrants' becoming nationalized to the point of zealotry? A powerful if literal illustration to the contrary is the organization by myriad ethnic groups of their members into volunteer units to fight in the Civil War: the "German 18th Regiment, the Polish Legion, the Cameron Rifle Highlanders, the Guard de La Fayette, the Netherlanders' Legion, and the [more multicultural] Garibaldi Guard, which was made up of Hungarians, French, Spaniards, and Croats, as well as Italians."[29]

Is there a singular "experience" to which Walzer can be referring when he says of the United States: "This is not Europe; we are a society of immigrants, and the experience of leaving a homeland and coming to this new place is an *almost* universal 'American' experience. It should be celebrated"?[30] Perhaps Walzer is not trying to refer to a common antecedent experience so much as he is trying to generate a new one: a thinly national sense of commonality around a not yet shared but perhaps now soon to be shared sense of immigrant journey. What could be wrong with that?

One problem is that the celebration of America's "almost universal" immigrant experience does not simply limit American nationalism; it is also a vehicle of it. The myth of an immigrant America is a nationalist narrative of choiceworthiness. In the American context, the pleasure and reinvigoration of having been chosen is illustrated and produced, for example, by the *New York Times*'s periodic publication of a photograph of new citizens taking the oath, right hands lifted, faces solemn or smiling. That pleasure is further protected by the failure of the United States to keep any continuous official statistics on remigration or emigration.[31] Everyone wants to come here.

---

[29] Frederick M. Binder and David M. Reimers, *All the Nations Under Heaven: An Ethnic and Racial History of New York City* (New York: Columbia University Press, 1995), p. 52.

[30] Walzer, *What it Means to be an American*, p. 17; emphasis added. On the supposed contrast to Europe, see Gerard Noiriel on France's true character as an immigrant nation ("Immigration: Amnesia and Memory," *French Historical Studies*, 19 (2), Fall 1995, pp. 367–380). In a later book, Walzer acknowledges that France is "Europe's leading immigrant society," but, he points out, it is different from the US in that it is not friendly to immigrants as such and demands their rapid assimilation (Michael Walzer, *On Toleration* [New Haven: Yale University Press, 1997], pp. 37ff.).

[31] Estimates are that 195,000 US residents emigrate annually. See Priscilla Labovitz, "Immigration: Just the Facts," *New York Times*, 25 March 1996, Op Ed. Regarding the first decades of the twentieth century: "Intelligent estimates of how many foreigners returned to their native countries range from a high of nearly 90 percent for the Balkan peoples to a low of 5 percent for the Jews. We do know that in the period between 1908 and 1914, immigration officials recorded 6,703,357 arrivals and 2,063,767 departures. During these years, more than half the Hungarians, Italians, Croatians, and Slovenes returned to Europe. For the most part returnees included a high percentage of single

Moreover, as Walzer's self-conscious "almost" indicates, the uni-versalization of America's immigrant "experience" has effects on those minorities whose membership in the regime does not map onto the immigrant trajectory to citizenship normatively privileged by Walzer. In particular, when landed and racial minorities "still remember the old places," the political import of their memory is quite different from the nostalgic yearnings of Walzer's immigrants. Unlike America's traditional ethnic groups, some blacks, Native Americans, and Hispanics have legitimate land-based claims. Unlike America's traditional ethnics, these groups have sometimes sought more than mere recognition. Contra Walzer, who says this never happens, these groups have at times sought secession, or even self-government.[32] It is no accident that these forms of political activism are obscured by Walzer's redeployment of the myth of an immigrant America.[33] Their demands might divide or fragment the nation-state rather than reanimate it from below. For Walzer, as for many on the left, the nation-state must be protected from such divisive claims because it is the most likely organizing force of any social democratic politics.

Landed and racial minorities are not the only ones whose claims are marginalized by Walzer's account, however. Also obscured from view are the many non-ethnic institutions for health, education, and welfare in the United States. Especially noteworthy in the last decade or two have been such groups as Planned Parenthood, ACT UP, and the Gay Men's Health Crisis. Why aren't the rather substantial democratic energies of such groups also granted a privileged place in Walzer's immigrant-invigorated civil society? If "citizens are not effective one by one but only when they are bound together in states or freely associated in parties, interest groups, or social movements," why not include as

men" who migrated back and forth, seasonally, until the 1920s quota system was put in place. Leonard Dinnerstein and David M. Reimers, *Ethnic Americans: A History of Immigration* (New York: Columbia University Press, 1999), pp. 46–47.

[32] On the black independence movement in Oklahoma, see Daniel F. Littlefield, *The Chickasaw Freedmen: A People without a Country* (Westport: Greenwood Press, 1980).

[33] Walzer does invite these other groups to become part of his immigrant America. One need not have entered the United States as an immigrant in order to imagine one's citizenship along an immigrant trajectory. Walzer asks whether his citizenship model "can successfully be extended to the racial minorities now asserting their own group claims." Noting recent adaptive moves by (some) black Americans to be called African-Americans, Walzer approves of the move. But he is not sure they will succeed. He worries that racism may get in the way and drive some groups to seek out the "anti-pluralist alternatives of corporate division and state-sponsored unification" (*What it Means to be an American*, p. 76). Walzer never asks whether his normative privileging of the immigrant-ethnic-citizen trajectory to membership, and the invitation to adapt to it, may itself obscure particular claims, injustices, and bases of organization for specific groups.

many groups as possible, as long as those groups contribute to the furtherance of social democratic projects?

Walzer's broad commitment to a vigorous civil society suggests he does support such groups. If he does not mention them explicitly, that may be because gay, lesbian, and feminist movements highlight the formation of secondary associations not just out of new migrations (Walzer's preferred source in the US case) but also (as in feminisms or gay rights movements, for example) out of *injuries* wrought by established, traditional groups.[34] Feminists, gays, and lesbians establish alternative institutional resources because their needs are not met and their ways of life are often not tolerated by the ethnic and civic communities with whom they might otherwise identify. In short, the autonomy of these extra-ethnic groups is itself a *symptom* of the sometime injustices of the various immigrant groups whose energies animate Walzer's civil society.

Others, more socially conservative than Walzer, share his concern about the rootlessness and mobility of late modern life, but they associate these explicitly with the loss of the very traditional family and community structures against which many feminist, gay, and lesbian groups often define themselves. For many pro-immigration conservatives, immigrants import the roles and expectations that maintain traditional, patriarchal structures. Here, new immigrants are mobilized symbolically to renormalize the native born into traditional heterosexual gender roles while "we" supposedly normalize "them" into a new national citizenship. This dynamic is powerfully illustrated in a popular fable of immigration and national renewal: the Australian film, *Strictly Ballroom*.

III.   Foreign brides, family ties, and new world masculinity

Strictly Ballroom, a campy comic Australian fable of immigration and national renewal, tells the story of an atrophied community of ballroom dancers saved from corruption by a Spanish immigrant, Fran, who brings new life and virtue to their practices and new energy to their flamenco.[35] Initially, Fran seeks assimilation. She assiduously studies

---

[34] For an analysis of new group formations out of injuries wrought by the old, see William Connolly, *The Ethos of Pluralization* (Minneapolis: University of Minnesota Press, 1995).

[35] *Strictly Ballroom*, directed by Baz Luhrmann (1992), is an Australian film, but it was very popular with US audiences. Its story of heteronormative national renewal is not unique to Australia. As Peter Weir's *Green Card* illustrates, the coupling of romance and

the forced steps that are the unquestioned ground upon which the community's dancers are judged. But her quest for inclusion is bound to fail. She has no connections in this corrupt community in which connections are necessary for success, and she has little to recommend her. Dancing "their" steps, she is awkward. She is also unattractive, weighed down by the thick glasses that film heroines have forever removed to reveal a stunning but somehow hitherto unsuspected beauty.

There is an opening for her, however. The powdery white, desiccated community is not only corrupt, it is also riven. One of its members, their star dancer, is a renegade who dares to depart from the community's fetishized steps. When Scott does his own thing, Fran is thrilled and impressed, but the community is aghast. From their perspective, he is too undisciplined, wild, all over the place. His dance seems to have no structure. The choice seems to be between the structure and discipline of a corrupt and unjust but orderly and established community, and a radical individualism that is irresponsible, chaotic, and nihilistic.[36] (In short, the film replays the most caricatured versions of contemporary political theory's liberal-communitarian debate.)

Scott's free dance style represents a self-seeking individualism that is symptomatic of the community's larger corruptions. Scott's mother, a disciplinary agent who consistently tries to renormalize Scott into the extant ballroom community, herself acts as a self-seeking individualist, too: she is cheating on Scott's father, having an affair with an oily man of superior standing in the dance community.

These corruptions are healed by the foreigner, Fran, and her family. Scott's individualism is tamed and structured by Fran's father, an Old World patriarch. This dark Spanish immigrant gives the couple lessons in

immigration themes on behalf of the nation travels well from Australia to the United States. There are several American immigration movies that would illustrate the same basic themes: *Big Night* is among the best. And since this chapter is focused on American immigration politics, it would have been less risky to offer a reading of one of them. I chose *Strictly Ballroom*, nonetheless, precisely because it is not usually seen as an immigration movie. Thus, in addition to deepening our understanding of the relation between the politics of foreignness and the politics of gender, reading this film in terms of its politics of foreignness is defamiliarizing and helps to show how the politics of foreignness is often at work in places where we least expect it. I am indebted to Samuel Fleishacker for first suggesting to me that *Strictly Ballroom* might be relevant to my argument (though I think he thought the movie would serve my purposes less well than it does).

[36] Interestingly, Scott, the individualistic renegade, is also a bearer of the community's standards. When he takes Fran as his partner, he begins by teaching her the basic steps upon which the community insists. Later, for the sake of a dance competition which Fran, a "nobody," obviously cannot win, he allows himself to be partnered with a pale blonde insider who knows how to dance properly. In the end, however, he returns to Fran.

authentic flamenco dancing.[37] (Fran's father used to dance with her mother[land], but his partner passed away.) At the same time, Fran's father teaches the youths two other lessons: his daughter learns to affirm her roots rather than deny them, and Scott learns that his dance and life choices are not exhausted by the options of the "strictly ballroom" community versus a renegade individualism. In the authentic flamenco of this immigrant community, Scott finds a Walzerian resource that provides his innovative dance (and his life) not only with the energy he craves but also with a shaping structure that distinguishes that newly energized dance from the chaotic individualism Scott's home community fears.[38]

At the final dance contest, Scott and Fran dance an energized and innovative flamenco that is not undisciplined and is capable, therefore, of finally felling the corrupt leaders of the strictly ballroom community whose lies and deceits are exposed. Scott's (Australian) individualism, now moderated and anchored by Fran's émigrée authenticity and familial bonds, refounds the dance community, rescuing it from its pallid fetishisms and restoring to it its original energy and its founding principles of elegance, honesty, creativity, and fairness.[39]

Fran functions as the communitarian/ethnic corrective of Scott's loveless individualism. But the film features a second supplementary relation as well: Fran's father, an empowered father-figure and a representative of the old patriarchal order, takes the place of Scott's father, a hopelessly henpecked, feeble, and feminized man who is utterly powerless to help his troubled son. Indeed, it often seems that Scott is more drawn to Fran's father than to Fran, that Scott values Fran because she is a way for Scott to get closer to a real father. This immigrant patriarch's foster fathering does not only benefit Scott; it also frees Scott's father from his dominating, castrating wife. The energies unleashed by these foreigners and, in particular, the example of Fran's Old World father benefit Scott's father: they make a man out of him.

---

[37] These immigrants are subtly depicted as good immigrants by contrast with the stereotypical Spaniard pictured in the background taking perpetual siestas with a bottle of alcohol nearby.

[38] Walzer himself uses dance to illustrate a similarly acceptable hybridity. In Gene Kelly's *An American in Paris*, Walzer finds a delightful fusion of Irish and American (African-American, to be precise) that is a synecdoche for the other admirable social, civic, and cultural fusions he admires.

[39] In effect, the film illustrates Louis Hartz's thesis about fragmented societies in the New World. The Australian dance community is like a Hartzian fragment. Separated from its organic origins and frozen in time, it is incapable of either innovation or restoration. The Old World, by contrast, is capable of innovation because it has dynamism, conflict, and multiplicity within it. See Louis Hartz, *The Founding of New Societies: Studies in the History of the United States, Latin America, South Africa, Canada and Australia* (New York: Harcourt, Brace and World, 1964).

In short, the supplement of foreignness works on at least two registers in *Strictly Ballroom*: through the agency of foreignness, proper virtue is restored to the social world of the ballroom and proper order is restored to the patriarchal family at Scott's house. With the proper containment of the feminine (in the form of Scott's outrageously ambitious mother), Scott's father can be a father again, and the world is made safe for the (re-)emergence of an Australian masculinity from within the confines of the feminized, suburban household. The agents of all this are the foreigners who import proper masculinity and proper femininity to a place that has lost its gender bearings. That is to say, *Strictly Ballroom* replays the classical republican identifications of corruption with female ambition and male emasculation and of refounding with a return to proper gender identities and roles.[40]

But the importation of a real masculinity from elsewhere does not only save Australian masculinity. It also stands as a perpetual reminder of the inadequacy of Australian masculinity. By comparison with Fran's father, who personifies an authentic, Old World masculinity, won't Australian masculinity always be a mere copy? And yet, without Fran's father, Australian masculinity will continue to be consumed by the feminized household of suburbia. There is no way out of this quandary.

Perhaps the point is that Australian masculinity needs not just the supplement of Fran's father but also that of Fran herself, who is enough of an Old World woman to provide Scott in marriage and in dance with the sort of adoring feminine prop that proper masculinity requires. The young couple's relationship, the film implies, will be different from Scott's parents' marriage because Scott's immigrant girlfriend comes from a family that values family more than the instrumental goods and status that led Scott's mother astray. By modeling immigration politics in terms of this new relationship, the film suggests that it may be possible for immigrants and members of the receiving regime to relate to each other without politics, as two Aristotelian friends somehow positioned on a single, unambiguous (and safely heterosexual) register of friendship.

The desire for an Old World wife to prop up New World masculinity and restore the patriarchal family is evident not only in film. American men are nowadays "introduced" to foreign women by companies such as Scanna International Worldwide Introductions. As one client, David Davidson of Fairlawn, Ohio, explains: "'There's an exodus of men

---

[40] Although, given Machiavelli's account of (male) *virtù* as the ability to be like (the female) *fortuna*, there is always some essential gender confusion at the base of republican politics. On *virago*, see my *Political Theory and the Displacement of Politics* (Ithaca: Cornell University Press, 1993), ch. 1.

leaving this country to find wives,' Davidson said. 'They're looking for women with traditional values like we had 40 years ago.[41] They're finding Russian women have those values. Family comes first for them – not work or the Mercedes or the bank account,' said Davidson who has been married and divorced four times." Of his own Russian fiancée, Davidson said, "'She is the most feminine young woman that I've been in the company of. She knows how to be a lady.'"[42]

Davidson's confident opposition between family values and rank materialism is called into question by another American man interviewed for the same article: "'In one form or another [American men] are sick and tired of the princess attitude of American women ... Russian women are old-fashioned ... Their husband and family come first.'" But he added that "'Russian women see marriage to U.S. men as a way to improve their impoverished lives.'"

The existence of a foreign bride *trade* already suggests that – the protests of American men notwithstanding – these marriages are not simply romantic. Indeed, the trade highlights the nature of the institution of marriage in general as not only an institutionalized form of heterosexual intimacy but also always a site at which all sorts of goods and services are exchanged, including citizenship, legal residence status, money, companionship, and sex.[43] Moreover, the fact that diverse American, Japanese, Taiwanese, and Arabic men locate a real femininity in places as diverse as Russia, Thailand, and the Philippines suggests that none of these places is a wellspring of true femininity. What if, instead, the foreignness of the imported brides functions to produce a set of relations and inequalities that are available to be (mis)read as femininity?[44] This would account for how it is that, somehow, the

---

[41] On the American fantasy of the traditional family, see Stephanie Coontz, *The Way We Never Were: American Families and the Nostalgia Trap* (New York: Basic Books, 1992).

[42] "More U.S. Men Look for Love Overseas," *Columbus Dispatch*, 30 December 1996, C2. See also Venny Villapando, "The Business of Selling Mail-Order Brides," in Asian Women of California (eds.), *Making Waves: An Anthology of Writing By and About Asian American Women* (Boston: Beacon Press, 1989) pp. 318–326.

[43] It is no accident that the term "foreign bride" has already floated over to the financial pages, where it operates as a metaphor for international merger: "A merger flurry in the Swedish banking sector continued on Tuesday and analysts forecast more reshuffling at home before banks cast their eyes overseas for foreign brides" ("Swedish Bank Merger Flurry Seen Continuing," *Reuters European Business Report*).

[44] The restoration of proper masculinity by way of the importation of truly feminine foreign brides is not exclusively practiced by American men. In Japan, Thai brides are a "sought-after commodity" for reasons that echo those given by the American men quoted here. Sonni Efron, "Here Come the Brides," *Newsday*, 3 March 1997, B04. And the same trend has been noted in Taiwan, where the government has recently set quotas "designed to slow the influx of foreign brides and boost the marriage prospects of Taiwanese women" (Lee Chuan-hsien, "Crackdown on Importing Foreign Brides,"

purchase of a foreign bride – for $7,500 and a residency permit – is said to put the romance back into an institution that is losing its charm.

Isolated from others and dependent upon her husband, the foreign bride is ignorant of local customs and languages. Her subject position mimes that of the traditional, feminine wife, but foreignness abets or trumps femininity as the real and reliable cause of a foreign bride's dependence and acceptance, her so-called family values. What is labeled "feminine" and eroticized is the foreign bride's would-be powerlessness, her confined agency, and her limited alternatives. That perceived powerlessness is why the husbands, who believe that their foreign wives are feminine and unmaterialistic, are undisturbed by the knowledge that these women – who are seeking to escape poverty and limited opportunities, after all – are actually quite interested in the very thing to which they are supposed to be indifferent: their husbands' proverbial "bank account" and the size of it. What is most important is not finally whether the woman is interested in money but whether she has the power to pursue that interest by way of employment for herself or ambition on her husband's behalf.

The xenophilic embrace of foreignness to re-enchant traditional family structures generates two xenophobic responses. Increasingly, the popular press has been publishing stories of foreign brides who turn out to have been using the husbands who sponsored their entry into the United States. Instead of self-sacrificing caregivers, these women are said to be untrustworthy takers who cheat their husbands, rob and leave them. More fundamentally, they wrong not only their husbands; they cheapen the institution of marriage by treating it instrumentally. An Aristotelian reading of the situation would say that it is because these wives relate to their husbands on the register of use rather than on the register of pleasure or virtue that the institution of marriage is politicized. Derrida would probably suggest, however, that it is the inevitable confusion of pleasure, virtue, and use (clearest here but attached to the institution of marriage as such) that is responsible for the politicization of marriage.

Such loveless marriages are seen as doubly dangerous (certainly more dangerous than all the other loveless marriages in the nation) because they disenchant two of the nation's most beloved institutions: the institution of marriage, which foreign brides are supposed to help prop up, as well as the institution of citizenship, which is supposedly damaged when immigrants acquire it improperly.[45] The affective

---

Chicago Tribune, 2 February 1997, p. 2). Business is flourishing as well in Saudi Arabia and elsewhere.

[45] This intersection of the institutions of marriage and citizenship is significant. Concerns about both came together in a 17 March 1997, Letter to the Editor in the

health of both institutions depends upon immigrants' being attracted to them not for the sake of money or other worldly goods but rather for the sake of a love, devotion, or virtue that is seen as prior to the institutions in question and not as one of their ideological effects. To the critical question, do these passions give legitimacy to the state (or marriage), or does the state (or marriage) itself generate and legitimate these passions?, this first xenophobic response has an emphatic if conventional answer: "First comes love, then comes marriage..."

The second xenophobic response generated by this particular xenophilia is audible in my own text. Here patriarchal immigrants are seen as threats to the rough (very rough) gender equalities that are American liberal democracy's ambiguous achievement.[46] The xenophilic deployment of foreignness on behalf of traditional family structures is particularly troublesome for social democrats because the foreign bride trade promises to resecure and revalorize female powerlessness and male power. The xenophilic deployment of foreignness to solve the problems of gender politics generates these xenophobic responses. This is what happens when foreigners are pressed, symbolically, into service on behalf of institutions – capitalism, community, family – that seem incapable of sustaining themselves. The deployment of foreignness as a restorative supplement itself positions foreigners also as the original cause of the very institutional illness they are supposed to be curing. Where foreign women are figured as exemplary wives who can save the institution of romantic marriage, they inevitably fail, and then they are also set up as betrayers of that and other ideals: the self-interested corrupters of increasingly devalued institutions whose downfall can now be safely attributed to the institutions' abuse at the hands of untrustworthy outsiders who never really loved us but were only out to use us all along.

New York Times. The author responded to the recent spate of marriages between immigrants and American citizens (reported by the paper as part of an effort by foreigners to acquire residency) by calling attention to the "irony" of the fact that Americans allow this abuse of marriage for instrumental purposes while continuing to deny marriage to those who really value it, gay couples in love. Two critics who examine this intersection are Michael Warner, *The Trouble with Normal* (New York: Free Press, 1999) and Lauren Berlant, "Face of America," in *Disciplinarity and Dissent in Cultural Studies,* ed. Cary Nelson and Dilip Parameshwar Gaonkar (New York: Routledge, 1996).

[46] Susan Okin makes this argument without apparent ambivalence in *Is Multiculturalism Bad for Women?*, ed. Joshua Cohen *et al.* (Princeton: Princeton University Press, 1999). See also my response to Okin, published in the same volume, "My Culture Made Me Do It."

**IV.   Dramatizing consent: the universal charms
of American democracy**

The demand that foreign women bring feminine romance to American
marriages is paralleled by the demand that immigrants romance
America and help to re-enchant another institution that many feel is in
danger of losing its affective charms: the institution of citizenship. The
fourth and final redeployment of the myth of an immigrant America, the
liberal version, looks to immigrants to reperform the official social
contract by naturalizing to citizenship. In the case of the United States,
this means (re-)enacting for established citizens the otherwise too
abstract universalism of America's democratic constitutionalism.[47]

Immigrants not only testify to the universality of American constitutional principles, they are also the only Americans who actually *consent*
explicitly to the regime. Since liberal democracies draw their legitimacy
from their consent base, the failure of the native born to consent
explicitly seems to pose a deep problem for liberal democracies. Some
liberals solve the problem by way of tacit consent. Others, like Peter
Schuck and Rogers Smith, have sought instead to provide heightened
opportunities for the native born to consent explicitly.

In *Citizenship without Consent: Illegal Aliens in the Polity*, Schuck and
Smith argue that native born citizens should be offered the opportunity
to self-expatriate at the age of majority.[48] Although a right of expatria-
tion now exists, few know about it and it is not easy to exercise. Schuck
and Smith favor routinizing the choice (by way of automatic mailings to
native born citizens at the age of majority) and lowering the costs
(citizens might choose permanent resident status, not necessarily emigration).[49] Why make these changes? "In a polity in which actual consent is expressed symbolically only through periodic elections, these
proposals can impart a new social meaning and integrity to the tacit
consent that must suffice during the intervening periods."[50]

It is possible that these changes may heighten consent for the native
born, and they may help relegitimate the liberal state, as Schuck and
Smith say.[51] But such changes may have other effects as well. For the

---

[47] As Kant was well aware, the universal cannot survive in the absence of particular
enactments of its law. Hence Kant's repeated, transgressive use in the *Groundwork of the
Metaphysics of Morals* of particular examples to represent the moral law on whose
unrepresentability he was otherwise insistent.
[48] Schuck and Smith, *Citizenship without Consent*, p. 130.
[49] Ibid., pp. 123–124.
[50] Ibid., pp. 131–132.
[51] Although it is beyond me why we should seek further to legitimate an institution whose
legitimacy ought properly always to be in question.

sake of a heightened affect and legitimacy, Schuck and Smith are willing to risk the creation of a rather substantial class of resident aliens, which is what will become of those who do not respond to a new invitation to consent. How will Schuck and Smith's revalorized citizenship benefit from the development of a potentially large class of persons willing to live here and consume goods and services without partaking of the rights (voting) and obligations (military service) of citizenship?[52] What will become of state citizenship when it is transformed from a supposedly universal category into a property of a self-chosen few? (This is not to say that citizenship should be preserved without change but rather to ask, genuinely, what would happen to its meaning and practice if the changes called for by Schuck and Smith were actually instituted.)

More to the point, what sort of power can we expect to come out of a mailed-in consent form? Consent by mail, an action, typically liberal, taken in private, is not likely ever to have the same affective symbolic-cultural effect as the public scene it is intended to mime: that of new citizens taking the oath of citizenship. As Sanford Levinson suggests, immigrant naturalization ceremonies function as a kind of "national liturgy."[53] With a hope and a prayer and an oath, the gap of consent is filled. Immigrant naturalization ceremonies – frequently publicized on the front pages of the nation's newspapers – testify to the fundamental consentworthiness of the regime by symbolically representing the consent that is effectively unattainable for native-born citizens of a liberal regime.

Does this mean that new citizen oath takers act as consenters by proxy, giving voice to the (supposed) silent, tacit consent of the native born? There is something odd about thinking that immigrants can fill the gap of consent when immigrants are so often infantilized (they can't speak English, they need help) and seen as desperate.[54] How could such (symbolic) persons be positioned to enact the mature, balanced, and reasonable reflection of rational consent? If the immigrant is desperate, infantile, or "too foreign," his speech act will misfire (it may look like parody to the native born). Indeed, liberals who want immigrants to help solve liberal democracies' legitimation problem are pressed by their own demands to distinguish impossibly between sincere and fraudulent speech acts, admirable immigrant idealism and rough practicality, and among virtue, pleasure, and use – is it true love or are they just

---

[52] These are the sort of people, "passport holders," that Benedict Anderson worries about in "Exodus," *Critical Inquiry*, 20 (2), Winter 1994, pp. 314–327.

[53] Sanford Levinson, *Constitutional Faith* (Princeton: Princeton University Press, 1988), p. 99.

[54] Schuck and Smith, *Citizenship without Consent*, p. 109.

using us?[55] As of 1 April 1997 elderly or mentally ill immigrants who cannot utter the words of the citizenship oath can no longer become US citizens. Is it the inaccessibility of immigrant intentions that drives the last decade's obsession with the quite literal performance of the speech act of citizenship? Or is that obsession, perched on the "paradox of intention and capacity," itself a symptom of the modern liberal effort to (in Elizabeth Wingrove's words) "theorize an individualism consistent with new standards of political legitimacy: consent"?[56]

The intractability of these problems (is the naturalizing immigrant sincere or is he just out for himself?) suggests that if immigrants and their swearing-in ceremonies are doing some symbolic-cultural-political work, that work must be something other than the simple provision of consent by proxy. What else might it be?

First, these ceremonies give the abstract universal value of consent a material and embodied form, thus addressing a problem that Elizabeth Wingrove identifies by way of Rousseau: "that consent makes sense only in its material enactments and that it remains unintelligible when divorced from worldly – institutional, bodily – conditions."[57] At a

---

[55] That is, new immigrants need to be taking on citizenship for the *right* reasons. In short, what we have here is an uneasy dependence of the performative (consent) on the constative (the right reasons). On the final unsustainability of Austin's distinction between these two, see Derrida's critical appreciation of Austin in "Signature, Event, Context," in *Limited, Inc.* (Evanston: Northwestern University Press, 1988). For my own extended reading of Derrida and Austin on this topic, see *Political Theory and the Displacement of Politics*, ch. 4.

[56] Elizabeth Wingrove, *Rousseau's Republican Romance* (Princeton: Princeton University Press, 2000), p. 23. As Wingrove rightly points out, the "perceived tension between structure and act – between determining conditions and undetermined choice – is not an epistemological crisis of social theory that arises in the wake of Marx and Freud." Instead, as in her quoted passage above, it is a result of liberal efforts to theorize an individualism capable of performing the consent that liberal legitimation requires. Wingrove's book came out just as I was putting the finishing touches on mine. I find her theorization of "consensual nonconsensuality" in Rousseau to be quite valuable for thinking about consent more generally, and wish I had had access to it earlier, so as to have been able to engage this work in more detail. As my own reading of Rousseau would suggest, however, the idea that the desires for freedom and domination are twinned (and not just connected, contra Wingrove, who in some moods, suggests that what consensual nonconsensuality comes down to is simply the fact that "the freedom [democratic politics] makes possible requires domination" [p. 23]) is worth pursuing not just through Rousseau's substantial writings on heterosexual romance (as Wingrove does). It is also worth pursuing through his figuration of the law as the both loved and feared paternal and alien figure of the lawgiver in *The Social Contract*, the text to which Wingrove pays the least sustained attention in her own reading of Rousseau. For more on this, see my *Democracy and the Foreigner*, chs. 2 and 5.

[57] Wingrove, *Rousseau's Republican Romance*, p. 22. French republicanism was founded with a similar turn to foreignness to testify to the power of France's would-be universal principles. The national legislative assembly approved granting the title of French citizen to Joseph Priestley, Thomas Paine, Jeremy Bentham, William Wilberforce,

deeper level, however, the rite of naturalization does not just re-enact or embody consent. It reperforms the origin of the regime *as* an act of consent. The oft-disseminated spectacle of new citizens taking the oath of citizenship – a scene in which the new citizen and the state embrace each other in an act of speech – recenters the regime on its fictive foundation of voluntarist consent. Two effects are achieved thereby:

(1) First, an emphatic answer is given to the question of who comes first, the law or the subject, by depicting a subject who exists as such prior to the law and is able therefore to consent to it without apparently being always already formed by it. In this regard, the iconic scene of new immigrants taking the pledge of citizenship has an ideological effect. It privileges a choosing subject as a natural subject prior to the law, and it grounds the law in a choice that is its foundation and its raison d'être.

(2) Second, rites of renaturalization re-enact the regime's ideologically approved origins, obscuring the non-consensual and ascriptive bases and present-day practices of American democracy. The broadcasting (on television, in the nation's newspapers) of this verbal, visible path to citizenship remarginalizes the varied, often violent, sources of the republic (slavery, conquest, appropriations, and constitutional conventions), and it recenters the regime on a voluntarism that most citizens and residents never experience directly. The scene may even excite in some citizens a sympathetic denaturalization that enhances their sympathetic renaturalization (just as many married couples effectively renew their vows when they go to other people's weddings, re-experiencing the pleasure of the gaze of the state and the community upon marital union).

But this (symbolic) "solution" to the problem of consent generates problems of its own. It places the legitimacy of the regime (and its claimed universality as a republic or a democracy) in the hands of

Thomas Clarkson, James MacKintosh, David Williams, George Washington, Alexander Hamilton, James Madison, and Kosciuszko, among others on 26 August 1792. (For the discussion, see *Archives parlementaires*, 24 and 26 August 1792.) This was in recognition of their writing or actions on behalf of "la liberté, de la humanité, et des bonnes moeurs." An interesting historical analysis of the xenophilic and xenophobic moments of the Revolution is provided by Virginie Giraudon, who says: "For the first time in French history, an integration status was granted in the name of the universality of ideas to those who had done the most for humanity." But later, "the need for proselytism was replaced after 1792 by the necessity to survive against foreign threats." Giraudon reports the shift from xenophilia to xenophobia but does not ask after the possible logic of their interrelation. "Cosmopolitanism and National Priority: Attitudes towards Foreigners in France between 1789 and 1794," *History of European Ideas*, 13 (5), 1991, p. 593.

foreigners who may or may not close the gap of consent for "us." This is a problem because many newcomers do not satisfy the national need to be chosen – many do not seek citizenship. And those who do naturalize do not simply solve the legitimacy problem; they also inadvertently highlight it by simultaneously calling attention to the fact that most American citizens never consent to the regime. (We saw the same dynamic at work in *Strictly Ballroom*, where Australian masculinity was both refurbished and also perpetually undone by the importation of masculinity from the Old World.)

In any case, even (or especially) when immigrants do prop up the national fantasy of consentworthiness, the regime's fundamental (unacknowledged) dependence upon foreigners produces an anxiety that finds expression in a displaced anxiety about foreigners' dependence upon us (an anxiety that, of course, erases the regime's dependence upon foreignness). Thus, it comes as no surprise that in Schuck and Smith's book (and in American political culture, more generally: the book is deeply symptomatic), the good, consenting immigrant, the model of proper, consensual American citizenship, is shadowed by the bad immigrant, the illegal alien who undermines consent in two ways: he never consents to American laws, and "we" never consent to his presence on "our" territory. Schuck and Smith's illegal takes things from us and has nothing to offer in return. He takes up residence without permission; he is interested in social welfare state membership (the proverbial bank account), not citizenship (except for instrumental purposes having to do with securing access to social welfare goods); she takes services without payment (the example repeatedly invoked is that of illegals' unpaid maternity bills at Los Angeles hospitals). In short, the "illegal" in Schuck and Smith's text slides from being a person defined by a juridical status that positions him as always already in violation of the (immigration) law into being a daily and willful lawbreaker.

The illegal's threat to consent is crystallized most vividly in *Citizenship without Consent* (a book widely touted at the 1996 Republican convention) by the American-born children of illegal aliens (hence, perhaps, the authors' [displaced] obsession with unpaid maternity bills). Schuck and Smith argue, against a century of Supreme Court decisions, that American-born children of illegals have no constitutional right to citizenship. The Fourteenth Amendment applies to people born in the "jurisdiction" of the United States. Illegal aliens, in the United States without the approval of the state or the consent of its citizens, are on American territory but not in its jurisdiction.[58] Schuck and Smith do not

---

[58] Schuck and Smith, *Citizenship without Consent*, p. 122.

argue that this means that these children should *not* receive birthright citizenship. It simply means that this right is not constitutionally entrenched and that the decision about whether or not to grant birthright citizenship to the children of illegal aliens is available for democratic (popular and legislative) debate and consent.[59]

The rhetorical weight of the rest of the book, however, is on the side of excluding children of the undocumented from birthright citizenship.[60] For Schuck and Smith, the goal is to revalue American citizenship, to (re)gain control over its distribution.[61] Schuck and Smith frame

---

[59] By stressing the right of the existing community of citizens to "consent" to newcomers, Schuck and Smith perversely turn Lockean consent from a device designed to limit state power into a device for its enhancement. A similar move is made by Levinson and by Walzer, though at least their way of making the point does not press into service the device of consent. Levinson: "A 'double choosing' is involved: An immigrant's choice to 'adopt' an American identity is coupled with that immigrant's need to be chosen by the United States itself as a suitable member of the political community" (Levinson, *Constitutional Faith*, p. 97). Cf. Michael Walzer, *Spheres of Justice: A Defense of Pluralism and Equality* (New York: Basic Books, 1983), pp. 31, 39.

[60] It should be noted, though, that Schuck and Smith also say that "children (and perhaps their parents as well) may have legitimate moral or humanitarian claims upon American society" (*Citizenship without Consent*, pp. 98, 100, and passim) apart from whether they have a claim to citizenship. "It is enough for present purposes to affirm that the Constitution need not and should not be woodenly interpreted either to guarantee their children citizenship or to cast them into outer darkness" (ibid., p. 100).

[61] Schuck and Smith, *Citizenship without Consent*, p. 107. One measure of the devaluation of citizenship is Supreme Court decisions such as *Graham* v. *Richardson*, which insists that social welfare benefits cannot be restricted to legal residents. In a later article, Schuck is more resigned to the "devaluation of citizenship." He rightly situates this development in the context of increased international integration and migration, and he thinks, four years after *Citizenship without Consent*, that recent changes in national citizenship are "probably irreversible." But he is unwilling to let citizenship go: "It provides a focus of political allegiance and emotional energy on a scale capable of satisfying deep human longings for solidarity, symbolic identification and community. Such a focus may be especially important in a liberal ethos whose centrifugal, cosmopolitan aspirations for global principles and universal human rights must somehow be balanced against the more parochial imperatives of organizing societies dominated by more limited commitments to family, locality, region, and nation." Schuck, "Membership in the Liberal Polity: The Devaluation of American Citizenship," in *Immigration and the Politics of Citizenship in Europe and North America*, ed. W. Rogers Brubaker (Lanham: University Press of America, 1989), pp. 64–65.

Schuck is right that the nation-state sometimes balances the drives towards globalization and localization. But the contrary is also true. The nation-state is often a *vehicle* of both globalization and localization as well, as was clear in the United States' move to found NAFTA and in ongoing efforts to localize the administration of social services. Moreover, it is also the case that global and local affiliations are not necessarily disempowering or undemocratic. They can provide helpful, democratizing checks against the coercive powers of the nation-state. It is therefore important to think about the ways in which the emotional "human" satisfactions of citizenship can be appropriated for non-national entities. Thus, I agree with the last line of Schuck's 1989 essay but take it as one of my *starting* points: "Today's conception of citizenship may not be adequate to meet tomorrow's needs" (ibid., p. 65).

the issue in terms of consent and depict the state as the non-consenting victim of wayward migrants, but it is not at all clear that the state does *not* consent to the presence on its territory of large numbers of illegal immigrants. Illegal migration is not only combatted by the state; it is also simultaneously enabled, covertly courted, often managed, and certainly tolerated by it.[62] Established citizens profit from the subsidies that cheap migrant labor provides to their childcare costs and food prices.[63]

More to the point, the liberal xenophilic deployment of the foreigner as the truest citizen because the only truly consenting one actually feeds the xenophobic backlash against the non-consenting immigrant – the illegal alien – to whom we supposedly do not consent and who does not consent to us.[64] If this analysis is correct, then the iconic good immigrant – the supercitizen – who upholds American liberal democracy is not accidentally or coincidentally partnered with the iconic bad immigrant who threatens to tear it down. Popular ambivalences about foreignness are not, as Rogers Smith has argued elsewhere, the product of distinct, nativist ideologies that are unconnected in any deep or significant way to American liberal democracy.[65] The co-presence in American political culture of xenophilia and xenophobia comes right out of America's fundamental liberal commitments, which map a normatively and materially privileged national citizenship onto an idealized immigrant trajectory to membership. This means that the undecidability of foreignness – the depiction of foreigners as good and bad for the nation – is partly driven by the logic of liberal, national consent, which, in the case of the United States, both produces and denies a fundamental dependence upon foreigners who are positioned symbolically so

[62] Kitty Calavita, *Inside the State: The Bracero Program, Immigration and the I.N.S.* (New York: Routledge, 1992), p. 167 and passim.
[63] This is a practice of which Michael Walzer was rightly critical in "Membership," ch. 2 of *Spheres of Justice*.
[64] It should be noted, however, that consent and voluntarism are not obviously nor necessarily enhanced by moving away from *jus soli*. Such a move makes citizenship (contrary to the authors' stated intentions) more ascriptive, not less so; it becomes a status that is more obviously inherited (or not) from one's parents. Moreover, the practice of *jus soli* is no less consensual than other mechanisms (tolerated by the authors) that accord children citizenship and nationality at birth.
[65] See Rogers Smith, "Beyond Tocqueville, Myrdal and Hartz: The Multiple Traditions Thesis in America," *American Political Science Review*, 87 (3), September 1993, pp. 549–566. Here and in his book, *Civic Ideals: Conflicting Visions of Citizenship in US History* (New Haven: Yale University Press, 1997), Smith positions himself as a critic of American exceptionalism so it might seem strange that I put him in the company of figures like Tocqueville, Myrdal, and Hartz when he wrote in opposition to them. As I argue in ch. 1 of *Democracy and the Foreigner*, however, Smith's liberalism is an exceptionalist's liberalism, unhaunted by doubts, otherness, or violences that touch it at its core. Smith departs from the more usual exceptionalists in his insistence that such a pure liberalism has not found itself fully at home in the United States – not yet.

that they must and yet finally cannot fill the gaps of consent and legitimacy for us.[66] That is, nativist ideologies may shape, direct, and accelerate the xenophobia in question. But, contra Rogers Smith, it is misleading to see them as the external corrupters of an otherwise fundamentally egalitarian and tolerant liberal tradition whose only weakness is its failure to inspire in communitarian terms.[67] Indeed, Smith's characterization of the problem as one of liberalism's corruption at the hands of an outside agitator itself replays the xenophobic script that Smith (in his most recent work) is out to criticize.

But xenophobia is not the only problem here. The iconic bad immigrant is also problematic because he distracts attention from democracy's real problems. Schuck and Smith's deployment of the figure of the illegal exceeds their apparent intent and highlights a different, more tenacious corruption than that of "illegal aliens in the polity" – that of the withdrawal of most American citizens and residents from political life.[68] The illegal imagined by Schuck and Smith turns out to stand for the much-rehearsed corruption of American citizenship from an active liberal voluntarism to a non-consenting, passive social welfare consumerism in which good citizens – "givers" – have been replaced by self-interested maximizers and freeriders, "takers." No more than a minority of American citizens votes in American elections; fewer still involve

---

[66] That is to say, I am hazarding a strong, logical claim, by contrast with Michael Rogin, who is wrongly charged by Rogers Smith with making claims about the logic of liberalism. Rogin's rather substantial arguments about America's history of exclusion and genocide are historical, not logical. See Smith's Response to "Beyond Tocqueville, Please!" by Jacqueline Stevens (*American Political Science Review*, 89 (4), December 1995, pp. 990 – 995) and Michael Rogin, *Ronald Reagan, the Movie: And Other Episodes in American Political Demonology* (Berkeley and Los Angeles: University of California Press, 1987).

[67] Smith, "Beyond Tocqueville, Myrdal and Hartz," and *Civic Ideals*.

[68] The authors unwittingly call attention to this deeper problem when they say that they are seeking to complement the "actual consent [that] is expressed symbolically only through periodic elections" in America. Concerned only about the periodicity of election-based consent, they do not mention the fact that no more than a minority of American citizens vote in American elections.This unselfconscious projection of the corruptions of American citizenship onto illegal aliens is paralleled by Michael Walzer's more self-conscious metaphorization of withdrawn American citizens as "psychological resident aliens." But Walzer's metaphor also misleads. Just as the metaphor of illegality slides from status to behavior in Schuck and Smith, so in Walzer, a juridical status assigned by the state (resident alien) slides into a political attitude imputed to the person (political withdrawalism). But there is no evidence to support the identification of resident alien status with political uninvolvement, at least not with any level of uninvolvement worthy of remark. Nor is there any evidence for the converse: that naturalizing immigrants are prone to political involvement. See Michael Walzer "Political Alienation and Military Service," in *Obligations*, ed. Michael Walzer (Cambridge, MA: Harvard University Press, 1970), pp. 99–100, 112–113, cited by Levinson, *Constitutional Faith*.

themselves directly in politics. Schuck and Smith externalize these corruptions of American democratic citizenship and project them onto a foreigner who can be made to leave. These Girardian scapegoats represent our best virtues and our worst vices. They become the occasion of a new social unity that Schuck and Smith hope, somehow, to achieve by way of some small policy changes, periodic mailings, constitutional reinterpretations, and better border policing. In short, Schuck and Smith's iconic foreigners, both good and bad, are problematic because they invite unfair treatment of foreigners but also because they mislead us into believing that the solution to liberal democracy's problems and the right response to heightened migrations is a politics of national retrenchment.

V.   Taking liberties: intimations of a democratic cosmopolitanism

> "To change a story signals a dissent from social norms as well as narrative forms."
> – Rachel Duplessis, *Writing Beyond the Ending* (1985)

Tracking the varied workings of the hegemonic myth of an immigrant America helps identify sites at which it may be possible to evaluate, interrupt, and reinhabit dominant figurations of foreignness. The next step is to ask: "How might the myth of an immigrant America be redeployed as part of a counterpolitics of foreignness?"

Fundamentally, the various versions of the myth of an immigrant America all seek to renationalize the state and to position it at the center of any future democratic politics. By pressing the foreign immigrant into service on behalf of the nation and its iconic economy, community, family, and liberal individual citizen, the myth positions the immigrant as either a *giver* to or a *taker* from the nation. Indeed, the xenophilic insistence that immigrants are givers to the nation itself feeds the xenophobic anxiety that they might really be takers from it. But the ostensibly pejorative symbolic depiction of immigrants as "takers" might have a positive dimension that democratic theorists could mobilize. In 1792, Madison said: "In Europe charters of liberty are granted by power [while] in America ... charters of power are granted by liberty." Madison's insight is that democracy is a form of politics in which power is not received by grateful subjects but rather is taken, redistributed, re-enacted, and recirculated by way of liberty, that is, by way of popular political action. Might the negative depiction of immigrants as those who take things from the nation (possibly a projection of a returning, repressed guilt for the original takings on which the regime is founded) be available for recuperation on the part of those who, like Madison, think democracy *always* involves some sort of taking?

Not all takings are performed by immigrants or foreigners, but they are all performed by subjects who are not fully included in the system of rights and privileges in which they live. The practice of taking rights and privileges rather than waiting for them to be granted by a sovereign power is, I would argue, a quintessentially democratic practice. Indeed, it is one of the practices whereby the American experiment in democracy itself began. As Alexis de Tocqueville points out in *Democracy in America*, American "settlers" began "exercising rights of sovereignty" without the prior knowledge or authorization of the "motherland." Says Tocqueville, "The new settlers, without denying the supremacy of the homeland, did not derive from thence the source of their powers, and it was only thirty or forty years afterward, under Charles II, that a royal charter legalized their existence."[69]

Jacques Rancière, in *Dis-agreement*, offers several other examples of the same sort of practice in which new rights and standing are taken and then recognized only later (if at all). Working with Pierre-Simon Ballanche's nineteenth-century retelling of Livy's tale of the Roman plebeians' secession on Aventine Hill, Rancière notes that, contra Livy, this is a battle not about poverty and anger but about who has the status of a speaking being and about how those who are denied such a status can nonetheless make their claims or make room for themselves. Rancière puts it beautifully: "Between the language of those who have a name and the lowing of nameless beings, no situation of linguistic exchange can possibly be set up, no rules or codes of discussion." Is armed battle, then, the only recourse for the nameless class? The plebeians found another way: "They do not set up a fortified camp in the manner of the Scythian slaves. They do what would have been unthinkable for the latter: they establish another order, another partition of the perceptible, by constituting themselves not as warriors equal to other warriors but as speaking beings sharing the same properties as those who deny them these." They mime the speech acts of their would-be superiors and "through transgression, they find that they too, just like speaking beings, are endowed with speech that does not simply express want, suffering or rage, but intelligence." All of this, Rancière refers to as the "staging of a nonexistent right."[70] Rancière gives another example of the practice when he cites the case of Jeanne Déroin who, in 1849, "presents herself

[69] Tocqueville, *Democracy in America*, pp. 40–41.
[70] Jacques Rancière, *Dis-agreement: Politics and Philosophy*, trans. Julie Rose (Minneapolis: University of Minnesota Press, 1999), pp. 24–25.

as a candidate for a legislative election for which she cannot run," thus staging the contradiction at the heart of the French republic which is a regime founded on both an "equality that does not recognize any difference between the sexes" and on "complementarity in laws and morals," where the latter is the proper sphere of women.[71] Yet another example, this one not in Rancière, is that of Victoria Woodhull, a nineteenth-century American feminist who, instead of campaigning to have women's right to vote added to the Constitution, asserted that the right to vote was already implicit and (along with other women) simply began voting and was arrested for it.

These examples of non-immigrant democratic takings invite a reassessment of the much-reviled figure of the bad immigrant taker. A positive valuation of the taking immigrant as a *democratic* taker anchors a fifth way of looking at the myth of an immigrant America, this one on behalf of a democratic cosmopolitanism. Here the myth is a narrative of democratic activism whose heroes are not nationals of the regime but insist, nonetheless, on exercising national citizen rights while they are here. Historically, such immigrants have banded together to take or redistribute power. Their demands were resisted, denied, misunderstood, sometimes grudgingly granted or yielded, often greeted with violence, once in a while ceded without fanfare. The people who made the demands were sometimes deported, imprisoned, or executed. Others sometimes stayed, sometimes left to go elsewhere, sometimes returned to their points of origin, sometimes died. The nation was not their telos. But they were all engaged in what Rancière calls, honorifically, "political activity," a form of activity that "shifts a body from the place assigned to it or changes a place's destination. It makes visible what had no business being seen, and makes heard a discourse where once there was only place for noise; it makes heard as discourse what was once only heard as noise."[72]

The democratic aspect of this version of the myth of an immigrant America lies not in its aspiration to tell a story of ever broadening *national* inclusion, nor in its effort to expose the "lie regarding the universal" enshrined in the nation's Constitution. The peculiarly democratic character of the reinhabited myth inheres in its character as a history and a continuing present of empowerment, frame-shifting, and world-building. We have here a story of illegitimate demands made by people with no standing to make them, a story of people so far outside the circle of who "counts" that they cannot make claims within the existing frames of claim-making. They make room for themselves by

[71] Rancière, *Dis-agreement*, p. 41.   [72] Ibid., p. 30.

staging non-existent rights, and by way of such stagings, sometimes, new rights, powers, and visions come into being.[73]

Because the myth of an immigrant America is a narrative of demands made by outsiders, it is not just a nationalist story; it is also, potentially, a myth of denationalization. Reinhabited as a democratic rather than a nationalist narrative, the recovered myth of an immigrant America might push late modern democratic actors to pursue two conflicting aims simultaneously: (1) to insist on the inclusion of immigrants and migrants in democracy's national future, while also (2) pressing for the (symbolic and institutional) denationalization of democracy at the same time.

One way to include immigrants in democracy's national future while resisting the recuperation of immigrant energies for the state's renationalization is to expand alien suffrage. Contrary to popular belief, the history of suffrage is not one of ceaseless expansion. The United States has a long history of alien suffrage ("Finally undone by the xenophobic nationalism attending World War I"), in which democratic participation is linked not to the juridical status of citizenship but to the fact of residence.[74] At present, several cities allow non-citizen residents to vote in local, school board (Chicago and New York), or municipal (several Maryland localities, such as Takoma Park) elections.[75]

Promoting social and worker movements might help win for presently unrepresented populations a voice in institutional self-governance as well as greater autonomy in daily life. One excellent example of such an effort is the Workplace Project, an organization that provides legal representation and advice to the undocumented while also training them to advocate and organize on their own behalf, representing themselves to bosses, landlords, school administrators, and state officials. The Workplace Project extends citizenship practices to non-citizens. It

[73] The word "counts" and the phrase quoted above are both from Rancière. Rancière recasts class struggle in terms of those who – from Plato forward – "count" and the uncounted.
[74] Jamin Raskin, "Legal Aliens, Local Citizens: The Historical, Constitutional, and Theoretical Meanings of Alien Suffrage," *University of Pennsylvania Law Review*, 141, April 1993, p. 1397.
[75] It should be noted, however, that residency can be a restrictive rather than a permissive requirement. Long Island uses stringent proof of residency requirements to keep immigrants out of public schools (Doreen Carvajal, "Immigrants Fight Residency Rules Blocking Children in L.I. Schools," *New York Times*, 7 August 1995, A1, B4). In a way, the move to residency harkens back to the legal practice in the eastern United States of treating settlement, not citizenship, as the decisive category of inclusion. However, settlement was hardly a benign category, no more than residence is now. On the legal use of the category of settlement to make blacks into "foreigners," see Parker, "Making Blacks Foreigners."

includes aliens in democracy's national future while also transforming citizenship from a state-granted juridical status to a civic practice.[76] Here is an education in democratic citizenship far worthier of the name than the citizenship classes offered by the state in preparation for naturalization. As Michael Walzer says, citizenship cannot be learned "just by watching."[77]

At the same time, the denationalization of democracy must be furthered by enacting transnational ties to empower local minorities. Groups like Women Living Under Islamic Law, Amnesty International, or Greenpeace press states and hold them accountable for their treatments of persons and public goods. In the name of fair and equal treatment of all persons, such groups provide state residents with alternative, not state-originated sites of support and power.[78]

The goal of a democratic cosmopolitanism is to offset the risks and vouchsafe the benefits of state (non-)membership by widening the resources and energies of an emerging international civil society to contest or support state actions in matters of transnational and local interest such as environmental, economic, military, cultural, and immigration policies. This is a *democratic* cosmopolitanism because democracy – in the sense of a commitment to local, popular empowerment, effective representation, and the generation of actions in concert across lines of difference – is its goal.

Movements need myths. Activists can make up new myths, or they can take those already in existence and recycle them. The latter strategy

---

[76] Another example of an organization devoted to immigrant worker empowerment is Choices, a domestic worker cooperative in the San Francisco Bay Area (Leslie Salzinger, "A Maid by Any Other Name: The Transformation of 'Dirty Work' by Central American Immigrants," in *Ethnography Unbound: Power and Resistance in the Modern Metropolis*, ed. Michael Burawoy et al. [Berkeley and Los Angeles: University of California Press, 1991], pp. 139–60). Other examples include Asian Immigrant Women's Advocates and UNITE. The LA Committee for the Protection of the Foreign Born may be seen as an ancestor of these and other groups seeking alien empowerment and rights protection.

[77] Walzer, *What it Means to be an American*, p. 33.

[78] Such groups are not usually state originated but they sometimes are, and perhaps they ought to be state supported. See Lester Salomon's discussion of NGOs and other third-sector associations: "Finally, perhaps the most decisive determinant of third sector growth will be the relationship that nonprofit organizations can forge with government. The task for third sector organizations is to find a *modus vivendi* with government that provides sufficient legal and financial support while preserving a meaningful degree of independence and autonomy" ("The Rise of the Nonprofit Sector," *Foreign Affairs*, 73 [4], 1994, p. 122). I would add only that in the event of such cohabitations, the third sector would do well to relate to its new partner – government – Gothically rather than romantically, that is to say, with healthy measures of caution, skepticism, and ambivalence. On the merits of a Gothic perspective for democratic politics, see *Democracy and the Foreigner*, Ch. 5.

is preferable because it takes advantage of existing cultural resources and simultaneously deprives opposing forces of the powerful narratives that would otherwise continue, uncontested, to support nationalist objectives. The myth of an immigrant America can be turned from its nationalist functions to serve a democratic cosmopolitanism in which citizenship is not just a juridical status distributed (or not) by states, but a *practice* in which denizens, migrants, residents, and their allies mobilize to hold states accountable for their definitions and distributions of goods, powers, rights, freedoms, privileges, and justice, while enacting and taking – inaugurating – new worlds.

Index

Aartsen, Jozia van, 357–358
Abbott, Lyman, 343
Aboriginals. *See* indigenous peoples
Abou Ramadan, Moussa, 134–135
Abu-Odeh, Lama, 124
ACT UP, 386
Acton, Lord, 3
Adams, John, 334–335
affirmative action, 45–46
Afghanistan, 87
African-Americans
  affirmative action, 45–46
  Battle of Little Rock, 316, 353
  racism, 98–100
  unique category, 37, 41, 42, 98–100
Africans, 95
agnostic democratic theory, 176
agonistics, 291
Albania, 3
Allen, Danielle, 19–20, 315–349, 353, 354, 368
An American in Paris, 389
Amish, 30, 38, 178, 255, 258
Amnesty International, 406
Anaya, James, 7
Appiah, Kwame Anthony, 94, 244, 256
approaches
  constitutionalism, 190–191, 197
  contextualism. *See* contextualism
  liberalism. *See* liberalism
  main approaches to diversity, 14–16
  meaning, 1, 14–15, 200
  modus vivendi approaches, 191–193
  political approaches. *See* politics
  relativism, 193–195
  universalism. *See* universalism
Arafat, Yassar, 198
archipelago view of society, 257–263
Arendt, Hannah
  The Human Condition, 319, 330, 331, 334, 342, 347
  Lessing Prize, 334

Little Rock Debate, 19–20, 316–325
Men in Dark Times, 330, 331–334, 336, 347
On Revolution, 334–335
social vs. political spheres, 319, 341–347
statelessness and human rights, 157
Aristotle, 176, 379, 392
Armitage, David, 110
asymmetry of power, 283–284, 285
Augustine, Saint, 298, 299, 300–303
Australia
  Aboriginals, 4, 57, 82, 95, 102, 108
  citizenship, 47, 107
  immigrants
    multiculturalism, 52, 57, 89
    racist policies, 107
    sexual myths, 387–390, 398
Austria, 3
Austro-Hungarian Empire, 3
autonomy
  group autonomy, 245–246, 257, 300
  personal autonomy, 356

Bakke, Alan, 103–104
Baldwin, James, 106
Balkans, 3
Balkenende, Jan-Peter, 360–361
Ballanche, Pierre Simon, 403
Barry, Brian, 15, 62–63, 65–66, 84, 86, 109, 152, 174–175, 187, 240, 243, 265, 269, 271–273, 274–275, 276, 288, 303
Basque Country, 6
Bates, Daisy, 322–324, 325, 338, 339–340, 344
Battle of Little Rock, 353
  Arendt-Ellison debate, 19–20, 316
  democratic sacrifice, 316–325
  invisibility and law, 329–341, 347–348
  related social and political spheres, 319, 341–347
  rule of law and sacrifice, 325–329

summary of events, 321–322
Bayle, Pierre, 19, 297–300, 301, 304
Behdad, Ali, 377–378, 379
Belgium, 35
Benhabib, Seyla, 78, 85–86, 135, 326, 347
Bentham, Jeremy, 179
Bercovitch, Sacvan, 375
Berlin, Isaiah, 155
Big Night, 388
Blackstone, William, 3
Blossom, Superintendent, 322–323, 324, 339
Blum, Lawrence, 96–97
Bluntschli, J. C., 315
Bohman, James, 342
Borstelmann, Thomas, 91
Bossuet, Jacques Bénigne, 299
Bouyeri, Mohammed, 20, 350, 351, 357, 358
Bretons, 41
Bridges, Harry, 381
Brilmayer, Lea, 154
Brink, Bert van den, 20–21, 350–372
Brown, Hazel, 353
Bulgaria, 3
Bush, George W., 87, 207

Canada *See also* Quebec
    Arbitration Act, 137
    Charter of Rights, 138
    citizenship, 47
    constitutional negotiations, 198, 206, 211
    Hartshorne case, 138–139
    Hutterites, 30, 38
    immigrants
        economic contribution, 56
        illegal immigrants, 53–54
        multiculturalism, 52, 89
        racist policies, 107
    indigenous peoples, 4, 38, 39, 113
    multi-societal culture, 35
    Muslim population, 55, 58
    Shari'a tribunals, 14, 117, 128–129, 136–145, 146
Caney, Simon, 15
capitalism, US immigration myth, 21, 379–382
Carens, Joseph, 78, 173, 183, 185, 195–196
Caribbeans, pigmentocracies, 107
Cassese, Antonio, 7
Castlereagh, Robert, Viscount, 3
Catalonia, 6, 26, 29
Catholic church, 309, 310, 346
CEE countries, 26, 184

Cherokees, 97–98
Chicanos, 41
children
    cultural accommodation and, 247, 253
    US illegal aliens, 394–395, 398–400
China, minorities, 4
Chinese migrants, 53–54
Christian culture, 309–310
cinema of immigration, 387–388
citizenship
    Arendt on, 157, 335
    Australia, 47, 107
    citizenization, 355–356
    civic integrity, 352–353, 355–356, 362, 366–371
    consensus, 361, 362
    differentiated citizenship, 129
    Dutch debate, 356–361
    erosion argument, 46–47
    features, 288–291
    France, 396–397
    human rights and, 157
    pluralism and concerted action, 366–367
    power relations, 367–369
    United States
        children of illegals, 394–395
        class mobility, 379–382
        consent, 394–407
        naturalization ceremonies, 396–398
        supercitizens, 378–379, 400
civic integrity, 352–353, 355–356, 362, 366–371
civic nations, 33, 34
civil society, vs. state, 80, 83–86, 405–407
class
    Marxism, 105
    race and, 105–106
    US immigrant mobility, 379–382
Cohen, G. A., 193, 273–277, 278
Cohen, Job, 358
Cold War, 4–5
colonialism
    legacy, 254
    liberalism and, 110–111
    national liberation movements, 5
    peoples' rights and, 2
    post-colonial feminism, 123–126
    racism, 91–92
    United States, 375, 397
common good, 315–316, 317
communicative democratic theory, 176
communitarianism
    immigrants, 379, 389
    liberal-communitarian debate, 27–28, 388

communitarianism (cont.)
  liberal-communitarianism, 360, 362,
    369–370
  minority rights and, 12, 27–28
  US immigration myth, 21, 374, 382–384
Condorcet, Marquis de, 197
consent, citizenship, 394–407
consequentialism, 176
Constant, Benjamin, 197
constitutionalism, 190–191, 197, 281, 285
contextualism
  cases and illustrations, 177–179
  conditions and circumstances, 180–184
  constitutionalism, 190–191
  elements, 195–196
  first wave, 173
  limits of justice, 186–190
  modus vivendi approaches, 191–193
  multiculturalism and, 15–16, 173–177
  relativism, 193–195
  second wave, 173–174
  stability theory, 185–186
  test cases, 179–180
cosmopolitanism, 262, 406
Council of Europe, Convention on
    National Minorities, 50
Crawford, James, 7
critical theory, 85, 106, 123, 307–311
Cubans, 41
cultural defense, 124–125
cultural diversity. See multiculturalism
cultural exemptions, 240–242, 289–290
culture
  authenticity, 225–226, 230–232, 238,
    240, 241, 389
  corruption, 225–226, 230–232
  cultural relativism, 195
  definitions, 126
  demarcation, 223, 227
  diversity. See multiculturalism
  essentialism. See essentialism of culture
  gender and, 87–88
  group representation, 233–235
  legitimate terminology, 93
  liberal culturalism, 12, 31–32
  normalization, 80, 86–88
  political uses of, 130–131
  politics of cultural difference, 74–88
  primary good, 270
  race and, 91–101
  racism and cultural difference, 80, 81–83
  recognition. See recognition
  societal culture, 34–36, 75, 78, 238, 274
  uniformity, 223, 225, 227–229
  ways of life, 224–225, 227–229, 230

Davidson, David, 390–391
deliberations
  claims as proto-reasons, 208–209
  claims of politics, 208–215
  conditions, 214–215
  deliberative democracy, 85–86,
    135–136, 245, 326
  logic, 209–215
democracy
  Battle of Little Rock and, 353
  civic nations, 34
  concepts, 257
  deliberative democracy, 85–86,
    135–136, 245, 326
  democratic cosmopolitanism, 406
  democratic sacrifice, 19–20, 316–325
  Dutch debate, 356–361
  famines and, 158, 167
  fundamental principle, 281, 285
  liberal democracy, 34, 244
    multicultural accommodation and,
      246–256
  other rights and, 167–168
  requirements, 161, 170
  United States, 374–375, 382–387,
    394–407
  universalism, 152, 154, 157, 394–407
Denton, Nancy, 100
Déroin, Jeanne, 403
Derrida, Jacques, 379, 396
Deveaux, Monique, 135
difference. See politics of difference
differential treatment
  affirmative action, 45–46
  liberalism and, 10–11
Diof, Semou, 98
disability, structural inequalities, 65–68
discovery doctrine, 107
domestic policy coherence constraint
    (DPCC), 154–155, 163–164
Doppelt, Gerald, 94
dresscodes, 40
Du Bois, W. E. B., 106
Duplessis, Rachel, 402
Dworkin, Ronald, 180, 181, 196, 269–270,
    273, 275, 276–277

East India Company, 111
Eckford, Elizabeth, 318, 321–322,
    323–324, 324, 339, 353–354
economic rights, 169
education
  Battle of Little Rock, 316, 353
  common language, 36
  curricula, 40

hijab debate, 128, 292, 306–307
internal minorities, 251–252
religious symbols in schools, 128,
   305–306
Ellison, Ralph
   Battle of Little Rock, 19–20, 316–325
   Invisible Man, 316–317, 325, 328, 330,
      333–334, 337–339, 348
Elster, Jon, 291
Enlightenment, 109–114, 297
environmental rights, 168, 169
equality
   See also structural inequalities
   deliberations and inequality, 214–215
   egalitarian liberal universalism, 151,
      152–153, 164–167
   equality of opportunity, 275–276
   equality of resources, 268–275
   luck-egalitarianism, 268–269, 277–279
   racial equality, 326–328
essentialism of culture
   critique, 1, 78, 226–232
   cultural exemptions, 240–242
   group prosperity argument, 237–240
   group representation argument, 233–235
   meaning, 16–17, 221–226
   recognition as human need, 236–237
ethnic nations, 33
ethnicity, race and, 101–104
Europe, multicultural debate, 90
exemptions, cultural exemptions, 240–242,
   289–290

Fabre, Cécile, 156
fair trial, 168–169
family law
   Canadian *Shari'a* tribunals, 14, 117,
      128–129, 136–145, 146
   Indian politics, 130
   Israeli federalism, 133–135
   Shari'a law in Western countries, 255
family life, cultural discrimination, 118
famines, 158, 167
Fanon, Frantz, 97
Faubus, Governor, 321, 322, 343–344
Feinberg, Joe, 253
female circumcision, 54, 55
feminism
   Canadian *Shari'a* tribunals and, 136–
      145, 146
   critique of multiculturalism, 115–117
   assessment, 145–147
   liberal feminism, 117–123, 140
   multicultural feminism, 126–129,
      140–142

post-colonial feminism, 123–126, 138,
   139–140
deliberative democracy, 135–136
legal systems and, 132–136
liberalism and, 110
political uses of culture, 130–131
politics of difference, 72, 73–74
theology, 131–132
US movement, 387
finality, 284–285, 286–287
Fine, Benjamin, 321, 339–340
Flanders, 26, 29
forced marriages, 54
Ford, Richard, 103–104, 263
foreign brides, 390–393
foreign policy coherence constraint
   (FPCC), 155–161
Forst, Rainer, 19, 292–311
Fortuyn, Pim, 356
Foucault, Michel, 355
France
   2005 riots, 98, 100
   Bretons, 41
   colonial rights over land, 2
   Edict of Nantes, 294
   Genocide Convention negotiations, 5
   hijab debate, 128
   immigrants, 57, 385
   minority languages, 57
   Muslims, 55, 100
   republicanism, 396–397
   Revolution, 296
Fraser, Nancy, 79–80, 105, 268
Fredrickson, George, 96
freedom of association, 152
freedom of conscience. *See* religious
   toleration
Freud, Sigmund, 396
friendship, 379
Frisians, 57
Fullinwider, Robert, 84
Furedi, Frank, 91

Galston, William, 249–250, 251, 252
Gay Men's Health Crisis, 386
gender equality
   immigrants and, 387–393
   foreign brides, 390–393
   movements, 6
   multiculturalism v, 14, 87–88, 251
   structural inequality, 14, 60–61, 72–74
genocide, cultural genocide, 5
Germany
   Danish minority, 57
   guest-workers, 42

Germany *(cont.)*
  hijab debate, 306–307
  homosexual marriage, 306
  Jews and, 331, 334
  religious symbols in schools, 305–306
  Turks, 41
Giraudon, Virginie, 397
Glazer, Nathan, 46
Goethe, Johann Wolfgang von, 293, 295,
    306
Gogh, Theo van, 20, 310, 350–353,
    356–357, 359
Goldman, Emma, 381
good faith, 212
Gray, John, 257
Greece, 3
Green, T. H., 3
Green Card, 387
Greenpeace, 406
Grotius, Hugo, 3, 176, 196
group autonomy
  assumptions, 257
  and liberalism, 246–256
group representation, 233–235
Gutmann, Amy, 71, 85

Habermas, Jürgen, 161, 170, 311
Hart, H. L. A., 166
Hartz, Louis, 373, 389
Hasidic Jews, 30
Hayek, Friedrich von, 176, 196
Hayes-Tilden Agreement, 346
Haymarket activists, 381
Heath Wellman, Christopher, 255
Hegel, Georg, 110, 202, 216
height and weight restrictions, 40
Held, David, 160
Hershovitz, Scott, 191
Heschel, Susannah, 131
hijab debate, 128, 292, 306–307
Hirsi Ali, Ayaan, 350–351, 356, 357, 359,
    360–361
Hobbes, Thomas, 202
Hobhouse, Leonard, 3
Hochschild, Jennifer, 374
Holmes, Steven, 381
Holocaust, 90, 112, 327, 330
Homer-Dixon, Thomas, 168
homosexuality. *See* sexual orientation
Honig, Bonnie, 21–22, 373–407
Honneth, Axel, 267, 268
honor killings, 54, 124, 126
human rights
  citizenship and, 157
  democracy and, 161

economic resources and, 170
immigrants' practices, 54–55
subsistence rights, 167
humanism, secular humanism, 356–357,
    359, 360, 369–370
Hume, David, 110, 176, 177, 196, 197
Hutterites, 30, 38

identity politics, 60
immigrants
  communitarianism, 379, 389
  economic burden, 55–56
  films, 387–388
  gender roles, 387–393
  illegal immigrants, 53–54, 398–402
  illiberal practices, 54–55
  individualism, 388–390
  liberalism and, 51–59
  modernity and, 29
  multiculturalism debate, 12
  nation-building, 39–41
  Netherlands. *See* Netherlands
  patriarchy, 21, 374, 388
  polyethnic rights, 300
  US immigrant myths
    alien suffrage, 405
    ambivalence, 377–378
    California's Proposition 382
    children of illegals, 398–400
    class mobility as citizenship,
        379–382
    communitarianism, 382–384
    consent to citizenship, 394–407
    exceptionalism, 373, 375, 379
    foreign brides, 390–393
    generally, 21–22, 373–379
    illegals, 398–402
    integration, 41
    naturalization ceremonies, 395, 396,
        396–398
    omissions, 375, 397
    patriotism, 384
    politics, 381–382
    racist policies, 107
    self-expatriation, 394–395
    sexuality, 387–393
    social movements, 405–407
    supercitizens, 378–379, 400
    threats, 376
    universalist democracy, 394–407
    Walzer's vision, 382–387
    Western backlash, 26, 51–59
India, 130, 195
indigenous peoples
  adaptability, 243

Australia, 4, 57, 82, 95, 102, 108
Canada, 4, 38, 39, 113
  Cherokees, 97–98
  cultural exemptions, 289–290
  group rights, 93
  Latin America, 82
  mobilization, 26
  North America, 6, 82, 94, 95
  politics of difference, 61
  progress, 50
  property rights, 181
  Quebec, 39
  recognition, 283
  United States, 41, 112
individualism
  common experience, 18
  immigrants, 388–390
  liberal individualism, 27–28, 259, 261
  secular humanism and, 356
  white individualism, 111
inequality. *See* equality
internal minorities
  archipelago view of society, 257–263
  assumptions, 257
    completeness assumption, 258–262
    independence assumption, 258,
      262–264
  children, 247, 253
  education, 251–252
  exit rights, 247–253, 261–262
  gender roles, 251
  institutional illiberalism, 255
  liberalism and, 17–18, 244–264
    multicultural accommodation
      theories, 246–256
  United States, 386–387
internal restrictions, 31, 302
International Labour Organization, 50
invisibility, 329–341, 347–348
Islam *See also* Muslims
  Canadian *Shari'a* tribunals, 14, 117,
    128–129, 136–145, 146
  caricatures of Prophet Muhammad, 292
  feminist theology, 132
  fundamentalism, 309
  interpretation of *Shari'a* law, 121–122,
    134–135
  radicalization, 135
  schools of law, 137
  treatment of women, 350–351
  Women Living Under Islamic Law, 406
Israel
  Oslo Accords, 198–199, 206
  personal law federalism, 133–135
Italy, Muslims, 55, 58

Jackson, Andrew, 98
Jagger, Alison, 117
Japan, Thai brides, 391
Japanese, 54
Jews
  anti-Semitism, 330
  feminist scholarship of Judaism, 131
  Germany, 331, 334
  Holocaust, 90, 112, 327, 330
  toleration, 295
Johnson Reagon, Bernice, 383
Joseph II, 294
justice
  civic integrity, 352, 370–371
  cultural difference and, 81–83
  discourse, 42–45
  Dutch civic debate, 370–371
  inequality, 214–215
  limits, 186–190
  priority, 176, 190
  redistribution vs. recognition, 18–19,
    79–80
  structural inequalities, 60–61
  theory of global justice, 153–163
  toleration and, 296

Kamm, Frances, 164
Kant, Immanuel, 19, 107, 110, 111, 114,
  166, 176, 179, 197, 293, 295, 301,
  302, 394
Kazakhs, 4
Kelly, Gene, 389
King, Desmond, 109
Klosko, George, 185–186
Kosovo, 48
Kristeva, Julia, 85
Kukathas, Chandran, 174, 175–176, 196,
  252, 253, 256–264
Kurds, 6
Kymlicka, Will, 5, 7, 12, 15, 17, 25–59,
  74–76, 76–78, 92, 93, 98, 125, 174,
  180–181, 182, 183–184, 238–240,
  268, 269, 270–271, 273–275, 276,
  300–301, 302

Laden, Anthony, 16, 18, 198–217, 266,
  279, 287, 288
Laitin, David, 189
languages
  culture and, 222
  education, 36
  France, 57
  minority rights, 9–10
  official languages, 33, 37, 39
  recognition, 30

languages *(cont.)*
   United States, 33, 34–35, 82
Latin America, pigmentocracies, 107
Latinos, 82
law. *See also* family law
   cultural bias, 124–125
   cultural defense, 124–125
   India, 130
   invisibility and, 329–341, 347–348
   multicultural approaches, 132–136
   privatizing justice, 141
   public vs. private sphere, 145, 319,
      341–347
   race and, 106–107
   rule of law, 339–340, 348–349
   rule of law and sacrifice, 325–329
   separation from religion, 118
League of Nations, 3, 4
Leopold II, King of the Belgians, 112
Lessing, Gotthold, 293, 331
Levellers, 296
Levi, Jacob, 248
Levinson, Sanford, 395, 399
Levy, Jacob, 15–16, 173–197
liberalism
   19th century, 3
   communitarianism, 360, 362, 369–370
   critique, 267
   difference blindness, 60–61, 67
   early liberalism, 109–114, 297
   egalitarian values, 151, 152–153,
      164–167
   illiberal liberalism, 109–111
   immigration and, 51–59
   individualism, 259, 261
   internal minorities and, 17–18,
      244–264
   liberal-communitarian debate, 27–28,
      388
   liberal culturalism, 12, 31–32, 51
   liberal democracy, 34, 244, 356
   liberal feminism, 117–123, 140
   limits of liberal tolerance, 77, 305, 307
      ambivalence, 295–297
   meaning, 244–245
   minority rights and, 7–11, 28–32
   multicultural accommodation theories,
      246–256
   Muslims and, 54–55
   neutral liberal states, 33–35
   politics of difference, 60–61, 63
   private and public sphere, 145
   race and, 108, 109–114
   religious tolerance, 8–9, 77–78, 297, 356
   self-ownership, 164, 166

   similar vs. differential treatment, 10–11
   state vs. civil society, 80, 84–86
   United States, 5, 21
   universalism. *See* universalism
Little Rock. *See* Battle of Little Rock
Livy, 403
Locke, John, 3, 110, 111, 113, 296, 297,
   298–299, 300, 310, 399
London bombings, 54
Longview Foundation, 318
luck egalitarianism, 268–269, 277–279
Luther, Martin, 296

Macedo, Stephen, 185
Machiavelli, Niccolò, 202, 390
MacKinnon, Catharine, 125
Madison, James, 402–403
Madrid bombings, 54
Makah Indians, 241–242
Malcomson, Scott, 98
Mansbridge, Jane, 340–341
Margalit, Avishai, 237–238
marriage *See also* patriarchy
   forced marriages, 54
   foreign brides, 390–393
   homosexual marriage, 292, 306
Marx, Karl, 110, 128, 396
Marxism, 105, 106, 107
Mason, Andrew, 17, 221–243
Massey, Douglas, 99
media, and immigrants, 40
Members of Parliament, 235
Mennonites, 250, 258
merit, 65–66
Methodists, 346
METRAC, 137
Mexico, 375
Mill, John Stuart, 3, 110, 111, 164, 196,
   300
Miller, David, 30, 184
Mills, Charles, 12–14, 89–114
minority rights *See also* politics of difference
   bad vs. good rights, 31–32
   citizenship erosion argument, 46–47
   communitarianism, 12, 27–28
   development of debate, 25–27
   external protections, 32
   group autonomy, 245–246
   group representation, 233–235
   immigrants. *See* immigrants
   in-between categories, 42
   internal minorities. *See* internal
      minorities
   internal restrictions, 31, 302
   justice discourse, 42–45

League of Nations regime, 4
liberal framework, 7–11, 28–32, 51
  limits of liberal tolerance, 77
  meaning, 25
  modernity, 29–30
  nation-building, 12, 33–42
  national minorities. *See* national
    minorities
  new debate, 42–48
  recognition. *See* recognition
  retreat from, 12, 49–59
  UN regime, 4
modernity
  minorities and, 29–30
  secular humanism, 356
modus vivendi approaches, 191–193
Muhammad, Prophet, 292
Montenegro, 3
Montesquieu, Charles-Louis de, 197, 297
Moore, Margaret, 188
morality
  ethics and, 303–305
  moral autonomy, 302
Mulroney, Brian, 198
multiculturalism *See also* minority rights
  anti-racism and, 13, 89–114
  approaches, 14–16
  arguments for, 232–242
    cultural exemptions, 240–242
    group prosperity, 237–240
    group representation, 233–235
    recognition as human need, 236–237
  debate, 11–22, 42–48, 90
  development of concept, 2–7, 90
  feminism. *See* feminism
  first wave, 115, 116, 187
  gender equality v, 14, 87–88
  justice discourse, 42–45
  liberalism. *See* liberalism
  meanings, 89–90
  retreat from, 12, 49–59
  second wave, 187–188, 189
Murray, Albert, 99
Musgrave, Thomas, 4, 7
Muslims *See also* Islam
  Canadian *Shari'a* tribunals, 14, 117,
    128–129, 136–145, 146
  Dutch debate about, 356–357
  France, 55, 100, 128
  gender discrimination, 87
  hijab debate, 128, 292, 306–307
  illiberal practices, 54–55
  Indian politics, 130
  intolerance, 310–311
  Netherlands, 351–372

racial discrimination, 83
Shari'a law in Western countries, 255

NAACP, 318, 321, 322, 324–325
Nagel, Thomas, 164
Nantes, Edict of (1598), 294
Narain, Vrinda, 130–131
Narayan, Uma, 123
nation-building
  immigrants, 39–41
  language rights and, 189
  minority rights and, 12, 33–42
  national minorities, 38–39, 50
nation-states. *See* states
national liberation movements, 5
national minorities
  European Framework Convention, 50
  meaning, 29
  modernity and, 29
  nation-building, 38–39
  progress, 50
nationalism, 2, 384
natural justice, 153
negotiations
  claims as vectors, 203–204
  logic, 204–208
  meaning, 204
  political theory, 201
  processes, 199
neo-Hegelianism, 197
neo-Kantianism, 197
neo-liberalism, 265
Netherlands
  anti-Muslim violence, 351–352, 354,
    360
  civic integrity and, 352–353, 355–356,
    362, 366–371
  consensus, 361, 362
  crisis of civic relations, 351–372
  Frisians, 57
  immigrants, 364–365
    failed integration, 352, 364–365
  multiculturalism, 52
  myth, 57, 354
  pillars, 362–364
  Revolution, 296
  secular humanism, 356–357, 359, 360,
    369–370
  van Gogh murder, 20–21, 310, 350–353
    public debate, 351–352, 356–361
    scapegoating, 354
neutral liberal states, 33–35
New World, 2, 7
New Zealand, 113
NGOs, 84, 405–407

Nickel, James, 156, 159
Nigeria, 129
Norman, Wayne, 39, 188
Nozick, Robert, 176, 181, 183

Okin, Susan, 73, 118–121, 123, 126, 393
O'Neill, John, 223
O'Neill, Onora, 152
Organization of American States, 50
orientalism, 124
OSCE, 50
Oslo Accords, 198–199, 206
Owen, David, 18–19, 265–291

Pagden, Anthony, 7
Palestine, 198–199, 206
Parekh, Bhikhu, 78, 272, 288
patriarchy
    foreign brides, 390–393
    immigrants, 388
    liberal feminist critique, 118–121
    religion and, 121–122
    US immigration myth, 21, 374
Patten, Alan, 239
peyote, 289–290
Phillips, Anne, 125
phobias, 276
pigmentocracies, 107
Planned Parenthood, 386
poiesis, 342
Poland, 3
political economy, race and, 104–109
politics
    asymmetry of power, 283–284, 285
    common good, 315–316, 317
    culture, political uses, 130–131
    definition, 201
    deliberations, 208–215
        claims as proto-reasons, 208–209
        conditions, 287–291
        logic, 209–215
        meaning, 204
        difference. See politics of difference
    forms of dialogue, 199, 204
    friendship politics, 379
    fundamental principles, 281–283
    negotiations
        claims as vectors, 203–204
        logic, 204–208
        meaning, 204
        processes, 199
        theory, 201
    pluralism and concerted action,
        366–367
    political approaches, 208–215, 280–286

    continuing dialogue, 284–285, 286–287
    vs. theory, 16, 18–19, 200–201,
        215–217, 266–267
    politics of recognition, 104
    public vs. private sphere, 145, 319,
        341–347
    related social and political, 319, 341–347
    representation, 235
    theory
        claims as vectors, 203–204
        negotiations, 201
        role, 215–217
        vs. political approaches, 16, 18–19,
            200–201, 215–217, 266–267
    US immigrants and, 381–382
politics of difference
    basis, 96
    cultural difference, 61, 74–88
        critical limits, 80–88
        justice issues, 81–83
        normalization of culture, 80, 86–88
        state vs. society, 80, 83–86
    generally, 10, 12–13, 60–88
    identity politics, 60
    liberalism and, 60–61, 63
    positional difference, 60–61, 64–74
        disability, 65–68
        gender inequality, 72–74
        racial inequality, 69–71
        vs. cultural difference, 60, 62–63
    redistribution vs. recognition, 18–19,
        79–80, 265–291
power
    asymmetries, 283–284, 285
    relations, 367–369
practical identities, 210
Proast, Jonas, 298
property rights
    indigenous people, 181
    self-ownership, 166
    universalism, 153
Prussia, 3
public holidays, 40
public vs. private sphere, 145, 319,
    341–347
Puerto Ricans, 41
Pufendorf, Samuel von, 3

Quebec, 6, 26, 29, 38
    constitutional negotiations, 198, 206, 211

Rabin, Yitzhak, 198
race
    class and, 105–106
    construction, 104, 105, 106

critical race theory, 106, 123
culture and, 91–101
ethnicity and, 101–104
liberalism and, 108, 109–114
non-existence, 101
political economy and, 104–109
social equality, 326–328
racism
colonialism, 91–92
cultural difference and, 13, 80, 81–83
discrediting, 93
equality movements, 6
legal systems, 106–107
liberalism and, 108, 109–114
multiculturalism and anti-racism, 13, 89–114
Muslims, 83
politics of difference, 69–71
racial states, 107
racialization process, 69–70
segregation, 70–71
slavery, 69–70
structural inequality, 60–61
Rancière, Jacques, 403–404, 404
Rawls, John, 5, 8, 65, 111–113, 114, 153, 176, 177, 179, 180, 181, 182, 183, 185–186, 191–193, 213, 216, 269, 269–270, 279, 284, 303, 304, 356, 366, 369
Raz, Joseph, 30, 237–238, 257
reactive culturalism, 263
recognition
continuing dialogue, 284–285, 286–287
human need, 236–237
indigenous people, 283
meaning, 266–267
politics of recognition, 104, 280–286
conditions, 287–291
principles, 281–283
vs. redistribution, 18–19, 79–80, 207, 265–291
redistribution
equality of resources, 268–275
neo-liberal policies, 265
vs. recognition, 18–19, 79–80, 207, 265–291
Reformation, 309
refugees, Western backlash, 26
Reich, Rob, 189
Reid, Bill, 92
relativism, 193–195
religion
exclusions, 247
faith and knowledge, 303–304
feminist theology, 131–132

institutional illiberalism, 255
Islam. See Islam
multicultural feminism, 128–129
patriarchy and, 120, 121–122
post-colonial feminism and, 139–140
separation from law, 118
tolerance. See religious toleration
religious toleration
autonomy and respect, 300
Bayle's justification, 297–300
development of concept, 2, 296–297
liberalism, 8–9, 77–78, 297, 356
Rawlsian approach, 192
religious symbols in schools, 128, 305–306
universalism, 152, 153
representation
group representation, 233–235
Members of Parliament, 235
respect, 295–297, 300, 304, 305, 307
Ridge, John, 97
right to life, 153
Rogin, Michael, 401
Roma, 5, 42
Romania, 3
Rorty, Richard, 165
Rousseau, Jean-Jacques, 197, 297, 374–375, 396–397
Roy, Oliver, 100
rule of law, 325–329, 339–340, 348–349
Russia, 3
Russian minorities, 42

Sacco, Nicola, 381
sacrifice
democratic sacrifice, 19–20, 316–325
rule of law and sacrifice, 325–329
Sample, Ruth, 107
Sandel, M. 183
Santa Clara Pueblo vs. Martinez, 178
Saward, Michael, 161
Scanlon, Thomas, 368–369
Scanna International Worldwide Introductions, 390
schools. See education
Schuck, Peter, 394–395, 398–402
Scotland, 6, 26, 57
Second World War, causes, 4
secular humanism, 356–357, 359, 360, 369–370
securitization, 55
segregation See also Battle of Little Rock
housing racism, 70–71
occupational gender segregation, 73
self-expatriation, 394–395

self-ownership, 164, 166
Sen, Amartya, 158
September 11 attacks, 54
Serbia, 3
sexual orientation
    right to marry, 292, 306
    structural inequality, 60–61
    US gay rights movements, 387
Shachar, Ayelet, 14, 15, 44–45, 115, 263
Sharp, Andrew, 7
Shih, Marty, 381
Shue, Henry, 156
Sikhs, 204, 240, 241
slavery
    anti-slavery white supremacists, 110
    Arendt on, 335
    legacy, 69–70, 94, 254
    legal systems, 107
    liberalism and, 111
    right to freedom from, 153
    United States, 69–70, 99, 113, 375, 397
Smith, Rogers, 376, 394–395, 398–402
social exclusion, 287–288
social movements
    deliberative democracy, 86
    new social movements, 105
    US immigrants, 405–407
societal culture, 34–36, 75, 78, 238, 274
South Africa, 107, 113, 135
Soviet Union, Russification, 4
Spain, 2, 35, 55
Spinner-Halev, Jeff, 30, 174, 184, 252,
    256–264
stability theory, 185–186, 206–207,
    213–214
states
    neutral liberal states, 33–35
    protection of women, 137–139
    racial states, 107
    self-conceived singularity, 78
    symbolism, 187
    vs. civil society, 80, 83–86, 405–407
Steiner, Hillel, 164
Sterba, James, 94
Strawson, John, 140
Street, Brian, 229
strict liability, 278
Strictly Ballroom, 387–390, 398
structural inequalities
    disability, 65–68
    gender, 14, 72–74
    politics of difference, 63
    positional difference, 60–61, 64–65
    race, 13, 60–61, 69–70
Submission, 350–351

subsistence rights, 167
Sundquist, Eric, 99
Switzerland, 5, 35

Taiwan, 391
Tamir, Yael, 7, 30, 184
Taylor, Charles, 7, 37, 61, 79, 95–96,
    96–97, 104, 184, 236, 267
terra nullius, 107
terrorism, Muslims and, 54
Tibet, 4
Tilly, Charles, 64
Tocqueville, Alexis de, 197, 373, 375, 403
Toews, Miriam, 250
toleration
    autonomy and respect, 300
    Bayle's justification, 297–300
    contested concept, 19, 292
    critical theory, 307–311
    ethics and morality, 303–305
    examples, 305–307
    limits of liberal tolerance, 77, 305, 307
        debate, 19
        gender issues, 87–88
        historic ambivalence, 295–297
    normalization of culture, 80, 86–88
    permission concept, 294–295, 304,
        307–308
    religious symbols in schools, 128,
        305–306
    respect concept, 295–297, 304, 307
Toleration Patents (1781), 294
truthfulness, civic integrity, 352, 355, 370
Tully, James, 7, 18–19, 92–93, 265–291,
    355
Turgot, Anne Robert Jacques, 197
Turks, 41

Uighurs, 4
UNESCO Declaration on Cultural
    Diversity, 51
United Kingdom
    colonial rights over land, 2
    devolution, 57
    Islamic Shari'a Council, 136
    parallel Islamic law, 135
    revolutions, 296
    Toleration Act 1689, 294
United Nations
    Draft Declaration on Indigenous
        Peoples, 26, 50
    minority rights, 4
United States
    affirmative action, 45–46
    American Dream, 374, 380–381

Americans with Disabilities Act, 67–68
annexations, 375
Bakke case, 103–104
black Americans. *See* African-Americans
conquests, 375
Constitution, 315–316, 398
crimes of passion, 124
critical race theory, 106
democratic legitimacy, 374–375
English language, 34–35, 82
exceptionalist belief, 373, 375, 379
foreign founders, 373–379
Genocide Convention negotiations, 5
Hayes-Tilden Agreement, 346
Haymarket activists, 381
immigrants. *See* immigrants
internal minorities, 386–387
Latinos, 82
legislators, 315–316, 373
liberalism, 5
Love Canal, 169
Mennonites, 250, 258
Mexican wars, 375
Native Americans, 41
    Cherokees, 97–98
    genocide, 112
neutral liberal state, 33, 34–35
patriotism, 384
race
    attitudes, 108
    Battle of Little Rock, 316, 353
    citizenship and, 107
    and ethnicity, 103–104
    racist policies, 108
    violence, 94
Revolution, 296
slavery, 69–70, 99, 113, 375, 397
universalism, 394–407
Universal Declaration of Human Rights, 4
universalism
    anti-universalism, 151, 152
    debate, 201
    domestic policy coherence constraint
        (DPCC), 154–155, 163–164
    egalitarian liberal values, 151, 152–153,
        164–167
    foreign policy coherence constraint
        (FPCC), 155–161
    liberal universalism, 15, 109, 151–172
    minimal universalism, 151, 153,
        161–162, 167–170
    theory of global justice, 153–163
    US democracy, 394–407
utilitarianism, 155, 176

Vanzetti, Bartolomeo, 381
Vattell, Emmerich de, 3
Vesta, Ellie, 102
Vienna, Congress of (1815), 3
Vietnam War, 94
Vitoria, Francisco de, 3, 196
Voltaire, 293, 297
Vuijsje, Herman, 358

Waldron, Jeremy, 21, 239, 262, 279–280,
    289, 366
Wales, 6, 57
Walzer, Michael, 33, 153, 183, 193, 373,
    375, 376, 377, 382–387, 399, 401
Warren, Ken, 328
Warren, Robert Penn, 318, 320, 325,
    329
Watson, C. W., 93
ways of life, 224–225, 227–229, 230
Weinstock, Daniel, 17–18, 189, 244–264
Weir, Peter, 387
welfare state
    crisis, 265
    equality of resources, 268–275
Wertheimer, Alan, 107
whaling, 241
Williams, Bernard, 155, 173, 277, 278
Williams, Robert, Jr, 7
Winant, Howard, 91
Wingrove, Elizabeth, 396–397
Wittgenstein, Ludwig, 222–223
Wolff, Jonathan, 278–280
Women *See also* feminism
    circumcision, 54, 55
    cultural accommodation and, 247, 251
    Islam and, 350–351
    politics of cultural difference, 63
Women Living Under Islamic Law, 406
Woodhull, Victoria, 404
World Bank, 50
Workplace Project, 405–406
Wu, Harry, 381

Young, Iris Marion, 7, 10, 12–14, 60–88,
    234

Zwagerman, Joost, 358